The Larger Moths of Warwickshire

by David C.G. Brown

Atropos
PUBLISHING

Dedication

To my dear parents, Margaret and Cuthbert, who had looked forward to reading this book but sadly did not live to see its completion.

Lepidopterists' field meeting, 1935. Left to right: P. Siviter-Smith, C. Wainwright, K. Davison (kneeling) and F.H. Lees. Photograph courtesy of L.J. Evans.

A section of the Warwickshire Moth Group at Grove Hill, near Alcester, 2 July 2005. Left to right: M. Astley, D.C.G. Brown (author), S. Taylor (back to camera), A. Visick and I.G.M. Reid. Photo: P. Nicholas.

The Larger Moths of Warwickshire

by David C.G. Brown

Atropos
PUBLISHING

Published by Atropos Publishing,
36 Tinker Lane, Meltham, Holmfirth, HD9 4EX.
www.atropos.info
Email atropos@atroposed.freeserve.co.uk
Tel. 01326 290287

Copyright © David C.G. Brown

First published 2006

ISBN 0-9551086-1-6

Front cover design by Robert Thompson
Typeset in Pennsylvania, USA, by Alcedo Publishing

Printed in Northern Ireland by Nicholson & Bass

All rights reserved. No part of this publication may be reproduced, stored in a retrieval system or transmitted in any form or by any means, electronic, mechanical, photocopying, recording or otherwise, without the prior written permission of the publisher or copyright holder.

Contents

Foreword
1 **Introduction**
    Former Warwickshire Lepidopterists 2
    Warwickshire—the County 7
    Geology of Warwickshire 8
    Habitats 10
    The Mixed Fortunes of Warwickshire's Moths 14
    Immigrants 21
    Conservation 23
27 **Introduction to Maps and Species Accounts**
    Terms and Abbreviations 33
    Featured Recorders 34
37 **Species Accounts**
    Hepialidae 37
    Cossidae 39
    Zygaenidae 40
    Limacodidae 43
    Sesiidae 43
    Lasiocampidae 48
    Saturniidae 53
    Drepanidae 54
    Thyatiridae 56
    Geometridae 61
    Sphingidae 177
    Notodontidae 187
    Lymantriidae 198
    Arctiidae 203
    Nolidae 214
    Noctuidae 215
345 Appendix 1. Doubtful or Imported species
348 Appendix 2. Abbreviations of Authors' Names
349 Appendix 3. Scientific Names of Plants
352 Appendix 4. Site Gazetteer
355 Appendix 5. Record Contributors
356 Appendix 6. Published Warwickshire Lists
357 Appendix 7. Lists from Neighbouring Counties
358 Appendix 8. Local Societies
359 Bibliography
365 Index of English Names
371 Index of Scientific Names
381 Acknowledgments

List of Illustrations

Figure 1	p.7	Major population centres in Warwickshire.
Figure 2	p.9	The solid geology of Warwickshire.
Figure 3	p.11	Woodland habitats.
Figure 4	p.13	Grassland, post-industrial, heathland and wetland habitats.
Figure 5	p.21	Warwickshire's central position.
Figure 6	p.27	Warwickshire and surrounding vice-counties.
Figure 7	p.28	Recorded tetrads (2 x 2km squares).
Figure 8	p.30	Regularly (nightly) recorded static garden moth trap sites referenced in the text.
Figure 9	p.94	Garden moth trap totals of *C. siterata* at Charlecote.
Figure 10	p.122	Garden moth trap totals of *E. intricata* in Rugby and Coventry.
Figure 11	p.126	Garden moth trap totals of *E. tripunctaria* at Hillmorton, Rugby.
Figure 12	p.145	Garden moth trap totals of *A. grossulariata* at Hillmorton, Rugby, illustrate a steady decline.
Figure 13	p.148	Garden moth trap totals of *M. wauaria* at Hillmorton, Rugby, illustrate the rapid fall in numbers during the 1980s.
Figure 14	p.156	Total numbers of *S. lunularia* in a garden moth trap at Charlecote.
Figure 15	p.163	Annual percentage frequency of the three forms of *B. betularia* in a garden moth trap at Hillmorton, Rugby.
Figure 16	p.198	The sharp decline of *D. caeruleocephala* in both rural and suburban districts.
Figure 17	p.209	The decline of *A. caja* in both rural and urban districts.
Figure 18	p.217	The decline of *E. nigricans* at Charlecote.
Figure 19	p.222	Fluctuations and recent decline of *R. simulans* in rural and urban districts.
Figure 20	p.226	The changes in fortune of *S. ravida* at Charlecote.
Figure 21	p.227	Diminishing population of *G. augur* at Charlecote.
Figure 22	p.229	Frequency of *P. saucia* in a suburban garden and a rural location.
Figure 23	p.247	Frequency of *H. compta* in urban, suburban and rural districts.
Figure 24	p.265	Annual garden moth trap figures of *A. nigra* at Charlecote and Rugby.
Figure 25	p.267	Increasing abundance in *L. ornitopus* at Hillmorton, Rugby.
Figure 26	p.268	Annual garden moth trap figures illustrating the establishment of *L. leautieri* in a rural and a suburban area.
Figure 27	p.273	The sudden decline of *A. chi* at Hillmorton, Rugby.
Figure 28	p.284	Annual totals of *A. aceris* in a garden moth trap at Hillmorton, Rugby.
Figure 29	p.296	Annual numbers of *C. affinis* in a garden moth trap at Charlecote.
Figure 30	p.297	Annual numbers of *C. diffinis* in a garden moth trap, Charlecote 1969–1979.
Figure 31	p.326	Increasing records of *P. prasinana* at Hillmorton, Rugby.

Table 1	p.14	Species which became extinct in Warwickshire before 1950.
Table 2	p.16	Species which have become extinct in Warwickshire since 1950 or are probably extinct.
Table 3	p.17	Species which have noticeably declined in Warwickshire during the last 30 years.
Table 4	p.18	Species which have significantly increased in Warwickshire since 1980.
Table 5	p.20	Species discovered to be resident in Warwickshire since 1970.
Table 6	p.21	Immigrant species recorded in Warwickshire.
Table 7	p.25	Nationally Scarce resident species in Warwickshire: Nationally Scarce A.
Table 8	p.25	Nationally Scarce resident species in Warwickshire: Nationally Scarce B.

Colour Plates

Plate 1	Species presumed to be extinct in Warwickshire.
Plate 2	Increasing species, recent colonisers and vagrants.
Plate 3	Immigrant species.
Plate 4	Immigrant species.
Plate 5	Nationally Scarce Warwickshire species.
Plate 6	Nationally Scarce Warwickshire species.
Plate 7	Woodland: Oversley Wood and woodland species.
Plate 8	Woodland: Ryton Wood and woodland species.
Plate 9	Woodland: Wappenbury Wood and woodland species.
Plate 10	Woodland: Snitterfield Bushes and woodland species.
Plate 11	Woodland species.
Plate 12	Woodland: Wolford Wood and woodland species.
Plate 13	Woodland: species found at Wolford Wood.
Plate 14	Calcareous grassland: Bishops Bowl & Grove Hill.
Plate 15	Calcareous grassland species.
Plate 16	Heathland: Sutton Park.
Plate 17	Heathland: species found at Sutton Park.
Plate 18	Heathland: Grendon Common.
Plate 19	Wetland: Alvecote Pools.
Plate 20	Wetland: Brandon Marsh and wetland species.
Plate 21	Wetland species.
Plate 22	Quarries: Judkins Quarry and associated species.
Plate 23	Larvae.
Plate 24	Aberrations and moths with mixed fortunes.

Foreword

Warwickshire, one of England's most geographically central counties, boasts an extremely good list of moth species recorded over the last 150 years.

In recent years the study of moths has been enhanced by naturalists developing a new interest in this group. The County of Warwickshire has maintained a hard core of entomologists, some pure lepidopterists, for a much longer time. This is reflected in the notes and records made in the Victoria County History (published in 1904). It seems that much has changed in the County with the expansion of cities, such as Birmingham and Coventry, and even towns swelling in size as the populations grow larger. Changes in land use have also put pressures on wildlife with the systematic removal of hedgerows and destruction of broadleaved woodland, often being replaced by rather more sterile conifer plantations. Fortunately, fragments of habitat rich in wildlife still exist under the protection of sympathetic landowners; now these are being properly managed, their potential for supporting a large diversity of species has increased. Previous industrial sites, now being returned to nature in the form of abandoned quarries and disused railway lines, are hosting a diversity of wildlife.

In the past recording of moths was rather an individual pastime, but nowadays most moth recorders are in close contact with the County Recorder and the collation of data means that the status of species distribution and populations are much better understood. The national media has become more aware of the growing popularity of invertebrates and moth recording now receives regular coverage. This has increased the amount of people involved in the subject. Group meetings now take place throughout the County with new and interesting sites being investigated, some for the first time.

The future for moths and moth recording in Warwickshire is certainly going in the right direction and hopefully those reading this book in years to come will appreciate the efforts and dedication of those involved in this study, both past and present. Over 450 contributors have submitted records and data for this book to be produced and the author should be congratulated for his devoted work, which will stand as a landmark for the study of entomology on a local basis.

Jim Porter, December 2005

Introduction

This book is the most comprehensive work ever produced on the larger moths of Warwickshire. It includes information on foodplants, flight periods, historic changes in distribution, population trends, habitat requirements and moth conservation. This wealth of information brings together the knowledge of local lepidopterists past and present, thereby providing for the first time a complete history of almost 600 species of macro-moths that have occurred since the nineteenth century. The enthusiastic participation of scores of individuals, who have contributed so many records over the years, and without which this book would not have been possible, is greatly appreciated.

The species covered in this book are the 'macrolepidoptera' or 'macro-moths', as defined in key works such as South (1907), Skinner (1984) and Waring, Townsend & Lewington (2003). In addition to macrolepidoptera there are a substantial number of mostly smaller 'micro-moths' (microlepidoptera); these have been subject to some attention during the last few decades but insufficient to merit inclusion in this volume. It is hoped that a separate book will follow in the near future to fulfil this aim.

The first comprehensive list of Warwickshire moths, compiled by H. Arthur Doubleday and William Page, was included in the *Victoria County History* of 1904. This publication contained brief notes on the distribution and status of all species of Lepidoptera in the Vice-County of Warwickshire (the biological county established in the nineteenth century based largely upon the old county boundary). In 1987, Warwickshire Museum published *The Lepidoptera of Warwickshire. Parts One & Two* by Roger Smith and David Brown (Eds. Hough, N. & Copson, P.). This included distribution maps and brief notes on the butterflies and larger moths of the County. A revised macro-moth checklist compiled by David Brown can be found in Roger Smith's 1998 publication *The Lepidoptera of Warwickshire 1900–1995. An Historical Summary*. These publications heightened the interest in Lepidoptera and created an upsurge in recording, which has in turn led to more detailed distribution maps. It is hoped that this book will trigger a similar response and provide a foundation for future studies on the moths of Warwickshire.

Former Warwickshire Lepidopterists

In the middle of the nineteenth century Warwickshire lepidopterists were building the foundations of our knowledge of the larger moths. The earliest known records in the County are from as far back as 1846, in which year W.C.E. Wheeler reported Convolvulus Hawk-moth *Agrius convolvuli* in numbers at Wolford. However, our knowledge of the former lepidopterists themselves is, in many cases, very slight. Information uncovered so far is summarised in this section and it is hoped that this will encourage others to come forward with more.

Most of the early lepidopterists were collectors, without whose interest we would have known very little about the moths of Warwickshire. It has to be remembered that they lacked modern monitoring tools such as mercury vapour light traps. Consequently, far more of their time was spent in the field diligently searching, sweeping and beating for larvae and pupa-digging at the foot of trees. Many hours would also be passed examining palings, posts or tree trunks for resting moths. After dark 'sugaring' was practised, as well as searching for moths feeding on natural blossoms such as sallow catkins in the springtime and Ivy bloom during the autumn. Tilley lamps, or their equivalent, would have been used for locating moths at night.

Nineteenth and Early Twentieth Century

The *Victoria County History* (1904) acknowledged F. Enock's local list for the Birmingham district, published in 1870. This appears to be the earliest known published list of Lepidoptera in Warwickshire.

The introduction to the Lepidoptera section of *Victoria County History* 1904 provides us with the first clear idea of the number of lepidopterists involved in Warwickshire at that time. Special mention is made of William G. Blatch, who was an active fieldworker and provided a vast number of records for the survey. Blatch, an early evangelist and secretary (later superintendent) of the Midland Counties Idiot Asylum, from its foundation in 1868 until his death in 1900, was undoubtedly an exceptional lepidopterist and coleopterist. He was also a co-founder of the Birmingham Entomological Society in 1888 with Colbran Wainwright and Ralph. C. Bradley. The latter made the first systematic assemblage of records for the *Lepidoptera of the Birmingham Plateau* survey in 1894 and maintained this for nearly 20 years. A tobacconist by trade, Bradley was primarily interested in the Diptera but formed a fine collection of microlepidoptera which has withstood critical examination and is now housed at the Birmingham Museum. Colbran Wainwright, a jeweller and watchmaker, was, like Bradley, particularly interested in the Diptera, being recognised as a European authority on the *Tachinidae*. He lived until 1948.

Many others supplied lists of Lepidoptera to the *Victoria County History* of 1904. Atherstone figured prominently in the publication and the provider of records for this district was a distinguished lepidopterist, Charles Baker, who had amassed a magnificent collection of butterflies and moths by the first decade of the twentieth century. He gave a lecture to the recently established 'Atherstone Archaeological Society and Field Club' in March 1913 at which he exhibited a large number of moths. He died on 6 May 1916, aged 79, after suffering a traumatic few months following the death of his beloved eldest son, the Reverend C.H. Baker in September 1915. Other principal recorders, about whom less information is available, were G.W. Wynn (Marston Green), H.W. Ellis (Knowle), W. Kiss (Knowle), Reverend Bree (Allesley), J. Furness (Overslade), N.V. Sidgwick (Rugby) and Reverend Wratislaw (Rugby). The southern half of Warwickshire was represented by Dr P.P. Baly (Warwick), W.C.E.

Wheeler and Mr Austen (Wolford), whilst Reverend J.H. Bloom and L.C. Keighley-Peach provided records from Whitchurch, Idlicote and Ettington.

First Half of the Twentieth Century

In the early decades of the twentieth century there was an increase in entomological activity with many accomplished lepidopterists contributing to knowledge of their own respective areas. Those born during this era were to become an exclusive band of individuals who, having begun their entomological lives using traditional collecting methods, would eventually live to witness and enjoy the early use of mercury vapour light at the beginning of the 1950s.

It is difficult to include all the enthusiastic and dedicated lepidopterists, but some of the more influential figures of Warwickshire who were active during the first half of the twentieth century are included here:

Lt Colonel William Bowater, MC, TD, DL, FRES (1880–1973) followed in the footsteps of his father and grandfather by becoming a dental surgeon. He was Bachelor of Dental Surgery, a member of the Royal College of Surgeons, Licentiate of the Royal College of Physicians and a life member of the British Dental Association.

William was a steadfast and loyal member of Birmingham Natural History Society and served as President in 1947, 1948 and again in 1967. His willingness to help and unfailing courtesy made him a tremendous asset to the Society. In the days before everyone had a car he was generous in the use of his vehicle for outings, and when unable to attend himself would often lend it to a friend. His own particular interest was in heredity and in earlier years much work was achieved with Scalloped Hazel *Odontopera bidentata*, a variety of which was named ab. *bowateri*.

Stuart E. Wace Carlier (1899–1962) was trained in field observation from the earliest years of his life by his father, Professor E. Wace Carlier; this early tuition remained an integral part of his outlook on Natural History. Stuart was a fine all round naturalist with an encyclopaedic knowledge of the insect world and for many years was Consulting Entomologist to the Birmingham Museum. He was one of the most energetic recorders in the Birmingham district and made most of his collecting trips by bicycle. His specialist interest in both micro and macrolepidoptera proved invaluable in providing a continuity of records for the first half of the twentieth century.

F.A. Noble in 'An appreciation of Stuart E. Wace Carlier' (*Birmingham Natural History Society Proceedings*, Vol. 20, No. 2, 1963) recalls how Stuart would always be keen and ready to venture forth on any field excursion, no matter how unexpected or irrespective of the time of day: 'The frugal meal was finished, the concert on the wireless switched off, his equipment hurriedly gathered and away we would go. Cannock Chase or Borth Bog, Wilmcote or Oversley Wood, winter or summer, it was all the same to him.'

H.E. Hammond (1902–1963) had a general interest in entomology but was primarily a lepidopterist. He was a most dedicated and meticulous field worker, conducting much of his valuable work in the Birmingham district.

J.M. Price, in his publication *Lepidoptera of the Midland (Birmingham) Plateau* (1993), pays special tribute to H.E. Hammond and reminds us how he was so instrumental in transforming what had become a very haphazard project into a viable proposition. 'Ted', as he was affectionately known, joined the Birmingham Natural History Society in 1938 and was an inspiration to fellow members. He was particularly interested in the life histories of Lepidoptera and added greatly to the County's knowledge on larvae and associated foodplants. He became a great expert in the preservation of larvae and amassed a tremendous collection. He perfected this art during the last 20 years of his life, 'blowing' thousands of larvae and distributing them to individuals, educational centres and museums at home and abroad, where the exquisitely preserved specimens have found permanent places. Many are still housed in Warwick museum. Ill health had forced Ted to give up active fieldwork in 1953, but he showed great courage and determination in the face of constant adversity and is remembered for his encouragement and kindness to both young and old.

Frederick Henry Latham (1913–1977) was born in Birmingham and on completing school education immediately joined the family business of industrial brush makers. Under the tuition of his father he started 'at the bottom of the ladder' as a bench-hand; this initiation proved invaluable when, in 1935 at the age of 22, he found himself in charge of the business following the death of his father.

For some years such circumstances left him little time to pursue any hobbies but he did manage to retain an interest in botany and ornithology. In future years he was to develop a great interest in Lepidoptera and in 1945 was elected a Fellow of the Royal Entomological Society.

He was widely regarded as the Midlands' expert on 'pugs' and in his collection, now housed in Warwick Museum, there are almost 700 specimens of this genus. All are immaculately set and mostly bred specimens, representing almost the entire British list.

Harry, as he was known to his friends, was a most valuable member of Birmingham Natural History Society and gave frequent talks, as well as contributing to various public exhibitions of Lepidoptera. In 1951 he introduced the *Bulletin* and subsequently gave much time editing and occasionally typing, as well as advising and carrying out research on behalf of the members. John M. Price in 'An appreciation of F.H. Latham' (*Birmingham Natural History Society Proceedings* Vol. 25, No. 1, 1983) recalls how members were occasionally inflicted with Harry's poetic verse. On one such occasion in an April editorial, Harry recounted investigating a reported roosting of House Martins in February at the Cross and Bowling Green Inn, and also referred to finding the Peach Blossom *T. batis* in the lighted porch of that inn, without making it clear that he was referring to another occasion at a different time of year. He was later taken to task by his great friend, Stuart Carlier, who wrote:

> 'Someone if in a mood, censorial,
> At least has read your editorial.
> April !??
> So early in the year this date is,
> I cannot 'swallow' your *T. batis*,
> The Cross and Green must have for sale,
> A very potent brew of ale —
> In fact, dear Sir, I wish I knew
> Which was lit-up, their porch or you.
>
> P.S.   If this makes neither rhyme or reason
> Remember Spring's the balmy season.'

To which Harry replied:

'I wish I had the space or time,
To write the whole of this in rhyme,
But after all, the whole world knows,
That amateurs are verse than prose.'

George Bertram Manly (Year of birth unknown) George, born and brought up in Birmingham, was a member of Birmingham Natural History Society from 1930 to 1955, acting as President of the Entomology section in 1951. He worked in the insurance industry, but spent most of his leisure time in pursuit of the larger moths and built up a fine collection. George was a dedicated and skilled fieldworker, adding greatly to our knowledge of the much under-recorded Sesiidae family (clearwings). His activities were concentrated mainly at sites in west Warwickshire, including Clowes Wood, Austy Wood, May's Wood, Snitterfield Bushes and Sutton Park. He was in his seventies when he died in 1955.

Francis Anthony Noble (1917–1985) was interested in natural history from early childhood and went on to become an excellent all-round naturalist and photographer with a main interest in entomology. After obtaining a degree at Birmingham University, Francis pursued a career in Social Services, firstly working at the Blind School in Harborne, before joining the Children's Department of the Local Authority in Birmingham. In 1972 he became a principal Officer in the newly formed Social Service Department with responsibility for co-ordinating and advising on all aspects of child care. He was deeply religious and a popular lay preacher, as a member of Carrs Lane Baptist Church.

Francis was a most dedicated fieldworker, much of which is reflected in this book, encountering some interesting species during a detailed study of Bannam's Wood. He was an important and highly valued member of Birmingham Natural History Society, of which he was General Secretary for 20 years. He spent much time rearranging the Society's Lepidoptera collections, which he found more attractive than collation of the accumulated records.

Francis contributed enormously to the *Lepidoptera of the Midland (Birmingham) Plateau* survey with a wealth of records from various collecting sites. Following the untimely deaths of Carlier and Hammond the task of directing the survey fell to him.

Sadly, he suffered long term ill health in the form of crippling arthritis which enforced early retirement from Social Services. In spite of the severe pain and difficulties encountered, he bravely managed to continue fieldwork until the time of his death in 1985.

Professor F.W. Shotton (1906–1990) was born in Coventry and quickly developed an enthusiasm for archaeology as a boy, going on to become a lecturer in geology at both Birmingham and Cambridge Universities. His life and work has been well documented in recent years and a local BBC radio station mentioned how he plotted the beaches for the D-Day landing.

His interests in Natural History were wide and he built up reference collections of Coleoptera (beetles), Hemiptera (plant and water bugs), Neuroptera (lacewings) and Diptera (flies), in addition to Lepidoptera.

Fred was a loyal and dedicated member of Coventry and District Natural History and Scientific Society for a record 70 years, in which time he served as both Vice President and President. He was a familiar figure on field excursions, invariably armed with his two favourite implements—a sweep net and a pond net. In the days before MV light, Fred's car headlamps were frequently shone onto a suspended white sheet attached to trees. On a number of occasions members of the Society remember having to push-start Fred's car at the end of each session as by then the battery was flat.

Arthur Norman Thomas (1914–2004) was an expert lepidopterist and photographer who lived in Coventry and spent many years of his long life studying the moths of Tile Hill Wood Nature Reserve. He added a number of new species of both micro- and macrolepidoptera to the reserve list. 'Tom', as he was affectionately known, was secretary of the Entomological section of Coventry and District Natural History and Scientific Society for five years and organised the section's meetings.

In addition to MV light or car headlights (in the days before generators) Tom would use his own sugar recipe. If it proved to be a poor night other members would make jokes about 'Tommy's moth repellent'—a teasing which he always took in good heart.

Trevor Trought (1891–1970) was a former County Recorder for the larger moths of Warwickshire. He was a famous and well respected lepidopterist who lived in the south of the County at Tysoe, where he added many interesting species to the County list in the early days of mercury vapour light traps. His extensive collection is housed in Warwick County Museum whilst his notebooks can be found in the British Natural History Museum in London.

Trevor Trought was employed by the Sudan Cotton Corporation and Jordan Government. He was an authority on the genetics of cotton growing and was interested in the butterflies of India and the Middle East. In 1947 he was elected a Fellow of the Royal Entomological Society of London.

In addition to the above there were many other former lepidopterists in the County who recorded during the first half of the twentieth century. The north Warwickshire contingent included G.A. Arnold, M.W. Beale, G.T. Bethune-Baker, K. Davison, W.H. Flint, J.H. Grant, Reverend K.E. Hood, A. King, H.T. King, F.H. Lees, E.H. Sills, F.V. Sills, P. Siviter-Smith, E.A.B. Stanton, G.P. Sutton, R.G. Warren and E.V. Whitby.

The Coventry and District Natural History and Scientific Society had a further band of keen lepidopterists, including M.E. Castle, J.E. Fawcett and J.W. Saunt, who contributed greatly to the Tile Hill Wood moth list.

East Warwickshire had been represented by, amongst others, Dr. K.C. Greenwood of Pailton, L. Raven, who actively worked the Princethorpe woodland complex, and A.H. Kennard, who contributed valuable work in the Long Itchington and Southam district.

Mid-Warwickshire had several former enthusiasts, including G.C. Grant, W.T. Taylor, W. Floyd, and E.P. Sharman, who assisted for many years with the processing of moth records for the Biological Records Centre at Warwick Museum.

Warwickshire—The County

Warwickshire is England's most central county and spans some 60 miles in length from the Staffordshire border in the north to the south where it meets Oxfordshire. It is roughly 40 miles from the Worcestershire and Gloucestershire borders in the west to the edges of Northamptonshire and Leicestershire in the east. Warwickshire is a lowland county at the watershed of two great river systems: the River Tame and its tributaries flowing north into the Trent and then the North Sea, and the River Avon and its tributaries flowing south-west towards the Severn and Irish Sea. Most of the County contains broad flood plains and gentle hills hardly rising above 150 metres (500 feet). Higher ground occurs in the north, where a ridge stretching from Nuneaton to Grendon almost reaches 180 metres (600 feet). In the south and east of the County higher ground (the Northamptonshire Wolds and Cotswolds) marks the boundary with Northamptonshire, Oxfordshire and Worcestershire. The highest point in the County is Ebrington Hill, near Ilmington on the edge of the Cotswolds, where the contour reaches 259 metres (850 feet). Warwickshire's geographical position, at the heart of England, and its generally low-lying nature makes the climate moderate, as south-westerly gales and northerly winds have usually lost some of their impact on reaching the district. Summer temperatures may be a degree or two higher than at the coast but frosts are more noticeable.

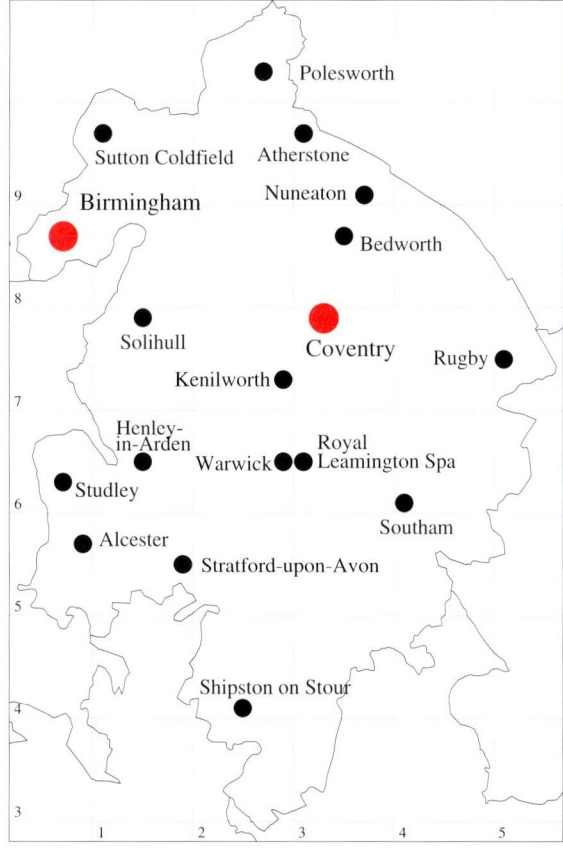

Figure 1. Major population centres in Warwickshire.

This central position results in a particularly interesting selection of moths as ranges of certain northern and southern species appear to overlap. It marks, for example, one of the most southerly stations for Angle-striped Sallow *Enargia paleacea* and yet contains one of the more northerly outlying populations of Great Oak Beauty *Hypomecis roboraria*.

Unfortunately, as with many English counties, a significant amount of the countryside has been lost to urban development in the last 200 years. Agricultural intensification and changes in woodland management have damaged the ecological value of much that remains. Habitats most affected have been species-rich grassland, heathland and coppiced broadleaved woodland. The population centres of Birmingham and Coventry dominate urban Warwickshire with populations of over 1 million and 300,000 respectively (Fig. 1). There are a further three towns with populations of around 60,000 people (Nuneaton, Rugby, and Royal Leamington Spa) and another three of about 20,000 (Kenilworth, Warwick and Stratford-upon-Avon).

The construction of the M40 motorway in the early 1990s considerably reduced the travelling time to London and the south-east, which has resulted in a huge demand for further housing in the south midlands and much recent development. Some of this demand is being met by building on 'brownfield' sites, though ironically many of these are much more species rich than the agricultural landscape now typically afforded more protection. Today the surviving habitats of Warwickshire tend to exist as small isolated patches within inhospitable farmland or townscapes (source: Habitat Biodiversity Audit map for Warwickshire, Coventry & Solihull). Losses have been counterbalanced to some extent by the gain of new valuable wildlife sites in abandoned quarries, railway lines and some old industrial sites. Gardens and urban habitats are also proving to be more interesting for moths than had been previously thought and local garden moth trapping is producing some interesting results in surprising places.

Geology of Warwickshire

by John Radley and Steven Falk—Warwickshire Museum

The County can be divided into three geological regions:
- The clay-dominated Jurassic terrain of the south and east, which is augmented by sandstones, ironstones and 'Cotswold' limestones.
- The Warwickshire coalfield, dominated by older sandstones and clays.
- The Triassic terrain, dominated by Mercia mudstone surrounding the coalfields to the north-west of the Jurassic terrain.

Jurassic geology, and the immediately adjacent late Triassic White Lias (exposed at sites such as Ufton Fields), has given rise to 'calcareous' (lime-containing) soils in many parts of the south and east, except where this is masked by thicker cappings of superficial sands and clays. The latter is particularly evident within sites like Whichford Wood and Oversley Wood, which are characterised by lime-hating bracken. Calcareous soils support the growth of 'calcicolous' (lime-loving) plants; moths associated with them include Ruddy Carpet *Catarhoe rubidata*, Pretty Chalk Carpet *Melanthia procellata* and Shaded Pug *Eupithecia subumbrata*. The best calcicolous communities tend to form in old limestone and Lias clay quarries and cuttings where pure limestone or lime-rich clays are exposed over extensive areas (e.g. the Harbury and Southam quarry complexes). A few of the woods in this part of Warwickshire, such as Wolford and Ufton, also support some shade-preferring calcicolous plants, including Wild Privet and Spurge Laurel with their associated insects.

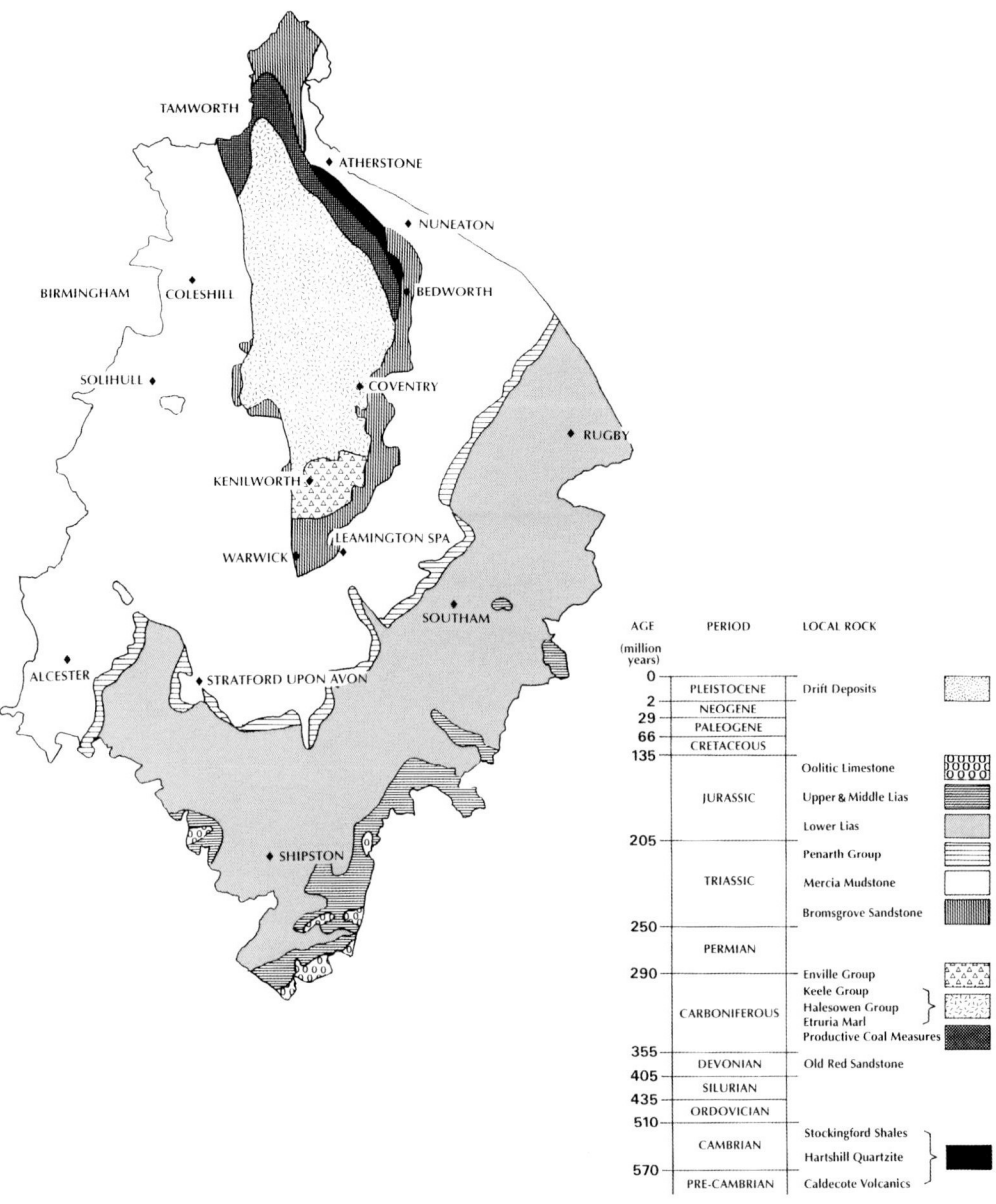

Figure 2. The solid geology of Warwickshire (courtesy of Warwickshire Wildlife Trust).

By contrast, the solid geology of the north and west, plus the extensive areas of glacial sands and gravels ('drift'), has resulted in somewhat acidic soils, in most parts lacking key minerals such as lime. This supports the growth of acidophilous (acid-loving) and calcifugous (lime-hating) plants; moths associated with these include Map-winged Swift *Hepialus fusconebulosa*, Barred Chestnut *Diarsia dahlii* and Beautiful Yellow Underwing *Anarta myrtilli*. The most acidic soils traditionally tended to exist within our heaths and bogs, though most of these have now been lost through agricultural improvement to produce better soils for crop growth and pasture. However, some small areas of new acidophilous vegetation can be found on some of the spoilheaps produced by the coal industry (e.g. at Grendon Common and Alvecote).

Interestingly, certain moth species can show distributions that are much more restricted than their foodplant(s), resulting in a seemingly calcicolous insect associated with a widespread foodplant. Classic examples of this are the Chalk Carpet *Scotopteryx bipunctaria cretata* and Six-Belted Clearwing *Bembecia ichneumoniformis*, which feed on trefoils (*Lotus* species). This may be linked to the need for particularly large and dense stands of *Lotus,* which tend to occur in old calcareous quarries, or the need for the foodplant to exist in particularly hot locations with plentiful bare soil. This is a rather different scenario to that where *Lotus* occurs within an old meadow or an exposed area of heathland.

In a number of cases, the cultivation of either calcicolous or acidophilous plants in gardens can extend their distributions significantly and sometimes those of the moths that feed on them; for example, Mullein *Shargacucullia verbasci* (garden mulleins), Streak *Chesias legatella* (ornamental brooms), True Lover's Knot *Lycophotia porphyrea* and Narrow-winged Pug *Eupithecia nanata* (both on garden heathers).

In essence, the effects of geology are pronounced, but have been rather diluted as we have introduced non-native foodplants and altered the natural distributions of native plant species that were formerly restricted to a particular soil type.

Habitats

Woodland

The natural broadleaved forest of Small-leaved Lime, elm, oak, Ash, Alder and birch (the 'wildwood'), which covered Warwickshire after the end of the last ice age, is now almost entirely gone. Although remnants of ancient woodland still exist, only about 5% of Warwickshire's land surface is wooded—one of the lowest proportions of any county in England. Unfortunately a significant amount of this consists of conifer plantation. Even where old woods have been spared coniferisation or felling, the widespread cessation of coppicing in the latter half of the twentieth century has resulted in many formerly fine woods, once full of flowery clearings, becoming densely shaded with a consequent reduction in moth diversity.

The woodlands in the south of the County (Fig. 3), such as Bowshot, Withycombe, Bannam's, Weethley, Rough Hill Wood, Old Park Wood, Whichford, Wolford, Hampton Wood, Snitterfield Bushes and Oversley Wood—many with a calcareous character—are particularly important for locally and Nationally Scarce species of moths. Despite extensive coniferisation and the clearance of large areas of Aspen and birch during the 1980s, Oversley Wood is without doubt the finest site for larger moths in the County today. Over 360 species have been recorded, including Light Orange Underwing *Archiearis notha*, False Mocha *Cyclophora porata*, Pinion-spotted Pug *Eupithecia insigniata*, Valerian Pug *Eupithecia valerianata*, Little Thorn *Cepphis advenaria*, Silver Cloud *Egira conspicillaris*, Dotted Chestnut *Conistra rubiginea*, Angle-striped Sallow *Enargia paleacea* and Mere Wainscot *Chortodes fluxa* (all of which are Nationally Scarce species). In addition to this splendid list of macro-moths, are several proposed Red Data Book (pRDB) species of micro-moths, including *Sciota hostilis*, *Salebriopsis albicilla*, and *Phyllonorycter sagitella*.

To the north-east of Royal Leamington Spa lies the Princethorpe woodland complex—the largest concentration of woodland in the County and an area famous for both butterflies and moths. The complex includes Ryton, Wappenbury, Old Nun, Waverley, Bubbenhall and Princethorpe Great Woods, all of which have retained at least some areas of ancient broadleaved woodland. Ryton Wood is a particularly fine example, containing Pedunculate

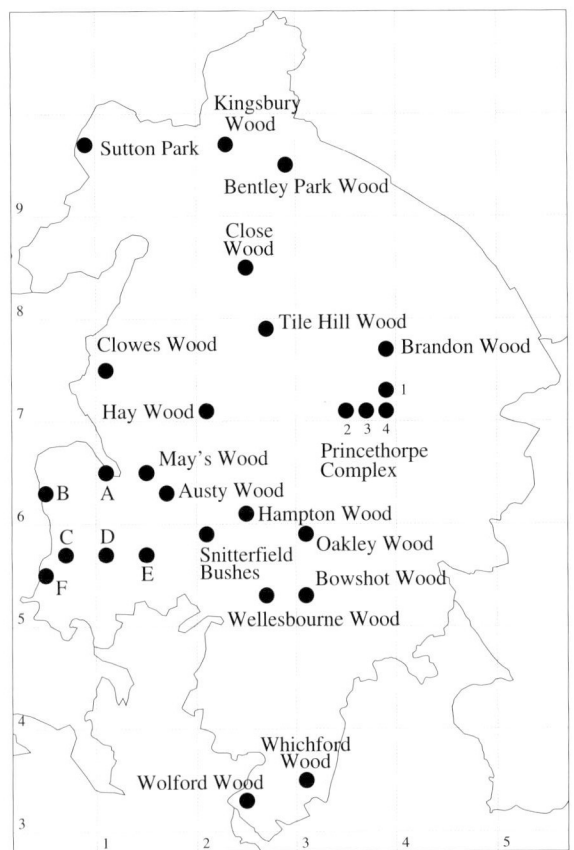

Figure 3. Woodland habitats.

Oak beneath which there is a Hazel understorey, some of which is being actively coppiced. Its species list is second only to Oversley Wood with an impressive 353 species of larger moth noted, including Light Orange Underwing *Archiearis notha*, Cloaked Carpet *Euphyia biangulata*, Great Oak Beauty *Hypomecis roboraria* and Mere Wainscot *Chortodes fluxa* (all of which are Nationally Scarce species).

The woods occurring in the north-west of the County are situated on acidic soils and many typically have a prolific ground cover of Bracken. Most contain remnants of ancient broadleaved woodland, including both Sessile Oak and Pedunculate Oak, Silver Birch and Downy Birch with an understorey of Rowan, Holly and to a lesser extent buckthorn. Kingsbury Wood and Monks Park/Bentley Park Woods are especially noted for a number of locally important species of moth, including the few surviving colonies of Clouded Magpie *Abraxas sylvata*. Other woodlands with a similar range of plants include Sutton Park, Hartshill Hayes, Windmill Naps, Hay Wood, Tile Hill Wood, Crackley Wood at Kenilworth and Binley Woods to the east of Coventry (comprising Piles Coppice and Brandon Wood).

The richest woodland for macro-moths in the north-west of the County is undoubtedly Clowes Wood, which has been well frequented by lepidopterists since the early years of the twentieth century. On its acid soils are areas of ancient oak and Beech plus small sections of heath, meadow and marsh. A clearing containing Bilberry supports a colony of Beautiful Snout *Hypena crassalis*, whilst other Nationally Local species include Blackneck *Lygephila pastinum*,

Barred Hook-tip *Watsonalla cultraria,* Triple-spotted Pug *Eupithecia trisignaria* and (Nationally Scarce) Light Orange Underwing *Archiearis notha.*

Hedges and the Loss of Elm Trees

The countryside of Warwickshire has been subject to enclosure with hedges for many centuries. The hedge systems of the Arden in the north and west are generally the oldest and richest, whilst those in the east and south tend to date from the Enclosure Acts of the seventeenth and eighteenth centuries and usually surround larger field systems. Many hedges have been grubbed out in post-war years, and Warwickshire suffered more than most counties from the ravages of Dutch elm disease, which profoundly affected our surviving hedgerows. The English Elm was formerly so common it was described as the 'Warwickshire Weed' and perhaps gave rise to the well-known saying 'Leafy Warwickshire'. Thousands of mature elm trees lining lanes and fields added both shelter and character to the countryside. Over 99% were lost to disease from the early 1970s onwards, radically altering the landscape. Several species were adversely affected by the epidemic. The White-spotted Pinion *Cosmia diffinis* suffered the most and is now almost certainly extinct. There are signs that its congener, the Lesser-spotted Pinion *C. affinis*, is managing to survive at low density on elm re-growth and it is hoped that populations will gradually recover. Other species to be adversely affected were Clouded Magpie *Abraxas sylvata*, Dusky-lemon Sallow *Xanthia gilvago* and rural populations of Lime Hawk-moth *Mimas tiliae*.

Grassland and Post-industrial Sites

Although Warwickshire does not contain any of the classic limestone downland characteristic of the Cotswolds, it is partly compensated by the valuable calcareous habitats, especially grasslands and early successional stages, created by limestone quarrying. These man-made habitats can be found in a broad band running south-west to north-east from the Cotswolds to Rugby (Fig. 4). Limestone has been quarried at places like Harbury, Ufton, Long Itchington, Bishops Itchington, Stockton and Rugby, leaving spoil heaps, embankments and railway cuttings as well as the quarry voids themselves. Some of these sites are Sites of Special Scientific Interest (SSSI) and a few are Warwickshire Wildlife Trust (WWT) reserves—carefully managed by regular cutting or grazing to prevent them from turning into dense scrub and eventually woodland.

Scrub encroachment is a major threat to these sites. Wilmcote Rough, which was an important wildlife site in the 1930s and 1940s, had lost much of its Lepidoptera value by the late 1970s due to scrub invasion. Nationally Scarce species such as Lace Border *Scopula ornata* and Ruddy Carpet *Catarhoe rubidata* are seemingly extinct there, and although some scrub clearance has taken place they have not reappeared. Fortunately there are surviving colonies of *Catarhoe rubidata* at Grove Hill near Alcester and Goldicote Cutting near Ettington, which are both managed by WWT volunteers. Other key sites such as Nelson's Quarry, Stockton, have also lost much of their scientific value due to scrub invasion; the Chalk Carpet *Scotopteryx bipunctaria cretata* and Light Feathered Rustic *Agrotis cinerea* (both Nationally Scarce) have disappeared as a consequence.

The Bishops Bowl/Bishops Hill complex, between Harbury and Bishops Itchington, is a vitally important site for moths but is threatened by building development. The area contains one of Warwickshire's last remaining populations of Chalk Carpet *Scotopteryx bipunctaria cretata.* Ashlawn Cutting Nature Reserve, an area of calcareous grassland located on the former Great Central Railway Line, contains the County's only surviving colony of the Forester

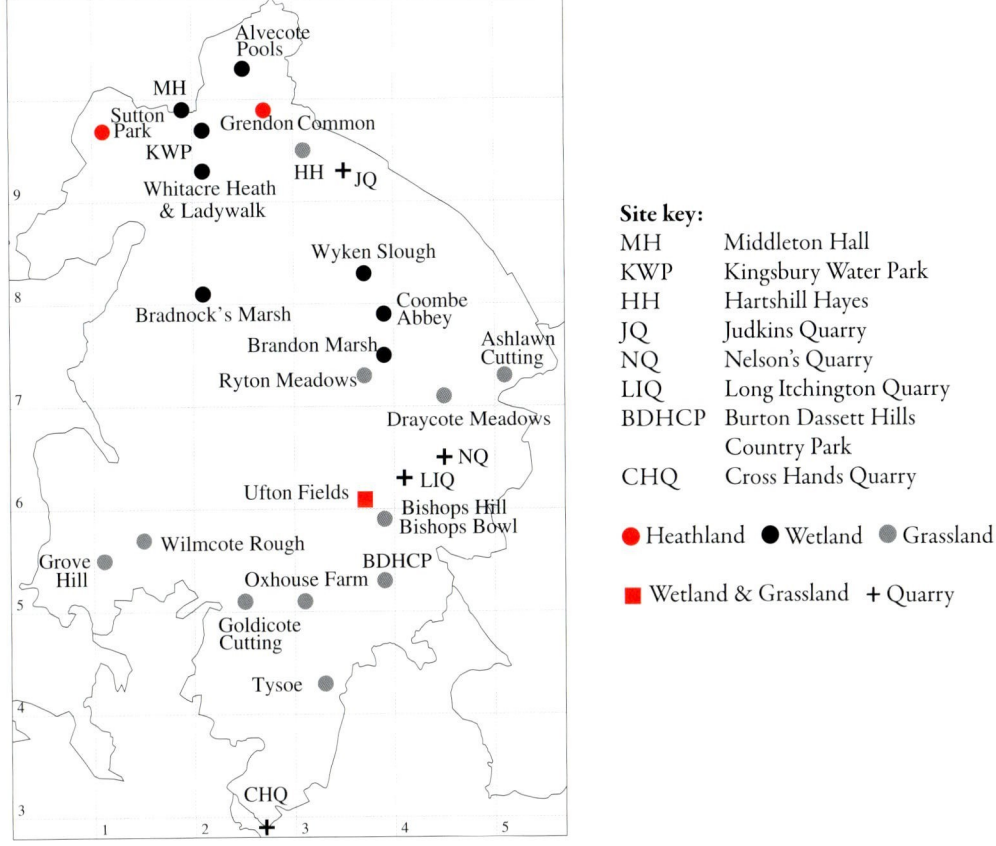

Figure 4. Grassland, post-industrial, heathland and wetland habitats.

Adscita statices (Nationally Local). Continuing site management by Butterfly Conservation members prevents the area being engulfed by scrub. Sites such as these reveal the importance of having plenty of volunteers and suitable equipment.

A good number of post-industrial sites and non-calcareous quarries occur in the north of our area and are important for many species. Colliery closures between the 1960s and 1980s left a legacy of spoil heaps and derelict land, and some huge tips were formed from waste minerals. Now vegetated, these areas are important sites for species such as Annulet *Charissa obscurata* and Pimpinel Pug *Eupithecia pimpinellata* (both Nationally Local).

Heathland

Heathland, characterised by heathers, Gorse, Broom and birch, was once widespread in the Midlands but has been largely destroyed by agricultural improvement and development. In Warwickshire this internationally important habitat is now confined to just two sites—Sutton Park and Grendon Common (Fig. 4). The latter site is too small and isolated to support a large diversity of heathland species but does contain Square-spot Dart *Euxoa obelisca grisea* (Nationally Scarce). Sutton Park, recently declared a National Nature Reserve, is the only heather terrain in the Vice-County extensive enough to support typical heathland moths such as Grass Wave *Perconia strigillaria*, Barred Chestnut *Diarsia dahlii* (both Nationally Local) and Beautiful Yellow Underwing *Anarta myrtilli*. However, the isolation of different habitats and increasing disturbance within the Park has led to a steady decline of significant species over the years.

Wetlands

Wetlands, including reedbeds and other areas dominated by sedges and rushes, are important habitats for many special moths. Brandon Marsh is undoubtedly the premier location, supporting an impressive array of wainscot species. Obscure Wainscot *Mythimna obsoleta*, Southern Wainscot *M. straminea*, Twin-spotted Wainscot *Archanara geminipuncta*, Brown-veined Wainscot *A. dissoluta*, Fen Wainscot *Arenostola phragmitidis* and Silky Wainscot *Chilodes maritimus*, all Nationally Local, occur at this site and were largely unknown in the County prior to the 1960s. The pools and marshes at Brandon originated from sand and gravel extraction, and the flooded areas were quickly colonised with reeds following the cessation of disturbance. WWT has extended the wetlands with a programme of excavations to form the Newlands reedbed. This is primarily to encourage Bitterns, but should also enhance the area for wainscot species. A chain of similar sites occurs within the Tame Valley, including Kingsbury Water Park, Middleton Hall, Ladywalk Bird Reserve and Whitacre Heath (Fig. 4).

Other key wetland sites, such as Alvecote Pools and Wyken Slough, resulted from mining subsidence, whilst wetlands at Nelson's Quarry, Stockton and Ufton Fields are the result of flooding within abandoned limestone workings. Some of the older lakes in private estates, including Coombe Abbey, Compton Verney, Farnborough Hall and Middleton Hall, contain suitable breeding territory for many interesting marshland species. Valuable wetland habitats can also be associated with water courses such as rivers and canals, but these are now much fewer due to drainage, river engineering, the effects of boat traffic and the use of banks for recreational purposes.

The Mixed Fortunes of Warwickshire's Moths

Extinct Species

Disappearances of many key species occurred in the late nineteenth and early twentieth centuries (Table 1). The reasons for extinctions at this time are rather difficult to understand. There may have been climatic causes for the loss of some, but from the Industrial Revolution onwards man started to have a major influence on the distributions and populations of moths and other wildlife. Extinctions of woodland species at the end of the nineteenth century in Warwickshire included Triangle *Heterogenea asella*, Waved Carpet *Hydrelia sylvata*, Small Chocolate-tip *Clostera pigra*, Light Crimson Underwing *Catocala promissa* and Dark Crimson Underwing *C. sponsa*. These are now graded as either Nationally Scarce or Red Data Book species.

Table 1. Species which became extinct in Warwickshire before 1950.

Vernacular Name	Scientific Name	Last Record	Habitat
Royal Mantle	*Catarhoe cuculata*	1869	Grassland
Lunar Yellow Underwing	*Noctua orbona*	1870	Open woodland/grassland
Scarce Vapourer	*Orgyia recens*	1880	Hedgerows/woodland
Dark Tussock	*Dicallomera fascelina*	1880	Heathland
Small Chocolate-tip	*Clostera pigra*	1888	Woodland
Light Crimson Underwing	*Catocala promissa*	1888	Woodland

Triangle	*Heterogenea asella*	1890	Woodland
Silvery Arches	*Polia trimaculosa*	1890	Heathland/woodland
Light Knot Grass	*Acronicta menyanthidis menyanthidis*	1899	Heathland
Dingy Mocha	*Cyclophora pendularia*	1904 (VCH)	Woodland
Marsh Carpet	*Perizoma sagittata*	1904 (VCH)	Wetland
Waved Carpet	*Hydrelia sylvata*	1904 (VCH)	Woodland
Brussels Lace	*Cleorodes lichenaria*	1904 (VCH)	Woodland/scrub
Bordered Gothic	*Heliophobus reticulata marginosa*	1904 (VCH)	Grassland
Beautiful Brocade	*Lacanobia contigua*	1904 (VCH)	Heathland/woodland
Silver Barred	*Deltote bankiana*	1904 (VCH)	Wetland/damp woodland
Dark Crimson Underwing	*Catocala sponsa*	1904 (VCH)	Woodland
Clouded Buff	*Diacrisia sannio*	1916	Heathland
Narrow-bordered Bee Hawk-moth	*Hemaris tityus*	1936	Open woodland

In the 1950s, as many important woodland sites became overgrown due to the cessation of coppicing and increasing coniferisation, further species became extinct (Table 2). These included Lead-coloured Pug *Eupithecia plumbeolata* and three day-flying moths—White-barred Clearwing *Synanthedon spheciformis*, Speckled Yellow *Pseudopanthera macularia* and Broad-bordered Bee Hawk-moth *Hemaris fuciformis*. Disappearances of others, such as Plain Clay *Eugnorisma depuncta* and Common Fan-foot *Pechipogo strigilata*, can be linked to a national decline.

The extinction of Barred Tooth-striped *Trichopteryx polycommata* in Warwickshire was due to habitat destruction on two occasions—firstly at Snitterfield Bushes to make way for a wartime aerodrome in the 1940s, and more recently at Wellesbourne Wood in 1975. Sadly this moth has not been rediscovered at these sites despite determined searches during the last 30 years.

The Argent & Sable *Rheumaptera hastata hastata,* which occupied 15 sites in the 1930s, is also feared extinct at its last remaining location. Former rotational coppicing had provided patchworks of regenerating birch in open sunny situations suitable for this day-flying moth. Although appropriate woodland management is now being practised at Hay Wood, it may have come too late to save this species from extinction in Warwickshire.

The disappearance of many hedgerows in post-war years adversely affected our Lepidoptera. The Small Eggar *Eriogaster lanestris*, a species prone to fluctuation, declined considerably in Britain during the twentieth century. Formerly larval webs had been recorded, not infrequently, in hawthorn hedgerows over a wide area of Warwickshire. A combination of indiscriminate hedge trimming, grubbing up of hedgerows, pollution from agricultural sprays, and climate change led to local extinction in the late 1940s.

Dutch elm disease in the 1970s and subsequent loss of mature English Elms from hedgerows and copses led to the disappearance of White-spotted Pinion *Cosmia diffinis*. The larvae prefer to feed on the epicormic foliage (shoots growing directly from the trunk) and until such time as the elms reach maturity there is little hope of this attractive species making a return.

Heathland, with its infertile sandy soils, was an early candidate for agricultural improvement and was later affected by urban expansion. Sutton Park became isolated and experienced local extinctions of Dark Tussock *Dicallomera fascelina* in the 1880s and Clouded Buff *Diacrisia sannio* in 1916. Since 1950 Beech Green Carpet *Colostygia olivata*, Grey Scalloped Bar *Dyscia fagaria*, Scarce Prominent *Odontosia carmelita*, Wood Tiger

Parasemia plantaginis plantaginis and Neglected Rustic *Xestia castanea* have followed suit. The loss of Sword-grass *Xylena exsoleta* would appear to be connected to a change in national distribution, having contracted northwards in recent decades, possibly in response to climate change.

Table 2. Species which have become extinct in Warwickshire since 1950 or are probably extinct.

Vernacular Name	Scientific Name	Last Record	Habitat
Small Eggar	*Eriogaster lanestris*	1950	Hedgerows
Sword Grass	*Xylena exsoleta*	1950	Heathland
White-barred Clearwing	*Synanthedon spheciformis*	1953	Woodland
Lead-coloured Pug	*Eupithecia plumbeolata*	1956	Woodland
Speckled Yellow	*Pseudopanthera macularia*	1956	Woodland
Broad-bordered Bee Hawk-moth	*Hemaris fuciformis*	1956	Woodland
Four-spotted	*Tyta luctuosa*	1957	Grassland
Beech Green Carpet	*Colostygia olivata*	1960s	Woodland/heathland
Grey Scalloped Bar	*Dyscia fagaria*	1960s	Heathland
Plain Clay	*Eugnorisma depuncta*	1960s	Woodland
Square-spotted Clay	*Xestia rhomboidea*	1960s	Woodland
Common Fan-foot	*Pechipogo strigilata*	1960s	Woodland
Neglected Rustic	*Xestia castanea*	1970s	Heathland
Wood Tiger	*Parasemia plantaginis plantaginis*	1971	Heathland
Lobster Moth	*Stauropus fagi*	1974	Woodland
Lace Border	*Scopula ornata*	1979	Grassland
White-spotted Pinion	*Cosmia diffinis*	1979	Hedgerows/copses
Galium Carpet	*Epirrhoe galiata*	1980	Grassland
Scarce Prominent	*Odontosia carmelita*	1987	Woodland
Stout Dart	*Spaelotis ravida*	1988	Grassland
Barred Tooth-striped	*Trichopteryx polycommata*	1989	Woodland
Light Feathered Rustic	*Agrotis cinerea*	1992	Grassland
Pale Shining Brown	*Polia bombycina*	1994	Grassland
Argent & Sable	*Rheumaptera hastata hastata*	1997	Woodland

Calcareous grassland species have fared particularly badly over the past 50 years through loss and deterioration of habitat. Lace Border *Scopula ornata*, Galium Carpet *Epirrhoe galiata*, Light Feathered Rustic *Agrotis cinerea* and Four-spotted *Tyta luctuosa* have been completely lost to Warwickshire. The Stout Dart *Spaelotis ravida* and Pale Shining Brown *Polia bombycina* have become nationally restricted in range during the last ten years. The former has always been prone to periodic fluctuations, but *bombycina* has undergone a more serious decline and is now rarely seen outside the Salisbury Plain area of Wiltshire.

Declining Species

Many species have shown significant declines in the last 30 years, but the reasons for this are not always understood (Table 3). In some cases, as with extinct species mentioned in the last section, factors could be directly linked to habitat deterioration/loss or climate change, whilst other causes of decline are obviously more complex. Light pollution may be a significant threat to moth populations. Artificial lighting may have many disruptive effects on moth behaviour

Table 3. Species which have noticeably declined in Warwickshire during the last 30 years.

Vernacular Name	Scientific Name	Habitat
Goat Moth	*Cossus cossus*	Hedgerows/parks
Lappet	*Gastropacha quercifolia*	Hedgerow/scrub/woodland
Lackey	*Malacosoma neustria*	General/hedgerows/gardens
Emperor Moth	*Saturnia pavonia*	Heathland
False Mocha	*Cyclophora porata*	Woodland
Dark Spinach	*Pelurga comitata*	Gardens/waste-ground
Spinach	*Eulithis mellinata*	Gardens/woodland
Autumn Green Carpet	*Chloroclysta miata*	Woodland
Tissue	*Triphosa dubitata*	Hedgerows/woodland
Juniper Pug	*Eupithecia pusillata pusillata*	Parks/gardens
Magpie	*Abraxas grossulariata*	Hedgerows/woodland/gardens
Clouded Magpie	*Abraxas sylvata*	Woodland
V-Moth	*Macaria wauaria*	Gardens
Lunar Thorn	*Selenia lunularia*	Woodland
Orange Moth	*Angerona prunaria*	Woodland
Brindled Beauty	*Lycia hirtaria*	General
Figure of Eight	*Diloba caeruleocephala*	General
Garden Tiger	*Arctia caja*	Gardens/general
Garden Dart	*Euxoa nigricans*	Gardens/general
Dotted Rustic	*Rhyacia simulans*	General
Double Dart	*Graphiphora augur*	General
Small Square-spot	*Diarsia rubi*	General
Triple-spotted Clay	*Xestia ditrapezium*	General
Glaucous Shears	*Papestra biren*	Heathland/grassland
Hedge Rustic	*Tholera cespitis*	Grassland
Blossom Underwing	*Orthosia miniosa*	Woodland
Powdered Quaker	*Orthosia gracilis*	Damp woodland/wetland/gardens
Deep-brown Dart	*Aporophyla lutulenta*	Grassland
Grey Chi	*Antitype chi*	Grassland
Brick	*Agrochola circellaris*	General
Flounced Chestnut	*Agrochola helvola*	Woodland
Brown-spot Pinion	*Agrochola litura*	General
Beaded Chestnut	*Agrochola lychnidis*	General
Dusky-lemon Sallow	*Xanthia gilvago*	Hedgerows/woodland
Lesser-spotted Pinion	*Cosmia affinis*	Hedgerows/copses
Golden Plusia	*Polychrysia moneta*	Gardens
Beautiful Golden Y	*Autographa pulchrina*	General
Plain Golden Y	*Autographa jota*	General
Gold Spangle	*Autographa bractea*	Grassland/woodland
Dark Spectacle	*Abrostola triplasia*	General
Small Purple-barred	*Phytometra viridaria*	Grassland/woodland

that in turn could impinge on reproductive success, as well as making moths more susceptible to predators (Parsons *et al.* 2005). Other factors might include land-use change, agricultural intensification (e.g. herbicide and insecticide use), urbanisation and eutrophication from air pollution by nitrates (Woiwod *et al.* 2005). The declines not only involve scarce species but common species too, and there is evidence that many formerly plentiful moths are now showing signs of diminishing populations.

Several garden species, including Dark Spinach *Pelurga comitata*, Spinach *Eulithis mellinata*, V-Moth *Macaria wauaria*, Garden Tiger *Arctia caja*, Garden Dart *Euxoa nigricans* and Golden Plusia *Polychrysia moneta*, have undergone severe declines in Warwickshire during the last 20 years. The decline of the Garden Tiger is general throughout much of southern Britain. Analysis has shown that wet winters and warm springs are particularly detrimental to this species, and that changes in distribution and abundance may be an unfortunate consequence of recent change in large-scale weather patterns over the North Atlantic (Conrad *et al.* 2003). The reasons for winter and spring weather being so critical for this species are not fully understood but are likely to be related to overwintering survival of the young hibernating larvae (Woiwod *et al.* 2005). Others suggest parasites to be the main cause of decline which would mean, judging from past events, that numbers may soon recover unless a warming climate continues (Pratt, in prep). The disappearance of many cottage gardens, the use of pesticides and a general lack of waste areas containing weeds could also have contributed to the decline of the Garden Tiger. In the case of V-Moth *Macaria wauaria* and Spinach *Eulithis mellinata* the decline in popularity of kitchen style gardens containing currant and Gooseberry may be one reason for their predicament. Other factors must be involved, however, as numbers of Phoenix *Eulithis prunata*, which has the same larval foodplants, have so far been less noticeably affected.

Increasing Species

Despite the large number of decreasing species in Warwickshire, there are a substantial number of moths that are exhibiting an upturn in fortunes, usually as part of a national pattern (Table 4). These moths are varied and frequent a diversity of habitats, though species that overwinter as adults feature well. This may be linked to milder winters in the last few decades. It is interesting that whilst moths like Red-green Carpet *Chloroclysta siterata* and Grey Shoulder-knot *Lithophane ornitopus lactipennis* have benefited, the Autumn Green Carpet *Chloroclysta miata,* which has a similar life cycle, has become much scarcer.

Table 4. Species which have significantly increased in Warwickshire since 1980.

Vernacular Name	Scientific Name	Habitat
Oak Hook-tip	*Watsonalla binaria*	Woodland/hedgerows
Pebble Hook-tip	*Drepana falcataria falcataria*	Woodland/general
Blotched Emerald	*Comibaena bajularia*	Woodland/hedgerows
Clay Triple-lines	*Cyclophora linearia*	Woodland/hedgerows
Treble Brown Spot	*Idaea trigeminata*	Woodland/hedgerows
Large Twin-spot Carpet	*Xanthorhoe quadrifasiata*	General
Blue-bordered Carpet	*Plemyria rubiginata rubiginata*	Woodland/hedgerows
Red-green Carpet	*Chloroclysta siterata*	Woodland/hedgerows
Spruce Carpet	*Thera britannica*	Woodland/parks/gardens
Juniper Carpet	*Thera juniperata*	Parks/gardens
Sandy Carpet	*Perizoma flavofasciata*	General
Double-striped Pug	*Gymnoscelis rufifasciata*	General
Satin Beauty	*Deileptenia ribeata*	Woodland
White-pinion Spotted	*Lomographa bimaculata*	Woodland/hedgerows
Clouded Silver	*Lomographa temerata*	Woodland/hedgerows

Alder Kitten	*Furcula bicuspis*	Woodland/heathland/river valleys
White Satin Moth	*Leucoma salicis*	Woodland/river valleys
Round-winged Muslin	*Thumatha senex*	Wetland/general
Orange Footman	*Eilema sororcula*	Woodland
Scarce Footman	*Eilema complana*	General
Obscure Wainscot	*Mythimna obsoleta*	Wetland
Black Rustic	*Aporophyla nigra*	General
Grey Shoulder-knot	*Lithophane ornitopus lactipennis*	Woodland/parks/gardens
Dotted Chestnut	*Conistra rubiginea*	Woodland/general
Barred Sallow	*Xanthia aurago*	Woodland/hedgerows
Sycamore	*Acronicta aceris*	General
Small Clouded Brindle	*Apamea unanimis*	Wetland/damp woodland
Large Nutmeg	*Apamea anceps*	Grassland/general
Dusky Sallow	*Eremobia ochroleuca*	Grassland/general
Small Rufous	*Coenobia rufa*	Wetland/damp woodland
Treble Lines	*Charanyca trigrammica*	Grassland/general
Green Silver-lines	*Pseudoips prasinana britannica*	Woodland
Straw Dot	*Rivula sericealis*	Grassland/general

The Black Rustic *Aporophyla nigra* has experienced one of the most dramatic increases. Following a virtual absence in the County between 1875 and 1975 it is now very common in both rural and suburban districts. Similarly, the Sycamore *Acronicta aceris*, having been recorded as singletons in 1870 and 1979, has become well-established in many areas since 1990. Two further species that have recently reappeared after a 100-year absence are Orange Footman *Eilema sororcula* and Dotted Chestnut *Conistra rubiginea*. The appearance of Orange Footman, as well as the increase of several other lichen-feeding species, could be due to a decrease in atmospheric pollution resulting in increased lichens and algae on trees and shrubs. The Dotted Chestnut experienced a national expansion in range during the 1990s. Formerly established on heathland in central southern England, it dispersed into Gloucestershire, Wiltshire and Oxfordshire, followed by Kent, Glamorgan, Essex, Hertfordshire, Buckinghamshire, Northamptonshire and Warwickshire in the early 2000s (Waring, 2003). A record seven individuals were recorded in the County during 2005.

New Additions

Moths have been added to the County list on a regular basis since recording began, and this continues into modern times with 29 new species since 1970 (Table 5). Sloe Pug *Pasiphila chloerata*, Svensson's Copper Underwing *Amphipyra berbera svenssoni* and Lesser Common Rustic *Mesapamea didyma* have recently been recognised as distinct from closely related species and no doubt existed here beforehand. Another small group of newcomers are associated with exotic trees and shrubs now grown more widely in parks and gardens. During the 1960s Juniper Carpet *Thera juniperata juniperata* was confirmed as resident in the County. It was initially spread through the sale of garden shrubs from a commercial nursery in Rugby and quickly became established in several widely separated localities. Blair's Shoulder-knot *Lithophane leautieri hesperica* has spread steadily northwards since the first British records on the Isle of Wight in 1951. Reaching Warwickshire in 1978, its dispersal was helped by widespread planting of *Cupressus* in both urban and rural districts. Freyer's Pug *Eupithecia intricata arceuthata*, a moth associated with various garden conifers, arrived during the early 1980s and quickly became established, but has never reached the high population densities of Blair's

Table 5. Species discovered to be resident in Warwickshire since 1970.

Vernacular Name	Scientific Name	Year First Noted
Varied Coronet*	Hadena compta	1970
Silky Wainscot	Chilodes maritimus	1970
Silver Cloud	Egira conspicillaris	1971
Mere Wainscot	Chortodes fluxa	1972
Southern Wainscot*	Mythimna straminea	1973
Pretty Chalk Carpet	Melanthia procellata	1974
Peacock Moth	Macaria notata	1974
Pale Oak Beauty	Hypomecis punctinalis	1975
Dwarf Cream Wave	Idaea fuscovenosa	1975
Vine's Rustic*	Hoplodrina ambigua	1976
Pimpinel Pug	Eupithecia pimpinellata	1977
Blair's Shoulder Knot*	Lithophane leautieri hesperica	1978
Freyer's Pug*	Eupithecia intricata arceuthata	1982
Sloe Pug	Pasiphila chloerata	1983
Pale Pinion*	Lithophane hepatica	1984
Waved Black*	Parascotia fuliginaria	1984
Twin-spotted Wainscot*	Archanara geminipuncta	1984
Red-necked Footman*	Atolmis rubricollis	1985
Campanula Pug	Eupithecia denotata denotata	1987
Buff Footman*	Eilema depressa	1987
Lesser Common Rustic	Mesapamea didyma	1988
Shaded Pug	Eupithecia subumbrata	1989
Valerian Pug	Eupithecia valerianata	1989
Beautiful Snout	Hypena crassalis	1989
Least Carpet	Idaea rusticata atrosignaria	1989
Svensson's Copper Underwing	Amphipyra berbera svenssoni	1990
Cloaked Carpet	Euphyia biangulata	1992
Cream-bordered Green Pea	Earias clorana	1994
Fen Wainscot	Arenostola phragmitidis	1996

* Has undergone a significant increase since first noted.

Shoulder-knot. A vagrant specimen of Cypress Pug *Eupithecia phoeniceata* was caught at Rugby in 1983 but there are no signs of this southern species becoming resident in the Midlands. The Varied Coronet *Hadena compta*, first noted breeding in Dover in 1948, is a garden species that feeds exclusively on the seeds of Sweet William throughout the larval stage. It spread quickly north and westward to become well established in Warwickshire during the 1970s. Peacock Moth *Macaria notata*, Red-necked Footman *Atolmis rubricollis*, Buff Footman *Eilema depressa*, Pale Pinion *Lithophane hepatica*, Vine's Rustic *Hoplodrina ambigua* and Waved Black *Parascotia fuliginaria* have all experienced a recent extension in range throughout southern England and become established in Warwickshire. The Least Carpet *Idaea rusticata atrosignaria* has also expanded its distribution but sporadic appearances suggest a transient population. A number of wetland species, such as Southern Wainscot *Mythimna straminea*, Twin-spotted Wainscot *Archanara geminipuncta*, Fen Wainscot *Arenostola phragmitidis*, Silky Wainscot *Chilodes maritimus* and Cream-bordered Green Pea *Earias clorana*, have spread into Warwickshire from the south and east to quickly colonise suitable marshland sites. Several other new species, such as Little Thorn *Cepphis advenaria*, Scarlet Tiger *Callimorpha dominula*, Feathered Ranunculus *Polymixis lichenea lichenea* and Marbled Green *Cryphia muralis muralis*, have been recorded in Warwickshire since 1970, but have yet to be confirmed as resident. Pine Hawk-moth *Hyloicus pinastri* is a possible future coloniser, following a substantial influx in 2005.

Immigrants

For such an inland county (Fig. 5) Warwickshire prospers well for immigrant Lepidoptera (Table 6). Species from as far afield as the Mediterranean and North Africa can sometimes make rapid incursions into our region. Sudden increases of Dark Sword-grass *Agrotis ipsilon*, Silver Y *Autographa gamma* and the pyralid Rush Veneer in local moth traps are often a quick and accurate indication of larger scale immigrations on the south coast. Long distance immigrants may follow the Bristol Channel and valleys of the higher and lower Avon for northward dispersal into the Midlands. Some of the rarer visitors to our shores, such as Blair's Mocha *Cyclophora puppillaria*, Oleander Hawk-moth *Daphnis nerii*, Silver-striped Hawk-moth *Hippotion celerio*, Cosmopolitan *Mythimna loreyi*, Ni Moth *Trichoplusia ni* and Slender Burnished Brass *Thysanoplusia orichalcea*, have occasionally reached Warwickshire.

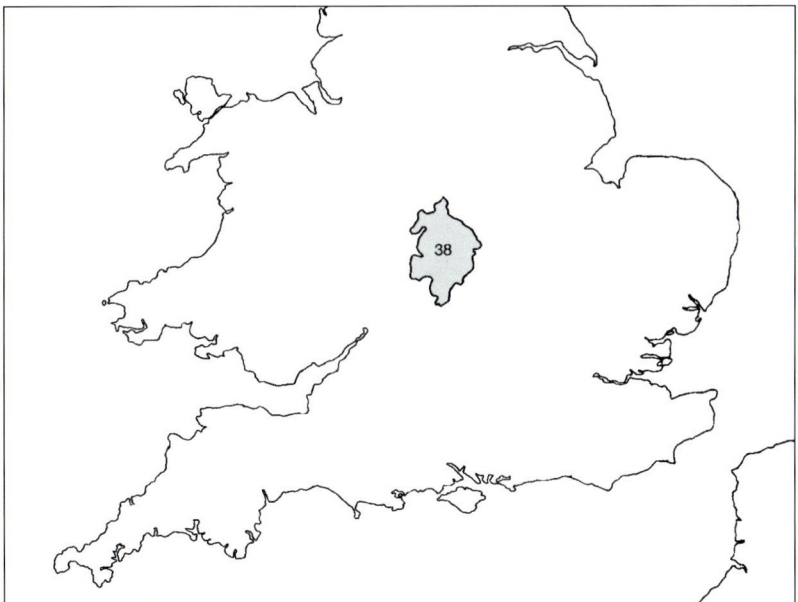

Figure 5. Warwickshire's central position.

Table 6. Immigrant species recorded in Warwickshire.

Vernacular Name	Scientific Name	First & Last Year	No. of Individuals
Blair's Mocha	*Cyclophora puppillaria*	1978	1
Vestal	*Rhodometra sacraria*	1908–2005	Approx. 200
Gem	*Orthonama obstipata*	1880–2003	71
Convolvulus Hawk-moth	*Agrius convolvuli*	1846–2004	50+
Death's-head Hawk-moth	*Acherontia atropos*	1867–2005	30+ adults & many larvae
Humming-bird Hawk-moth	*Macroglossum stellatarum*	Almost annual	Sometimes numerous

Oleander Hawk-moth	*Daphnis nerii*	1869–1961	8
Bedstraw Hawk-moth	*Hyles gallii*	1870–2003	8 adults & a few larvae
Striped Hawk-moth	*Hyles livornica*	1870–2004	9 adults, 1 larva
Silver-striped Hawk-moth	*Hippotion celerio*	1868–1977	4
Dark Sword-grass	*Agrotis ipsilon*	Annual	Sometimes numerous
Eversmann's Rustic	*Actebia fennica*	1983	1
Pearly Underwing	*Peridroma saucia*	Almost annual	Generally low numbers
Great Brocade	*Eurois occulta*	1927–1997	15
Delicate	*Mythimna vitellina*	1977–2005	18
White-speck	*Mythimna unipuncta*	1978–2000	9
Cosmopolitan	*Mythimna loreyi*	2000–2005	3
Golden-rod Brindle	*Lithomoia solidaginis*	1969–1982	5
Small Mottled Willow	*Spodoptera exigua*	1956–2005	64
Scarce Bordered Straw	*Helicoverpa armigera*	1859–2005	40
Bordered Straw	*Heliothis peltigera*	1947–2004	86
Ni Moth	*Trichoplusia ni*	1982–1996	11
Slender Burnished Brass	*Thysanoplusia orichalcea*	1983	1
Dewick's Plusia	*Macdunnoughia confusa*	1977–1991	3
Silver Y	*Autographa gamma*	Annual	Often common
Scarce Silver Y	*Syngrapha interrogationis*	1995	1
Clifden Nonpareil	*Catocala fraxini*	1880–2002	2
Paignton Snout	*Hypena obesalis*	1973	1
Plumed Fan-foot	*Pechipogo plumigeralis*	2005	1

Since 1980 there has been a noticeable increase in many of the regular immigrants from the south. The Humming-bird Hawk-moth *Macroglossum stellatarum* has now become a familiar annual visitor; Warwickshire Museum has received dozens of sightings in recent years from members of the public. The Vestal *Rhodometra sacraria*, Gem *Orthonama obstipata*, Small Mottled Willow *Spodoptera exigua*, Scarce Bordered Straw *Helicoverpa armigera* and Bordered Straw *Heliothis peltigera* have all become more frequent in the last two decades. Surprisingly, Death's-head Hawk-moth *Acherontia atropos*, which, due to its extraordinary size and habits, is often reported by members of the general public, has so far not been reported from a single moth trap in Warwickshire.

Immigrants from Scandinavia and Northern Europe are less frequent but Warwickshire has received a small selection over the years. The Great Brocade *Eurois occulta* is the most frequent, but rarer species such as Scarce Silver Y *Syngrapha interrogationis* and Clifden Nonpareil *Catocala fraxini* have very occasionally been noted. The most spectacular example of this group, however, was the sixth British record of Eversmann's Rustic *Actebia fennica* at Rugby in August 1983. The more unusual immigrants from Central Europe are only rarely observed in Warwickshire; the occurrence of the third British record of Paignton Snout *Hypena obesalis* at Charlecote in August 1973 was exceptional. A backtracking technique using wind and pressure field information from the point and time of observation found the potential source of origin to be Germany (Peter Davey pers. comm., 1990). Equally surprising was the capture of a Plumed Fan-foot *Pechipogo plumigeralis* in July 2005 at Rugby—the first to be recorded in the British Isles away from the Kent and Sussex coast.

Conservation

The conservation of Warwickshire's moths must be achieved on a landscape scale, paying particular attention to the management and protection of individual sites and habitats. Thanks largely to English Nature, WWT and the various local authorities of the area, most of the prime woodland sites in Warwickshire are either nature reserves, Sites of Special Scientific Interest (SSSIs) or both. WWT, the largest woodland landowner, has led the way in reviving traditional woodland coppicing methods. Other woodland owners have followed their lead so that many key sites are actively managed following years of neglect. Forest Enterprise now has a policy to replace conifers with broadleaved native trees in replanted ancient woodland, which may help to reverse much of the damage done during the twentieth century. The majority of large wetlands, including reedbeds, are also nature reserves or situated in well-managed estates. A number of nature reserves, country parks and public amenity areas have been established along watercourses, e.g. Kingsbury Water Park, Leamington's Leam Valley Nature Reserve and Alcester's River Arrow Nature Reserve, and water quality in streams and rivers is much improved. Calcareous grassland is a particularly vulnerable habitat in Warwickshire as so much of it is found within sites that have traditionally been classified as 'brownfield', such as disused quarries, spoil heaps and railway cuttings. This means that many such sites have been subject to development pressure. The two main heathland sites in Warwickshire are relatively secure. Sutton Park is now a National Nature Reserve; Grendon Common is being carefully managed by the Merevale Estate with the support of the Department for Environment, Food and Rural Affairs (Defra) and English Nature.

The value of the wider agricultural landscape for moths deteriorated markedly during the second half of the twentieth century due to agricultural improvement. Government incentives, designed to make Britain more self-sufficient following the Second World War, encouraged farmers to drain land and increase the size of fields at the expense of hedgerows, ditches and flowery, uncultivated corners. Much unimproved, permanent grassland was ploughed up and there was an increase in the use of fertilisers and pesticides to produce greater crop yields. Warwickshire is thought to have lost more than 95% of its species-rich grassland since 1900. Since the 1980s the Countryside Stewardship Scheme (CSS) and designation of Environmentally Sensitive Areas (ESAs) have been helping biodiversity in farmed environments. There are currently over 250 CSS agreements in Warwickshire and many of these are benefiting moths. Recent examples include scrub and grassland management along a disused railway cutting at Wolfhampcote and at Grove Hill, near Alcester.

Since 2005, CSS and ESA have been replaced by Environmental Stewardship, a two-tiered approach which offers payments to farmers for basic environmental land management under an Entry Level Scheme (ELS) and/or a Higher Level Scheme (HLS) requiring more ambitious land improvement. Both are administered by Defra's Rural Development Service (RDS). It is expected that upwards of 70% of farmers in England will enter ELS. Sensitive hedgerow management, the establishment of buffer strips and reduced agricultural inputs over a large part of the countryside should benefit moths substantially. Grants for woodland coppicing and ride management, scrub control and heathland management also have the potential to benefit many high priority moths. However, close liaison between RDS advisers, Butterfly Conservation and landowners will be crucial if agri-environment resources are to be targeted most efficiently.

Conserving Warwickshire's Scarcer Moths

Butterfly Conservation has done much to help protect key species and monitor population changes. By systematic recording, the contractions and expansions of many species have been well documented. In 1997, following the appointment of a volunteer Warwickshire Moth Officer, Regional Action Plans were implemented with the following aims:

- To identify moth species most at risk within the region.
- To understand management requirements of these species.
- To identify the most important sites for moths in the region.
- To highlight areas where there are large gaps in local knowledge and where surveying should receive priority attention.

In August 1997 the West Midlands Regional Action Plan (RAP) was published. This was a collaborative effort by three Butterfly Conservation branches—Gloucestershire, Warwickshire and West Midlands (the latter covering part of the Vice-County of Warwickshire). It was the first regional plan to be published in the UK and has served as a model for other regions to follow. The plan reflected national and regional priorities for butterflies and moths, and offered a framework from which sound conservation policies could be developed by both Butterfly Conservation and other conservation bodies. It is encouraging a more consistent approach to the conservation of Lepidoptera. RAPs highlight the main conservation considerations for 'high priority' and 'medium priority' moths and habitats in the region. For each priority species information is provided on known status, perceived threats, recent survey and monitoring work, and a description of current management measures. In each case a series of actions have been identified with target dates and the range of possible partners to be involved.

By 1999 an initial list of 53 UK Biodiversity Action Plan (UK BAP) species was formed. These are considered to be some of our most threatened moths. In that same year, Butterfly Conservation's Action for Threatened Moths Project was launched. Part of the project's remit was to oversee the implementation of the plans for the majority of the species on the UK BAP list. Surveys, monitoring work and advice to landowners have been incorporated into the programme. The National Scarce Moth Recording Scheme has also been co-ordinated by Butterfly Conservation, with the support of the Joint Nature Conservation Committee, to enable a fuller understanding of the overall distribution in the British Isles of scarce and threatened species of macro-moth. Unfortunately, these projects may have come too late to save Warwickshire's Argent & Sable *Rheumaptera hastata hastata* and Barred Tooth-striped *Trichopteryx polycommata* populations, but could help the only remaining UK BAP species in the County—the Chalk Carpet *Scotopteryx bipunctaria cretata*.

Moth conservation in Warwickshire does not operate in isolation. The Warwickshire, Coventry and Solihull Local Biodiversity Action Plan (LBAP) has action plans for 24 habitats and 26 species, including two UK BAP moths—the Argent & Sable *Rheumaptera hastata hastata* and Chalk Carpet *Scotopteryx bipunctaria cretata*. The targets in these plans are harmonised with those in the RAP and ensure that Lepidoptera gains coverage in this important process being driven by a large and exciting partnership of organisations. Their decision making could be subsequently helped by Butterfly Conservation's comprehensive coverage and documentation of the County's scarce moth species (Table 7 & 8).

Nationally Scarce Resident Species in Warwickshire

Table 7. Nationally Scarce A.
Recorded from 16–30 10km squares in Great Britain since 1 January 1980 (Waring 1994, reviewed 1999b).

Vernacular Name	Scientific Name	County Distribution
Campanula Pug	*Eupithecia denotata denotata*	Whichford Wood, Red Hill Wood.
Silver Cloud	*Egira conspicillaris*	South-west VC 38.

Table 8. Nationally Scarce B.
Recorded from 31–100 10km squares in Great Britain (Waring 1994, reviewed 1999b).

Vernacular Name	Scientific Name	County Distribution
Goat Moth	*Cossus cossus*	Very local. Last record Stoneleigh, 1993.
Hornet Moth	*Sesia apiformis*	Only two records since VCH. Last record Oxhouse Farm, 1979.
Currant Clearwing	*Synanthedon tipuliformis*	Very local.
Yellow-legged Clearwing	*Synanthedon vespiformis*	Packington Park.
Orange-tailed Clearwing	*Synanthedon andrenaeformis*	Burton Dassett Hills Country Park.
Red-belted Clearwing	*Synanthedon myopaeformis*	Central and south-west VC 38.
Red-tipped Clearwing	*Synanthedon formicaeformis*	Brandon Marsh.
Large Red-belted Clearwing	*Synanthedon culiciformis*	Sutton Park, Snitterfield Bushes. Last record 1988.
Six-belted Clearwing	*Bembecia ichneumoniformis*	Very local.
Light Orange Underwing	*Archiearis notha*	Clowes Wood, Snitterfield Bushes, Oversley, Ryton, Wappenbury and Ufton Woods.
Mocha	*Cyclophora annularia*	Only three records. Last Wolverton 1983.
False Mocha	*Cyclophora porata*	Weethley Wood, Oversley Wood.
Chalk Carpet *	*Scotopteryx bipunctaria cretata*	Bishops Hill, Long Itchington Quarry.
Ruddy Carpet	*Catarhoe rubidata*	Grove Hill, Goldicote Cutting.
Cloaked Carpet	*Euphyia biangulata*	Ryton Wood, Oakley Wood.
Pinion-spotted Pug	*Eupithecia insigniata*	South-west VC38 and Rugby.
Valerian Pug	*Eupithecia valerianata*	Very local.
Broom-tip	*Chesias rufata rufata*	Only two records. Last Bidford 1995.
Great Oak Beauty	*Hypomecis roboraria*	Ryton Wood.
Square-spot Dart	*Euxoa obelisca grisea*	Rugby, Coventry, Grendon Common.
Wormwood	*Cucullia absinthii*	Very local.
Dotted Chestnut	*Conistra rubiginea*	South-west VC38.
Angle-striped Sallow	*Enargia paleacea*	Sutton Park, Old Park Wood, Oversley Wood.
Mere Wainscot	*Chortodes fluxa*	Princethorpe Woodland Complex, Ladywalk, Bowshot Wood and Oversley Wood.
Cream-bordered Green Pea	*Earias clorana*	Brandon Marsh. Very local in southern half of VC38.
Waved Black	*Parascotia fuliginaria*	Very local in southern half of VC38.

* UK BAP Priority Species.

Promoting Interest in Moths

The level of interest in moths within Warwickshire is currently greater than at any time, and the data being generated is proving highly valuable in detecting trends within individual species and individual sites. Moth data and its management is critical in supporting conservation work; to this end, efforts are currently being made to computerise the entire moth dataset for Warwickshire using MapMate software. This will ease the production of county atlases in the future and help with checking moth data against planning applications, agri-environment grant applications and wildlife site management plans.

Warwick University has been particularly instrumental in creating an interest in moths throughout the region during the last 20 years. The University's Open Studies department sets out to bring as wide a range of learning opportunities as possible to the local community. The course 'Winged Splendour' has introduced the subject of moths and butterflies to a large number of people. It covers many aspects of Lepidoptera, including conservation and habitat management. Many of the participants have become sufficiently inspired to devote future years to the pursuit of moth recording, forming an integral part of the large team of recorders in the County.

Warwickshire Museum and Coventry's Herbert Art Gallery & Museum have also been supporting moth recorders by managing fine voucher collections. These are crucial for gaining a full understanding of the County's moths. They provide hard evidence for the past distributions of many species which have a changed status, or the presence of species that are difficult to distinguish without dissection or critical examination under a microscope. Warwickshire Museum also publishes County atlases (The Benchmark Atlas series) and two key works covering macro-moths are still available: *The Lepidoptera of Warwickshire Parts One & Two,* by Roger Smith and David Brown (Eds. Hough, N. & Copson, P., 1987) and *The Lepidoptera in Warwickshire 1900–1995 An Historical Summary,* by Roger Smith (1998).

A programme of moth trapping nights is arranged each year in conjunction with the RINGS initiative (Research Recording and Recreation in Nature Groups) co-ordinated by Warwickshire Museum (this is referred to as Warks Moth Group in the species accounts). National Moth Night, launched by the entomological journal *Atropos* in 1999, has also stimulated a wider interest in moths and provides impetus for further concentrated recording.

Maps and Species Accounts

Distribution Maps

As the borders of many counties are constantly changing it is essential for natural history purposes that there is some form of continuity to recording boundaries. Potential new county records can thus be directly compared with lists created many years ago. In Victorian times the Watsonian vice-counties were devised by Hewett Cotterell Watson using 112 vice-counties of approximately equal size to cover the United Kingdom. In the map below (Fig. 6) an outline of the Watsonian Vice-County 38 (Warwickshire) is shown, together with the position of the neighbouring vice-counties.

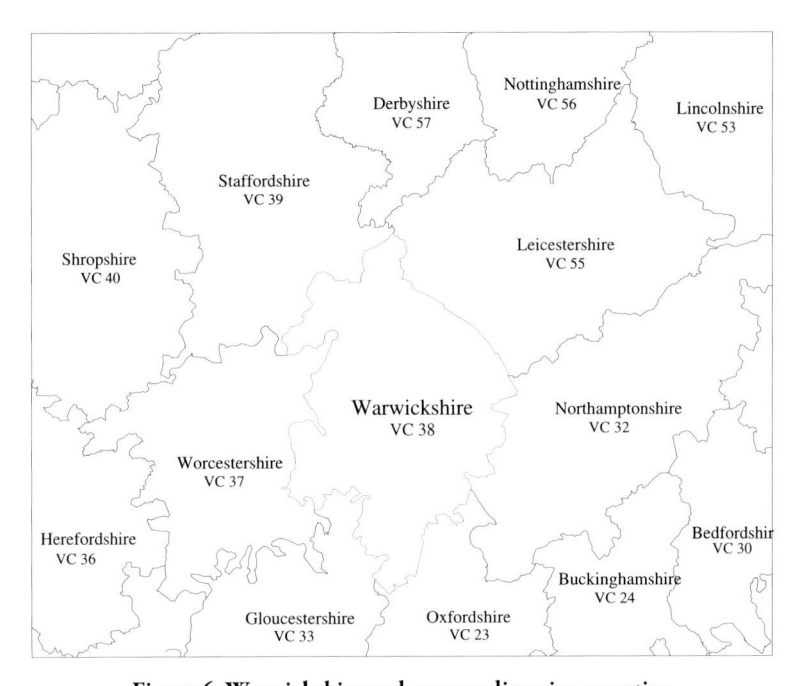

Figure 6. Warwickshire and surrounding vice-counties.

The individual distribution maps in the species accounts show an outline of VC38 and areas of the immediately bordering counties. Warwickshire lies mostly within the SP 100km Ordnance Survey square; only its most northerly regions are in the SK 100km square.

The map gridlines are shown at 10km intervals. Each species is recorded at the level of a 2km square or tetrad, and the grid references for all sites specifically noted in the text are given to the 1km square level in the Site Gazetteer.

The larger moths of Warwickshire have been extensively recorded over the years and more than 125,000 records are now stored in the County Database. The map (Fig. 7) shows the geographic coverage of the recordings at a tetrad level.

Although every effort has been made to obtain a full and even coverage of records throughout the County there are still a small number of areas which lack in-depth coverage. One such key area is the more rural southern extent of Warwickshire, containing many potentially rich habitats, many on calcareous soil. Although the Warwickshire Moth Group and other individuals have held occasional moth trapping sessions it has generally lacked an all

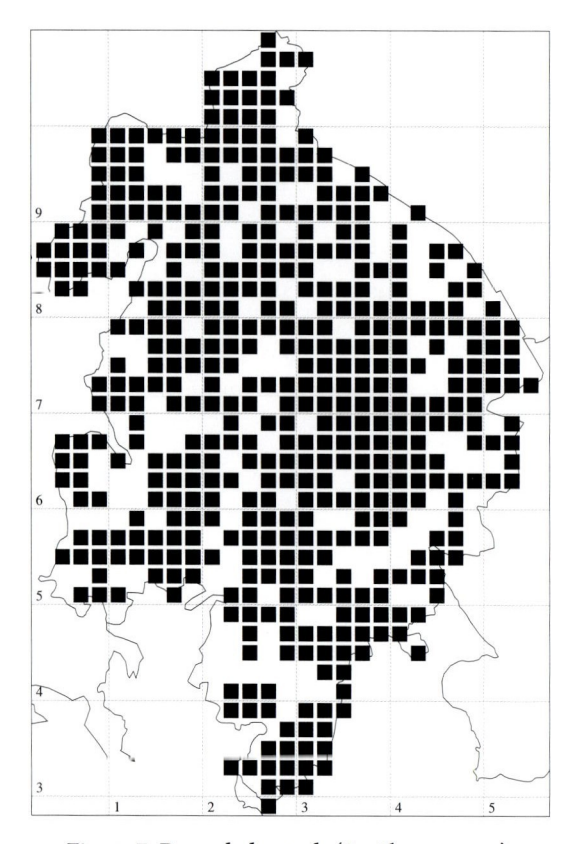

Figure 7. Recorded tetrads (2 x 2km squares).

year round coverage. As there are no static moth traps south of Pillerton Priors (Fig. 8) the distribution maps may give an unbalanced perspective for some species.

Five different symbols are used on the maps:

+ Nineteenth century records, up to 1904
● records dated between 1905 and 1930
■ records dated between 1931 and 1955
■ records dated between 1956 and 1979
■ records from 1980 onwards

On the distribution maps, symbols for modern day records automatically supersede symbols for historic records when located in the same 2km tetrad.

Maps are not included for immigrant species.

Species Accounts

Accounts are given for each species recorded naturally in the County (including pre-1900 records). A list of species having only been recorded doubtfully, or as a result of artificial introduction, is given in Appendix 1.

National Status

National status of the less common species is given according to the system devised by Waring (1994, reviewed 1999 b):

- Red Data Book (RDB). All species known from 15 or fewer 10km squares in Great Britain. (No current Warwickshire species of larger moth apply).
- pRDB. Species proposed for inclusion in the next Red Data Book listing.
- Nationally Scarce A. Recorded from 16–30 10km squares in Great Britain since 1980.
- Nationally Scarce B. Recorded from 31–100 10km squares in Great Britain since 1980.
- Nationally Local. Recorded from 101–300 10km squares in Great Britain since 1960.
- Nationally Uncommon. Recorded from less than 100 10km squares in Great Britain since 1980 but all known larval foodplants are non-native.

County Status

The county status for each species is given and the terminology used for resident species is summarised by the following:

County Status	Number of 10km squares in VC38 in which each species has been recorded since 1980
Widespread	20+
Fairly widespread	15–19
Local	10–14
Very local	Less than 10

Estimate of frequency (post-1980)

Abundant	Over 100 individuals usually seen per visit
Common	15 + individuals usually seen per visit
Fairly common	3–15 individuals usually seen per visit
Uncommon	Odd individuals observed
Scarce	Infrequent sightings

Flight Times

Adult flight times have been derived using observations in Warwickshire from records spanning the past 30 years. Special reference is made to bivoltinism where this is known to occur. This is particularly important as, in the case of some species, it has only previously been noted from southern England. Examples of extremely early or late individuals are quoted in the species accounts.

Larval Foodplants

Foodplants are included and have been obtained principally from Skinner (1984), Porter (1997) and Waring, Townsend & Lewington (2003). Observations pertaining to Warwickshire are marked with an asterisk * and refer to finding the larvae on the plant with firm evidence of the host plant being eaten by the species in question. The vast majority of records for this book are of adult Lepidoptera; consequently our knowledge of recorded foodplants for Warwickshire is incomplete.

Habitats

Habitat types for each species are included in the text and have been derived from field observation records in Warwickshire over the last 100 years.

Verification of Rare, Unusual and Critical Species

In order to maintain a high level of accuracy records have only been accepted having met certain criteria. Depending on the species concerned, one of the following is required to verify correct identification.

- Live moth carefully scrutinised by County Recorder.
- Voucher specimen retained and genitalia dissection if required.
- Good quality photograph.

Records

Records are listed chronologically for the County's scarce, very local and immigrant species. Where no indication of quantity is given it is representative of a single specimen. Light trapping is the general method of observation for modern day records unless otherwise stated.

Garden Moth Data

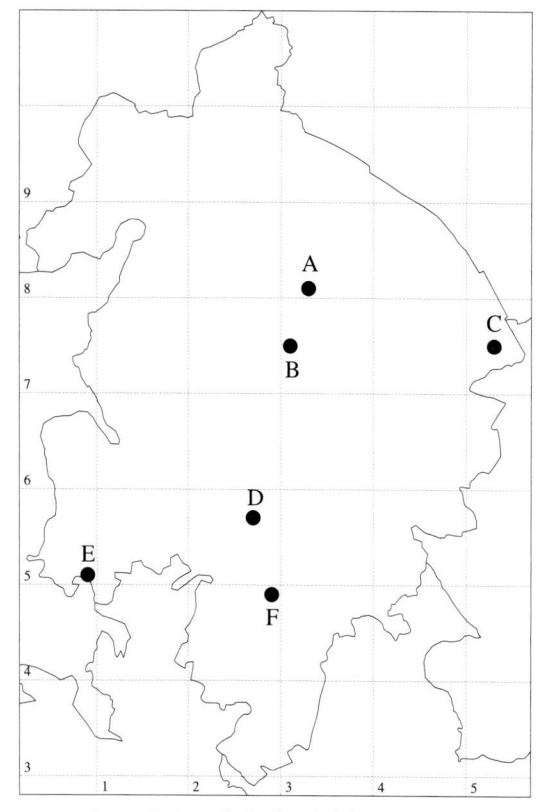

Site Key:
A Radford, Coventry
B Kenilworth Road, Coventry
C Hillmorton, Rugby
D Charlecote
E Bidford-on-Avon
F Pillerton Priors

Figure 8. Regularly (nightly) recorded static garden moth trap sites referenced in the text.

Garden moth trap data, taken from regularly monitored sites, has been included for some species to provide not only a picture of abundance, but also to compare rural and urban locations (Fig. 8). It has not been possible to include such information for some of the most common species, which are difficult to monitor accurately due to their extreme abundance; for example, Large Yellow Underwing and Dark Arches. It is recognised that variation in trapping effort and equipment will influence the annual totals recorded at each site, but nevertheless it is felt that this information provides an historical snapshot that may be of interest for both present and future generations.

Radford, Coventry

125 watt Robinson MV trap operated from 1969 (M.C. Vice).

This is a truly urban site situated only a mile from Coventry city centre. The trap is operated in a small garden in a residential district. The house has a main road at the front and a factory to the rear. In the species accounts long sequences of annual garden moth trap totals have been used to illustrate population trends for selected species. Otherwise yearly totals are taken from regular 5 or 10 year periods.

Kenilworth Road, Coventry

Two 125 watt Skinner MV traps operated from 1992 (M. Astley).

Situated on the wooded outskirts of Coventry and Kenilworth, in a select district containing large detached houses with extensive and well-established gardens. Immediately to the west is a large expanse of countryside with mainly arable fields. In the species accounts, garden moth trap totals for this site are taken from the years 2001–2005.

Hillmorton, Rugby

Two 125 watt Robinson MV traps and one 30 watt actinic trap operated from 1982 (D.I. Porter).

Situated in a typical suburban district of Rugby, where properties contain large mature gardens with a mixture of native and exotic trees and shrubs. Neighbouring streets are generally tree-lined and the nearest open countryside is approximately 1km away. In the species accounts garden moth trap totals for this site are generally taken from the years 1982, 1985, 1990, 1995, 2000, 2004 and 2005. Longer sequences of annual totals have also been used to illustrate population trends for selected species.

Charlecote (two adjacent gardens used)

125 watt Robinson MV trap operated from 1968 (D.C.G. Brown).
125 watt Robinson MV trap operated from 1975–2004 (A.F.J. Gardner).
(NB. None of the annual totals are combined)

Charlecote is a small rural village containing extensive National Trust parkland and situated midway between Warwick and Stratford-upon-Avon. It is positioned in the valley of the Avon and the surrounding land is generally flat and used for arable farming. The two gardens are well-established and sheltered with a good variety of trees and shrubs. In the species accounts long sequences of annual garden moth trap totals have been used to illustrate population trends for selected species. Otherwise yearly totals are taken mainly from regular 5 or 10 year periods.

Bidford-on-Avon

125 watt Robinson MV trap operated from 1982 (R.M. Cox).

Bidford-on-Avon is a large village lying to the west of Stratford-upon-Avon. The garden in which the trap is operated is situated on the very edge of the village overlooking large arable fields with hedgerows and only isolated trees. In the species accounts garden moth trap totals for this site are generally taken from the years 1988–1996.

Pillerton Priors

125 watt Robinson MV trap operated from 1991 (C. Ivin).

This is the most southerly and rural garden used in the survey. It is situated mid-way between two hamlets—Pillerton Priors and Pillerton Hersey. The garden contains an old orchard and overlooks open countryside which consists mainly of permanent pasture and old hay meadows enclosed by mature hedgerows. In the species accounts garden moth trap totals for this site are taken from the years 1992, 1993, 1994, 2002, 2003, 2004 and 2005.

Use of Data From Other Habitats

Single night moth trap figures for a selection of locally interesting species at key sites highlight some unusually large catches. However, as several of these involve 1970s and 1980s data they may not necessarily reflect present population levels.

Victoria County History Records

For the interest of the reader, and as a comparison with the present day, the VCH 1904 records and brief status for each species is quoted (H. Arthur Doubleday and William Page, 1904). This is only given for species that are mentioned in that work.

Nomenclature

The nomenclature accords with that of Bradley (2000). The checklist numbers, also from the same source, conform to the first number given for each species in *Field Guide to the Moths of Great Britain and Ireland* by Waring, Townsend & Lewington (2003).

References

As this book, through necessity, contains much information taken from a variety of sources it is not practical to individually cite these within the text. A full bibliography, however, appears at the back of the book. Where references are of particular relevance to important records in the County these may be quoted.

Terms and Abbreviations Used in Text

Recording Methods

actinic light—a low wattage fluorescent tube coated to emit ultra-violet light. This can be operated off a 12v D.C. battery or mains electricity.

Heath trap—a collapsible moth trap using a vertically held 6 watt fluorescent ultra-violet tube.

MV—mercury vapour light (lamp). This can either be operated on a tripod over a sheet or incorporated into a moth trap. There are now a number of commercially produced traps, of which Robinson and Skinner types have been widely used in Warwickshire.

static trap—moth trap operated in the same position every night.
Note: In the species accounts the abbreviation 'attracted to light' is used to cover all sources of light generally used for light trapping.

assembling—method by which males of a species are attracted to a virgin female contained within a net cage or netted bag. The scent from the female, known as a pheromone, evaporates into the air and is carried off on the breeze. The males detect this scent using their antennae. The moths fly upwind towards increasing concentrations of the scent which brings them to the female.

pheromone lures—synthetically manufactured pheromones hung in net bags and secured to branches can attract males of specific species, depending on the artificial pheromone used. This is a particularly effective method of monitoring clearwings.

sugar—sugaring is an alternative way of attracting and studying moths that is only occasionally used by Warwickshire lepidopterists but was formerly very popular before the advent of mercury vapour lights. A sticky, syrupy concoction of black treacle, brown sugar and rum or beer is painted in vertical strips onto tree trunks and fence posts and inspected at regular intervals throughout the evening with a torch.

wine roping—a similar, more recently used technique, in which ropes such as sash cord are soaked in a mixture of red wine and white sugar and then hung on foliage.

beating—a term used by lepidopterists to describe the method by which larvae may be obtained by gently tapping branches of trees and shrubs with a stick. An upturned umbrella, sheet or purpose-built beating tray is held underneath to catch the falling larvae.

sweeping—sweeping is the equivalent technique used for species feeding on low-growing plants. A strong framed net with a cloth bag is swept vigorously through such plants as heather and grass.

pupa-digging—a method by which pupae are found underneath the ground at the foot of trees after the soil has been loosened with a trowel.

larva blowing—a method of preserving larvae. The emptied skin is inflated by blowing through a glass tube as the carcass is dried over a flame.

---

voltinism—the number of broods a species has in any one year.

univoltine—a single brood occurring in any one year.

bivoltine—two broods occurring in any one year.

gen. det.—genitalia determinations. There are a number of species only reliably identified or separated from closely related species by genitalia determination or dissection.

Featured Recorders

PWA	Abbott, P.W.	BENHS	British Entomological and Natural History Society
DA	Allen, D.		
RA	Allen, R.	WWB	Brookes, W.W.
JA	Allton, J.	DB	Brown, D.C.G.
GAA	Arnold, G.A.	MDB	Bryan, M.D.
MAA	Arnold, M.A.	CC	Cadogan, C.
MA	Astley, M.	DCbll	Campbell, D.
ANHS	Atherstone Natural History Society	EWC	Carlier, E.W.
		SEWC	Carlier, S.E.W.
PA	Atherton, P.	DCsh	Cash, D.
WA	Atkins, W.	MEC	Castle, M.E.
A	Austen	IC	Challcey, I.
JSB	Badmin, J.S.	MC	Clarke, M.C.
CB	Baker, C.	RHC	Clinton, R.H.
GTB	Baker, G.T.	PC	Cooke, P.
MB	Ball, M.	DC	Couchman, D.
PPB	Baly, P.P.	MHC	Court, M.H.
AB	Barber, A.	CDNHSS	Coventry & District Natural History & Scientific Society
ACB	Barlow, A.C.		
BB	Barnett, B.	RMC	Cox, R.M.
DWB	Barnett, D.W.	DCr	Creeber, D.
LB	Barnett, L.K.	WC	Creeber, W.T.
RJB	Barnett, R.J.	JC	Culpin, J.
JBt	Bates, J.	SC	Cunningham, S.
BBr	Baxter, B.	HCl	Cuttell, H.
MWB	Beale, M.W.	PBD	Darch, P.B.
JBd	Beards, J.	CD	Davis, C.F.
DHB	Beech, D.H.	RD	Dawson, R.
AGB	Beers, A.G.	AWD	Divett, A.W.
TB	Besterman, T.	SD	Dix, S.
GTBB	Bethune-Baker, G.T.	MD	Doughty-Lee, M.
PAB	Betts, Sgt. P.A.	AD	Drewett, A.
BNHS	Birmingham Natural History Society	HE	Eccles, H.
		WSE	Edmonds, W.S.
WHB	Blaber, W.H.	REd	Edmunds, R.
WGB	Blatch, W.G.	CEd	Edwards, C.
RGB	Bliss, R.G.	JHE	Edwards, J.H.
JHB	Bloom, J.H.	BE	Elliott, B.
DBlr	Blower, D.	HWE	Ellis, H.W.
PBdm	Boardman, P.	CE	Emms, C.
SB	Bodnar, S.	FE	Enock, F.
PB	Bolton, P.	LJE	Evans, L.J.
JB	Booth, J.	RE	Evans, R.
WB	Bowater, Col. W.	SFa	Falk, S.
RCB	Bradley, R.C.	JEF	Fawcett, J.E.
LBr	Brare, Mrs. L.	G&AF	Finch, G. & A.
RFB	Bretherton, R.F.	DSF	Fletcher, D.S.

WHF	Flint, W.H.	AJK	Kolaj, A.J.
WF	Floyd, W.	JL	Landon, J.
HF	Fowkes, H.H	SAL	Lane, S.A.
SF	Fowkes, S.	BL	Laney, B.
Mrs G	Gallagher, Mrs.	HL	Langley, H.
AFG	Gardner, A.F.J.	FHL	Latham, F.H.
PG	Gardner, P.	EAL	Laxon, E.A.
AG	Garner, A.	NL	Lear, N.
TEG	Giles, T.E.	RL	Ledbury, R.
NG	Gill, N.	HML	Lee, H.M.
LFBG	Gillespy, L.F.B.	MJL	Leech, M.J.
TRG	Gosling, T.R.	FHLs	Lees, F.H.
GCG	Grant, G.C.	GBL	Lees, G.B.
JG	Grant, J.	KAL	Livings, K.A.
KCG	Greenwood, Dr. K.C.	CL	Lloyd, C.
DTG	Griffiths, D.T.	WL	Ludlow, W.
Mr Grubb	Grubb, Mr.	GBM	Manly, G.B.
DG	Grundy, D.	DM	Mann, D.
EIG	Guyner, E.I.	AHM	Martineau, A.H.
CH	Hall, C.	KM	McGee, K.
HEH	Hammond, H.E.	IM	McLenagham, I.
MHk	Hancock, M.	BM	Mitchell, B.R.
JAH	Hardman, J.A.	JM	Moore, J.
WH	Harrison, W.	LEM	Moore, L.E.
HDNHS	Hinckley and District Natural History Society	KAM	Moseley, K.A.
		JMd	Mountford, J.
KEH	Hood, Reverend K.E.	DMn	Musson, D.
EAH	Hopkins, E.A.	MGN	Nash, M.G.
MH	Housey, M.	CN	Neville, C.
NWH	Hudson, N.W.	PN	Nicholas, P.F.
VRH	Hughes, V.R.	FAN	Noble, F.A.
ADI	Imms, A.D.	AN	Normand, A.
ITE	Institute of Terrestrial Ecology, Monks Wood.	PAP	Pain, P.A.
		PJP	Parr, P.J.
CI	Ivin, C.	RKP	Parson, R.K.
ATJ	Jacques, A.T.	HHP	Patrick, H.H.
EWJ	Jephcott, E.W.	RGP	Payne, R.G.
CJ	Johnson, C.	NJP	Peckett, N.J.
RJ	Johnson, R.	MP	Perkins, M.
RJs	Juckes, R.	AP	Pollard, A.
RCK	Kendrick, R.C.	DP	Porter, D.
AHK	Kennard, A.H.	DIP	Porter, Dr. D.I.
MK	Kennard, M.	PhP	Porter, P.
AK	King, A.	CP	Potter, C.
HTK	King, H.T.	APll	Powell, A.
HDK	Kirk, H.D.	JMP	Price, J.M.
JK	Kirk, J.	AJP	Prior, A.J.
WK	Kiss, W.	WTR	Raine, W.T.
AKn	Knapton, A.	KR	Randall, K.A.

LR	Raven, L.
JRwn	Rawson, J.
HR	Redfern, H.
JGR	Reeve, J.G.
IGMR	Reid, I.G.M.
JR	Robbins, J.
PJR	Robbins, P.J.
JRR	Roberts, J.R.
GR	Robson, G.
PR	Rogers, P.
RR	Ruban, R.
RNHS	Rugby Natural History Society
RPP	Rugby Past & Present
EMR	Rumary, E.M.
J.Rush	Rush, J.
ES	Sadler, E.
A.Sale	Sale, A.
S	Sandford, Archdeacon
JWSt	Saunt, J.W.
TS	Saville, T.S.
DWS	Scott, D.W.
A.Seats	Seats, A.
WTES	Seeley, W.T.E
ASeg	Seggie, A.
EPS	Sharman, E.P.
PS	Sharp, P.
FWS	Shotton, F.W.
ASk	Sidgwick, A.
NVS	Sidgwick, N.V.
EHS	Sills, E.H.
FVS	Sills, F.V.
JWS	Simmonds, J.W.
HS	Skelcher, H
BS	Skinner, B.
MS	Slater, M.J.
DkS	Smith, D.
JTS	Smith, J.T
KGVS	Smith, K.G.V.
RHS	Smith, R.H.
RS	Southwell, R.
EABS	Stanton, E.A.B.
DS	Stone, D.A.
NJS	Stone, N.J.
RJS	Stone, R.J.
SS	Stroud, S.P.
GPS	Sutton, G.P.
DT	Taylor, D.
HT	Taylor, H.
PAT	Taylor, P.A.
SDT	Taylor, S.D.
WTT	Taylor, W.T.
MT	Telfer, Dr. M.
ANT	Thomas, A.N.
RJT	Thomas, R.J.
STm	Thomas, S.
PTn	Thompson, Peter
PT	Thompson, Phil
CT	Timms, C.
TT	Trought, T.
FWT	Tunbridge, F.W.
KT	Turner, K.
DV	Vallance, D.
MCV	Vice, M.C.
VCH	Victoria County History
AV	Visick, A.T.
JW	Waddell. J.
JWW	Wagstaff, J.W.
CJW	Wainwright, C.J.
CJWd	Wakefield, C.J.
CW	Wale, C.A.
MWsh	Walsh, M.
DWn	Walton, D.
AEW	Ward, A.E.
MJW	Waring, M. J.
KW	Warmington, K.
DW	Warren, D.
RGW	Warren. R.G.
Warks Moth Group	Warwickshire Moth Group
R&SW	Wasley, R. & S.
JWkn	Watkins, J.
RAW	Watson, R.A.
VW	Weston, V.
SW	Wharam, S.
WCEW	Wheeler, W.C.E.
EVW	Whitby, E.V.
GW	Wilkinson, G.
CWy	Willey, C.
MW	Williams, M.
MPW	Willmott, M.P.
BW	Withers, B.
WI Survey	Women's Institute survey
MGW	Woodhams, M.G.
TWW	Wratislaw, T.W.
RW	Wright, R.
GWW	Wynn, G.W.
MRY	Young, M.R.

Family: Hepialidae—The Swifts

This family of moths is represented by five resident species, all of which occur in Warwickshire. The members of this primitive group are medium to large sized with elongate wings, very short antennae and no proboscis. Both sexes come to light, mainly at dusk or during the first hour of darkness. The females scatter eggs at random over areas of the foodplant whilst in flight and the whitish larvae live underground feeding on the roots.

Ghost Moth
14 *Hepialus humuli humuli* (L.)

County status: Widespread and fairly common.
Flight: Early June to mid-August.
Larval foodplants: Polyphagous on the roots of grasses and herbaceous plants, including Wormwood*.

The white males of this species are a familiar sight as they hover at dusk in grassy locations. The female is a frequent visitor to light. Recorded over a wide area of Warwickshire from open grassland, woodland rides and clearings to marshy areas.

VCH 1904: *'Common everywhere.'*

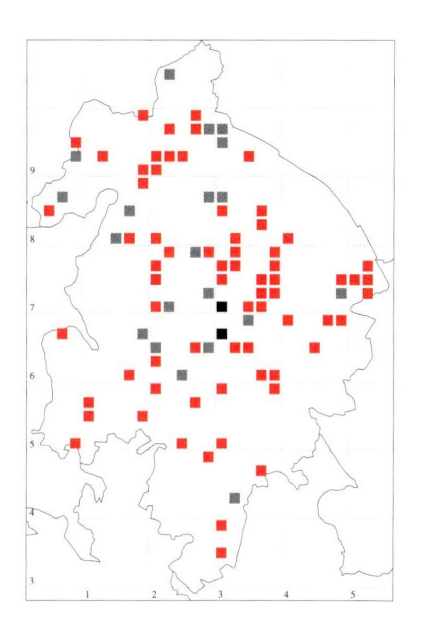

Orange Swift
15 *Hepialus sylvina* (L.)

County status: Widespread and fairly common.
Flight: Late June to mid-September.
Larval foodplants: Polyphagous on the roots of Bracken and many herbaceous plants.

The Orange Swift is found widely across the County in a variety of habitats, including open woodland, heathland, road and railway embankments, rough waste ground and gardens.

VCH 1904: *'Generally distributed but not common.'*

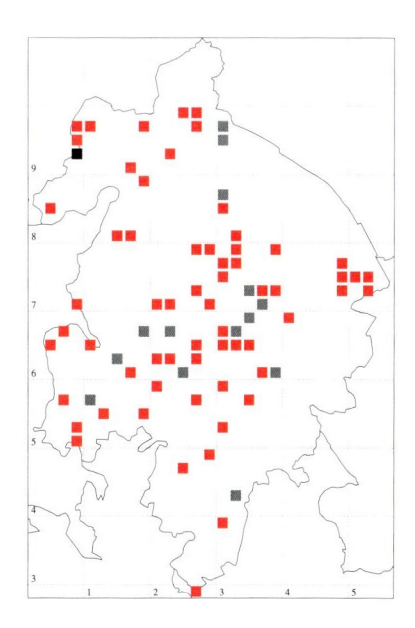

Gold Swift
16 *Hepialus hecta* (L.)

Nationally Local

County status: Local but fairly common.
Flight: Late May to late July.
Larval foodplants: The roots of Bracken and possibly herbaceous plants and grasses.

The Gold Swift is locally plentiful in woodlands, where it is often observed flying at dusk. Occasionally visits garden moth traps where there is little or no Bracken, suggesting the use of other foodplants.

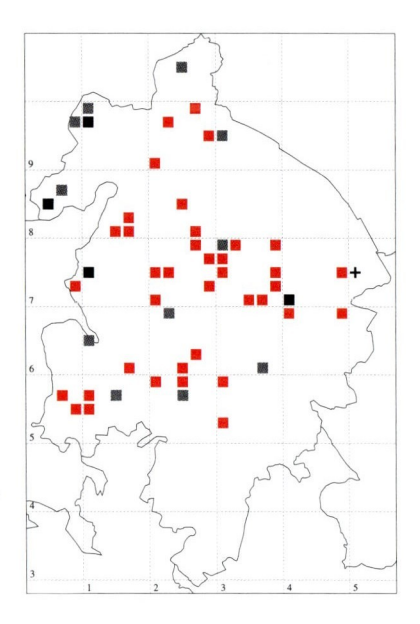

VCH 1904: *'Common everywhere.'*

Common Swift
17 *Hepialus lupulinus* (L.)

County status: Widespread and common, sometimes abundant.
Flight: May to late August.
Larval foodplants: Polyphagous on the roots of grasses* and herbaceous plants, including Geranium* and Garden Mint*.

As its name implies, this is the commonest species of the genus, being found in all types of habitat in rural and urban areas.

The following moth trap totals give an idea of frequency in a suburban garden:
Hillmorton, Rugby: 1982 (30), 1985 (5), 1990 (5), 1995 (16), 2000 (14), 2004 (94) (DIP).

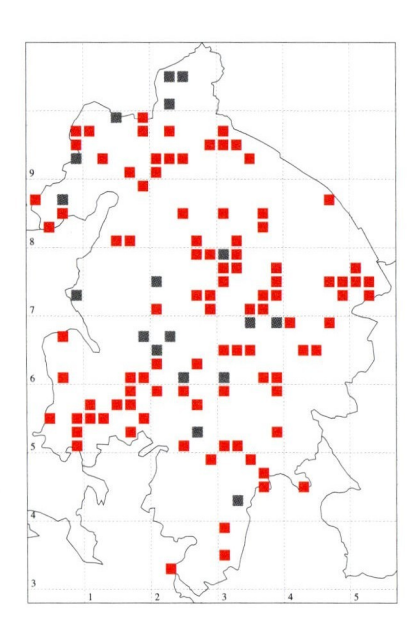

VCH 1904: *'Common everywhere.'*

Map-winged Swift
18 *Hepialus fusconebulosa* (DeG.)

Nationally Local

County status: Very local and generally scarce, but fairly common at one site.
Flight: June and July.
Larval foodplants: The roots of Bracken and possibly other plants.

In contrast to other members of this family, the Map-winged Swift is decidedly scarce in Warwickshire and largely restricted to acidic soils in the north-west. It appears to survive at low density in a few sites but is fairly common at Clowes Wood.

Records:
Long Lawford, 1948 (AGB); **Clowes Wood**, 1956 seen annually (BNHS), 23/6/1979 (14) (DB, RHS, AFG), 18/6/1993 four (Warks Moth Group); **Sutton Park**, 1970s (LJE); **Oakley Wood**, June 1979 (AFG); **Crackley Wood**, 13/7/1996 (RMC).

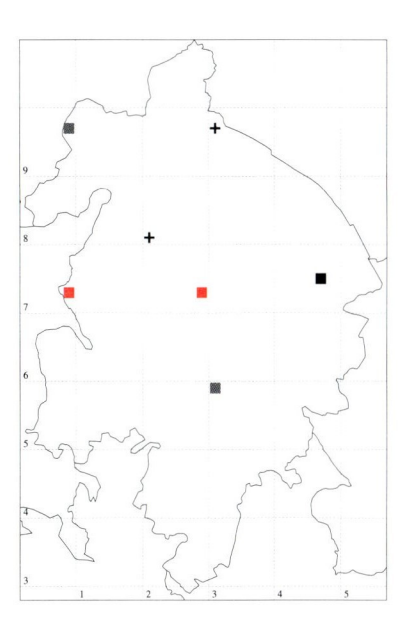

VCH 1904: *'Not uncommon at Sutton Park.'* Also recorded from Hampton-in-Arden and Atherstone.

Family: Cossidae—Leopards and Goat Moth

Although this family consists of approximately 700 species throughout the world, only three are found in the British Isles, of which two are resident in Warwickshire. The adults are nocturnal, do not feed and are only occasionally attracted to light. The maggot-like larvae feed internally in living wood or pith, often taking several years to mature.

Leopard Moth
161 *Zeuzera pyrina* (L.)

County status: Widespread and fairly common.
Flight: Late June to mid-August.
Larval foodplants: Polyphagous on trees and shrubs, including birches* and sallows*, feeding inside the stems and branches.

The males of the Leopard Moth are frequently recorded in moth traps but the female is seldom encountered.

Recorded from many wooded habitats, including parks, orchards and gardens throughout much of the County.

VCH 1904: *'Odd specimens turn up throughout the district.'*

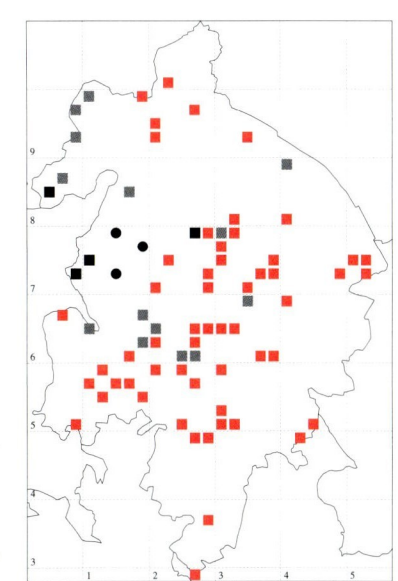

Goat Moth
162 *Cossus cossus* (L.)

Nationally Scarce B

County status: Very local and scarce.
Flight: June to August.
Larval foodplants: Many deciduous trees, including Ash*. The larvae feed inside the trunks and branches.

The true status of this species is difficult to determine as the adult is not normally attracted to light and the larvae are not easy to find. Formerly more frequently recorded, but with only two records since 1980 the indications are that it is now scarce.

Records:
May's Wood, 1913 larvae on Ash (GBM); **Rugby**, 25/9/1930 larva (RNHS); **New Fallings Coppice and Clowes Wood**, 1938–53 (BNHS); **Baginton**, 1942 (LR); **Tysoe**, 2/8/1948 female at rest on gate post (R. Oliver per TT); **Long Itchington**, 17/9/1948 larva (AHK); **NVRS, Wellesbourne**, 3/5/1955 bred from full grown larva (JAH), 29/3/1965 larva (JAH); **Marston Green**, 1965 W.I Survey; **Oakley Wood**, 1969 two larvae in felled Ash (WF); **Weston Park**, 1985 larva—imago bred; **Stoneleigh**, June 1993 adult found (per SD).

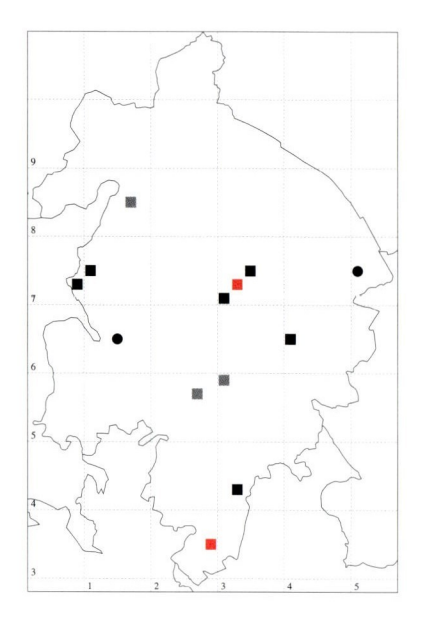

VCH 1904: *'Seems to occur throughout the County but is not often seen, and few specimens exist in collections. Infested trees are, however, reported from many places.'*

Family: Zygaenidae—Foresters and Burnets

There are ten resident British species of Zygaenidae, of which three presently exist in Warwickshire. This family contains many brightly coloured, colonial, day-flying species. The burnet moths, with bright colours and club-like antennae, could be confused with butterflies but resting posture with forewings held at a steep angle close to the body provide the vital difference. The adult's aposematic colouration allows individuals to rest openly on low herbage and chemical defences include the release of poisons such as hydrogen cyanide through joints on the thorax and legs when attacked. The larvae are mostly green with black and sometimes yellow markings and mainly feed on plants of the Leguminosae family. The silken cocoons of Six-spot Burnet and Narrow-bordered Five-spot Burnet are a familiar sight at their Warwickshire strongholds, being conspicuously attached to grass and plant stems.

    The early stages of the Forester are more difficult to locate, whilst the adults display a cryptic green colouration which was likened to the Lincoln green worn by medieval foresters in Sherwood Forest, giving rise to the English name of the species.

Forester
163 *Adscita statices* (L.)

Nationally Local

County status: Very local and occasionally fairly common at one site.
Flight: Day-flying. Early June to early July.
Larval foodplants: Common Sorrel, Sheep's Sorrel.

The Forester was found at a handful of sites in the 1960s, but is now restricted to just one location at Ashlawn Cutting, Rugby. The population is small and occupies a limited area. Numbers of adults are monitored regularly by Butterfly Conservation members and site management is practised to prevent scrub encroachment.

Records:
Rugby district, 1872, (A. Sidgwick, 1893); **Clowes Wood**, 1938–56 (BNHS); **Wappenbury Wood**, 20/6/1941 common (RFB), 1970s (RHS); **Bubbenhall Glade**, 12/6/1943 & annually until 1949 (LR); **Easenhall**, 1949 (LR); **Coleshill**, 1960s (JB); **Ashorne Wood**, 1968 (WF); **Marston Green**, 1976 (DMn); **Hillmorton Ballast Pits**, 1987 (PJP); **Ashlawn Cutting**, 1980s–2005 annually observed (PJP, DB, IGMR, AFG, PN).

VCH 1904: *Sutton, Marston Green, Wolford, Coombe Woods.*

Six-spot Burnet
169 *Zygaena filipendulae stephensi* Dupont

County status: Fairly widespread and sometimes locally fairly common.
Flight: Day-flying from late June to mid-August.
Larval foodplants: Common Bird's-foot-trefoil*.

The Six-spot Burnet is locally plentiful over a large area of Warwickshire. It favours vegetated spoil heaps from limestone quarrying and road and railway embankments with a calcareous flora. There are particularly large populations at Grove Hill, Bishops Hill, Ufton Fields, and the Navigation Cutting, Willoughby.

Occasional confluent forms have been recorded and six ab. *chrysanthemi* Borkh. (blackish-brown spots instead of red) were noted in Solihull, 1920 (HDK).

VCH 1904: *'Commonest of the genus – local'*

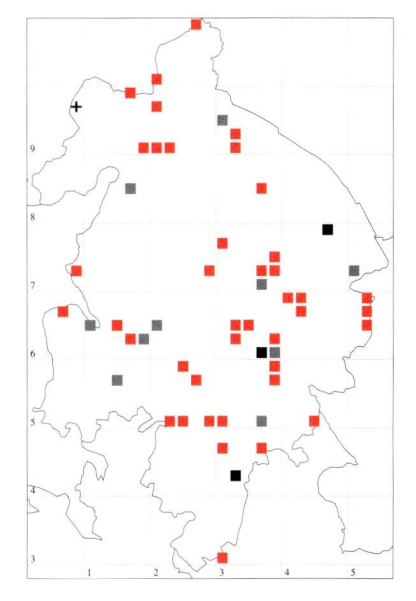

Five-spot Burnet
170 *Zygaena trifolii decreta* Ver.

Nationally Local

County status: No fully confirmed records. The status as a Warwickshire insect remains doubtful.
Flight: July to early August.
Larval foodplants: Greater Bird's-foot-trefoil.

This species and the following are subject to a considerable degree of confusion.

Waring (2003) states that ssp. *decreta* is very difficult to distinguish from the much more widespread Narrow-bordered Five-spot Burnet ssp. *latomarginata* Tutt, even using features of genitalia, but other experts claim that the typical forms, given the relevant habitat and presence of the foodplant, make separation possible.

Although respected authorities such as H.E Hammond reported *trifolii* from Clowes Wood in 1938–53, including ab. *glycirrhizae* Hb. with the middle and outer spots confluent and the inner spots united (J. M. Price, 1990), it remains doubtful whether this species still exists in Warwickshire.

All specimens examined over the last 30 years, both in the field and from scrutinising old collections, have revealed only Narrow-bordered Five-spot Burnet (RHS, DB).

VCH 1904: *'I doubt if this species is properly distinguished from* **lonicerae** *and merely give the records as I received them.' Knowle, Olton, Coventry, Atherstone, Wolford.*

Narrow-bordered Five-spot Burnet
171 *Zygaena lonicerae latomarginata* Tutt

County status: Widespread and locally fairly common.
Flight: Day-flying. Mid-June to late July.
Larval foodplants: Greater Bird's-foot-trefoil*, Meadow Vetchling, clovers and vetches.

The Narrow-bordered Five-spot Burnet is found over a large part of Warwickshire in road and railway cuttings, woodland rides and many post-industrial brownfield sites, including quarries, colliery spoil heaps and goods-yards. Alvecote Pools, Stonebridge Meadows, Ryton Meadows and Ettington Road cutting contain good populations.

An extreme confluent form with the markings similar to Transparent Burnet *Zygaena purpuralis* (Brünn.) was caught at Oxhouse Farm, Combrook, 20/6/2004 (DB; Brown, 2005)

VCH 1904: *Marston Green, Hay Wood, Rugby, Wolford.*

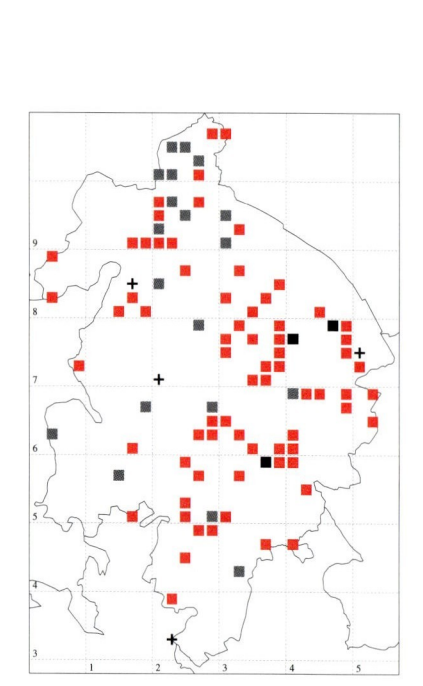

Family: Limacodidae

Although this family contains approximately 1,000 species throughout the world just two are found in the British Isles, the Festoon and Triangle. Both occur in southern England and are associated with broadleaved woodland. The Triangle has been recorded in Warwickshire, but not since Victorian times.

Triangle
174 *Heterogenea asella* ([D. & S.])

RDB

County status: Extinct
Flight: June.
Larval foodplants: Oaks and Beech.

This oak and Beech woodland species was recorded at Brandon Wood, 27/6/1890 (RNHS).

Family: Sesiidae—Clearwing Moths

In Britain there are an accepted 14 resident species of 'clearwing,' of which 10 have been found in Warwickshire. This family consists of small to medium sized moths which have scale-free areas on the wings. The adults resemble Hymenoptera and are diurnal, flying rapidly in the sunshine but also spending much time resting on the vegetation. The majority of species in this group are most elusive and consequently very much under-recorded in Warwickshire, which is reflected in the distribution maps. Recording may be improved in the future with the use of synthetic pheromone lures to attract the males. The whitish maggot-like larvae feed in stems, trunks and roots of plants, often leaving little or no evidence of their presence.

Hornet Moth
370 *Sesia apiformis* (Cl.)

Nationally Scarce B

County status: Very local and scarce.
Flight: Day-flying from mid-June to July.
Larval foodplants: The inner wood of poplars, especially Black Poplar and Aspen.

This species is associated with poplars growing in open habitats. Exit holes may be located near the base of the trunk and could be a clue to occupied trees.

Records:
Alvecote, 20/6/1975 (ANHS); **Oxhouse Farm, Combrook,** 17/7/1979 (AKn).

VCH 1904: *Salford Priors, Warwick, Atherstone.*

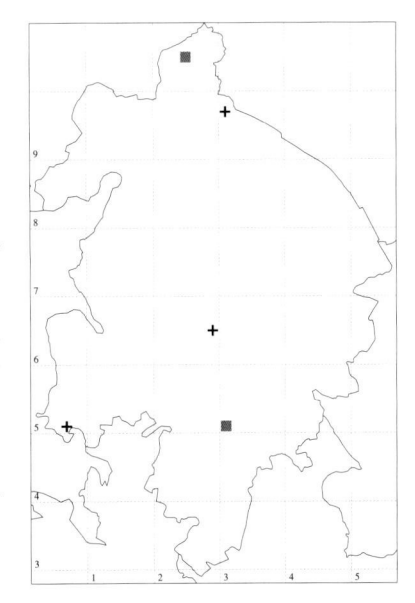

Lunar Hornet Moth
371 *Sesia bembeciformis* (Hb.)

County status: Very local and sometimes fairly common.
Flight: Day-flying from late June to July.
Larval foodplants: Various species of sallows*, willows* and poplars, feeding on the inner wood.

The Lunar Hornet Moth is more frequently noted than the preceding species. It shows a preference for damp woodland where sallows abound.

Records:
Rugby district, pre-1893, (A. Sidgwick, 1893); **Princethorpe Wood,** 1903; **Clowes Wood,** 1938–56 (HEH, BNHS); **May's Wood,** 1940 ten larvae and one imago in sallow (GBM); **Tile Hill Wood, Coventry,** July 1952 pair in cop. (WFES); **Snitterfield Bushes,** 1988 larvae in tunnels when cutting sallow trees (JAH); **Malpass Quarry, Rugby,** 28/6/1992 two imagines (RHS); **Ryton Organic Garden Centre, car park,** 15/3/1999 tunnels and caps in cut willows (SC), larvae plentiful in April 1999 (AFG); **Solihull,** 2001 (RL); **Bath Place, Royal Leamington Spa,** 25/6/2004 imago (SF).

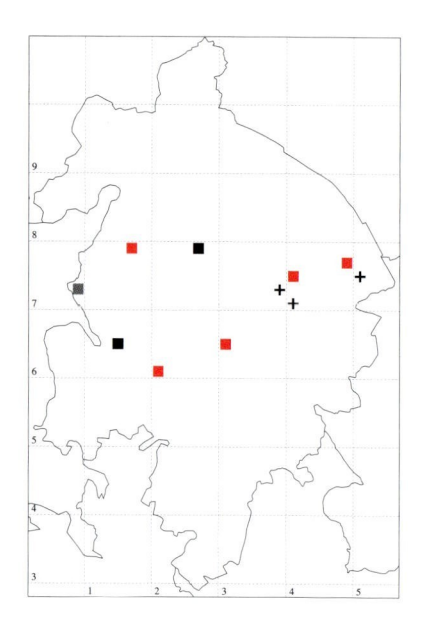

VCH 1904: *Rugby.*

Currant Clearwing
373 *Synanthedon tipuliformis* (Cl.)

Nationally Scarce B

County status: Very local and occasionally fairly common.
Flight: Day-flying. June and July.
Larval foodplants: Feeding inside the stems of Black Currant*, Red Currant* and Gooseberry*.

The Currant Clearwing is now less common than in the earlier part of the twentieth century, but is probably also under-recorded. At Birmingham during 1946 it was considered a pest species in gardens and allotments.

Records:
Rugby district, pre-1893 (A. Sidgwick, 1893); **Harbury and Bishops Itchington Quarries,** 25/6/1950 (AHK); **Lillington, Royal Leamington Spa,** 1950s–1990s (EPS); **NE Birmingham,** 1960s–1970s (LJE); **Earlsdon, Coventry,** 27/6/1965, 6/6/1976 (PC); **Marton,** July 1977 (RA); **Charlecote,** 20/6/1993–16/6/2004 (DB); **Water Orton,** 29/6/1993, 2/7/1993 (KM); **Pillerton Priors,** 1993–2004, 18/6/2005 30 males to pheromone lure (CI); **Tamworth Road, Coventry,** 15/6/2003 (MT); **Holbrooks, Coventry,** June 2005 (DP); **Canley Ford allotments, Coventry,** 10/7/2005 male to pheromone lure (MJW).

VCH 1904: *'Common on currant bushes in some of the suburbs of Birmingham. Not many records of the species, but probably common everywhere.'*

Yellow-legged Clearwing
374 *Synanthedon vespiformis* (L.)

Nationally Scarce B

County status: Very local and scarce.
Flight: Day-flying from late June to July.
Larval foodplants: Oaks*, birches, Sweet Chestnut and others. The larvae feed on the inner bark of stumps.

The Yellow-legged Clearwing has been found in a variety of habitats in Warwickshire, including woodland, parkland and overgrown quarries. There is only one recent record.

Records:
Knowle, 1890 (HWE); **Austy Wood**, 1914 three larvae (GBM); **Clowes Wood**, 1914 and 1949 several larvae in oak stumps (GBM, HEH), 25/5/1949 one larva in oak stump (BNHS); **May's Wood**, 1914 three larvae (GBM); **Wilmcote**, 1929 (SEWC); **Earlswood**, 1930 (SEWC); **Harbury and Bishops Itchington Quarries**, 25/6/1950 (AHK); **Packington Park**, 11/7/1998 imago beaten from oak branch (DM).

VCH 1904: *Sutton and Knowle.*

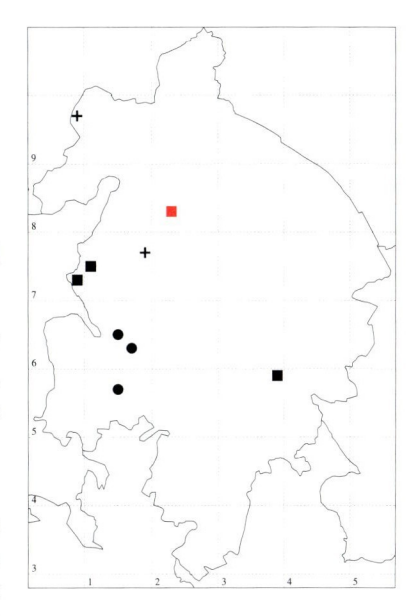

White-barred Clearwing
375 *Synanthedon spheciformis* ([D. & S.])

Nationally Scarce B

County status: No recent records. Presumed extinct.
Flight: Day-flying. June.
Larval foodplants: Birches and Alder. The larvae feed on the inner wood.

There is a possibility this species could still exist in the County. Fieldwork at former sites and on heathland is needed.

Records:
Clowes Wood, 1938–1956 small numbers annually (HEH, KGVS, BNHS); **Windmill Naps**, 1938–1953 small numbers annually (HEH, KGVS); **Bickenhill**, 1944 (DA); **Earlswood**, 1944–45 seven recorded (SEWC, GBM); **Austy Wood**, 1948 (HEH); **May's Wood**, 1949 (HEH).

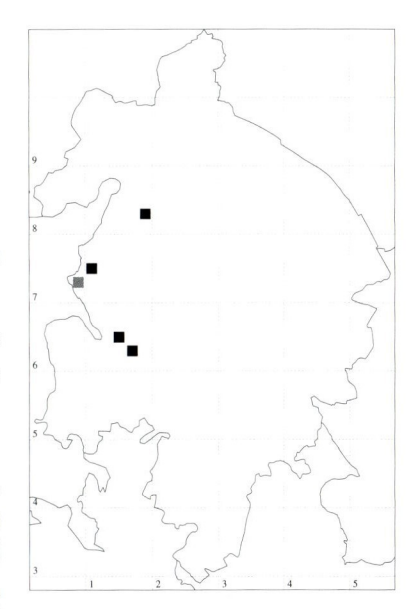

Orange-tailed Clearwing
378 *Synanthedon andrenaeformis* (Lasp.)

Nationally Scarce B

County status: Very local and scarce.
Flight: Day-flying. June.
Larval foodplants: Wayfaring Tree* and Guelder Rose. The larvae feed inside the stems.

The Orange-tailed Clearwing was discovered in Warwickshire as recently as 2001 at Burton Dassett Hills C.P. (NL). This species is associated with Wayfaring Trees in hedgerows and woodland edges on calcareous grassland. Pheromone lures could be an effective method of monitoring in the future.

Records:
Burton Dassett Hills C.P., 27/5/2001 half a dozen 'larval caps' noted on Wayfaring Tree. Male imago emerged 12/6/2001 (NL), 29/3/2002 old emergence holes and vacated larval tunnels were noted on Wayfaring Tree. No larvae or pupae found (DB).

Red-belted Clearwing
379 *Synanthedon myopaeformis* (Borkh.)

Nationally Scarce B

County status: Very local and scarce.
Flight: Day-flying from late June to July.
Larval foodplants: Crab Apple, cultivated Apple, pear, cherry, Rowan, hawthorns and Almond. The larvae feed on the inner bark.

A species found in orchards, gardens, hedgerows and avenues of trees in suburban districts. The same trees are used for many years and clues to tenancy are frass in bark crevices, protruding pupal cases and exit holes.

Records:
May's Wood, 1913 (GBM); **Shipston on Stour**, 2/7/1988 imago found in an old orchard (ACB); **Milverton, Royal Leamington Spa**, 28/6/1992 imago found in a shop window (RHS); **Pathlow**, 5/7/1997 imago netted (PC).

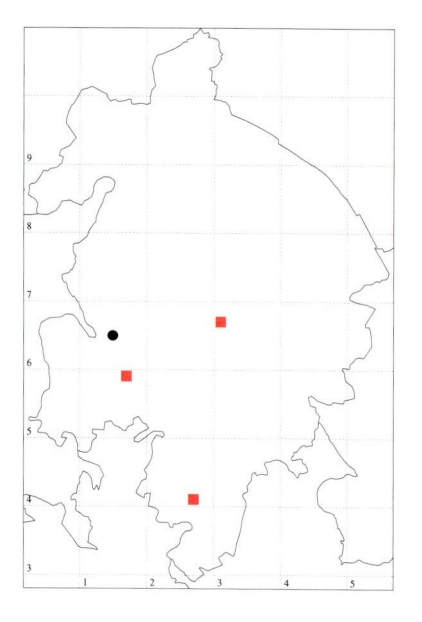

Red-tipped Clearwing
380 *Synanthedon formicaeformis* (Esp.)

Nationally Scarce B

County status: Very local and sometimes fairly common.
Flight: Day-flying in June to early July.
Larval foodplants: Osier, sallows and willows. The larvae feed in the trunks and stems.

The Red-tipped Clearwing should be searched for amongst *Salix* in wetland areas and in the vicinity of watercourses.

Winter-time inspection of the stems for swellings can often be a clue to presence of the species. Pheromone lures after mid-day are an effective method of attracting males.

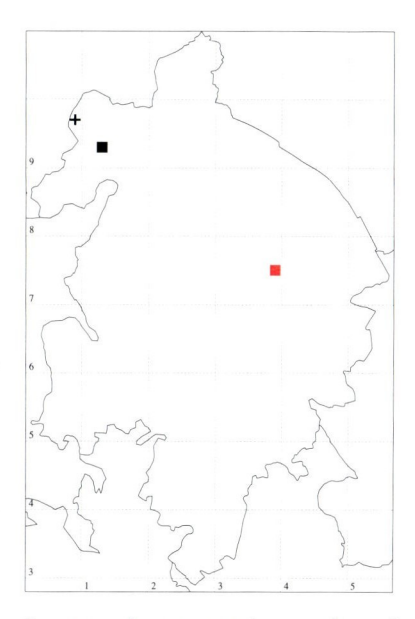

Records:
Sutton Park, 1891 (WHF); **Erdington**, 1934 (GPS); **Brandon Marsh**, 7/7/1986 a number of imagines around one willow tree (DM), 30/6/1988 (AB), June 1993 imago netted feeding on flowers (DM), 18/6/2005 four males attracted to pheromone lure (CI), 22/6/2005 male attracted to pheromone lure (DB), 25/6/2005 male, 26/6/2005 three males attracted to pheromone lure (AJK).

Large Red-belted Clearwing
381 *Synanthedon culiciformis* (L.)

Nationally Scarce B

County status: Very local and scarce.
Flight: Day-flying. May and June.
Larval foodplants: Birches*. The larvae feed on the inner bark and wood.

Most Warwickshire records of Large Red-belted Clearwing are as larvae found in birch stumps from trees cut within the previous two or three years. Frass extruding between the inner bark and main wood of the stump and old exit holes are a clue to occupancy. Pheromone lures could be an effective method of monitoring.

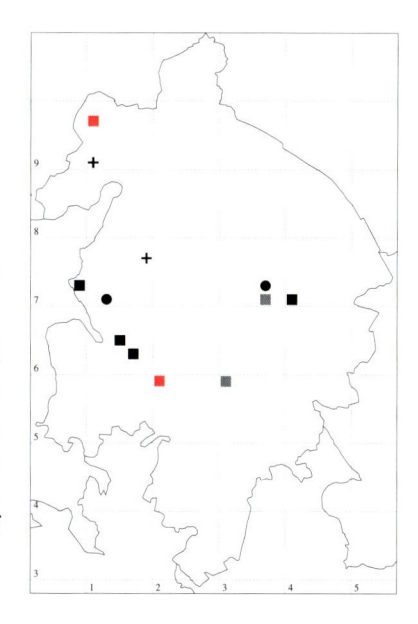

Records:
Austy Wood, 1913 (SEWC), 1947 (KGVS); **May's Wood**, 1914, 1934 (GBM, SEWC, FHL); **Clowes Wood**, 1914, 1940 (GBM, HEH), 4/5/1940 three larvae in birch stump (BNHS); **Bubbenhall**, 1919 (FHL); **Umberslade**, 1923 (SEWC); **Princethorpe**, 1950 (AHK); **Wappenbury Wood**, 1959 (SEWC); **Oakley Wood**, 1968 several larvae in birch stumps (WF); **Snitterfield Bushes**, 1980s (JAH); **Sutton Park**, 1988 (LJE).

VCH 1904: *Sutton Coldfield and Knowle.*

Six-belted Clearwing
382 *Bembecia ichneumoniformis* ([D. & S.])

Nationally Scarce B

County status: Very local but sometimes fairly common.
Flight: Day-flying. Mid-June to late August.
Larval foodplants: Common Bird's-foot-trefoil and Kidney Vetch. The larvae feed in the roots.

This is the most frequently recorded clearwing, the majority having been noted by sweeping or searching well-established areas of bird's-foot-trefoil. Locally plentiful on road and railway embankments, disused quarries, spoil heaps and other post-industrial brownfield sites.

Records:
May's Wood, 1914 (GBM); **Bearley**, 1917 (5), 1921 (2) (SEWC); **Harbury and Bishops Itchington Quarries**, 21/7/1951 (AHK); **Harbury Spoilbank**, 11/7/1964 (6) (FWS); **Wilmcote Rough**, plentiful 1980s (Anon); **Bishops Hill**, 3/7/1988 (RJB, DM), 12/7/2004 specimen at rest on Bird's-foot-trefoil (DB), 30/6/2005 (AD); **Stockton Cutting**, 19/7/1988 (SAL), 1/7/1993 (AFG); **Stockton Quarry**, 19/7/1988 (SAL); **Newbold Quarry**, 3/7/1990 (RW); **Malpass Quarry, Rugby**, 28/6/1992 (RHS, PP); **Navigation Cutting, Willoughby**, 16/7/1995 (SF); **Dordon**, 15/7/1995 swept off Bird's-foot-trefoil along roadside verge in good numbers (DB, BM), 14/7/2002 one swept (BM); **Pooley Fields, Alvecote**, 13/6/1997 (RW), 8/8/1998, 20/8/1999 male and female swept off Bird's-foot-trefoil, 24/7/2001 one swept off Knapweed, 14/7/2002 (BM); **Ashlawn Cutting**, 8/7/1997 (RW), 28/6/2000 (DB); **Ufton Fields**, 7/8/1997 (RW).

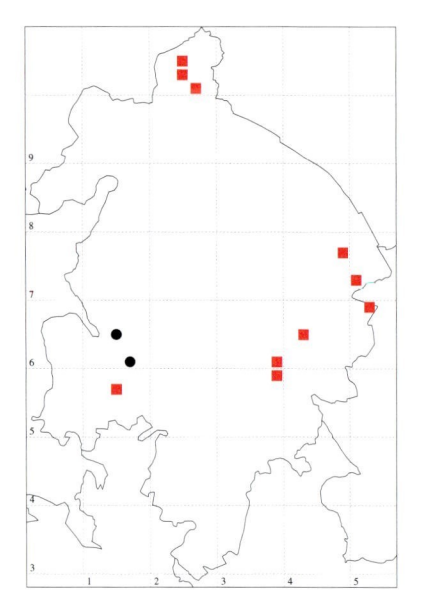

Family: Lasiocampidae—Eggars

This family of medium to very large sized moths contains about 1000 species worldwide, ten occurring in the British Isles, of which seven are resident in Warwickshire. The moths are mostly nocturnal but the males of Oak Eggar and Fox Moth fly by day with a very fast and erratic flight as they search for the resting females. The latter fly at night and come to moth traps. The adults have vestigial mouthparts and so do not feed. The larvae are densely hairy and many are often seen basking in the sun, the most familiar in Warwickshire being the Drinker. Pupation of some species occurs in substantial egg-shaped cocoons which give rise to the name 'eggar'.

December Moth
1631 *Poecilocampa populi* (L.)

County status: Fairly widespread and fairly common.
Flight: Late October to early January.
Larval foodplants: Polyphagous on deciduous trees, including oaks*, birches, poplars, hawthorns and Blackthorn.

Due to its extremely late flight period the December Moth is under-recorded. In areas where there are mature deciduous trees and well-established hedgerows, moth traps operated on mild nights in November and December will usually attract good numbers of males and the occasional female.

Garden moth trap totals at **Hillmorton, Rugby,** are as follows: 1982 (10), 1985 (20), 1990 (8), 1995 (20), 2004 (24) (DIP).

VCH 1904: *'Not common.'*
Sutton Park, Yardley, Knowle, Rugby, Atherstone.

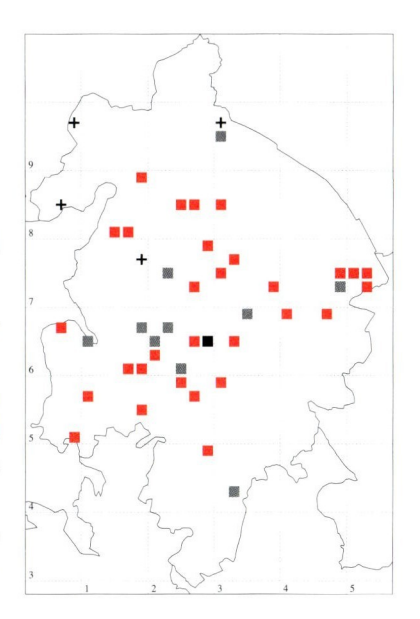

Pale Eggar
1632 *Trichiura crataegi* (L.)

County status: Fairly widespread but becoming uncommon.
Flight: August and September.
Larval foodplants: Oaks*, birches*, sallows*, Blackthorn*, hawthorns*, Hazel, Crab Apple.

The Pale Eggar is well represented over a large part of central and south Warwickshire but there is a dearth of records from the north-west. Most frequent in woodland and well established at Oakley Wood, Hampton Wood, Oversley Wood, Snitterfield Bushes, Chesterton Wood, Ryton Wood, Waverley Wood and Wolford Wood.

VCH 1904: *'Rare.'*
Atherstone and Rugby.

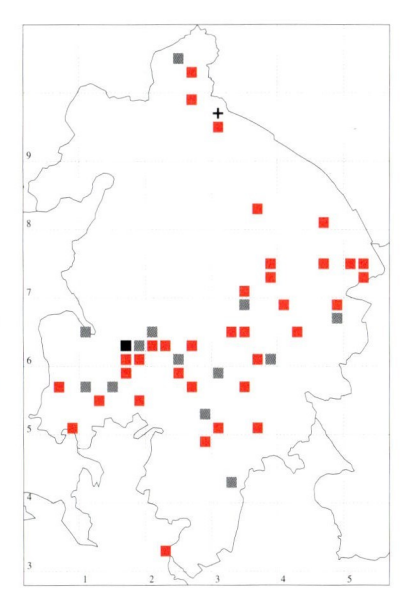

Small Eggar
1633 *Eriogaster lanestris* (L.)

Nationally Scarce B

County status: Presumed extinct.
Flight: February and March.
Larval foodplants: Hawthorns* and Blackthorn, living in a large web.

Linked to a national decline, the Small Eggar disappeared from Warwickshire during the 1950s. This species was badly affected by the removal and indiscriminate trimming of hedgerows in post-war years.

Records:
Rugby district, 1874 (RNHS); **Church Lawford**, 26/7/1890 larvae (RNHS); **Cathiron Canal**, 27/6/1894 larvae (RNHS); **Newbold on Avon**, 10/6/1896 larvae (RNHS); **May's Wood**, 1912 adult at light, larval web in hawthorn (GBM); **Great Wolford Parish**, 13/5/1949 larval web (TT).

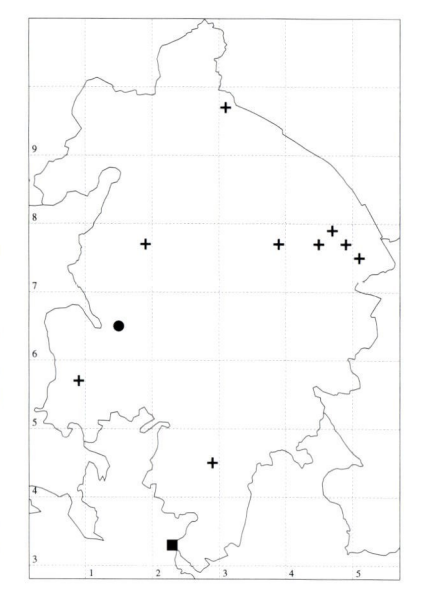

VCH 1904: *'Not common.'*
Alcester, Knowle, Brandon Woods, Atherstone, Wolford (larvae sometimes common WCEW)), Idlicote.

Lackey
1634 *Malacosoma neustria* (L.)

County status: Fairly widespread and fairly common.
Flight: July and August.
Larval foodplants: A wide variety of trees and shrubs, including hawthorns*, oaks*, cherry*, birches*, Blackthorn* and Aspen*.

The Lackey is fairly widespread although more frequently reported from the south of the County. The distinctive black, red, white and blue striped larvae are gregarious and their nests often noticed.

Found in a variety of habitats including woodland clearings, railway cuttings, scrub and gardens. The adult displays a wide variation in ground colour, ranging from straw to reddish-brown.

Most long term recorders report a reduction in numbers in recent years, as illustrated by the following garden moth trap totals:
Pillerton Priors: 1992 (20), 1993 (26), 1994 (10), 2002 (17), 2003 (9), 2004 (7) 2005 (8) (CI).
Hillmorton, Rugby: 1982 (53), 1985 (108), 1990 (28), 1995 (24), 2000 (1), 2004 (0) (DIP).

VCH 1904: *'By no means a pest in Warwickshire as it seems to be in many places further south. It is rather an uncommon insect with us as a rule.'*

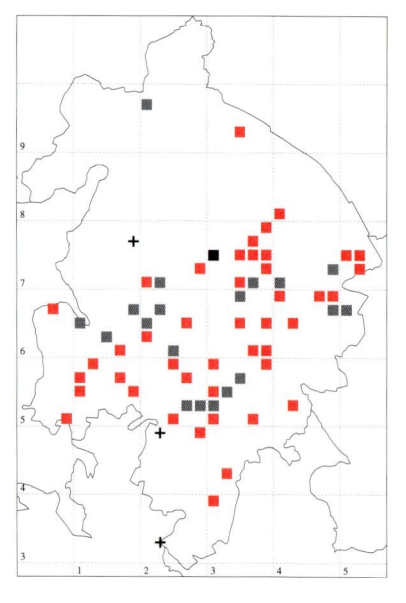

Oak Eggar
1637 *Lasiocampa quercus* (L.)

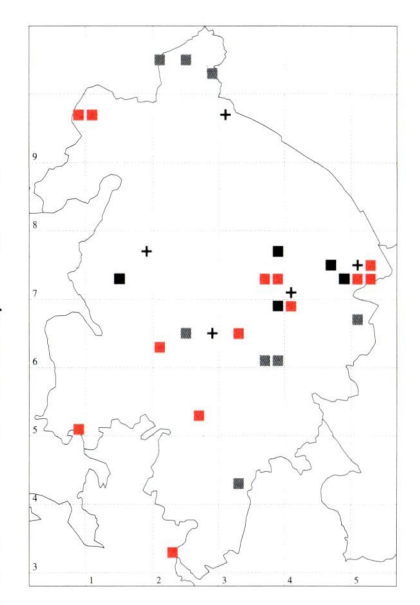

County status: Very local and uncommon.
Flight: July and August. The males fly in sunshine and the females from dusk.
Larval foodplants: A variety of trees and shrubs, including oaks, sallows, brambles, Broom*, hawthorns*, Blackthorn*.

The Oak Eggar has been noted from a number of habitats, ranging from disused railway embankments and heathland to rides and clearings in broadleaved woodland. The males fly rapidly during the daytime, whilst females occasionally visit MV.

Records:
Rugby district, pre-1893, (A. Sidgwick, 1893); **Sutton Park**, 12/5/1928, 16/6/1928, 11/7/1928 (LJE), 1960–83 (JB, AN), 1990s (DWS); **Tysoe**, 1940–60 (TT); **Bubbenhall**, Aug. 1944, 1947 (LR); **Hockley Heath**, 1947 (HEH); **Long Lawford**, 1948 (AGB); **Brandon Wood**, 1950 (LR); **Bilton**, 1950s (BB); **Eathorpe**, 1955 (WTT); **Alvecote**, 3/8/1968 (RGW); **Bonehill**, 1970s (RJT); **Willoughby Railway**, 1970s (BB); **Marton**, 1970s (GR), 21/6/1984 (RA); **Ryton Wood**, 1970s (LEM); **Ufton Fields**, 19/8/1972 (LM), 30/6/1973 female at MV, 11/8/1973 female at MV (DB); **Tamworth**, 2/7/1975 (ANHS); **Austrey**, 30/7/1977 female taken (WA); **Wolverton Hill**, 17/7/1983 at rest on shrub near oak trees (FWT); **Wellesbourne Wood**, 19/8/1985 (JL); **Hillmorton, Rugby**, 12/7/1986, 1994, 20/7/1996, 22/7/1999, 8/7/2002, females at MV (PN), 29/7/2000, 11/8/2000 (DIP); **Wolford Wood**, 13/7/1997 (KR); **Ashlawn Cutting, Rugby**, 15/6/2002 larva (MK); **Sydenham, Royal Leamington Spa**, 11/7/2005 & 13/7/2005 male assembled to a reared female (MK), **Ryton Meadows**, 16/7/2005 three females at MV (Warks Moth Group); **Bidford-on-Avon**, 20/7/2005 female at MV (RMC).

VCH 1904: *'Common at Sutton Park, where the larvae are sometimes abundant.'* Princethorpe, Atherstone, Wolford.

Fox Moth
1638 *Macrothylacia rubi* (L.)

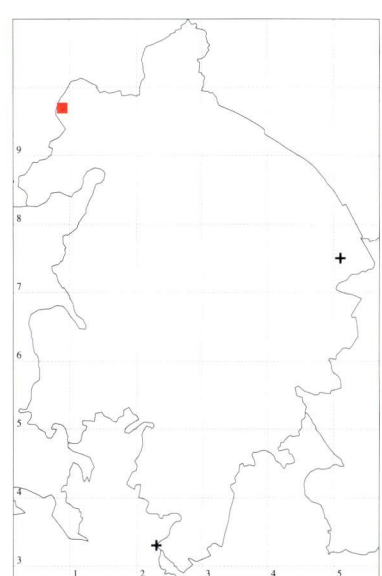

County status: Confined to one site and scarce.
Flight: Late April to June.
Larval foodplants: Many plants, including Heather, brambles, and Bilberry.

The Fox Moth is restricted to the heathland of Sutton Park where it is observed very occasionally. More fieldwork is needed to ascertain the precise status of this species. Males are day-flying and can be observed until dusk in warm weather. Females fly at night and respond to MV. Fully grown larvae can be found basking in sunshine after hibernation in late March and April.

Records:
Sutton Park, 30/5/1929, 8/6/1929, 24/4/1931, 18/6/1936, 1970s (LJE), 1960s (JB) and 3/6/1992 (AP).

VCH 1904: *Sutton Park—'common.'*
Rugby and Wolford.

Drinker
1640 *Euthrix potatoria* (L.)

County status: Widespread and common.
Flight: Late June to August.
Larval foodplants: Many species of grasses*, including Cock's-foot*, and reeds.

The Drinker is frequently attracted to light in large numbers and the caterpillar is often observed amongst coarse grasses. This species displays a predilection for damp habitats and is very plentiful at Brandon Marsh, Ryton Pools Country Park, Alvecote Pools, Kingsbury Water Park, Coombe Abbey and Ufton Fields.

VCH 1904: *'Common everywhere.'*

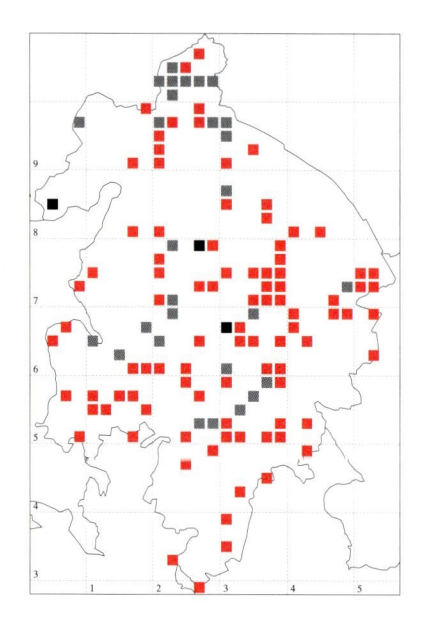

Lappet
1642 *Gastropacha quercifolia* (L.)

County status: Very local and becoming scarce.
Flight: Late June to mid-August.
Larval foodplants: Hawthorns*, Blackthorn*, Crab Apple and cultivated Apple.

The Lappet was stated to be '*very rare*' in the VCH 1904 with records from five locations. There were no further sightings until the 1940s when a few were reported at Tysoe (TT) and Long Lawford (AGB). During the 1950s there was a gradual resurgence which continued to the 1980s, by which time the species had become locally well established in the southern half of the County. Frequenting open woodland and scrub, it was noted at Oakley Wood (WF, DB), Chesterton Wood (DB), Hampton Wood (AFG), Ettington Park (DB) and Ufton Fields (DB, PC). The adult visited garden moth traps at Marton (RA), Pailton (KCG), Rugby (DIP), Claverdon (IGMR), Wolverton (DS), Charlecote (DB),

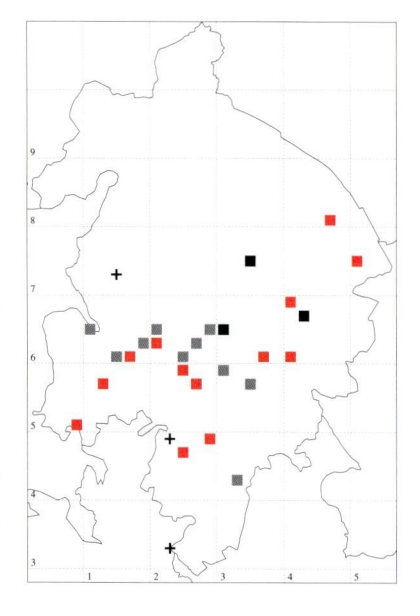

Bearley Station (IGMR), Pillerton Priors (CI), Red Hill, near Alcester (JAH) and Bidford-on-Avon (RMC).

During the 1990s a decline occurred and there have been no records of this species since 1995.

VCH 1904: *'Very rare.'* Bidford-on-Avon, Hockley Heath, Rugby, Warwick, Wolford.

Family: Saturniidae—Emperors

This family comprises about 1,300 species worldwide including many spectacular giant silkmoths from India and the Far East. However, Warwickshire, and indeed Britain, is represented by only one example.

Emperor Moth
1643 *Saturnia pavonia* (L.)

County status: Very local and scarce.
Flight: Late April to mid-May.
Larval foodplants: Brambles*, Blackthorn*, hawthorns, Heather* and many other woody plants.

In the VCH 1904, this attractive species was reported to be '*common*' in Sutton Park. It was stated that '*considerable numbers of males had been obtained by assembling to females*'. Numbers gradually declined at the site and it is now only very rarely observed. Sporadic records from other widely separated locations, chiefly open woodland and railway cuttings, suggest the species may survive at low density.

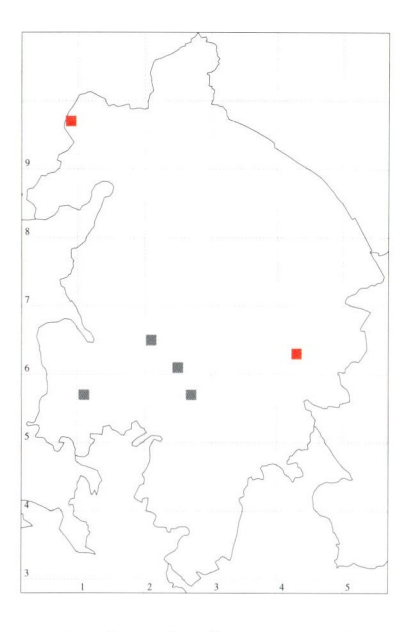

Records:
Sutton Park, 25/4/1928–1970s (LJE), 1970s (KEH, JB), 8/7/1997 larva (SFa), 1/9/2002 larva (HS); **Oversley Wood**, 1960 four larvae on Blackthorn (DWS); **Claverdon railway station**, 23/7/1964 larvae on Bramble (RE); **Hampton Wood**, 5/5/1973 male assembled to female (AFG); **Charlecote**, 14/5/1974 male assembled to female (DB); **Southam**, 7/5/1981 (JWW).

VCH 1904: *Sutton Park—'common.'*

Family: Drepanidae—Hook-tips

All but one of the six resident British species in this family have ample forewings hooked at the apex. Primarily inhabitants of broadleaved woodland, the Warwickshire contingent of five have all shown an increase during the last 20 years. The larvae feed on the foliage of trees and rest in a characteristic manner with the front and tail ends of the body raised. The tapering of the hind section is accentuated by an absence of properly developed rear claspers.

Scalloped Hook-tip
1645 *Falcaria lacertinaria* (L.)

County status: Widespread and fairly common.
Flight: Possibly three generations. Late April to late June, July to August, and occasional specimens in late September to October.
Larval foodplants: Birches*.

The Scalloped Hook-tip is more widely distributed than in the mid-1900s with small colonies now existing even in suburban districts containing birch. Well established in Sutton Park, Brandon Wood, Waverley Wood, Ryton Wood, Wappenbury Wood, Hay Wood and Oakley Wood. Brandon Marsh also contains good populations and large numbers are sometimes attracted to MV; for example, 30/7/2005 (20) (Warks Moth Group).

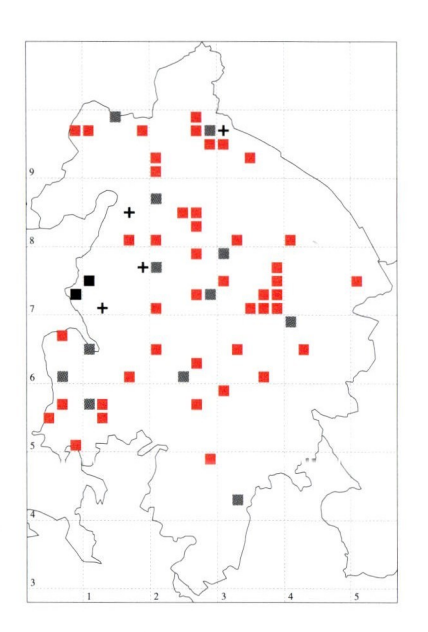

VCH 1904: *'With falcataria but not quite so common.'*
Marston Green, Knowle, Sutton Park, Umberslade, Brandon Wood and Atherstone.

Oak Hook-tip
1646 *Watsonalla binaria* (Hufn.)

County status: Widespread and fairly common.
Flight: Two overlapping generations. May to June and July to September.
Larval foodplants: Oaks*.

The Oak Hook-tip has increased in range and frequency since 1980 to become fairly common in woodlands, hedgerows, parks and gardens. It has two overlapping generations and may be seen anytime from early May until late September with peaks occurring at the end of May and late July.

VCH 1904: *'Rare.'*
Knowle and Rugby 1877, 1888.

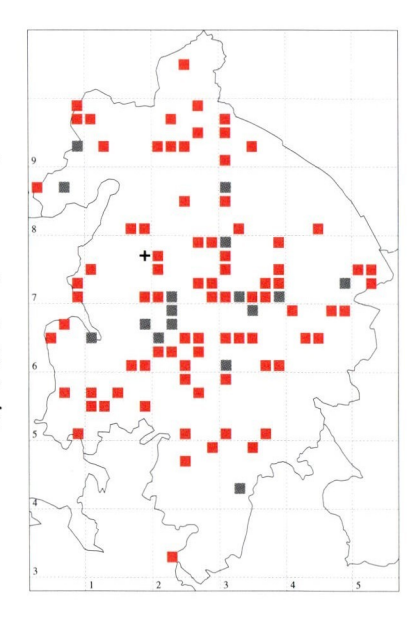

Barred Hook-tip
1647 *Watsonalla cultraria* (Fabr.)

Nationally Local

County status: Very local and uncommon.
Flight: May and June.
Larval foodplants: Beech*.

The Barred Hook-tip has never been plentiful in the County, but there has been an increase in records since 1990. It is found in mature broadleaved woodland containing Beech.

Records:
Clowes Wood, 12/10/1940 two larvae beaten from Beech (HEH), 1956 listed as 'rare' (BNHS), 15/7/1997 larva beaten from oak, moth bred (MCV); **Austy Wood**, 1940 several larvae beaten from Beech (HEH); **Mappleborough Green**, 1952–56 a few larvae and imagines (FHL); **Charlecote**, 1/5/1990 (AFG); **Oversley Wood**, 25/5/1991 (DB); **Hay Wood**, 14/5/2004 (AJP, VW, NJS); **Meigh's Wood**, 16/5/2004 (NJS); **Meriden Shafts**, 6/5/2005 (2) (NJS, AJP).

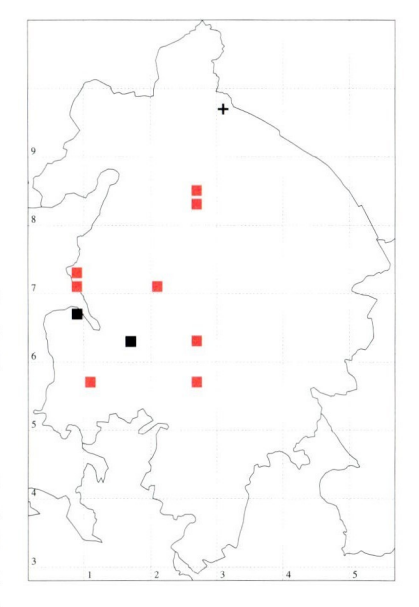

VCH 1904: *Atherstone.*

Note: A larva beaten off oak in Clowes Wood 15/7/1997 (MCV) was reared successfully on oak to the adult stage, showing a reluctance to feed on Beech. This individual could possibly have originally wandered from an adjacent supply of Beech. This phenomenon has subsequently been observed elsewhere (Platts, 2005).

Pebble Hook-tip
1648 *Drepana falcataria falcataria* (L.)

County status: Widespread and fairly common.
Flight: Two overlapping generations. Early May to late September.
Larval foodplants: Birches*.

The Pebble Hook-tip has shown a considerable increase since 1980 and is now established in many built-up districts containing isolated birches. It is most plentiful in birch woodland and often attracted to light in numbers: Oversley Wood, 7/6/2004 (17) (RMC, DG, AJP).

Healthy populations are also present on the heathland of Sutton Park and Grendon and the wetlands of Brandon Marsh and Ufton Fields.

A particularly late individual was recorded at Charlecote on 5/10/1997 (AFG).

VCH 1904: *'Not rare.'*
Knowle, Marston Green, Coventry, Coleshill, Brandon Wood, Atherstone and Frankton.

Chinese Character
1651 *Cilix glaucata* (Scop.)

County status: Widespread and fairly common.
Flight: Two generations which sometimes overlap. Mid-April to mid-June and July to mid-September.
Larval foodplants: Hawthorns* and Blackthorn*.

The Chinese Character is found in a wide range of habitats containing hawthorns and Blackthorn. The imago may be seen any time from April to September with recorders reporting peaks in mid-May and again at the end of July to mid-August. A regular visitor to garden moth traps, often remaining on the outside and successfully avoiding predation due to its uncanny resemblance to a bird dropping.

VCH 1904: *'Generally distributed.'*

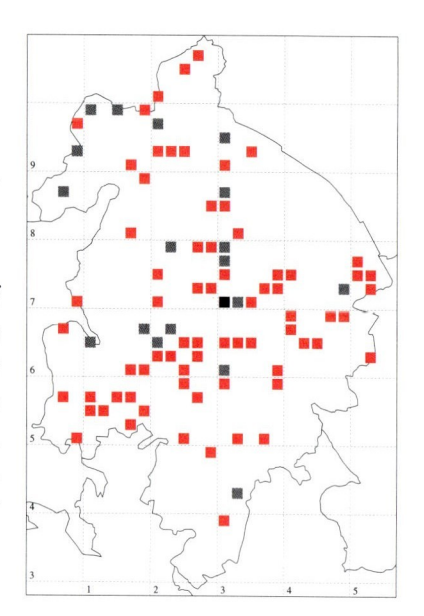

Family: Thyatiridae—Lutestrings

A small family of nine British species, all of which have been recorded in Warwickshire.
The adults visit light freely and many also come to the sugar patch. Members of this family resemble the noctuid moths but are slightly slimmer in build and rest with wings close to the body.

Peach Blossom
1652 *Thyatira batis* (L.)

County status: Widespread and locally fairly common.
Flight: Late May to mid-August.
Larval foodplants: Brambles*.

This attractive species is found throughout the County, usually in small numbers but fairly commonly in open deciduous woodland containing a good ground cover of brambles. It visits garden moth traps occasionally. Unusually late examples were noted on 28/8/1983 and 3/9/1987 at Hillmorton, Rugby (DIP).

VCH 1904: *'More numerous than the Buff Arches and equally distributed.'*

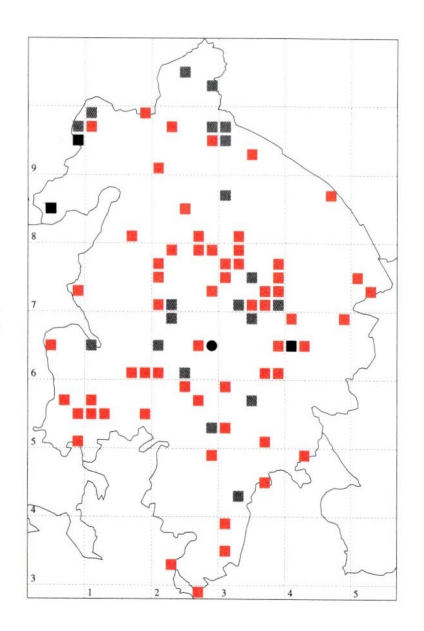

Buff Arches
1653 *Habrosyne pyritoides* (Hufn.)

County status: Widespread and fairly common.
Flight: Mid-June to mid-August.
Larval foodplants: Brambles*.

Generally more plentiful and widely distributed than the preceding species. The Buff Arches similarly feeds on brambles during the larval stage yet is found more frequently outside woodland. Garden moth trap totals at **Pillerton Priors** (CI) are as follows:
1992 (3), 1993 (13), 1994 (8), 2002 (12), 2003 (1), 2004 (6), 2005 (18).

VCH 1904: *'Occurs throughout the County but not abundantly.'*

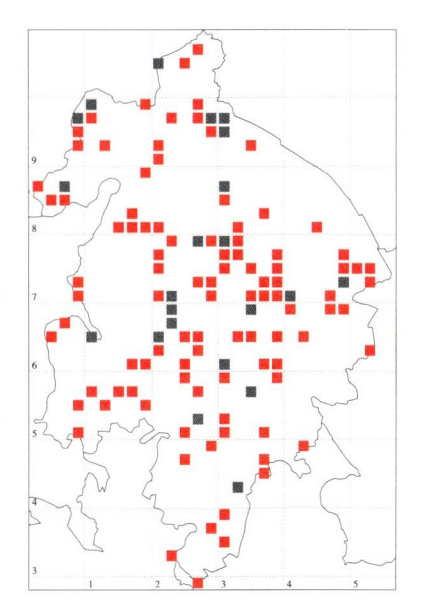

Figure of Eighty
1654 *Tethea ocularis octogesimea* (Hb.)

County status: Widespread and fairly common.
Flight: Late May to July.
Larval foodplants: Aspen* and poplars*.

In the VCH 1904 this species was considered to be a rarity with only two records from Waverley Wood. The next known sighting was at Coventry on 18/6/1938 (LR). From the 1940s *ocularis* began to spread across the County. It is now found in many damp woodlands containing Aspen. Waverley Wood, Ryton Wood, Oakley Wood, Snitterfield Bushes, Oversley Wood, Clowes Wood, Whichford Wood and Wolford Wood all have good colonies. Former gravel extraction sites with poplars by the edges of pools, as at Ufton Fields and Brandon Marsh, provide ideal breeding conditions. Often noted in garden moth traps.

VCH 1904: *Waverley Wood*

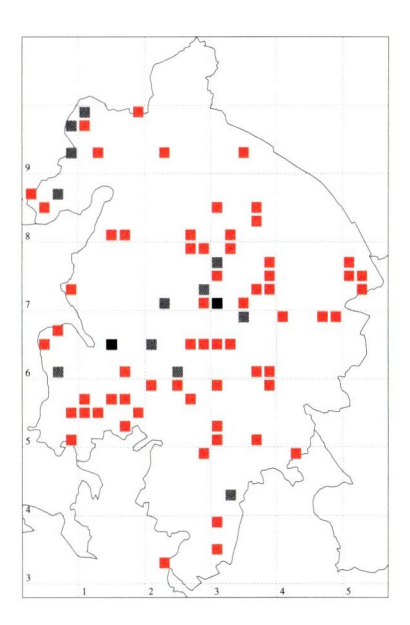

Poplar Lutestring
1655 *Tethea or or* ([D. & S.])

Nationally Local

County status: Very local but fairly common.
Flight: Early May to late August.
Larval foodplants: Aspen* and poplars.

The Poplar Lutestring is restricted to an Aspen-rich group of woodlands in the Stratford-upon-Avon and Redditch districts. It is well established and plentiful at Oversley Wood as the following moth trap totals illustrate:
30/5/1978 (21), 27/5/1980 (18), 14/5/1982 (20) (DB), 21/5/1982 (35) (DB, AFG), 19/5/1989 (23) (DB, AFG, IGMR), 17/6/1996 (20) (DB, AFG, RMC), 7/6/2004 (18) (RMC, AJP, DG), 26/5/2005 (21) (J. Rush).

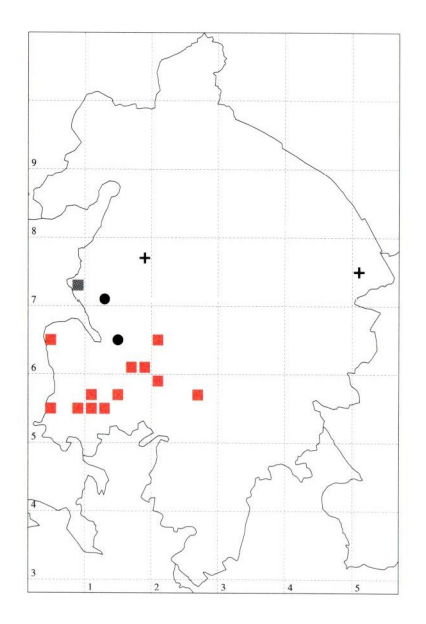

Records:
May's Wood, 1911 (GBM); **Umberslade**, 1919, 28/5/1927 (SEWC); **Clowes Wood**, 1939 a few at light (HEH), 12/9/1951 three larvae on Aspen (HEH), 1956 frequent (BNHS); **Oversley Wood**, 1970 2005 (Warks Moth Group), **Claverdon**, 1985 (IGMR), **Snitterfield Bushes**, 14/5/1988 (2) (DB, AFG, RMC), 16/6/1989 (6) (DB, RGB), 1/6/1990 (3) (DB, AFG, IGMR), 12/6/1995 (2) (DB, BS & Warks Moth Group), 23/6/1998 (2) (DB, MA, RGB); **Charlecote**, 22/6/1989 (DB); **Weethley Wood**, 5/5/1990 (SD), 22/5/1999 (Warks Moth Group); **Bearley**, 10/6/1993, 19/6/1995 (IGMR); **Rough Hill Wood**, 15/6/1994 (CE, LB); **Withycombe Wood**, 31/5/1997 (2) (AJK, DB, Warks Moth Group); **Temple Grafton**, 11/7/2005 (AFG).

VCH 1904: *'Rare.'*
Knowle, Rugby (once only in 1888)

Satin Lutestring
1656 *Tetheella fluctuosa* (Hb.)

Nationally Local

County status: Uncertain.
Flight: June to early August.
Larval foodplants: Birches.

There are only three records of this species in Warwickshire. The Marton specimen was possibly a stray from the nearby Princethorpe woodland complex, which may contain undiscovered colonies.

Records:
Tysoe, 16/7/1956 (TT); **Hillmorton, Rugby**, 12/6/1966 (IGMR); **Marton**, 1/8/1975 (RA).

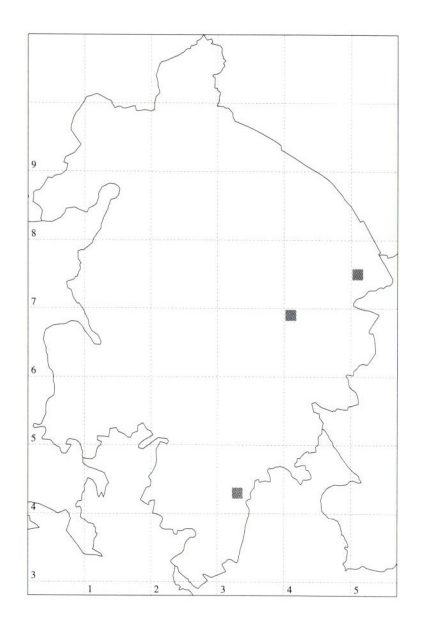

Common Lutestring
1657 *Ochropacha duplaris* (L.)

County status: Fairly widespread and locally fairly common.
Flight: Mid-June to late August.
Larval foodplants: Birches*, Alder, Hazel and oaks.

The Common Lutestring is found locally over a large part of Warwickshire, frequenting open woodland and heathland. The imago may sometimes be attracted to light in good numbers as the following records show: Tile Hill Wood, 25/7/1975 (12) (DB, PC, LEM); Oversley Wood, 28/7/1975 (20) (DB); Sutton Park, 5/8/2000 (15) (Warks Moth Group). Occasionally noted in garden moth traps. The uniform grey-brown f. *obscura* Tutt tends to be dominant but blackish-brown melanic specimens are often encountered in woodland and urban districts.

VCH 1904: *'Not common.'*
Sutton Park, Hay Wood, Knowle, Rugby and Wolford Wood.

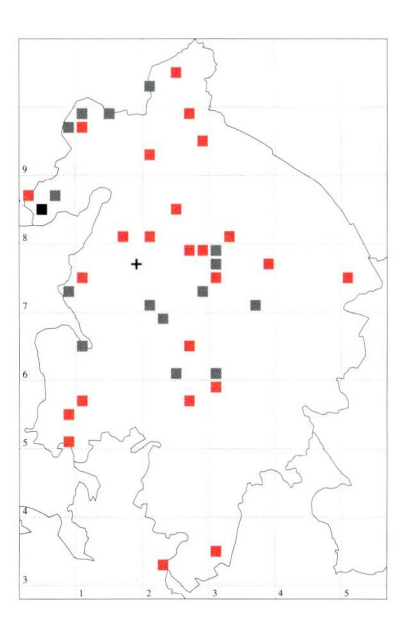

Oak Lutestring
1658 *Cymatophorima diluta hartwiegi* (Reisser)

Nationally Local

County status: Very local and usually scarce, but common at one site.
Flight: Late August to September.
Larval foodplants: Oaks.

There was a dearth of records for this oak woodland species between the 1960s and 1990s. In September 1990 an unusual dispersal appeared to take place with individuals visiting garden moth traps at widely separated sites.

A large population was subsequently discovered in Rough Hill Wood in 1996.

Records:
Rugby district, pre-1893, (A. Sidgwick, 1893); **May's Wood**, 1914 (GBM); **Umberslade**, 1919–21 (SEWC); **Tile Hill Wood**, 1934–37 (CDNHSS); **Clowes Wood**, 1950s annually (BNHS); **Wainbody Wood**, 1955, 13/9/1961 (MEC); **Ufton Wood**, 1959 Survey; **Crackley Wood**, 2/9/1964 two at sugar (CDNHSS); **Bidford-on-Avon**, 1/9/1990 (RMC); **Hampton Magna**, 2/9/1990 (PJR); **Shottery, Stratford-upon-Avon**, 3/9/1990 (RGB); **Rough Hill Wood**, 31/8/1996 (80) (Warks Moth Group).

VCH 1904: *Knowle, Marston Green, Wolford, Whitchurch, Chelmsley Wood.*

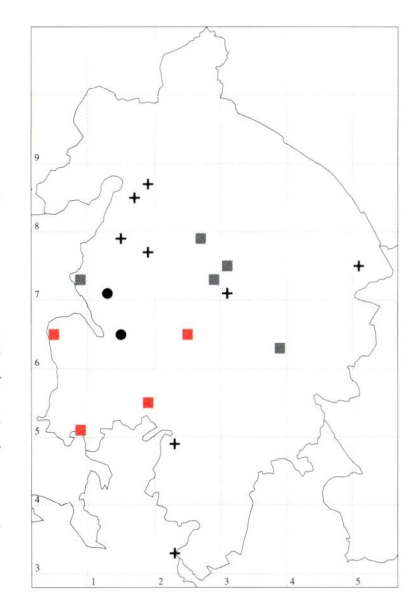

Yellow Horned
1659 *Achlya flavicornis galbanus* (Tutt)

County status: Local and fairly common.
Flight: Late February to late April.
Larval foodplants: Birches*.

The Yellow Horned is an attractive early spring species occurring locally on heathland and in woodland with an abundance of birch.

It is a common visitor to light at some sites as the following figures show: Oakley Wood 9/4/1979 (42) (DB); Snitterfield Bushes 4/3/1989 (25) (DB, AFG); Oversley Wood 5/3/1992 (63) (DB, AFG, RMC).

Occasionally noted in garden moth traps: Tysoe, 20/4/1946 (TT); Charlecote, 18/3/1972 (DB), 16/3/1992 (2) (AFG); Shottery, Stratford-upon-Avon, 26/2/1992 (RGB); Bearley Station, 15/3/1991, 14/3/1992, 7/3/1994 (IGMR).

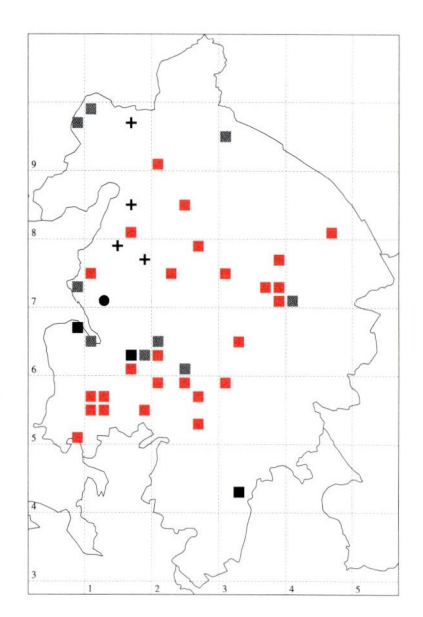

VCH 1904: *'Not common.'*
Sutton Park, Middleton Woods, Solihull, Marston Green and Knowle.

Frosted Green
1660 *Polyploca ridens* (Fabr.)

Nationally Local

County status: Local but fairly common.
Flight: April and May.
Larval foodplants: Oaks*.

The Frosted Green is locally plentiful in broadleaved woodland containing mature oak. Well established in Ryton Wood, Ufton Wood, Oakley Wood, Chesterton Wood, Hampton Wood, Snitterfield Bushes, Oversley Wood and Rough Hill Wood.

Hedgerow oaks also provide suitable breeding conditions. Consequently *ridens* is more frequently encountered outside woodland than the previous species.

VCH 1904: *'Rare.'* Only one record at Wolford Wood.

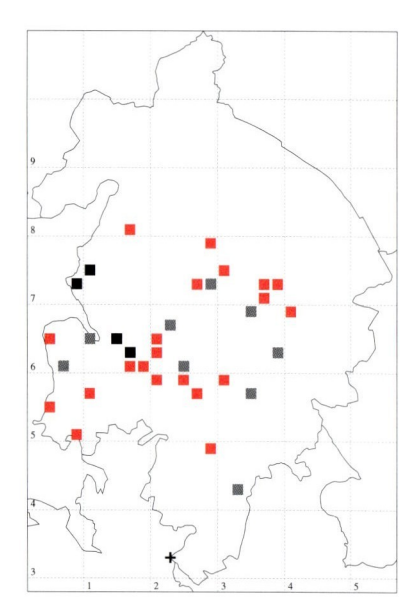

Family: Geometridae

This is the second largest family of macrolepidoptera, consisting of over 300 species in the British Isles, of which 200 are resident in Warwickshire. A diverse group, but most have broad forewings, ample hindwings and light, slender bodies enabling low energy flight. As a result, very few species in this family regularly migrate and only two, Vestal and Gem, are observed in Warwickshire with any frequency. Several species fly by day whilst many others are readily disturbed from herbage, fly at dusk and later respond to light in varying numbers. A few species overwinter as adults but the majority do so as eggs, larvae or pupae.

The family Geometridae is unevenly divided into six sub-families, the largest of which is the Larentiinae (carpets, pugs and allies) consisting of nearly 170 species. The smallest groups are the Archiearinae (orange underwings) with two species and the Alsophilinae containing just one (March Moth). Of the other sub-families the Ennominae (thorns, beauties and umbers) contains over 80 resident species, of which 57 are currently known to occur in Warwickshire. This is a particularly attractive and diverse group. The late autumn to early spring species have wingless females enabling them to remain active on cold winter nights withstanding sub-zero temperatures. The Geometrinae (emeralds) are a striking group displaying wings of a bright green colouration with intricate cross-lines. This subfamily is well represented in Warwickshire with six out of the ten British species. The Sterrhinae (mochas and waves) consist of nearly 40 British species, many of which are small and delicate, and although some of the less distinctive species may still be under-recorded in Warwickshire 19 are known to exist in the County.

The larvae of the Geometridae mostly lack the first three pairs of prolegs, which means that the central area of the body has no legs and is looped up when the caterpillar moves forward. Consequently, the larvae in this group are often termed as loopers, stick caterpillars or inch worms. The name 'Geometer', originated from the word 'geometrid', which means 'ground measurer' in Greek.

Orange Underwing
1661 *Archiearis parthenias* (L.)

Nationally Local

County status: Very local and sometimes fairly common.
Flight: Day-flying in mid-March to late April.
Larval foodplants: Birches*.

The Orange Underwing flies in sunshine during March and April and frequents open birch woodland. It has a rapid flight around the tops of birch trees and is often observed feeding on sallow catkins or basking on the ground. It is found in a number of woodlands and is especially plentiful at Oakley Wood, Oversley Wood, Clowes Wood and Wappenbury Wood.

Records:
Sutton Park, 1928–1931, 1970s (LJE), 1960's (JB); **Austy Wood**, 1940 (GBM); **Forshaw Heath**, 1940 (HEH); **Waverley Wood**, 13/4/1941 (RFB), 1950 (AHK); **Brandon Wood**, 7/4/1947 (6) (LR); **Tile Hill Wood**, 1950 several larvae & imagines (CDNHSS); **Clowes Wood**, 1956 scarce but constant (BNHS), 9/4/1991 (3), 11/4/1991,

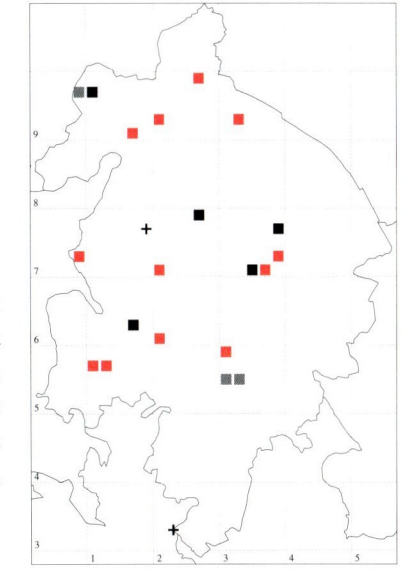

17/3/1992 (6), 31/3/1992, 9/4/1992 (4), 10/4/1992 (10) (MCV); **Oversley Wood**, 30/3/1974 plentiful (DB, AFG), 2/4/1974, 4/4/1974 (3) (DB), 22/3/1980, 5/4/1980 (DB, AFG), 1990s (IGMR), 30/3/2004 (DB, DG, AJP); **Wappenbury Wood**, April 1974 (RHS), 10/4/1976 (DB, RHS), 3/4/1980 (20+) (DB, AFG), 10/4/1985 plentiful (DB, AFG), 1990s (EPS); **Lighthorne**, 1978 plentiful (AKn); **Oakley Wood**, 14/4/1979 (3), 22/3/1980, 3/4/1980 (30+) (DB, AFG), 1990s (DB); **Moreton Morrell**, 11/8/1979 larvae (JRR); **Red Hill, Alcester**, 3/4/1982 (JAH); **Hay Wood**, 18/4/1985 (3) (AFG); **Grendon Common**, 5/4/1987, April 1988 (BM); **Water Orton**, 17/3/1991 (2), 14/3/1993, 20/3/1993 (3), 8/3/1994, 21/3/1994 (KM); **Ryton Wood**, 1992 (LB, CF.); **Ladywalk**, 13/3/1993 (KM), 24/3/2005 (JBr); **Bubbenhall Wood**, April 1997 (LB); **Snitterfield Bushes**, 17/3/1997 (3) (RS); **Whittleford Park**, 17/3/2004 (RR).

VCH 1904: *'Rare.'*
Wolford Wood, Brandon Wood and Knowle.

Light Orange Underwing
1662 *Archiearis notha* (Hb.)

Nationally Scarce B
County status: Very local and sometimes fairly common.
Flight: Day-flying. Late March to early May.
Larval foodplants: Aspen*.

The Light Orange Underwing is on the wing marginally later than its congener the Orange Underwing, and similarly flies above head height in woodland rides and clearings. It occasionally basks on the ground or settles to take moisture and nutrients from muddy paths, especially on sunny mornings following an April rain shower. This species is far more local than *parthenias* and restricted to woods containing Aspen. It is plentiful at Wappenbury Wood and Oversley Wood, where on the evening of 16/4/1983 a male imago was unusually attracted to MV (DB, RMC).

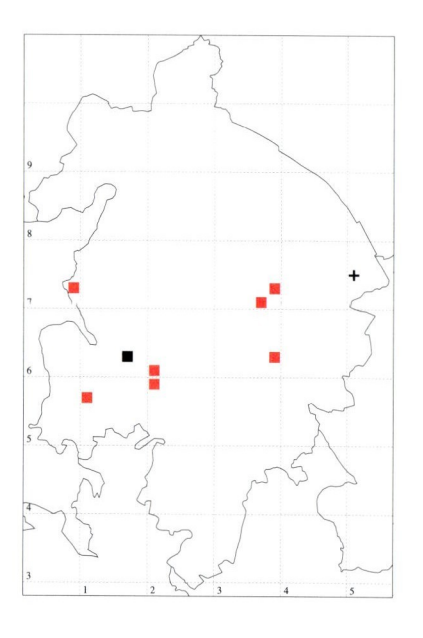

Records:
Wappenbury Wood, 1942 (RFB), 10/4/1976 common (RHS, DB), 13/4/1977 (5) (DB), 17/4/1977 (2) (DB), 10/4/1985 common (AFG, DB), 5/5/1985 (DB); **Austy Wood**, 1946 (FHL); **Windmill Naps**, 1950 (FAN), 1960 three larvae beaten from Aspen (FAN); **Oversley Wood**, 1960–70, 9/4/1980 (DB), 12/4/1980 common, 18/4/1980 (IGMR), 16/4/1983 MV (DB, RMC), 23/4/1984 common (DB), 10/4/1995 plentiful (DB, IGMR), 31/3/1997 (DB), 30/3/2004 (3) (DB, DG, AJP), 28/3/2005 (4) (DB, IGMR); **Ufton Wood**, 4/4/1980 (8), 7/4/1980 (15) (DB, AFG); **Ryton Wood**, May 1985 (RHS), 3/4/1991 (RCK), 1993 (LB, CE); **Clowes Wood**, 9/4/1991 (2), 9/4/1992 (2), 10/4/1992 (2), 19/5/1992, 9/6/1992 larvae on Aspen saplings (MCV); **Snitterfield Bushes**, 29/4/1996 (DB), 11/3/1997, 17/3/1997 (2) (RS).

VCH 1904: *'One record from Rugby district in 1867.' (RNHS)*

March Moth
1663 *Alsophila aescularia* ([D. & S.])

County status: Widespread and fairly common.
Flight: Early February to late April.
Larval foodplants: Polyphagous on deciduous trees, including hawthorns*, Ash*, Wild Privet*, Blackthorn*, Field Maple* and oaks*.

The March Moth breeds on a large number of broadleaved trees and shrubs, enabling the species to be found in many habitats. It occurs plentifully in woodland, where the wingless females may be seen on tree trunks in the early evening. Males are strongly attracted to MV; for example, Oakley Wood, 9/4/1979 (16) (DB); Oversley Wood, 14/3/1986 (26) (DB, AFG, RMC); Snitterfield Bushes, 4/3/1989 (32) (DB, AFG, PJR).

The flight period has normally finished by the end of April but an unusually late individual was caught at Hillmorton, Rugby, on 10/5/1981 (DIP).

VCH 1904: *'Generally distributed and fairly common.'*

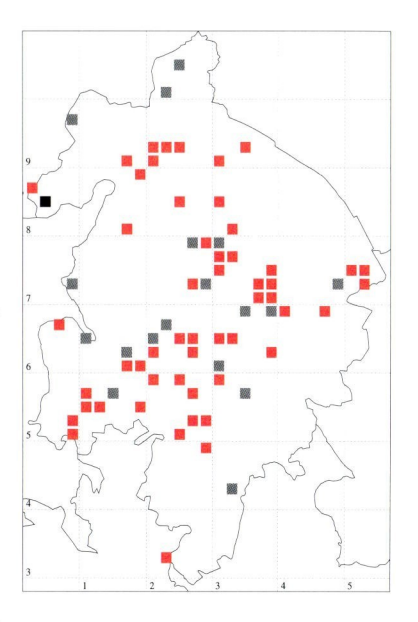

Grass Emerald
1665 *Pseudoterpna pruinata atropunctaria* (Walk.)

County status: Local and fairly common on heathland.
Flight: Late June to mid-August.
Larval foodplants: Gorse and Broom*.

The Grass Emerald is generally scarce in south Warwickshire with sporadic records from static moth traps and evidence of a substantial decline since 1980. In the north of the County, however, it is more frequent and reasonably plentiful on heathland. Sutton Park contains the largest colonies where the adult comes freely to light; for example, 5/8/2000 (12) (DB, DG).

VCH 1904: *'Not uncommon.'*
Sutton Park, Knowle, Rugby, Atherstone and Wolford.

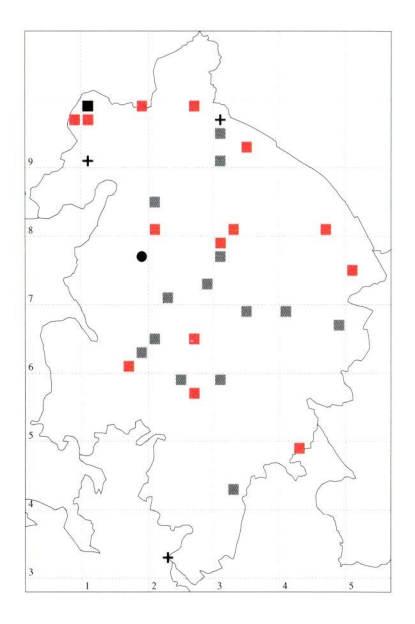

Large Emerald
1666 *Geometra papilionaria* (L.)

County status: Widespread and fairly common.
Flight: Mid-June to late August.
Larval foodplants: Birches*, Alder* and Hazel.

This attractive species is widely distributed and plentiful in broadleaved woodland. Ryton Wood, Oversley Wood and Waverley Wood contain the largest populations. The adult responds well to light; for example, Waverley Wood 20/7/1990 (22) (Warks Moth Group). An occasional visitor to garden moth traps.

VCH 1904: *'Not common.'*
Brandon Wood, Bubbenhall Wood, Frankton Wood, Marston Green, Knowle and Atherstone.

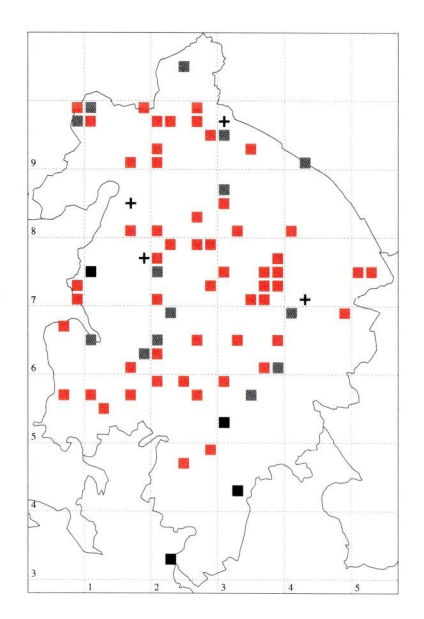

Blotched Emerald
1667 *Comibaena bajularia* ([D. & S.])

Nationally Local

County status: Fairly widespread and locally common.
Flight: Mid-June to early August.
Larval foodplants: Oaks.

The Blotched Emerald has increased since 1980 in both range and frequency. It is now well established in many oak woodlands where good numbers of adults may be attracted to light; for example, Ryton Wood 29/6/1990 (15) (DB, RGB); Waverley Wood 6/7/1991 (35) (Warks Moth Group). Ancient hedgerows containing isolated oaks also provide suitable areas for colonisation. Occasionally recorded in garden moth traps.

VCH 1904: *'Not common and local.'*
Waverley Wood, Bubbenhall Wood, Knowle, Solihull and Atherstone.

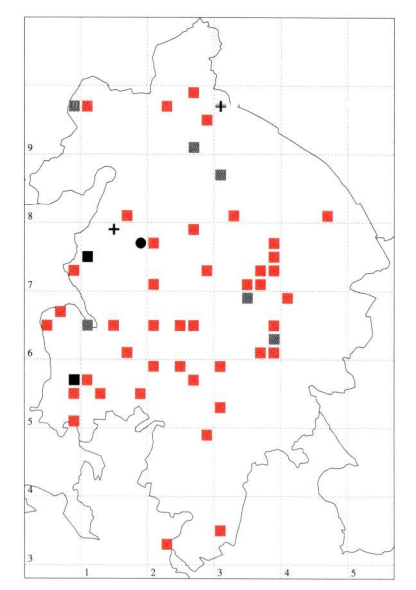

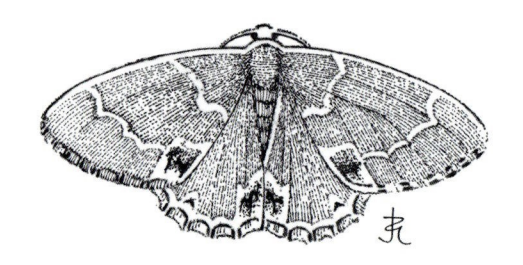

Common Emerald
1669 *Hemithea aestivaria* (Hb.)

County status: Widespread and fairly common.
Flight: June to early August.
Larval foodplants: Polyphagous on deciduous trees and shrubs, including Blackthorn*, hawthorns*, oaks*, Field Maple*, birches* and Bilberry*.

The Common Emerald is a widespread species frequenting woods, parks, hedgerows and scrub on disused railway cuttings or road embankments. It is found plentifully in both rural and urban districts.

Garden moth trap totals from **Hillmorton, Rugby,** are as follows: 1982 (21), 1985 (25), 1990 (27), 1995 (31), 2000 (33), 2004 (6) (DIP).

VCH 1904: *'Not common'.*
Hampton-in-Arden, Knowle, Brandon Wood, Wolford Wood and Atherstone.

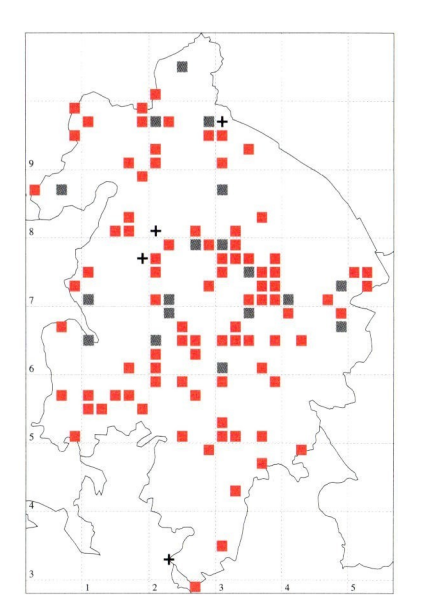

Small Emerald
1673 *Hemistola chrysoprasaria* (Esp.)
Nationally Local

County status: Local and uncommon.
Flight: June to early August.
Larval foodplants: Traveller's-joy* and cultivated species of clematis.

The Small Emerald was first recorded in Warwickshire on 13/7/1946 at Tysoe (TT). This species is found locally in the southern half of the County, in both rural and urban districts. Cultivated species of clematis are possibly used for breeding in urban areas. It is most often observed amongst Traveller's-joy on calcareous soils, especially in disused railway cuttings and woodland edges. An unprecedented 45 were recorded during 2005 in a garden moth trap at Temple Grafton (AFG).

Garden moth trap totals at **Pillerton Priors** are generally low as the following figures indicate: 1992 (1), 1993 (1), 2002 (1), 2003 (5), 2004 (2) (CI).

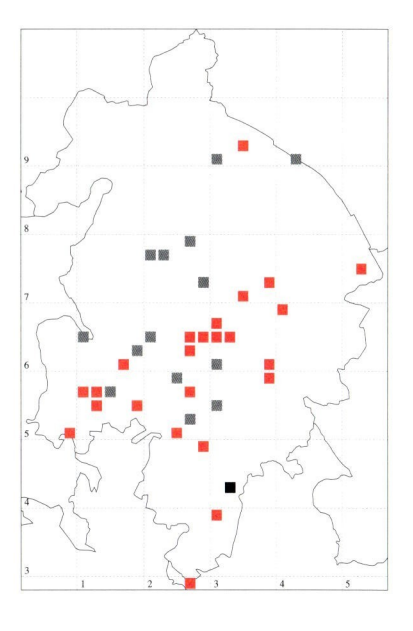

Little Emerald
1674 *Jodis lactearia* (L.)

County status: Fairly widespread and locally fairly common.
Flight: May to July.
Larval foodplants: Polyphagous on trees and shrubs, including hawthorns*, sallows* and Bilberry*.

The Little Emerald is well established in a large number of deciduous woodlands throughout the County. The adult is often noted at dusk flying in sheltered woodland rides. It is less frequently noted in open countryside.

VCH 1904: *'Common everywhere.'*

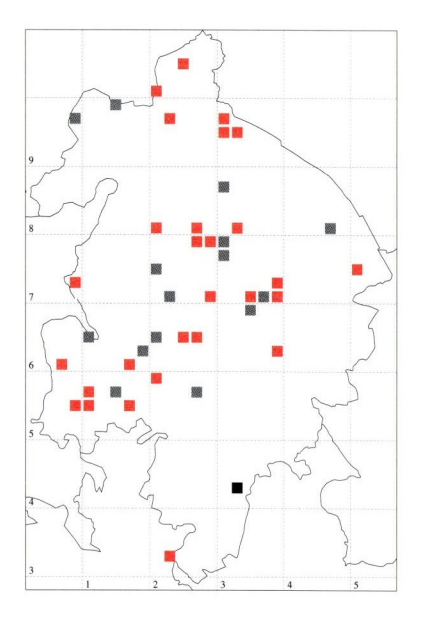

Dingy Mocha
1675 *Cyclophora pendularia* (Cl.)

RDB

County status: Extinct.
Flight: No dates available.
Larval foodplants: Sallows, especially the small-leaved species.

VCH 1904: *Knowle, Erdington, Brandon Wood.*

Mocha
1676 *Cyclophora annularia* (Fabr.)

Nationally Scarce B

County status: Very local and scarce.
Flight: Generally bivoltine in the British Isles, but has to date only been recorded during July and August in Warwickshire.
Larval foodplants: Field Maple.

There are no recent records of this species, which is associated with ancient hedgerows and woodland.

Records:
Lillington, Royal Leamington Spa, 10/7/1950 (WTT); **Wolverton**, 23/8/1983 (RMC).

VCH 1904: *Brandon Wood.*

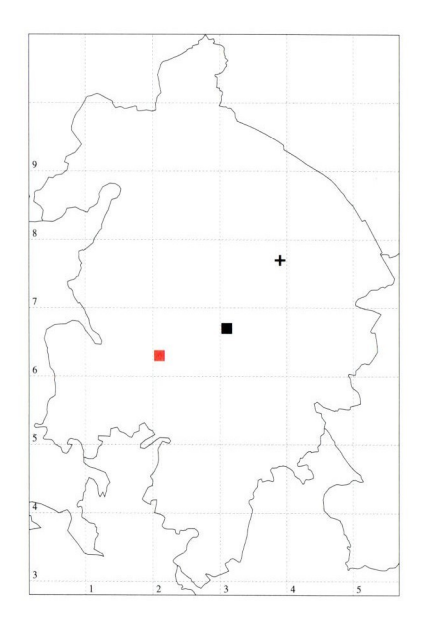

Birch Mocha
1677 *Cyclophora albipunctata* (Hufn.)

Nationally Local

County status: Very local and occasionally fairly common.
Flight: Early May to mid-June and mid-July to late August in two broods.
Larval foodplants: Birches*.

The main populations of Birch Mocha are centred around a group of woodlands in the Coventry district, including Waverley Wood, where it may sometimes be fairly plentiful; for example, 20/7/1990 (12) (Warks Moth Group). Occasionally recorded outside normal woodland habitats in suburban gardens.

Records:
Henley-in-Arden, 2/6/1914 (GBM); **Brandon Wood**, 8/5/1946 (LR), 9/6/1998, 5/7/1998 (2) (DB, DG); **Waverley Wood**, 1954 (AHK), 1960s (JB), 1976 (MCV), 19/8/1989 (6), 20/7/1990 (12) (Warks Moth Group), 26/8/1995 larvae (2) (MCV), 17/5/2003 (2) (Warks Moth Group); **Tile Hill Wood**, 1/7/1959 larva (GW); **Coughton Park**, 1968 (KEH); **Wappenbury Wood**, 10/7/1972 (DB), 30/7/1999 (CDNHSS); **Hillmorton**, **Rugby**, 14/6/1986, 1990s (DIP), 14/8/1986 (PN); **Tile Hill**, **Coventry**, 1991 (AJK); **Brandon Marsh**, 27/8/1991 (DB); **Ryton Wood**, 1992–93 (LB), 12/6/1992 (AJK), 6/6/1996 (RCK), 8/8/1997 (PC, MA); 16/5/2005 (RR); **Royal Leamington Spa**, 1992 (PhP); **Steetley Meadows**, 7/8/1992 (PC, CW); **Bearley Station**, 19/8/1993 (IGMR).

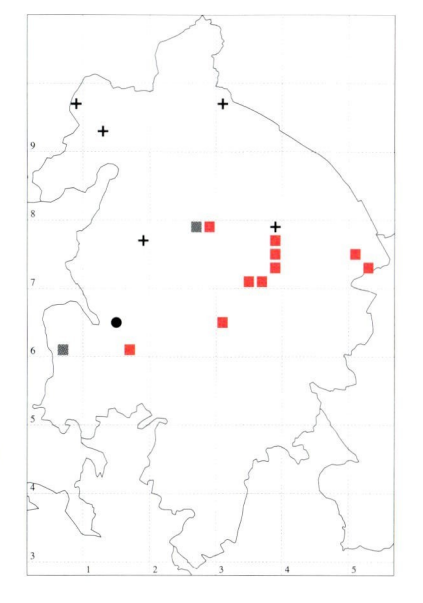

VCH 1904: *'Not common.'*
Knowle, Erdington, Brandon Wood, Atherstone, Coombe Wood, Sutton Park.

Blair's Mocha
1678 *Cyclophora puppillaria* (Hb.)

Scarce and irregular immigrant: Southern Europe, Mediterranean and North Africa

County status: Very scarce immigrant.
Larval foodplants: Evergreen Oak.

A male of this scarce immigrant was caught in a garden moth trap at Alveston, Stratford-upon-Avon on 13/10/1978 (DB). It was the northernmost of six *puppillaria* recorded in southern Britain during that week (Brown, 1979a).

False Mocha
1679 *Cyclophora porata* (L.)
Nationally Scarce B

County status: Very local and scarce.
Flight: Two generations. Early May to June, and August.
Larval foodplants: Oaks.

This Nationally Scarce species is associated with young oak re-growth following coppicing. Such conditions existed in Weethley Wood during 1990 when the moths could be observed in small numbers at dusk and later at light. Following subsequent changes in woodland management there have been no further sightings. Similarly at Oversley Wood appearances have dwindled in the last decade.

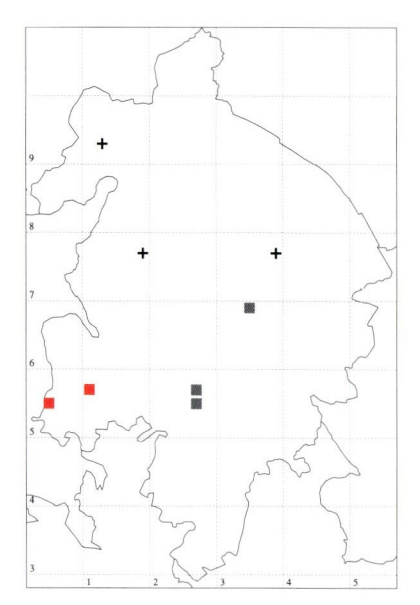

Records:
Charlecote, 23/8/1969, 18/8/1979 (DB); **Cubbington**, 9/6/1970 (AFG); **NVRS**, **Wellesbourne**, 6/8/1970 (RAW); **Oversley Wood**, 16/6/1984 (AFG), 1/8/1992 (Warks Moth Group); **Weethley Wood**, 3/5/1990 a few at dusk (SD), 12/5/1990 (2) (DB, AFG, PJR, SD).

VCH 1904: '*Not common.*'
Erdington, Knowle, Brandon Wood.

Maiden's Blush
1680 *Cyclophora punctaria* (L.)
Nationally Local

County status: Fairly widespread and fairly common.
Flight: Two generations. May to early July and August to September.
Larval foodplants: Oaks*.

Another oak-feeding species found locally over a large part of the County but with a dearth of records from the south. The Maiden's Blush is well established in broadleaved woodlands at Ryton Wood, Waverley Wood, Brandon Wood, Kingsbury Wood, Hay Wood, Snitterfield Bushes, Oversley Wood, Weethley Wood, Rough Hill Wood and Old Park Wood.

It is occasionally recorded from gardens in the vicinity of oak trees.

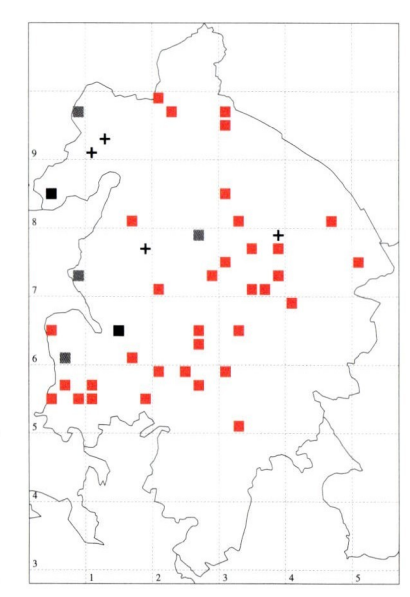

VCH 1904: '*Not common*'.
Sutton Park, Knowle, Erdington, Brandon Woods, Coombe Wood, Atherstone.

Clay Triple-lines
1681 *Cyclophora linearia* (Hb.)

Nationally Local

County status: Local and uncommon, but gradually increasing.
Flight: Late May to July with occasional individuals in August.
Larval foodplants: Beech*.

First recorded in 1948 at Austy Wood (HEH), the Clay Triple-lines has slowly expanded its range in the County. As with most species feeding exclusively on Beech in Warwickshire colonisation of new areas is difficult, but *linearia* has gradually spread into built-up areas by using garden Beech hedges. Occasionally recorded at garden moth traps.

Woodland sites include Purley Chase, Temple Grafton, Wolford Wood, Rough Hill Wood, Bowshot Wood and Oakley Wood. Particularly strong colonies have developed in recent years at Ryton Wood and Oversley Wood where a record 38 imagines were attracted to light on 7/6/2004 (RMC, DG, AJP).

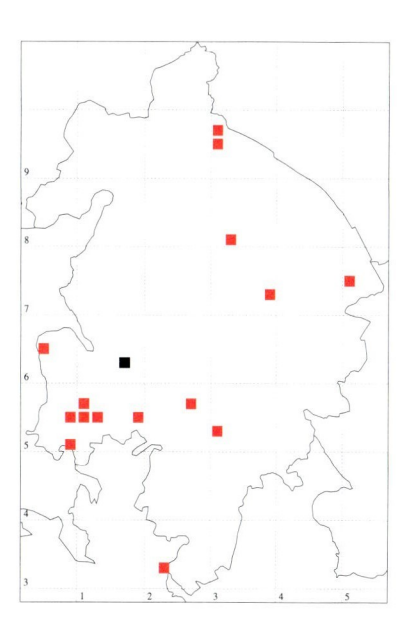

Blood-vein
1682 *Timandra comae* (Schmidt)

County status: Widespread and fairly common.
Flight: Two or three overlapping generations. Mid-May to early October.
Larval foodplants: Docks, sorrels and Knotgrass.

The Blood-vein is found throughout the County in a diversity of habitats, but has a particular penchant for damp meadows and waste-ground. It is frequently disturbed during the daytime from low herbage. Three generations may be produced in warm years.

VCH 1904: *'Not common but generally distributed.'*

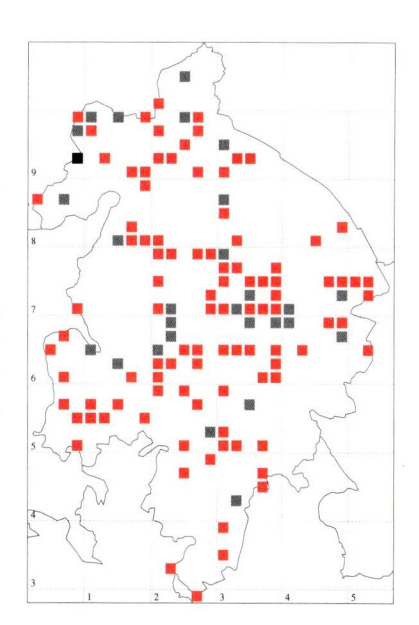

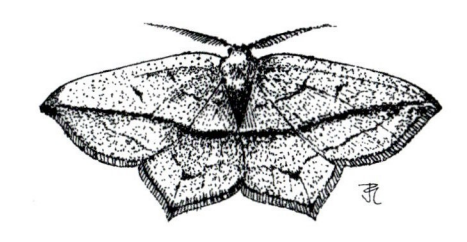

Lace Border
1687 *Scopula ornata* (Scop.)

Nationally Scarce A

County status: Presumed extinct.
Flight: June. Often observed by day.
Larval foodplants: Wild Thyme and Wild Marjoram.

This Nationally Scarce species, associated with calcareous grassland, was found in small numbers (four or five each year) at Wilmcote Rough between 1977 and 1979 (JMP). Recent visits to the site have failed to produce further examples and it is feared this attractive moth has become extinct.

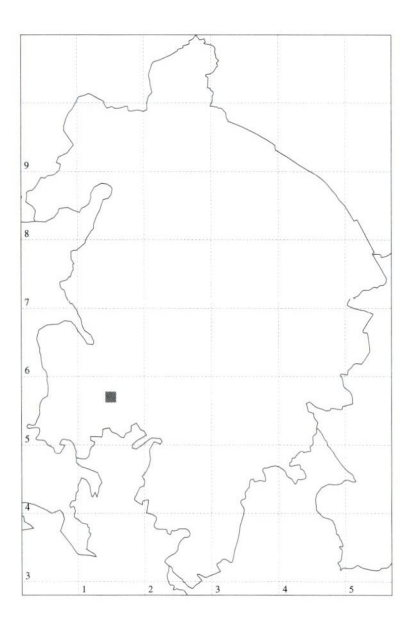

Mullein Wave
1689 *Scopula marginepunctata* (Goeze)

Nationally Local

County status: Status uncertain. Very local and scarce.
Flight: Possibly two generations. June to August.
Larval foodplants: Mugwort, Wood Sage, Wild Marjoram, plantains and other low-growing plants.

The status of this elusive species in Warwickshire is not clear as 100 years separated the first two records. During 2005 four specimens were caught in a garden moth trap at Hillmorton, Rugby, suggesting local colonisation, perhaps on a nearby railway embankment.

Records:
Rugby district, pre-1893, (A. Sidgwick, 1893); **Hillmorton, Rugby**, 26/8/1991 (DIP), 12/8/2005, 23/8/2005, 31/8/2005, 1/9/2005 (PN); **Ufton Fields**, 8/6/1997 specimen netted in daytime (DB).

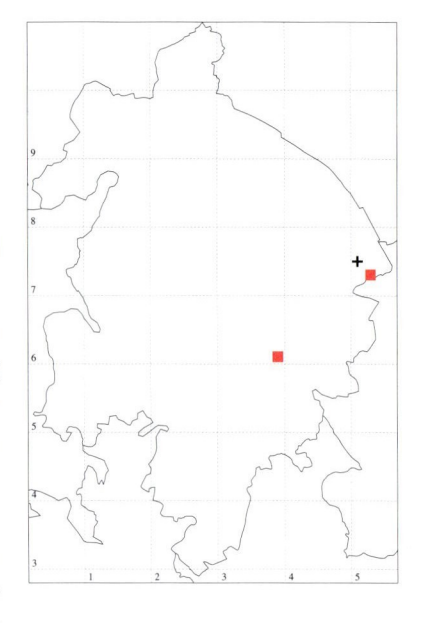

Small Blood-vein
1690 *Scopula imitaria* (Hb.)

County status: Widespread and fairly common.
Flight: Late June to August, with a partial second generation in September.
Larval foodplants: Privet, Honeysuckle and probably a variety of low-growing plants.

The Small Blood-vein is found throughout the County in a number of habitats in both rural and suburban areas. It visits light in variable numbers as the following figures illustrate:
Pillerton Priors: 1992 (4), 1993 (8), 1994 (6), 2002 (2), 2003 (7), 2004 (4) (CI);
Hillmorton, Rugby: 1982 (6), 1985 (7), 1990 (10), 1995 (31), 2000 (23), 2004 (22) (DIP).

VCH 1904: *'Not common'.*
Yardley, Atherstone, Wolford and Overslade.

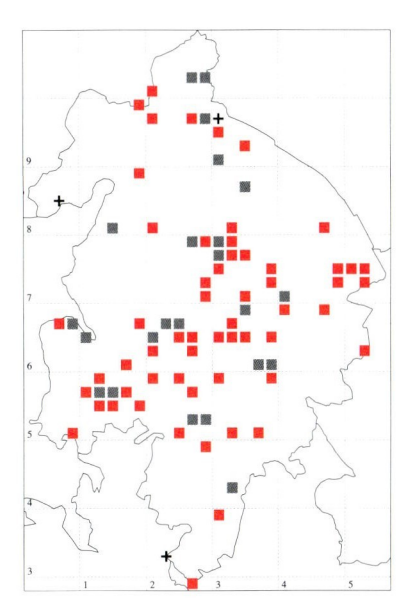

Lesser Cream Wave
1692 *Scopula immutata* (L.)

Nationally Local

County status: Very local and scarce.
Flight: July.
Larval foodplants: Common Valerian and Meadowsweet.

This rare Warwickshire species is associated with damp meadows and marshy areas in river valleys. The two recent records are from garden moth traps, which may indicate the presence of undiscovered colonies in the vicinity.

Records:
May's Wood, 1940–50 'a few each year' (GBM); **Austy Wood**, 1946 (HEH); **Tile Hill Wood**, 1950s, 1960 (CDNHSS); **Ryton Wood**, 12/6/1987, 19/5/1989 (CDNHSS); **Charlecote**, 15/7/2000 (AFG); **Hampton Magna**, 2001 (PJR).

VCH 1904: *Wolford.*

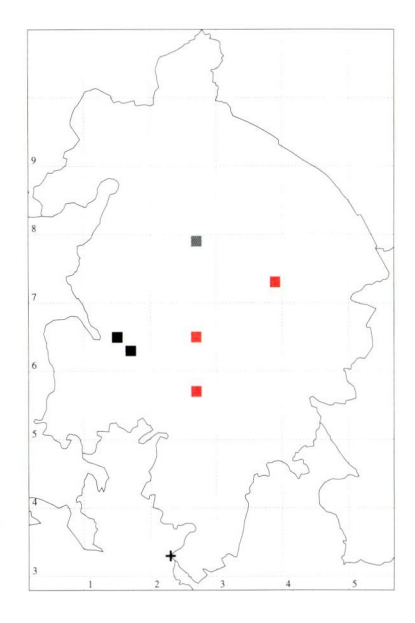

Cream Wave
1693 *Scopula floslactata* (Haw.)

Nationally Local

County status: Local and fairly common.
Flight: May to July.
Larval foodplants: Bedstraws, Knotgrass and probably a variety of low-growing plants.

The Cream Wave is found locally over a large area of central Warwickshire. Although it has occasionally been recorded in gardens, woodland is the main habitat. This species is well established in Waverley Wood, Ryton Wood, Brandon Wood, Ufton Wood, Hay Wood, Snitterfield Bushes, Oakley Wood, Oversley Wood, Weethley Wood and Old Park Wood.

VCH 1904: *'Common.'*
Sutton Park, Knowle, Brandon Wood and Wolford Wood.

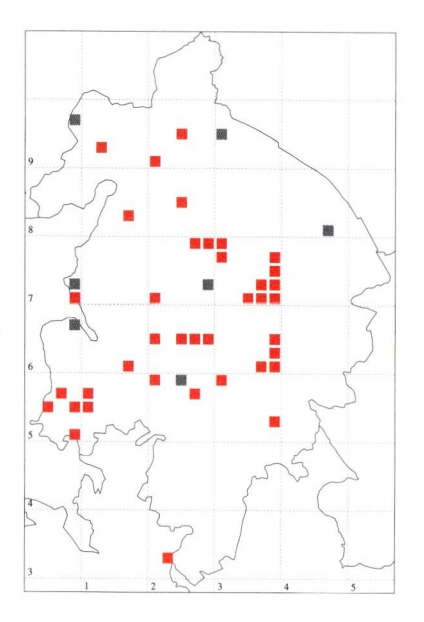

Least Carpet
1699 *Idaea rusticata atrosignaria* Lempke

Nationally Local
Resident and possible immigrant

County status: Status uncertain.
Flight: July and early August.
Larval foodplants: Ivy, Traveller's-joy, Golden Alyssum and probably many other plants.

The Least Carpet was first recorded in Britain in 1831 from the London area; populations continued to be centred around the Thames Estuary until a recent expansion north and westward during the 1980s and 1990s. It was first noted in Warwickshire on 17/7/1989 at Coventry (MB). The County status of this species is now uncertain following a lack of records since 1996.

Records:
Parkside, Coventry, 17/7/1989 (MB); **Hillmorton, Rugby,** 1/8/1991, 20/7/1995 (DIP); **Charlecote,** 2/8/1991, 20/7/1996 (DB).

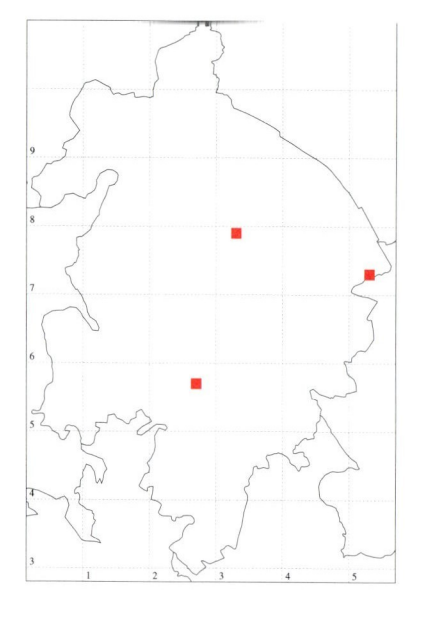

Small Fan-footed Wave
1702 *Idaea biselata* (Hufn.)

County status: Widespread and fairly common.
Flight: Late June to late August.
Larval foodplants: Little known in the wild, but in captivity will eat Dandelion, Knotgrass, plantains and brambles.

The Small Fan-footed Wave is frequently observed during the daytime. It is found in a variety of wooded habitats and regularly recorded from garden moth traps. Totals at **Kenilworth Road, Coventry,** are as follows: 2001 (35), 2002 (25), 2003 (28), 2004 (40) 2005 (24) (MA).

VCH 1904: *'Common'.*
Knowle, Yardley, Overslade, Atherstone, Wolford.

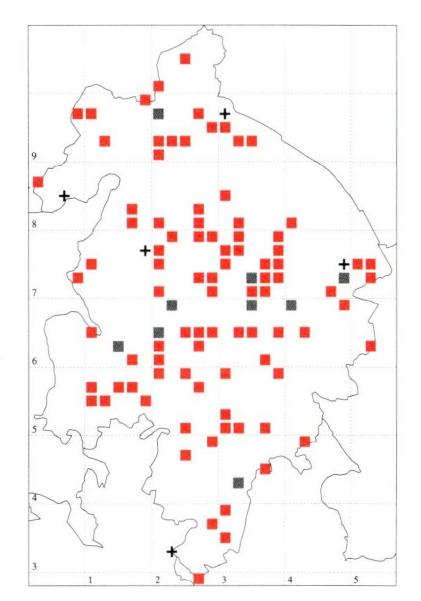

Dwarf Cream Wave
1705 *Idaea fuscovenosa* (Goeze)

Nationally Local

County status: Very local and uncommon.
Flight: June to August.
Larval foodplants: Little known in the wild, but in captivity will eat Dandelion, Knotgrass and brambles.

The Dwarf Cream Wave has been noted in wooded habitats, as well as gardens in both rural and urban districts. With no mention in the VCH 1904 and a lack of records during the first half of the twentieth century it is not clear if this species had simply been overlooked or is a recent coloniser.

Records:
Hartshill Hayes, 1975–79 (RJT); **Fen End**, **Kenilworth**, 1977–79 (DC); **Wootton Green**, 26/7/1980 (CDNHSS); **Charlecote**, 1980–2000 annually (DB, AFG); **Hampton-in-Arden**, 16/7/1983 (MCV); **Snitterfield Bushes**, 1986 (JMP); **Hillmorton**, **Rugby**, 16/7/1986, 19/8/1986, 12/7/1996, 5/7/1998, 23/6/1999, 14/8/2001, 14/7/2002, 26/7/2005 (PN), 25/7/1997, 6/7/1999, 7/7/2001, 30/7/2002, 2/8/2002 (DIP); **Ryton Wood**, 1992 (RCK, LB, CE), 11/6/2002 (NJS); **Hampton Magna**, 2001 (PJR); **Central Rugby**, 19/7/2004 (IGMR); **Sydenham**, **Royal Leamington Spa**, 15/7/2005 (MK).

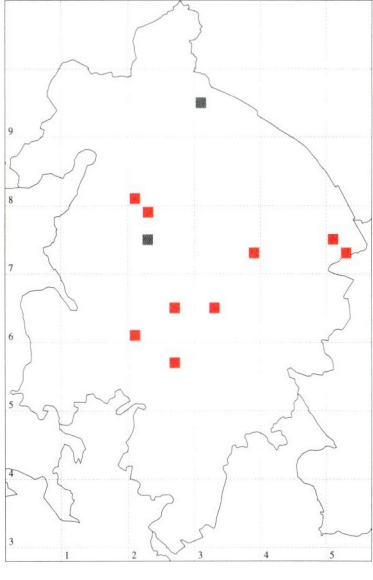

Small Dusty Wave
1707 *Idaea seriata* (Schr.)

County status: Widespread and fairly common in urban districts.
Flight: Possibly two generations. Early June to late September.
Larval foodplants: Ivy and, in captivity, Dandelion, docks and Knotgrass.

The Small Dusty Wave appears to have two overlapping broods from early June to late September. Recorders report peaks during the third week of June and again in mid-September.

This tiny moth is very much an urban species as the following comparative garden moth trap totals illustrate:

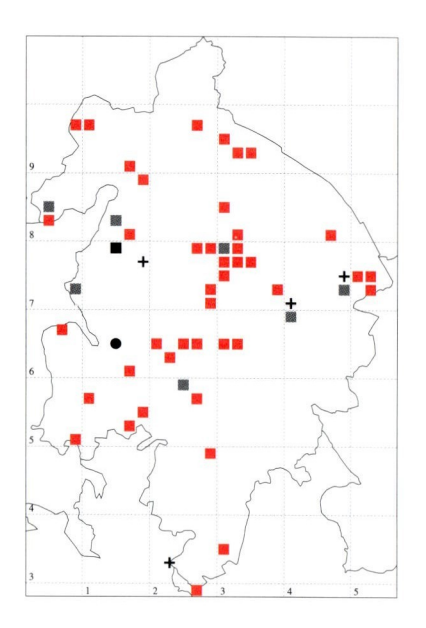

Habitat	Location	1983	1985	1989	1990	1992	1995	1999	2001	2003	2004
Urban	Radford, Coventry (MCV)	11	6	8	14	12	13	11	19	19	15
Suburban	Hillmorton, Rugby (DIP)	29	4	18	32	37	64	44	55	50	38
Rural	Charlecote (DB)	0	0	0	4	6	4	1	3	2	0

VCH 1904: *Solihull, Knowle, Princethorpe, Overslade, Wolford.*

Single-dotted Wave
1708 *Idaea dimidiata* (Hufn.)

County status: Widespread and fairly common.
Flight: June to September.
Larval foodplants: Cow Parsley, Burnet-saxifrage, Hedge Bedstraw and probably many other herbaceous plants.

The Single-dotted Wave is found throughout Warwickshire in a wide range of habitats, but shows a preference for damp woodland and marshy areas.

VCH 1904: *'Common.'*
Knowle, Hampton-in-Arden, Atherstone, Overslade, Wolford.

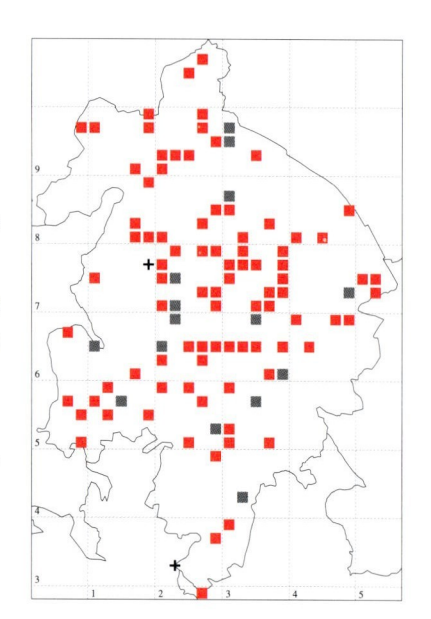

Satin Wave
1709 *Idaea subsericeata* (Haw.)

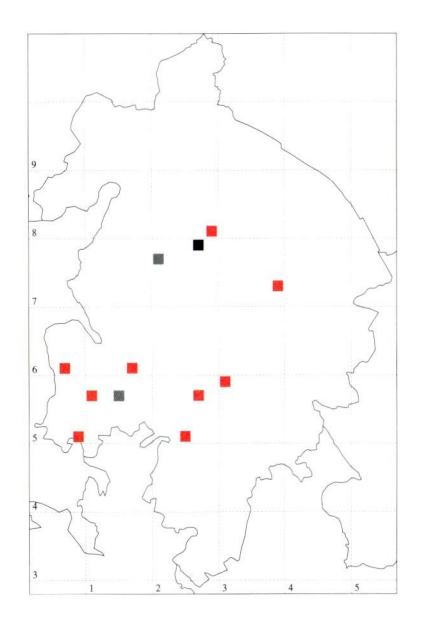

County status: Very local and uncommon.
Flight: June and July.
Larval foodplants: Little known in the wild, but in captivity will eat Dandelion, Knotgrass and plantains.

Before 1980 there were very few records of this species and it is not certain if numbers have increased substantially, or whether the moth had previously been overlooked. The Satin Wave frequents woodland, scrub and rough calcareous grassland, including disused railway embankments. It is occasionally noted in garden moth traps.

Records:
Tile Hill Wood, 5/6/1937, 5/7/1937, 30/5/1953 (CDNHSS); **Temple Balsall**, 9/7/1977 (FWS); **Wilmcote Rough**, 1977–80 three or four each year (JMP); **Allesley, Coventry**, 26/7/1980 (MW); **Charlecote**, June 1981, 2/7/1981, 23/6/1991, 20/6/1996, 27/6/1996, 9/6/1997, 12/6/1998, 11/8/1999 (DB, AFG); **Bearley Station**, 10/6/1988 (IGMR); **Ryton Wood**, 1991–92 (RCK, LB, CE); **Bidford-on-Avon**, 30/6/1991, 3/7/1991, 4/7/1991, 1992 (6), 1993 (2) (RMC); **Oakley Wood**, 21/6/1992 (DB); **Coughton Park**, 29/6/1996 (DB, AFG); **Oversley Wood**, 16/6/2000 (Warks Moth Group), 14/6/1995 (AFG, BS, BE); **Goldicote Cutting**, 25/6/2004 (CI).

Treble Brown Spot
1711 *Idaea trigeminata* (Haw.)

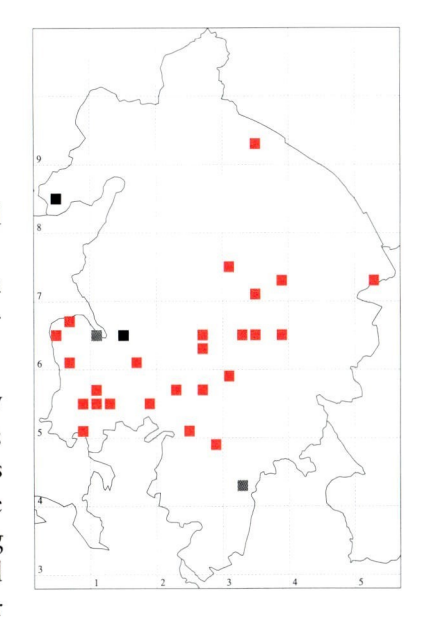

Nationally Local

County status: Local and fairly common. Increasing.
Flight: June to August with an occasional partial second generation in September.
Larval foodplants: Little known in the wild, but in captivity will eat Ivy, Knotgrass, plantains and other low-growing plants.

The Treble Brown Spot was first recorded in the County during the 1940s: May's Wood (annually) (GBM); Edgbaston, Birmingham, August 1946 (MWB). It has undergone a dramatic increase since 1980 and the species has become established at many sites containing open woodland and old hedgerows. Sheltered rural and suburban gardens also provide suitable conditions for breeding.

Small Scallop
1712 *Idaea emarginata* (L.)

Nationally Local

County status: Fairly widespread and locally fairly common.
Flight: Late June to early September.
Larval foodplants: Bedstraws and a variety of low-growing plants.

The Small Scallop is now found over a large part of the County, having become established since the VCH 1904. It shows a distinct preference for damp woodlands and marshy areas. There are particularly good populations at Waverley Wood, Ryton Wood, Brandon Marsh, Whitacre Heath, and Newbold Comyn near Royal Leamington Spa. The adult is not strongly attracted to light but is more often observed flying in numbers at dusk on warm, calm evenings.

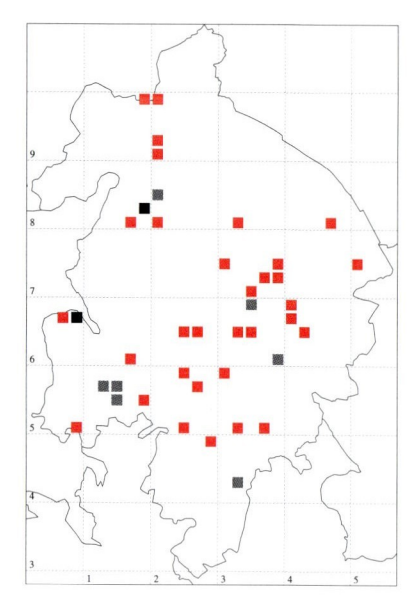

VCH 1904: *'Doubtfully recorded from Rugby.'*

Riband Wave
1713 *Idaea aversata* (L.)

County status: Widespread and abundant.
Flight: June to late August; occasionally a partial second generation in September and October.
Larval foodplants: Various low-growing plants, including docks, Dandelion and bedstraws.

The Riband Wave is an abundant summertime species throughout the County. The imago is readily disturbed during the daytime and is dominant in moth traps.

There is evidence of a partial second generation in some years: Hillmorton, Rugby, 29/8–2/10/1989 (6), 22/9/1992 (DIP); Charlecote, 29/9/1999 (DB).

The plain form ab. *remutata* (L.) is generally more plentiful than the banded typical form. At Charlecote, during 2005, out of a total of 164 specimens only 23 were of the banded form—a ratio of 6:1 (DB). Similarly, results from a garden moth trap in a suburban district of Rugby (Hillmorton) show a ratio of 5:1 (PN):

Form	1999	2005
Typical banded	24	55
Plain (ab. *remutata*)	131	294

VCH 1904: *'Common everywhere.'*

Plain Wave
1715 *Idaea straminata* (Borkh.)

Nationally Local

County status: Local and occasionally fairly common.
Flight: Late June to early August.
Larval foodplants: Little known in the wild but in captivity will eat Dandelion and Knotgrass.

The Plain Wave is found mainly in the northern half of Warwickshire where it frequents heathland, woodland rides and clearings. Well established at Ryton Wood, Wappenbury Wood, Alvecote Pools, Sutton Park and Grendon Common. This species is generally observed at light in small numbers with the following exceptions: Bentley Park Wood 20/7/1996 (12) (Warks Moth Group); Waverley Wood 4/7/1992 (15) (Warks Moth Group).

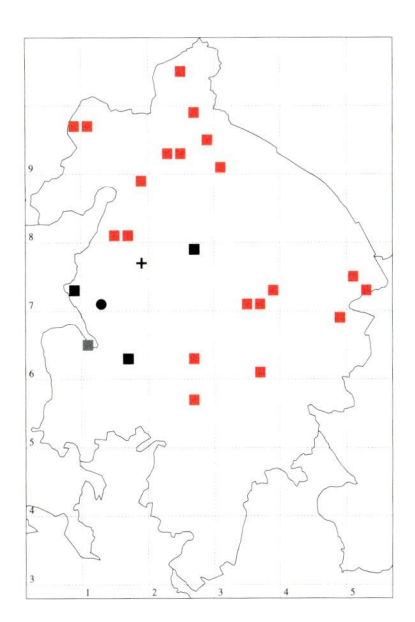

Occasionally recorded in garden moth traps:
Hillmorton, Rugby, 23/6/1982, 13/7/1986, 17/7/1988, 7/7/1992 (DIP), 1986 (21) (PN); **Charlecote**, 7/7/1992 (AFG); **Solihull**, 1994 (AP), 2002, 14/7/2003 (RL); **Nuneaton**, 1996 (PT); **Warwick**, 2/8/2003 (SDT).

VCH 1904: *'Not common.'*
Sutton Park, Rugby, Knowle.

Vestal
1716 *Rhodometra sacraria* (L.)

Frequent immigrant: Southern Europe and North Africa

County status: A regular immigrant.
Flight: July to October.
Larval foodplants: Knotgrass. In captivity the larvae will eat many low-growing plants, including docks and Dandelion.

The Vestal has become a regular visitor in recent decades. 1983 was an exceptional year when in excess of 100 examples were noted, some of which may have originated from local breeding.

Records:

1908—**Saltley, Birmingham**, (AEW).
1947—**Olton, Birmingham**, (FAN).
1973—**Radford, Coventry**, 8/9 (MCV).
1977—**Marton**, 28/10 (RA).
1978—**Charlecote**, 10/10 (2) (DB), 14/10 (2), 24/10 (AFG);
    Hampton Lucy, 14/10 (2) (DB).

1980—**Charlecote**, 26/9 (DB).
1981—**Charlecote gravel pit**, 4/10 flushed in daytime (DB, AFG).
1983—**Marton**, 24/9–30/9 (10+) (RA);
    Bidford-on-Avon, 24/9–30/9 (10+) (RMC);

Hillmorton, Rugby, 15/6, 27/9 to 5/10 (14) (DIP);
Charlecote, 5/8–19/10 (80+ including uniform pink specimens) (AFG);
Radford, Coventry, 30/9 (MCV);
Charlecote gravel pit, 2/10 (AFG, DB);
Hampton Wood, 6/10 (AFG, RGB).
1984—Charlecote, 2/9 (DB), 13/9 (AFG);
Pailton, 7/9, 8/9 (2) (KCG).
1987—Pailton, (KCG);
Charlecote, 31/8, 2/9, 9/9 (2), 16/9, 22/9 (AFG, DB).
1989—Charlecote, 12/9, 15/9, 25/9, 27/10 (AFG, DB);
Hillmorton, Rugby, 2/10 (DIP).
1990—Charlecote, 16/10 (AFG).
1992—Charlecote, 23/7 (AFG);
Bearley Station, 29/9 (IGMR).
1994—Bidford-on-Avon, 4/8 (RMC);
Charlecote, 4/8, 27/8 (DB);
Hillmorton, Rugby, 6/8 (DIP).
1995—Bidford-on-Avon, 9/8 (RMC);
Charlecote, 12/10 (3) (AFG).
1996—Charlecote, 14/10 (DB), 20/10 (AFG);
Solihull, 15/10 (AP);
Pillerton Priors, 24/10 (CI).
1998—Bidford-on-Avon, 14/8 (RMC);
Charlecote, 30/8, 1/9 (2), 5/9, 20/9, 14/10 (AFG, DB);
Hillmorton, Rugby, 31/8 (DIP);
Kenilworth, 6/9, 25/9 (PA).
2000—Charlecote, 24/6, 25/8–28/8 (3), 26/9 (DB, AFG);
Hillmorton, Rugby, 30/8 (PN).
2001—Tile Hill, Coventry, 5/10 (AJK);
Charlecote, 13/10 (2), 17/10 (AFG), 20/10 (DB).
2002—Charlecote, 17/8 (DB).
2003—Charlecote, 22/6, 17/8, 19/9–29/9 (4), 2/10, 13/10 (AFG, DB);
Bidford-on-Avon, 25/6, 2/10 (RMC);
Kenilworth Road, Coventry, 17/8, 21/9 (MA);
Pillerton Priors, 22/9 (CI).
2005—Charlecote, 23/7 (DB);
Solihull, 2/10 (RL).

Oblique Carpet
1719 *Orthonama vittata* (Borkh.)

Nationally Local

County status: Very local and scarce.
Flight: June. No evidence of a second generation in Warwickshire.
Larval foodplants: Bedstraws.

The Oblique Carpet, an inhabitant of marshy places, is only very occasionally recorded in Warwickshire. There are no recent records, but fieldwork in suitable undisturbed habitats in river valleys may reveal new sites.

Records:
Rugby, 1893 (PWA); **Hampton Wood**, 1973 (AFG); **Charlecote**, 16/6/1974 (AFG).

VCH 1904: *'Once taken in Sutton Park.'*

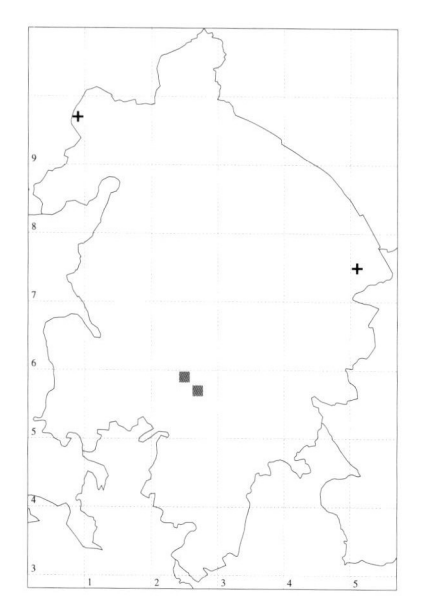

Gem
1720 *Orthonama obstipata* (Fabr.)
Regular immigrant: Southern Europe and North Africa

County status: Fairly regular immigrant.
Flight: May to November.
Larval foodplants: Little known in the wild, but in captivity will eat docks, Dandelion, groundsels, ragworts and many other herbaceous plants.

The Gem is now recorded almost annually, but usually in small numbers. 1996 was the most prolific year on record with 21 individuals reported.

Records:

1880—**Knowle**, (WGB).
1949—**Tysoe**, 10/10 (TT).
1959—**Wilmcote**, (FAN).
1973—**Hampton Wood**, 31/8, 3/9 (AFG).
1975—**Charlecote**, 23/8 (AFG).
1976—**Fen End, Kenilworth**, (DC).
1977—**Charlecote**, 21/10 (AFG).
1978—**Charlecote**, 14/10 (AFG).
1979—**Charlecote**, 8/9, 8/10 (DB, AFG); **Marton**, 9/10 (RA).
1980—**Charlecote**, 26/10 (AFG).
1981—**Charlecote**, 29/7 (DB).
1982—**Charlecote**, 2/10 (DB); **Bidford-on-Avon**, (RMC).
1983—**Radford, Coventry**, 7/8 (MCV); **Charlecote**, 7/9 (AFG); **Hillmorton, Rugby**, 4/11 (DIP).
1987—**Charlecote**, 17/9, 31/10 (AFG); **Bearley Station**, 31/10 (IGMR).
1991—**The Island, Tysoe**, 18/7 (RCK).
1992—**Charlecote**, 29/5, 14/7, 28/7, 3/10 (AFG).
1993—**Charlecote**, 28/7 (AFG); **Hillmorton, Rugby**, 6/8, 25/9 (DIP).
1994—**Charlecote**, 23/10 (DB), 12/11 (2) (AFG).
1995—**Charlecote**, 13/11 (AFG).
1996—**Charlecote**, 7/6, 28/7–13/8 (9), 30/9, 19/10, 1/11 (AFG, DB).
Bidford-on-Avon, 17/6, 7/8 (RMC).
Radford, Coventry, 20/7, 28/7, 27/8 (MCV).
Hillmorton, Rugby, 12/8, 16/8, 21/10 (DIP).
1998—**Charlecote**, 8/5, 13/5, 20/5, 15/7–29/8 (4), 10/9 (DB, AFG); **Bidford-on-Avon**, 2/7, 20/7, 25/7 (RMC); **Wilmcote Rough**, 10/7 (Warks Moth Group).
2000—**Charlecote**, 9/9 (AFG).
2002—**Charlecote**, 22/10 (DB).
2003—**Hillmorton, Rugby**, 4/8, 7/8 (DIP).

Flame Carpet
1722 *Xanthorhoe designata* (Hufn.)

County status: Widespread and fairly common.
Flight: Two overlapping generations, late April to late September.
Larval foodplants: Little known in the wild but in captivity will eat Wallflower and other species of Cruciferae.

A widely distributed species with the largest populations in woodland. Numbers in garden moth traps are generally low.

VCH 1904: *'Not common.'*
Sutton Park, Brandon Wood, Middleton, Solihull, Frankton, Wolford Wood.

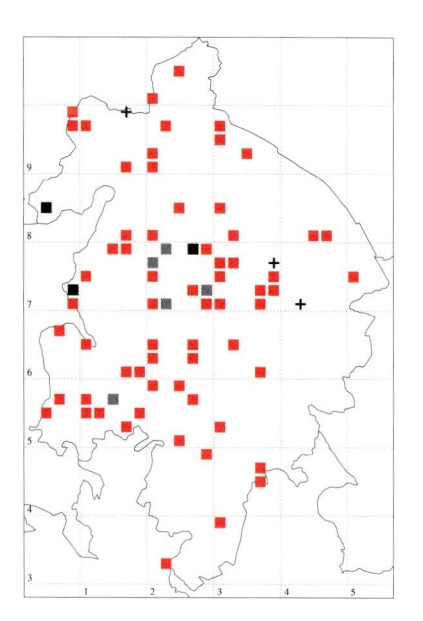

Red Twin-spot Carpet
1724 *Xanthorhoe spadicearia* ([D. & S.])

County status: Widespread and fairly common.
Flight: Two generations. Late April to mid-June and late July to early September.
Larval foodplants: Bedstraws and a variety of other low-growing plants.

The Red Twin-spot Carpet is widely distributed in the southern half of the County but records become sporadic further north. This species frequents a wide range of habitats, including woodland, marshland, road and railway embankments, waste-ground and gardens.

VCH 1904: *'Common.'*

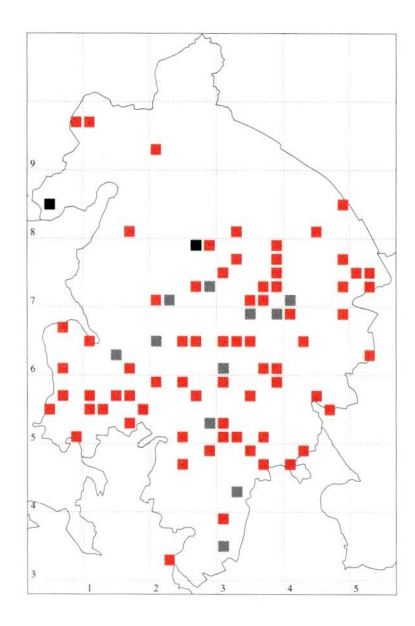

Dark-barred Twin-spot Carpet
1725 *Xanthorhoe ferrugata* (Cl.)

County status: Widespread and fairly common.
Flight: Two overlapping generations. May to September.
Larval foodplants: Polyphagous on low-growing plants.

The Dark-barred Twin-spot Carpet is more evenly distributed than the preceding species, frequenting similar habitats. There are two overlapping generations with peak numbers reported in late May and early to mid-August. Out of season specimens were caught at Hillmorton, Rugby, on 3/4/1997 (PN) and 18/10/1984 (DIP).

VCH 1904: *'Common.'*

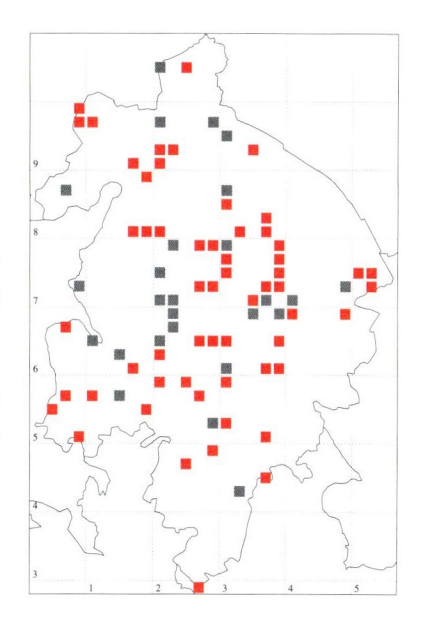

Large Twin-spot Carpet
1726 *Xanthorhoe quadrifasiata* (Cl.)

Nationally Local

County status: Widespread and fairly common.
Flight: June to August.
Larval foodplants: A range of herbaceous plants, including bedstraws, violets and Primrose.

The Large Twin-spot Carpet was first recorded in Warwickshire in 1869 at Birmingham (FE) and Knowle in 1890 (RCB). During the next 80 years there was a paucity of records: Clowes Wood 1947, one imago disturbed from herbage in daytime (BNHS); Tysoe 28/6/1949 (TT); Wilmcote 26/7/1959 (2) (FAN).

From the 1960s to the present day a huge increase in range and frequency has been experienced. It is now widely distributed and plentiful in a diversity of habitats, including woodlands, marshland and gardens.

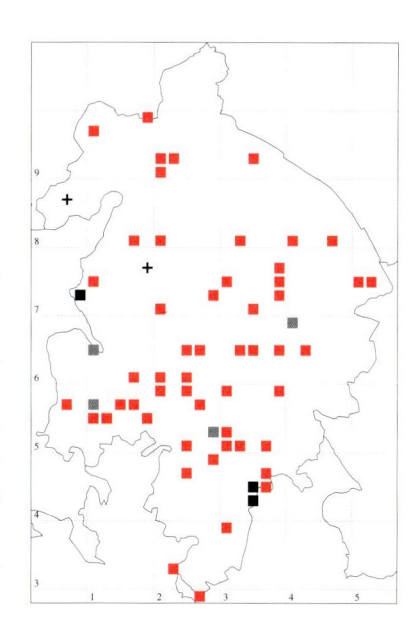

Silver-ground Carpet
1727 *Xanthorhoe montanata montanata* ([D. & S.])

County status: Widespread and common.
Flight: Mid-May to late July.
Larval foodplants: Polyphagous on low-growing plants.

The Silver-ground Carpet is a common moth in every type of habitat, but particularly in damp woodland where open areas provide a variety of herbaceous plants on which to breed. Easily disturbed during the daytime and after dark responds well to light.

VCH 1904: *'Very common in all woods.'*

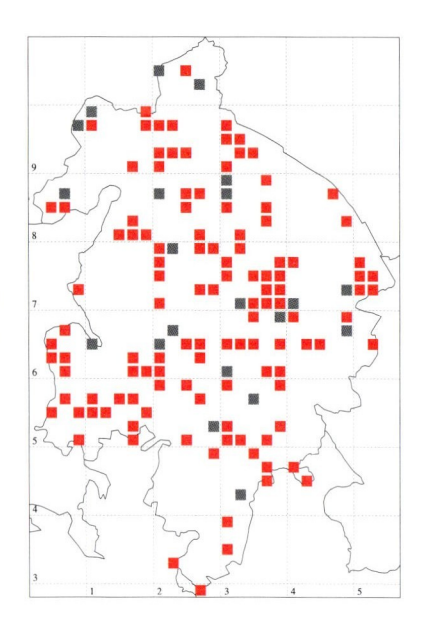

Garden Carpet
1728 *Xanthorhoe fluctuata fluctuata* (L.)

County status: Widespread and common.
Flight: Two or perhaps three overlapping generations from April to October.
Larval foodplants: Various crucifers, including garden Nasturtium, cultivated brassicas, Garlic Mustard and Alyssum.

The Garden Carpet is found in a range of habitats where herbaceous plants of the cabbage family grow. As its vernacular name suggests, however, gardens are preferred. Vegetable allotments provide additional food sources for the larvae in the form of cultivated brassicas.

This species is particularly plentiful in urban and suburban districts, as the following garden moth trap figures illustrate:
Radford, Coventry: 1979 (171), 1985 (201), 1991 (336), 1997 (305), 2000 (110) (MCV);
Hillmorton, Rugby: 1982 (273), 1985 (330), 1990 (229), 1995 (243), 2000 (255) (DIP).

VCH 1904: *'Very common everywhere.'*

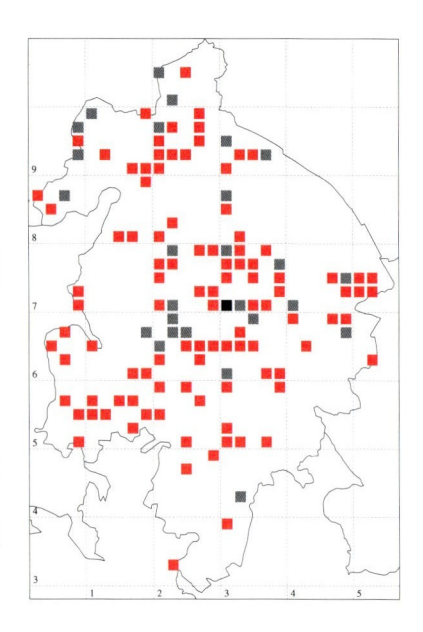

Chalk Carpet
1731 *Scotopteryx bipunctaria cretata* (Prout)

Nationally Scarce B

County status: Very local, but fairly common at one site.
Flight: Late June to mid-August.
Larval foodplants: Trefoils, clovers and vetches.

This Nationally Scarce species is restricted to calcareous soils where colonies have formed in quarries and on vegetated spoil heaps. The Chalk Carpet formerly occurred at six sites but is now restricted to just two, one of which is threatened by development.

Records:
Wilmcote Rough, 1928 (SEWC), 1939 (3) (HEH), 1953 several (SEWC); **Harbury Quarry**, 21/7/1951 (AHK); **Ufton Fields**, 20/7/1963 (ANT), 1963 a few, 26/7/1969 (LEM); **Kite's Hardwick**, 1972 (KT per RHS); **Nelson's Quarry**, **Stockton**, 1970s–1980 (DB); **Bishops Hill**, 3/8/1988 (SAL), 14/7/1996 (DB), 27/7/2002 (4) (AJK), 12/7/2004 (15) (DB, P. Bdm, AD), 20/6/2005 (2 at MV) (DB), 14/7/2005 (90+ at MV) (MA, DB, AD, AJP, NJS); **Long Itchington Quarry**, 17/7/2005 (DB, MS).

Shaded Broad-bar
1732 *Scotopteryx chenopodiata* (L.)

County status: Widespread and common.
Flight: Late June to early September.
Larval foodplants: Vetches and clovers.

The Shaded Broad-bar is a common and widely distributed species, found in a diverse range of grassland habitats. Plentiful in woodland rides and clearings, marshy areas, meadows, road and railway embankments, heathland and areas of waste-ground in urban districts. It is frequently encountered during the daytime and is a regular visitor to garden moth traps.

VCH 1904: *'Common throughout the County.'*

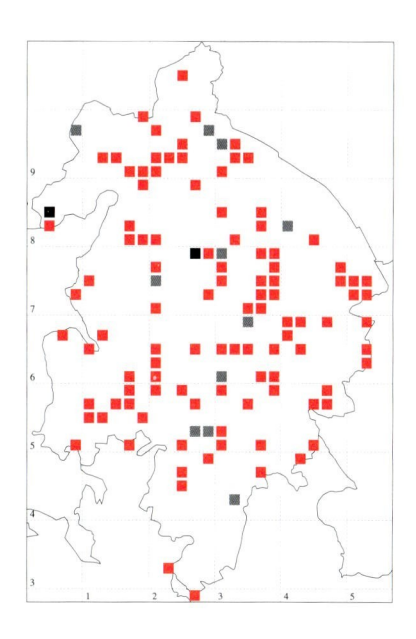

Lead Belle
1733 *Scotopteryx mucronata umbrifera* (Heydemann)
Nationally Local

County status: Very local and scarce.
Flight: Late May and June.
Larval foodplants: Gorse, Broom, Petty Whin and Dyer's Greenweed.

Formerly locally plentiful at sites in the south of the County on calcareous soil, and on acid heathland and woodland at Sutton Park and Tile Hill in the north. With a dearth of recent records the present status is uncertain. Renewed fieldwork is needed in areas containing an abundance of Gorse and Broom.

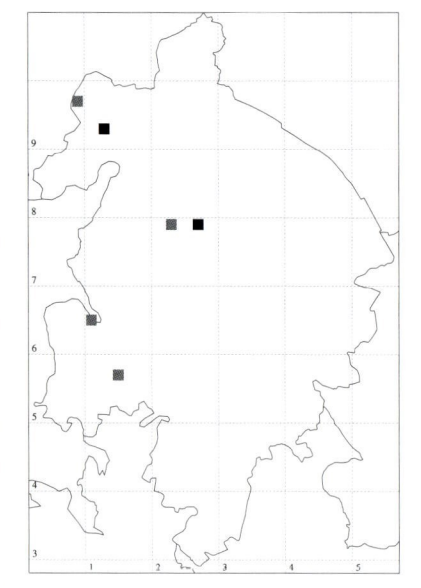

Records:
Tile Hill Wood, 3/6/1950 (CDNHSS); **Erdington, Birmingham**, 14/7/1955 (LJE); **Sutton Park**, 1960s (JB), 17/7/1965, 21/6/1966, 29/6/1966, 1970s (LJE); **Bannam's Wood**, 1964–79 (FAN); **Wootton Grange, Wootton Green**, 10/7/1965 (CDNHSS); **Wilmcote Rough**, 17/6/1972 several (DB, RHS), 1977 (JMP).

July Belle
1734 *Scotopteryx luridata plumbaria* (Fabr.)

County status: Very local and scarce.
Flight: Mid-June to July.
Larval foodplants: Gorse, Dyer's Greenweed, Petty Whin.

As with the previous species, due to a lack of recent records the status of July Belle is uncertain. It is possible that undiscovered colonies could exist in the south of the County on calcareous escarpments and in the north on acid heathland or post-industrial brownfield sites containing Gorse.

Records:
Wilmcote Rough, 17/6/1972 several (DB, RHS), 1977 (JMP); **Sutton Park**, 8/7/1983 AN); **Hillmorton, Rugby**, 12/8/1986 (PN); **Windmill Hill, Nuneaton**, 19/7/1997 (BBr, CWy).

VCH 1904: *'Very common in Sutton Park.'*
Also recorded from Overslade, Brownsover, Atherstone.

Note: In the VCH the Lead Belle and July Belle were collectively known as *Ortholitha plumbaria* (Fabr.), 'The Belle'. The separation into distinct species came in 1941.

Ruddy Carpet
1735 *Catarhoe rubidata* ([D. & S.])

Nationally Scarce B

County status: Very local and scarce.
Flight: June to August.
Larval foodplants: Hedge Bedstraw and Lady's Bedstraw.

This Nationally Scarce species is presently found in very small numbers at two sites on steep grassy slopes with a calcareous flora.

Records:
Knowle, 1869 one larva found (WGB); **Tile Hill Wood**, 13/6/1936 (CDNHSS); **Clowes Wood**, 11/8/1952 female found on oak trunk (HTK); **Wilmcote Rough**, 18/7/1959 (GCG), 12/7/1979 (JMP); **Goldicote Railway Cutting**, 27/7/1991, 12/6/1992 (CI); **Grove Hill**, 6/6/1992 (3) (DB, Warks Moth Group); **Pillerton Priors**, 14/7/1993 (CI).

VCH 1904: *'Very rare.'*

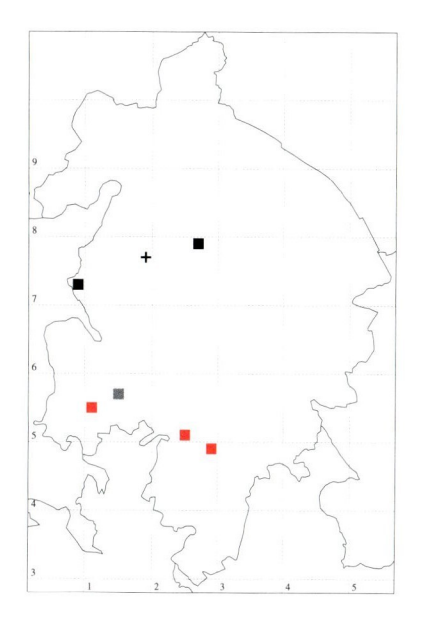

Royal Mantle
1736 *Catarhoe cuculata* (Hufn.)

Nationally Local

County status: Extinct.
Flight: No dates available.
Larval foodplants: Lady's Bedstraw and Hedge Bedstraw.

VCH 1904: *Knowle, 1869.*

Common Carpet
1738 *Epirrhoe alternata alternata* (Müll.)

County status: Widespread and common.
Flight: Two overlapping generations. May to September.
Larval foodplants: Bedstraws.

The Common Carpet is a widespread species. It occurs in an enormous range of habitats in both urban and rural areas. Garden moth trap totals are as follows:
Radford, Coventry: 1982 (9), 1985 (7), 1990 (36), 1995 (46), 2000 (8), 2004 (19) (MCV);
Hillmorton, Rugby: 1982 (46), 1985 (51), 1990 (102), 1995 (96), 2000 (63), 2004 (82) (DIP).

VCH 1904: *'Very common.'*

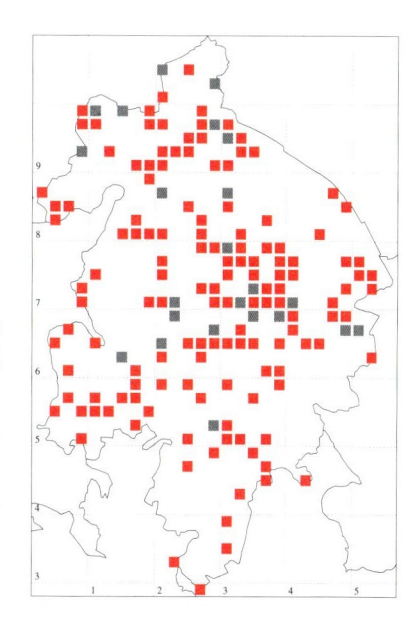

Wood Carpet
1739 *Epirrhoe rivata* (Hb.)
Nationally Local

County status: Very local and scarce.
Flight: June to August.
Larval foodplants: Hedge Bedstraw and Lady's Bedstraw.

The exact status of the Wood Carpet is hard to determine due to the identification difficulties in trying to distinguish it from the Common Carpet *Epirrhoe alternata*. It is certainly a scarce species in Warwickshire and confined to well-wooded areas, heathland and calcareous outcrops.

Records:
Marston Green and **Sutton Park**, 1890 (GWW); **Knowle**, 1890 (WGB); **Lower Hillmorton Road, Rugby**, 26/5/1893 (RNHS); **Tile Hill Wood, Coventry**, 30/5/1931, 30/6/1951, 1930–1960 occasional (CDNHSS); **May's Wood**, 1940–50 (GBM); **Clowes Wood**, 1940, 1947 (HEH); **Austy Wood**, 1946 (HEH); **Bickenhill**, 1947–50 (GPS); **Tysoe**, 1950s (TT); **Sutton Park**, 1960s (JB); **Charlecote**, 4/8/1972 (DB); **Hampton Wood**, 1972–1975 (AFG); **Temple Balsall**, 21/8/1976, 1978 (FWS); **Wilmcote Rough**, 1977–80 (JMP); **Bowshot Wood**, 26/6/1992 (DB); **Ryton Wood**, 1992 (RCK, LB, CE); **Pillerton Priors**, 4/7/1992, 14/7/1992 (CI); **Steetley Meadows**, 18/8/1993 (PC, CW); **Windmill Hill, Nuneaton**, 22/7/1995 (CWy, BB); **Oxhouse Farm, Combrook**, 1998 (DT).

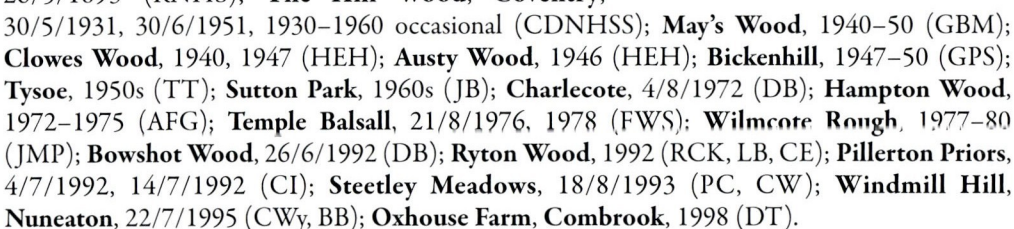

VCH 1904: *'There are numerous records of both **rivata** and **sociata (alternata)** but I am of the opinion that most if not all of the specimens are of **sociata**; **rivata** may occur, but I think it is rare if it does.'*

Galium Carpet
1740 *Epirrhoe galiata* ([D. & S.])
Nationally Local

County status: No recent records. Presumed extinct.
Flight: June to mid-July.
Larval foodplants: Bedstraws.

The Galium Carpet is mainly associated with coastal districts but occurs on calcareous grasslands inland. It was last seen at Wilmcote Rough in 1980.

Records:
Tysoe, 1950s (TT); **Wilmcote Rough**, 1977–80 two or three each year (JMP).

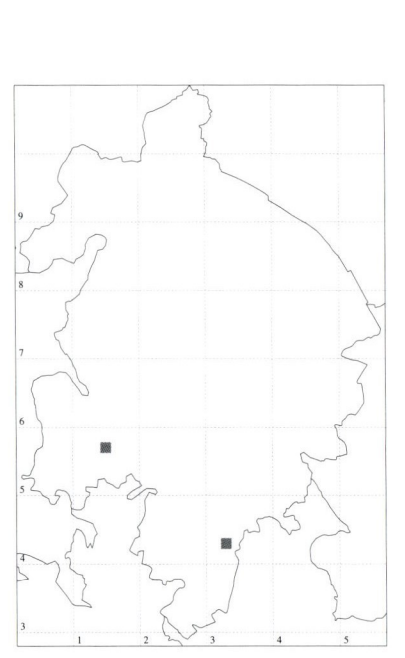

Yellow Shell
1742 *Camptogramma bilineata bilineata* (L.)

County status: Widespread and fairly common.
Flight: June to early September.
Larval foodplants: Polyphagous on low-growing plants.

The Yellow Shell has been found in a variety of habitats, including railway cuttings, meadows, wetlands, heathland, woodland rides and clearings over a large part of the County.

Often disturbed by day, but generally responds poorly to light as the following garden moth trap figures illustrate:
Radford, Coventry: 1992 (9), 1993 (5), 2002 (2), 2003 (3), 2004 (8) (MCV);
Pillerton Priors: 1992 (6), 1993 (12), 2002 (7), 2003 (4), 2004 (8) (CI).

VCH 1904: *'Common everywhere.'*

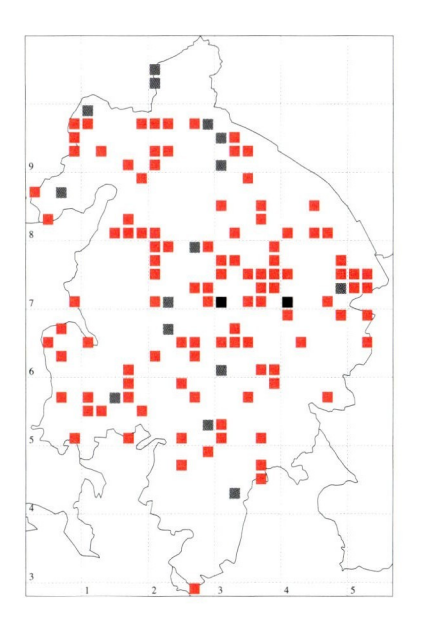

Mallow
1745 *Larentia clavaria* (Haw.)

County status: Very local and uncommon.
Flight: September to late October.
Larval foodplants: Common Mallow and Hollyhock.

The Mallow appears to be restricted to the south-west quarter of the County. Apart from an isolated 1991 record at Rugby (DIP) this species has not been noted from the northern half of the County since 1980. It frequents gardens with Hollyhock and areas where Common Mallow grows, such as field edges and roadside verges.

The following garden moth trap totals give an idea of frequency at **Charlecote**: 1971 (10), 1978 (43), 1991 (7), 1998 (20), 2003 (25) (DB).

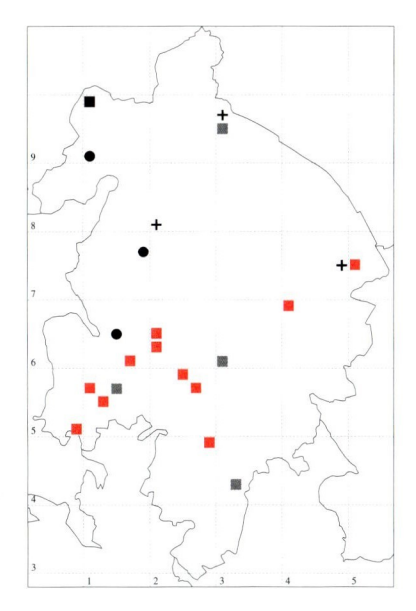

Records:
May's Wood, 6/8/1911 (4) (GBM); **Knowle**, 1923 (SEWC); **Four Oaks, Little Aston and Sutton Coldfield**, 1925–53 'few' (FHL, GPS, EVW); **Tysoe**, 1946 (TT); **Long Lawford**, 1948 (AGB); **Compton Wynyates**, 1948 (TT); **Wilmcote**, 14/9/1958 (FAN); **Charlecote**, 1970–2004 annually (DB); **Marton**, 1970–1989 (RA); **Hampton Wood**, 1972–1975 a few annually (AFG), 1985 (RGB); **Hartshill Hayes**, 1975–1979 (RJT); **Claverdon**, 24/9/1985 (IGMR); **Bidford-on-Avon**, 1980s–2004 annually (RMC); **Wolverton**, 1980s (DS); **Hillmorton, Rugby**, 11/10/1991 (DIP); **Pillerton Priors**, 7/10/1992, 3/10/2003, 14/10/2003 (CI); **Bearley**

Station, 18/9/1993, 11/10/1993 (IGMR); **Temple Grafton**, 25/9/2004, 28/9/2004, 13/9/2005, 15/9/2005 (2), 6/10/2005 (AFG).

VCH 1904: *'Not common.'*
Sutton, Knowle, Atherstone, Rugby, Overslade and Hampton-in-Arden.

Shoulder Stripe
1746 *Anticlea badiata* ([D. & S.])

County status: Widespread and fairly common.
Flight: Early March to mid-May.
Larval foodplants: Dog-rose* and other wild rose species.

The Shoulder Stripe is a fairly common springtime species which is found throughout Warwickshire.

It is particularly plentiful in old hedgerows and open woodland; for example, Oversley Wood, 12/5/1979 (42 at MV) (DB, AFG).

A regular visitor to garden moth traps in rural districts as the following figures illustrate:
Pillerton Priors: 1992 (25), 1993 (13), 1994 (3), 2002 (1), 2003 (9), 2004 (7), 2005 (14) (CI).

VCH 1904: *'Common everywhere.'*

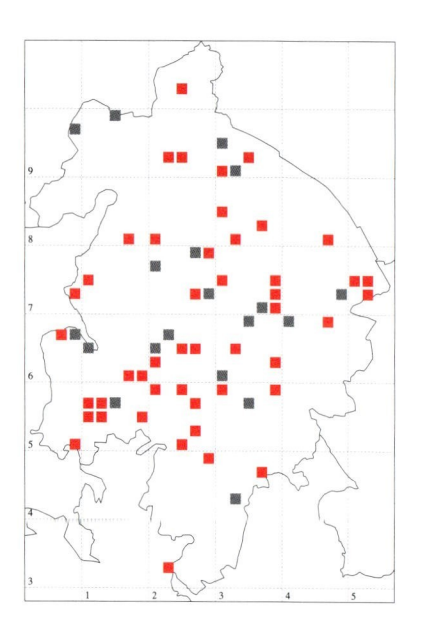

Streamer
1747 *Anticlea derivata* ([D. & S.])

County status: Widespread and fairly common.
Flight: Late March to end of May.
Larval foodplants: Dog-rose* and other wild rose species.

The Streamer has a very similar distribution to the preceding species and shares the same habitats. It is perhaps slightly more confined to woodland, where good numbers of adults may sometimes visit light; for example, Snitterfield Bushes, 11/4/1992 (20) (DB, RMC, AJK, IGMR).

Garden moth trap totals are generally low:
Pillerton Priors: 1992 (7), 1993 (1), 1994 (1), 2002 (1), 2003 (0), 2004 (0) (CI);
Hillmorton, Rugby: 1982 (2), 1985 (2), 1990 (2), 1995 (1), 2000 (0), 2004 (2) (DIP).

VCH 1904: *'Much less common than **badiata**'*

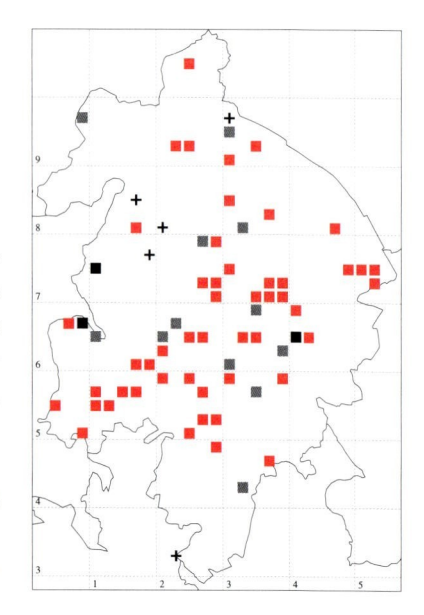

Beautiful Carpet
1748 *Mesoleuca albicillata* (L.)

County status: Very local and uncommon.
Flight: Late May to early August.
Larval foodplants: Brambles, Raspberry and Hazel.

The Beautiful Carpet is a very local species, frequenting the more open parts of woodland where there is a good ground cover of brambles. It is rarely seen in numbers; the three specimens recorded at light in Kingsbury Wood 23/6/1989 (RGB, DB & Warks Moth Group) were exceptional.

Records since 1980:
Tile Hill Wood, **Coventry**, 20/6/1980 (PC); **Clowes Wood**, 24/7/1986 (RJB); **Oversley Wood**, 8/8/1986, 16/6/1989 (AFG), 16/6/2000 (DG), 19/7/2000 (MA), 29/6/2002 (DB), 7/6/2004 (RMC, DG, AJP), 4/6/2005 (Warks Moth Group), 18/6/2005 (AJP, VW); **Snitterfield Bushes**, 16/6/1989 (2), 19/6/1992 (DB); **Kingsbury Wood**, 23/6/1989 (3) (RGB, DB & Warks Moth Group); **Grendon Common**, 6/7/1990 (DB); **Rough Hill Wood**, 25/6/1993 (CI, RGB); **Brandon Marsh**, 24/6/1994 (PC, NWH, CW); **Hay Wood** 8/7/1995 (DB); **Crackley Wood**, 13/7/1996 (AJK), 8/7/1999 (MA); **Withycombe Wood**, 31/5/1997 (AJK); **Windmill Hill**, **Nuneaton**, 19/7/1997 (BBr, CWy).

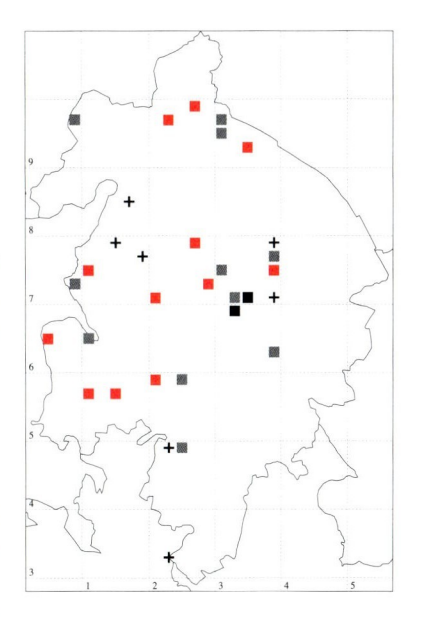

VCH 1904: *Sutton Park (abundant), Marston Green, Knowle, Solihull, Coombe Wood, Brandon Wood, Princethorpe Wood, Atherstone, Whitchurch, Wolford Wood.*

Dark Spinach
1749 *Pelurga comitata* (L.)

County status: Very local and scarce.
Flight: July and August.
Larval foodplants: Goosefoots and oraches.

The Dark Spinach has declined since 1980 and is now scarcely recorded. Although it has occasionally been noted in rural districts, *comitata* is essentially a species of the larger conurbations of Birmingham and Coventry and the smaller satellite towns. Fieldwork in derelict areas or post-industrial brownfield sites may uncover new populations.

Records:
Edgbaston, **Birmingham**, 1950s (FAN); **Lillington**, **Royal Leamington Spa**, 1957 (GCG, WTT); **Birmingham**, 1961 (LJE); **Canley**, **Coventry**, 2/8/1963 (LEM); **Earlsdon**, **Coventry**, 1/8/1969 (LEM); **Radford**, **Coventry**, 1970 (2), 1980, 1981, 1983 (2), 1984, 1988 (MCV); **Kingsbury**, 1970 (RJT); **Charlecote**, 5/8/1970, 24/7/1972, 14/8/1979, 19/8/1979, 2/8/1980, 18/8/1981, 8/8/1988, 21/7/1989 (DB, AFG); **Cubbington Wood**, 1970

(AFG); **Hampton Wood**, 1972–75 occasionally (AFG); **Hartshill Hayes**, 1975–79 (RJT); **Bilton**, 1979 (2) (R. Johnson); **Bidford-on-Avon**, 1980 (RMC); **Dosthill**, 1980 (RJT); **Hillmorton, Rugby**, 3/8/1981 (DIP); **Hampton-in-Arden**, 1983 (MCV); **Pailton**, 1984 (2) (KCG); **Royal Leamington Spa**, 1992 (PhP).

VCH 1904: *Atherstone, Overslade.*

Water Carpet
1750 *Lampropteryx suffumata* ([D. & S.])

County status: Fairly widespread and locally fairly common.
Flight: Late March to the end of May.
Larval foodplants: Bedstraws.

The Water Carpet is locally plentiful over a wide span of the County, but records are fewer in the extreme north and south. This may, in part, be due to under-recording as the species flies early in the season. It occasionally responds well to MV; for example, Snitterfield Bushes 12/4/1991 (23) (DB, AFG, IGMR), Ryton Wood 10/5/1991 (30) (DB, RGB). The adults are more readily attracted to actinic light or may be found by torchlight in the denser parts of damp woods.

VCH 1904: *'Common.'*
Sutton Park, Knowle, Brandon Wood, Overslade, Atherstone, Wolford.

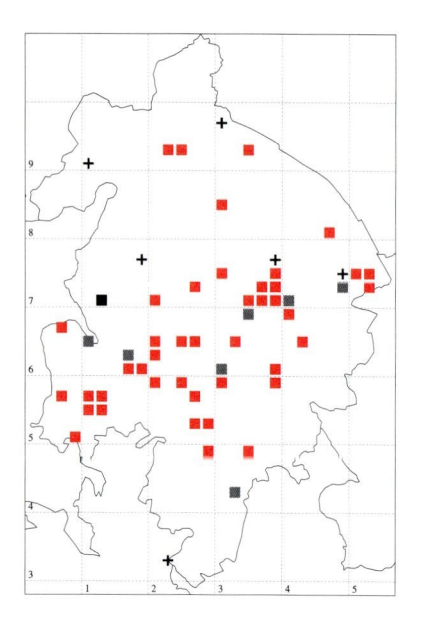

Purple Bar
1752 *Cosmorhoe ocellata* (L.)

County status: Widespread and fairly common.
Flight: Two overlapping generations. May to late September.
Larval foodplants: Bedstraws.

A widely distributed species utilising a range of habitats, including open woodland, heathland, marshland and disused railway cuttings. Most commonly observed on calcareous grassland.

VCH 1904: *'Common everywhere.'*

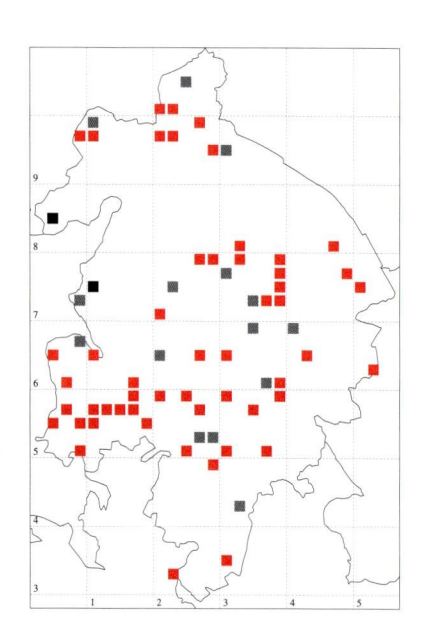

Phoenix
1754 *Eulithis prunata* (L.)

County status: Fairly widespread and fairly common.
Flight: June to mid-August.
Larval foodplants: Black Currant, Red Currant and Gooseberry.

A species recorded mainly in gardens especially in suburban districts. Lesser numbers have been noted in woodland and wetland habitats. Although the Phoenix has not experienced such a drastic decline as the Spinach and V-Moth, which have similar larval foodplants, numbers are nevertheless beginning to dwindle.

The following moth trap records compare rural and suburban gardens:

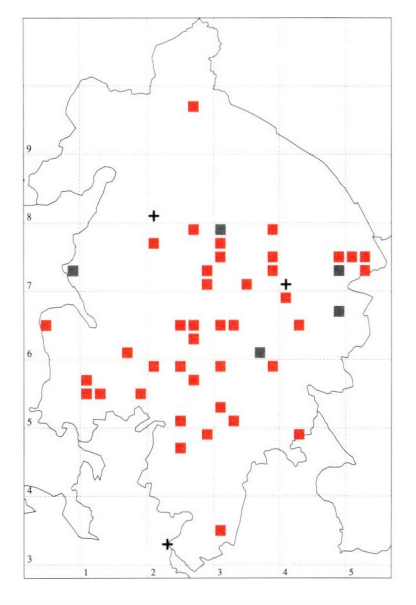

Habitat	Location	1982	1985	1990	1995	2000
Suburban	Hillmorton, Rugby (DIP)	12	17	24	73	16
Rural	Charlecote (AFG)	3	12	2	4	1

VCH 1904: *'Not common'.*
Hampton-in-Arden, Overslade, Princethorpe, Wolford.

Chevron
1755 *Eulithis testata* (L.)

County status: Local and fairly common at a few sites.
Flight: July to mid-September.
Larval foodplants: Sallows*, willows, birches and Aspen.

The Chevron is found in damp woodland, marshes and heathland at widely separated sites.

More fieldwork is needed to ascertain the precise status of this species in the County. It is currently known to occur at Wolford Wood, Oakley Wood, Ryton Wood, Ufton Fields and Whitacre Heath. Larger populations exist at Brandon Marsh: 30/7/2005 (25) (Warks Moth Group), and Sutton Park: 17/8/2002 (10) (DB, DG), 13/8/2005 (12) (Warks Moth Group).

Occasional specimens have appeared in static garden moth traps:
Radford, Coventry, 8/8/1982, 4/8/1994 (MCV);
Bearley Station, 9/8/1988, 7/7/1989 (IGMR);
Bidford-on-Avon, 31/8/1996 (2) (RMC);
Charlecote, 1/9/1996 (DB).

VCH 1904: *'Not very common but occurs throughout the County.'*

Northern Spinach
1756 *Eulithis populata* (L.)

County status: Very local and occasionally fairly common.
Flight: Late June to August.
Larval foodplants: Bilberry*.

This species has a scattered distribution in the County. It has been recorded from a number of woodlands in the north and west, the majority of which do not host the only known larval foodplant, Bilberry. The largest populations occur amongst Bilberry in Clowes Wood.

Occasional specimens in garden moth traps suggest the presence of undiscovered colonies.

Records since 1980:
Hartshill Hayes, 1/8/1980 (RJT); **Charlecote**, 1980s, 1990s occasional (DB, AFG); **Tile Hill Wood**, 3/7/1987 (PC); **Kingsbury Wood**, 23/6/1989 (Warks Moth Group); **Grendon Common**, 6/7/1990 (12) (Warks Moth Group), 24/8/1990 (DB, RMC, BM); **Whichford Wood**, 11/7/1991 (DB, AFG, RMC), 20/6/1992 (Warks Moth Group); **Clowes Wood**, 11/7/1992 (10) (Warks Moth Group), 30/7/2002 (2) (DG); **Rough Hill Wood**, 25/6/1993 (CI, RGB); **Alvecote Pools**, 9/7/1993 (Warks Moth Group); **Windmill Hill, Nuneaton**, 9/7/1994 (RCK); **Crackley Wood**, 13/7/1996 (Warks Moth Group); **Tile Hill, Coventry**, 13/7/1996 (AJK); **Bentley Park Wood**, 20/7/1996 (Warks Moth Group).

VCH 1904: *'Not uncommon.'*
Sutton Park, Knowle, Solihull, Rugby and Atherstone.

Spinach
1757 *Eulithis mellinata* (Fabr.)

County status: Widespread but becoming uncommon.
Flight: Mid-June to late August.
Larval foodplants: Red Currant and Black Currant.

The Spinach is evenly distributed throughout the County. It is generally a garden species, where the larvae feed on currant, but it is also established in a few woodlands; for example, Ryton Wood, Waverley Wood, Clowes Wood, Kingsbury Wood and Whichford Wood. There is evidence of a decline in numbers over the last 20 years.

Garden moth trap totals at **Hillmorton, Rugby,** are as follows: 1982 (15), 1985 (15), 1990 (3), 1995 (6), 2000 (10), 2004 (1), 2005 (1) (DIP).

VCH 1904: *'Common in gardens'.*
Yardley, Sutton, Hampton-in-Arden, Overslade, Atherstone, Wolford.

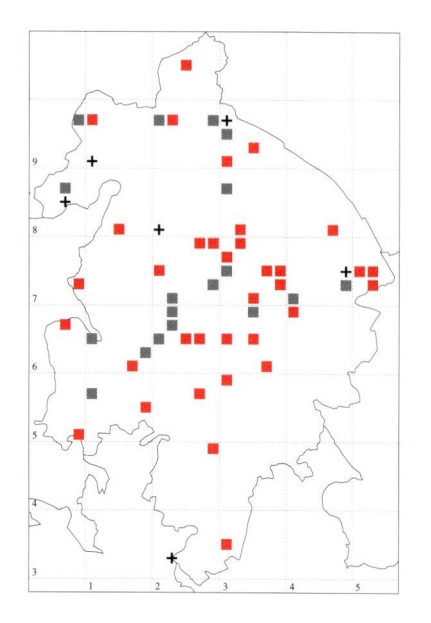

Barred Straw
1758 *Eulithis pyraliata* ([D. & S.])

County status: Widespread and fairly common.
Flight: Late May to early August.
Larval foodplants: Goosegrass* and other species of bedstraw.

The Barred Straw has an extensive distribution across Warwickshire and is generally more plentiful in rural areas. This species is found in a number of grassland habitats, including woodland rides and clearings, road and railway embankments, waste-ground, and gardens.

Garden moth trap totals at **Pillerton Priors** give an idea of frequency: 1992 (27), 1993 (32), 1994 (24), 2002 (15), 2003 (13), 2004 (22), 2005 (47) (CI).

VCH 1904: *'Common.'*
Knowle, Solihull, Overslade, Atherstone, Wolford.

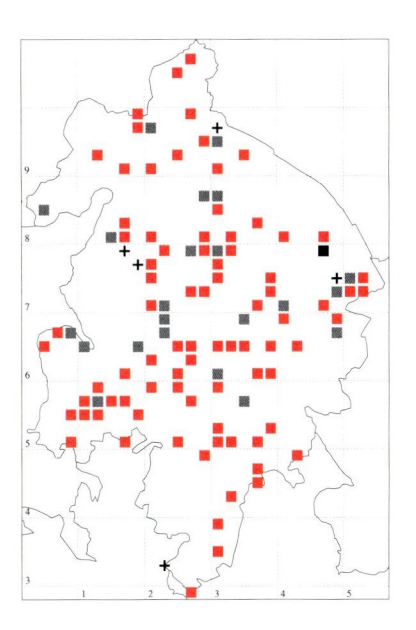

Small Phoenix
1759 *Ecliptopera silaceata* ([D. & S.])

County status: Widespread and fairly common.
Flight: Two overlapping generations from early May to September.
Larval foodplants: Willowherbs.

A fairly common moth in all types of habitats containing willowherbs. The adult has been reported each week from May to September with peaks in late May and mid-August.

VCH 1904: *'Not common, from only Rugby, Wolford and Brandon Wood.'*

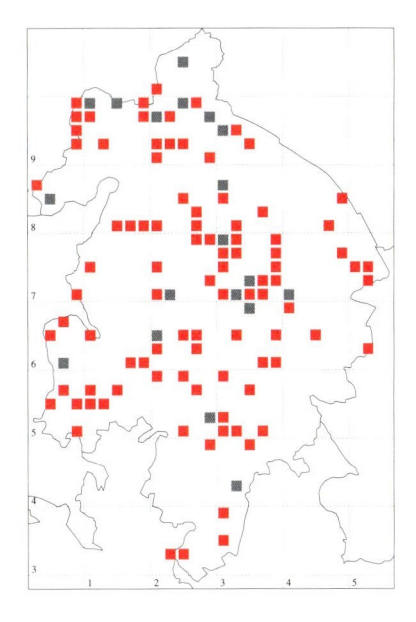

Red-green Carpet
1760 *Chloroclysta siterata* (Hufn.)

County status: Widespread and becoming fairly common.
Flight: September to November and, after hibernation, March to late May.
Larval foodplants: Oaks* and various other broadleaved trees.

The Red-green Carpet was a notable species in the County during the early twentieth century. The first known records were from Sutton Park where it was reported to be 'fairly common' between 1925 and 1938 (FHL). Sporadic sightings at Tile Hill Wood in the 1930s (CDNHSS) and Sutton Park 1960s (JB) concluded recordings until the 1980s. From that decade to the present day the moth has continued to increase, being discovered in many woodlands, including Oakley Wood (DB), Snitterfield Bushes (DB), Oversley Wood (RMC), Clowes Wood (DB), Ryton Wood (RMC) and Wolford Wood (MK). Now also regularly observed in many garden moth traps.

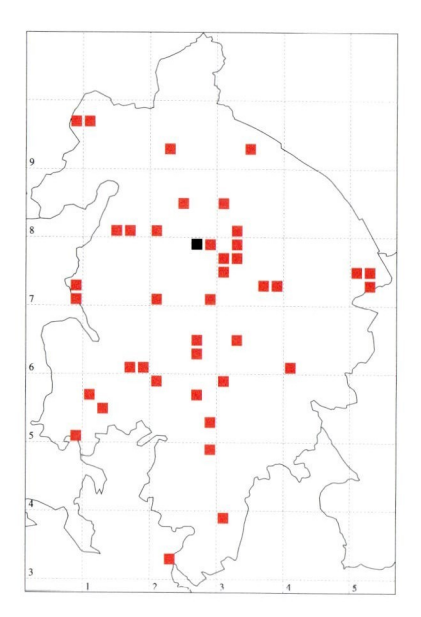

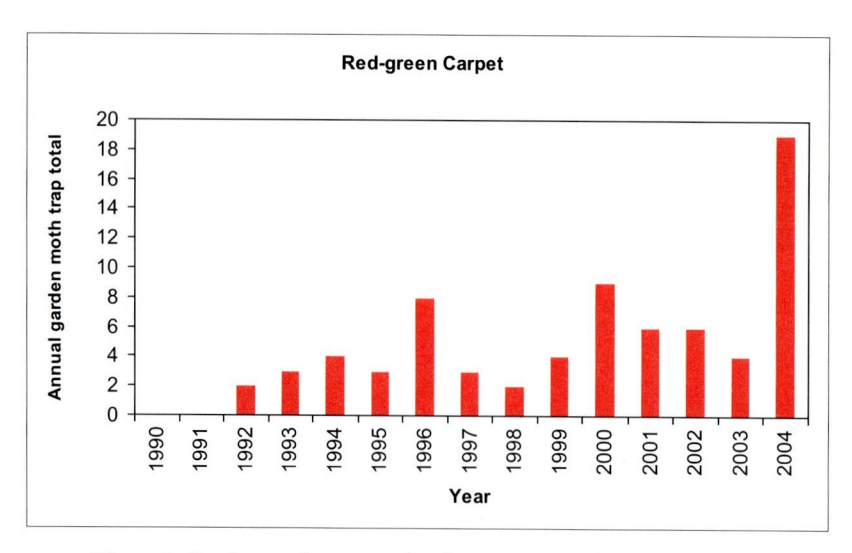

Figure 9. Garden moth trap totals of *C. siterata* at Charlecote (DB).

Autumn Green Carpet
1761 *Chloroclysta miata* (L.)

Nationally Local

County status: Very local and becoming scarce.
Flight: September to late October. No Warwickshire records in the spring.
Larval foodplants: Sallows, birches, Alder, oaks, limes, Rowan and other broadleaved trees.

The Autumn Green Carpet, in contrast to the preceding species, has dramatically decreased since 1980 and is now very rarely seen. Preferred habitats are woodland, scrub and sheltered gardens.

Records since 1980:
Hillmorton, **Rugby**, 22/10/1982, 22/10/1986 (DIP); **Claverdon**, 7/10/1984 (IGMR); **Charlecote**, 12/10/1984 (DB), 8/10/1985, 14/10/1986, 22/10/1988 (AFG), 3/10/1991 (DB), 23/10/2001 (AFG); **Bearley Station**, 18/9/1988 (IGMR); **Hampton Magna**, Oct. 1988 (PJR); **Bidford-on-Avon**, 14/10/1988, 12/10/1990 (RMC); **Bishopton, Stratford-upon-Avon**, 24/10/1991 (JMP).

VCH 1904: *'Not uncommon.'*
Knowle, Overslade, Atherstone, Wolford.

Dark Marbled Carpet
1762 *Chloroclysta citrata citrata* (L.)

County status: True status uncertain. Very local and scarce.
Flight: July and August.
Larval foodplants: Many broadleaved trees and woody plants, including Bilberry and heathers.

The status of this species is not easy to determine due to the difficulties in separation from the Common Marbled Carpet. The Dark Marbled Carpet is single brooded and appears between the two broods of *truncata*, although there is a degree of overlap. The acutely angled postmedian lines of both fore- and hindwings help to separate the two. The Dark Marbled Carpet is undoubtedly scarce in Warwickshire compared to its congener. Woodland, heathland and gardens are the preferred habitats.

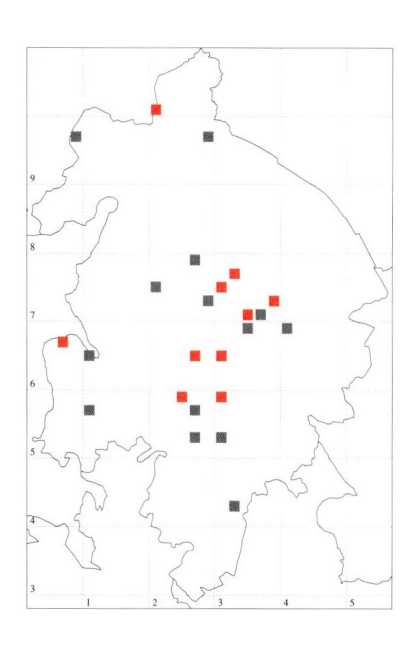

VCH 1904: *'Both this species and* **truncata** *are, I believe, common throughout the County and occur in all their known forms; they are doubtless, however, much mixed up in collections and records.'*

Common Marbled Carpet
1764 *Chloroclysta truncata* (Hufn.)

County status: Widespread and common.
Flight: Two generations, sometimes overlapping. May to June and August to October.
Larval foodplants: Polyphagous, mainly on deciduous trees and shrubs, including Blackthorn*, elms* and Bilberry*.

The Common Marbled Carpet is a common species in many different habitats. Dark melanic forms predominate but a wide range of colour variations occur, especially a tawny-orange centred form. At Mancetter a colony along the railway line consists of steel blue/grey forms that perfectly match the paint on the metal bridges upon which they rest (RJT per JMP; Price, 1990).

The first generation normally reaches a peak by mid-June and stragglers continue through part of July, adding to the confusion in separating this species from *citrata*.

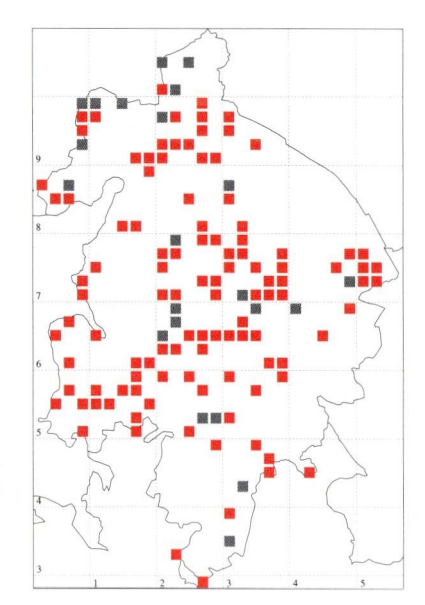

Moth trap totals in urban districts may sometimes be large as the following figures show:
Radford, Coventry: 1988 (61), 1994 (86), 1999 (94), 2000 (192), 2003 (71) (MCV).

VCH 1904: *'Common throughout the County.'*

Barred Yellow
1765 *Cidaria fulvata* (Forst.)

County status: Widespread and fairly common.
Flight: June to early August.
Larval foodplants: Dog-rose*, Burnet Rose* and probably cultivated roses.

This attractive species occurs over a large part of the County, frequenting open woodland and scrub. It is very plentiful amongst wild rose growing on calcareous soils at Grove Hill, Ufton Fields and Bishops Bowl.

Barred Yellow is a regular visitor to garden moth traps, even in urban areas, strongly suggesting that cultivated roses are used for breeding.

An idea of frequency can be derived from the following garden moth trap figures:
Pillerton Priors: 1992 (5), 1993 (18), 1994 (13), 2002 (2), 2003 (2), 2004 (5), 2005 (10) (CI);
Hillmorton, Rugby: 1982 (4), 1985 (0), 1990 (4), 1995 (12), 2000 (8), 2004 (8) (DIP).

VCH 1904: *'Common everywhere.'*

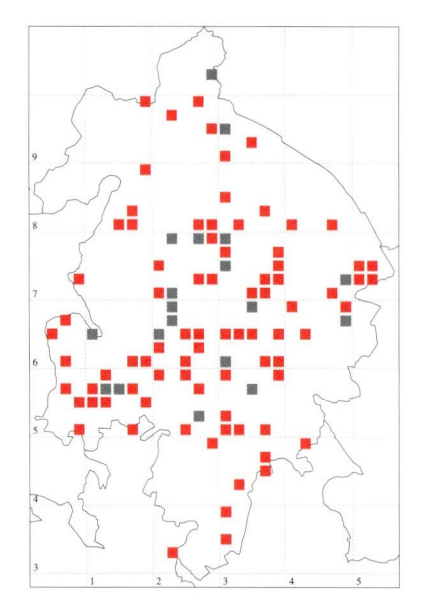

Blue-bordered Carpet
1766 *Plemyria rubiginata rubiginata* ([D. & S.])

County status: Fairly widespread and sometimes fairly common.
Flight: June to early August.
Larval foodplants: Alder and Blackthorn, but also apple, plum and hawthorns.

The Blue-bordered Carpet has increased in range and frequency since 1980. Good populations occur at Brandon Wood, Brandon Marsh, Ryton Wood, Clowes Wood, Whitacre Heath, Bowshot Wood, Old Park Wood and Oversley Wood. It is also plentiful on the railway cuttings of Bearley and Combrook and the flood meadows at Newbold Comyn, Royal Leamington Spa, where on 30/6/2001 large numbers were observed flying over Blackthorn at dusk (DB, JWkn). A frequent visitor to many garden moth traps.

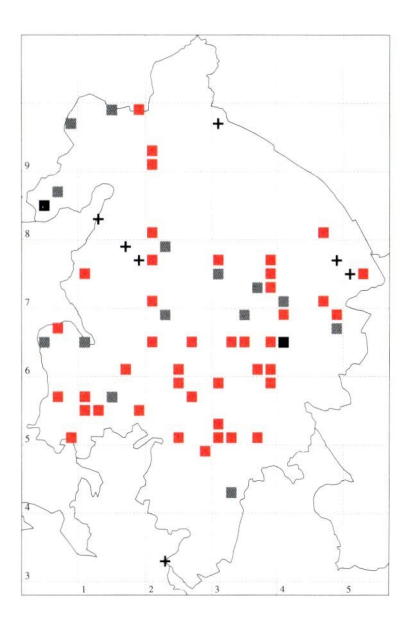

VCH 1904: *'Not common.'*
Sutton Park, Knowle, Olton, Solihull, Rugby, Atherstone, Wolford.

Pine Carpet
1767 *Thera firmata* (Hb.)

County status: Local and uncommon.
Flight: Late June to November.
Larval foodplants: Scots Pine* and Corsican Pine.

Records of this species are erratic and usually of singletons from both rural and suburban districts containing isolated mature pines. It is only occasionally noted from larger areas of woodland.

The flight period is long and extends well into the autumn. There is an unusually late record of Pine Carpet at Shottery, Stratford-upon-Avon, on 26/11/1993 (RGB).

VCH 1904: *'Rare—a few larvae have been taken in Sutton Park and it is recorded twice in Rugby lists.'*

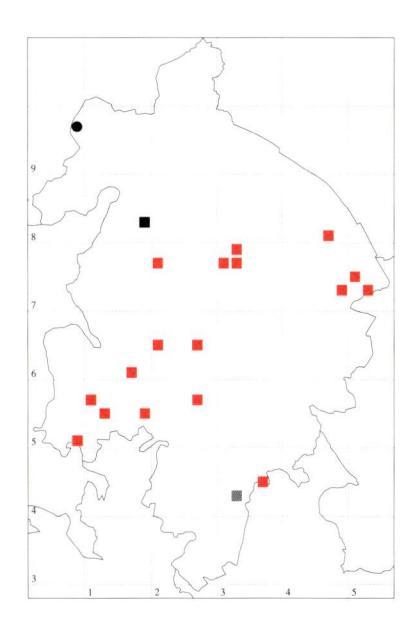

Grey Pine Carpet
1768 *Thera obeliscata* (Hb.)

County status: Widespread and fairly common.
Flight: Two overlapping generations. Early May to November.
Larval foodplants: Polyphagous on coniferous trees and shrubs, including Leyland Cypress*.

In contrast to the last species, the Grey Pine Carpet is found in generally good numbers over a large area. Whilst *firmata* is associated with pines, *obeliscata* also utilises a large number of firs, spruces and cypresses, enabling colonisation of woodlands, parks, cemeteries and gardens.

VCH 1904: *'Common locally.'*
Sutton Park, Knowle, Hampton-in-Arden, Overslade.

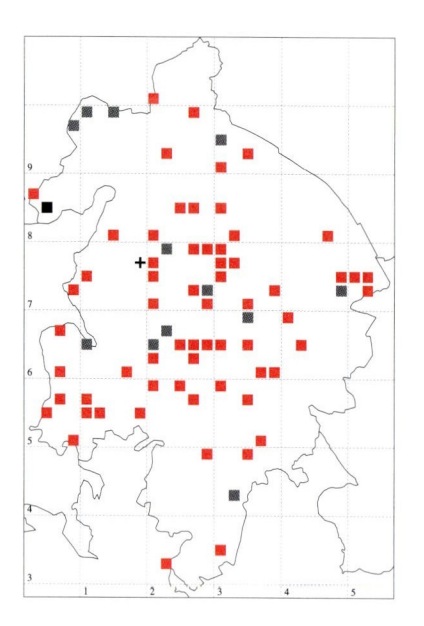

Spruce Carpet
1769 *Thera britannica* (Turn.)

County status: Widespread and fairly common.
Flight: Two generations. May to mid-July and mid-August to November.
Larval foodplants: Polyphagous on coniferous trees and shrubs.

This species has increased considerably in recent years to become widespread and numerous. Found in many woodlands, parks and gardens.

VCH 1904: *'Very common in Sutton Park.'*
Also recorded from Knowle, Hampton-in-Arden and Overslade.

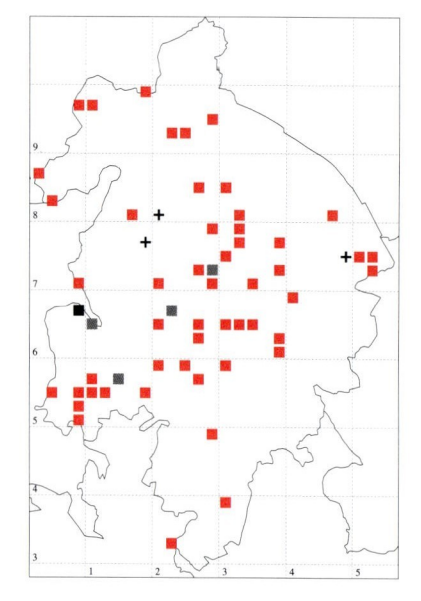

Juniper Carpet
1771 *Thera juniperata juniperata* (L.)

County status: Local and sometimes fairly common.
Flight: Late September to late November.
Larval foodplants: Cultivated junipers*.

The main populations of Juniper Carpet are concentrated in the conurbations of Birmingham, Coventry, Nuneaton, Rugby, Warwick and Royal Leamington Spa. The moth breeds on cultivated junipers in domestic gardens, parks and cemeteries. The earliest known record is from Rugby in October 1963 (RGW), after which year numerous colonies became established, many being introduced inadvertently by the nursery trade.

An out of season example was caught at Hillmorton, Rugby, on 29/7/2005 (PN).

Garden moth trap counts at **Hillmorton, Rugby,** are: 1982 (24), 1985 (20), 1990 (14), 1995 (42), 2004 (51), 2005 (41) (DIP).

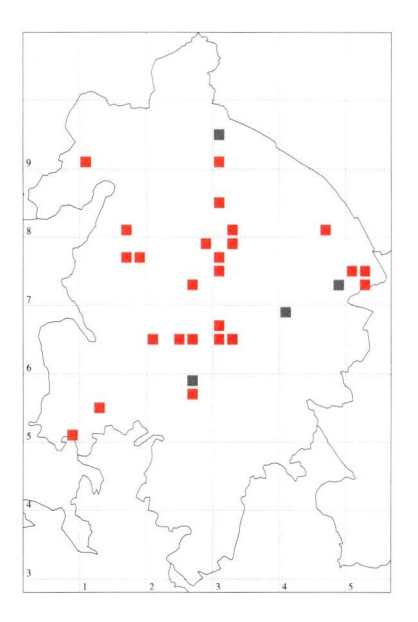

Broken-barred Carpet
1773 *Electrophaes corylata* (Thunb.)

County status: Widespread and fairly common.
Flight: May to mid-July.
Larval foodplants: A variety of broadleaved trees, including hawthorns*, Blackthorn*, birches*, Beech* and oaks.

A fairly common species throughout the County but fewer recent records from the north. Found in a number of wooded habitats, as well as parks and gardens.

Typical numbers to light at Oversley Wood are: 4/6/1976 (12), 3/5/1980 (7) (DB, AFG).

Garden moth trap counts at **Hillmorton, Rugby,** are as follows: 1982 (29), 1985 (4), 1990 (6), 1995 (4), 2000 (3), 2004 (4) (DIP).

VCH 1904: *'Common throughout the County.'*

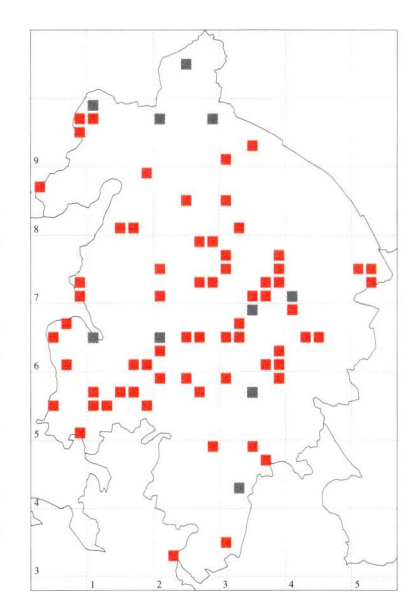

Beech-green Carpet
1774 *Colostygia olivata* ([D. & S.])

Nationally Local

County status: No recent records. Presumed extinct.
Flight: July and August.
Larval foodplants: Bedstraws.

This Nationally Local species was resident in Sutton Park during the 1960s but no indication of frequency is given. Despite diligent fieldwork at this site in subsequent years, no further sightings have been made and it is now presumed to be extinct.

Records:
Sutton Park, 1960s (JB).

VCH 1904: *Atherstone, Whitchurch.*

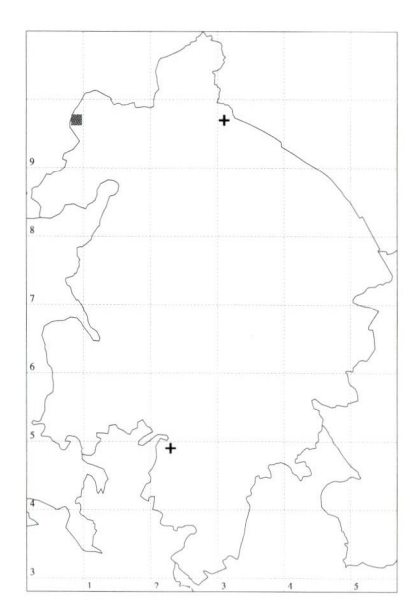

Mottled Grey
1775 *Colostygia multistrigaria* (Haw.)

County status: Very local and scarce.
Flight: Late March to April.
Larval foodplants: Bedstraws.

The Mottled Grey is a species of damp woodland and heathland. It is only very occasionally noted in Warwickshire but may be under-recorded due to the early flight period.

Records:
Austy Wood, 1945 (HEH); **Oakley Wood**, 1949 (TT); **Waverley Wood**, 15/4/1952 (AHK); **Four Oaks**, 1956 (EVW); **Windmill Naps**, 1956–60 (DWS), 9/4/1956 (FAN); **Sutton Park**, 1960s (JB); 1970s (LJE); **Charlecote**, 18/4/1979 (DB), 15/4/1987 (AFG), 28/3/1992 (DB), 31/3/1999 (AFG), 2/5/2004 (DB); **Ryton Wood**, 1991 (LB, CE); **Nether Whitacre**, 18/3/2000 (JBt).

VCH 1904: *'Common.' in Sutton Park, also recorded from Knowle, Marston Green, Small Heath, Princethorpe Wood.*

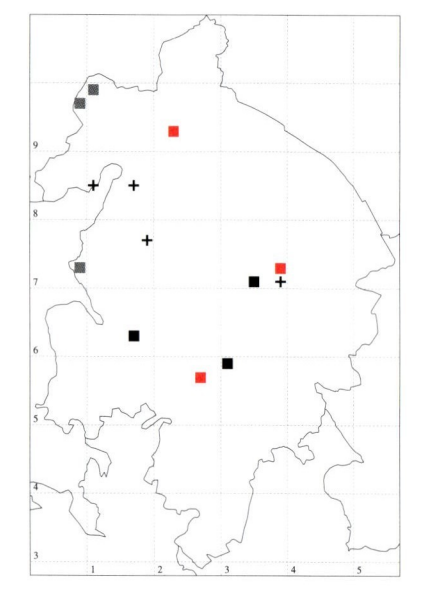

Green Carpet
1776 *Colostygia pectinataria* (Knoch)

County status: Widespread and fairly common.
Flight: Two generations. Early May to late July and mid-August to September.
Larval foodplants: Bedstraws.

The Green Carpet is a widespread moth; it is found in a variety of habitats, but most commonly in deciduous woodland.

Annual numbers at a garden moth trap on the wooded outskirts of Coventry show a steady increase; for example, **Kenilworth Road, Coventry:** 2001 (31), 2002 (34), 2003 (112), 2004 (136), 2005 (186) (MA).

VCH 1904: *'Common everywhere.'*

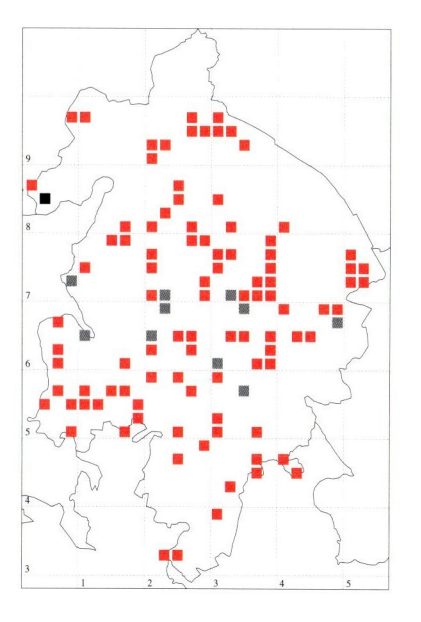

July Highflyer
1777 *Hydriomena furcata* (Thunb.)

County status: Widespread and common.
Flight: June to August, occasionally September.
Larval foodplants: Willows*, sallows*, Aspen* and Bilberry*.

A very common species in broadleaved woodland, heathland and many other habitats, including gardens. Nationally an extremely variable species, but in Warwickshire the predominant forms are dark green or blackish.

Even in built-up districts garden moth trap totals can sometimes be fairly good; for example, **Radford, Coventry:** 1979 (26), 1987 (18) (MCV); **Hillmorton, Rugby:** 1982 (17), 1985 (6) (DIP).

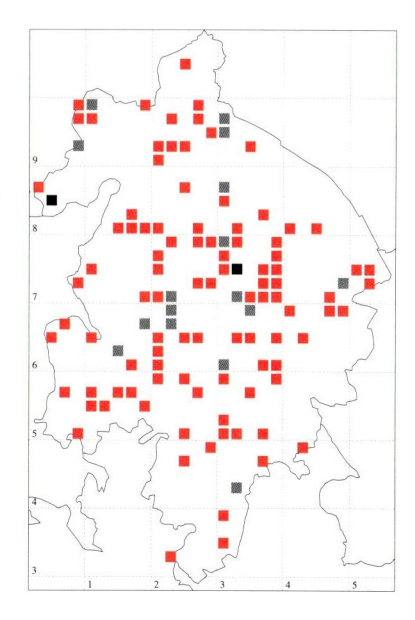

VCH 1904: *'Common everywhere.'*

May Highflyer
1778 *Hydriomena impluviata* ([D. & S.])

County status: Widespread and locally fairly common.
Flight: Late April to July.
Larval foodplants: Alder*.

The May Highflyer is associated with Alder and is locally plentiful in damp woodlands, marshes and river valleys over a large part of the County. It is established at Ufton Fields, Brandon Marsh, Newbold Comyn, Snitterfield Bushes, Hampton Wood and Oversley Wood. This species has occasionally been noted in urban districts.

VCH 1904: *'Not common.'*
Sutton Park, Marston Green, Knowle, Solihull, Rugby and Atherstone.

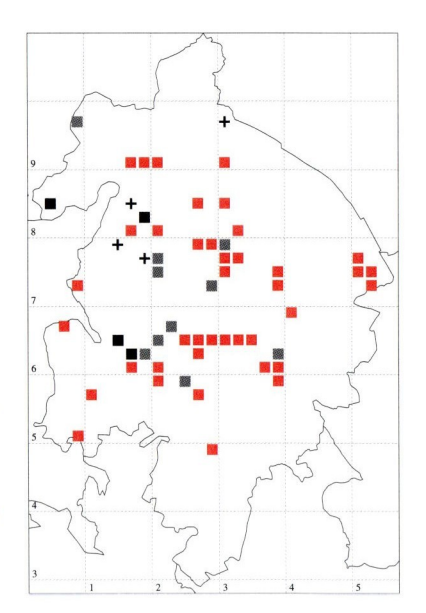

Ruddy Highflyer
1779 *Hydriomena ruberata* (Freyer)

Nationally Local

County status: Very local and scarce.
Flight: May and June.
Larval foodplants: Sallows*.

The Ruddy Highflyer is only very occasionally caught in Warwickshire. Difficulties have arisen with this species due to its similarity to May Highflyer and there are few unequivocally recorded examples.

The following records are of carefully scrutinized specimens.

Records:
Umberslade, 26/5/1919, 22/5/1927 (SEWC); **Chapelfields, Coventry**, 1965 (ANT); **Coombe Fields**, 1973 (MCV); **Bidford-on-Avon**, 1981 (RMC); **Hillmorton, Rugby**, 1986 (DIP), 11/6/2000 (PN); **Parkside, Coventry**, 26/6/1987 (MB); **Pailton**, 1987 (KCG); **Matchborough, Redditch**, 1989, 12/5/1990 (SD); **Ryton Pools Country Park**, 24/6/2000 (RGB).

VCH 1904: *'Has been recorded many times but I do not believe it occurs with us at all.'*

Small Waved Umber
1781 *Horisme vitalbata* ([D. & S.])

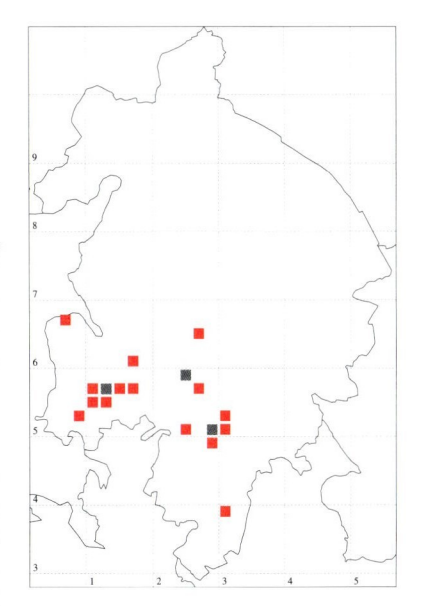

County status: Very local but sometimes fairly common.
Flight: Two generations. May to June, and August.
Larval foodplants: Traveller's-joy*.

The Small Waved Umber is found in the south-west of Warwickshire, on or near calcareous soils. It frequents open woodland, disused railway cuttings, scrub and well-established gardens. There is evidence of an increase in range and frequency over the last decade.

Records:
Wilmcote Rough, 1959 (2) (SEWC, FAN), 23/5/1998 (AFG, Warks Moth Group); **Oversley Wood**, 1960 (DWS), 1/8/1992 (Warks Moth Group), 15/6/2004 (DG), 26/5/2005 (J. Rush), 10/8/2005 (MA, JWkn); **Walton**, 17/8/1971 (DB); **Hampton Wood**, 12/6/1974 (AFG); **Redhill, Alcester**, 16/8/1974 (JAH); **Charlecote**, 18/8/1978, 17/7/1979, 1/9/1980, 29/7/1981, 11/8/1982, 1984 (2), 1985 (2), 1986 (2), 1987 (2), 17/6/1989, 24/8/1991, 1992 (6), 1996 (2), 6/8/1997, 11/8/2002, 15/5/2004 (DB, AFG); **Billesley**, 30/9/1984 larva (MCV); **Broom**, 1985 (RMC); **Bidford-on-Avon**, 1980–2004 annually (RMC); **Matchborough, Redditch**, 12/8/1988, 1992 (SD); **Grove Hill**, 6/6/1992 (2), 20/5/1995 (Warks Moth Group), 18/6/2005 (MK); **Pillerton Priors**, 2/8/1993, 19/8/1993, 23/8/2001, 25/8/2001, 25/5/2004, 6/8/2004 (CI); **Goldicote Cutting**, 1990s–2000s plentiful (CI); **Oxhouse Farm, Combrook**, 14/8/1993 (CI), 26/6/1994 (DB); **Bearley Station**, 14/8/1993 (IGMR); **Compton Verney**, 7/8/1999 (Warks Moth Group); **Hillmorton, Rugby**, 18/8/2002 (DIP); **Brailes**, 10/8/2003 (CI); **Temple Grafton**, 2004 (23), 2005 (9) (AFG).

Fern
1782 *Horisme tersata* ([D. & S.])

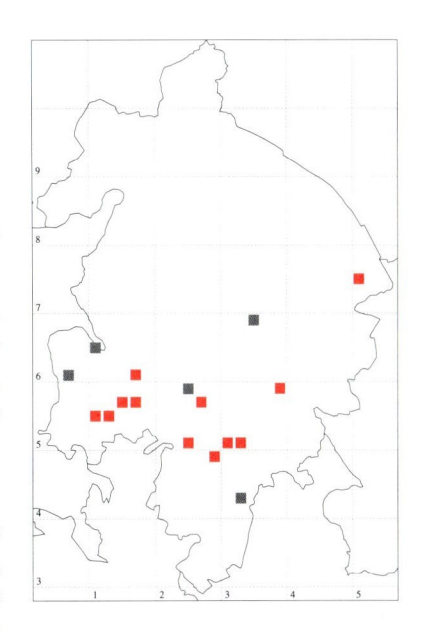

County status: Very local and generally uncommon.
Flight: Late May to early September.
Larval foodplants: Traveller's-joy* and probably cultivated clematis.

The Fern has a slightly wider distribution in the southern half of the County than the preceding species. This may suggest cultivated clematis is used as a larval foodplant. Favoured habitats are open woodland, disused railway cuttings, scrub and well-established gardens.

Records:
Wilmcote Rough, 1959–1998 annually in small numbers (SEWC, FAN, JMP, AFG), 23/5/1998, 10/7/1998 (DG, AFG, Warks Moth Group); **Tysoe**, 1964 (TT); **Bannam's Wood**, 1964–1979 (FAN); **Coughton Park**, 1966 (KEH);

Cubbington, 20/7/1971 (AFG); **Charlecote**, 30/6/1974, 9/7/1983, 22/6/1994 (DB, AFG); **Hillmorton, Rugby**, 1980s–2000s sporadic (DIP), **Bowshot Wood**, 22/6/1992 (3) (DB), 10/6/1988 (AFG); **Bidford-on-Avon**, 9/6/1992, 29/6/1992, 7/7/1992, 30/6/1993, 19/7/1994, 22/6/1995 (RMC); **Goldicote Cutting**, 2/7/1992, 17/6 2005 (CI); **Pillerton Priors**, 8/7/1993 (CI); **Bearley Station**, 29/6/1992 (IGMR); **Bishops Bowl**, 14/6/1997 (MA, Warks Moth Group); **Oxhouse Farm, Combrook**, 28/6/1998, 19/6/2005 (2) (DB); **Temple Grafton**, 22/5–2/9/2004 (27) (AFG); **Grove Hill**, 18/6/2005 (5), 2/7/2005 (2) (Warks Moth Group), 15/7/2005 (DB); **Brick Kiln Coppice, Compton Verney**, 9/7/2005 (3) (MA, MK, JWkn).

VCH 1904: *Rugby*.

Pretty Chalk Carpet
1784 *Melanthia procellata* ([D. & S.])

County status: Very local and occasionally fairly common.
Flight: June to August.
Larval foodplants: Traveller's-joy.

Pretty Chalk Carpet is a relatively recent coloniser of Warwickshire, which first came to notice during the 1970s. It is another moth associated with Traveller's-joy and is similarly centred around the south-west of the County on calcareous soils, sharing the same habitat types as the last two species.

Records:
Oversley Wood, 12/7/1974, 27/7/1974, 4/7/1976 (6), (AFG), 8/7/1977, 31/7/1980 (DB), 4/7/1982 (AFG), 19/6/1984 (AFG, RMC), 16/6/2000 (DG), 24/6/2003 (DB), 18/6/2005 (4) (DG); **Red Hill, Alcester**, 2/8/1974 several tapped out of Traveller's-joy along roadsides (DB), 26/7/1983 (JAH); **Wilmcote Rough**, 31/7/1974 several tapped out of Traveller's-joy (DB), 1977–80 two or three each year (JMP), 10/7/1998 (2) (DB); **Bannam's Wood**, 1979 (3) (FAN); **Tile Hill Wood**, 10/8/1984 (ANT, CW); **Bowshot Wood**, 26/6/1992 (5) (DB); **Snitterfield Bushes**, 8/7/1992 (AFG); **Bearley Station**, 3/7/1994 (IGMR).

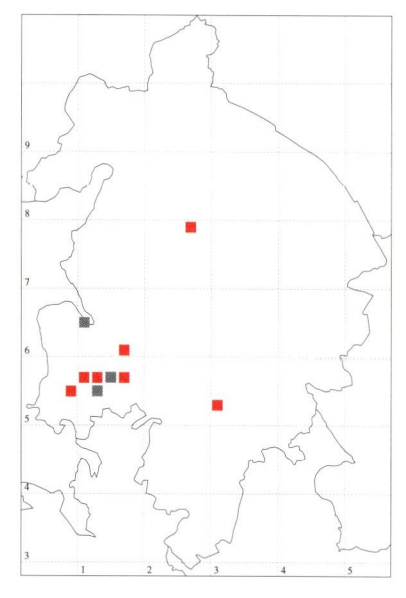

Argent & Sable
1787 *Rheumaptera hastata hastata* (L.)

Nationally Scarce B

County status: Presumed extinct.
Flight: May and June.
Larval foodplants: The low re-growth of Downy Birch and Silver Birch.

Formerly found in a number of birch woodlands in Warwickshire but now reduced to one site at Hay Wood, where numbers had declined to a seriously low level by 1997. Extinction is feared following inappropriate woodland management in 2002.

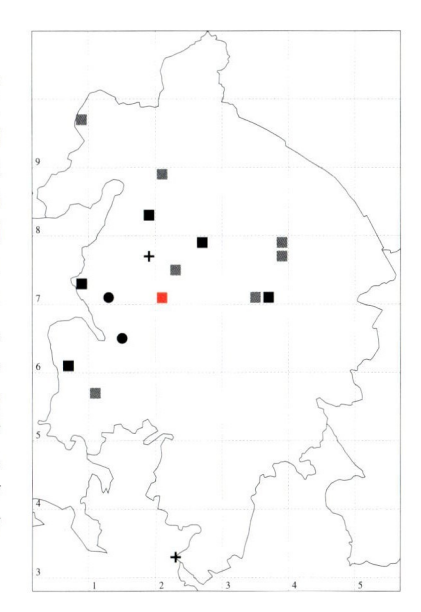

Records:
Umberslade, 1919, 1921 (SEWC); **May's Wood,** 1925–38 (FHL); **Tile Hill Wood, Coventry,** 13/6/1931 (FWS), 25/5/1935 (JWS), 17/5/1936 (JWS), 4/6/1938 (FWS), 26/5/1940 (FVS), 31/5/1947 (GW), 24/5/1952 (HHP), 22/5/1953 (FWS), 23/5/1953 (GW), 30/5/1953 (FWS), 8/6/1954, 5/6/1955 (CDNHSS); **Bubbenhall Glade,** 30/5/1937 (LR); **Wappenbury Wood,** 20/6/1941 (RFB); **Clowes Wood,** 9/8/1941 (FHL), 1949, 1951 (BNHS); **Austy Wood,** 1940s (HEH); **Brandon Wood,** 30/5/1948 (LR), 1951, 8/6/1954 (AHK); **Bickenhill,** 1950s annually (GPS); **Tile Hill Wood, Coventry,** 8/6/1954, 5/6/1955 (CDNHSS); **Coughton Park,** 1954 (Anon); **Oversley Wood,** 1961–70 (WTT); **Sutton Park,** 1960s (JB); **Coleshill,** 11/6/1965 (Anon); **Waverley Wood,** 28/5/1966 (LEM); **Hay Wood,** 1989–1997 very small numbers (PJR, AFG).

VCH 1904: *'Rare.'*
Knowle, Brandon Woods, Wolford Wood.

Scarce Tissue
1788 *Rheumaptera cervinalis* (Scop.)

Nationally Local

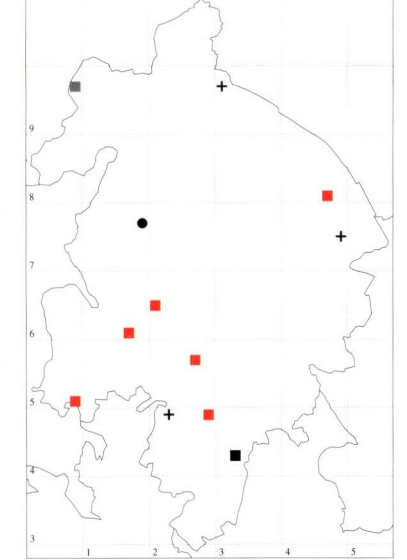

County status: Very local and uncommon.
Flight: Late April to June.
Larval foodplants: Barberry and cultivated species of *Berberis*.

The Scarce Tissue is largely restricted to the southern half of the County. Apart from twentieth century records at Knowle and Sutton Park all observations of this species are from domestic gardens. This suggests that many Warwickshire populations are supported by cultivated varieties of *Berberis*.

Records:
Knowle, 1908–25 (5) (SEWC); **Tysoe,** 4/5/1946 (TT); **Sutton Park,** 1960s (JB); **Charlecote,** 15/5/1979, 5/5/1986, 12/6/1986, 17/5/1989, 4/5/1992, 7/5/1992, 18/5/1992, 24/4/1993, 27/4/1996, 5/6/1996, 19/5/1997, 29/5/1997, 14/5/1998, 18/5/1998, 9/5/2000, 13/5/2001, 12/5/2004 (DB, AFG); **Pailton,** 1984, 1985, (KCG); **Claverdon,** 4/6/1984, 25/5/1985 (IGMR); **Bidford-on-Avon,** 18/6/1986, 20/5/1992 (RMC); **Pillerton Priors,** 29/4/1992, 30/4/1992, 4/5/1992, 12/5/1992, 10/5/1994, 25/4/2004 (CI); **Bearley Station,** 23/4/1993 (IGMR).

VCH 1904: *'Rare.'*
Atherstone, Overslade, Whitchurch.

Scallop Shell
1789 *Rheumaptera undulata* (L.)

Nationally Local

County status: Very local and uncommon.
Flight: June and July.
Larval foodplants: Sallows*, Aspen and Bilberry.

The Scallop Shell is found very locally in damp woodlands where there is an abundance of sallow. Populations are presently confined to three distinct areas—the woodlands and wetlands of north Warwickshire, the Princethorpe complex, and woodlands in the Stratford-upon-Avon and Redditch districts.

Records:
Clowes Wood, 1910 (WB); **Sutton Park**, 1912–26 (SEWC, GPS); **Umberslade**, 1920 (SEWC); **Wappenbury Wood**, 1970s (DB); **Hampton Wood**, 1972 (AFG); **Oversley Wood**, 3/7/1976 (5), 2/8/1980 (4), 8/7/1981, 11/6/1984 (DB, AFG), 20/7/1990 (Warks Moth Group), 15/6/2002 (MA), 29/6/2002 (DB), 7/6/2004, 15/6/2004 (DG), 20/7/2004 (DG, NJS, AJP), 18/6/2005 (DG); **Red Hill, Alcester**, 30/6/1984 (JAH); **Dosthill**, 25/7/1984 (PBD, MAA); **Ryton Wood**, 18/7/1986 (CDNHSS); 26/6/1987 (SAL), 1997 (LB), 14/6/2003 (NJS); **Waverley Wood**, 20/7/1990 (6) (Warks Moth Group); **Alvecote Pools**, 11/6/1992 (BM), 18/7/1994 (RCK, DB); **Rough Hill Wood**, 25/6/1993 (CI, RGB); **Water Orton**, 17/6/1995 (KM); **Coughton Park**, 12/8/1995 larvae on Sallow (2) (MCV); **Bentley Park Wood**, 20/7/1996 (Warks Moth Group); **Brandon Wood**, 5/7/1998 (Warks Moth Group); **Temple Grafton**, 24/7/2004 (AFG).

VCH 1904: *Sutton Park, Knowle, Brandon Woods, Cut Throat Coppice (Solihull).*

Tissue
1790 *Triphosa dubitata* (L.)

Nationally Local

County status: Local and becoming scarce.
Flight: Mid-July to September and, after hibernation, April to May.
Larval foodplants: Buckthorn*, and Alder Buckthorn.

The Tissue is found in open woodland and scrub, railway embankments and well-established gardens, chiefly on calcareous soil, but it has steadily declined in the County since the 1970s.

Records since 1970:
Red Hill, Alcester, 26/7/1970 (JAH); **Oversley Wood**, 1970s (DB, AFG); **Bilton**, 1970s (BB); **Royal Leamington Spa Railway station**, 1970s (AFG); **Nuneaton**, 1970s (RJT); **Sutton Park**, 1970s (LJE); **Walton**, 1970s (DB, AFG); **Oakley Wood**, 1970s (DB, AFG); **Hampton Wood**, 17/4/1972 (AFG); **Wilmcote Rough**, 1977 (JMP);

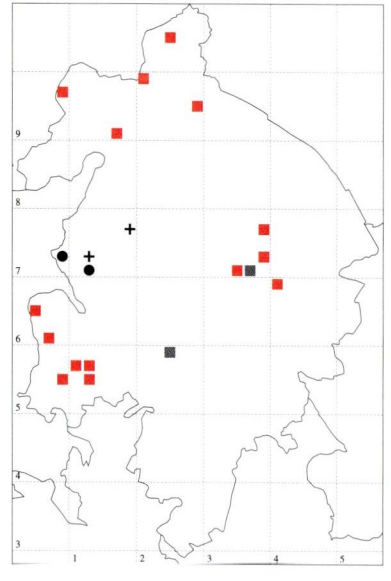

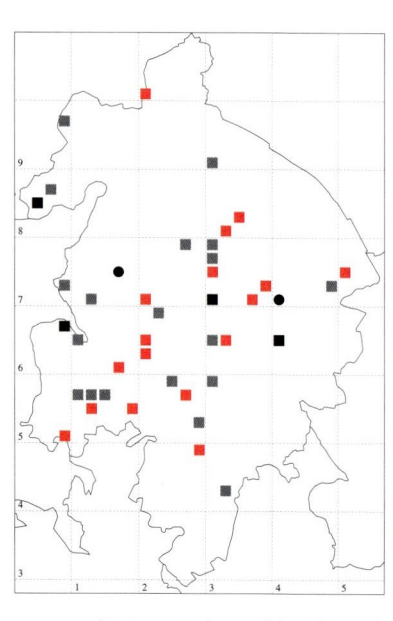

Coombe Fields, 13/6/1978, 20/6/1978, 25/6/1978 larvae (MCV); **Hillmorton, Rugby**, 13/8/1980, 21/8/1987 (DIP); **Dosthill**, 1981 (RJT); **Wolverton**, 1983 (DS); **Charlecote**, 18/8/1983, 25/4/1987, 8/8/1987, 21/8/1987, 28/7/1997 (AFG, DB); **Claverdon**, 10/8/1985, Aug. 1997 (IGMR); **Bidford-on-Avon**, 30/8/1985, 9/9/1986 (RMC); **Pillerton Priors**, 27/7/1992 (CI); **Shottery, Stratford-upon-Avon**, May 1994 (RGB); **Radford, Coventry**, 25/7/1995 (MCV); **Baddesley Clinton N.T**, 24/7/1999 (AJK); **Hall Green, Coventry**, 23/8/2001 (SS); **Sydenham, Royal Leamington Spa**, 9/8/2005 (MK).

VCH 1904: *'Common everywhere.'*

Brown Scallop
1791 *Philereme vetulata* ([D. & S.])

Nationally Local

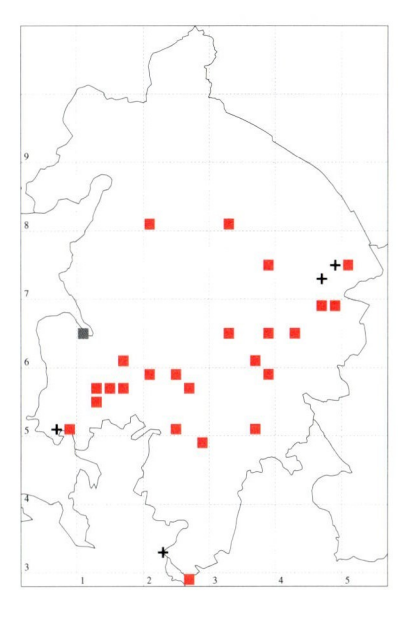

County status: Local and uncommon.
Flight: Late June to July.
Larval foodplants: Buckthorn*.

The Brown Scallop is an inhabitant of disused railway cuttings, woodland edges, scrub and hedgerows, particularly on calcareous soils. Sites include Goldicote Cutting, Bearley Station, Snitterfield Bushes, Chesterton Wood, Ufton Fields, Wilmcote Rough, Nelson's Quarry and Draycote Water. This species generally responds poorly to MV and as a rule only faded specimens are noted. During May and early June more effective recording methods are to search the foodplant at night with a torch for feeding larvae, or alternatively check in the daytime for purses of spun leaves in which they are contained.

VCH 1904: *Salford Priors, Rugby—Cawston, Overslade, Wolford.*

Dark Umber
1792 *Philereme transversata britannica* (Lempke)

Nationally Local

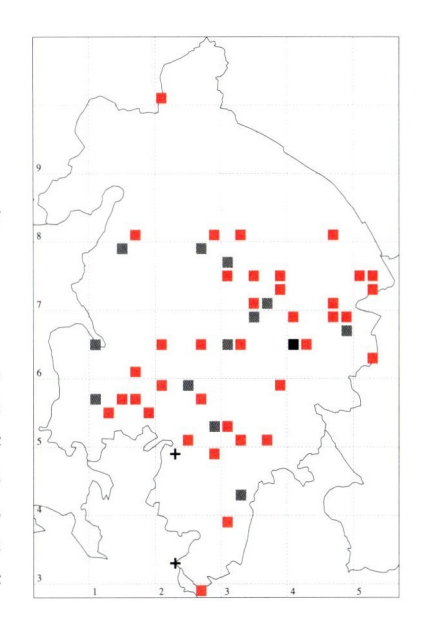

County status: Fairly widespread but generally uncommon.
Flight: Late June to late August.
Larval foodplants: Buckthorn* and Alder Buckthorn.

The Dark Umber is found in woodland, scrub, overgrown quarries and disused railway cuttings on chalky soils. Colonies presently occur at Wilmcote Rough, Bearley Station, Flecknoe disused railway, Bowshot Wood, Snitterfield Bushes, Waverley Wood, Ryton Wood and Draycote Water. A good population exists at Goldicote Cutting where 21 individuals were observed during 2004 (CI). Occasional wanderers appear in garden moth traps from time to time, especially in hot weather.

VCH 1904: *'Not common.'*
Overslade, Wolford.

Cloaked Carpet
1793 *Euphyia biangulata* (Haw.)

Nationally Scarce B

County status: Very local and uncommon.
Flight: Late June to early August.
Larval foodplants: Stitchworts.

The Cloaked Carpet is a recent addition to the Warwickshire list with examples first being recorded in Ryton Wood and Oakley Wood during the 1990s. Although seemingly well established at both locations it has only been observed in small numbers.

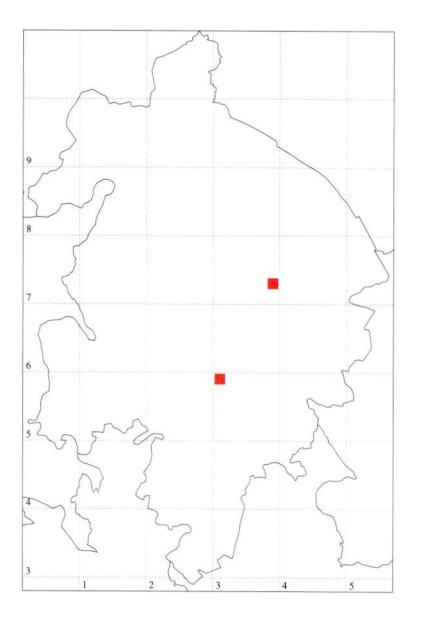

Records:
Ryton Wood, 27/6/1992 (RCK, CW), 8/7/1993 (RCK, LB), 6/7/1995 (PC, NWH, CW); 5/8/1996 (DT) 15/7/2003 (MA); **Oakley Wood**, 11/7/1995 (AFG, PAP), 28/6/2005 (3) (DB, PAP).

Sharp-angled Carpet
1794 *Euphyia unangulata* (Haw.)

Nationally Local

County status: Local and occasionally fairly common.
Flight: Late June to early August.
Larval foodplants: Unknown in the wild but in captivity will feed on chickweeds and stitchworts.

The Sharp-angled Carpet is found in areas of damp woodland and pockets of moist sheltered waste-ground. It is usually observed in low numbers but occasionally attracted to light in greater quantity: Haseley Knob, 10/7/1971 (24) (DB, PC, LEM, CW); Waverley Wood, 4/7/1992 (15) (Warks Moth Group).

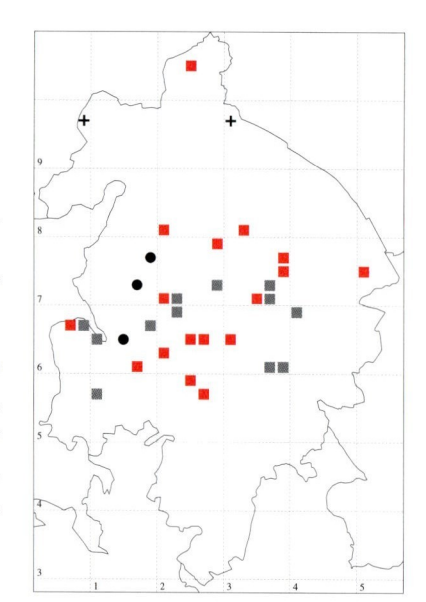

Records since 1980:
Wolverton, 9/7/1982 (DS); **Charlecote**, 29/7/1983, 9/7/1987 (AFG); **Hampton Wood**, July 1985, 1986 (RGB); **Hampton-in-Arden**, 23/7/1985 (MCV); **Hillmorton, Rugby**, 13/7/1986, 14/7/1987, 28/7/1991 (DIP); **Tile Hill, Coventry**, 4/7/1987, 7/7/1995 (AJK); **Matchborough, Redditch**, 3/8/1988 (SD); **Hampton Magna**, 1989 (PJR); **Alvecote Pools**, 21/6/1991 (RCK); **Waverley Wood**, 6/7/1991 (12), 4/7/1992 (15) (Warks Moth Group); **Royal Leamington Spa**, 1992 (PhP); **Brandon Marsh**, 25/7/1992 (Warks

Moth Group); **Bearley Station**, 27/6/1994, 29/6/1994 (IGMR); **Radford, Coventry**, 28/6/1994 (MCV); **Hay Wood**, 8/7/1995 (Warks Moth Group).

VCH 1904: *'Rare.'*
Sutton Park, Knowle, Rugby, Atherstone.

Genus: *Epirrita*—November Moths

This genus consists of four species, three of which occur in Warwickshire. The trio are very similar and require genitalic dissection to achieve certain separation. Knowledge on the distribution of *christyi* and *autumnata* is very limited, as reflected in the distribution maps. Due to the subsequent separation of the three *Epirrita* species the VCH comment that *dilutata* was 'very common everywhere' can only now be regarded as a comment on the genus.

November Moth
1795 *Epirrita dilutata* ([D. & S.])

County status: Fairly widespread and common.
Flight: Early October to late November.
Larval foodplants: Polyphagous on deciduous trees, including oaks*, birches*, Field Maple*, Blackthorn* and Alder*.

The November Moth is a common species in well-wooded habitats, including urban gardens. An exceedingly early specimen was taken at Grendon Common on 18/8/1990 (DB, AFG, RGB).

Dark forms predominate in Warwickshire.

VCH 1904: *'Very common everywhere.'*

Pale November Moth
1796 *Epirrita christyi* (Allen)

County status: Very local and sometimes fairly common.
Flight: October and November.
Larval foodplants: Polyphagous on deciduous trees.

Due to identification difficulties the distribution of this moth is not well known. From the limited number of records available it appears to favour areas of broadleaved woodland. Perhaps more plentiful than previously thought, as from a random sample of 59 male *Epirrita* specimens retained from Oversley Wood on 1/11/2004 for genitalia dissection 41 proved to be *christyi* (NJS).

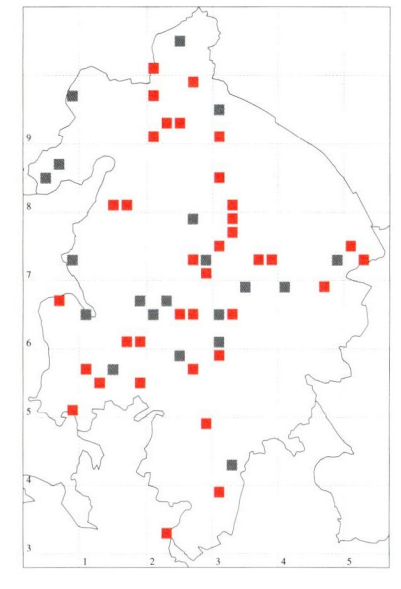

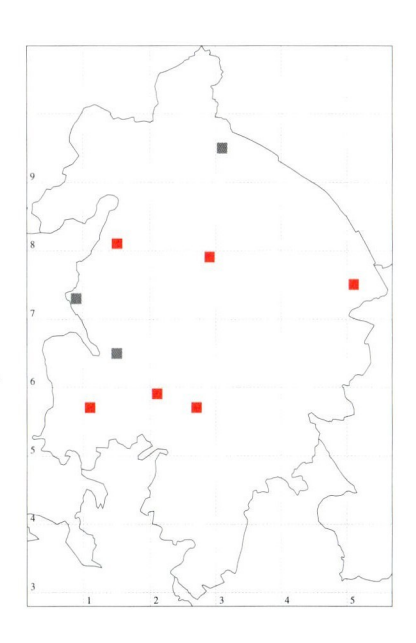

Records:
May's Wood, 1968 (DWS); **Charlecote**, 1970–2004 occasional (DB); **Clowes Wood**, 31/10/1972 (DB); **Hartshill Hayes**, 1975 (RJT); **Hillmorton, Rugby**, 9/10/1983 (DIP); **Solihull**, 1994 (AP); **Snitterfield Bushes**, 10/11/1989 (DB); **Tile Hill, Coventry**, 10/10/1992, 12/10/1992 (AJK); **Oversley Wood**, 1/11/2004 (41) (NJS, AJP, MK) (NJS gen. det).

Autumnal Moth
1797 *Epirrita autumnata* (Borkh.)

County status: Very local and occasionally fairly common.
Flight: October and November.
Larval foodplants: Polyphagous on deciduous and coniferous trees and shrubs, including birches*.

The status of this species is uncertain due to the similarity to both *dilutata* and *christyi*. The preferred habitats appear to be broadleaved woodland and sheltered gardens.

Records:
Sutton Park, 1928–88 frequent (LJE gen. det.), 25/5/1966 two larvae beaten from birch (LJE); **Tysoe**, 16/10/1947 (TT); **Ufton Wood**, 1959 survey; **Windmill Naps**, 1960 (FAN); **Birmingham**, 1965 (LJE gen. det.); **Clowes Wood**, 31/10/1972 (DB); **Snitterfield Bushes**, 10/11/1989 (DB); **Hillmorton, Rugby**, 6/10/2002 (PN); **Pillerton Priors**, 1/11/2002 (CI) (gen. det. M. Bailey); **Meriden Shafts**, 26/10/2004 (10 males) (AJP, VW, NJS) (NJS gen. det.); **Wolford Wood**, 30/10/2004 (MK) (NJS gen. det.) **Close Wood**, 8/11/2004 (NJS, AJP) (NJS gen. det.);

Winter Moth
1799 *Operophtera brumata* (L.)

County status: Widespread and common.
Flight: Late October to mid-January.
Larval foodplants: Polyphagous on deciduous and coniferous trees and shrubs, including Blackthorn*, hawthorns*, Field Maple*, oaks*, sallows*, birches*, poplars*, Alder*, Rowan*, Beech*, Sweet Chestnut*, Wild Rose* and Bilberry*.

Although this species is fairly well represented on the distribution map, it is undoubtedly under-recorded due to the late autumn and winter flight period. The larvae are perhaps more frequently encountered than the imago and utilise a huge range of trees and shrubs.

VCH 1904: *'Common everywhere.'*

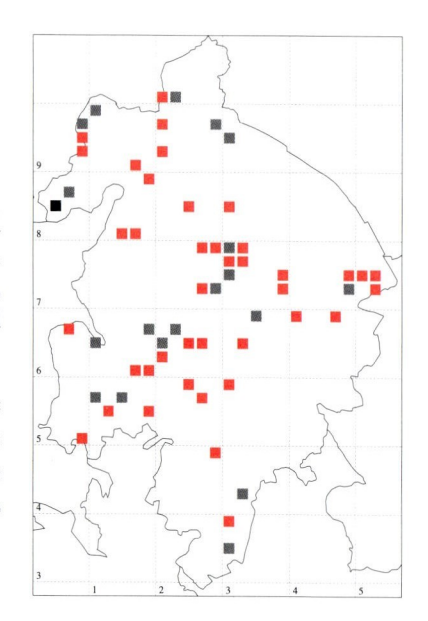

Northern Winter Moth
1800 *Operophtera fagata* (Scharf.)

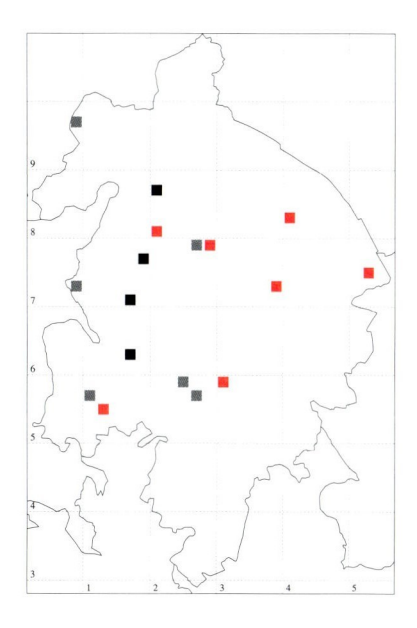

County status: Very local but fairly common.
Flight: Late October to November.
Larval foodplants: Birches*, Hazel*, Alder, Beech, apple, plum and cherry.

The Northern Winter Moth is decidedly more local than its congener and appears to be restricted to well-wooded districts.

Records:
May's Wood, 1930s annually (GBM); **Clowes Wood**, 1938–53 (BNHS); **Knowle**, 1938 (HEH); **Lapworth**, 1938 (HEH); **Coleshill Bog**, 1949 (HEH); **Austy Wood**, 1951 several larvae on Hazel (HEH); **Tile Hill Wood**, 1960s (LEM), 31/5/1954 larva, 2/11/1957, 11/11/1960, 25/10/1964 (ANT); **Sutton Park**, 1960s (LJE); **Charlecote**, 24/10/1971 (DB); **Hampton Wood**, 1972–75 (AFG); **Oversley Wood**, 1970s, 1980s (DB); **Ansty**, 30/5/1983 larva (JR); **Hampton-in-Arden**, 1983 (MCV); **Oakley Wood**, 11/11/1989 plentiful at rest on herbage, 27/11/1991 (8) (AFG); **Hillmorton, Rugby**, 17/11/1997 (PN); **Ryton Wood**, 22/11/2002 specimen disturbed in daytime (DkS), 16/11/2004 (AJP, NJS); **Temple Grafton**, 4/12/2004 (AFG).

Rivulet
1802 *Perizoma affinitata* (Steph.)

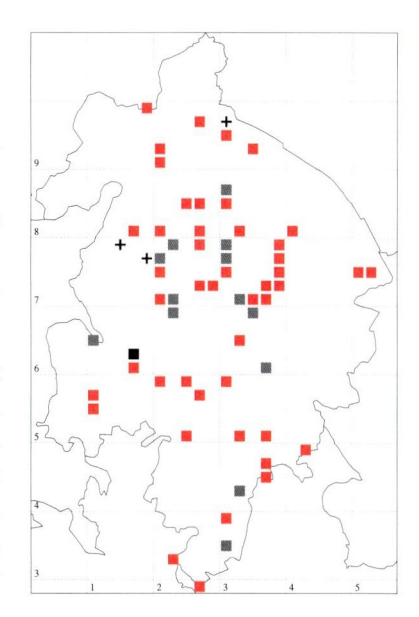

County status: Fairly widespread and occasionally fairly common.
Flight: Possibly two generations. Early May to late June and July to late August.
Larval foodplants: The flowers and seeds of Red Campion.

The Rivulet is found in well-wooded districts over a large part of the County. The imago occasionally visits light in fairly large numbers; for example, Hampton Wood 11/5/1990 (15) (DB, RGB). Well established at Snitterfield Bushes, Oversley Wood, Oakley Wood, Ryton Wood, Waverley Wood, Crackley Wood, Brandon Marsh and Whitacre Heath. Sporadically reported from garden moth traps in both rural and urban districts.

VCH 1904: *'Common.'*
Solihull, Knowle, Rugby, Atherstone, Wolford.

Small Rivulet
1803 *Perizoma alchemillata* (L.)

County status: Widespread and fairly common.
Flight: May to late August.
Larval foodplants: The flowers and seeds of Common Hemp-nettle.

The Small Rivulet is fairly common in a variety of habitats, including woodland rides and clearings, meadows, marshes, road and railway cuttings and gardens.

Garden moth trap totals at **Hillmorton, Rugby**, are as follows: 1982 (15), 1985 (12), 1990 (17), 1995 (44), 2000 (10), 2004 (62) (DIP).

VCH 1904: *'Common.'*
Knowle, Solihull, Overslade.

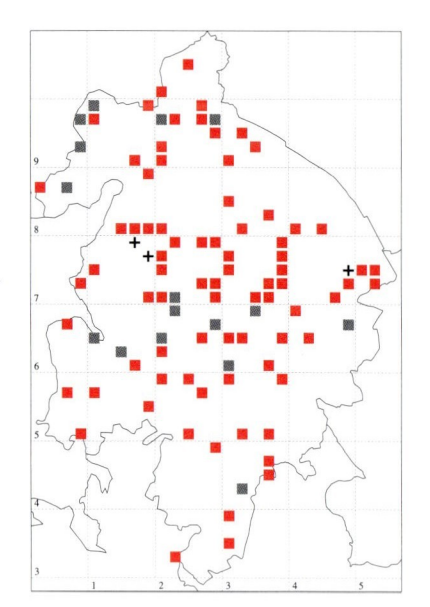

Barred Rivulet
1804 *Perizoma bifaciata* (Haw.)

Nationally Local

County status: Very local and uncommon.
Flight: Late June to August.
Larval foodplants: The ripening seeds of Red Bartsia* and occasionally eyebright.

The Barred Rivulet was first recorded in Warwickshire at Wilmcote Rough in 1959 in good quantity. A species most often seen on or near chalky soil in a range of open habitats, including woodland rides, clearings and railway cuttings.

Records:
Wilmcote Rough, 1959 (18) (SEWC, HTK, FAN); **Tysoe**, 1960s (TT); **Bilton**, 1970s (BB); **Woodrow, Redditch**, 30/6/1973 (ATJ); **Hampton Wood**, 1/8/1973 (AFG); **Walton**, 8/8/1973 (PR); **Oversley Wood**, 6/8/1976 (AFG); **Charlecote**, 27/7/1976, 12/8/1983, 21/7/1994, 31/7/1994, 10/8/1988 (DB, AFG); **Bearley Station**, 10/8/1987, 9/9/1987, 6/8/1988, 7/8/1988 (2); 13/8/1988, 9/8/1989 (IGMR); **Ufton Fields**, 21/8/1987 (CDNHSS); 20/8/1988 (Warks Moth Group); **Matchborough, Redditch**, 28/7/1988 (SD); **Oakley Wood**, 8/8/1988 (DB); **Hillmorton, Rugby**, 11/8/1991, 17/8/1996, 10/8/1998, 5/8/2000 (DIP); **Bidford-on-Avon**, 12/8/1991, 9/8/1998 (RMC); **Bannam's Wood**, 12/8/1995 (6) (Warks Moth Group); **Galley Common, Nuneaton**, 1995 (PT); **Radford, Coventry**, 16/8/1998 (MCV).

Grass Rivulet
1807 *Perizoma albulata albulata* ([D. & S.])

Nationally Local

County status: Local and occasionally fairly common.
Flight: Mid-May to mid-July.
Larval foodplants: The ripening seeds of Yellow-rattle*.

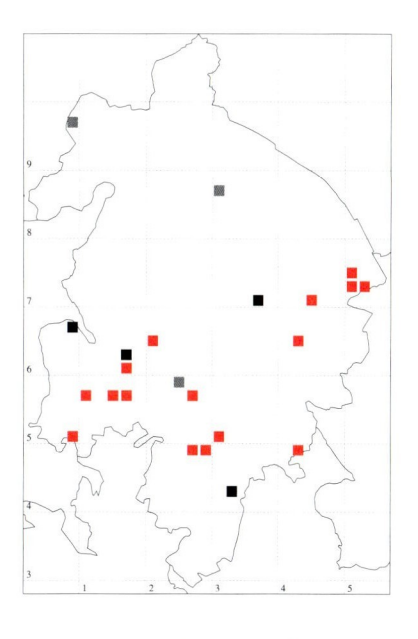

The Grass Rivulet is associated with calcareous grassland, especially road and railway embankments, disused quarries, and occasionally woodland rides or clearings. Locations include Ashlawn Cutting, Nelson's Quarry, Draycote Water, Bearley Station, Wilmcote Rough, Oversley Wood, Ettington Road Embankment and Oxhouse Farm, Combrook. The adult may be disturbed in small numbers by day and is attracted to light. It is a regular visitor to garden moth traps, especially in rural areas. Garden moth traps totals at **Pillerton Priors** (CI) reflect a healthy population: 2003 (63), 2004 (174), 2005 (24).

Described as '*common everywhere*' in the VCH 1904, when there was an abundance of flower-rich meadows containing Yellow-rattle.

VCH 1904: *'Common everywhere.'*

Sandy Carpet
1808 *Perizoma flavofasciata* (Thunb.)

County status: Widespread and fairly common.
Flight: Mid-May to early August.
Larval foodplants: The flowers and ripening seeds of Red Campion and less often, White Campion and Bladder Campion.

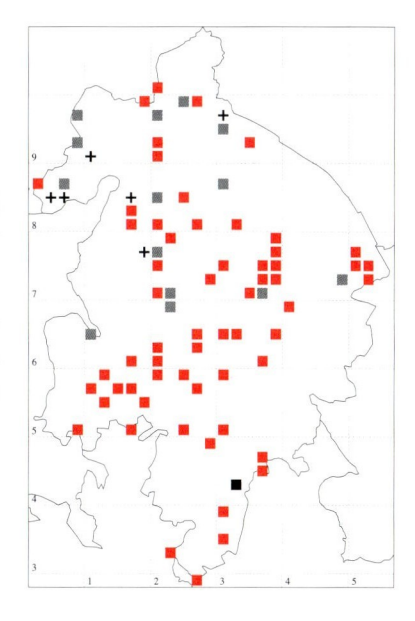

The Sandy Carpet has increased since 1980 to become distributed over a wide area of the County. It frequents a diversity of habitats and has been recorded at most regularly operated garden moth traps.

VCH 1904: *'Not uncommon.'*
Edgbaston, Yardley, Marston Green, Sutton, Knowle, Rugby, Atherstone.

Twin-spot Carpet
1809 *Perizoma didymata didymata* (L.)

County status: Fairly widespread and fairly common.
Flight: Late June to early August.
Larval foodplants: Polyphagous on low-growing plants and trees, including sallows, pines, heathers, Bilberry*, Blackthorn*, Field Maple*, Honeysuckle*, docks, willowherbs and campions.

The Twin-spot Carpet is fairly common in many of the larger deciduous woodlands. It is found less commonly in hedgerows, copses, well-established orchards and gardens. The imago has often been noted flying at dusk and later visits light in generally low numbers. Dark forms regularly occur at some sites.

VCH 1904: *'Very common everywhere.'*

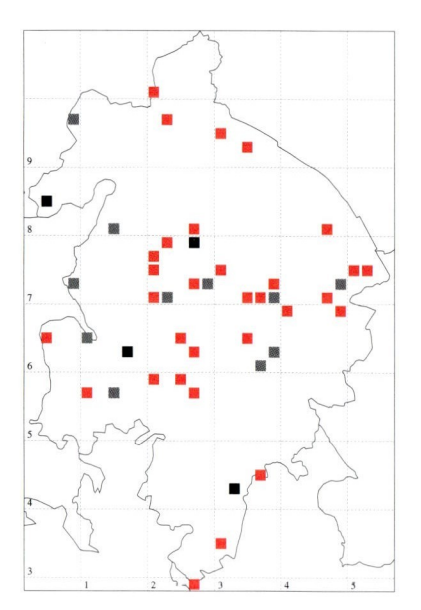

Marsh Carpet
1810 *Perizoma sagittata* (Fabr.)

Nationally Scarce A

County status: Extinct.
Flight: No dates available.
Larval foodplants: The ripening seeds of Common Meadow-rue.

VCH 1904: *Rugby*

Genus: *Eupithecia*—Pugs

There are almost 50 species of *Eupithecia* in the British Isles, of which 39 have been recorded in Warwickshire. Generally the 'pugs', with their small but distinctively shaped narrow forewings, are not difficult to distinguish from other groups but can be difficult to identify to species level, particularly when dealing with worn light trap examples. This has resulted in a number of lepidopterists not even attempting to tackle the more obscure species. The *Eupithecia* are consequently a very much under-recorded genus in Warwickshire. There is a need for greater fieldwork as the larvae are often more distinctive than the adults and in many cases are confined to particular foodplants, leading to more reliable identification.

Slender Pug
1811 *Eupithecia tenuiata* (Hb.)

County status: Local and occasionally fairly common.
Flight: June to August.
Larval foodplants: The catkins of sallows*.

The Slender Pug is associated with sallow growing in damp areas and was first noted in Warwickshire in 1928 at Umberslade (SEWC). Populations are known to occur at a number of locations, including Alvecote Pools, Kingsbury Wood, Whitacre Heath, Middleton Hall, Coombe Abbey, Ryton Wood, Brandon Wood, Sutton Park, Oversley Wood and Snitterfield Bushes. Individuals have been noted in garden moth traps in both rural and urban districts.

Assiduous searching could prove this species to have a wider distribution than the map shows. The larvae are easily obtainable by beating sallow catkins into a tray or collecting them from the ground during March and April.

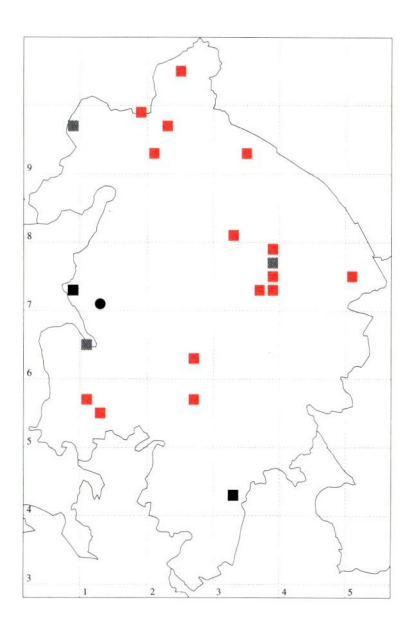

Maple Pug
1812 *Eupithecia inturbata* (Hb.)

Nationally Local

County status: Local and occasionally fairly common.
Flight: July and August.
Larval foodplants: The flowers of Field Maple*.

The Maple Pug was first recorded in Warwickshire during the 1960s at Wilmcote Rough (FAN). There were no further records until the mid-1980s and 1990s when the species was discovered in a number of woodlands and well-established hedgerows. Sites included Chesterton Wood, Snitterfield Bushes, Rough Hill Wood, Oversley Wood and Tocil Wood. The largest colony, however, appears to be at Bannam's Wood where over 70 specimens were attracted to light on 12/8/1995 (Warks Moth Group). Occasional individuals are noted in garden moth traps in both rural and urban districts.

This species may yet prove to be more widespread than is realised through diligent fieldwork to obtain larvae by tapping the lower branches of Field Maple.

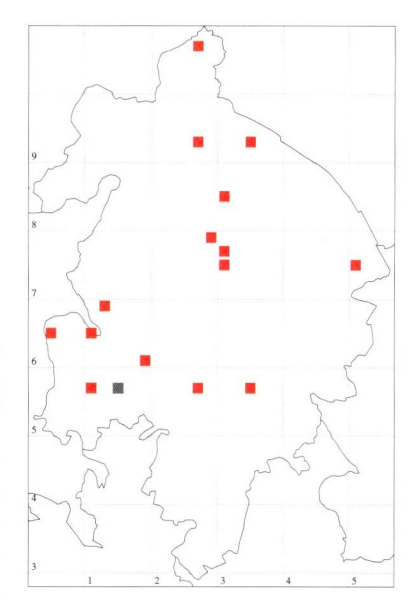

Haworth's Pug
1813 *Eupithecia haworthiata* Doubl.

Nationally Local

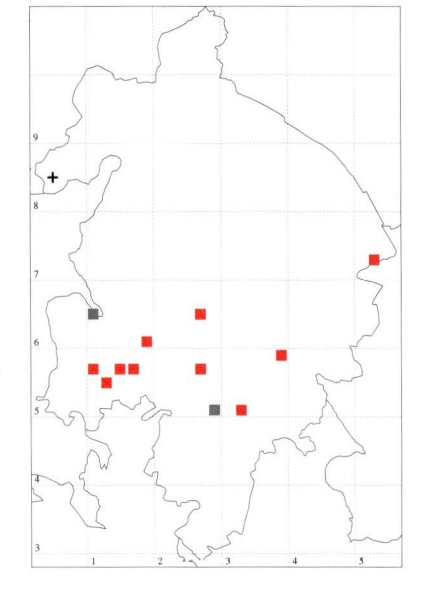

County status: Very local and sometimes fairly common.
Flight: Late June to early August.
Larval foodplants: The flower buds of Traveller's-joy* and cultivated species of clematis.

Haworth's Pug is confined to calcareous districts with an abundance of Traveller's-joy. Although the adult visits light in small numbers, a far more effective method of monitoring is to tap the foodplant during the daytime.

Records:
Edgbaston, Birmingham, 1900 (3) (EWC); **Bannam's Wood**, 1964–79 (FAN); **Wilmcote Rough**, 31/7/1974 numbers tapped from Traveller's-joy (DB), 10/7/1998 (3) (Warks Moth Group); **disused railway, Walton Wood**, 27/8/1978 (2) (DB, AFG, RHS); **Red Hill, Alcester**, 9/8/1986, 20/8/1988 larvae (MCV); **Snitterfield Bushes**, 23/6/1994 (BS); **Charlecote**, 20/7/1996, 10/7/2003, 10/7/2005 (DB); **Hillmorton, Rugby**, 1992 (2), 2001, 2004 (3) (DIP); **Temple Grafton**, 17/6/2004, 30/6/2004, 13/7/2004 (AFG); **Oversley Wood**, 15/6/2004 (DG); **Brick Kiln Coppice, Compton Verney**, 9/7/2005 (MA, MK, JWkn); **Bishops Hill**, 14/7/2005 (5) (Warks Moth Group).

Lead-coloured Pug
1814 *Eupithecia plumbeolata* (Haw.)

Nationally Scarce B

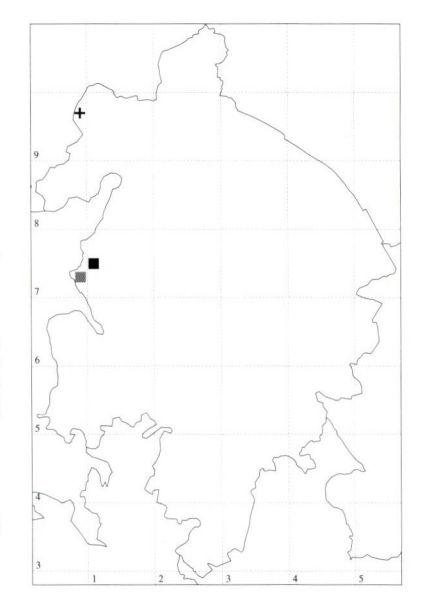

County status: Presumed extinct.
Flight: June.
Larval foodplants: Common Cow-wheat and occasionally Yellow-rattle.

This species is associated with open woodland where coppicing benefits the foodplant. It was once well established at Clowes Wood but is now presumed extinct.

Records:
Earlswood, 6/7/1944 (SEWC); **Clowes Wood**, 1956 common (BNHS).

VCH 1904: *'Sutton Park.' 1900 (GWW)*

Cloaked Pug
1815 *Eupithecia abietaria* (Goeze)

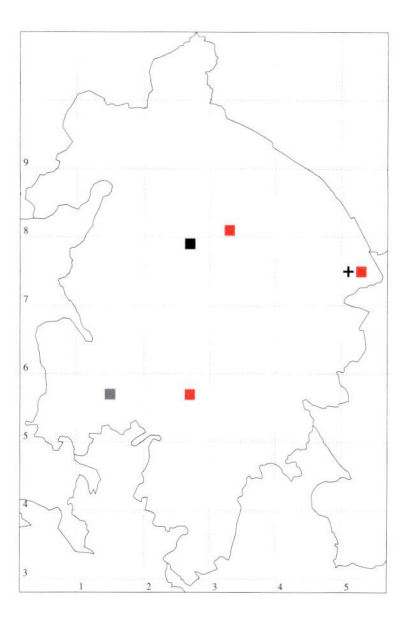

Nationally Uncommon; suspected immigrant.

County status: Status uncertain; possible vagrant/immigrant.
Flight: June and July.
Larval foodplants: Inside the cones of Norway Spruce and occasionally other spruces and firs of sufficient age to produce good numbers of large cones.

The Cloaked Pug, a species associated with mature spruce plantations, formerly occurred at Tile Hill Wood and Wilmcote Rough. Detailed searches of these sites in recent years have proved negative and there is no evidence this moth exists in the region.

The three isolated records at garden moth traps are presumed vagrants or immigrants.

Records:
Rugby district, pre-1893, (A. Sidgwick, 1893); **Tile Hill Wood, Coventry**, 30/5/1953, 5/6/1953 (CDNHSS); **Wilmcote Rough**, 1977–80 'a well-established colony' (JMP); **Radford, Coventry**, 13/7/1986 (MCV); **Charlecote**, 17/6/2000 (DB; Brown, 2000); **Hillmorton, Rugby**, 4/7/2001 (DIP).

Toadflax Pug
1816 *Eupithecia linariata* ([D. & S.])

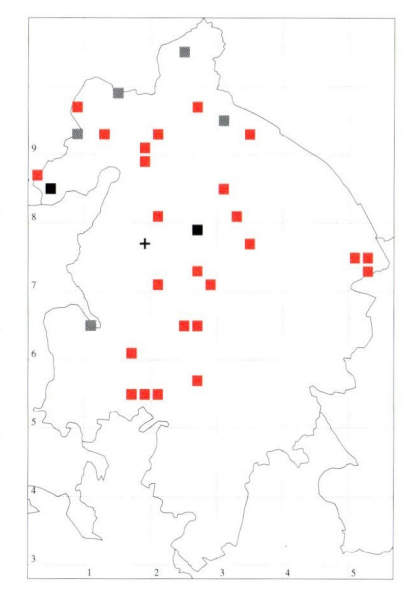

County status: Fairly widespread but generally uncommon.
Flight: Late June to August.
Larval foodplants: The flowers and seed capsules of Common Toadflax* and Pale Toadflax*.

The Toadflax Pug is fairly evenly distributed in the north and west of the County, but there is a curious lack of records from much of the south and east. It frequents rough, open grassland, roadside verges and railway cuttings where the foodplant occurs. The majority of records for this species are from static garden moth traps. Also noted in recent years from Alvecote Pools, Water Orton, Whitacre Heath, Windmill Hill, Baddesley Clinton and Bearley Station. In August 1988 larvae were found in the seed-heads of toadflax plants growing on waste-ground and roadside verges at Stratford-upon-Avon (JMP). The distribution may prove to be greater with further diligent fieldwork in other districts.

VCH 1904: *'Not common.'*

Foxglove Pug
1817 *Eupithecia pulchellata pulchellata* Steph.

County status: Widespread and fairly common.
Flight: May to early August.
Larval foodplants: The flowers of Foxglove*.

This species is fairly common in a number of habitats where Foxgloves grow, especially woodland rides and clearings.

The following moth trap counts give an idea of numbers in a suburban garden: **Hillmorton, Rugby:** 1982 (3), 1985 (8), 1990 (27), 1995 (57), 2000 (57), 2004 (41) (DIP).

VCH 1904: *'Not uncommon.'*
Sutton Park, Knowle, Marston Green, Edgbaston, Rugby.

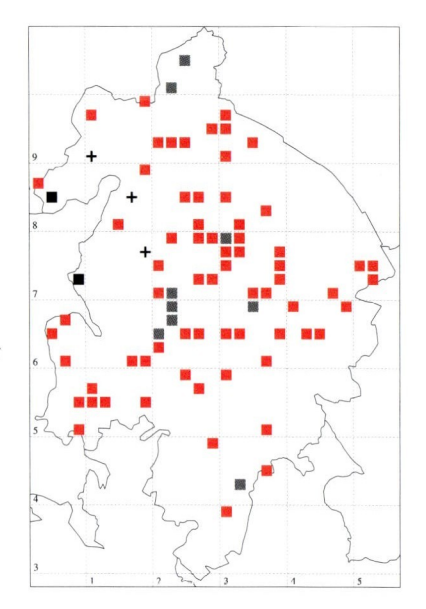

Mottled Pug
1819 *Eupithecia exiguata exiguata* (Hb.)

County status: Widespread and fairly common.
Flight: May to early July.
Larval foodplants: Hawthorns*, oaks* and Blackthorn*.

A widespread and fairly common early summer species of pug which is relatively easy to identify. It frequents broadleaved wooded areas, waste-ground and gardens.

Plentiful in suburban districts, as the following garden moth trap counts illustrate: **Hillmorton, Rugby:** 1982 (107), 1985 (43), 1990 (102), 1995 (271), 2000 (371), 2004 (328) (DIP).

VCH 1904: *Knowle and Overslade.*

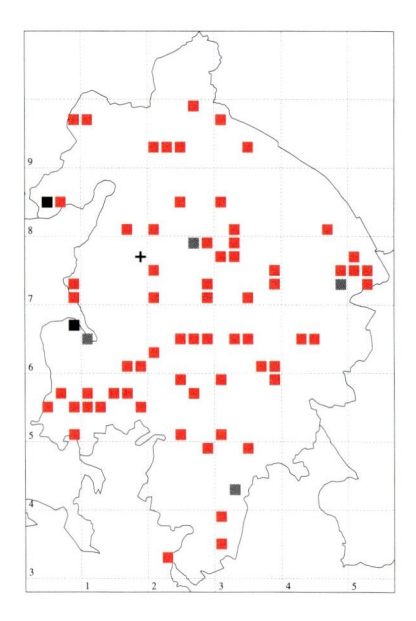

Pinion-spotted Pug
1820 *Eupithecia insigniata* (Hb.)

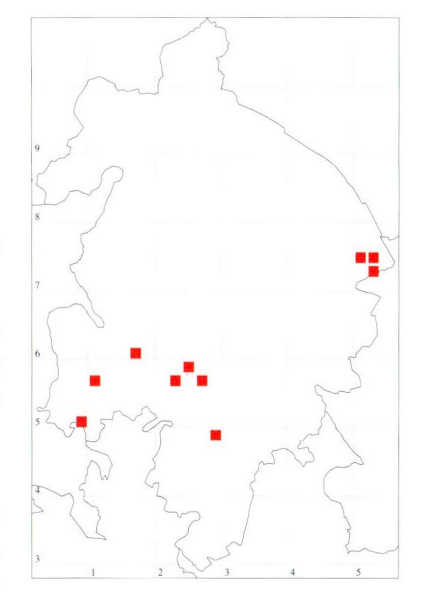

Nationally Scarce B

County status: Very local and uncommon.
Flight: May to early June.
Larval foodplants: Hawthorns, and occasionally Crab Apple and cultivated Apple.

The first record of this species in Warwickshire was from Oversley Wood in 1960 (FAN). Now sporadically recorded at a number of garden moth traps, chiefly in the south-west of the County.

Records:
Oversley Wood, 1960 (FAN), 31/5/1980 (DB, AFG); **Charlecote**, 1980 (3), 20/5/1982, 1984 (6), 1985 (3), 1986 (2), 1987 (2), 1989 (2), 1992 (2), 10/5/2001 (DB, AFG); **Hillmorton, Rugby**, 1982 (1), 1984 (3), 1991 (2), 2001 (1) (DIP), 18/5/1997, 1/5/2000, 28/5/2002, 30/4/2005, 3/5/2005, 4/5/2005 (PN); **Hampton Wood**, 1985–1986 (RGB); **Bidford-on-Avon**, 2/5/1990, 2/5/1997, 6/5/1999 (RMC); **Bearley Station**, 13/5/1992 (IGMR); **Pillerton Priors**, 24/5/1992 (CI); **Alveston Youth Hostel**, 14/5/2001 (DB).

Valerian Pug
1821 *Eupithecia valerianata* (Hb.)

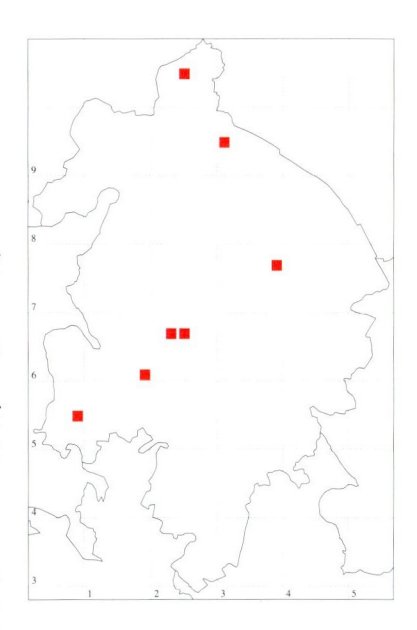

Nationally Scarce B

County status: Very local and uncommon.
Flight: June.
Larval foodplants: The flowers and ripening seeds of Common Valerian and Marsh Valerian*.

The Valerian Pug was first recorded in the County as recently as 1989 at Hatton (MCV).

Assiduous searching for larvae in the flower-heads of valerian plants, during July in wetland habitats, may find the species to be more plentiful than is realised.

Records:
Hatton (by canal), 1/7/1989 larva, 8/7/1989 larva, 14/7/1990 two larvae (MCV); **Alvecote Pools**, 21/6/1991 imago (RCK); **Piles Coppice, Brandon Wood**, 6/6/1993, imago (TRG); **Haseley**, 16/7/1994 larvae common (MCV); **Snitterfield Bushes**, 19/7/1994 larva (MCV); **Purley Chase, Mancetter**, 8/6/2004 imago (DB); **Oversley Wood**, 13/6/2005 (DG, gen. det. NJS).

Marsh Pug
1822 *Eupithecia pygmaeata* (Hb.)
Nationally Scarce B

County status: Very local and uncommon.
Flight: Day-flying. May and June.
Larval foodplants: The flowers and seed capsules of Field Mouse-ear.

The first fully confirmed record of Marsh Pug in Warwickshire was at Edgbaston, Birmingham, in 1971 (MRY). It has since been noted at a further eight widely separated sites. Detailed searches of damp meadows and marshy waste-ground during May and June could reveal further colonies.

Records:
Edgbaston, **Birmingham**, 1971 (MRY) (Determined by R.F. Bretherton); **Hartshill Hayes**, 1980 (anon.); **Kingsbury Water Park**, 4/6/1983 (GAA, MAA, RJT); **Charlecote**, 16/6/1985 (2) (AFG), 27/5/1989 (DB); **Whitacre Heath**, 1986 small colony (KW, MAA); **Stonebridge Meadows**, 6/6/1988 (SAL); **Coughton Park**, 19/5/1989 (RJB); **Water Orton**, 11/6/1994 (KM); **Castle Hills**, **Solihull**, 2/6/2005 (gen. det. NJS), 8/6/2005 (5) (RL).

Netted Pug
1823 *Eupithecia venosata venosata* (Fabr.)
Nationally Local

County status: Very local and scarce.
Flight: June to early July.
Larval foodplants: The ripening seed capsules of Bladder Campion.

A large and instantly recognisable species of pug, which has always been scarce in Warwickshire. Larval searches amongst the seed capsules of Bladder Campion in calcareous districts may add further knowledge to the distribution of this elusive moth.

Records:
Rugby district, pre-1893, (A. Sidgwick, 1893); **Sutton Park**, 1880–1938 (PWA, WHF, WGB, FHLs); **Four Oaks**, 1960 (EVW); **Dorridge**, 1970 (FWS); **Marton**, 20/6/1983 (RA); **Hillmorton**, **Rugby**, 5/7/1987 (DIP); **Bidford-on-Avon**, 27/6/1988 (RMC); **Oakley Wood**, 17/6/1989 (AFG); **Bishops Hill**, 14/7/2005 (AJP gen. det.).

VCH 1904: *Sutton Park.*

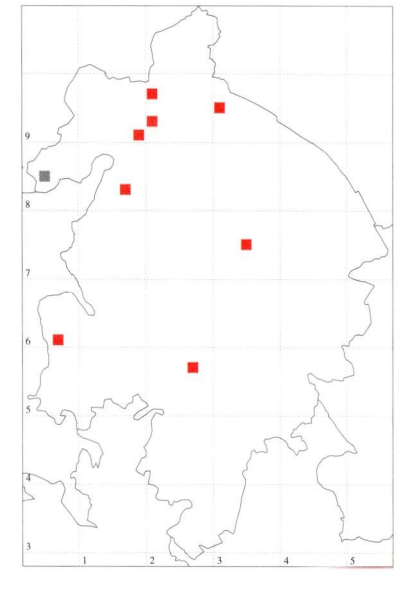

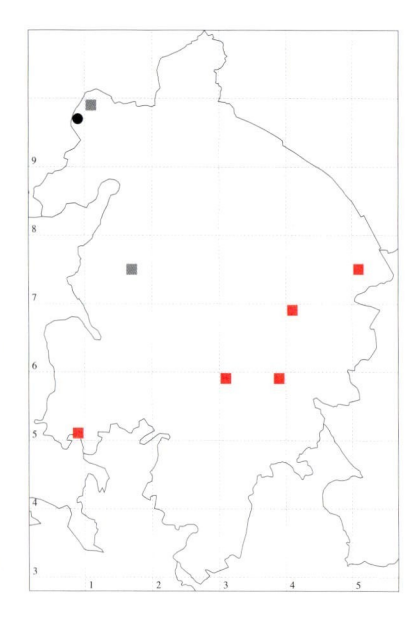

Lime-speck Pug
1825 *Eupithecia centaureata* ([D. & S.])

County status: Widespread and fairly common.
Flight: Possibly two generations in warm years. May to September.
Larval foodplants: The flowers of ragworts*, Common Knapweed* and many other low-growing plants.

The Lime-speck Pug is one of the most easily identified of the genus and also one of the most widespread in the County. It is found in a wide range of open habitats, including woodland rides and clearings, road and railway cuttings, disused quarries and gardens. The imago is continually noted from May to the early autumn with peak numbers in mid-August.

Steady populations are found in urban districts, as the following garden moth trap records illustrate: **Radford, Coventry:** 1973 (31), 1983 (67), 1993 (15), 2003 (36) (MCV).

VCH 1904: *'Not common.'*
Atherstone, Wolford, Knowle, Hampton-in-Arden, Yardley, Overslade, Frankton.

Triple-spotted Pug
1826 *Eupithecia trisignaria* H.-S.

Nationally Local

County status: Very local and sometimes fairly common.
Flight: July to early August.
Larval foodplants: The flowers and ripening seeds of Wild Angelica* and Hogweed.

The Triple-spotted Pug, having first been recorded at Sutton Park in 1895 (CJW), was not recognised again in Warwickshire for almost a century.

Recent fieldwork involving searches for the larvae on the heads of Wild Angelica plants has provided vital knowledge on the distribution of this easily overlooked species. The largest populations have been located in damp, sheltered woodland rides.

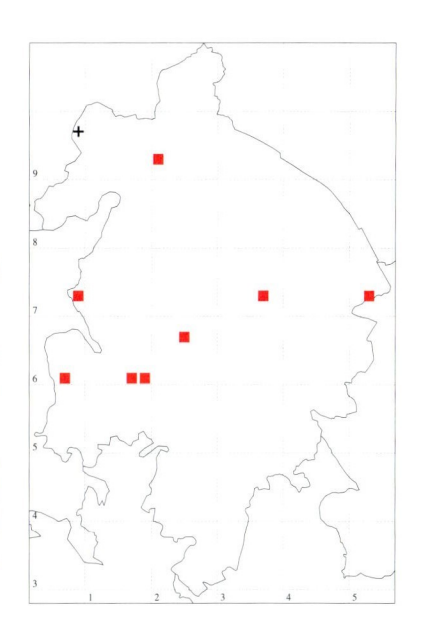

Records:
Sutton Park, 1895 (CJW); **Hatton**, 15/9/1990 two larvae (MCV); **Clowes Wood**, 9/9/1991 larvae common, 22/9/1992 four larvae (MCV), 27/9/1993 larvae plentiful (MCV, DB), 2/10/1993 twelve larvae (DB, AFG); **Bearley**, 13/9/1991 three larvae (MCV); **Coughton Park**, 21/9/1991 four larvae (MCV); **Snitterfield Bushes**, Sep. 1993 larvae plentiful (AJK); **Ryton Pools Country Park**, 16/7/1999 adult (AJP); **Whitacre Heath**, 17/7/1999 four adults (Warks Moth Group); **Hillmorton, Rugby**, 7/7/1986 adult (PN), 2/8/2001 adult (DIP).

Freyer's Pug
1827 *Eupithecia intricata arceuthata* (Freyer)

County status: Widespread and fairly common.
Flight: May to July.
Larval foodplants: Cypresses, including Leyland Cypress*, junipers and other introduced conifers.

This large and rather distinctive pug is a recent colonist of the County, associated with cypresses, exotic junipers and other introduced conifers in gardens, parks and woodlands. It was first noted at Charlecote and Rugby in 1982 (DB, DIP). By the late 1980s populations had developed in many rural and urban districts.

The graph below depicts the swift establishment in urban Coventry and suburban Rugby:

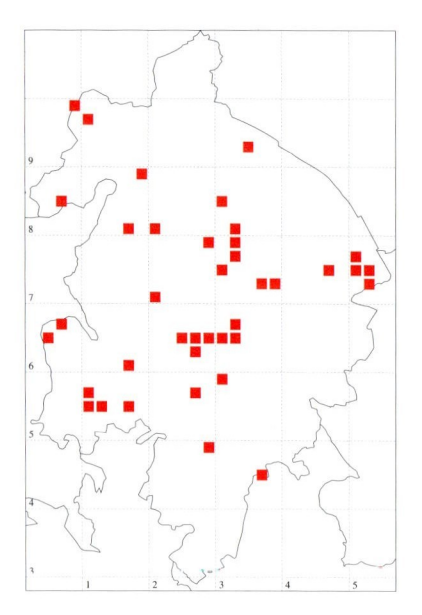

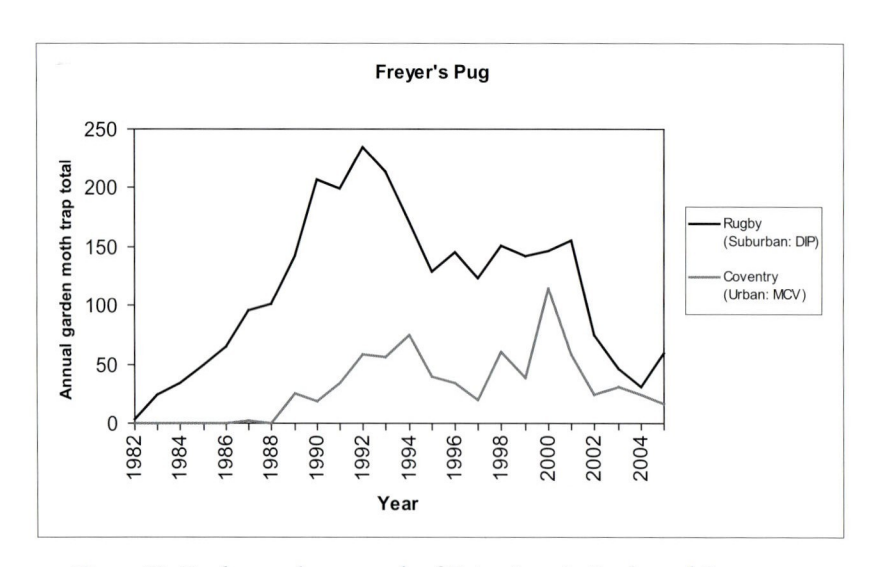

Figure 10. Garden moth trap totals of *E. intricata* in Rugby and Coventry.

NB. No recording took place at the Rugby site during the flight period in 1994, so an assumed value has been used.

Satyr Pug
1828 *Eupithecia satyrata satyrata* (Hb.)

Nationally Local

County status: Very local and scarce.
Flight: Early June to early July.
Larval foodplants: The flowers of a wide range of herbaceous plants, including Mugwort, knapweeds, ragworts and hawkweeds.

This easily overlooked species is only occasionally recorded. It shows a preference for open woodland and calcareous grassland.

Records:
Clowes Wood, 1947 (3) (BNHS); **Bannam's Wood**, 1964–79 (FAN); **Oversley Wood**, 1960s (FAN), 27/6/2000 (DB), 26/6/2001 (DB, RGB, PJR); **Snitterfield Bushes**, 7/7/1990 (RMC, DB); **Grove Hill**, 6/6/1992, 18/6/2005 (3), 2/7/2005 (2) (Warks Moth Group); **Hillmorton**, **Rugby**, 19/6/1993–1999 sporadic (DIP); **Wolford Wood**, 23/6/2001 (Warks Moth Group).

VCH 1904: *Knowle, Rugby, Atherstone.*

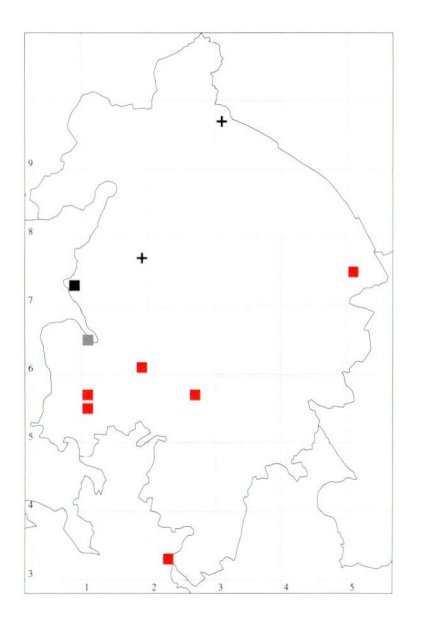

Wormwood Pug
1830 *Eupithecia absinthiata* (Cl.)

County status: Fairly widespread and fairly common.
Flight: June to August.
Larval foodplants: The flowers of a wide range of herbaceous plants, including ragworts*, Wild Angelica* and Meadowsweet*.

The Wormwood Pug is found fairly commonly in a diversity of habitats, from woodlands to gardens. The following garden moth trap totals from **Hillmorton, Rugby**, give an idea of frequency: 1982 (8), 1985 (7), 1990 (3), 1995 (10), 2000 (31), 2004 (28) (DIP).

VCH 1904: *Rugby only.*

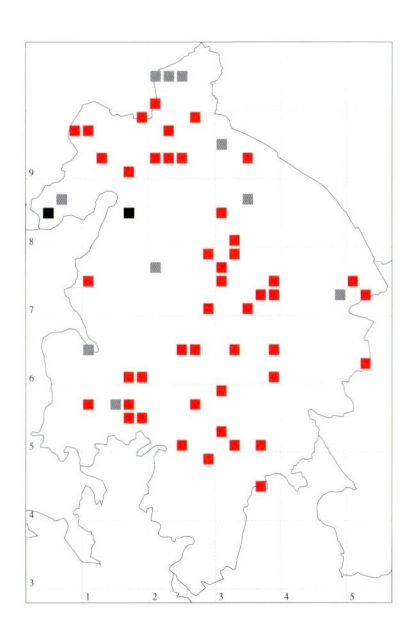

Ling Pug
1831 *Eupithecia absinthiata* f. *goossensiata* Mab.

Nationally Local

County status: Very local but common.
Flight: August.
Larval foodplants: The flowers of Heather*.

The Ling Pug is considered by some to be merely a heathland form of the preceding species. However, its generally smaller size with slightly narrower wings, greyer colouration (often with a mauvish tint), and its distinctive ecology set it apart.

Restricted to heather areas at Grendon Common and at Sutton Park, where a huge population exists.

Records:
Sutton Park, 1920–60 (SEWC, GPS, FAN, LJE), 1960s (JB), 5/8/2000 (80+ at MV) (DB, DG), 17/8/2002 (40+ at MV), 13/8/2005 (13 at MV) (Warks Moth Group); **Grendon Common**, 18/8/1990 singleton (DB, AFG, RGB), 19/8/1994 singleton (DB, BS).

VCH 1904: *Sutton Park.*

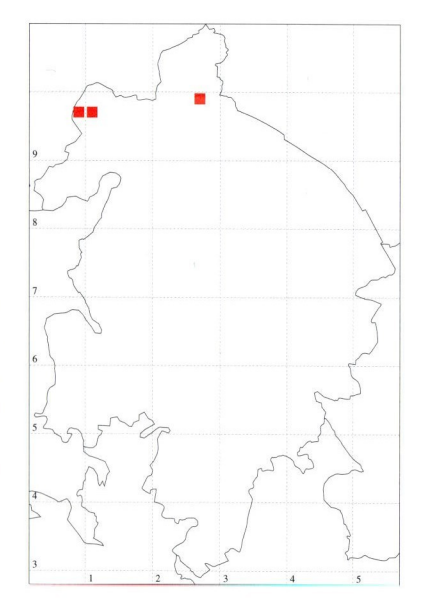

Currant Pug
1832 *Eupithecia assimilata* Doubl.

County status: Local and generally uncommon.
Flight: Two generations. May, and late July to early September.
Larval foodplants: Hop*, Black Currant* and Red Currant*.

This species of pug is easily overlooked due to its similarity to others. Since the 1960s there has been a general decline, perhaps in some part due to the lack of currant bushes in gardens. Larvae have, however, been found commonly on Hop growing in hedgerows at Little Alne 12/6/1990 (MCV).

Garden moth trap totals at **Hillmorton, Rugby**, are as follows: 1982 (1), 1985 (1), 1990 (10), 1995 (2) 2000 (2), 2005 (1) (DIP).

VCH 1904: *'Common in gardens on currant bushes around Birmingham, also Atherstone and Overslade.'*

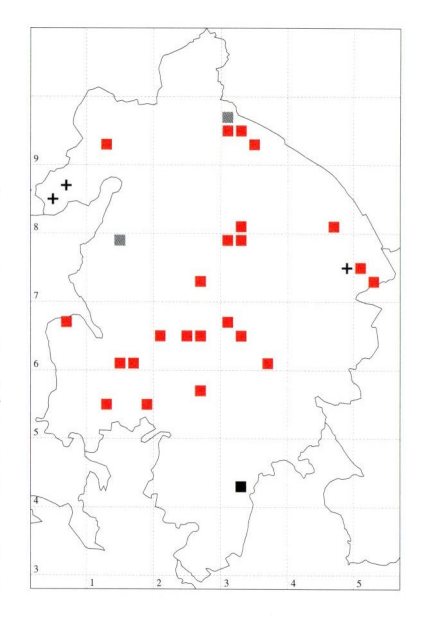

Bleached Pug
1833 *Eupithecia expallidata* Doubl.

Nationally Scarce B

County status: Status uncertain. Scarce.
Flight: July and August.
Larval foodplants: The flowers of Goldenrod.

There is no firm evidence that this woodland species is resident in Warwickshire. The handful of garden records may merely represent vagrant individuals.

Records:
Hillmorton, Rugby, 26/7/1986 (PN); **Pailton,** 1987 (KCG); **Charlecote,** 27/8/1988 (DB) (gen. det. RJB); **Pillerton Priors,** 1/8/1992 (CI).

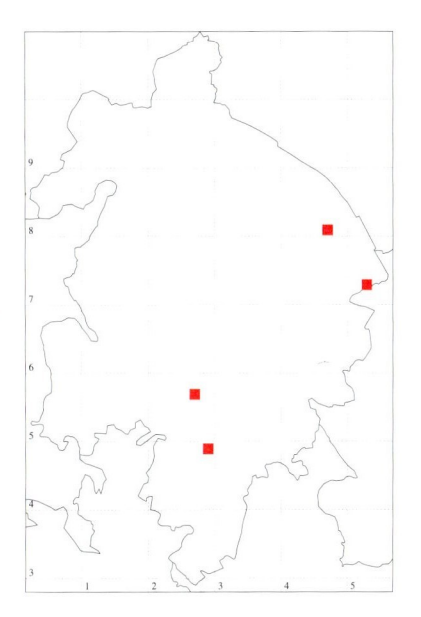

Common Pug
1834 *Eupithecia vulgata vulgata* (Haw.)

County status: Widespread and fairly common.
Flight: Two overlapping generations. Late April to the end of August.
Larval foodplants: The leaves of a wide range of trees and shrubs, including hawthorns, sallows and the flowers and leaves of low-growing plants, including ragworts* and Mugwort*.

One of the commonest of the pugs and found in a wide range of habitats. It is most often recorded in wooded districts, but numbers may also be reasonably high in urban areas as the following moth trap figures illustrate:
Radford, Coventry: 1980 (42), 1985 (15), 1990 (11), 1995 (46), 2000 (68), 2004 (34) (melanic forms predominant) (MCV).

Exceptionally early and late specimens were caught in 2005 at Solihull 16/2/2005 (JGR), Charlecote 26/3/2005 (DB), Hillmorton, Rugby 19/10/2005 (PN) and Solihull 20/10/2005 (RL).

VCH 1904: *'Common everywhere.'*

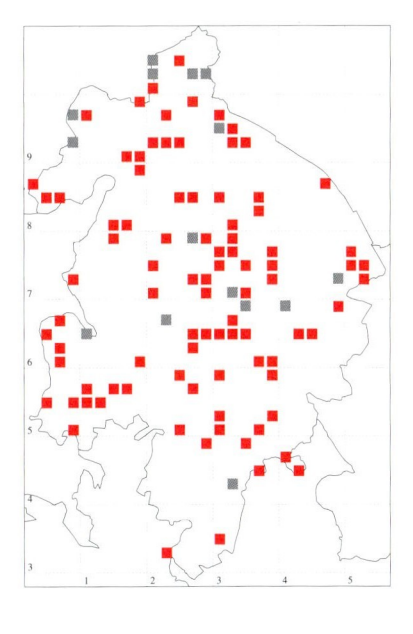

White-spotted Pug
1835 *Eupithecia tripunctaria* H.-S.

Nationally Local

County status: Widespread and fairly common.

Flight: Two generations. Early May to early July, and late July to the end of August.

Larval foodplants: First generation on Elder flowers*, the second on the developing fruits of Wild Angelica*, Cow Parsley, Hogweed, Wild Parsnip and Wild Carrot.

The White-spotted Pug was first recorded in the County at Tile Hill Wood on 28/5/1932 (CDNHSS). This species has shown a general increase since 1980. Favoured habitats include open woodland, road and railway cuttings, disused quarries, river flood plains and gardens.

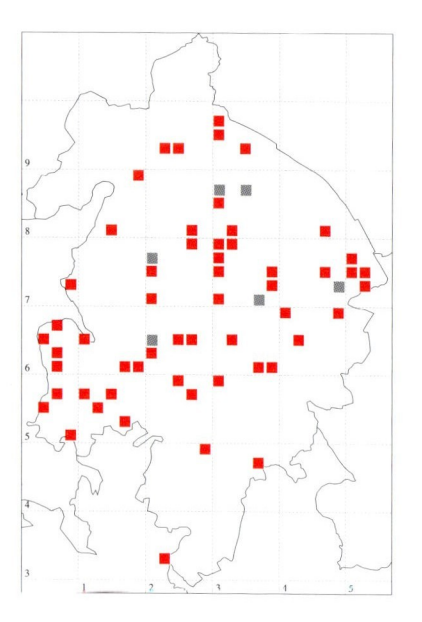

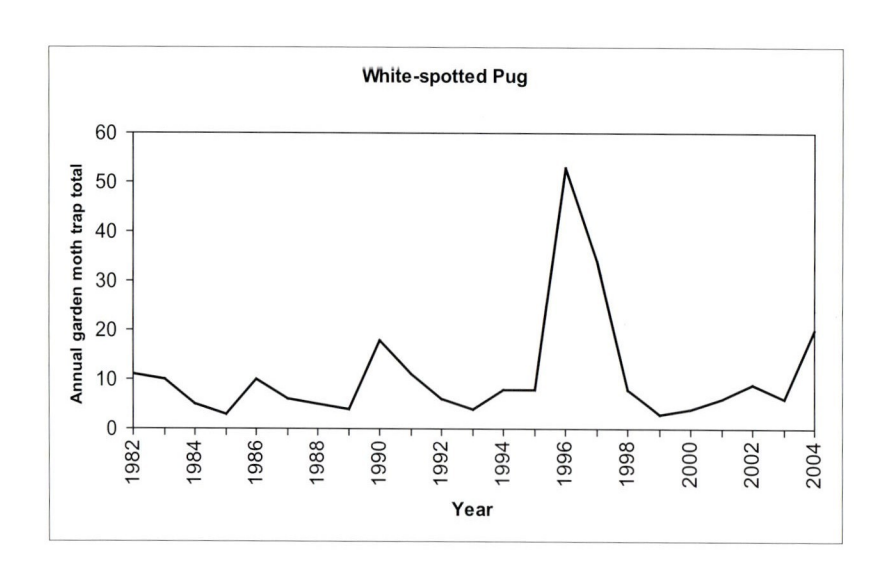

Figure 11. Garden moth trap totals of *E. tripunctaria* at Hillmorton, Rugby (DIP).

Campanula Pug
1836 *Eupithecia denotata denotata* (Hb.)

Nationally Scarce A

County status: Very local and sometimes fairly common.
Flight: Late June.
Larval foodplants: The seed capsules of Nettle-leaved Bellflower* and Giant Bellflower.

The Campanula Pug was discovered in Redhill Wood, near Alcester, in 1987 (MCV) and has only been found at one additional location since. Further fieldwork may well uncover more colonies.

Records:
Redhill Wood, **nr Alcester**, 22/8/1987 three larvae on seedheads of Nettle-leaved Bellflower (MCV); **Whichford Wood**, 28/7/1990 larvae numerous on the seedheads of Nettle-leaved Bellflower (MCV), 20/6/1992 female at light (Warks Moth Group).

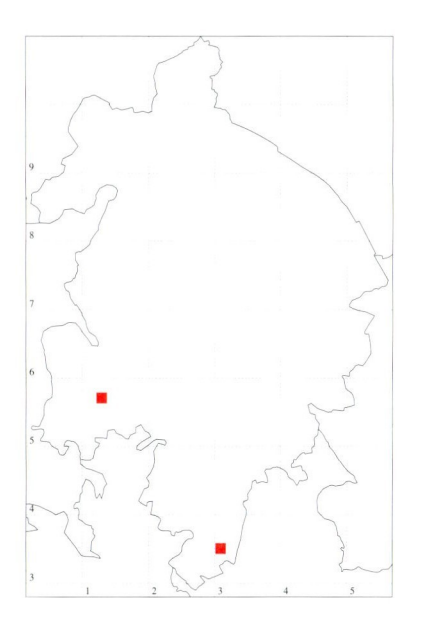

Grey Pug
1837 *Eupithecia subfuscata* (Haw.)

County status: Widespread and fairly common.
Flight: May to mid-July and occasionally a partial second generation in August.
Larval foodplants: The flowers and leaves of many herbaceous plants and broadleaved shrubs. Plants include Wild Angelica*, St. John's-wort*, Heather*, Broom*, Mugwort*, ragworts*, knapweeds*, hawthorns*, Blackthorn*, sallows*, oaks* and Field Maple*.

The Grey Pug is found plentifully throughout Warwickshire, especially in woodland and wetland locations. It occurs in both rural and urban gardens. The melanic form *f. obscurissima* Prout is more frequent in the latter.

VCH 1904: *'Fairly common.'*
Sutton, Knowle, Rugby, Brandon.

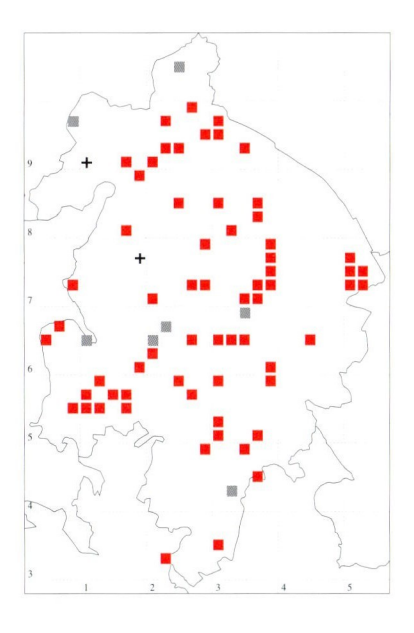

Tawny Speckled Pug
1838 *Eupithecia icterata subfulvata* (Haw.)

County status: Widespread and fairly common.
Flight: Late June to early September
Larval foodplants: The flowers and leaves of Yarrow and Sneezewort.

The Tawny Speckled Pug has been recorded from most parts of the County. It frequents a large range of habitats, including heathland, woodland, railway cuttings, rough waste-ground, parks and gardens. A particularly late specimen was caught at Pillerton Priors on 13/10/2001 (CI).

It is attracted to light in small numbers, as the following figures reflect:
Radford, Coventry: 1975 (4), 1980 (8), 1985 (7), 1990 (2), 1995 (2), 2000 (1) (MCV).

VCH 1904: *'Not uncommon.'*
Yardley, Hampton-in-Arden, Sutton, Knowle, Rugby, Atherstone.

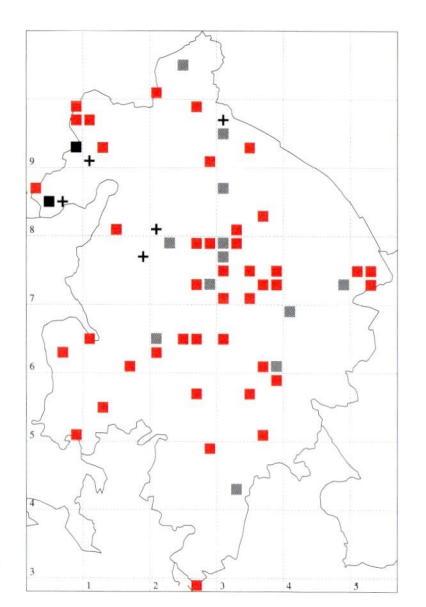

Bordered Pug
1839 *Eupithecia succenturiata* (L.)

County status: Widespread and fairly common.
Flight: June to the end of August.
Larval foodplants: Mugwort.

The Bordered Pug is one of the easier species to recognise in the genus. It frequents open habitats, such as railway cuttings, disused quarries, woodland clearings and rough waste-ground. An unusually late example was captured at Hillmorton, Rugby, on 17/9/1985 (DIP).

Rural garden moth trap counts are as follows:
Charlecote: 1990 (6), 1995 (11), 2000 (7) (AFG).

VCH 1904: *'Enock 1869 says common, but only one Rugby record.'*

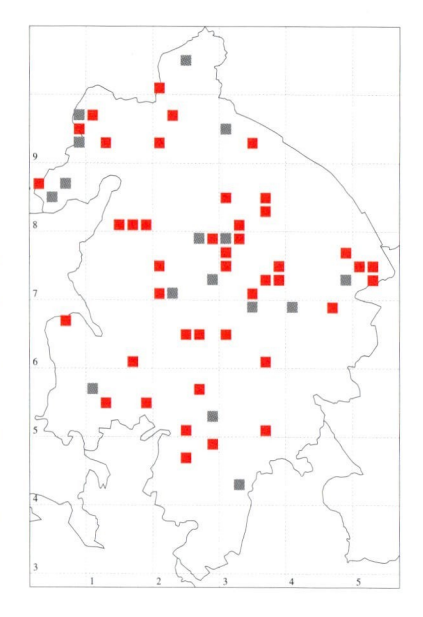

Shaded Pug
1840 *Eupithecia subumbrata* ([D. & S.])

Nationally Local

County status: Very local and common at one site.
Flight: June.
Larval foodplants: The flowers of many herbaceous plants, including ragworts, hawk's-beards, St. John's-wort, Field Scabious and Wild Marjoram.

In Warwickshire the Shaded Pug is restricted to a small but threatened site at Bishops Itchington, on vegetated spoil heaps from limestone quarrying. Moth trapping suggests the population is large; for example, 14/6/1997 (30+) (Warks Moth Group).

A specimen in a garden moth trap at Charlecote on 13/6/1989 (AFG) represents the only other County record.

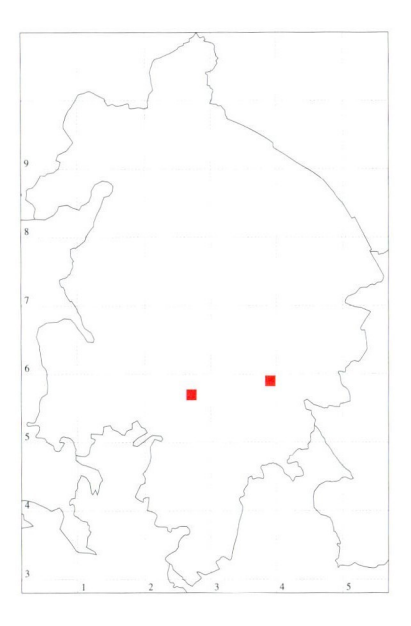

Plain Pug
1842 *Eupithecia simpliciata* (Haw.)

Nationally Local

County status: Local and uncommon.
Flight: Mid-June to early August.
Larval foodplants: The ripening seedheads of goosefoots and oraches.

Records of this species cover a large area of the County, yet it remains distinctly uncommon. Occasionally noted in garden moth traps. Fieldwork to find the beautifully cryptic larvae on the seedheads of the foodplant, situated on areas of rough, open waste-ground, could provide a clearer indication of the status.

VCH 1904: *No sites quoted but reference is given to Enock's 1869 Birmingham list in which the species was described as 'common'.*

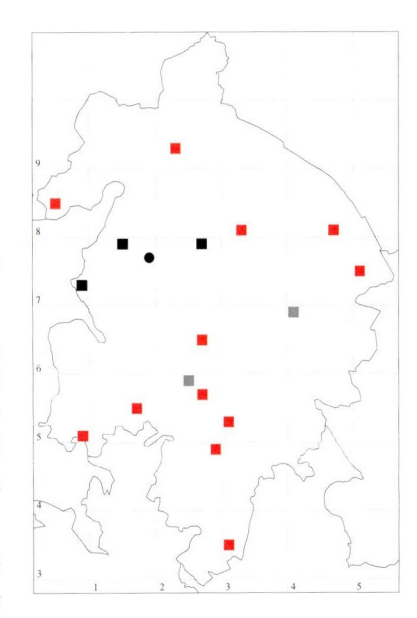

Ochreous Pug
1844 *Eupithecia indigata* (Hb.)

County status: Local and uncommon.
Flight: Late April to June.
Larval foodplants: The buds and fresh shoots of Scots Pine* and occasionally Lodgepole Pine and Larch.

The Ochreous Pug is a pine species that occurs in small numbers over a fairly large area of Warwickshire. Colonies are established at Oakley Wood, Snitterfield Bushes, Weethley Wood, Wilmcote Rough and Sutton Park. It is occasionally recorded in gardens with very few pines in the vicinity, suggesting the possible use of other coniferous trees.

Suburban garden moth trap figures at **Hillmorton, Rugby,** reflect low density levels: 1982 (1), 1985 (1), 1990 (0), 1995 (0), 2000 (1), 2004 (3) (DIP).

VCH 1904: *'Fairly common in Sutton Park.'*

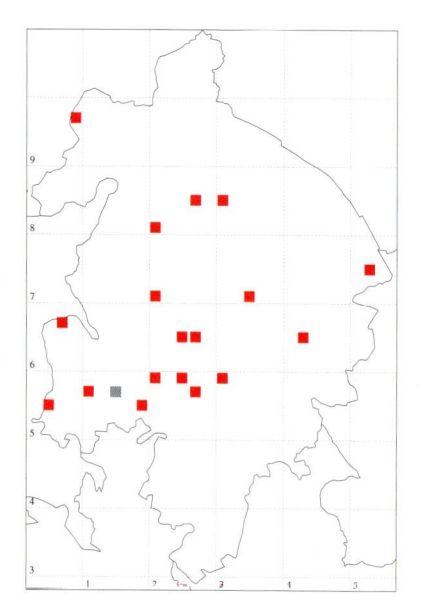

Pimpinel Pug
1845 *Eupithecia pimpinellata* (Hb.)

Nationally Local

County status: Very local and scarce.
Flight: July.
Larval foodplants: The ripening seed-capsules of Burnet-saxifrage*.

This Nationally Local species has been recorded in the derelict quarries of north Warwickshire and on the calcareous escarpment at Wilmcote in the south-west of the County. No recent fieldwork has been conducted to ascertain the present status of this moth.

Records:
Wilmcote Rough 1977–80 'two or three most years' (JMP); **Hartshill, Woodlands Quarry,** 15/9/1981 larva on Burnet-saxifrage (RJT) (confirmed by S. Church, M. Hadley); **Dosthill** 25/7/1984 adult (PBD).

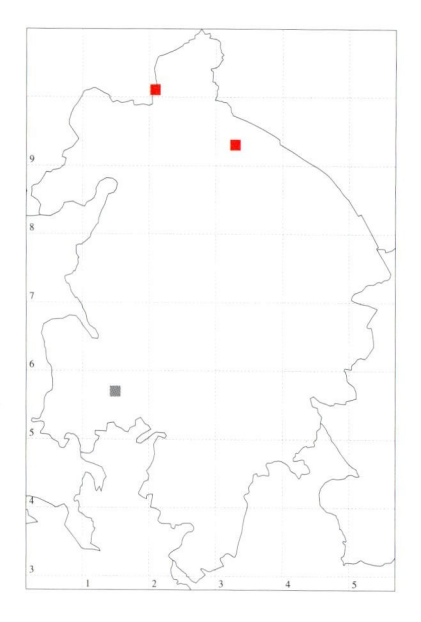

Narrow-winged Pug
1846 *Eupithecia nanata* (Hb.)

County status: Very local and fairly common on heathland.
Flight: July to late August.
Larval foodplants: The flowers of Heather*.

The Narrow-winged Pug is found in good numbers at Sutton Park and Grendon Common. Sporadic garden records suggest the use of ornamental heathers.

Records:
Sutton Park, 1960s (JB), 1970s (LJE), 1980s (AN), 5/8/2000 (2) (DB, DG), 17/8/2002 (6), 13/8/2005 (6) (Warks Moth Group); **Bannam's Wood**, 1964–79 (FAN); **Charlecote**, 1970s, 1990s occasional (DB, AFG); **Temple Balsall**, 19/8/1978 (FWS); **Hillmorton, Rugby**, 20/6/1984, 14/7/1986, 23/6/1989, 23/7–11/8/1991 (6), 15/7/1992, 9/8/1995, 1997 (2), 2003 (2), 2004 (2) (DIP), 17/7/1997 (PN); **Grendon Common**, 6/7/1990 (10) (Warks Moth Group), 18/8/1990 (4) (DB, AFG, RGB), 24/8/1990 (DB, RMC); **Radford, Coventry**, 26/7/1991, 1992 (3) (MCV); **Hampton Magna**, 7/8/1991 (PJR); **Ryton Wood**, 1992 (LB, CE); **Brandon Marsh**, 25/6/1993 (PC, NWH, CW); **Print Wood**, 2/7/1993 (PC, CW); **Solihull**, 1994–1995 (3) (AP); **Canley, Coventry**, 28/7/1995 (PC, CW); **Keresley, Coventry**, 28/7/2002 (NJS).

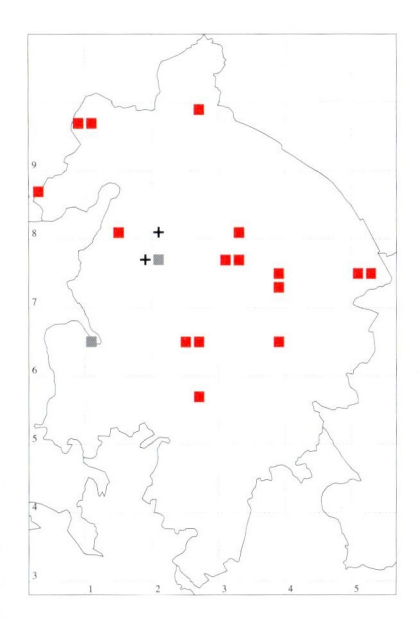

VCH 1904: *'Common at Sutton Park.'* Knowle and Hampton-in-Arden.

Ash Pug
1849 *Eupithecia innotata* f. *fraxinata* Crewe

County status: Very local and uncommon.
Flight: Two generations. Late May to June, and August.
Larval foodplants: Ash*.

This easily overlooked species, which appears to survive at low density in the vicinity of the larval foodplant, Ash, is infrequently recorded. Numbers in rural and urban districts are about equal.

Records:
Minworth, 1950s (GPS); **Arley Wood**, 23/6/1962 (EABS); **Bannam's Wood**, 1964–79 (FAN); **Hillmorton, Rugby**, 1980–2004 annual in recent years (DIP), 23/5/1986, 1/5/2005 (PN); **Charlecote**, 2/8/1981, 14/7/1987, 2/8/1987, 19/5/1992 (DB, AFG); **Holbrooks, Coventry**, 22/6/1985 (JR); **Radford, Coventry**, 28/5/1990, 1991, 1992 (2) (MCV); **Hampton-in-Arden**, 12/6/1990 (MCV); **Royal Leamington Spa**, 1992 (PhP); **Ryton Wood**, 1992 (LB, CE); **Steetley Meadows**, 10/7/1992

(CDNHSS); **Ufton Fields**, May 1994 (RCK); **Compton Verney**, 7/8/1999 (Warks Moth Group); **Tile Hill, Coventry**, 3/6/2000 (AJK).

VCH 1904: *'Common on Ash in suburbs of Birmingham. Larvae on Ash trees at Wylde Green.'*

Golden-rod Pug
1851 *Eupithecia virgaureata* Doubl.

Nationally Local

County status: Very local and uncommon.
Flight: Two generations. May to June, and August.
Larval foodplants: The flowers of Goldenrod and ragworts. Foodplants of the first generation are not yet known.

The Golden-rod Pug is probably more widespread than records suggest. It is easily mistaken for the Grey Pug. Genitalia dissection of specimens in 2005 has provided evidence of the continued existence of the species in the County. Larvae should be searched for during September in the flowers of ragworts and Goldenrod growing on open waste-ground or in open woodland.

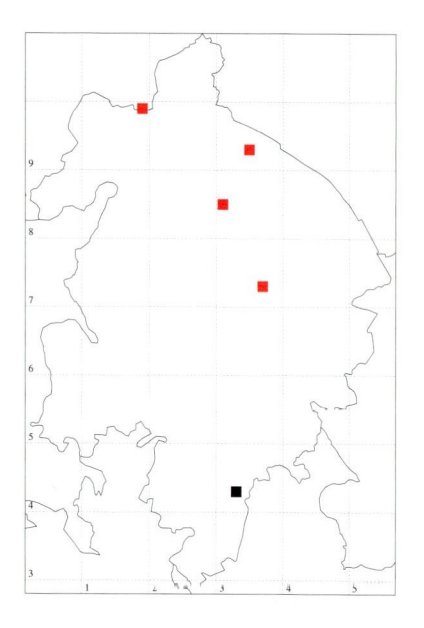

Records:
Tysoe, 10/5/1948, 27/5/1948 (TT); **Windmill Hill, Nuneaton**, 10/5/2003 (DG, gen. det. AJP); **Ryton Meadows**, 29/4/2005 (AJP, VW); **Middleton Hall**, 6/8/2005 (AJP, VW); **Keresley, Coventry**, 11/8/2005 (NJS).

Brindled Pug
1852 *Eupithecia abbreviata* Steph.

County status: Widespread and locally common.
Flight: March to May.
Larval foodplants: Oaks* and hawthorns.

This species occurs over most of the County. Very large populations exist in many broadleaved woodlands and the adult is sometimes attracted to light in profusion: Oversley Wood, 23/4/1982 (42) (DB, AFG); Snitterfield Bushes, 11/4/1992 (54) (DB, AJK, RMC, IGMR).

Also found abundantly amongst hawthorn scrub on calcareous soils. Regularly operated garden moth traps throughout the County annually record the species; examples of the melanic f. *hirschkei* Bast. are occasionally observed.

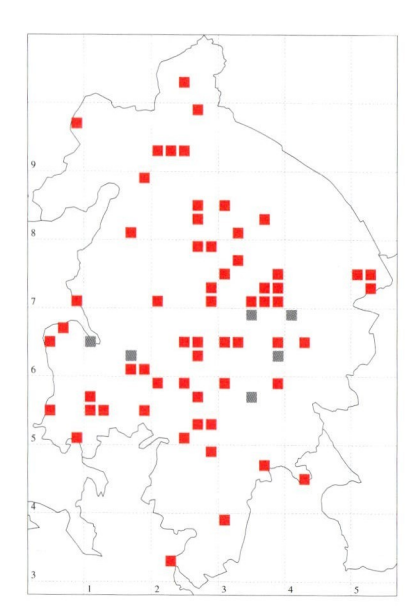

VCH 1904: *'Fairly common everywhere in woods.'*

Oak-tree Pug
1853 *Eupithecia dodoneata* Guen.

County status: Widespread and becoming fairly common.
Flight: Mid-April to early June.
Larval foodplants: Hawthorns, feeding mainly on the calyx of the hips*, but also on the leaves of mature hawthorns and oaks.

The earliest known County record of this species is from Tile Hill Wood in 1931 (CDNHSS). The Oak-tree Pug has subsequently increased its range to become established in a number of woodlands, including Ryton Wood, Tile Hill Wood, Wainbody Wood, Hay Wood, Oakley Wood, Snitterfield Bushes, Weethley Wood, Oversley Wood and Old Park Wood. It is also found in hawthorn scrub and visits garden moth traps occasionally.

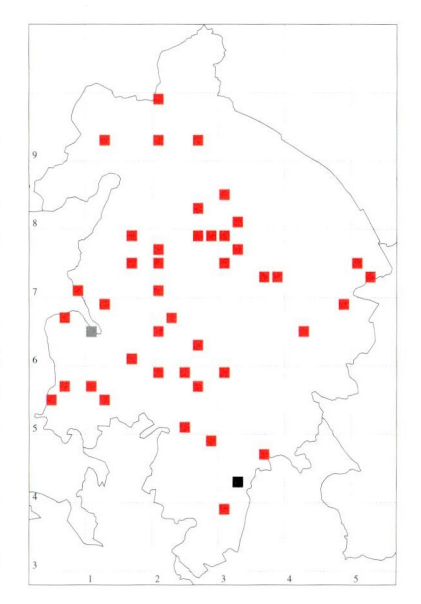

Juniper Pug
1854 *Eupithecia pusillata pusillata* ([D. & S.])

County status: Very local and uncommon.
Flight: July to September.
Larval foodplants: Common and cultivated junipers and possibly other cultivated conifers such as cypresses.

The Juniper Pug is associated with cultivated junipers growing in parks and gardens. It is confined mainly to the conurbations of the larger towns and cities in the northern half of the County. Recorders all report a decline in numbers during the last 15 years.

Records:
Tysoe, 8/7/1946, 20/9/1947, 11/7/1948 (TT); **Hillmorton, Rugby**, 1982 (6), 1983 (18), 1984 (13), 1985 (2), 1987 (9), last seen 1993 (DIP), 2/7/1986 (PN); **Hampton-in-Arden**, 1984 (MCV); **Dosthill**, 25/7/1984 (PBD, MAA); **Radford, Coventry**, 1984 to 1987 (11), 1990 (2) (MCV); **Sutton Coldfield**, 1987, (LJE); **Solihull**, 1994–1995 (3) (AP); **Earlsdon, Coventry**, 25/6/2004 (PC); **Windmill Hill, Nuneaton**, 17/7/2004 (AJP, NJS gen. det.).

VCH 1904: *'Not common.'*
Knowle, Overslade.

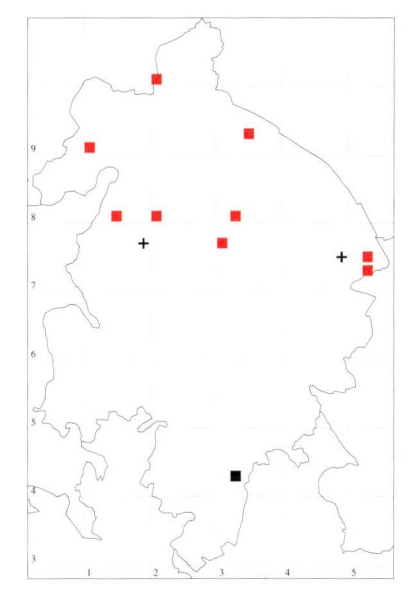

Cypress Pug
1855 *Eupithecia phoeniceata* (Ramb.)

Nationally Uncommon

County status: Vagrant/immigrant.
Flight: August and September.
Larval foodplants: Monterey Cypress and probably Lawson's Cypress and Leyland Cypress.

A specimen of this distinctive species was caught in a garden moth trap at Hillmorton, Rugby, 23/8/1983 (DIP). It was during a month of intense immigrant activity which included Eversmann's Rustic at the same site (DIP) and Slender Burnished Brass in Stratford-upon-Avon (RGB). The Cypress Pug was first recorded in Britain at Lamorna, Cornwall, in 1959 and has since spread along the south coast. The possibility of the species becoming resident in Warwickshire is unlikely with climatic factors weighing heavily against the success of its winter-feeding larvae.

Larch Pug
1856 *Eupithecia lariciata* (Freyer)

County status: Very local and sometimes fairly common.
Flight: May to July.
Larval foodplants: Larch.

The Larch Pug is a relatively easy species to recognise with a conspicuous raised white spot on the back of the thorax. It is locally plentiful in larch plantations within woodlands and is easily disturbed during the daytime by gently tapping the larch branches. It occasionally visits MV in reasonable numbers; for example, Waverley Wood, 28/7/2001 (15) (Warks Moth Group).

Records:
Umberslade, 9/5/1929, 16/5/1936 (SEWC); **Tile Hill Wood**, 7/5/1934 (JWS), 2/6/1962, 8/6/1963, 1/6/1968 (ANT); **Sutton Park**, 1950s annually (GPS); **Bannam's Wood**, 1964–79 (FAN); **Hillmorton, Rugby**, 1980–99 sporadic (DIP); **Hartshill Hayes**, 13/6/1980 (RJT); **Hampton-in-Arden**, 28/7/1985 (MCV); **Waverley Wood**, 20/7/1990 (6), 28/7/2001 (15) (Warks Moth Group); **Oakley Wood**, 1991 (AFG); **Whichford Wood**, 20/6/1992 (Warks Moth Group); **Oversley Wood**, 18, 22, 25 & 26/6/1994 (BS), 1/8/1992, 16/6/2000, 29/6/2002 (Warks Moth Group), 24/6/2003 (DB), 20/7/2004 (DG, AJP, NJS), 26/5/2005 (3) (J. Rush), 18/6/2005 (AJP, VW); **Bentley Park Wood**, 20/7/1996 (12) (Warks Moth Group); **Oxhouse Farm, Combrook**, 28/6/1998 (DB); **Brandon Wood**, 5/7/1998 (2) (Warks Moth Group); **Tile Hill, Coventry**, 23/6/2003 (AJK); **Close Wood**, 4/9/2004 (AJP, VW, MK, NJS); **Meriden Shafts**, 6/5/2005 (2) (AJP); **Radford, Coventry**, 12/7/2005 (MCV).

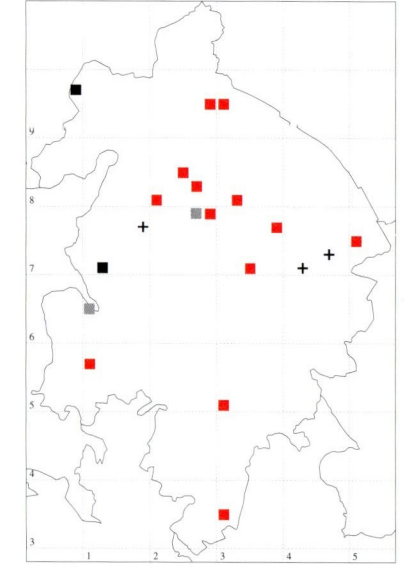

VCH 1904: *'Common in fir woods.'*
Sutton Park, Rugby, Knowle, Frankton Wood, Cawston Spring.

Dwarf Pug
1857 *Eupithecia tantillaria* Boisd.

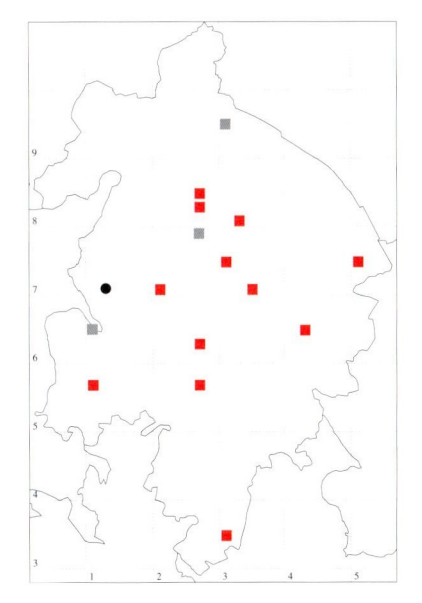

County status: Very local and occasionally fairly common.
Flight: May to early July.
Larval foodplants: A number of firs and spruces, but especially Norway Spruce and Douglas Fir.

The Dwarf Pug was first noted in Warwickshire at Umberslade in 1927 (SEWC). A species associated with fir and spruce plantations, it is sometimes recorded in good numbers by tapping the branches.

Records:
Umberslade, 1927–36 (SEWC); **Tile Hill Wood**, 1934–70 (CDNHSS, JWS, FWS, ANT); **Wainbody Wood**, 23/5/1951 (CDNHSS); **Bannam's Wood**, 1964–79 (FAN); **Hartshill Hayes**, 1975–79 (RJT); **Hillmorton, Rugby**, 1980–2004 sporadic (DIP); **Oversley Wood**, 5/6/1981, 25/5/1991 (DB), 1/5/2004 (J.Rush), 7/6/2004 (DG, AJP), 26/5/2005 (J.Rush), 4/6/2005 (2) (Warks Moth Group); **Radford, Coventry**, 15/5/1982 (MCV); **Nelson's Quarry, Stockton**, 6/5/1990 (DB); **Whichford Wood**, 11/7/1991 (DB); **Hay Wood**, 4/6/1994 (Warks Moth Group), 25/5/2004 (DB); **Charlecote**, 28/5/1996 (DB); **Waverley Wood**, 17/5/2003 (Warks Moth Group); **Meigh's Wood**, 16/5/2004 (NJS); **Meriden Shafts**, 6/5/2005 (2) (AJP); **Warwick**, 10/6/2005 (AV, SDT).

V-Pug
1858 *Chloroclystis v-ata* (Haw.)

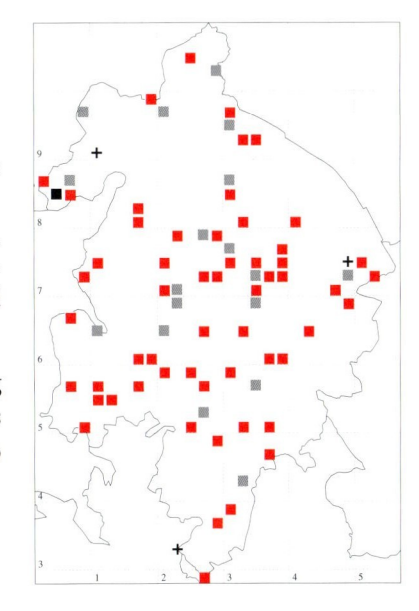

County status: Widespread and fairly common.
Flight: Two generations. May to mid-June, and July to late August.
Larval foodplants: The flowers of various plants, including Dog-rose, hawthorns, Traveller's-joy, Hemp-agrimony, brambles, Elder, Wild Angelica*, Mugwort and Meadowsweet*.

The V-Pug is found in a variety of habitats, including woodland, wetlands, railway embankments, scrub areas and gardens. This species generally responds poorly to MV and the majority of records are of singletons.

VCH 1904: *'Rare.'*
Sutton, Wolford, Overslade.

Sloe Pug
1859 *Pasiphila chloerata* (Mab.)

County status: Very local and sometimes fairly common.
Flight: May to July.
Larval foodplants: The flowers of Blackthorn*.

The Sloe Pug was not recognised in Britain until 1971, but examination of specimens in Surrey collections are proof that it had been resident and overlooked for many years previously (Collins, 1997).

It was first sought and discovered in Warwickshire in 1975, when larvae were beaten from Blackthorn blossom at All Oaks Wood, 27/4/1975 (MCV). Since then further fieldwork and genitalia dissections of specimens has found this species to be established in many other areas.

The larvae can be obtained during April by beating blossom from the higher branches of mature Blackthorn stands.

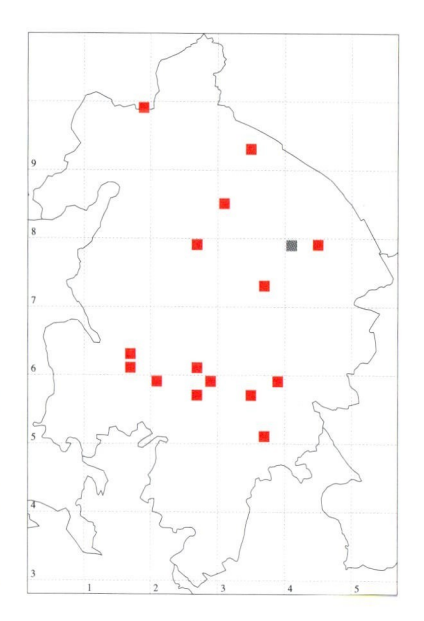

Records:
All Oaks Wood, 27/4/1975, 18/4/1976, 20/4/1991, 10/4/1993 larvae beaten from Blackthorn blossom (MCV); **Coombe Fields**, 14/5/1978 larvae (MCV); **Chesterton Wood**, 17/4/1983, 28/4/1985 larvae (MCV); **Barford**, 5/4/1988 larvae (MCV); **Ashorne Wood**, 7/4/1988 larvae (DB); **Pailton**, April 1988 larvae (KCG); **Austy Wood**, 7/4/1988 larvae (DB); **Snitterfield Bushes**, 1/7/1989 (AFG; gen. det. M. Bailey); **Bearley**, 4/4/1990 larvae (MCV); **Charlecote**, May 1995 (AFG; gen. det. M. Bailey); **Flints Green, Coventry**, Apr 2004 larvae (AJK); **Temple Grafton**, 18/6/2005, 21/6/2005 (AFG); **Keresley, Coventry**, 19/6/2005 (NJS gen. det.); **Middleton Hall**, 9/7/2005 (4) (gen. det. AJP, NJS); **Bishops Hill**, 14/7/2005 (AJP gen. det.); **Ryton Meadows**, 16/7/2005 (2) (NJS gen. det.); **Windmill Hill, Nuneaton**, 23/7/2005 (AJP gen. det.).

Green Pug
1860 *Pasiphila rectangulata* (L.)

County status: Widespread and fairly common.
Flight: June to early August.
Larval foodplants: The flowers of Crab Apple*, cultivated Apple*, pear, hawthorns and Blackthorn*.

The Green Pug has been recorded from a large number of habitats, including woodland, heathland, railway cuttings, marshes, gardens and orchards.

The following moth trap figures give an idea of frequency in an urban garden at **Radford, Coventry**: 1975 (4), 1980 (6), 1985 (12), 1990 (7), 1995 (10), 2000 (11) (MCV).

Dark and melanic forms occur in both rural and urban districts.

VCH 1904: *'Common in gardens and orchards.'*

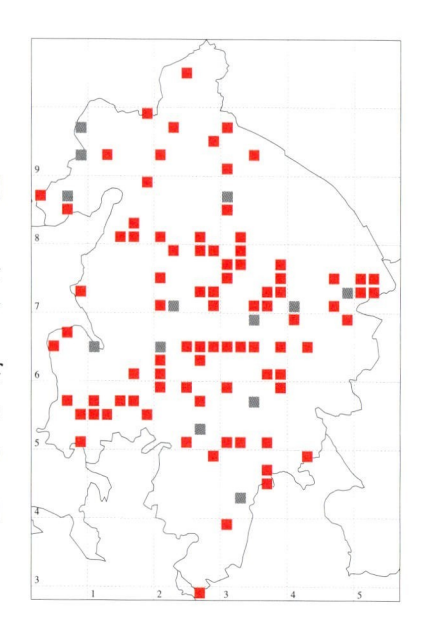

Double-striped Pug
1862 *Gymnoscelis rufifasciata* (Haw.)

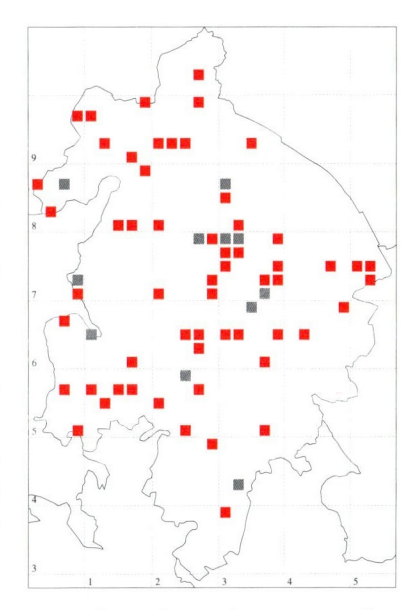

County status: Widespread and fairly common.
Flight: Two overlapping generations. March to August. Occasionally a partial third generation in September to October.
Larval foodplants: The flowers of many plants, including Heather*, Broom, Gorse, Holly, Ivy, Traveller's-joy, buddleias, ragworts* and Meadowsweet*.

There appear to be no records of Double-striped Pug in Warwickshire prior to 1964, in which year it was seen at Bannam's Wood (FAN). Since 1980 this species has been observed over a large part of the County suggesting a major expansion in range. Favoured habitats are woodland, heathland, road and railway cuttings, wasteground and gardens.

The adult has been noted during every month of the year with peak numbers reported in mid-July and August. Out of season dates for the moth are: Brailes, 23/1/2004, Pillerton Priors, 16/2/2004 (CI); Hillmorton, Rugby, 20/11/2004 (DIP); Tanworth-in-Arden, 19/12/2004, 11/2/2005 (SW).

Streak
1864 *Chesias legatella* ([D. & S.])

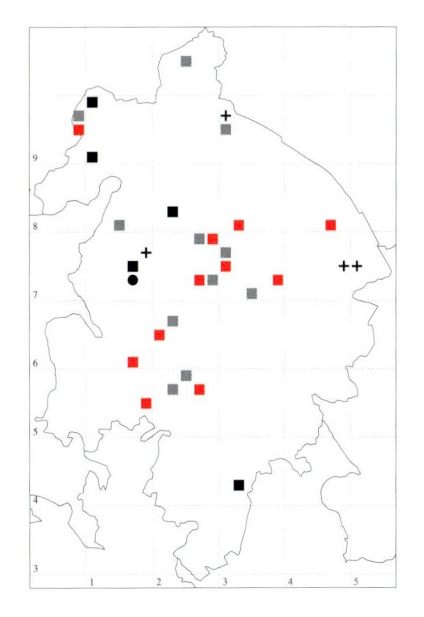

County status: Very local and sometimes fairly common.
Flight: September to early November.
Larval foodplants: Broom*.

This late autumn species has occasionally been found in good numbers at night, resting on the foodplant in open woodland and heathland. Isolated individuals in garden moth traps suggest the use of ornamental Broom and other related plants for breeding.

Records:
Packwood, 24/9/1910 (SEWC); **Dorridge**, 9/10/1921, 13/10/1935 (SEWC); **Tysoe**, 23/10/1947 (TT); **Sutton Park**, 1950s (GBM), 1970s (LJE); **Packington**, 1951 twenty larvae on Broom (GBM); **Four Oaks**, 11/10/1951 (EVW); **Tile Hill Wood**, 1964 (LEM); **Earlsdon, Coventry**, 7/10/1965 (LEM); **Alvecote & Hartshill Hayes**, 1970s (RJT); **Hampton Wood**, 29/10/1972, 27/9/1980 (AFG); **Waverley Wood**, 4/11/1972 twenty at rest on Broom (DB, AFG); **Charlecote**, 31/10/1973, 24/10/1982, 23/10/1984, 24/10/1992, 3/10/1994, 22/10/2000, 13/10/2001 (DB, AFG); **Fen End, Kenilworth**, 1974–1976 (DC); **Hatton Green**, 23/9/1977 (AP); **Alveston**, 20/10/1978 (DB); **Solihull**, 1978 (CD); **Claverdon**, 1982–1985 (IGMR); **Pailton**, 1984–1986 (KCG); **Kenilworth**, 20/10/1987 (P.A); **Tile Hill, Coventry**, 26/9/1988 (AJK); **Bearley**, 12/10/1990, 8/11/1994 (IGMR); **Radford, Coventry**, 28/10/1991

(MCV); **Shottery, Stratford-upon-Avon**, 28/10/1991 (RGB); **Ryton Wood**, 1992 (LB, CE); **Kenilworth Road, Coventry**, 11/9/2001 (MA).

VCH 1904: *'Very local.'*
Sutton Park, Knowle, Rugby, Atherstone, Overslade.

Broom-tip
1865 *Chesias rufata rufata* (Fabr.)

Nationally Scarce B

County status: Very local and scarce.
Flight: May.
Larval foodplants: Broom.

A rather elusive species in the County with just two records from garden moth traps at widely separated locations. It is thought these specimens are strays from undetected colonies as *rufata* is associated with established stands of Broom.

Records:
Earlsdon, Coventry, 2/5/1964 (LEM), Bidford-on-Avon, 24/5/1995 (RMC).

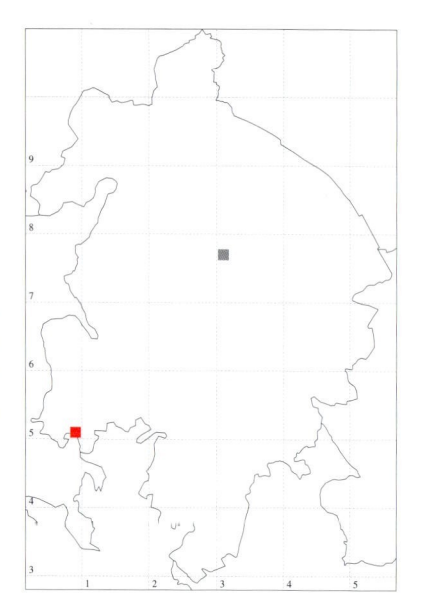

Treble-bar
1867 *Aplocera plagiata plagiata* (L.)

County status: Fairly widespread and fairly common.
Flight: Two generations. Mid-May to early July, and early August to late September.
Larval foodplants: St. John's-wort.

The Treble-bar is most frequently observed on calcareous grassland in a variety of open habitats, such as road and railway cuttings, disused quarries, rough stony waste-ground and wide woodland paths and clearings. It is easily disturbed during the daytime and embarks on short rapid flights. Wanderers are occasionally noted in garden moth traps.

VCH 1904: *'Not uncommon, occurs throughout the County.'*

N.B. As the two species of treble-bar were not confirmed to be separate until 1923 (Jordon) the VCH report would have combined records of both.

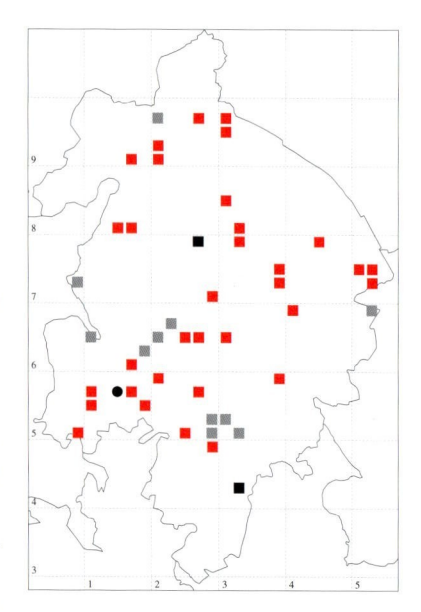

Lesser Treble-bar
1868 *Aplocera efformata* (Guen.)

County status: Fairly widespread and fairly common.
Flight: Two generations. Mid-May to June, and early August to early October.
Larval foodplants: St. John's-wort.

The Lesser Treble-bar is often confused with the Treble-bar and there may be a margin of error in some of the records. The two species are found in the same habitats and have a similar distribution within the County.

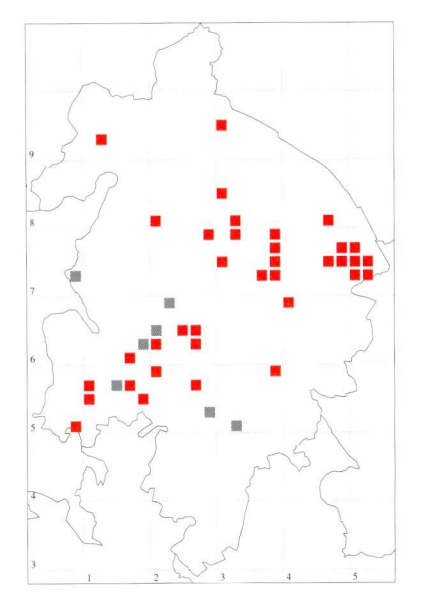

Chimney Sweeper
1870 *Odezia atrata* (L.)

County status: Fairly widespread and locally common.
Flight: Day-flying. Late May to the end of July.
Larval foodplants: The flowers and seeds of Pignut.

Colonies of this conspicuous day-flying moth have been found over most of Warwickshire with the largest concentration of records in the north. The moth has a lazy, fluttering flight and frequently settles on grass and plant stems to show its subtle white wing tips. It is found in a variety of open situations, including a number of post-industrial sites, such as gravel pits, disused quarries, mine spoil and railways, in addition to woodland edges, marshy areas, commons, meadows and churchyards. Large colonies have recently been discovered at Bedworth Slough, 26/6/2000 and Whittleford Park, Nuneaton, 12/6/2001 (JW).

VCH 1904: *'Very local, but given in all lists, and is usually common where found.'*

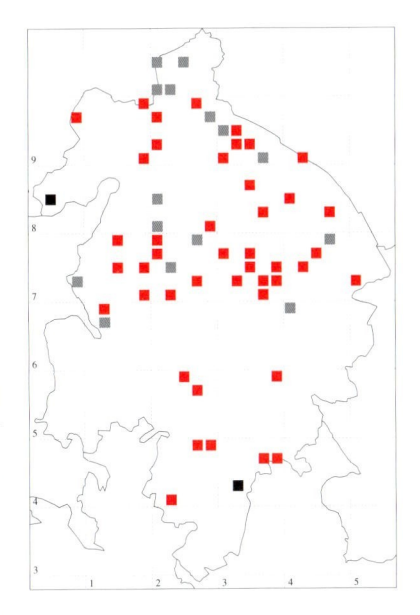

Dingy Shell
1874 *Euchoeca nebulata* (Scop.)

Nationally Local

County status: Local and occasionally fairly common.
Flight: Late May to early August.
Larval foodplants: Alder*.

The Dingy Shell frequents damp woodland, wetlands and river valleys containing Alder, chiefly in the northern half of Warwickshire. Established sites include Kingsbury Water Park, Middleton Hall, Water Orton, Bentley Park Wood, Whitacre Heath, Tocil Wood, Ufton Fields, Waverley Wood and Brandon Marsh. This species is immediately recognised as it rests with wings folded in butterfly-fashion.

VCH 1904: *'Not common.'*
'Occurs at Sutton amongst the Alders and at Marston Green, Knowle, Solihull, and Atherstone.'

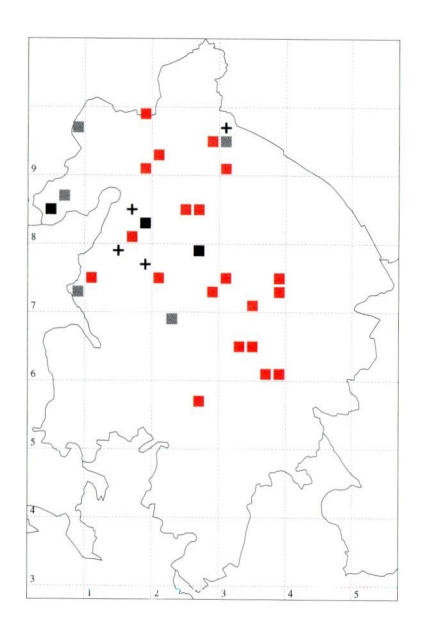

Small White Wave
1875 *Asthena albulata* (Hufn.)

County status: Fairly widespread and locally fairly common.
Flight: Mid-May to early August.
Larval foodplants: Various trees, including Hazel, birches and Hornbeam.

The Small White Wave is fairly common in a number of ancient broadleaved woodlands. Ryton Wood contains the largest populations, where it may be seen flying along the rides at dusk in great quantity, and later visiting light; for example, 22/5/1993 (35) (DB). Established colonies also exist in Wappenbury Wood, Waverley Wood, Wainbody Wood, Brandon Wood, Crackley Wood, Kingsbury Wood, Snitterfield Bushes, Oakley Wood, Oversley Wood, Rough Hill Wood and Old Park Wood. It is found in smaller numbers in the wetland habitats of Brandon Marsh and Ufton Fields. Occasionally noted in garden moth traps.

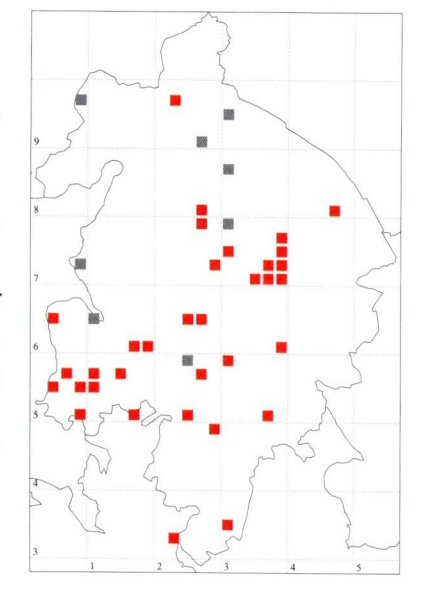

VCH 1904: *'Common everywhere in woods.'*

Small Yellow Wave
1876 *Hydrelia flammeolaria* (Hufn.)

County status: Widespread and fairly common.
Flight: Late May to early August.
Larval foodplants: Alder*, Field Maple* and Sycamore.

The Small Yellow Wave is found in many damp wooded habitats, including Ryton Wood, Wappenbury Wood, Brandon Wood, Coombe Abbey, Brandon Marsh, Clowes Wood, Bentley Park Wood, Ufton Fields, Waverley Wood, Oversley Wood, Hampton Wood and Wolford Wood. This species is generally a more regular visitor to garden moth traps than *albulata*.

VCH 1904: *'Not common.'*
Knowle, Brandon Wood, Atherstone.

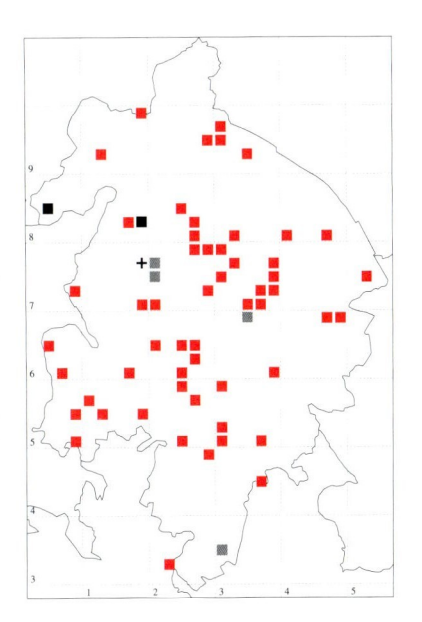

Waved Carpet
1877 *Hydrelia sylvata* ([D. & S.])

Nationally Scarce B

County status: Extinct.
Flight: No dates available.
Larval foodplants: Alder, birches, sallows and Sweet Chestnut.

VCH 1904: *'Rare.',* Knowle, Chalcot Wood, Wolford Wood, Coombe Wood.

Seraphim
1879 *Lobophora halterata* (Hufn.)

Nationally Local

County status: Fairly widespread and locally fairly common.
Flight: Early May to June.
Larval foodplants: Aspen* and poplars.

The Seraphim occurs locally in a number of damp woodlands where Aspen is plentiful. Occasionally found on the tree trunks in numbers. Healthy populations occur in Cubbington Wood, Ryton Wood, Snitterfield Bushes, Weethley Wood, Rough Hill Wood and Brandon Marsh. Sometimes attracted to light in large numbers: Oversley Wood, 20/5/1977 (35) (DB, RHS) and Wappenbury Wood, 20/5/2003 (26) (DB, RGB,

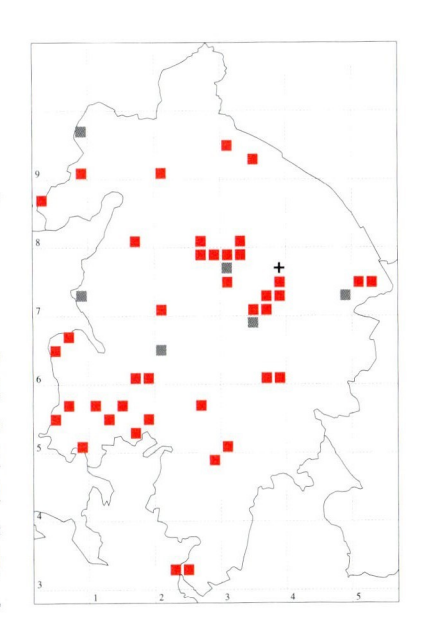

JWkn). Sporadic records from urban districts indicate the possible use of cultivated poplars for breeding.

VCH 1904: *'Brandon Wood only.'*

Barred Tooth-striped
1880 *Trichopteryx polycommata* ([D. & S.])

Nationally Scarce A.

County status: Status uncertain. Possibly extinct.
Flight: Late March to April.
Larval foodplants: Wild Privet and Ash.

The Barred Tooth-striped has suffered greatly through habitat destruction over the last 60 years. A colony existed at Snitterfield Bushes until the early 1940s when the habitat was cleared to create a runway for aircraft. During the 1960s specimens were recorded at a garden moth trap in Tysoe (TT) but no indication of frequency is given. In April 1972 a thriving colony was discovered at Wellesbourne Wood (DB). Tragically the area containing the essential Wild Privet was cleared and bulldozed in February 1975. Thus *polycommata* succumbed to the same fate here as had the Snitterfield colony 30 years previously. Subsequent searches at these locations have proved fruitless.

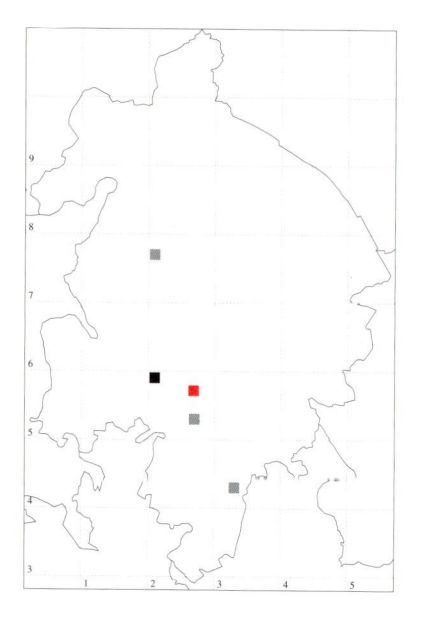

The species was feared extinct in the County until a slightly worn male specimen was caught in a garden moth trap at Charlecote, 29/3/1989 raising hopes of an extant population somewhere in the vicinity.

Records:
Snitterfield Bushes, 1930s, 6/4/1939 (2) (HEH, GBM); **Tysoe**, 1960s (TT); **Temple Balsall**, 1970 (FWS) This was reported to RHS in 1971 but never confirmed nor further recorded; **Wellesbourne Wood**, 5/4/1972 (4) (DB), 6/4/1972 (DB, RHS), 7/4/1972 (AFG, DB), 12/4/1972 (AFG), 31/3/1973 (AFG), 25/3/1974 (6) (AFG), 30/3/1974 (DB, BW); **Charlecote**, 29/3/1989 (DB).

Early Tooth-striped
1881 *Trichopteryx carpinata* (Borkh.)

County status: Fairly widespread and sometimes locally common.
Flight: Early April to late May.
Larval foodplants: Honeysuckle, sallows, birches* and Alder.

A locally plentiful springtime species at Ryton Wood, Wappenbury Wood, Brandon Wood, Bubbenhall Wood, Oakley Wood, Wolford Wood and other woodlands. Large numbers at light in Oversley Wood, 19/4/1974 (80), 12/5/1979 (105) (DB, AFG) and Snitterfield Bushes, 31/3/1989 (26) (DB) reflect extremely healthy populations. Increasingly noted in garden moth traps.

VCH 1904: *'Rare.'* Knowle.

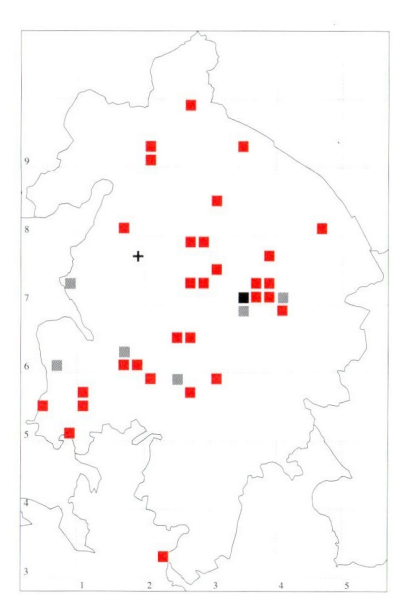

Small Seraphim
1882 *Pterapherapteryx sexalata* (Retz.)

Nationally Local

County status: Very local and sometimes fairly common.
Flight: Only one generation has so far been noted in Warwickshire. Mid-June to late July.
Larval foodplants: Sallows*.

This species, which was first recorded in the County in 1932 at Tile Hill Wood (CDNHSS), is found in damp woodland and railway cuttings containing an abundance of sallow.

Occasionally fairly common at light; for example, Oversley Wood, 3/7/1976 (10) (DB, AFG); Wolford Wood, 17/6/1989 (5) (DB).

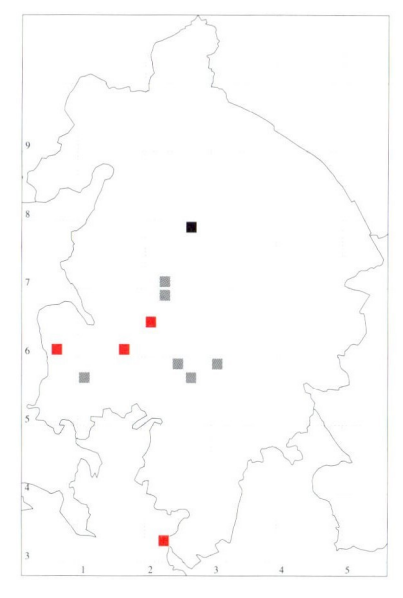

Records:
Tile Hill Wood, 25/6/1932 (CDNHSS); **Haseley Knob**, 10/7/1971 (DB); **Hampton Wood**, 2/8/1972, 2/7/1973, 5/7/1973 (AFG); **Oakley Wood**, 1972 (DB); **Charlecote**, 22/6/1973, 11/7/1973, 21/7/1974, 28/6/1976, 15/7/1977 (DB, AFG); **Oversley Wood**, 22/7/1974, 27/7/1974, 3/7/1976 (10), 15/7/1977, 13/7/1979 (DB, AFG); **Claverdon**, 3/6/1980 (IGMR); **Bearley Station**, 7/6/1988 (2), 15/6/1988, 5/5/1990 (IGMR); **Wolford Wood**, 17/6/1989 (5) (DB), 23/6/2001 (3) (DB, MA, Warks Moth Group); **Coughton Park**, 12/8/1995 two larvae on sallow (MCV).

Yellow-barred Brindle
1883 *Acasis viretata* (Hb.)

Nationally Local

County status: Widespread and occasionally fairly common.
Flight: Two generations. May to early June, and mid-July to late August.
Larval foodplants: Holly, Ivy, Wild Privet*, Dogwood, Guelder Rose and hawthorns.

The Yellow-barred Brindle is usually observed in small numbers but is found over a large part of Warwickshire. It frequents woodlands, parks, gardens, hedgerows and heathland. The VCH 1904 reported the species to be found at Sutton Park in considerable numbers in some years. Small populations still occur at this locality.

Garden moth trap totals are as follows: **Charlecote:** 1985 (6), 1990 (4), 1992 (11), 2000 (2) (AFG).

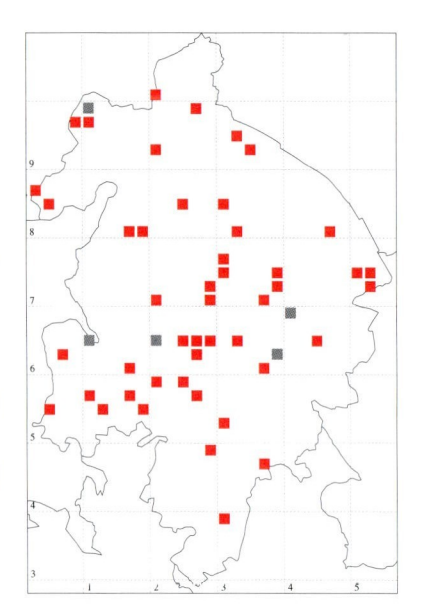

VCH 1904: *Sutton Park. 'In some years it has been taken there in considerable numbers.'*

Magpie
1884 *Abraxas grossulariata* (L.)

County status: Widespread but becoming uncommon.
Flight: Late June to early September.
Larval foodplants: Hawthorns*, Gooseberry*, Blackthorn*, sallows*, roses*, Red Currant*, Black Currant*, Portugal Laurel*.

The Magpie is found throughout the County in urban and rural gardens, woodlands and hedgerows. There is, however, evidence of a general decline during the last 20 years (Fig. 12).

A species subject to considerable variation in the extent of black and yellow wing markings. An entirely black specimen was bred from a larva found on Gooseberry at Erdington in 1945 (GPS). The larvae have been noted on an extensive range of trees and shrubs, the most unusual being Portugal Laurel *Prunus lusitanica* at Bishopton, Stratford-upon-Avon, 11/6/1999 (JMP).

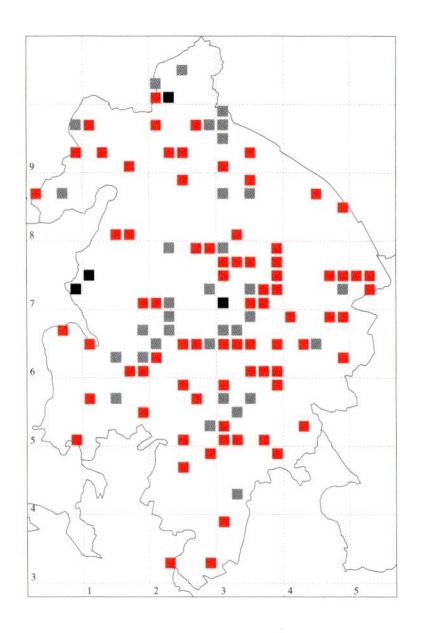

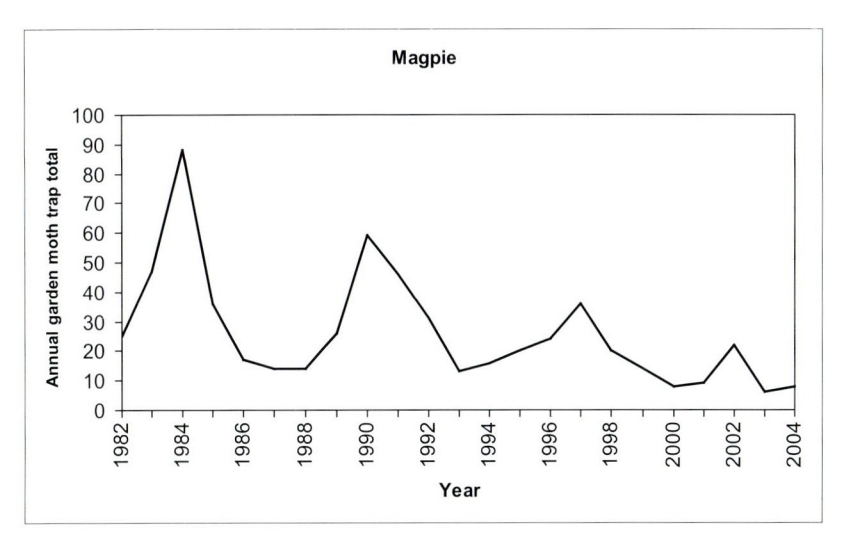

Figure 12. Garden moth trap totals of *A. grossulariata* at Hillmorton, Rugby (DIP), illustrate a steady decline.

NB. No recording took place during the flight period of this species in 1994 so an assumed value has been used.

VCH 1904: *'Exceedingly abundant in gardens.'*

Clouded Magpie
1885 *Abraxas sylvata* (Scop.)

Nationally Local

County status: Very local and uncommon.
Flight: June to mid-August.
Larval foodplants: Wych Elm and English Elm.

The Clouded Magpie has always been very local and uncommon in Warwickshire, and the ravages of Dutch elm disease during the 1970s added further to its demise. Colonies at this time were lost from Clowes Wood and New Park Wood. However, some woodland populations have survived and the appearance of occasional specimens in garden moth traps over a wide radius gives hope of further undetected colonies.

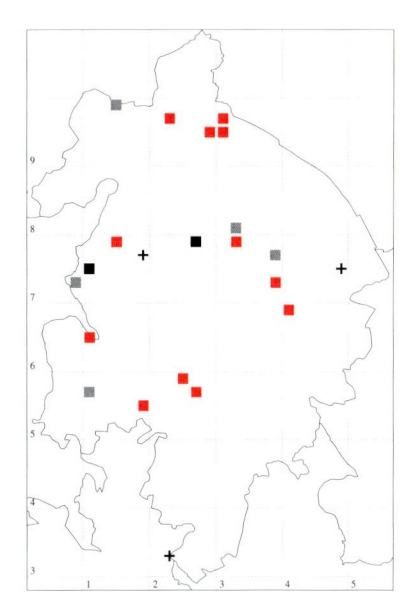

Records since 1980:
Oversley Wood, 11/6/1984 (AFG); **Parkside, Coventry**, 25/6/1988 (SAL); **Charlecote**, 25/6/1988 (DB), 9/7/2003 (AFG); **Kingsbury Wood**, 23/6/1989 (5) (Warks Moth Group); **Shottery, Stratford-upon-Avon**, 28/6/1993 (RGB); **Marton**, June 1994 (RA); **Bannam's Wood**, 12/8/1995 (Warks Moth Group); **Bentley Park Wood**, 20/7/1996 (Warks Moth Group); **Solihull**, 16/6/1999 (AWD); **Hampton Wood**, 17/7/1999 (RGB); **Ryton Meadows**, 15/7/2003 (MA); **Purley Chase, Mancetter**, 8/6/2004 (DB, RR).

VCH 1904: *'Not common and very local.'* Knowle, Brandon Wood, Overslade, Atherstone, Wolford Wood.

Clouded Border
1887 *Lomaspilis marginata* (L.)

County status: Widespread and common.
Flight: May to early August with occasional second generation individuals in late August and September.
Larval foodplants: Aspen*, poplars*, sallows* and Hazel.

The Clouded Border is a widespread species and particularly common in damp woodland amongst sallow. Peak numbers are usually reported in late June and during the first half of July.

It is subject to a considerable degree of variation in the intensity of wing markings. The brownish-black borders vary in width and some specimens possess extra spots or a band into the centre of the wing. A remarkable white aberration with only rudimentary markings around the costa, was taken in Waverley Wood, 28/7/2001 (DB).

VCH 1904: '*Common in woods.*'

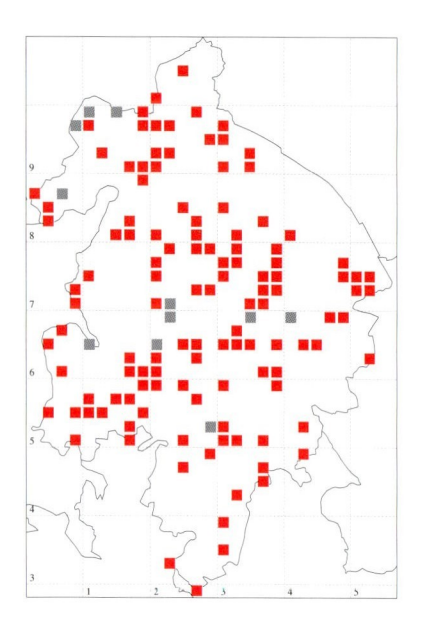

Scorched Carpet
1888 *Ligdia adustata* ([D. & S.])

Nationally Local

County status: Local and uncommon.
Flight: Two generations. Late April to early July, and August.
Larval foodplants: Spindle.

The Scorched Carpet is found chiefly in the southern half of the County, especially on calcareous soils. Preferred habitats are broadleaved woodland, scrub, disused quarries, railway cuttings and sheltered gardens. Typical sites include Wilmcote Rough, Bannam's Wood, Oversley Wood, Weethley Wood, Bowshot Wood, Grove Hill and Goldicote Cutting.

VCH 1904: '*Rare.*'
Sutton Park, Rugby, Wolford Wood.

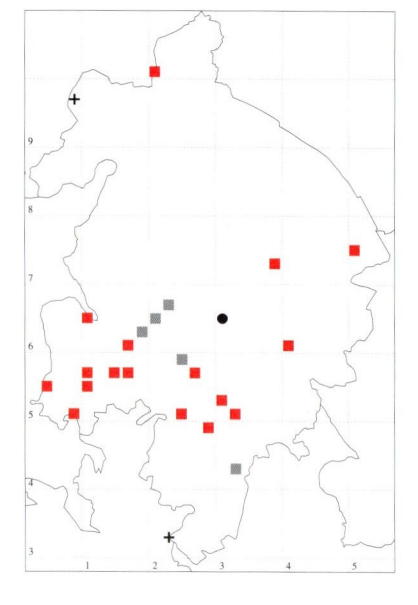

Peacock Moth
1889 *Macaria notata* (L.)

Nationally Local

County status: Very local and scarce.
Flight: Two generations. May, and July to August.
Larval foodplants: Birches.

A relatively recent addition to the County list, this Nationally Local species has so far been observed only very rarely in the County. Apart from a wanderer caught in a garden moth trap at Rugby, all records have been from extensive areas of broadleaved woodland containing a wealth of birch.

Records:
Oversley Wood, 22/7/1974 (DB); **Waverley Wood**, 6/7/1991 (RMC); **Hillmorton**, **Rugby**, 28/5/1992 (DIP); **Ryton Wood**, 4/8/2004 (MA).

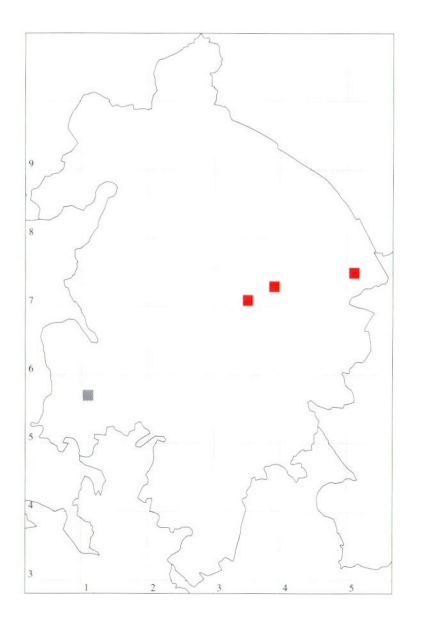

Tawny-barred Angle
1893 *Macaria liturata* (Cl.)

County status: Widespread and fairly common.
Flight: Mid-May to late August.
Larval foodplants: Scots Pine and Norway Spruce.

The Tawny-barred Angle is found over a large area of Warwickshire and seems able, like many other pine feeders, to exist in districts containing minimal numbers of trees. It is plentiful in woodlands with well-established coniferous plantations; for example, Bentley Park Wood, 20/7/1996 (43 at light) (Warks Moth Group).

The melanic f. *nigrofulvata* predominates in urban districts but represents only a small percentage of rural populations.

VCH 1904: *'Common in Sutton Park, also recorded from Brandon Wood, Knowle and Frankton.'*

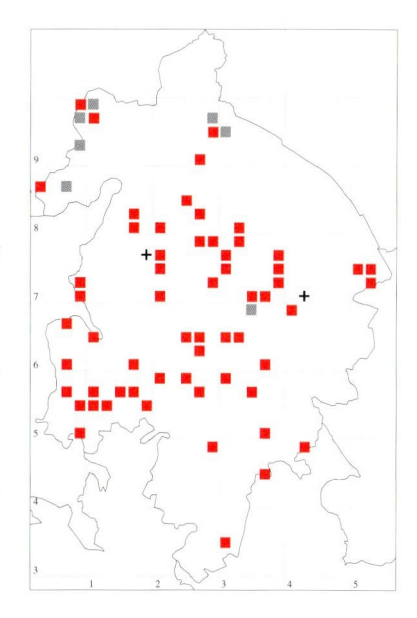

V-Moth

1897 *Macaria wauaria* (L.)

Nationally Local

County status: Very local and becoming scarce.
Flight: July and August.
Larval foodplants: Black Currant, Red Currant and Gooseberry.

The V-Moth, a garden species, has been declining in Warwickshire for many decades.

By the mid-1980s appearances had become sporadic at regularly operated garden moth traps in the conurbations of Birmingham, Coventry and smaller towns and villages throughout the County. There have been no records since 1996.

This trend may be attributed to an increase in pesticide spraying or to the decline in popularity of the old style kitchen gardens containing currant and Gooseberry bushes. Climatic change relating to global warming could also have played a part.

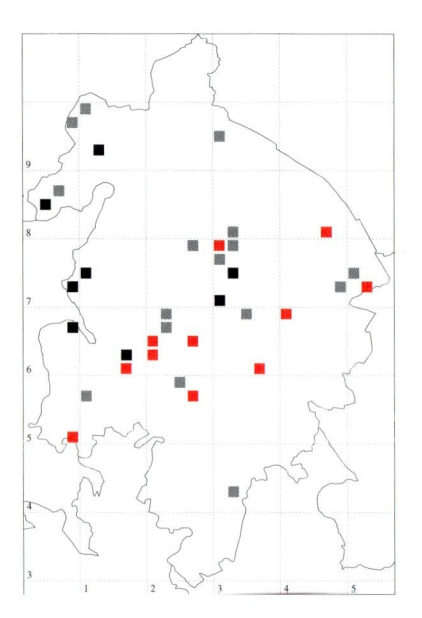

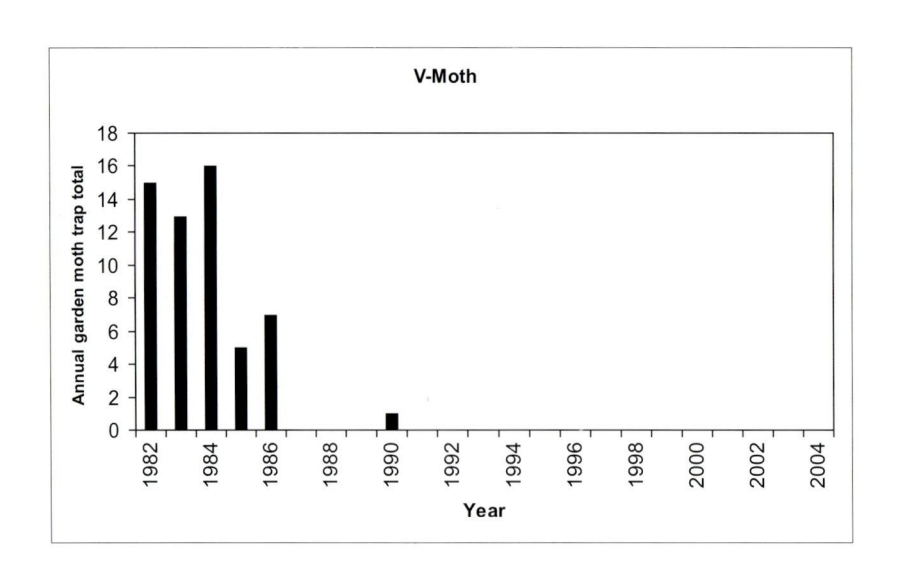

Figure 13. Garden moth trap totals of *M. wauaria* at Hillmorton, Rugby (DIP), illustrate the rapid fall in numbers during the 1980s.

Records since 1990:
Hillmorton, Rugby, 28/7/1996 (PN).

VCH 1904: *'Common' especially in gardens.*

Latticed Heath
1894 *Chiasmia clathrata clathrata* (L.)

County status: Widespread and common.
Flight: Two overlapping generations. Early May to late September.
Larval foodplants: Clovers, trefoils and lucerne.

The Latticed Heath has been recorded from most areas of the County in a range of grassland habitats, including railway cuttings, disused quarries, marginal wetland, woodland rides and clearings. Frequently noted flying during the daytime, it also responds to MV.

A specimen of *f. alboguttata* Fettig (wings plain dark brown with wide chequered borders) was caught at Ufton Fields 27/5/1977 (DB).

VCH 1904: *'Seems to occur in the southern half of the County but not in the north.'*

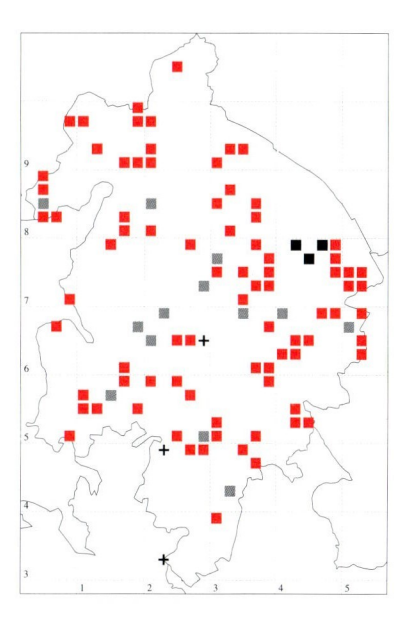

Little Thorn
1901 *Cepphis advenaria* (Hb.)

Nationally Scarce B

County status: Status uncertain.
Flight: June.
Larval foodplants: Bilberry. Alternative foodplants in the wild unknown.

A specimen of this Nationally Scarce species was captured in Oversley Wood on 7/6/2004 (RMC). Further research is required to ascertain the status of the moth at this site and to establish the larval foodplant in the absence of Bilberry.

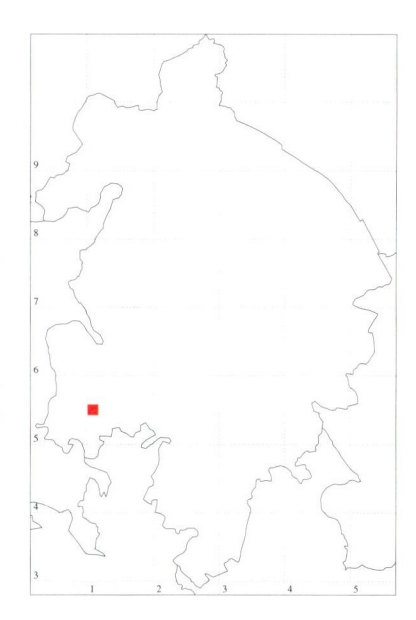

Brown Silver-line
1902 *Petrophora chlorosata* (Scop.)

County status: Widespread and common.
Flight: May to mid-July.
Larval foodplants: Bracken.

The Brown Silver-line is a very common moth in woodland clearings, where enormous numbers can sometimes be disturbed from Bracken during the daytime. Also found less plentifully in areas containing very little Bracken, including gardens, where it possibly utilises ornamental ferns.

VCH 1904: *'Fairly common.'*
Sutton Park, Brandon Wood, Princethorpe Wood, Wolford Wood, Knowle, Atherstone.

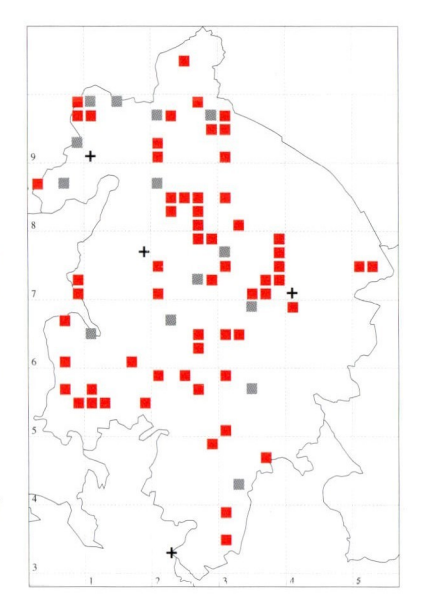

Barred Umber
1903 *Plagodis pulveraria* (L.)
Nationally Local

County status: Very local and occasionally fairly common.
Flight: May to early July.
Larval foodplants: Hazel*, birches, sallows and hawthorns.

The presence of Barred Umber at a site is usually an indication that there are remnants of ancient woodland. The largest populations of this species in the County are found in Ryton Wood and Oversley Wood.

Records:
Packwood, 4/6/1909 (EWC); **Umberslade**, 1/6/1922, (SEWC); **Tile Hill Wood**, 1934–1980 (CDNHSS, FVS, ANT, PC); **Bubbenhall Glade**, 4/6/1939 (LR); **Wappenbury Wood**, 1940s (APll), 20/5/2003 (DB); **Windmill Naps**, 1955–56 (FAN, HTK); **Ufton Wood**, 1959 survey; **Wainbody Wood**, 1960 (ANT); **Bannam's Wood**, 1964 (FAN); **Cubbington Wood**, 1970s (AFG); **Oversley Wood**, 1970s–1990s (DB, AFG, RMC), 26/5/2005 (2) (J.Rush), 4/6/2005 (2) (Warks Moth Group); **Brandon Wood**, 2/9/1973 larva on Hazel (MCV); **Hampton Wood**, 19/6/1974 (AFG); **Fen End, Kenilworth**, 1975 (DC); **Ryton Wood**, 1980–2005 (Warks Moth Group); **Wolverton**, 31/5/1982 (DS); **Hampton-in-Arden**, 1983 (MCV); **Kenilworth**, 2/6/1987 (PA); **Matchborough, Redditch**, 1989 (SD); **Weethley Wood**, 12/5/1990, 22/5/1999 (Warks Moth Group); **Hay Wood**, 30/5/1991 (DB); **Ufton Fields**, 5/7/1991 (RCK); **Waverley Wood**, 15/5/1993 (Warks Moth Group), 17/5/2003 (NJS); **Bubbenhall Wood**, 1997 (LB, CE); **Old Nun Wood**, 21/5/2004 (3) (AJP, VW, MK, NJS).

VCH 1904: *'Not common.'* Brandon Wood, Hampton-in-Arden, Atherstone, Knowle.

Scorched Wing
1904 *Plagodis dolabraria* (L.)

Nationally Local

County status: Widespread and fairly common.
Flight: Mid-May to early July.
Larval foodplants: Oaks*, Beech*, birches and sallows.

The Scorched Wing is widespread over the greater part of the County but thins towards the north.

It is found in a diversity of habitats and is plentiful in many broadleaved woodlands. Numbers of adults visiting light can sometimes be large; for example, Oversley Wood, 7/6/2004 (47) (RMC, DG, AJP).

Observed at many garden moth traps, even in suburban districts.

VCH 1904: *'Not common.'*
Sutton Park, Brandon Wood, Knowle, Wolford Wood.

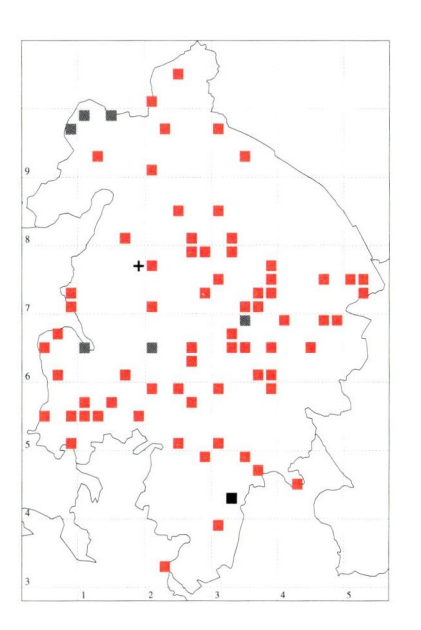

Brimstone Moth
1906 *Opisthograptis luteolata* (L.)

County status: Widespread and common.
Flight: Two, or possibly even three generations, from late April to early October.
Larval foodplants: Polyphagous on deciduous trees, including hawthorns*, Blackthorn* and cherry*.

The Brimstone Moth is a common and familiar species that is frequently encountered both in the daytime and at moth traps. It occurs in a wide range of habitats, especially woodland, and may be seen in any month from April to October with peaks reported in late May, mid-July and late August. A particularly late individual was caught at Temple Grafton on 2/11/2005 (AFG).

The voltinism of this species is rather complicated and difficult to assess as it can overwinter either as a larva or pupa. Some authors believe there is a regular pattern of three generations over two years.

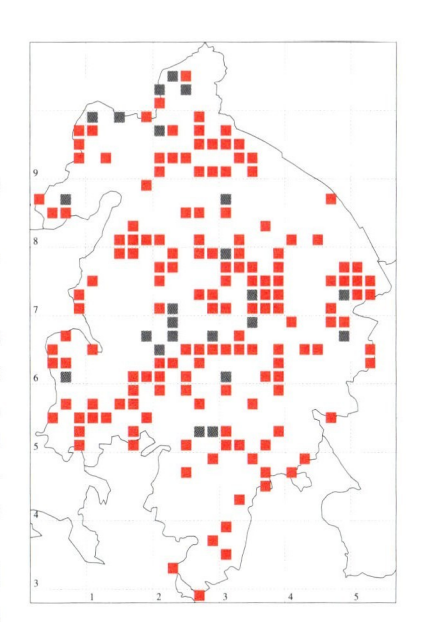

An idea of frequency in urban districts can be gained from the following trap counts:
Radford, Coventry: 1970 (14), 1980 (13), 1990 (18), 2000 (64) (MCV).

VCH 1904: *'Very common everywhere.'*

Bordered Beauty
1907 *Epione repandaria* (Hufn.)

County status: Fairly widespread but usually uncommon.
Flight: July to September.
Larval foodplants: Sallows*, Alder*, Black Poplar and Hazel.

The Bordered Beauty is found locally in damp areas containing sallows over a large part of the County but is never common.

The following garden moth trap totals reflect this: **Bidford-on-Avon:** 1990 (1), 1992 (1), 1993 (3) (RMC); **Charlecote:** 1997 (2), 2000 (1), 2003 (1) (DB); **Pillerton Priors:** 1992 (2), 1993 (1), 2002 (1) (CI).

VCH 1904: *'Occurs throughout the County but is far from common.'*

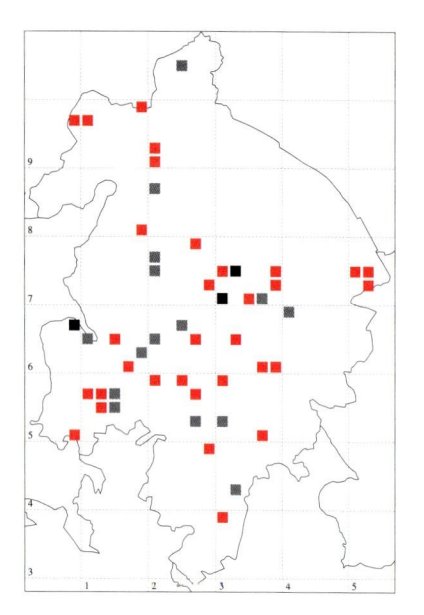

Speckled Yellow
1909 *Pseudopanthera macularia* (L.)

County status: Presumed extinct. Formerly very local and uncommon.
Flight: Day-flying in May and June.
Larval foodplants: Wood Sage.

This attractive day-flying species sadly disappeared from Warwickshire during the late 1950s. It was associated with open areas of woodland where coppicing was practised. The Speckled Yellow is still known to exist in several of the adjoining counties.

Records:
Clowes Wood and New Fallings Coppice, 1938–1956 a few seen annually (BNHS); **Austy Wood,** 1950s a few seen annually (HEH); **Windmill Naps,** 1950s a few seen annually (HEH).

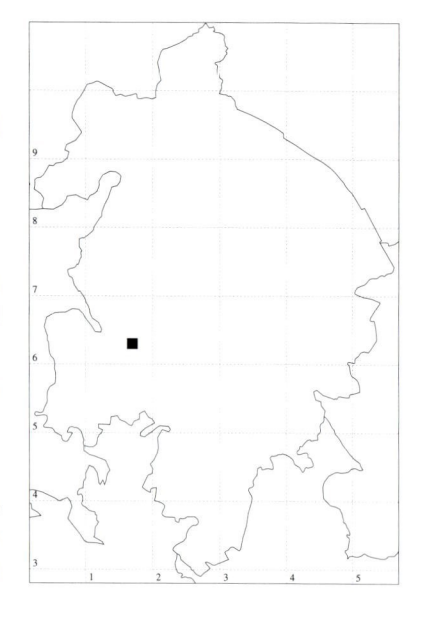

Lilac Beauty
1910 *Apeira syringaria* (L.)

Nationally Local

County status: Fairly widespread and fairly common.
Flight: June to late July. Sometimes individuals of a partial second generation occur from August to October.
Larval foodplants: Honeysuckle*, Ash, Wild Privet.

The Lilac Beauty is a fairly widespread species found in broadleaved woodlands and mature gardens. There is evidence of a partial second generation in some years as the following records indicate: Oversley Wood: 10/9/1982 (AFG); Hillmorton, Rugby: 26/9/1989, 3/10/1992, 23/8/2003 (DIP); Charlecote: 9/9/1982, 12/9/1989, 12/9/1990, 26/9/1994, 12/9/1999, 10/9/2003, 13/9/2003 (DB, AFG); Bidford-on-Avon: 15/9/1995 (RMC); Goldicote Cutting: 17/9/2004 (CI).

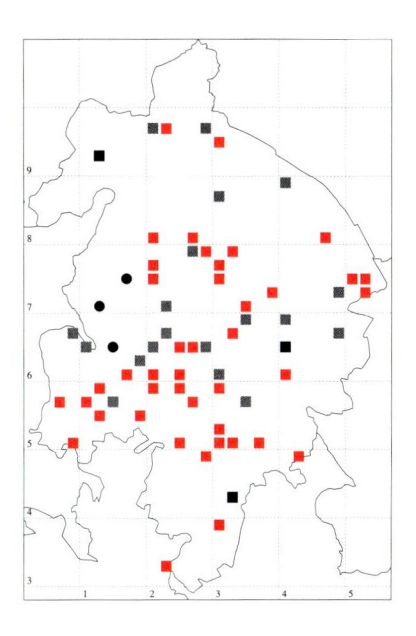

VCH 1904: *'Occurs throughout the County but is far from common.'*

August Thorn
1912 *Ennomos quercinaria* (Hufn.)

Nationally Local

County status: Fairly widespread and uncommon.
Flight: Late July to late September.
Larval foodplants: Polyphagous on deciduous trees, including Beech* and hawthorns*.

The August Thorn is found in small numbers in broadleaved woodlands, scrub, hedgerows and well-established gardens. It is less frequently recorded from the north of the County.

The following garden moth trap records reflect generally low frequency: **Charlecote:** 1992 (1), 1993 (2), 1996 (1), 2001 (4), 2004 (2), 2005 (5) (DB).

VCH 1904: *'Not common.'*
Knowle, Rugby, Overslade, Frankton Wood, Wolford Wood.

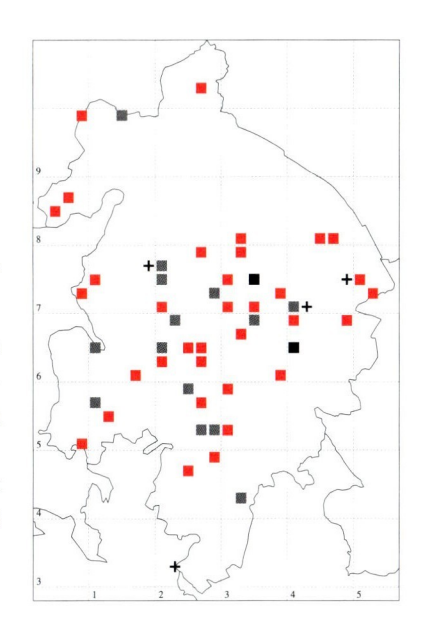

Canary-shouldered Thorn
1913 *Ennomos alniaria* (L.)

County status: Widespread and fairly common.
Flight: Late July to mid-October.
Larval foodplants: Polyphagous on deciduous trees, including birches* and Alder*.

This finely featured species has been recorded from a diversity of wooded habitats in both rural and urban districts.

The following garden moth trap figures give an idea of frequency: **Pillerton Priors:** 1992 (20), 1993 (10), 2002 (8), 2003 (15), 2004 (6), 2005 (8) (CI); **Hillmorton, Rugby:** 1982 (22), 1985 (32), 1990 (46), 1995 (31), 2000 (40), 2004 (9) (DIP).

VCH 1904: *'Fairly common and generally distributed.'*

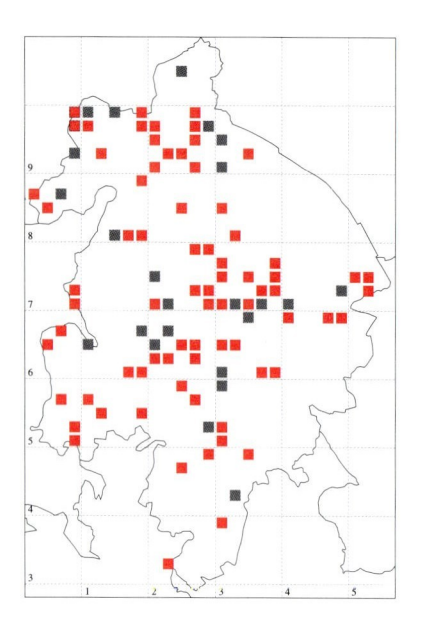

Dusky Thorn
1914 *Ennomos fuscantaria* (Haw.)

County status: Widespread and fairly common.
Flight: Late July to mid-October.
Larval foodplants: Ash*.

The Dusky Thorn is widespread and fairly common in woodlands where Ash is present. It has been recorded from most regularly operated garden moth traps, even in urban districts. Fox (2006) reports a dramatic national decline of this species over the last 35 years, but so far this has been less noticeably reflected in Warwickshire.

The following garden moth trap totals compare urban and rural districts:

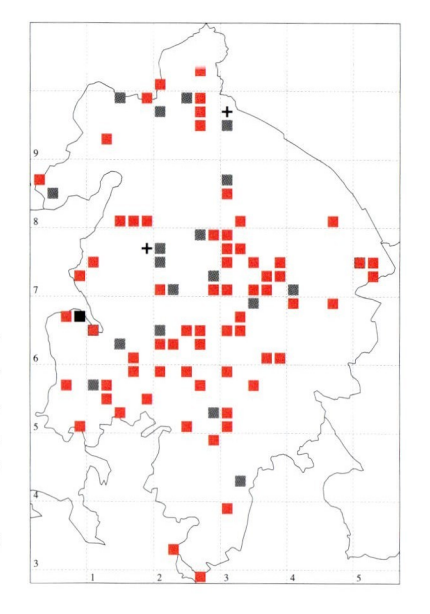

Habitat	Location	1978	1990	1991	2000	2002	2005
Urban	Radford, Coventry (MCV)	4	4	3	4	4	0
Rural	Charlecote (DB)	17	67	31	41	17	18

VCH 1904: *'Not common.'*
Knowle, Rugby, Atherstone.

September Thorn
1915 *Ennomos erosaria* ([D. & S.])

County status: Widespread and fairly common.
Flight: July to September.
Larval foodplants: Oaks*, birches, limes and Beech.

The September Thorn occurs fairly commonly in broadleaved woodland containing an abundance of mature oak, and less plentifully in parks and mature gardens. As with *quercinaria* there have been fewer sightings in north Warwickshire.

Garden moth trap records at **Charlecote** are as follows: 1992 (13), 1993 (4), 2001 (6), 2004 (2), 2005 (5) (DB).

VCH 1904: *'Rare.'*
Marston Green, Leamington, Knowle, Rugby.

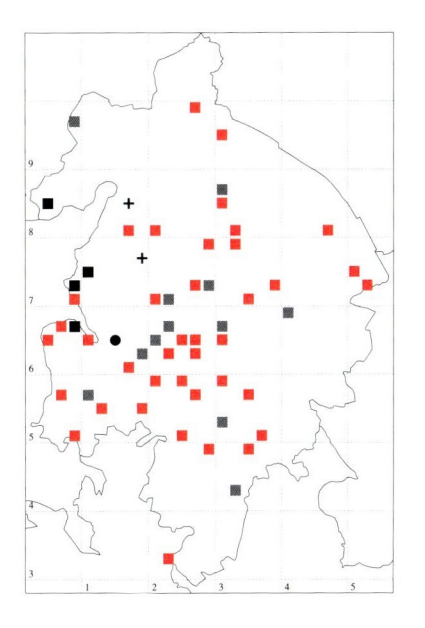

Early Thorn
1917 *Selenia dentaria* (Fabr.)

County status: Widespread and fairly common.
Flight: Two generations. Mid-March to early May, and early July to late August, with individuals occasionally in September.
Larval foodplants: Polyphagous on deciduous trees, including hawthorns*, Blackthorn*, Alder* and oaks*.

The Early Thorn is widely distributed in a vast range of urban and rural habitats but is especially plentiful in broadleaved woodland. Melanic forms are frequent in built-up areas.

Comparative rural and urban garden moth trap totals are as follows:

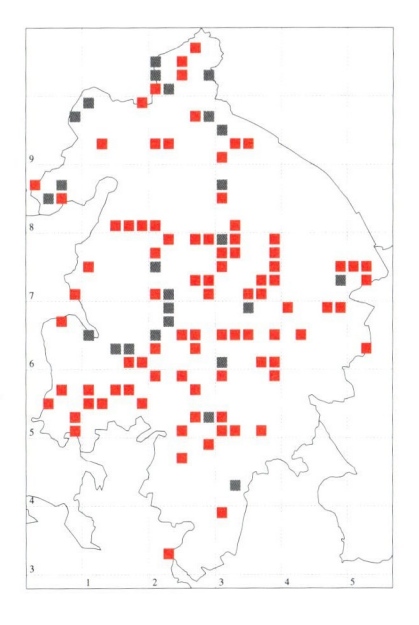

Habitat	Location	1981	1987	1988	1994	2003
Urban	Radford, Coventry (MCV)	5	8	6	15	8
Rural	Charlecote (DB)	50	57	28	14	16

VCH 1904: *'Occurs throughout the County not uncommonly'.*

Lunar Thorn
1918 *Selenia lunularia* (Hb.)
Nationally Local

County status: Very local and scarce. Overall decline.
Flight: May to early July.
Larval foodplants: Sallows*, oaks, birches, Blackthorn, elms, Ash, Dog-rose and other deciduous trees and shrubs.

This species has been recorded from a number of different habitats, including open woodland, parks and gardens. The Lunar Thorn experienced a dramatic population crash in Warwickshire during the late 1970s from which it has never recovered.

The graph below depicts the decline and subsequent disappearance at Charlecote.

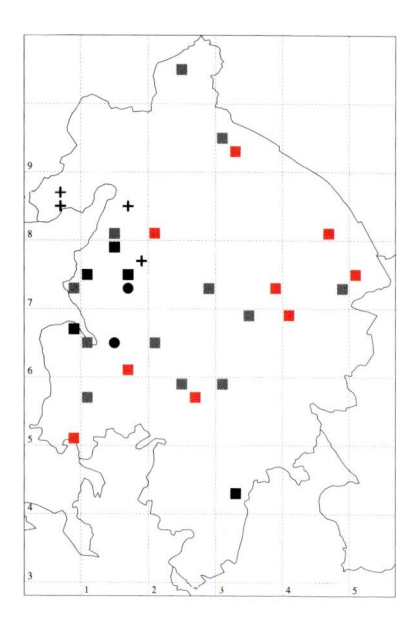

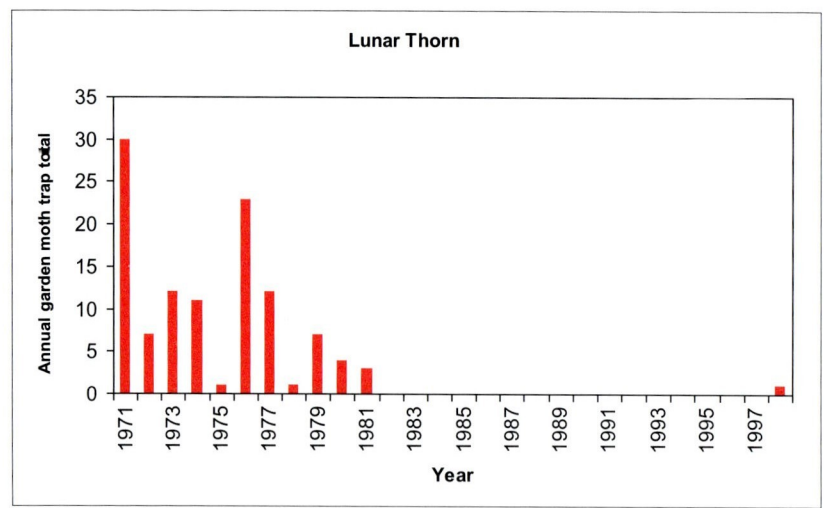

Figure 14. Total numbers of *S. lunularia* in a garden moth trap at Charlecote (DB).

Records:
May's Wood, 5/5/1910 (GBM); **Packwood**, 10/6/1917 (SEWC); **Dorridge**, 5/6/1935 (SEWC); **New Fallings Coppice**, 1938 (BNHS); **Solihull**, 8/6/1946 (SEWC); **Tysoe**, 13/6/1950 (TT); **Mappleborough Green**, 1950–60 (FHL); **Forshaw Heath**, 5/6/1959 (FAN); **Morton Bagot**, 1964 (FAN); **Charlecote**, 1968–80, 1998 (DB, AFG); **Cubbington Wood**, 1970 (AFG); **Oakley Wood**, 1970s (DB); **Marton**, 1970s (RA); **Bilton**, 1970s (RJ); **Fen End, Kenilworth**, 1970s (DC); **Hartshill Hayes**, 1970s (RJT); **Oversley Wood**, 1970s (DB, AFG); **Hampton Wood**, 1972–75 (AFG); **Claverdon**, 14/6/1978, 21/6/1979, 27/6/1979, 4/6/1980, 9/6/1984 (IGMR); **Solihull**, 1978 (CD); **Alvecote Cottages**, 22/6/1979 (NJP); **Bidford-on-Avon**, 1980s, 22/7/1991 (RMC); **Hillmorton, Rugby**, 12/6/1980, 1/6/1981, 26/6/1986 (DIP); **Hampton-in-Arden**, 1983 (MCV); **Pailton**, 1985 (KCG); **Ryton Wood**, 1993 (LB, CE).

VCH 1904: *'Far less common than* **dentaria**'.
Knowle, Yardley, Marston Green, Birmingham, Rugby.

Purple Thorn
1919 *Selenia tetralunaria* (Hufn.)

County status: Widespread and fairly common.
Flight: Two generations. April to the end of May, and July to mid-August.
Larval foodplants: Polyphagous on deciduous trees and shrubs, including hawthorns* and Alder*.

The Purple Thorn is widespread and locally fairly common in broadleaved woodland, copses and scrub. Second generation specimens are much smaller and paler. A very late individual was caught in September 1985 at Hampton Wood (RGB).

Garden moth trap totals are generally fairly low: **Hillmorton, Rugby:** 1982 (0), 1985 (3), 1990 (1), 1995 (3), 2000 (0), 2004 (2) (DIP); **Pillerton Priors:** 1992 (12), 1993 (4), 1994 (0), 2002 (4), 2003 (7), 2004 (2), 2005 (2) (CI).

VCH 1904: *'Not common.'*
Knowle, Rugby.

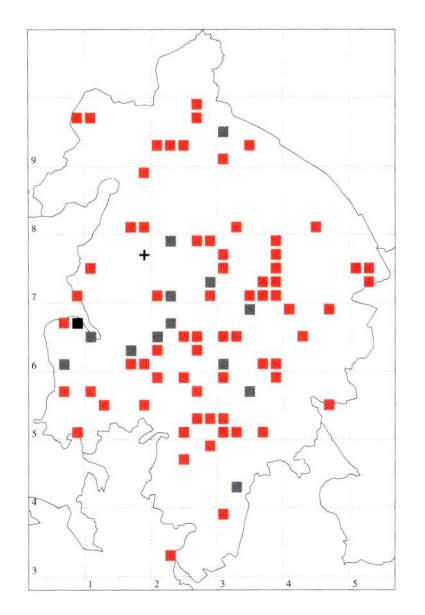

Scalloped Hazel
1920 *Odontopera bidentata* (Cl.)

County status: Widespread and fairly common.
Flight: Late April to early July with occasional individuals of a partial second generation in late August and September.
Larval foodplants: Polyphagous on deciduous and coniferous trees, including oaks* and birches*.

The Scalloped Hazel is fairly common in urban areas but becomes far less frequent in rural districts. In the conurbations of Coventry and Birmingham dark forms are seen regularly with the occasional ab. *nigra* Prout.

Unusually early and late sightings of this species are: Ipsley Alders Marsh, Redditch, 13/3/1989 (SD); Pretty Pigs pub, Shuttington, 22/9/1968 (anon.) and Hillmorton, Rugby, 24/8/2005 (DIP).

Garden moth trap totals in an urban district are as follows: **Radford, Coventry:** 1970 (21), 1980 (5), 1990 (11), 2000 (26) (MCV).

VCH 1904: *'Common everywhere.'*

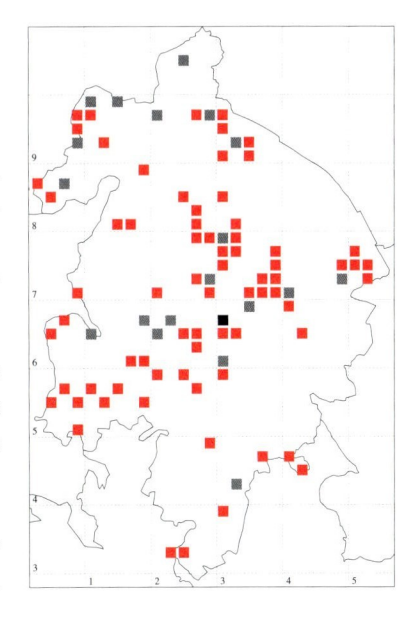

Scalloped Oak
1921 *Crocallis elinguaria* (L.)

County status: Widespread and fairly common.
Flight: Late June to end of August.
Larval foodplants: Polyphagous on deciduous trees and shrubs, including apple* and Blackthorn*.

The Scalloped Oak is a widespread species found in a diversity of habitats, especially woodland. It also occurs in built-up districts, where dark banded and melanic forms are sometimes noted. At Snitterfield Bushes on 3/8/1991 amongst 15 normal specimens was a spectacular aberration with a reduced unicoloured central band and the marginal area of the forewing rayed with blackish-brown (AJK; Kolaj, 1993).

Garden moth trap totals are as follows: **Pillerton Priors:** 1992 (32), 1993 (38), 1994 (10), 2002 (21), 2003 (22), 2004 (19) (CI); **Radford, Coventry:** 1975 (8), 1980 (13), 1985 (3), 1990 (6), 1995 (16), 2000 (10) (MCV); **Hillmorton, Rugby:** 1982 (30), 1985 (55), 1990 (46), 1995 (73), 2000 (42), 2004 (37) (DIP).

VCH 1904: *'Generally distributed and fairly common.'*

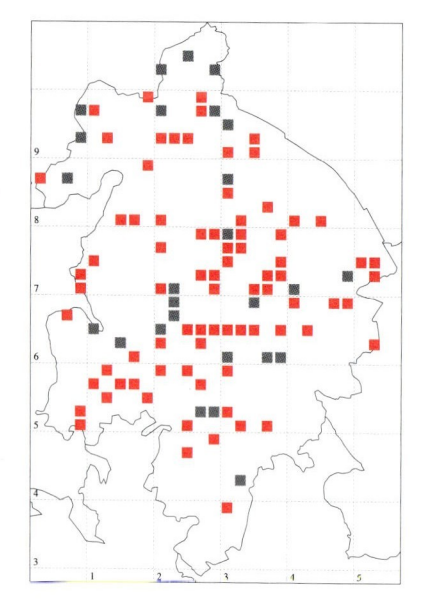

Swallow-tailed Moth
1922 *Ourapteryx sambucaria* (L.)

County status: Widespread and fairly common.
Flight: Late June to mid-August with an occasional partial second generation in September and October.
Larval foodplants: Polyphagous on trees and shrubs, including Ivy*, hawthorns* and Honeysuckle*.

The Swallow-tailed Moth is found over most of Warwickshire in an enormous range of habitats.

It is freely attracted to light with numbers peaking in mid-July. There is an occasional partial second generation during the autumn which was formerly preceded by hot summers but is now becoming more regular, perhaps due to climate change.

Garden moth trap totals in urban and suburban districts are as follows: **Radford, Coventry:** 1982 (16), 1985 (21), 1990 (35), 1995 (57), 2000 (21), 2004 (14) (MCV); **Hillmorton, Rugby:** 1982 (46), 1985 (92), 1990 (78), 1995 (159), 2000 (66), 2004 (46) (DIP).

VCH 1904: *'Common everywhere.'*

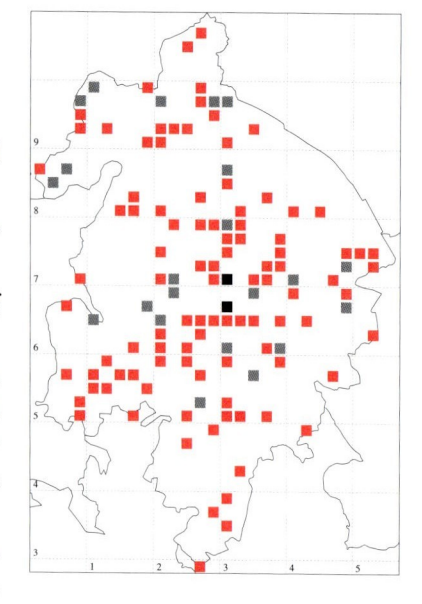

Feathered Thorn
1923 *Colotois pennaria* (L.)

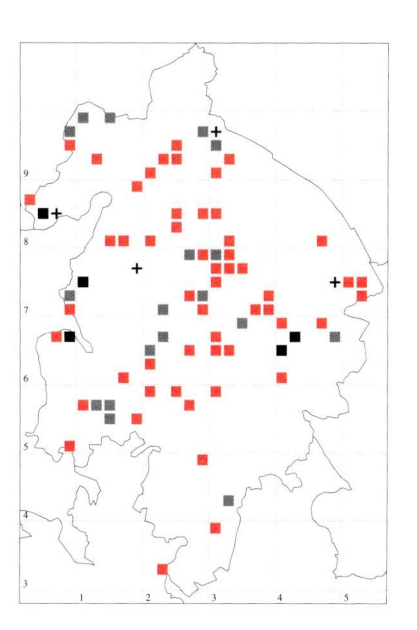

County status: Widespread and locally common, sometimes abundant.
Flight: Late September to late November.
Larval foodplants: Polyphagous on deciduous trees and shrubs, including Field Maple*, Alder*, Beech*, Wild Privet*, oaks*, hawthorns* and poplars*.

This late autumn species is well-recorded from a variety of habitats. It is freely attracted to MV and very large numbers have been recorded in woodland on mild nights; for example, Oversley Wood, 3/11/1979 (450) (DB, AFG), Oakley Wood, 11/11/1990 (155) (DB). A highly variable species, ranging from plain brick red to heavily speckled orange forms.

An unusually dark melanic specimen was caught in Oakley Wood on 11/11/1989 (DB).

VCH 1904: *'Not common.'*
Sutton Park, Knowle, Yardley, Overslade and Atherstone.

Orange Moth
1924 *Angerona prunaria* (L.)

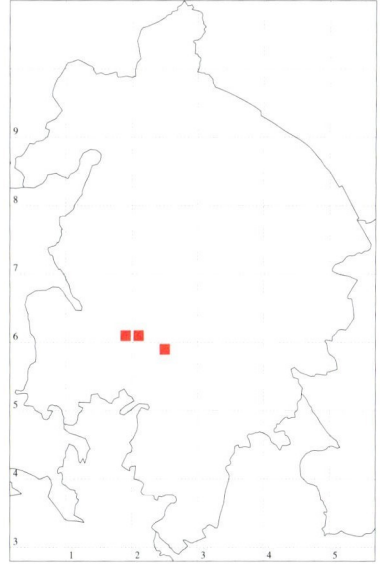

Nationally Local

County status: Very local and generally scarce.
Flight: June and July.
Larval foodplants: A wide range of broadleaved trees and shrubs, including Blackthorn, hawthorns, birches and also Broom and Traveller's-joy.

Apart from a solitary example at Hampton Wood in 1985 (RGB), all records of Orange Moth are confined to Snitterfield Bushes, where appearances have been very intermittent over the years. There were no reports of this species between 1940 and 1985, after which there was a marked resurgence culminating in a record 23 individuals in 1989. The ensuing years saw a rapid decline once again and there have been no sightings since 1994.

Records:
Snitterfield Bushes, 1939 (3) (GBM), 10/7/1986 (JMP), 19/6/1988 (3) (AFG), 29/6/1988 (6) (RMC, AFG), 2/7/1988 (RMC, DB), 13/6/1989 (6) (AFG), 16/6/1989 (16) (DB, RGB, RHS), 1/7/1989 (DB, AFG), 13/6/1990 (DB, RMC), 15/6/1990 (6) (DB, RGB, IGMR), 9/6/1993 (3) (AJK, TRG), 22/6/1994 (DB, RMC, BS), 24/6/1994 (4) (AJK); **Hampton Wood**, 5/7/1985 (RGB).

Small Brindled Beauty
1925 *Apocheima hispidaria* ([D. & S.])
Nationally Local

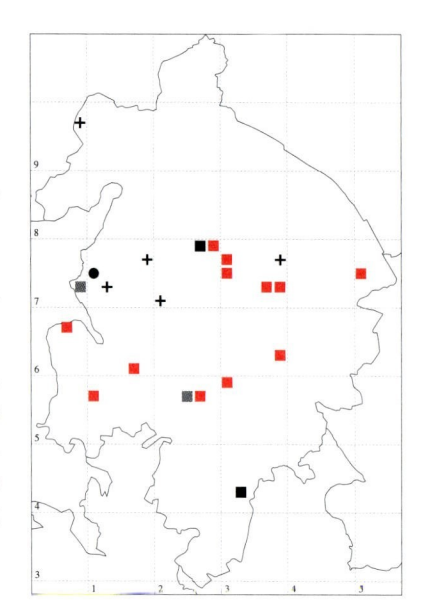

County status: Very local. Common and sometimes abundant at one site, but scarce elsewhere.
Flight: February to mid-April.
Larval foodplants: Oaks* and occasionally Hazel, English Elm, Silver Birch, Hornbeam and Sweet Chestnut.

The Small Brindled Beauty is common in Ryton Wood where the male sometimes arrives at MV in prodigious numbers; for example, 19/2/1977 (60) (DB, AFG, BE), 23/2/1991 (400) (DB, PJR). Occasionally singletons are recorded in garden moth traps in the vicinity of old oak trees.

Records:
Oakley Wood, Mar 1910 male & female (Chadwick), 11/3/1991 (DB, AFG, RMC); **Earlswood**, 1916 (GBM); **Tysoe**, 10/2/1948, 29/2/1948, 9/3/1948 (TT); **Tile Hill Wood**, 1950 (CDNHSS); **Clowes Wood**, 1956 (BNHS); **Charlecote**, 1/3/1970, 11/4/1970, 16/3/1972, 29/2/1980, 15/3/1982, 15/3/1986, 1/3/1987, 4/3/1989, 4/3/1991, 16/3/1991, 23/2/1992, 4/3/1992, 16/3/1992, 27/2/1994, 9/3/1997, 1999 (1), 10/3/2001, 15/3/2005 (DB, AFG); **Ryton Wood**, 14/2/1971 (3), 19/2/1971 (9), 12/3/1971 (13) (DB, AFG), 28/3/1971 (6), (DB, LEM), 17/3/1972 (16) (DB, LEM), 19/2/1977 (60) (DB, AFG, BE), 23/2/1991 (400) (DB, PJR), 1/3/1991 (4) (DB, RMC, IGMR), 7/3/1992, 15/3/1992, 19/3/1992 (AJK), 1993 (CE, LB); **Ufton Wood**, 4/3/1984 (NG); **Earlsdon, Coventry**, 15/3/1986 (PC); **Oversley Wood**, 11/3/1991 (DB, AFG); **Hillmorton, Rugby**, 4/3/1992 (DIP); **Matchborough, Redditch**, 14/3/1992 (SD); **Pig Wood, Tile Hill, Coventry**, 17/3/1992 female on oak trunk (AJK); **Bearley Station**, 28/2/1995 (IGMR); **Kenilworth Rd, Coventry**, 7/3/2001 (MA); **Ryton Meadows**, 18/3/2005 (14) (JWkn, NJS).

VCH 1904: *Sutton Park, Chalcot Wood, Hay Wood, Brandon Wood, Knowle.*

Pale Brindled Beauty
1926 *Phigalia pilosaria* ([D. & S.])

County status: Widespread and fairly common.
Flight: Late December to early April.
Larval foodplants: Polyphagous on deciduous trees and shrubs, including limes*, birches*, oaks*, Field Maple*, hawthorns*, Beech* and sallows*.

This species is very much under-recorded due to its early flight period. It is found in a variety of habitats but is most plentiful in areas of broadleaved woodland. The males can sometimes be prolific at MV; for instance, Oversley Wood, 6/2/1981 (125) (DB, AFG); Ryton Wood, 23/2/1991 (45) (DB, PJR).

The dark form *monacharia* has become less frequent in the last 30 years. Moth trap counts at rural **Charlecote** (DB) illustrate how this form has seemingly disappeared:

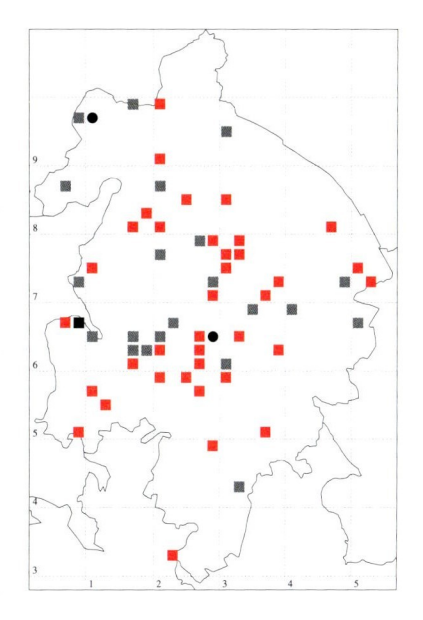

Form	1970	1971	1972	1982	1987	1998	1999	2001	2003	2004
Usual	11	39	8	19	9	27	4	4	9	3
monacharia	2	3	3	0	0	0	0	0	0	0

VCH 1904: *'Common. All are of the usual form; the black form has not yet been noticed.'*

Brindled Beauty
1927 *Lycia hirtaria* (Cl.)

County status: Widespread but becoming less common.
Flight: Mid-March to late May.
Larval foodplants: Polyphagous on deciduous trees and shrubs, including limes*, sallows*, oaks*, Alder*, Ash*, hawthorns*, Blackthorn* and apple*.

The status of the Brindled Beauty has changed considerably since the VCH 1904, at which time it was described as *'very rare'*, with only a solitary pre-1900 record from Knowle (WGB). There were no subsequent records until 1960 when small numbers were attracted to light at Tysoe (TT) and Oversley Wood (SEWC).

During the next 20 years the species underwent an extremely rapid expansion in range and frequency. It is now widespread across Warwickshire in a diversity of rural and urban habitats, but there is evidence of a decline as the the MV figures (over the page) illustrate:

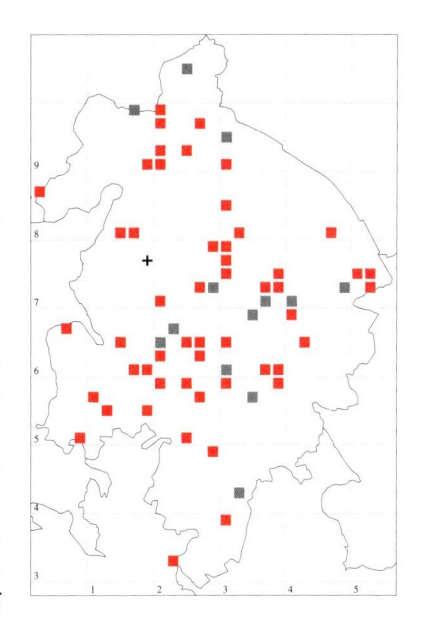

Pillerton Priors: 1992 (13), 1993 (23), 1994 (10), 2002 (6), 2003 (1), 2004 (1) 2005 (4) (CI);
Charlecote: 1972 (106), 1975 (50), 1980 (105), 1985 (30), 1990 (51), 1995 (14), 2000 (8), 2004 (1) 2005 (2) (DB).

An unusually early specimen was caught at Ryton Wood on 15/1/2005 (NJS, AJP, VW).

VCH 1904: *'Very rare.'* Knowle (1).

Oak Beauty
1930 *Biston strataria* (Hufn.)

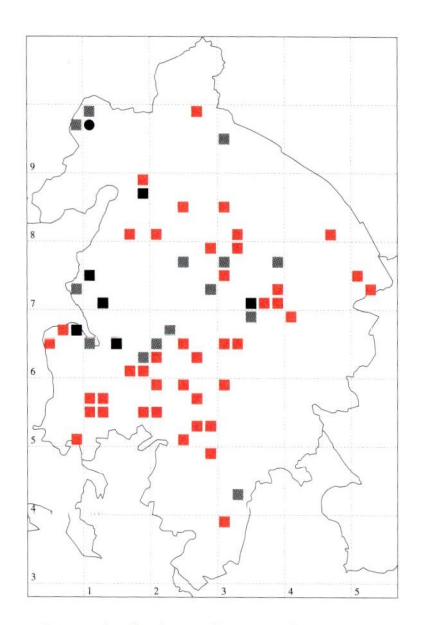

County status: Fairly widespread and common in oak woodland.
Flight: February to late April.
Larval foodplants: Polyphagous on deciduous trees and shrubs, including oaks* and birches*.

The Oak Beauty, despite its specific vernacular name, breeds on a wide range of broadleaved trees and shrubs, enabling the species to exist in a diversity of habitats. It is most plentiful in woodlands containing mature oaks. Vast numbers of males can be attracted to light in suitable weather conditions, but the female is rarely noted. Examples of large quantities of males at light are: Oversley Wood, 11/3/1991 (82) (DB, AFG, RMC); Oakley Wood, 16/3/1992 (44) (DB). The widespread use of MV light has shown this species to be far more plentiful than at the beginning of the twentieth century when it was considered 'rare'.

VCH 1904: *'Rare, but I think it occurs throughout the district.'*

Peppered Moth
1931 *Biston betularia* (L.)

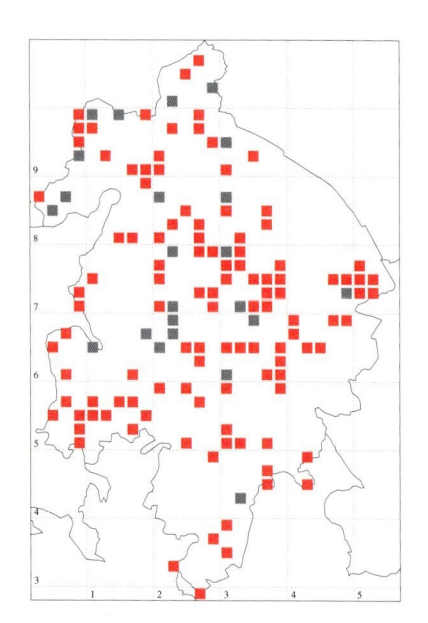

County status: Widespread and fairly common.
Flight: One protracted generation. Early May to mid-August.
Larval foodplants: Polyphagous on deciduous trees, shrubs and herbaceous plants, including limes*, birches*, sallows*, oaks*, Field Maple*, poplars*, hawthorns*.

The Peppered Moth is found fairly commonly in a wide range of open and wooded habitats but is far less plentiful than formerly. Populations in Warwickshire include the melanic form *carbonaria* Jordan and f. *insularia* Thierry-Mieg, which is intermediate in appearance between the melanic and typical forms. There has been a marked decline in the melanic form, thought to be due to decreasing levels of air pollution. For example, Charlecote: 1968 (23 *carbonaria*, 3 typical), 1969 (25 *carbonaria*, 9 typical), 2004 (0 *carbonaria*, 4 typical), 2005 (2 *carbonaria*, 11 typical) (DB).

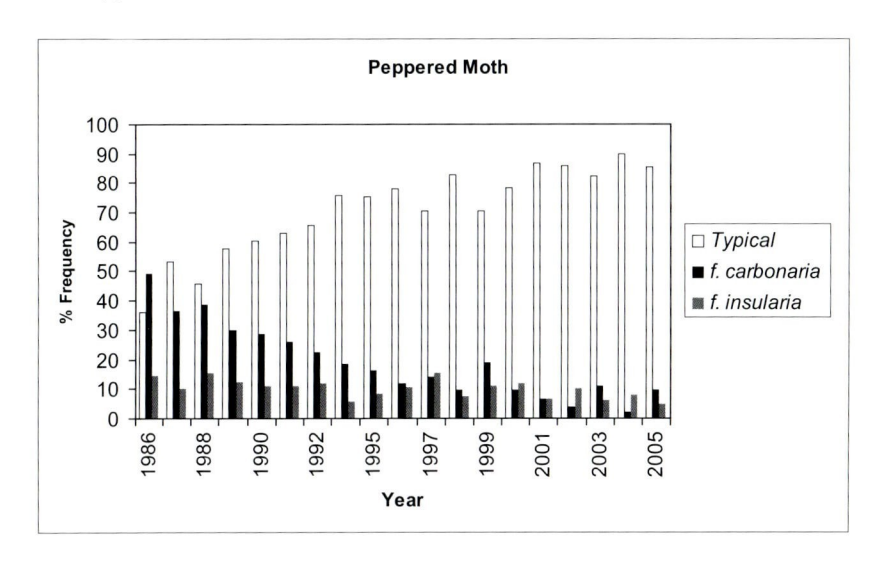

Figure 15. Annual percentage frequency of the three forms of *B. betularia* in a garden moth trap at Hillmorton, Rugby (DIP).

NB. No recording took place during the flight period of this species in 1994 so an assumed value has been used.

VCH 1904: '*Common throughout the district.*'

Spring Usher
1932 *Agriopis leucophaearia* ([D. & S.])

County status: Widespread, locally common and sometimes abundant.
Flight: Mid-January to early March.
Larval foodplants: Oaks*.

The Spring Usher is found over most of the County, in woodlands, parks, hedgerows and gardens with mature oaks. The greatest populations occur in broadleaved woodlands, where on mild February nights large quantities of males can sometimes be attracted to light; for example, Oversley Wood, 6/2/1981 (45) (DB, AFG); Ryton Wood, 23/2/1991 (650) (DB, PJR).
Dark banded forms are frequent but melanic forms are rare.

VCH 1904: '*Generally distributed and fairly common.*'

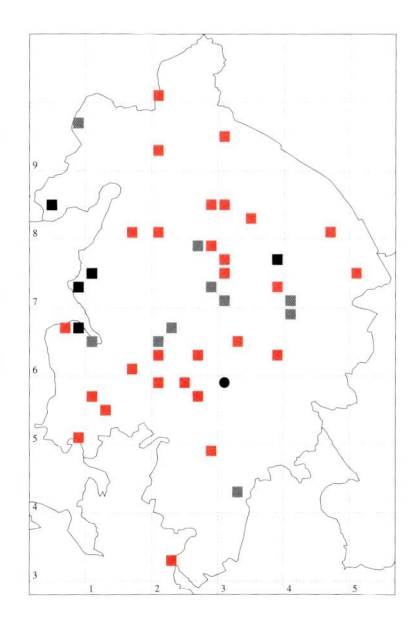

Scarce Umber
1933 *Agriopis aurantiaria* (Hb.)

County status: Local and sometimes fairly common.
Flight: October to December.
Larval foodplants: Polyphagous on deciduous trees and shrubs, including hawthorns*, sallows*, oaks* Alder* and Beech*.

The Scarce Umber frequents broadleaved woodland, mature hedgerows and sheltered gardens. Although local in Warwickshire it is not as scarce as its English name implies and may sometimes be observed commonly; for example, Ryton Wood, 16/11/2004 (22) (NJS, AJP). Males of this species are attracted to light but do not appear to fly long distances. An effective method of monitoring both males and wingless females is to search bare twigs and tree trunks at night with a torch.

VCH 1904: *'Not common.' Sutton Park, Yardley, Knowle, Atherstone, Wolford.*

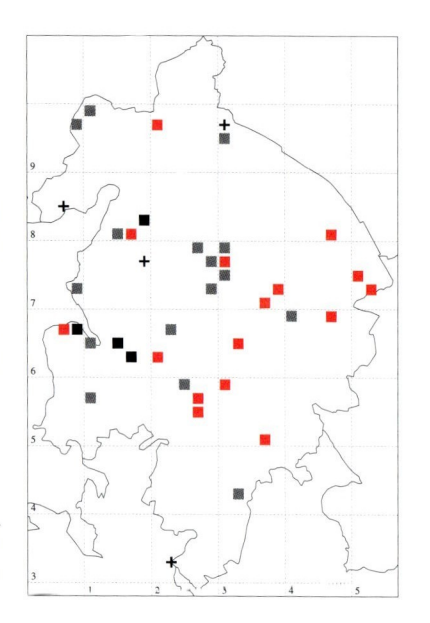

Dotted Border
1934 *Agriopis marginaria* (Fabr.)

County status: Widespread and fairly common.
Flight: January to late April.
Larval foodplants: Polyphagous on deciduous trees and shrubs, including Beech*, Field Maple*, Alder*, Aspen*, Rowan*, hawthorns* and limes*.

The Dotted Border is one of the first woodland species of Geometer to occur in the year. The adults have been noted in early January during mild winters; for example, Temple Grafton, 12/1/2005 (AFG). Searching hedgerow branches and tree trunks at night with a torch is a good method of observing both males and wingless females. The former may sometimes be attracted to light in large numbers: Ryton Wood, 23/2/1991 (55) (DB, PJR).

This species is prone to considerable variation with the uniformly dark-brown f. *fuscata* Mosley being found in most populations.

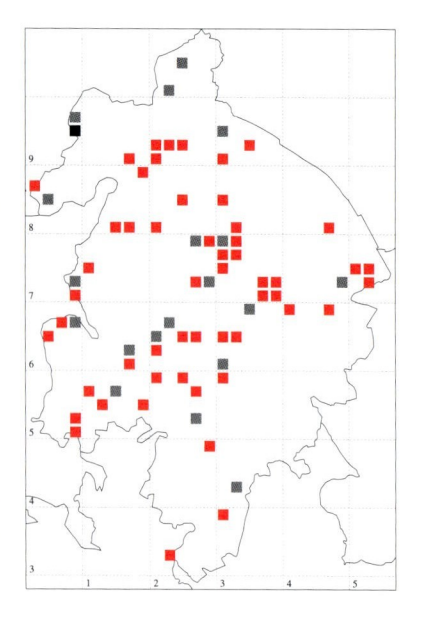

VCH 1904: *'Very common everywhere. Dark forms are frequent, both the unicolorous var.* **fuscata** *and also specimens more or less richly clouded with dark colour, the markings remaining as usual.'*

Mottled Umber
1935 *Erannis defoliaria* (Cl.)

County status: Widespread and fairly common.
Flight: October to February.
Larval foodplants: Polyphagous on trees and shrubs, including hawthorns*, oaks*, sallows*, Field Maple*, Alder*, Rowan*, Beech* and birches*.

The Mottled Umber is found in a wide range of habitats, but is most plentiful in woodland. Many forms occur within the same populations with dark orange-brown and unmarked brown forms being most frequent in urban districts. An attractive strongly marked black and yellow form is not uncommon in woodlands.

VCH 1904: *'Very common everywhere. The oaks in Sutton Park are in some seasons nearly stripped of their foliage by the larvae of this species. The perfect insects show great variation from a unicolorous brown to pale specimens richly marked with dark bars.'*

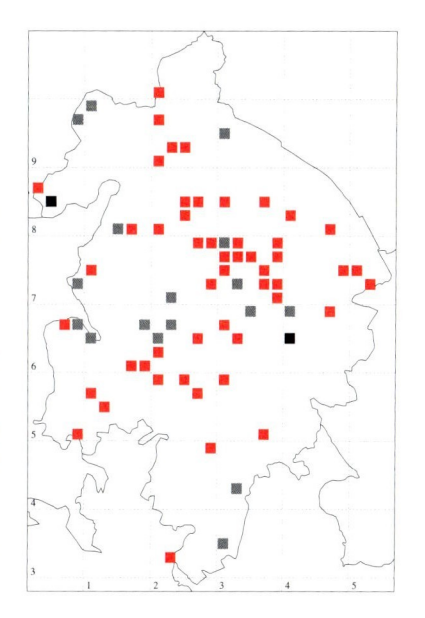

Waved Umber
1936 *Menophra abruptaria* (Thunb.)

County status: Widespread and fairly common.
Flight: Mid-April to late June.
Larval foodplants: Privet and Lilac.

The Waved Umber is found in many rural and urban districts. It is especially plentiful in woodlands, disused railway cuttings and quarries where there is a good growth of privet. The dark-brown f. *fuscata* Tutt, which has faint markings, is occasionally noted in urban parts of Coventry and Birmingham.

VCH 1904: *'Not common, but generally distributed. Comes to "light" sometimes in the suburbs of Birmingham.'*

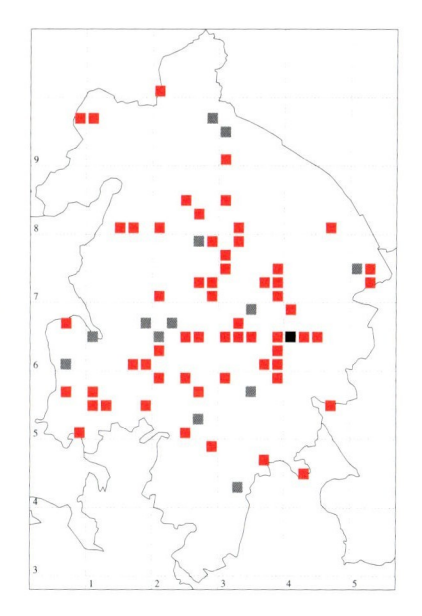

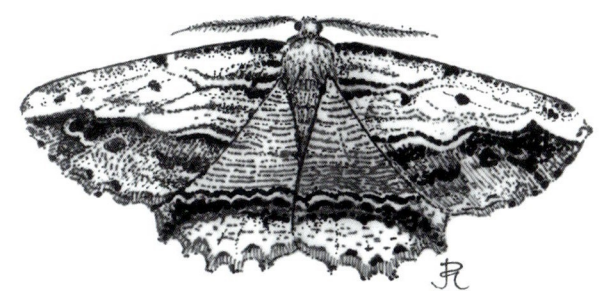

Willow Beauty
1937 *Peribatodes rhomboidaria* ([D. & S.])

County status: Widespread and common.
Flight: Early June to October. Probably bivoltine.
Larval foodplants: Polyphagous on deciduous and coniferous trees and shrubs, including Blackthorn*, Ivy* and Leyland Cypress*.

The Willow Beauty is a common and widely distributed species found in a vast range of habitats. The adult has been noted each week from early June to late October with peak numbers from mid-July to mid-August. It is a highly variable moth with specific colour forms in different districts. A light-brown form is consistently observed in many rural areas, whilst in urban parts of Coventry and Birmingham the slate-grey f. *perfumaria* Newm. is dominant with occasional melanic specimens.

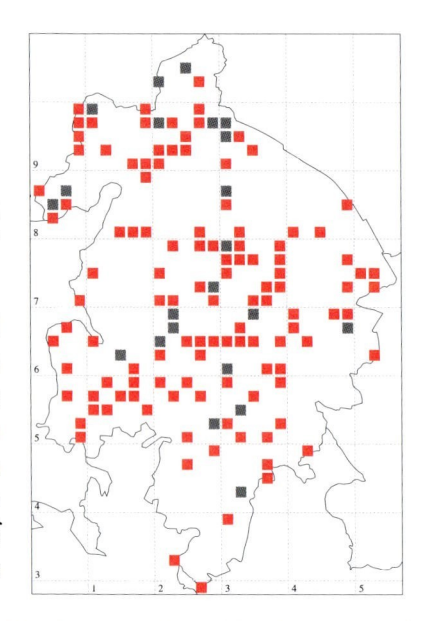

Moth trap totals in an urban Coventry garden at **Radford** give an idea of the frequency of *rhomboidaria*: 1975 (101), 1980 (154), 1985 (100), 1990 (126), 1995 (106), 2000 (117) (MCV).

VCH 1904: *'Common everywhere, especially gardens.'*

Satin Beauty
1940 *Deileptenia ribeata* (Cl.)

County status: Very local and sometimes fairly common.
Flight: Late June to mid-August.
Larval foodplants: Polyphagous on various conifers and also birches and oaks.

The Satin Beauty, having first been recorded at Frankton Wood in the early part of the twentieth century (VCH 1904), was not observed again until 31/7/1986 in Oversley Wood (DB). It is possible that this species may have been overlooked in the intervening years, but the large-scale planting of conifers during the 1950s and 1960s could have enabled *ribeata* to spread.

Records:
Oversley Wood, 31/7/1986 (DB), 8/8/1986 (AFG), 8/8/1987, 29/6/2002 (DB), 19/7/2000, 24/7/2001 (MA), 21/6/2004 (DG, AJP, NJS), 20/7/2004, 30/7/2004 (DG, AJP, VW, MA, RMC, R&SW, NJS), 18/6/2005 (DG); **Oakley Wood**, 15/7/1989 (4) (DB, AFG), 17/7/1990 (AFG), 23/6/2005 (DB); **Waverley Wood**, 19/8/1989, 6/7/1991, 28/7/2001 (AFG, Warks Moth Group), 10/7/2004 (2) (NJS, AJP); **Windmill Hill**, **Nuneaton**, 9/7/1994 (RCK); **Sutton Park**, 5/8/2000 (DB, DG); **Hillmorton**, **Rugby**, 4/7/2001 (DIP).

VCH 1904: *Frankton Wood*

Mottled Beauty
1941 *Alcis repandata repandata* (L.)

County status: Widespread and common.
Flight: Early June to late August.
Larval foodplants: Polyphagous on deciduous and coniferous trees and shrubs, including Gorse*, Blackthorn*, Honeysuckle*, oaks*, Field Maple*, Bilberry* and Heather*.

The Mottled Beauty is a common species, found in a diverse range of habitats. It is abundant in woodland but far less plentiful than *rhomboidaria* in urban districts. Brownish-grey forms are predominant in rural areas but almost entire urban populations are made up of dark forms. There appear to be no records of the banded form ab. *conversaria* Hübner, other than a singleton to MV at Bishops Hill on 20/6/2005 (SDT).

Garden moth trap totals are as follows: **Pillerton Priors:** 1992 (24), 1993 (18), 1994 (20), 2002 (9), 2003 (10), 2004 (5), 2005 (13) (CI); **Hillmorton, Rugby:** 1982 (12), 1985 (8), 1990 (12), 1995 (22), 2000 (7), 2004 (3) (DIP).

VCH 1904: *'Common everywhere.'*

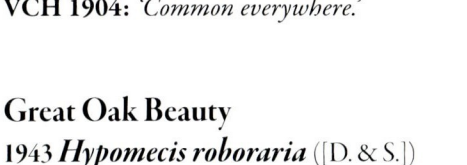

Great Oak Beauty
1943 *Hypomecis roboraria* ([D. & S.])

Nationally Scarce B

County status: Very local and uncommon.
Flight: Late June to July.
Larval foodplants: Pedunculate Oak.

There is a relict population of this magnificent species in Ryton Wood. Former colonies in Frankton Wood, Brandon Wood, Wolford Wood, Princethorpe Wood, Waverley Wood, Bubbenhall Glade and Snitterfield Bushes have all been lost due to critical woodland clearances during the first half of the twentieth century.

Ryton Wood therefore represents Warwickshire's final extant colony of this Nationally Scarce species, which has only a handful of outlying populations at protracted distances from the main strongholds in southern England.

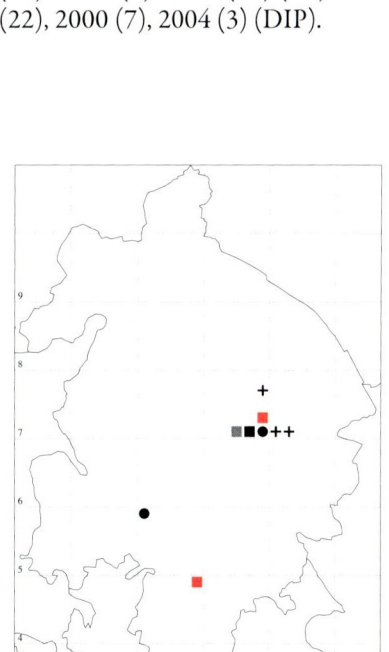

Records:
Princethorpe Wood, 1902 (f. *infuscata* Stdgr. taken), July 1907 (HL), recorded not uncommonly until 1940s (Lloyd, Chadwick, HL); **Snitterfield Bushes**, 1916 (MWB); **Bubbenhall Glade**, 6/7/1947 (LR); **Waverley Wood**, 3/7/1954 (2), 9/7/1954 (AHK), 1956, 1957 (CDNHSS); **Ryton Wood**, 27/7/1972 (DB), 24/6/1981 (2), 1/7/1981 (2), 26/7/1985 (PC, CW), 28/6/1987

(AFG), 21/6/1992 (5) (MA, DB, DW), 1992, 1993 (LB, CE); **Pillerton Priors**, 27/6/1994 presumed to have been a vagrant (CI).

VCH 1904: *'Very rare.'*
Wolford Wood, Frankton Wood, Brandon Wood, 15/7/1886, 2/7/1896 (RNHS).

Pale Oak Beauty
1944 *Hypomecis punctinalis* (Scop.)

County status: Very local and fairly common at two sites.
Flight: Late May to June.
Larval foodplants: Oaks, birches, sallows, hawthorns, Hazel.

This is another very local woodland species, which, unlike its congener, was only added to the Warwickshire list in the 1970s. It has a greater range of larval foodplants, enabling the moth to be found in a variety of wooded habitats.

Records:
Hartshill Hayes, 19/5-1979 (ANHS), 1976, 28/5/1977, 29/5/1977 (RJT); **Ryton Wood**, 28/5/1988, 10/6/1988 (DB, AFG), 1992 (LB, CE), 29/5/1992 (DB, RGB); **Oakley Wood**, 11/6/1993 (AFG, PAP); **Oversley Wood**, 8/6/1995 (DB), 7/6/2004 (RMC), 15/6/2004 (2) (DG), 26/5/2005 (7) (J. Rush), 4/6/2005 (7) (Warks Moth Group); **Charlecote**, 16/6/1995 (DB); **Temple Grafton**, 31/5/2004 (AFG).

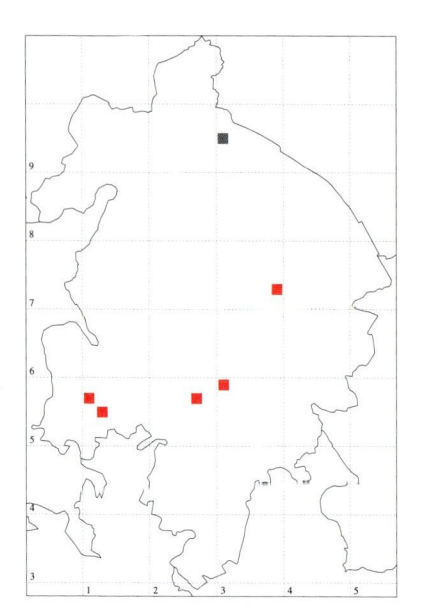

Brussels Lace
1945 *Cleorodes lichenaria* (Hufn.)

Nationally Local

County status: Extinct.
Flight: No dates available.
Larval foodplants: Lichens growing on branches and stems of woody plants and walls.

Rugby, pre-1893 (A. Sidgwick, 1893).

VCH 1904: *Wolford.*

Engrailed
1947 *Ectropis bistortata* (Goeze)

County status: Widespread and fairly common.
Flight: Two generations. February to mid-May, and late June to early September.
Larval foodplants: Polyphagous on deciduous trees and shrubs, including oaks*, Ash*, Blackthorn*, brambles* and sallows*.

This species and the Small Engrailed are the subject of much controversy and confusion. Continental authorities maintain the two are synonymous since it has recently been found they cannot be distinguished on wing markings or genitalia (Waring, Townsend & Lewington, 2003). Consequently, records of distribution and frequency in Warwickshire may be inaccurate.

Large populations of Engrailed are established in many woodlands, first generation specimens arriving copiously at MV; for example, Oversley Wood, 5/3/1992 (43) (DB, AFG, RMC). Second generation imagines are smaller in size and lower in abundance. A particularly late specimen was caught at Temple Grafton, 7/10/2005 (AFG). Melanic forms occur in most woodland populations.

VCH 1904: *'Fairly common and generally distributed. The commoner form has slight markings and is evenly dusted with grey.'*

Small Engrailed
1948 *Ectropis crepuscularia* ([D. & S.])

Nationally Local

County status: Fairly widespread and fairly common.
Flight: Mid-May to mid-June.
Larval foodplants: Polyphagous on deciduous trees and shrubs, including Alder*, sallows* and hawthorns*.

The Small Engrailed flies in a single brood between those of the preceding species. Records suggest that it is distinctly less widespread and numerous, although found in similar well-wooded habitats. This may in part be due to the fact that identification difficulties arise frequently and, as with *bistortata*, much of the resulting data may be inaccurate.

VCH 1904: *'I am told that all our specimens are **bistortata** and that **crespuscularia** is not a Midland insect. I confess, however, that I cannot follow the distinctions or synonymy of this pair of species.'*

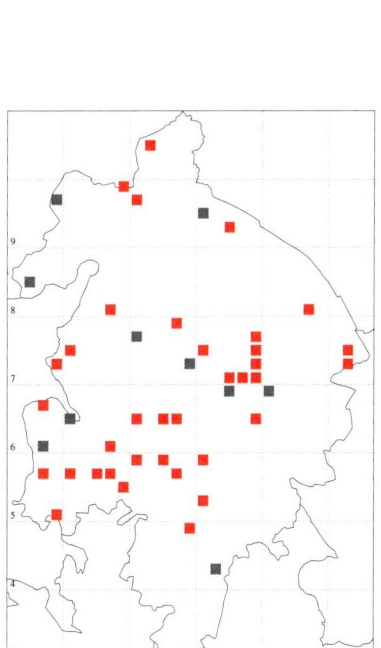

Square Spot
1949 *Paradarisa consonaria* (Hb.)

Nationally Local

County status: Very local and fairly common at one site.
Flight: Late April to late May.
Larval foodplants: Oaks, birches, Beech, Hornbeam, pines and Yew.

The Square Spot is a relatively recent addition to the Warwickshire list, being first noted during the 1960s in Sutton Park (JB). There are, however, no recent records from this location. The only existing population of this Nationally Local woodland species is at Oversley Wood, where it may sometimes be plentiful.

Records:
Sutton Park, 1960s (JB); **Oversley Wood**, 16/5/1987 (3) (DB, RMC); 29/5/1987 (2) (AFG), 12/5/1989 (DB, RGB), 19/5/1989 (DB, AFG, IGMR, PJR), 25/5/1991 (15) (Warks Moth Group), 30/4/1992 (3), 21/5/1994 (3) (DB, RMC), 1/5/2004 (11), 26/5/2005 (6) (J. Rush).

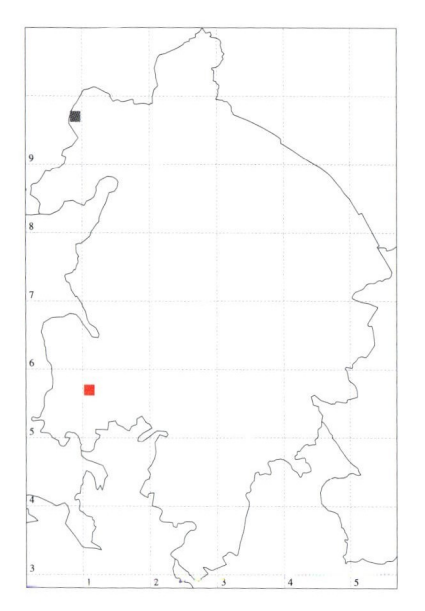

Brindled White-spot
1950 *Parectropis similaria* (Hufn.)

Nationally Local

County status: Fairly widespread and fairly common.
Flight: Early May to late June.
Larval foodplants: Pedunculate Oak, Hazel, Common Hawthorn, Midland Hawthorn, birches and sallows*.

The Brindled White-spot is well established and fairly plentiful at a number of ancient woodland sites. There are good populations in Ufton Wood, Ryton Wood, Wappenbury Wood, Brandon Wood, Tile Hill Wood, Kingsbury Wood, Snitterfield Bushes, Oversley Wood, Rough Hill Wood and Wolford Wood.

VCH 1904: *'Rare.'*
Wolford Wood, Brandon Wood, Rugby area, Whitchurch.

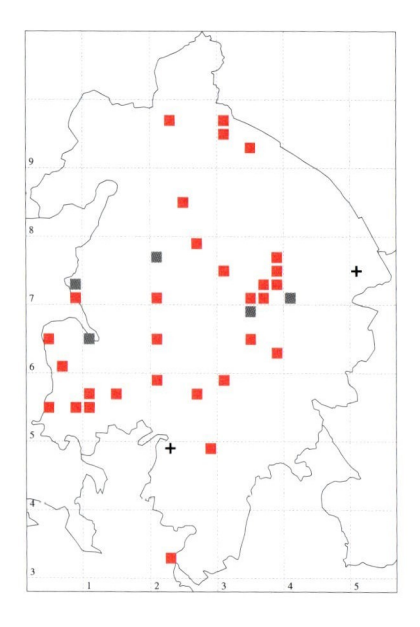

Grey Birch
1951 *Aethalura punctulata* ([D. & S.])

County status: Fairly widespread and fairly common.
Flight: Mid-April to June and occasionally July to early August.
Larval foodplants: Birches* and Alder*.

The Grey Birch is locally fairly plentiful in broadleaved woodlands containing birches. It has been recorded from a large number of sites; healthy populations exist at Hay Wood, Bubbenhall Wood, Oakley Wood, Snitterfield Bushes, Old Park Wood and Wolford Wood.

This species is also found at lower density in rural and suburban districts with isolated birch trees.

VCH 1904: *'Not common.'*
Coventry, Atherstone, Brandon Wood.

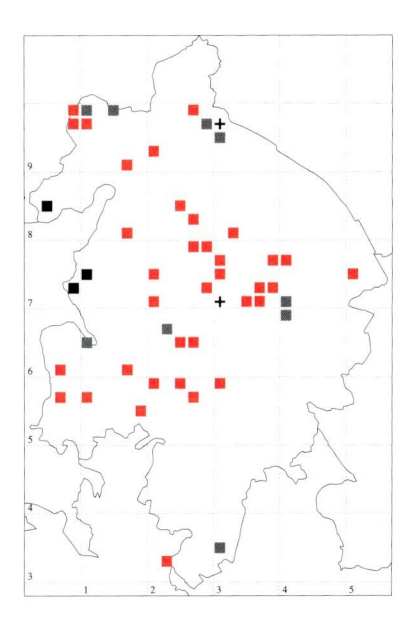

Common Heath
1952 *Ematurga atomaria atomaria* (L.)

County status: Very local and scarce.
Flight: Day-flying in May and June.
Larval foodplants: Heather on heathland; trefoils, clovers and vetches elsewhere.

The Common Heath is rarely encountered, being restricted to heathland in the north of the County and calcareous grassland in the south.

Records:
Sutton Park, 1929 (LJE), 1960s (JB), 1970s (LJE), 1980s (AW, RJB), 23/5/1998 (MS), 25/5/1999 (HF); **Clowes Wood & New Fallings Coppice**, 1939 (BNHS); **Brandon Wood**, 3/6/1962 (LEM); **Oxhouse Farm, Combrook**, 13/6/1976 (JRR); **Bidford-on-Avon**, 1981–84 (RMC); **Hampton Magna**, 16/6/1985 (PJR); **Shipston-on-Stour (railway cutting)**, 17/5/1988 (SAL); **Goldicote Cutting**, 10/5/1992, 25/5/1992 (CI); **Ashlawn Cutting**, 4/6/1997, 18/6/1997 (MS); **Shotteswell**, 9/6/1997 (MS); **Bishops Bowl**, 11/6/1997 (MS); **Hartshill**, 7/6/1998 (VW).

VCH 1904: *Sutton Park, Atherstone, Wolford.*

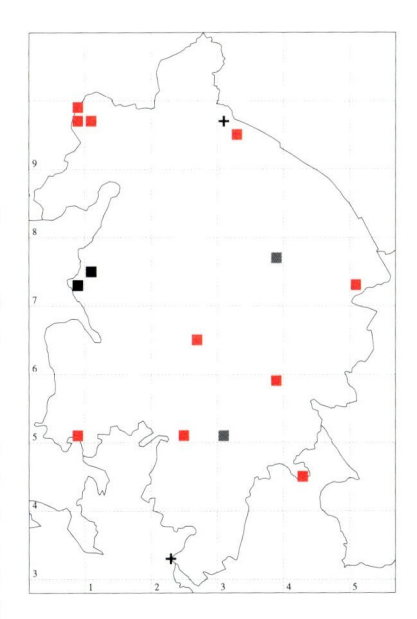

Bordered White
1954 *Bupalus piniaria* (L.)

County status: Widespread and fairly common.
Flight: Late May to early August.
Larval foodplants: Mainly mature Scots Pine*; also other pines, spruces and Larch.

The Bordered White is generally plentiful in woodlands where there are well-established pine plantations. On warm, sunny days the males have been observed flying around tree-tops. There are particularly strong colonies in Hay Wood, Brandon Wood, Waverley Wood, Oakley Wood, Oversley Wood and Coughton Park.

Garden moth traps in districts with isolated pines record the occasional specimen.

Univoltine with a protracted flight period, peak numbers occurring in late-June to mid-July.

VCH 1904: *'Very common'* in Sutton Park, also recorded from Brandon Wood, Frankton Wood, Princethorpe Wood and Knowle.

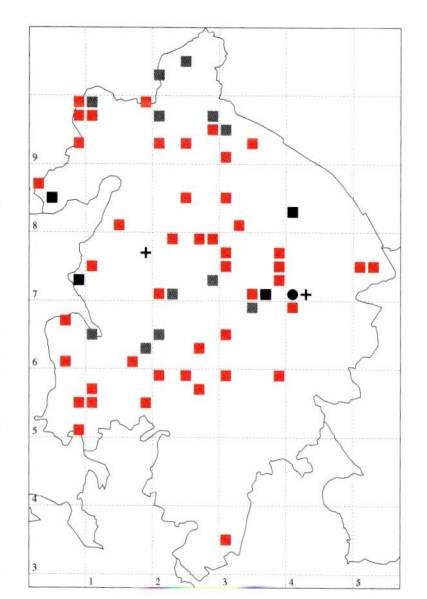

Common White Wave
1955 *Cabera pusaria* (L.)

County status: Widespread and fairly common.
Flight: Early May to August with occasional individuals in September.
Larval foodplants: Birches*, Alder* and sallows*.

The Common White Wave is a widely distributed species. It is particularly abundant in deciduous woodland and scrub. The imago has been observed continuously between May and September with peaks reported in late June and July. It is possibly double-brooded, although there is no firm evidence from larval records to prove this.

The following garden moth trap totals give an idea of the frequency in a well-wooded garden:
Kenilworth Rd, Coventry: 2001 (17), 2002 (24), 2003 (15) (MA).

VCH 1904: *'Common everywhere.'*

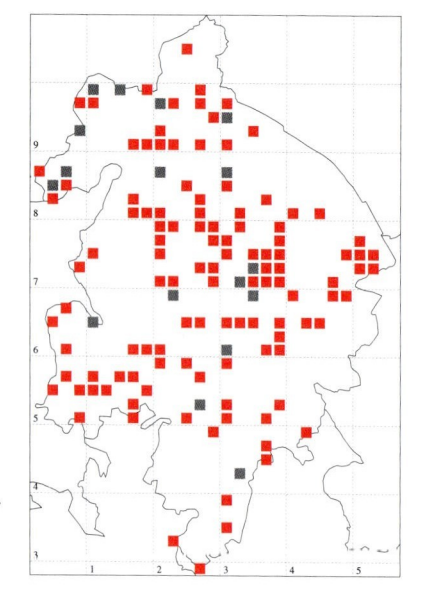

Common Wave
1956 *Cabera exanthemata* (Scop.)

County status: Widespread and occasionally fairly common.
Flight: Early May to August with occasional individuals in September.
Larval foodplants: Willows, sallows*, Aspen and poplars.

The Common Wave shows a preference for damper habitats. It is found in a number of woodland and wetland sites but is generally less plentiful than *pusaria*.

The following garden moth trap counts provide a comparison of numbers:
Kenilworth Rd, Coventry: 2001 (6), 2002 (2), 2003 (9) (MA)

VCH 1904: *'Common everywhere.'*

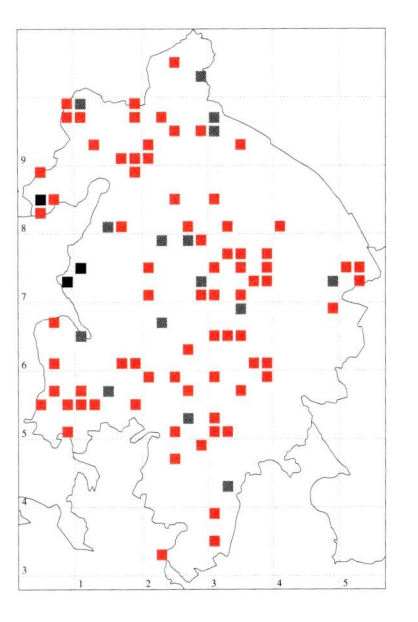

White-pinion Spotted
1957 *Lomographa bimaculata* (Fabr.)

County status: Widespread and fairly common.
Flight: May to late June.
Larval foodplants: Blackthorn and hawthorns*.

A relatively recent coloniser of Warwickshire, first noted at Bannam's Wood during the 1960s (FAN).

The White-pinion Spotted has increased dramatically since 1970. It now occurs over much of the County and often in very good quantity, especially in deciduous woodland and hawthorn scrub. For example, Oversley Wood, 7/6/2004 (24) (RMC, DG, AJP).

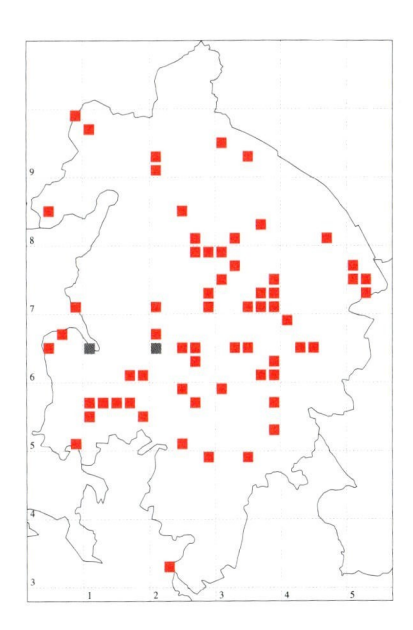

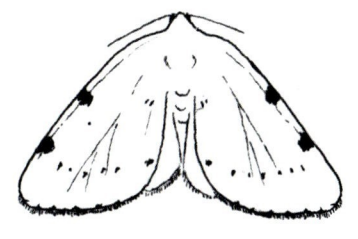

Clouded Silver
1958 *Lomographa temerata* ([D. & S.])

County status: Widespread and fairly common.
Flight: Mid-May to late July.
Larval foodplants: Common Hawthorn*, Midland Hawthorn, Blackthorn*, plum, cherry, Crab Apple and cultivated Apple.

This species has increased enormously since the VCH 1904. The Clouded Silver is now widely distributed and plentiful in woodlands, scrub and mature gardens in both rural and built-up districts. It is often disturbed during the daytime from herbage.

Garden moth trap counts are as follows: **Pillerton Priors:** 1992 (24), 1993 (28), 1994 (25), 2002 (9), 2003 (21), 2004 (19), 2005 (45) (CI); **Hillmorton, Rugby:** 1982 (28), 1985 (25), 1990 (22), 1995 (16), 2000 (19), 2004 (27) (DIP).

VCH 1904: *'Rare.'*
Frankton Wood and Wolford Wood only.

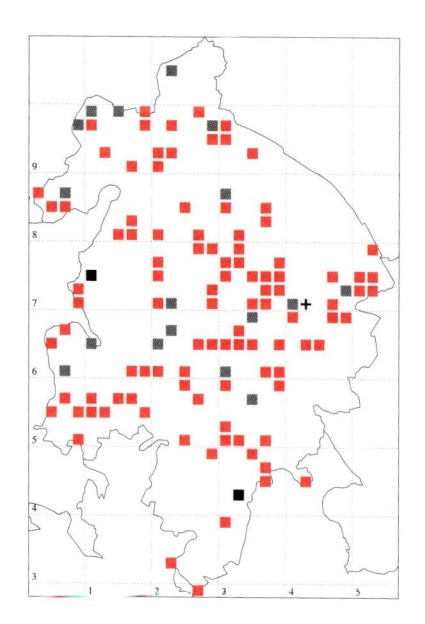

Early Moth
1960 *Theria primaria* (Haw.)

County status: Fairly widespread and locally common.
Flight: January to mid-March.
Larval foodplants: Hawthorns*, Blackthorn*, Crab Apple*, wild roses*.

As its English name implies, the Early Moth is generally the first species to appear in the New Year. It can be found after dark, resting on bare twigs of Blackthorn and hawthorn hedges; for example, Wellesbourne Wood, 8/2/1971 (over 80 found resting on hawthorns) (DB).

The moth is sluggish and consequently moth traps do not give an accurate assessment of frequency; however, the scattered records of specimens recorded by this method in open woodland and isolated hedgerows do cover quite a large area of the County.

Interestingly larvae have been found in Warwickshire on previously unrecorded plants: Coombe Fields, 3/6/1973 larvae on wild rose (MCV); Gospel Oak, 8/5/1983 larvae on Crab Apple (MCV).

VCH 1904: *'Common throughout the County.'*

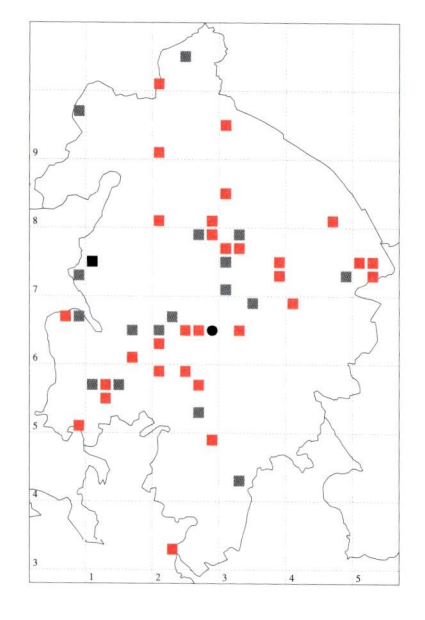

Light Emerald
1961 *Campaea margaritata* (L.)

County status: Widespread and common.
Flight: June to mid-August. A partial second generation in September and early October is becoming almost annual.
Larval foodplants: Polyphagous on deciduous trees and shrubs, including Ash*, apple*, birches*, Beech*, Alder*, Field Maple*, plum*, Blackthorn* and oaks*.

The Light Emerald has been reported throughout the County but less frequently in urban districts. It is found in a number of habitats, including woodland, parks, railway embankments, wetlands and gardens. This species may often be disturbed during the daytime or detected at rest on the undersides of leaves.

The last decade has produced almost annual records of second generation individuals during September and October.

The table below shows a comparison of annual moth trap totals in urban, suburban (wooded) and rural gardens:

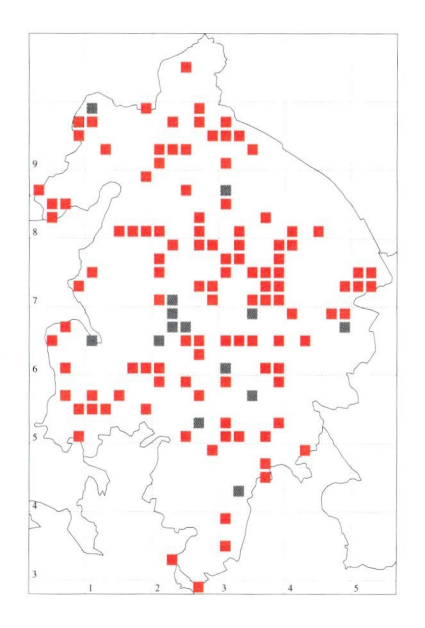

Habitat	Location	2001	2002	2003
Urban	Radford, Coventry (MCV)	9	0	6
Wooded Suburban	Kenilworth Rd, Coventry (MA)	68	66	118
Rural	Charlecote (DB)	10	24	41

VCH 1904: *'Common and generally distributed.'*

Barred Red
1962 *Hylaea fasciaria* (L.)

County status: Widespread and fairly common.
Flight: June to mid-August.
Larval foodplants: Scots Pine*, Douglas Fir, Norway Spruce and other conifers.

The Barred Red is locally plentiful in woodlands containing fir and pine plantations, such as Brandon Wood, Hay Wood, Oakley Wood, Waverley Wood, Coughton Park, Bentley Park Wood and Oversley Wood. It is occasionally noted in districts with solitary conifers.

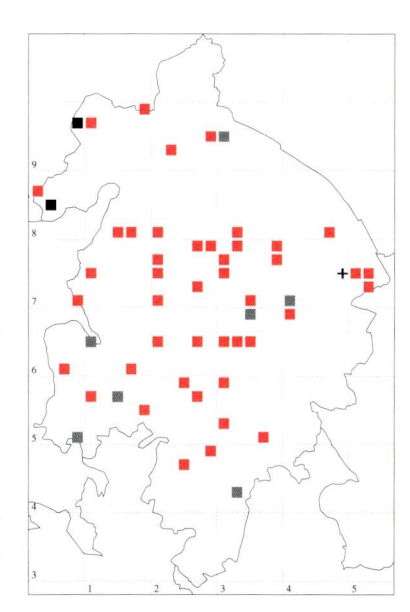

The table below compares garden trap totals in urban and rural districts:

Habitat	Location	1967–77	1978–88	1989–99	2000–04
Urban	Radford, Coventry (MCV)	1	13	5	3
Rural	Charlecote (DB)	0	8	4	4

VCH 1904: *'Occurs in Sutton Park, but not commonly, the only other record is from Overslade.'*

Annulet
1964 *Charissa obscurata* ([D. & S.])

Nationally Local

County status: Very local and uncommon.
Flight: Late July to August.
Larval foodplants: Common Bird's-foot-trefoil, Kidney Vetch, Wild Strawberry, Wild Thyme, Salad Burnet, Heather and many other herbaceous plants.

Formerly recorded on the heathland at Sutton Park populations have more recently been discovered in the quarries and abandoned tips of the Nuneaton area.

Records:
Sutton Park, 1940 (HEH); **Hartshill Hayes**, 1975–79 frequent (RJT); Woodlands Quarry, 10/8/1977, 19/8/1978, 25/8/1978, 1/8/1980, 13/8/1980 (2) (RJT); **Camp Hill**, Nuneaton, 1978 (AG); **Dosthill**, 7/8/1982 (PBD); **Waverley Wood**, 18/8/1983 (CW); **Judkins Quarry**, Nuneaton, 23/7/2005 (2) (MK, RR).

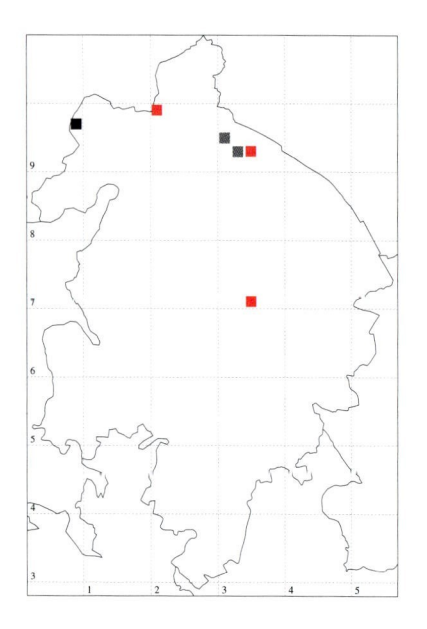

Grey Scalloped Bar
1969 *Dyscia fagaria* (Thunb.)

Nationally Local

County status: Presumed extinct.
Flight: June and July.
Larval foodplants: Heathers.

This Nationally Local heathland species was recorded from Sutton Park during the 1960s (JB). There have been no records since and it is assumed that this attractive moth is now extinct.

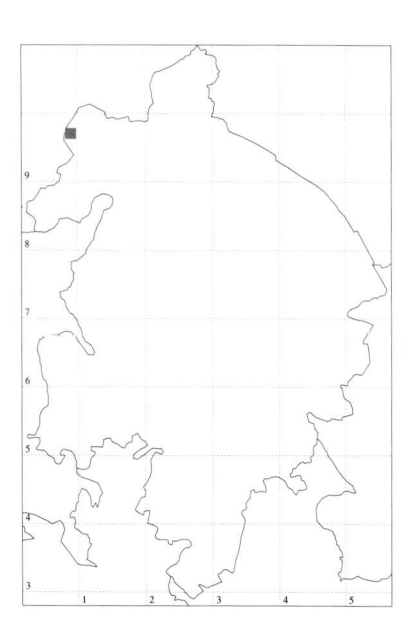

Grass Wave
1970 *Perconia strigillaria* (Hb.)

Nationally Local

County status: Very local and uncommon.
Flight: May, June and August.
Larval foodplants: Heathers, Broom and Petty Whin.

This heathland species has existed in Sutton Park for many years, latterly at very low density. It is easily disturbed from the heather by day.

Records:
Clowes Wood, 1938–53 occasionally flushed from herbage (BNHS); **Austy Wood**, 1947 (2) (HEH); **Sutton Park**, 1940–1970 (JB, LJE), 5/8/2000 (4) (DG).

VCH 1904: *Sutton Park*

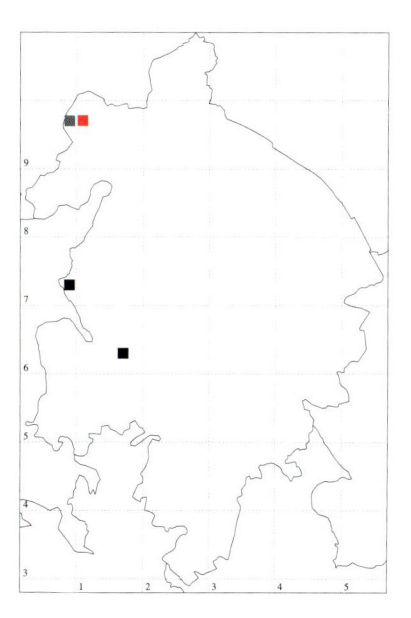

Family: Sphingidae—Hawk-Moths

A family of generally large and impressive moths, powerfully built and strong flyers. There are eight immigrants in addition to the nine resident British species. A noteworthy 16 members of this family have been recorded in Warwickshire during the last 70 years, two of which have unfortunately become extinct. Some possess a long proboscis, enabling nectar to be taken in flight as they hover close to flowers, whilst the Smerinthinae have a proboscis of reduced length and do not feed at all.

The name, 'Sphingidae' refers to the sphinx-like attitude that some caterpillars adopt with the head and front segments reared up. Many of the larvae are brightly coloured and can be distinguished by a horn on the eleventh segment.

Convolvulus Hawk-moth
1972 *Agrius convolvuli* (L.)

Regular immigrant, sometimes common: Mediterranean and North Africa

County status: Occasional immigrant.
Flight: August to October.
Larval foodplants: Bindweeds.

The Convolvulus Hawk-moth is recorded in Warwickshire every few years. It is occasionally found at rest on vertical objects, but the majority are recorded at light during the late summer and autumn.

Records:

1846—**Wolford,** numbers recorded (WCEW).
1868—**Birmingham,** common in the district (FE).
1872—**Warwick** (PPB).
1875—**Solihull,** 24/9 (WL).
1876—**Rugby,** September (WSE).
1877—**Kingswood,** 20/9 (Recorder unknown).
1886—**Wolford,** (WCEW).
1887—**Birmingham,** (WTR).
1888—**Rugby,** (WSE).
1898—**Birmingham,** (ADI); **Solihull,** (AHM).
1901—**Hampton-in-Arden,** (GWW).
1903—**Atherstone,** 26/9 male found at rest on a door (Recorder unknown) (Baker, 1903).
1922—**Knowle,** (SEWC).
1950—**Middle Tysoe,** 28/8 (TT); **Tysoe,** 6/9 (TT).
1951—**Long Itchington,** 7/9 (AHK); **Baginton,** 30/9 (Recorder unknown).
1953—**Solihull,** 15/8 (SEWC).
1956—**Radford Semele,** 5/9 (Recorder unknown).
1970—**Chrysler factory, Ryton-on-Dunsmore,** 5/10 (LEM).
1972—**Harbury,** 12/9 (MrsG).
1974—**Hampton Wood,** 18/8 (AFG).
1976—**Amington, Tamworth,** 23/9 (GAA); **Woodloes, Warwick,** 2/10 (EIG); **Marton,** (GR).
1979—**Marton,** 11/9 (RA).
1982—**Charlecote,** 20/9 (AFG).
1983—**Charlecote,** 3/9 (DB), 4/10 (AFG).
1984—**Pailton,** 26/7 (KCG); **Kenilworth,** 26/7 female found by Mrs. T. Douthwaite (LEM).
1985—**Claverdon,** 28/8 (IGMR); **NVRS, Wellesbourne,** 30/9 (JAH).
1986—**Hillmorton, Rugby,** 13/10 (DIP).
1989—**Packwood,** 15/8 specimen brought in dead by cat (JMd).
1990—**Charlecote,** 22/9 (DB);
1991—**Wellesbourne,** 24/9 (TS); **Tysoe,** 1/10 specimen found at rest on garage door (JAH); **CAD Kineton,** 14/10 (MGW); **Oversley Wood,** specimen on Pine trunk (RJs).
1995—**Weddington, Nuneaton,** September (IC, PTn).
1996—**Bidford-on-Avon,** 2/9 (RMC).
1997—**Knowle,** 6/9 specimen at rest on door frame (LBr).
1998—**Charlecote,** 10/9 (DB); **Bishops Tachbrook,** 24/8 (MHk).
2003—**Pillerton Priors,** 18/8 (CI); **Norton Lindsey,** 31/8 specimen at rest on fence post (HCl).
2004—**Temple Grafton,** 22/9 (AFG).

VCH 1904: *'Only odd stragglers in Convolvuli years, several have been recorded in Birmingham and its suburbs.'*

Death's-head Hawk-moth
1973 *Acherontia atropos* (L.)

Regular immigrant: Mediterranean and North Africa

County status: Occasional immigrant.
Flight: June to early July and September to October.
Larval foodplants: Potato*, Woody Nightshade*, Jasmine*.

The Death's-head Hawk-moth is sometimes noticed by members of the general public, but strangely there have been no records of the adult in moth traps. The majority of sightings are as larvae, formerly in potato fields, but with changing farming practices it is more frequently noted on small allotments, gardens or amongst clumps of nightshade.

Records:

1867—**Chalcot Wood**, (WH).
1872—**Rugby**, (RNHS).
1874—**Solihull**, (AHM).
1889—**Water Orton**, (RCB);
Hillmorton, Rugby, 16/8 larva (RNHS).
1900—**Whitchurch**, very common (JHB);
Atherstone, (CB);
Warwick, (PPB);
Wolford Wood, (A);
Knowle, (HWE).
1910—**Packwood**, pupae (SEWC).
1949—**Long Itchington**, 4/10, 7/10, 8/10 pupae (AHK).
1950—**Tysoe**, 9/8 larva feeding on Woody Nightshade (TT, DWn);
Walton, 18/9 larva (MHC);
Long Itchington, 2/10, 23/10 pupae (AHK).
1951—**Meriden**, 13/10 pupa (VRH).
1955—**Atherstone**, Sept. (JWS).
1956—**Birmingham**, 9/9 adult (CN);
Coventry, (3) (MEC);
Royal Leamington Spa, (WTT).
1957—**Kineton & Charlecote**, larvae (recorder unknown).
1963—**Lower Haselor**, 21/10 adult (EWJ);
1976—**College Farm, Princethorpe**, 5/8 a few pupae in potato field (GR, RA).
1980—**Southam**, 28/9 specimen found in a drive being poked by a cat.
1983—**Regal Road, Stratford-upon-Avon**, 12/7 adult dropped out of Whitbread's warehouse doorway (DHB);

Pailton, 1/9 worn female (KCG);
Kingsbury Water Park 12/10 specimen found dead in grass field (EAH).
1984—**Loxley**, 20/10 (2) larvae feeding on Jasmine (JRwn).
1985—**Barton**, 8/7 adult (DHB).
1986—**Fen End, Kenilworth** , 2/9 pupa (IGMR).
1990—**Fenny Compton churchyard**, 5/9 (7) larvae feeding on Woody Nightshade (AFG).
1991—**Welford-on-Avon**, 15/9 (12) pupae on allotment (DHB).
Long Itchington, 24/11 pupa found under potatoes (Mr Grubb).
1996—**Sutton-under-Brailes**, 29/9 fully-grown larva on garden potato plant (MP).
1998—**Wasperton Hill Farm, Barford**, 16/9 larva on garden potato plant (CC).
2003—**Stockton**, 14/8 a few larvae (recorder unknown);
Stratford-upon-Avon post sorting office, 9/9 adult found, reported to Stratford Butterfly House.
2004—**Haselor**, larva (CH);
Polesworth, adult found on lamp-post (JA).
2005—**Cheylesmore, Coventry**, 13/7 adult found at Quinton Pool and taken to the local Vet (MC; confirmed NJS).

VCH 1904: *'In the years when this species is common in England, we get our share and hear of its occurrence in the larval stage in potato fields.'*

Privet Hawk-moth
1976 *Sphinx ligustri* (L.)

County status: Very local and uncommon.
Flight: June and July.
Larval foodplants: Privet*, Ash, Lilac.

Favoured habitats of this species include disused railway cuttings, open woodland and scrub, especially on calcareous soils. Wilmcote Rough was a well-known site during the first half of the twentieth century (SEWC, GBM). In the 1950s the Privet Hawk-moth enjoyed a period of comparative plenty. The ensuing years witnessed a steady fall in numbers throughout the County, followed by an even sharper decline from the 1970s onwards. There are encouraging signs, however, of a recent resurgence in south Warwickshire.

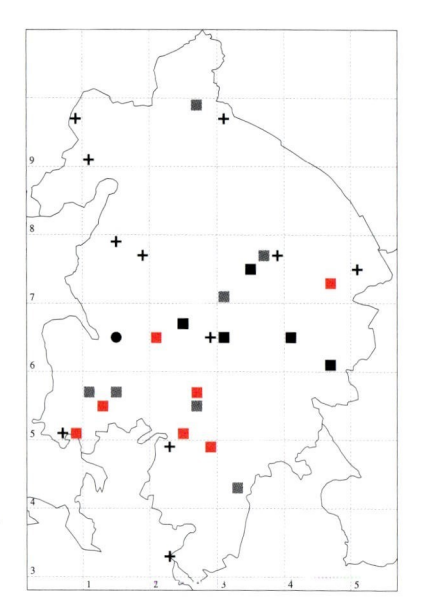

Records since 1970:
Charlecote, 11/7/1971, 21/6/2005 (DB); **Hinckley district**, 1970s (RJT); **Claverdon**, 29/6/1982 (IGMR); **Cawston, Rugby**, 1984 larva (DCsh); **Bearley Station**, 30/5/1989 (IGMR); **Bidford-on-Avon**, 24/6/1992, 1/7/2004 (RMC); **Goldicote Cutting**, 11/6/2004 (CI); **Pillerton Priors**, 23/6/2005 (CI); **Temple Grafton**, 14/7/2005 (AFG).

VCH 1904: *'Not common.'*
Odd specimens at Knowle, Salford Priors, Solihull, Rugby, Sutton Coldfield, Brandon Wood, Warwick, Atherstone, Whitchurch, and Wolford.

Pine Hawk-moth
1978 *Hyloicus pinastri* (L.)
Nationally Local

County status: Vagrant.
Flight: June to late July.
Larval foodplants: Scots Pine.

This species is resident in southern England and East Anglia with outlying populations in Bedfordshire and Oxfordshire; these are the nearest known stations to Warwickshire. Since the 1980s there have been occasional appearances of vagrant Pine Hawk-moth in the County. During 2005 the number of sightings more than doubled, making permanent establishment a distinct possibility in the near future.

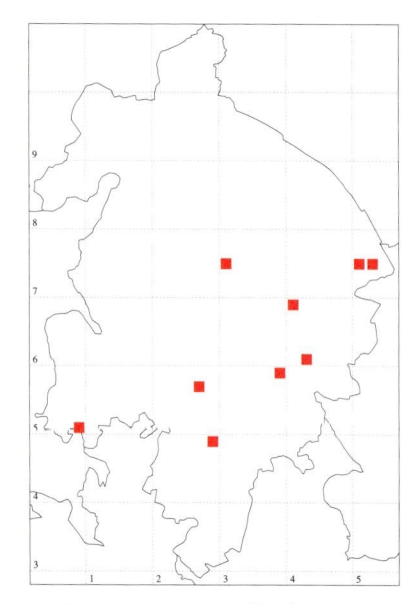

Records:
Charlecote, 28/6/1982, 17/7/1991 (AFG); **Welsh Road, Southam**, 30/7/1991 (IM); **Marton**, 18/7/1995 (RA); **Pillerton Priors**, 7/6/2004 (CI); **Central Rugby**, 23/6/2005 (IGMR); **Hillmorton, Rugby**, 23/6/2005, 19/7/2005 (DIP); **Kenilworth Rd, Coventry**, 24/6/2005 (MA); **Bishops Hill**, 14/7/2005 (NJS); **Bidford-on-Avon**, 25/7/2005 (RMC).

Lime Hawk-moth
1979 *Mimas tiliae* (L.)

County status: Widespread and fairly common.
Flight: Late April to early July.
Larval foodplants: Limes*, elms*, Alder* and birches*.

The Lime Hawk-moth is found throughout Warwickshire, but since the advent of Dutch elm disease rural districts have seen a reduction in numbers. Populations have remained constant in urban areas; in Warwick, Royal Leamington Spa, Coventry and Birmingham fully grown larvae are frequently observed crawling on tarmac pavements beneath lime trees.

The following annual garden moth trap totals at **Charlecote** (DB) illustrate how this species was suddenly affected by Dutch elm disease:
1970 (24), 1971 (15), 1972 (2), 1973 (4), 1974 (0), 1975 (0), 1976 (10), 1977 (1), 1978 (4), 1979 (0), 1980 (2).

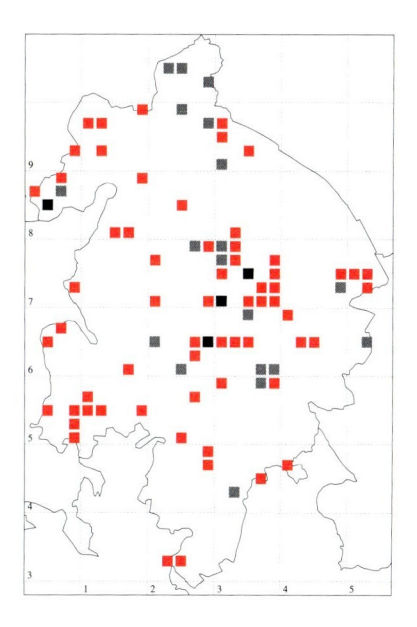

Note: The sequence of decline was halted temporarily during the extraordinary heat wave of 1976, which triggered dispersal and an unexpected influx of *tiliae* during late June and July.

VCH 1904: '*Less common than the Eyed Hawk but generally distributed.*'

Eyed Hawk-moth
1980 *Smerinthus ocellata* (L.)

County status: Widespread and fairly common.
Flight: May to mid-July with an occasional partial second generation in late August and September.
Larval foodplants: Sallows*, willows* and apple*.

The Eyed Hawk-moth is widely distributed but is not found as plentifully as the Poplar Hawk-moth. It frequents open woodland, wetlands, river valleys, railway embankments, orchards and sheltered gardens. The adult has been noted as early as 25/4/1997 at Hillmorton, Rugby (PN), and as late as 13/9/1971 at Wasperton (REd).

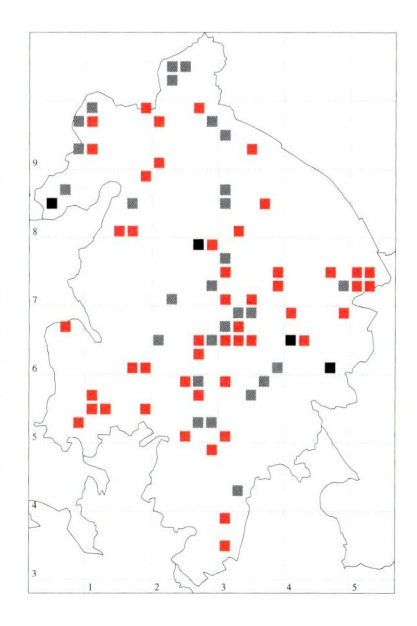

Comparative moth trap totals show numbers of adults to be greatest in sheltered suburban gardens:

Habitat	Location	1982	1985	1990	1995	2000
Urban	Radford, Coventry (MCV)	0	0	3	1	8
Suburban	Hillmorton, Rugby (DIP)	9	10	20	2	3
Rural	Charlecote (DB)	4	0	5	0	3

VCH 1904: *'Fairly common, but less so than Poplar Hawk-moth.'*

Poplar Hawk-moth
1981 *Laothoe populi* (L.)

County status: Widespread and fairly common.
Flight: Late April to August with individuals occasionally representing a partial second generation during September.
Larval foodplants: Poplars*, Aspen*, sallows* and willows*.

The Poplar Hawk-moth is a widespread species occurring in urban, suburban and rural districts. In built-up areas poplars tend to be the larval foodplant, but in woodland Aspen and sallows are favoured. Adults may sometimes be very common at MV; for example, Oversley Wood 22/7/1974 (64), 8/7/1977 (62), 5/6/1981 (48) (DB).

This moth is a regular visitor to garden moth traps and like the preceding species is plentiful in suburban districts, as the table below illustrates:

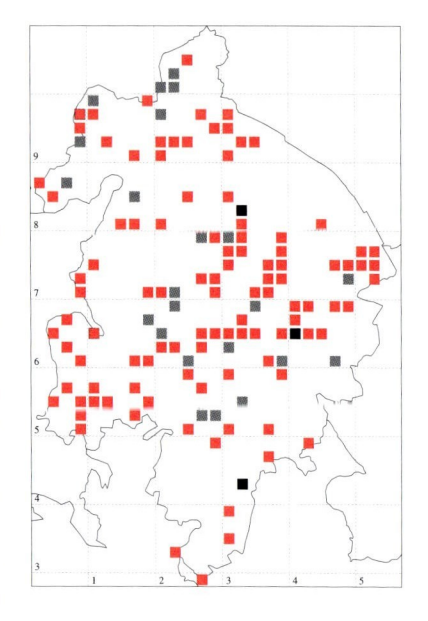

Habitat	Location	1982	1985	1990	1995	2000
Urban	Radford, Coventry (MCV)	7	9	5	4	12
Suburban	Hillmorton, Rugby (DIP)	81	77	89	77	33
Rural	Charlecote (DB)	33	6	15	19	43

VCH 1904: *'Common everywhere.'*

Narrow-bordered Bee Hawk-moth
1982 *Hemaris tityus* (L.)

Nationally Scarce B

County status: Extinct.
Flight: June.
Larval foodplants: Devil's-bit Scabious.

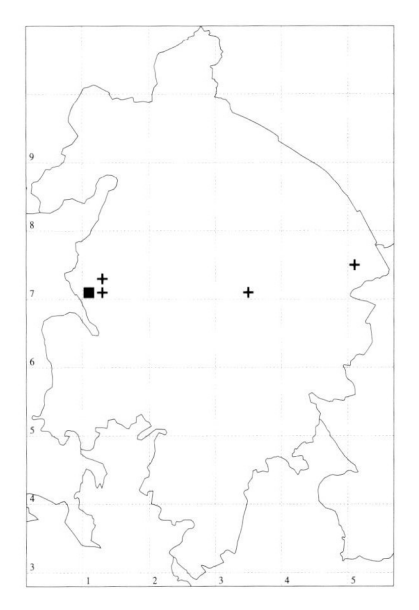

The last Warwickshire record of this now Nationally Scarce species was on 10/6/1936 at Tanworth-in-Arden (WB).

VCH 1904: *Chalcot Woods, Knowle, Umberslade, Waverley Wood and Rugby.*

Broad-bordered Bee Hawk-moth
1983 *Hemaris fuciformis* (L.)

Nationally Scarce B

County status: Extinct.
Flight: May to mid-July.
Larval foodplants: Wild Honeysuckle.

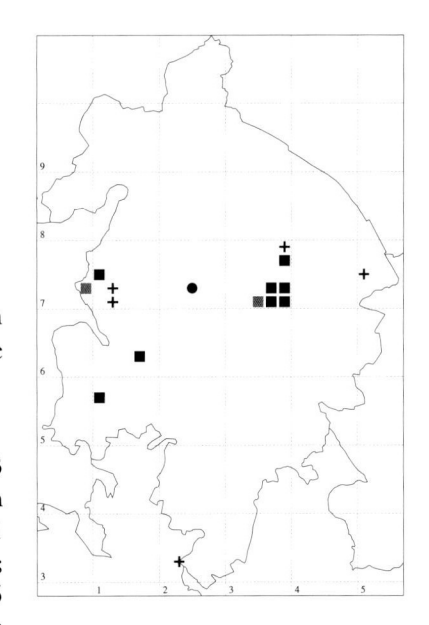

The cessation of coppicing and increasing coniferisation at key woodland sites in the County contributed to the demise of this impressive moth.

Records:
Umberslade, 1900–07 (EWC); **Chase Wood,** 3/6/1923 (FHL); **Bubbenhall Glade,** 21/5/1938 (LR); **Ryton Wood,** 1940s (FHL); **Wappenbury Wood,** 20/5/1941 (TT); **Waverley Wood,** 20/5/1941, 15/7/1956 (TT); **Oversley Wood,** 1/6/1942 (FHL); **Clowes Wood,** 1945 (3) (HEH), 1947 (3) (KGVS), 1956 scarce (BNHS); **Princethorpe Wood,** 13/6/1948 (AHK); **Austy Wood,** 1949 two at Bugle flowers (HEH); **Brandon Wood,** 17/6/1951, 24/6/1951, 1/7/1951, 8/6/1954 (AHK).

VCH 1904: *Waverley Wood, Brandon Wood, Bubbenhall Glade, Chalcot Woods, Coombe Wood, Umberslade and Wolford Wood.*

Humming-bird Hawk-moth
1984 *Macroglossum stellatarum* (L.)

Frequent immigrant, sometimes common: Southern Europe and North Africa

County status: Regular immigrant.
Flight: Day-flying. Mid-June to mid-November.
Larval foodplants: Hedge Bedstraw, Lady's Bedstraw* and Wild Madder.

The Humming-bird Hawk-moth was fairly regularly observed in Warwickshire from the 1940s to the 1960s and since 1970 has become an almost annual visitor. 2003 was a particularly good year, the adult's spectacular hovering flight being witnessed by many members of the general public for the first time. It was reported to be feeding from a number of flowers, including buddleia, valerian, Honeysuckle, Petunia and Jasmine. A record 10 larvae were found on Lady's Bedstraw in the garden of Ashorne House (Ashorne village) on 31/7/2003 (BL).

There is evidence of the occasional specimen attempting to overwinter; for example, 24/12/1947 Tysoe (CEd) and in Coventry on 21/1/1977 (RJT) and 13/3/1993 (CL).

VCH 1904: *'This species could occur anywhere in good migration years and is not uncommon sometimes locally.'*
Sutton (PWA), Aston (CJWd), Solihull (AHM), Hampton-in-Arden (one 1900) (GWW), Knowle (HWE, WK), Small Heath Park (HT), Overslade (RNHS), Warwick (most years) (PPB), Atherstone (CB), Wolford (common some years) (WCEW), Whitchurch (very common in 1900) (JHB).

Oleander Hawk-moth
1985 *Daphnis nerii* (L.)

Rare immigrant: North Africa and Mediterranean

County status: Very rare immigrant.
Flight: September and October.
Larval foodplants: Oleander and Lesser Periwinkle.

This spectacular Hawk-moth has been recorded eight times in Warwickshire, but not since 1961.

Records:

1869—**Edgbaston, Birmingham,** 24/9 (WGB).
1870—**Birmingham,** (FE).
1903—**Atherstone,** 9/10, adult at rest on Yew hedge (A. Sale; Baker, 1903).
1909—**Saltley, Birmingham,** 13/10 specimen housed in the collection of Mr Buckingham at Warwick Museum.
1930—**Ward End, Birmingham,** one adult (JG).
1953—**Erdington, Birmingham,** 13/9 specimen exhibited at BENHS annual meeting by JB (French, 1953).
1959—**Bell Green, Coventry,** 3/10 one adult found by workmen cleaning street lamp (DBlr).
1961—**Crackley Wood, Kenilworth,** one adult found (CDNHSS).

Bedstraw Hawk-moth
1987 *Hyles gallii* (Rott.)

Frequent but erratic immigrant: central, eastern and southern Europe

County status: Scarce immigrant.
Flight: June and July.
Larval foodplants: Lady's Bedstraw*, Rosebay Willowherb*, madders and fuschias.

The Bedstraw Hawk-moth has occasionally been recorded in the County. There was evidence of short term breeding during the early 1970s.

Records:

1870—**Birmingham,** 2/8 one adult (JL); **Edgbaston, Birmingham,** August (FE).
1872—**Rugby,** one adult (WGB).
1888—**Overslade,** one taken in a cottage window (NWH).
1943—**Castle Bromwich,** September; larva on Rosebay Willowherb (CT).
1973—**Alvecote Pools,** larvae and pupae (GAA, MAA).
1977—**Charlecote,** 25/6 female at MV (DB); **Whitley, Coventry,** 6/9 three larvae on Lady's Bedstraw (schoolboys; confirmed DB, AFG).
1989—**Ryton Wood,** 5/7 male at MV (DW, KCG).
2001—**Stoke, Coventry,** 23/7 female at MV (TRG).
2003—**Pillerton Priors,** 6/7 female at MV (CI).

Striped Hawk-moth
1990 *Hyles livornica* (Esp.)

Frequent but erratic immigrant: Mediterranean and North Africa

County status: Scarce immigrant.
Flight: May to November.
Larval foodplants: Willowherbs, bedstraws and other plants.

This splendid moth is a very occasional visitor to Warwickshire, usually during major immigration years.

Records:

1870—**Edgbaston, Birmingham,** female on vine leaf (FE).
1912—**Coventry,** 'One circling electric stand, knocked down with umbrella' (EHS).
1931—**Coleshill,** one adult (WWB); **Sutton Park,** one adult (LFBG).
1949—**Long Lawford, Rugby,** August, (AGB); **Solihull,** 1/10 (DA); **Kenilworth,** larva reared to imago on Knotgrass (CDNHSS).
1994—**Knowle, Solihull,** 26/11 female at MV (AWD).
1996—**Hillmorton, Rugby,** 30/5 male at MV (DIP).
2004—**Warwick,** 9/6 male at MV (SDT).

Elephant Hawk-moth
1991 *Deilephila elpenor* (L.)

County status: Widespread and fairly common.
Flight: May to early August.
Larval foodplants: Rosebay Willowherb*, Great Willowherb*, Himalayan Balsam*, bedstraws*, fuchsias*, Purple-loosestrife* and many other plants.

The Elephant Hawk-moth occurs in a variety of habitats where willowherb grows, including railway cuttings, roadside verges, waste-ground, woodland rides, clearings and gardens. Larvae can be a pest on garden fuchsias.

The adult is attracted freely to moth traps and can sometimes be observed in abundance; for example, Wolford Wood, 17/6/1989 (22) (DB, PJR).

Garden moth trap figures show larger numbers in suburban Rugby compared to rural Pillerton Priors:
Hillmorton, Rugby: 1982 (101), 1985 (175), 1990 (120), 1995 (52), 2000 (44), 2004 (53) (DIP);
Pillerton Priors: 1992 (6), 1993 (21), 1994 (8), 2002 (10), 2003 (15), 2004 (20), 2005 (62) (CI);

VCH 1904: *'Not common.'*
Marston Green, Shirley, Sutton Park, Knowle, Solihull, Hockley Heath, Rugby, Atherstone, Whitchurch, Wolford.

Small Elephant Hawk-moth
1992 *Deilephila porcellus* (L.)

Nationally Local

County status: Fairly widespread and becoming locally fairly common.
Flight: Mid-May to late July.
Larval foodplants: Bedstraws, including Heath Bedstraw* and Lady's Bedstraw*.

The Small Elephant Hawk-moth is more restricted than its congener, showing a preference for lighter, well-drained soils. Frequenting disused quarries, railway cuttings and heathland, this attractive moth is most often seen in the south of the County, on or near calcareous soils.

There is evidence of an increase both in range and frequency during the last two years. An unprecedented 47 specimens were attracted to light at Bishops Hill on 20/6/2005 (MA, DB, AD, SDT, JWkn).

Garden moth trap counts at **Pillerton Priors** are as follows: 1992 (0), 1993 (2), 1994 (10), 2003 (4), 2004 (9), 2005 (23) (CI).

VCH 1904: *'Not common. Sutton Park is the best known locality for this species but it is rare there.' Atherstone, Rugby, Wellesbourne, Wolford.*

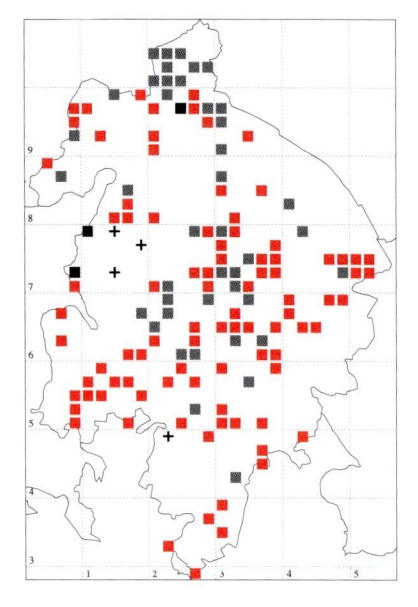

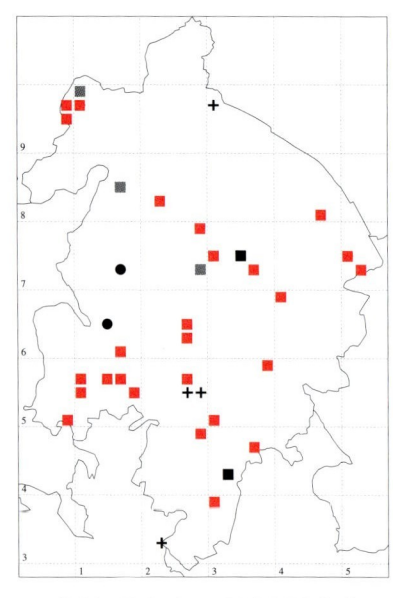

Silver-striped Hawk-moth
1993 *Hippotion celerio* (L.)

Rare immigrant: North Africa and Mediterranean

County status: Very rare immigrant.
Flight: October to November.
Larval foodplants: Grape-vine and Virginia Creeper.

The majority of Warwickshire sightings are from the nineteenth century.

Records:
1868—**Birmingham,** (FE).
1880—**Edgbaston, Birmingham,** November (GTB).
1892—**Dunchurch,** 15/10 (S).
1977—**Marton,** 28/10 (RA) (Gardner, 1978).

Family: Notodontidae—Prominents

In Britain there are currently an accepted 22 species of resident Notodontidae, of which 20 have been noted in Warwickshire since 1880.

The majority of species in this family of medium to large sized moths are attractively marked and distinctive. The adults do not possess a proboscis and are unable to feed. The males of most species in this group respond freely to light but the females are far less frequently attracted.

The 'prominents' are so named because the trailing edge of the forewing on some species contains a triangular tuft of long scales which form a prominent projection raised over the back when the moth is at rest. The larvae also possess prominent lobe-like projections and humps on their backs, whilst the Puss Moth and kittens have whip-like tails.

Puss Moth
1995 *Cerura vinula* (L.)

County status: Fairly widespread and fairly common.
Flight: Late April to mid-July.
Larval foodplants: Willows*, sallows*, poplars* and Aspen.

The Puss Moth is found in wooded and marshy areas and is also an annual visitor to many garden moth traps, especially in the southern half of the County. The spectacular larva is less frequently noticed than formerly.

Garden moth trap totals are generally low, as reflected in the following figures:
Hillmorton, Rugby: 1982 (0), 1985 (1), 1990 (5), 1995 (3), 2000 (0), 2004 (1) (DIP).

VCH 1904: *'Common everywhere.'*

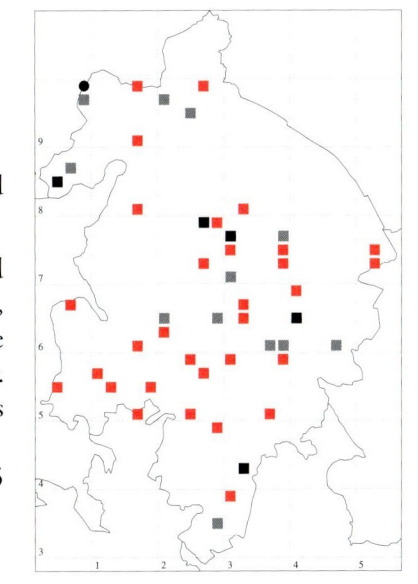

Alder Kitten
1996 *Furcula bicuspis* (Borkh.)

Nationally Local

County status: Local and uncommon.
Flight: May to mid-June.
Larval foodplants: Alder and birches.

The Alder Kitten is found on heathland in the north of the County, and in woodland and river valleys in the south. It was first noted during the 1940s at Mappleborough Green (FHL). Woodland sites include Oversley Wood, Hampton Wood and Snitterfield Bushes. Populations in Sutton Park and Hay Wood appear to be recent colonisations, probably becoming established during the 1980s. Individuals occasionally noted in garden moth traps could be wanderers from undetected colonies.

Two specimens caught in Oversley Wood on 2/8/1976 (DB) may have represented a partial second generation during an exceptionally hot summer.

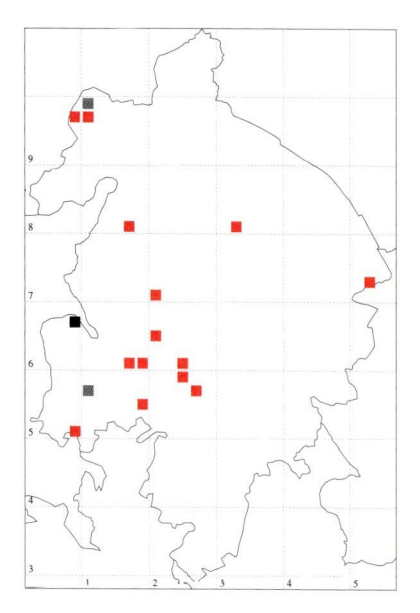

Sallow Kitten
1997 *Furcula furcula* (Cl.)

County status: Fairly widespread and fairly common.
Flight: Two generations. May to June, and mid-July to late August.
Larval foodplants: Willows*, sallows*, Aspen and poplars.

The Sallow Kitten is the commonest and most widely distributed member of the genus. It is found in a diversity of habitats containing the foodplants, including woodland, wetland, heathland and waste-ground. The second generation is more numerous. Use of mercury vapour light has revealed this species to be more plentiful than was thought in the early part of the twentieth century.

VCH 1904: '*Rare.*'
Sutton Park, Rugby, Knowle.

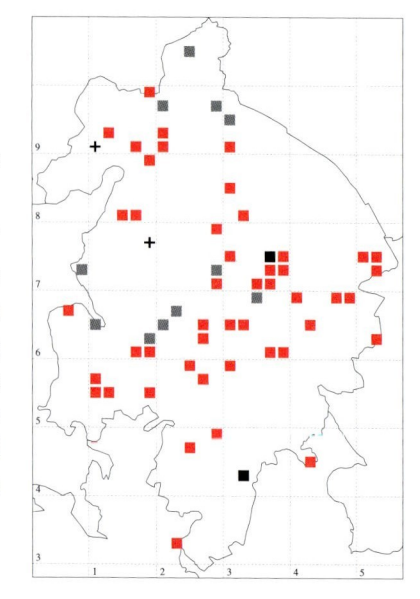

Poplar Kitten
1998 *Furcula bifida* (Brahm)

Nationally Local

County status: Fairly widespread and sometimes fairly common.
Flight: May to July with a possible partial second generation in August.
Larval foodplants: Aspen*, poplars* and sallows.

This species is found locally over a large area of the County. It is sometimes recorded in urban districts. Larger populations occur at Waverley Wood, Ryton Wood, Clowes Wood, Brandon Marsh, Oakley Wood and Snitterfield Bushes. Occasionally observed in numbers at light in Oversley Wood: 28/5/1976 (6), 21/5/1982 (5) (DB, AFG).

Records at Hillmorton, Rugby (DIP), during 1990, included an early example on 29/4 followed by a gravid female on 14/8, suggesting a second generation.

VCH 1904: *'Not uncommon in the larval stage on poplars and Aspen.'* Yardley, Handsworth, Hampton-in-Arden, Marston Green, Knowle, Brandon Wood.

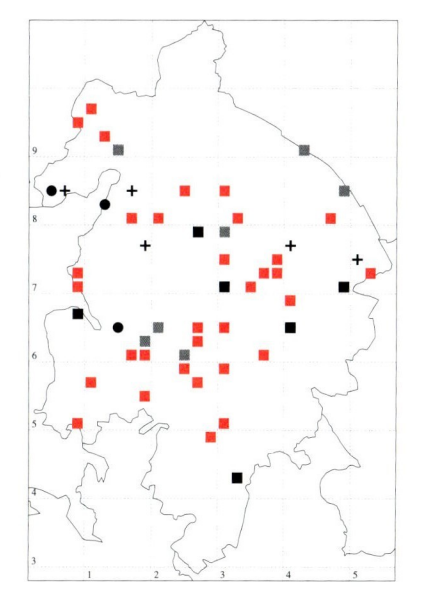

Iron Prominent
2000 *Notodonta dromedarius* (L.)

County status: Widespread and fairly common.
Flight: Two generations. May to June, and July to August.
Larval foodplants: Birches*, Alder* and sometimes Hazel and oaks.

The Iron Prominent is found in a wide range of habitats but is especially numerous on heathland containing a plentiful supply of birch. It is noted in garden moth traps in both rural and built-up districts:
Pillerton Priors: 1992 (0), 1993 (2), 1994 (0), 2002 (3), 2003 (4), 2004 (1), 2005 (2) (CI);
Hillmorton, Rugby: 1982 (12), 1985 (2), 1990 (5), 1995 (5), 2000 (18), 2004 (12), 2005 (5) (DIP).

VCH 1904: *'Not uncommon.'*
Sutton Park, Knowle, Marston Green, Solihull.

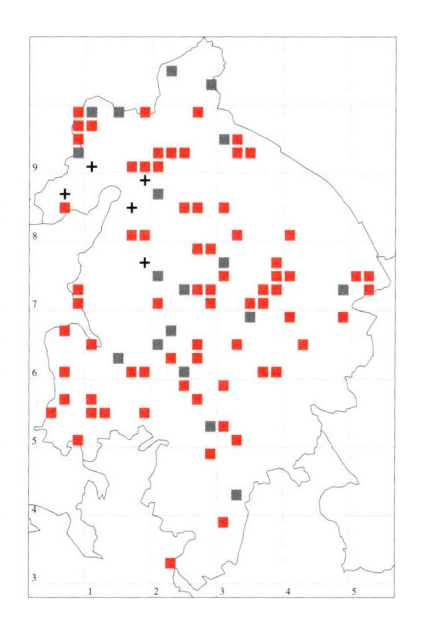

Species appearing in Plate 1 (opposite)

1. Wood Tiger *Parasemia plantaginis plantaginis*
2. Dark Tussock *Dicallomera fascelina*
3. Lunar Yellow Underwing *Noctua orbona*
4. Scarce Vapourer *Orgyia recens*
5. Dark Crimson Underwing *Catocala sponsa*
6. Speckled Yellow *Pseudopanthera macularia*
7. Dingy Mocha *Cyclophora pendularia*
8. Silver Barred *Deltote bankiana*
9. Brussels Lace *Cleorodes lichenaria*
10. Sword-grass *Xylena exsoleta*
11. Marsh Carpet *Perizoma sagittata*
12. Grey Scalloped Bar *Dyscia fagaria*
13. Beautiful Brocade *Lacanobia contigua*
14. Small Eggar *Eriogaster lanestris*
15. Square-spotted Clay *Xestia rhomboidea*
16. Bordered Gothic *Heliophobus reticulata marginosa*
17. Clouded Buff *Diacrisia sannio*
18. Stout Dart *Spaelotis ravida*
19. Broad-bordered Bee Hawk-moth *Hemaris fuciformis*
20. Pale Shining Brown *Polia bombycina*
21. Plain Clay *Eugnorisma depuncta*
22. Silvery Arches *Polia trimaculosa*
23. Four-spotted *Tyta luctuosa*
24. Lace Border *Scopula ornata*
25. Small Chocolate-tip *Clostera pigra*
26. Royal Mantle *Catarhoe cuculata*
27. Lobster Moth *Stauropus fagi*
28. White-spotted Pinion *Cosmia diffinis*

All specimens figured on this plate are represented at life size.

SPECIES PRESUMED TO BE EXTINCT IN WARWICKSHIRE

(Photography: G.B. Senior)

PLATE 1

INCREASING SPECIES

Red-green Carpet *Chloroclysta siterata*
Robert Thompson

Grey Shoulder-knot *Lithophane ornitopus lactipennis*
David Porter

RECENT COLONISERS

Red-necked Footman *Atolmis rubricollis*
Robert Thompson

Vine's Rustic *Hoplodrina ambigua*
David Porter

VAGRANT SPECIES

Scarlet Tiger *Callimorpha dominula*
Roy Leverton

Pine Hawk-moth *Hyloicus pinastri*
David Brown

IMMIGRANT SPECIES

Slender Burnished Brass *Thysanoplusia orichalcea*
Mark Tunmore

Ni Moth *Trichoplusia ni*
Paul Harris

Gem *Orthonama obstipata*
David Porter

Convolvulus Hawk-moth *Agrius convolvuli*
Robert Thompson

Vestal *Rhodometra sacraria*
Robert Thompson

IMMIGRANT SPECIES

Larva of Death's-head Hawk-moth *Acherontia atropos*
Robert Thompson

Death's-head Hawk-moth *Acherontia atropos*
Robert Thompson

Striped Hawk-moth *Hyles livornica*
Robert Thompson

NATIONALLY SCARCE WARWICKSHIRE SPECIES

Silver Cloud *Egira conspicillaris*
Robert Thompson

Square-spot Dart *Euxoa obelisca grisea*
David Porter

Wormwood *Cucullia absinthii*
Roy Leverton

Goat Moth *Cossus cossus*
Robert Thompson

PLATE 5

NATIONALLY SCARCE WARWICKSHIRE SPECIES

Dotted Chestnut *Conistra rubiginea*
Paul Harris

Waved Black *Parascotia fuliginaria*
Paul Harris

Orange-tailed Clearwing *Synanthedon andrenaeformis*
Paul Harris

Yellow-legged Clearwing *Synanthedon vespiformis*
Paul Harris

WOODLAND

Oversley Wood, near Alcester. Warwickshire's prime woodland site where over 360 species of larger moth have been recorded. This mixed woodland contains important stands of Aspen *Populus tremula*, Beech *Fagus sylvatica* and Silver Birch *Betula pendula*.
David Brown

Rosy Footman *Miltochrista miniata*
David Brown

Angle-striped Sallow *Enargia paleacea*
Roy Leverton

Clay Triple-lines *Cyclophora linearia*
Roy Leverton

Pinion-spotted Pug *Eupithecia insigniata*
Jim Porter

PLATE 7

WOODLAND

Ryton Wood, near Coventry. A magnificent ancient broadleaved woodland consisting of Pedunculate Oak *Quercus robur* with Hazel *Corylus avellana* understorey. An impressive 353 species of larger moth have been recorded here.
John Roberts

Great Oak Beauty *Hypomecis roboraria*
Roy Leverton

Orange Footman *Eilema sororcula*
Roy Leverton

Cloaked Carpet *Euphyia biangulata*
Jim Porter

WOODLAND

Wappenbury Wood, part of the Princethorpe Woodland complex. The site contains a good mixture of oak *Quercus* spp., birch *Betula* spp. and Aspen *Populus tremula*, supporting many important species.
David Brown

Light Orange Underwing *Archiearis notha*
Paul Harris

Pebble Hook-tip *Drepana falcataria falcataria*
David Porter

Great Prominent *Peridea anceps*
Robert Thompson

PLATE 9

WOODLAND

Snitterfield Bushes, near Stratford-upon-Avon. An area of damp woodland containing mainly oak *Quercus* spp., Ash *Fraxinus excelsior*, birch *Betula* spp. and Aspen *Populus tremula*. The site contains Warwickshire's only population of Orange Moth *Angerona prunaria*.
David Brown

Green Arches *Anaplectoides prasina*
Robert Thompson

Scarce Silver-lines *Bena bicolorana*
David Porter

WOODLAND

Lappet *Gastropacha quercifolia*
Robert Thompson

Poplar Lutestring *Tethea or or*
Jim Porter

Orange Moth *Angerona prunaria*
Paul Harris

Lunar Hornet Moth *Sesia bembeciformis*
Roy Ledbury

PLATE 11

WOODLAND

Wolford Wood, situated in the south of the County on the Gloucestershire border. An area of damp broadleaved woodland; it is managed by traditional methods and contains a number of Nationally Local species.
David Brown

White Satin *Leucoma salicis*
Robert Thompson

Larva of White Satin *Leucoma salicis*
Robert Thompson

WOODLAND

Lilac Beauty *Apeira syringaria*
Robert Thompson

Small Seraphim *Pterapherapteryx sexalata*
Robert Thompson

Blotched Emerald *Comibaena bajularia*
Paul Harris

Puss Moth *Cerura vinula*
Robert Thompson

CALCAREOUS GRASSLAND

Bishops Bowl, near Southam. An important brown-field site created by limestone quarrying, where a rich mosaic of grasslands and wetlands are framed by cliffs of blue lias limestone.
Steven Falk

Grove Hill, near Alcester. An important area of calcareous grassland where active site management is practised to prevent scrub encroachment. A number of nationally and locally important species have been found here.
David Brown

CALCAREOUS GRASSLAND SPECIES

Chalk Carpet *Scotopteryx bipunctaria cretata*
David Brown

Bordered Sallow *Pyrrhia umbra*
Jim Porter

Ruddy Carpet *Catarhoe rubidata*
Roy Leverton

Blackneck *Lygephila pastinum*
Paul Harris

Small Elephant Hawk-moth *Deilephila porcellus*
Robert Thompson

Six-belted Clearwing *Bembecia ichneumoniformis*
Paul Harris

PLATE 15

HEATHLAND

Sutton Park, now a National Nature Reserve, is Warwickshire's only remaining extensive area of heathland. It supports a number of local and nationally important species.
Steven Falk

Emperor *Saturnia pavonia*
Robert Thompson

HEATHLAND SPECIES

Beautiful Yellow Underwing *Anarta myrtilli*
Roy Leverton

Grass Wave *Perconia strigillaria*
Roy Leverton

True Lover's Knot *Lycophotia porphyrea*
Robert Thompson

Barred Chestnut *Diarsia dahlii*
Roy Leverton

HEATHLAND

Grendon Common, near Atherstone. A restricted area of heathland that is home to a number of locally important species.
Keith Warmington

Heath Rustic *Xestia agathina agathina*
Robert Thompson

Autumnal Rustic *Eugnorisma glareosa*
Roy Ledbury

PLATE 18

WETLAND

Alvecote Pools, near Tamworth, consists of a series of shallow lakes formed by mining subsidence. Reedbeds subsequently developed and a number of wainscot species have now colonised.
Steven Falk

Bulrush Wainscot *Nonagria typhae*
Robert Thompson

WETLAND

Brandon Marsh, near Coventry, contains a number of pools which were created by gravel extraction. This rich wetland area contains extensive reedbeds and willow carr, supporting a large number of important marshland species.
Steven Falk

Red-tipped Clearwing *Synanthedon formicaeformis*
Paul Harris

Fen Wainscot *Arenostola phragmitidis*
Roy Ledbury

Cream-bordered Green Pea *Earias clorana*
Paul Harris

PLATE 20

WETLAND SPECIES

Larva of Drinker *Euthrix potatoria*
David Brown

Gold Spot *Plusia festucae*
Robert Thompson

Crescent *Celaena leucostigma leucostigma*
Paul Harris

PLATE 21

QUARRIES

Judkins Quarry, near Nuneaton. One of several important brown-field sites in north Warwickshire. Disused areas quickly become appropriate for the colonisation of species such as Annulet *Charissa obscurata*.
Steven Falk

Annulet *Charissa obscurata*
Roy Leverton

Rosy Minor *Mesoligia literosa*
Roy Ledbury

Bird's Wing *Dypterygia scabriuscula*
Paul Harris

Broad-barred White *Hecatera bicolorata*
Paul Harris

PLATE 22

LARVAE

Goat Moth *Cossus cossus*
The larva of this species has been found more often in Warwickshire than the adult moth.
Robert Thompson

Puss Moth *Cerura vinula*
A spectacular larva that is now less frequently encountered than formerly in the County.
Jim Porter

Cinnabar *Tyria jacobaeae*
An easily recognisable larva; it is found on ragwort *Senecio* spp. at its Warwickshire strongholds.
Jim Porter

Lime Hawk-moth *Mimas tiliae*
A familiar sight in built-up districts; often observed on the ground below lime trees when fully grown.
Jim Porter

Sprawler *Asteroscopus sphinx*
This larva has been discovered in Warwickshire on a previously unrecorded foodplant.
Jim Porter

ABERRATIONS AND MOTHS WITH MIXED FORTUNES

Narrow-bordered Five-spot Burnet
Zygaena lonicerae latomarginata
This unusual confluent form was found at Oxhouse Farm,
Combrook, on 20 June 2004.
David Brown

Barred Tooth-striped *Trichopteryx polycommata*
A species feared extinct in the County following the loss of
colonies through habitat destruction in the 1940s and 1970s.
Jim Porter

Marbled Beauty *Cryphia domestica*
Unlike many other species this attractive moth has been unaffected by urbanisation; some of the largest populations
in the County exist in town and city centres.
Robert Thompson

Pebble Prominent
2003 *Notodonta ziczac* (L.)

County status: Widespread and fairly common.
Flight: Two generations. May to June, and July to August.
Larval foodplants: Willows*, sallows*, Aspen* and poplars.

The Pebble Prominent is widespread and fairly common in a number of habitats, from woodlands to gardens. It can be particularly plentiful in the former, as moth trap counts at Oversley Wood reflect: 15/8/1974 (10), 2/8/1980 (12), 14/5/1982 (18), 21/5/1982 (21) (DB, AFG).

Garden moth trap figures at **Pillerton Priors** (CI) are as follows: 1992 (12), 2002 (9), 2003 (14), 2004 (12), 2005 (9).

VCH 1904: *'Not common.'*
Sutton Park, Knowle, Yardley, Overslade, and Wolford Wood.

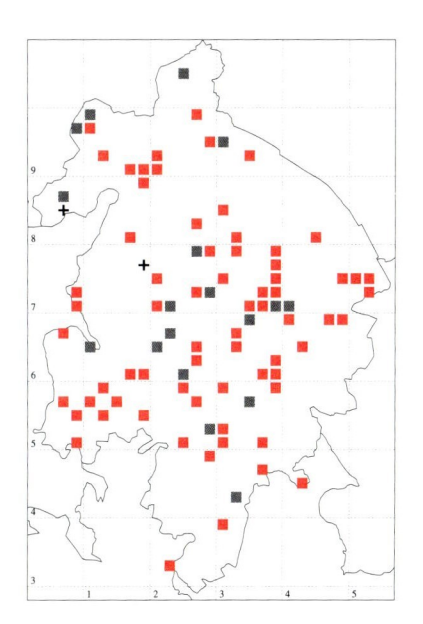

Lesser Swallow Prominent
2006 *Pheosia gnoma* (Fabr.)

County status: Widespread and fairly common.
Flight: Two generations. Mid-April to June, and July to August.
Larval foodplants: Birches*.

The Lesser Swallow Prominent is present in most areas where birches are well-established. It can be numerous in broadleaved woodland as the following moth trap counts indicate: Hay Wood, 30/8/1972 (12) (DB); Oversley Wood, 4/6/1976 (22) (DB), 2/8/1980 (25) (AFG, DB); Oakley Wood, 6/8/1988 (20) (DB).

Occasionally recorded at garden moth traps in rural and suburban districts.

VCH 1904: *'Locally more common than* **tremula***.'*
Brandon Wood, Sutton Park, Knowle and Atherstone.

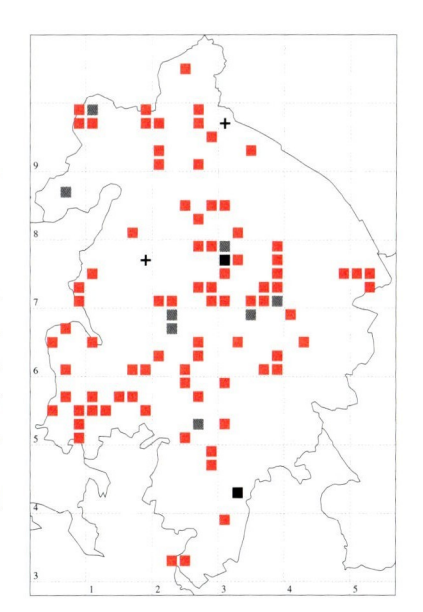

Swallow Prominent
2007 *Pheosia tremula* (Cl.)

County status: Widespread and fairly common.
Flight: Two generations. Early May to June, and July to early September.
Larval foodplants: Aspen*, poplars*, willows and sallows.

The Swallow Prominent is widely distributed and in the vicinity of its foodplant can be fairly common. It is a familiar species at moth traps in both woodlands and gardens. An unusually early specimen was caught at Charlecote on 29/3/1990 (DB).

Garden moth trap totals at **Charlecote** give an idea of frequency: 1985 (7), 1990 (18), 1995 (14), 2000 (16), 2005 (11) (DB).

VCH 1904: *'Not common but probably generally distributed.'*
Knowle, Rugby, Wolford,

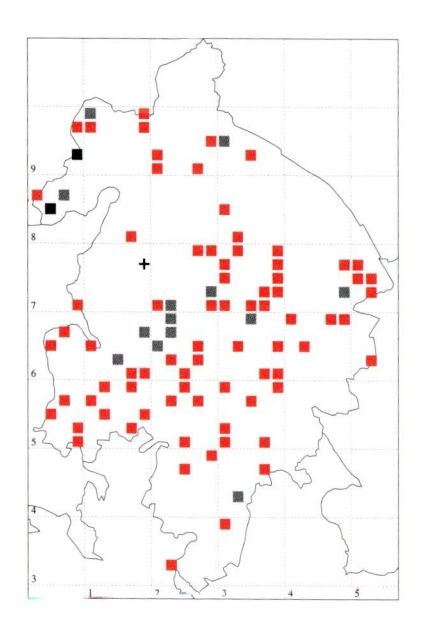

Coxcomb Prominent
2008 *Ptilodon capucina* (L.)

County status: Widespread and fairly common.
Flight: Two overlapping generations. May to mid-September.
Larval foodplants: Polyphagous on deciduous trees, including oaks*, birches*, Beech*, Small-leaved Lime*, Alder*, Hazel* and hawthorns*.

This is one of the most widespread of the 'prominents'. The larvae feed on a large variety of broadleaved trees, which allows the species to utilise a diversity of habitats. It is most frequently encountered in woodland. Garden moth trap numbers at **Charlecote** are generally low but consistent: 1980 (6), 1985 (3), 1990 (3), 1995 (4), 2000 (3) (DB).

VCH 1904: *'A common species everywhere.'*

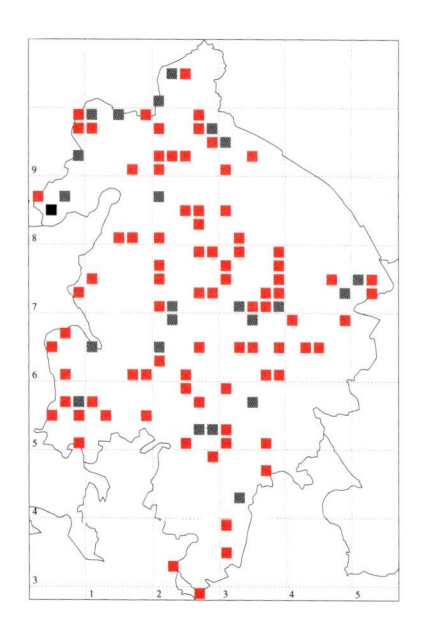

Scarce Prominent
2010 *Odontosia carmelita* (Esp.)

Nationally Local

County status: Possibly extinct. Formerly very local.
Flight: April and May.
Larval foodplants: Birches.

The status of this birch woodland species is uncertain. It was present in Sutton Park during the 1970s, but there have been no recent sightings. Similarly, at Oversley Wood no specimens have been forthcoming following the initial capture in 1987, despite much fieldwork.

Records:
Sutton Park 1970s (LJE); **Oversley Wood** 25/4/1987 (DB, PJR).

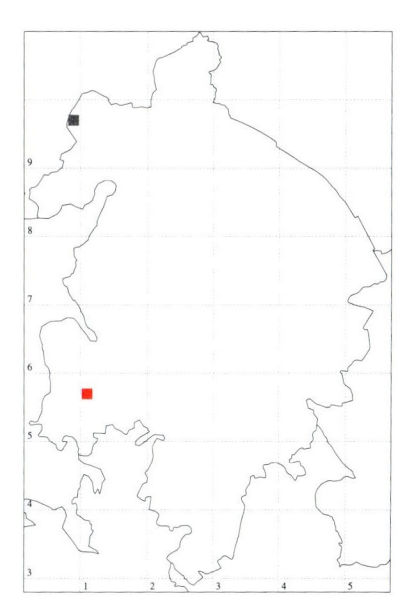

Pale Prominent
2011 *Pterostoma palpina* (Cl.)

County status: Widespread and fairly common.
Flight: Two generations. May to June, and July to August.
Larval foodplants: Aspen*, poplars, willows and sallows*.

A well-recorded species from a wide range of habitats. The Pale Prominent is plentiful in woodlands, marshes and river valleys containing the foodplants. It is also fairly frequent in rural and suburban gardens, as the following moth trap figures show:
Pillerton Priors: 1992 (6), 1993 (15), 1994 (3), 2002 (5), 2003 (18), 2004 (10), 2005 (5) (CI);
Hillmorton, Rugby: 1982 (4), 1985 (14), 1990 (12), 1995 (10), 2000 (3), 2004 (15) (DIP).

VCH 1904: *'Not uncommon on Aspen.'*
Knowle, Small Heath, Overslade and Wolford Wood.

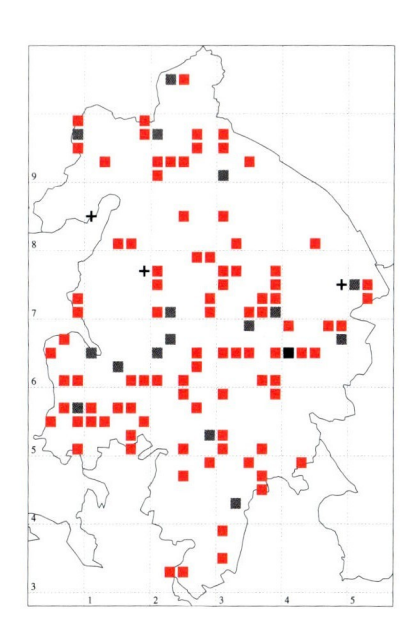

Marbled Brown
2014 *Drymonia dodonaea* ([D. & S.])

Nationally Local

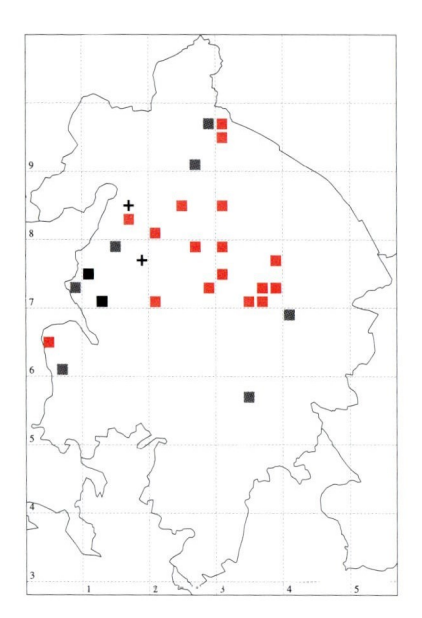

County status: Very local, but fairly common at one site.
Flight: Early May to early July.
Larval foodplants: Oaks.

The Marbled Brown is restricted to oak woodland in the north and west of the County. The largest populations occur at Ryton Wood where the moth is numerous most years; for example, 28/5/1988 (12), (DB, AFG), 22/5/1993 (14) (MA, RMC, DB, RCK).

Records:
Umberslade, 1928 (SEWC), 30/5/1955 (FAN); **Tile Hill Wood**, 1930–1990 (CDNHSS, PC, AJK); **Clowes Wood**, 1939–51 (BNHS, GBM, HEH); **Wainbody Wood**, 8/5/1955 (JEF, MEC), 14/5/2002 (DB); **Windmill Naps**, 1955 (FAN); **Arley Wood**, 1962 (EABS); **Solihull**, 1963 (JSB); **Coughton Park**, 1968 (6) (KEH); **Marton**, 1970 (RA); **Merevale**, 1970 (KEH); **Chesterton Wood**, 29/5/1970 (DB); **Monks Park Wood**, 27/5/1974 (RJT); **Ryton Wood**, 1970–2005 annually in numbers (Warks Moth Group); **Chapelfields, Coventry**, 15/5/1981 (CW); **Hampton-in-Arden**, 1982 (MCV); **Elmdon Manor**, 10/7/1982 (CDNHSS); **Waverley Wood**, 15/5/1993 (Warks Moth Group); **Crackley Wood**, 14/6/1996 (DB); **Rough Hill Wood**, 4/5/1997 (DB, RMC); **Bubbenhall Wood**, 1997 (LB, CE); **Brandon Wood**, 9/6/1998 (Warks Moth Group); **Kenilworth Rd, Coventry**, 22/5/2001, 7/6/2004 (MA); **Hay Wood**, 14/5/2004 (NJS, AJP, VW); **Close Wood**, 3/6/2004 (NJS, AJP, VW); **Purley Chase, Mancetter**, 8/6/2004 (JWkn, DB, RR); **Keresley, Coventry**, 26/5/2005 (NJS).

VCH 1904: *'Rare.'*
Marston Green, Atherstone, Knowle.

Lunar Marbled Brown
2015 *Drymonia ruficornis* (Hufn.)

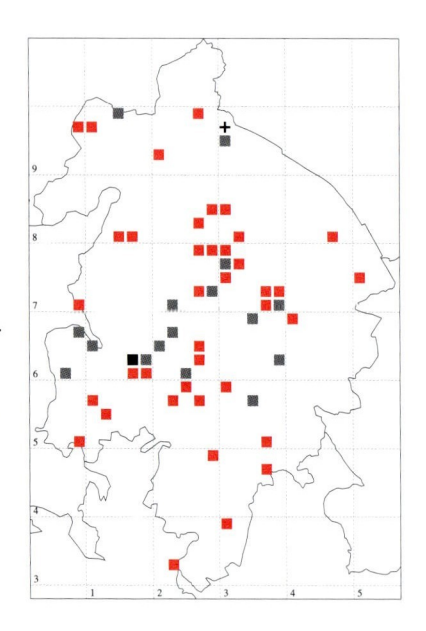

County status: Widespread and fairly common.
Flight: April and May.
Larval foodplants: Oaks*.

The Lunar Marbled Brown is found in a larger range of habitats than the preceding species. It occurs in open terrain where oaks grow in hedgerows, parkland and gardens.

The annual garden moth trap counts (over the page) illustrate how the Charlecote aspect, with nearby National Trust parkland containing ancient oaks, could be the reason for higher numbers:

Bidford-on-Avon: 1992 (2), 1993 (2), 1994 (2), 1995 (3) (RMC);
Charlecote: 1992 (7), 1993 (12), 1994 (8), 1995 (4) (DB).

VCH 1904: *'Rare.'*
Atherstone (one record) (C.B), Wolford (one record) (WCEW).

Small Chocolate-tip
2017 ***Clostera pigra*** (Hufn.)

Nationally Scarce B

County status: Extinct.
Flight: No dates available.
Larval foodplants: Aspen, willows and sallows.

Rugby, 1888, (A. Sidgwick, 1893).

VCH 1904: *'The only claim of this species to inclusion in the County list rests on a record in the Rugby lists 1888. It has however, probably been overlooked elsewhere.'*

Chocolate-tip
2019 ***Clostera curtula*** (L.)

Nationally Local

County status: Fairly widespread and sometimes locally common.
Flight: Two generations. April to early June, and late July to late August.
Larval foodplants: Aspen*, poplars*, sallows* and willows.

The largest populations of Chocolate-tip are found in woodlands containing poplars and Aspen. Notable sites are Oversley Wood, Snitterfield Bushes, Weethley Wood, Bowshot Wood, Oakley Wood, Waverley Wood and Ryton Wood. The moth is generally distributed at low density over the rest of the County. It is an occasional visitor to garden moth traps in the vicinity of the larval foodplants.

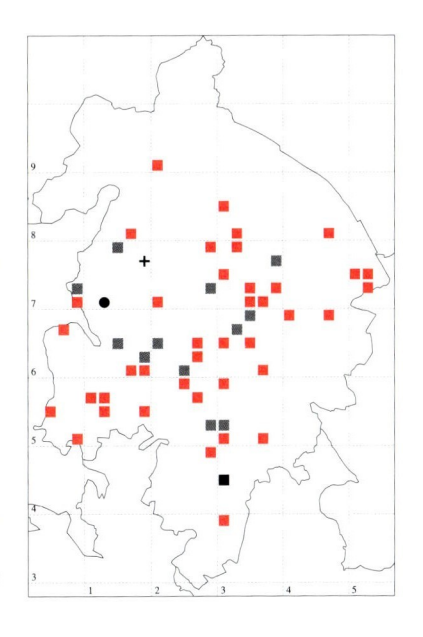

The first brood is generally more plentiful, as indicated by the following moth trap counts at Oversley Wood: 27/5/1974 (32), 24/5/1980 (34), 14/5/1982 (51) (DB, AFG). Second brood figures show lower numbers: 22/8/1974 (4), 1/8/1975 (2), 17/8/1979 (3), 31/7/1980 (3) (DB).

VCH 1904: *'Very rare.'*
One record only, Knowle.

Buff-tip
1994 *Phalera bucephala* (L.)

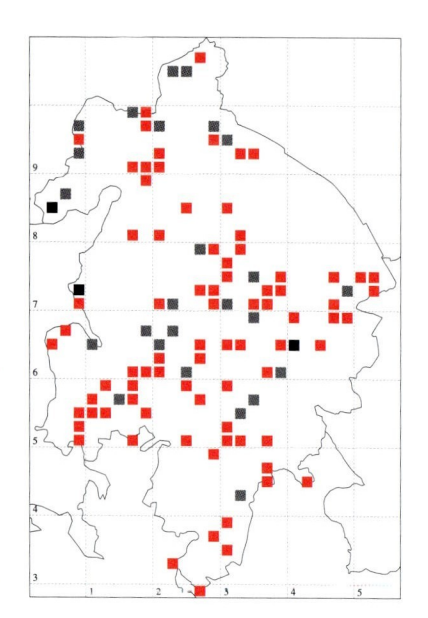

County status: Widespread and fairly common.
Flight: Mid-May to late July.
Larval foodplants: Birches*, oaks*, limes*, sallows*, willows*, English Elm*, Garden Rose* and many other broadleaved trees and shrubs.

The Buff-tip occurs in a variety of habitats, but most commonly in deciduous woodland. The gregarious larvae are often observed on birches and oaks.

Garden moth trap totals vary considerably from year to year:
Pillerton Priors: 1992 (41), 1993 (38), 1994 (12), 2002 (3), 2003 (1), 2004 (15), 2005 (28) (CI);
Hillmorton, Rugby: 1982 (6), 1985 (69), 1990 (36), 1995 (3), 2000 (1), 2004 (16) (DIP);
Charlecote: 1970 (33), 1980 (70), 1985 (37), 1990 (20), 1995 (12), 2000 (17), 2004 (27) (DB).

VCH 1904: *'Very common everywhere.'*

Lobster Moth
1999 *Stauropus fagi* (L.)

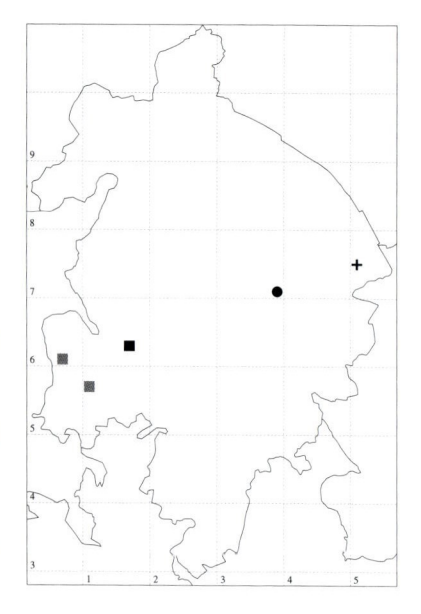

County status: Presumed extinct. Formerly very local.
Flight: June.
Larval foodplants: Beech*, birches, oaks and Hazel.

This species has not been observed in the County since 1974 and there is doubt whether it still exists.

The Lobster was always a special find, even in Victorian times when a Rugby schoolboy found the first larva in the district in 1888. The species was next seen at Princethorpe Wood on 5/6/1907 (HL) and subsequently prevailed here until the 1920s.

In 1939 five imagines were attracted to car headlights in a gateway at Austy Wood (HEH) and there was a solitary record at Coughton Park in 1968 (KEH). Oversley Wood, however, remained the only viable population and a colony seemed well-established from 1960, in which year an initial seven were recorded (DWS), until the mid-1970s when single examples were attracted to light on 12, 14 and 29 June 1974 (DB), with the last record on 14/6/1975 (AFG). Despite much fieldwork during the next 30 years no further examples have been seen.

VCH 1904: *'Rugby 1888 larva.'*

Great Prominent
2005 *Peridea anceps* (Goeze)

Nationally Local

County status: Very local and sometimes fairly common.
Flight: Late April to mid-June.
Larval foodplants: Oaks*.

The Great Prominent is an inhabitant of mature oak woodland with populations in the Princethorpe woodland complex. Numbers of adults attracted to light in Ryton Wood can sometimes be large: 10/5/1991 (25), 3/5/1993 (20) (DB, RGB, CI, RCK).

A well-established but isolated colony exists at Old Park Wood, in the west of the County. Fieldwork in south Warwickshire may result in the discovery of further colonies.

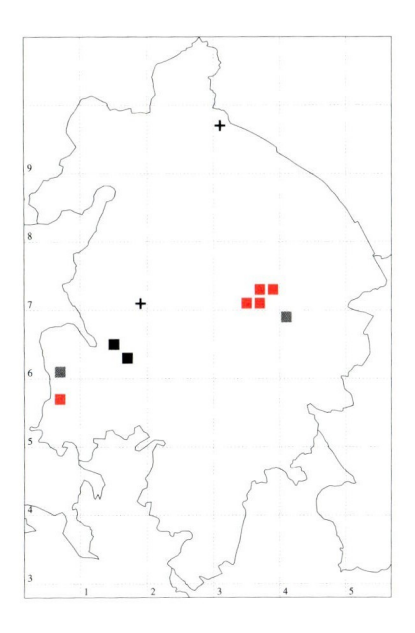

Records:
May's Wood, 1939 (2) (HEH); **Austy Wood**, 1952 two larvae on oak (HEH); **Brandon Wood**, 1950s (HEH); **Coughton Park**, 1968 (5) (KEH); **Marton**, 4/6/1979 (RA); **Old Park Wood**, 30/5/1985 (RMC, DB); **Waverley Wood**, 15/5/1993 (Warks Moth Group), 17/5/2003 (NJS); **Bubbenhall Wood**, 1997 (LB, CE); **Wappenbury Wood**, 20/5/2003 (12) (DB, JWkn); **Ryton Wood**, 1970–2005 annually in numbers (Warks Moth Group).

VCH 1904: *Atherstone, Kingswood.*

Figure of Eight
2020 *Diloba caeruleocephala* (L.)

County status: Local and becoming uncommon.
Flight: Late September to mid-November.
Larval foodplants: Blackthorn*, hawthorns*, apple*, Wild Rose*, Bullace, cherry, plum.

The late flight period of this species undoubtedly results in under-recording, consequently the majority of sightings are from garden moth traps. Woodland populations are known at Snitterfield Bushes, Oakley Wood, Oversley Wood, Hampton Wood, Ryton Wood, Tocil Wood and Clowes Wood.

All long-term recorders report a serious decline in numbers (Fig. 16).

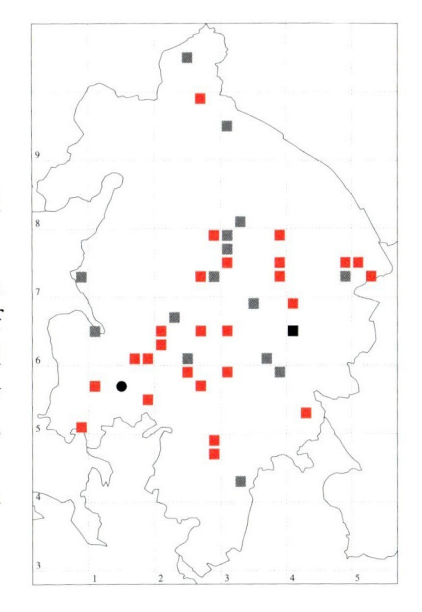

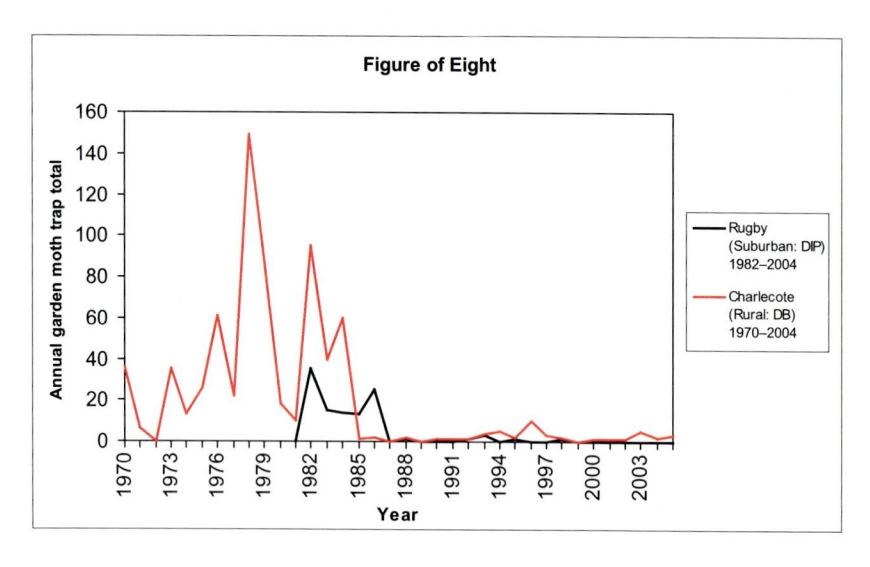

Figure 16. The sharp decline of *D. caeruleocephala* in both rural and suburban districts.

VCH 1904: *'Found throughout the County. Recorded in every list.'*

Family: Lymantriidae—Tussocks

Eleven species of this family have been recorded in the British Isles, of which nine have been noted in Warwickshire since 1880. Only five, however, are presently known to exist in the County. Most species in this family are moderately sized, furry-bodied moths with broad, rounded wings. The males possess well developed feathered antennae. Members of this family regularly come to light but do not feed as adults. The *Orgyia* species consist of day-flying males and large bodied, wingless females. The family name of 'tussocks' is derived from the caterpillars, some of which have colourful toothbrush-like tufts of hair on their backs.

Scarce Vapourer
2025 *Orgyia recens* (Hb.)

RDB

County status: Extinct.
Flight: No dates available.
Larval foodplants: Mainly hawthorns, oaks and sallows.

VCH 1904: *Coombe Wood, Coventry; Rugby, 1888.*

Vapourer
2026 *Orgyia antiqua* (L.)

County status: Widespread and fairly common.
Flight: Day-flying. July to early November.
Larval foodplants: Many deciduous trees and shrubs, including hawthorns*, brambles*, cherry*, oaks*, Alder*, birches*, wych hazel*, poplars*, Broom*, Field-rose, cultivated Rose*, apple*, Beech*, Elder*, Swamp Cypress*, Golden Hop* and Water Lily*.

The males of this species are especially conspicuous on sunny days during the early autumn, flying erratically along hedgerows, woodland edges and in gardens. The adult male has occasionally been noted at light.

This moth is on the wing between July and November, the latest record of the imago being 8/11/1999 at Knowle (AWD). The voltinism is difficult to determine. Waring, Townsend & Lewington (2003) suggest one protracted generation, which must mean late examples of adults are the result of a prolonged hatching of the ova or pupae.

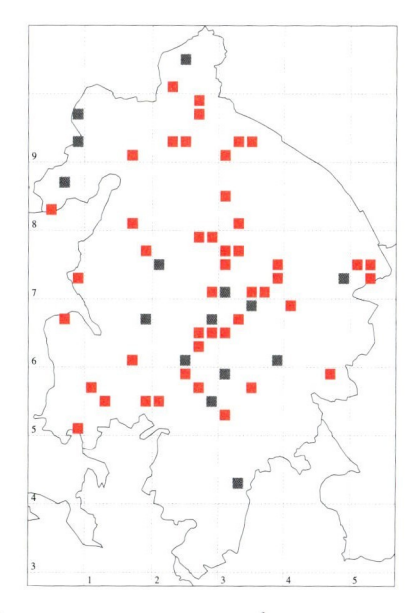

Numbers of the Vapourer are normally fairly constant, but in July 1975 a huge population explosion was witnessed in Coventry city centre. Every leafless branch of pavement trees was enveloped with a haze of cocoons, some forks having up to 20 spun one on the other. An army of caterpillars marched across pavements and buildings in a quest for food. The nearby telephone exchange building was smothered with eggs from wingless females, which themselves hung in scores from windows and ledges (Brown, 1975).

VCH 1904: *'Common everywhere.'*

Dark Tussock
2027 *Dicallomera fascelina* (L.)

Nationally Local

County status: Extinct.
Flight: No dates available.
Larval foodplants: Heather, Broom, sallows, brambles and many other plants.

VCH 1904: *Sutton Park, 1880.*

Pale Tussock
2028 *Callitearia pudibunda* (L.)

County status: Widespread and fairly common.
Flight: May and June.
Larval foodplants: Many deciduous trees and shrubs, including cultivated Apple*, oaks*, birches* Alder*, sallows*, Field Maple*, Hop*, hawthorns*, poplars*, Aspen*, and Traveller's-joy*.

The Pale Tussock is found over most of the County in a number of habitats, including woodland, scrub, parks and gardens. It occurs in rural and suburban districts. The males predominate at light but the female is only occasionally seen.

A melanic specimen was taken in Oakley Wood on 12/6/1993 (AFG).

Typical garden moth trap figures are:
Kenilworth Road, Coventry: 2001 (5), 2002 (10), 2003 (8), 2004 (19), 2005 (9) (MA).

VCH 1904: *'Not uncommon.'*
Brandon Wood, Princethorpe Wood, Knowle, Solihull, Atherstone, Wolford Wood

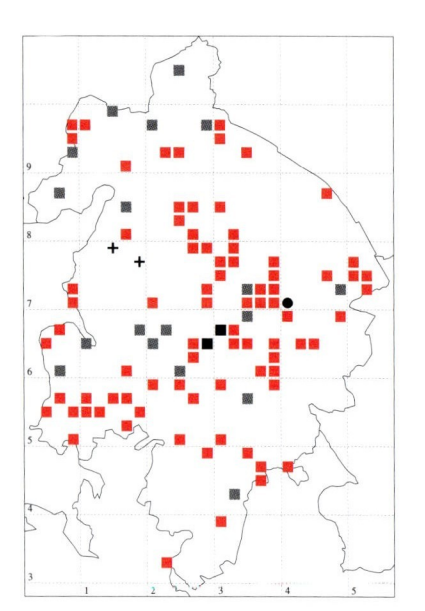

Brown-tail
2029 *Euproctis chrysorrhoea* (L.)

Nationally Local

County status: Status uncertain. Suspected vagrant.
Flight: July to early August.
Larval foodplants: Polyphagous on deciduous trees and shrubs.

This species was first observed in Warwickshire in the nineteenth century at Birmingham and Wolford. The close proximity of the next records on 4/8/1951 and 26/7/1952 (CDNHSS) in the Coventry district, suggest local colonisation. However, no further sightings were made until the 1990s:
Shottery, Stratford-upon-Avon, 26/7/1991 (RGB); Charlecote, 15/7/1992 (DB); Rugby, 11/7/1997 (DIP), 2/7/1999 (IGMR); Royal Leamington Spa, 16/7/2004 (JWkn); Oversley Wood, 20/7/2004 (DG, AJP).

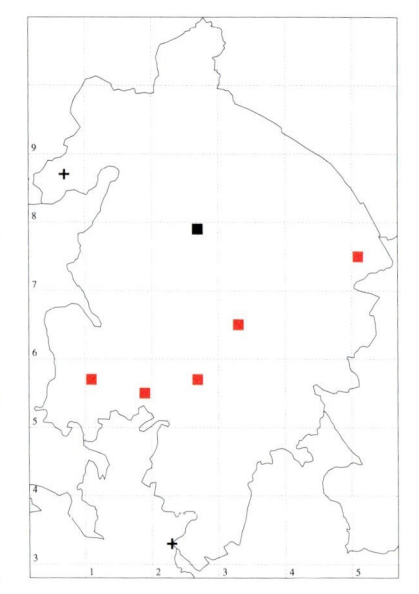

As records are now more frequent there is a possibility that this species may become established. The larvae can devastate large areas of foliage, and also possess hairs that are strongly urticating.

VCH 1904: *Birmingham, Wolford.*

Yellow-tail
2030 *Euproctis similis* (Fuessl.)

County status: Widespread and common.
Flight: Late June to August with individuals of a partial second generation in September to October.
Larval foodplants: Hawthorns*, Blackthorn*, dogwoods*, cultivated Apple*, oaks*, sallows* and many other deciduous trees and shrubs.

This species is widespread and generally common throughout the County in a variety of habitats. In some years there is evidence of a partial second generation; a particularly late example was noted at Hillmorton, Rugby, on 10/10/1986 (DIP).

A fairly regular visitor to garden moth traps as the following figures show:
Bidford-on-Avon: 1989 (11), 1990 (15), 1991 (15), 1992 (24) (RMC);
Hillmorton, Rugby: 1982 (46), 1985 (14), 1990 (20), 1995 (13), 2000 (2), 2004 (5) (DIP).

VCH 1904: *'Very common, often abounds.'*

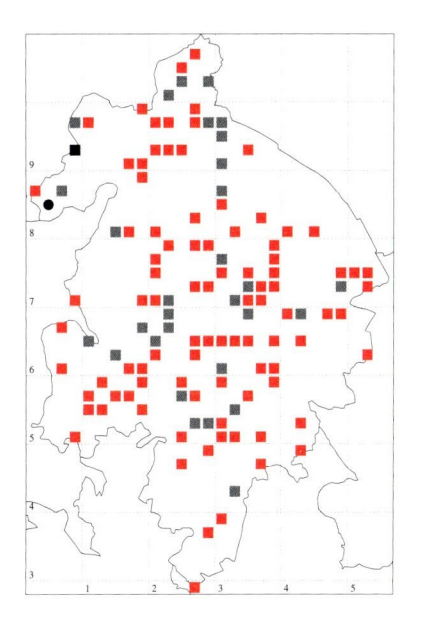

White Satin Moth
2031 *Leucoma salicis* (L.)
Nationally Local

County status: Widespread and locally fairly common.
Flight: Late June to mid-August.
Larval foodplants: Aspen, poplars*, sallows and willows.

The White Satin Moth has increased in both range and frequency over the last 30 years and is now found in many parks and gardens within close proximity of poplars and sallows. The species even became established in urban parts of Coventry during the 1970s and 1980s, 26 individuals being recorded at a regularly operated moth trap in Radford between 1970 and 1989 (MCV). However, none have been seen in the ensuing years.

It is especially plentiful in river valleys and floodplains, but deciduous woodland provides the most favoured habitat and typical sites include Wolford Wood, Wappenbury Wood, Oakley Wood, Oversley Wood, and Brandon Marsh.

VCH 1904: *'Not common.'*
Coventry, Rugby, Edgbaston, Knowle.

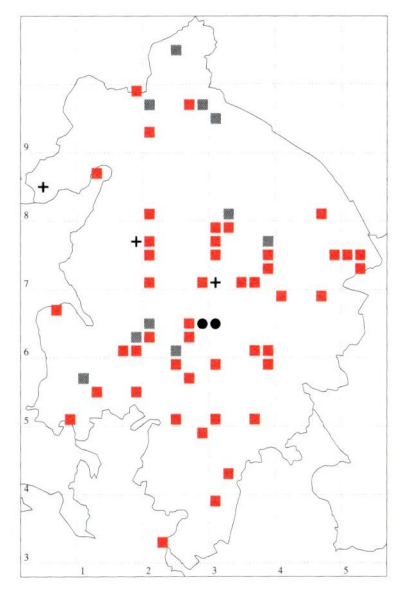

Black Arches
2033 *Lymantria monacha* (L.)

Nationally Local

County status: Local and sometimes fairly common.
Flight: July to early September.
Larval foodplants: Mainly oaks, but also recorded from many other deciduous and coniferous trees.

The Black Arches frequents oak-rich woodland. Choice sites include Ryton Wood, Wappenbury Wood, Waverley Wood, Hay Wood, Clowes Wood, Oakley Wood, Snitterfield Bushes, Oversley Wood and Sutton Park.

It is occasionally recorded outside woodlands, particularly in ancient hedgerows with isolated oaks.

VCH 1904: *Sutton Park, Brandon Wood, Coombe Wood, Wolford Wood.*

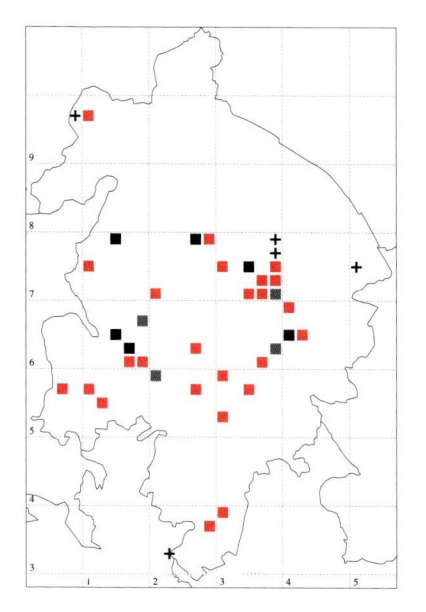

Gypsy Moth
2034 *Lymantria dispar* (L.)

Immigrant from Europe; former resident

County status: Extinct.
Flight: No dates available.
Larval foodplants: A variety of broadleaved trees and shrubs. The extinct British population fed on Bog-myrtle and Creeping Willow.

Rugby, 1885, (WHB) (Sidgwick, 1893).

Family: Arctiidae—Tigers and Footman Moths

This attractive family is represented by 29 resident species, 21 of which have been seen in Warwickshire. The 'tiger' moths are highly colourful with stripes and bands forming patterns which are often highly cryptic. Red and yellow colours warn predators they may be distasteful, or even poisonous in some cases. The adults do not possess a proboscis and thus never feed. Several species are partially diurnal, but all those that fly at night are strongly attracted to light.

The 'footman' moths are generally small with elongated forewings. The larvae of the Arctiidae are generally covered with tufts of hairs arising from raised warts. The Lithosiinae eat lichens and are consequently found in slightly damper habitats.

Round-winged Muslin
2035 *Thumatha senex* (Hb.)

Nationally Local

County status: Local and sometimes fairly common.
Flight: Late June to August.
Larval foodplants: Various mosses and lichens.

This wetland species was first recorded in Warwickshire during the 1960s, when specimens were noted in Oversley Wood (1961) and May's Wood (1962) (DWS). The early 1980s saw an expansion in range and an increase in frequency, culminating in an unprecedented 30 imagines to MV at Brandon Marsh on 3/7/1992 (DB, RGB). Colonies were subsequently discovered at Coombe Abbey, Bradnock's Marsh and Middleton Hall. A succession of records during the 1990s, from garden moth traps in both rural and urban districts, appeared to be part of a general dispersal to drier habitats.

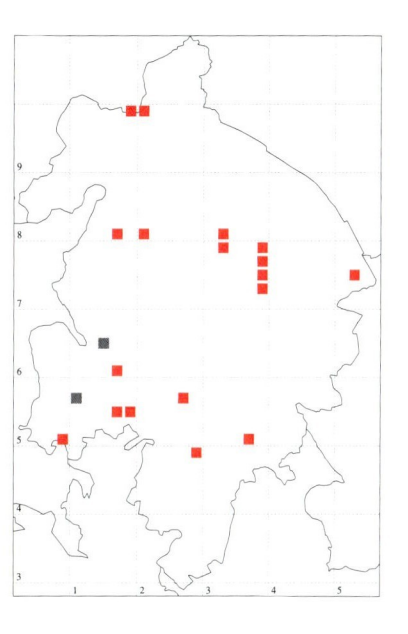

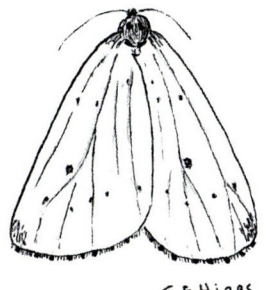

Rosy Footman
2037 *Miltochrista miniata* (Forst.)

Nationally Local

County status: Very local and occasionally fairly common.
Flight: Mid-June to early August.
Larval foodplants: Lichens growing on trees.

This species now appears to be confined to the south-west quarter of the County. Oversley Wood is the main stronghold; for example, 22/7/1974 (10) (DB); 17/7/1986 (12) (DB, RMC); 27/6/2000 (14) (MA, DB, RGB).

Records:
Rugby district, 1874 (RNHS); **Bubbenhall Glade**, 2/7/1938 (LR), 6/7/1947 (KGVS); **Princethorpe Wood**, 6/7/1953 (AHK); **Waverley Wood**, 1956 (2), 1960 (JB); **Brandon Wood**, 1959 (AHK); **Charlecote**, 12/7/1969 (DB); **Wolford Wood**, 17/6/1989 (DB, PJR); **Temple Grafton**, 1/8/2004 (AFG); **Oversley Wood**, 1970–2005 annually recorded (Warks Moth Group).

VCH 1904: *Brandon Wood.*

Muslin Footman
2038 *Nudaria mundana* (L.)

Nationally Local

County status: Very local and generally uncommon.
Flight: July to early August.
Larval foodplants: Lichens on stone walls, posts and branches.

The Muslin Footman is almost entirely confined to the south-west quarter of the County, where it is associated with open terrain demarcated by walls and hedgerows. Unprecedented numbers were recorded at Cross Hands Quarry, 9/7/2005 (CI, RGB).

Records:
Tysoe, 16/7/1958 (TT); **Charlecote**, 25/7/1984, 25/7/1985, 11/7/1986, 21/7/1987, 13/7/1995, 28/6/2000, 9/7/2000 (DB, AFG); **CAD Kineton, Old Mineral Line**, 10/7/1992, (AFG, RGB, CI); **Bidford-on-Avon**, 10/7/1992, 6/7/2004 (RMC); **Pillerton Priors**, 1992, 1993, 1994 (3), 2002 (6), 2003 (9), 2004 (11), 2005 (39) (CI); **Oakley Wood**, 11/7/1995 (AFG); **Brailes**, 4/8/2002, 6/7/2003, 28/7/2003, 29/6/2004, 3/7/2004, 10/7/2004 (2), 17/7/2004 (2), 25/6/2005, 27/6/2005, 2/7/2005 (CI); **Hillmorton, Rugby**, 20/7/2003 (DIP); **Temple Grafton**, 11/7/2004, 15/7/2004 (AFG); **Cherington**, 9/7/2005 (5) (CI); **Cross Hands Quarry**, 9/7/2005 (200) (CI, RGB).

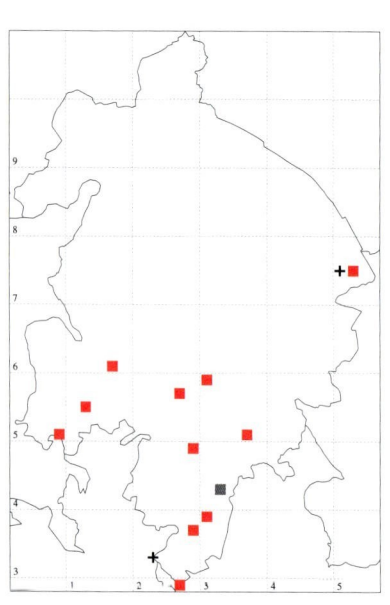

VCH 1904: *'Not common.' Wolford, Rugby.*

Red-necked Footman
2039 *Atolmis rubricollis* (L.)

Nationally Local

County status: Very local and becoming fairly common.
Flight: June and July.
Larval foodplants: Lichens and green algae growing on oaks, birches, Beech, Larch, spruces and other trees.

The Red-necked Footman is a recent coloniser of Warwickshire. Since 2000, large populations have quickly become established in Oversley Wood and Oakley Wood. It has dispersed widely and wanderers have been noted in garden moth traps. A 'yellow-necked' specimen was caught at Kenilworth Road, Coventry, on 24/6/2005 (MA).

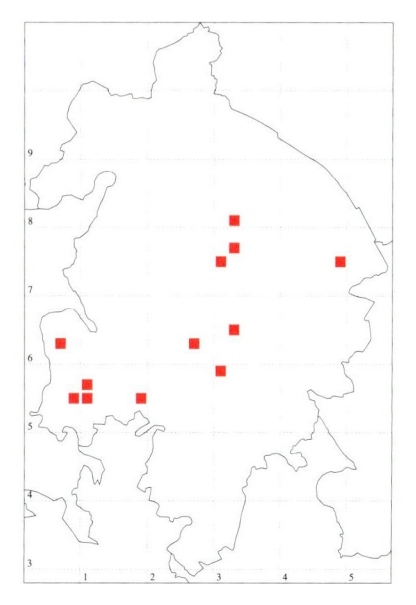

Records:
Radford, **Coventry**, 10/7/1985 (MCV); **Rugby (cricket ground)**, 23/6/1996 specimen caught in sunshine (IGMR); **Shottery**, **Stratford-upon-Avon**, 23/6/2001 (RGB); **Oversley Wood**, 26/6/2001 (MA), 29/6/2002 (DB), 7/6/2004 (2) (RMC, DG, AJP), 15/6/2004 (5) (DG), 18/6/2005 (19) (DG, G&AF, AJP, VW); **Grove Hill**, 18/6/2005 (SDT & Warks Moth Group); **Royal Leamington Spa**, 19/6/2005 (JWkn); **Cheylesmore**, **Coventry**, 22/6/2005 (MD); **Oakley Wood**, 23/6/2005 (19) (DB, PAP); **Studley**, 23/6/2005 (JK); **Kenilworth Rd**, **Coventry**, 24/6/2005 (MA); **Warwick**, 24/6/2005 (SDT).

Four-dotted Footman
2040 *Cybosia mesomella* (L.)

Nationally Local

County status: Very local and scarce.
Flight: Late June and July.
Larval foodplants: Algae and lichens on the stems of trees and woody plants.

This species is associated with damp woodland and was recorded several times during the late nineteenth century at Brandon Wood. There were no further records in the County until 2004, when an individual was caught in a small wood at Temple Grafton (AFG). No subsequent examples were found during 2005, despite regular trapping.

Records:
Temple Grafton, 25/6/2004 (AFG).

VCH 1904: *'Brandon Wood, 2/7/1887, 8/7/1895, 11/7/1896, 21/6/1890.'*

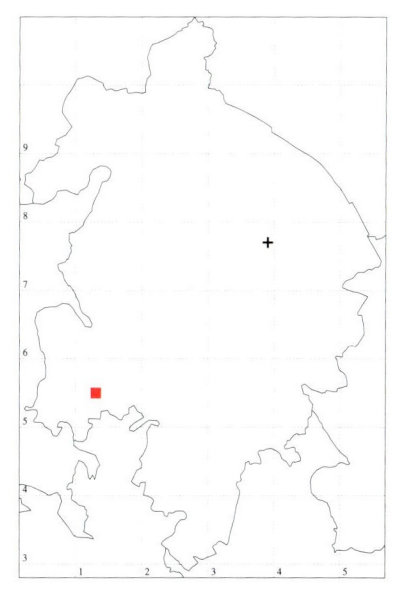

Orange Footman
2043 *Eilema sororcula* (Hufn.)

Nationally Local

County status: Very local and becoming fairly common.
Flight: May and June.
Larval foodplants: Lichens growing on oaks, Beech, Larch, Blackthorn and other trees.

Connected to a national expansion in range during the early part of the twenty-first century, this species has become re-established in Warwickshire after an absence of 100 years. A large population has quickly formed in Oversley Wood and, as with *rubricollis*, dispersal has occurred through rural and urban areas.

Records:
Princethorpe Wood, 1/6/1901, 14/6/1902 (RNHS); **Oversley Wood**, 15/6/2002 (PS), 15/5/2004 (4) (MA, JWkn), 7/6/2004 (2) (RMC, DG, AJP), 12/6/2004 (3) (MK, AJP, VW, DG), 15/6/2004 (2) (DG), 26/5/2005 (31) (J. Rush), 4/6/2005 (22) (Warks Moth Group), 18/6/2005 (DG); **Ryton Wood**, 11/5/2004 (JWkn); **Temple Grafton**, 4/6/2004, 2/6/2005 (AFG); **Pype Hayes, Birmingham**, 24/5/2005 (SB); **Central Rugby**, 25/5/2005 (IGMR); **Charlecote**, 17/6/2005 (DB); **Brailes**, 19/6/2005 (CI).

Dingy Footman
2044 *Eilema griseola* (Hb.)

County status: Local and occasionally fairly common.
Flight: July and August.
Larval foodplants: Lichens and algae growing on trees and bushes.

This species was first recorded in the County at Tysoe on 16/7/1949 (TT). The Dingy Footman is local and chiefly restricted to the southern half of Warwickshire, where it frequents river valleys, marshes and damp woodland. There is recent evidence of a northward extension in range.

The following garden moth trap figures give an idea of numbers in rural south Warwickshire:
Pillerton Priors: 1992 (8), 1993 (16), 1994 (3), 2002 (25), 2003 (26), 2004 (23), 2005 (152) (CI).

Note: The plain straw yellow f. *stramineola* (Doubleday) represented 13% of the above totals.

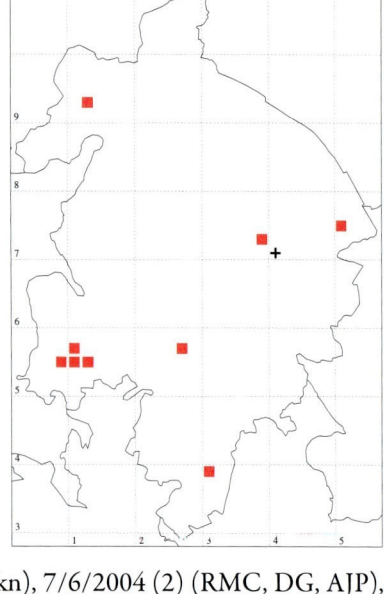

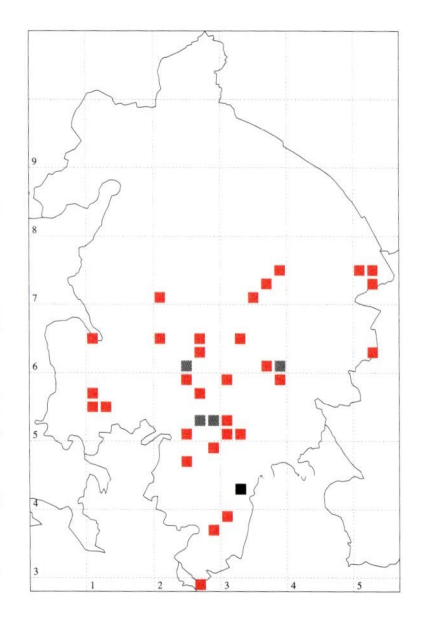

Scarce Footman
2047 *Eilema complana* (L.)

Nationally Local

County status: Widespread and fairly common.
Flight: July to mid-August.
Larval foodplants: Lichens and green algae* growing on branches, walls and fence posts*.

Although initially recorded at Rugby in 1872 (RNHS), this species remained absent for almost 100 years before the next sighting at Wainbody Wood in 1964. The Scarce Footman now belies its English name by being well distributed and increasingly plentiful in Warwickshire. It is found in a number of habitats including woodland, heathland, wetlands, waste-ground and gardens, but is only occasionally noted in urban districts.

Garden moth trap totals at **Hillmorton, Rugby**, are as follows: 1982 (6), 1985 (8), 1990 (19), 1995 (16), 2000 (9), 2004 (14) (DIP).

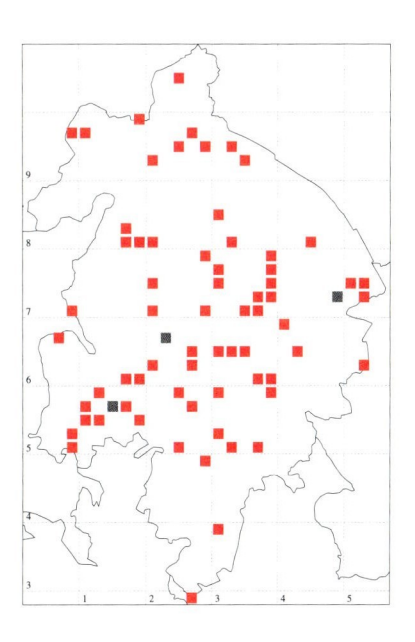

Buff Footman
2049 *Eilema depressa* (Esp.)

Nationally Local

County status: Fairly widespread and sometimes common.
Flight: Late June to mid-August.
Larval foodplants: Lichens and algae* on the branches of trees and shrubs, including oaks, birches, hawthorns, spruces, pines* and Yew*.

The Buff Footman was first observed in Warwickshire on 6/8/1987 when a solitary specimen was recorded at light in Oversley Wood (DB). During the 1990s the species dispersed rapidly to colonise numerous woodland and grassland locations throughout the County. Sites include Bentley Park Wood, Middleton Hall, Crackley Wood, Clowes Wood, Hay Wood, Oakley Wood, Bishops Hill, Wilmcote Rough and Cross Hands Quarry. Huge populations have quickly developed and a record 80 specimens were recorded at Waverley Wood on 28/7/2001 (Warks Moth Group).

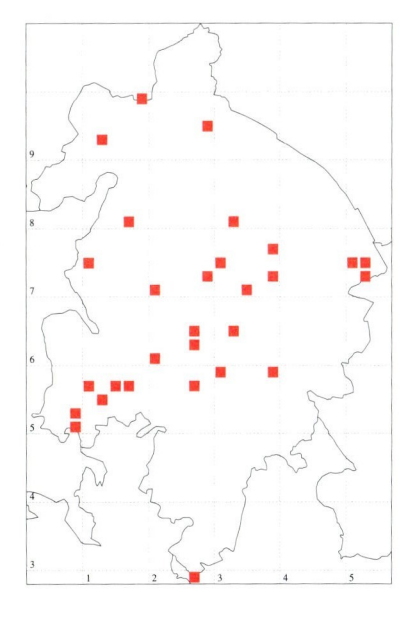

Common Footman
2050 *Eilema lurideola* (Zinck.)

County status: Widespread and common.
Flight: Late June to August.
Larval foodplants: Lichens* and green algae* on trees, bushes (including Honeysuckle*), posts*, walls* and rocks.

The Common Footman is more abundant than *complana* and occurs in rural and, less plentifully, in urban districts. The attractive black and orange caterpillar is frequently seen on wooden fence posts and walls. Hundreds were noted on a farmland gate opposite Waverley Wood on 13/4/1979 and similar numbers in subsequent years (MCV).

The following garden moth trap figures compare frequency in urban, suburban and rural districts:

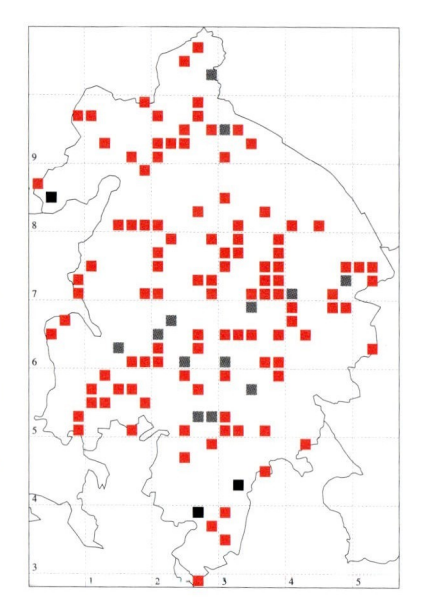

Habitat	Location	1982	1985	1990	1995	2000
Urban	Radford, Coventry (MCV)	3	0	0	5	2
Suburban	Hillmorton, Rugby (DIP)	98	57	64	106	29
Rural	Charlecote (DB)	450	184	132	325	74

VCH 1904: *'Generally distributed but not very common.'*

Wood Tiger
2056 *Parasemia plantaginis plantaginis* (L.)

Nationally Local

County status: Presumed extinct. Formerly very local and scarce.
Flight: Late May to July. Partial day-flyer.
Larval foodplants: Polyphagous on herbaceous plants.

This delightful species was last recorded in the County during 1971 at Sutton Park (LJE).

Records:
Olton, May 1929 (MWB); **Sutton Park,** 1911–15 (SEWC), 1960s (LJE), last record 1971 (LJE).

VCH 1904: *'Fairly common in Sutton Park.'*
Wolford Wood.

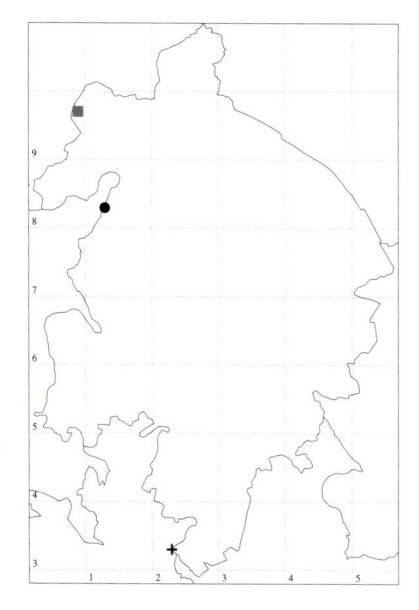

Garden Tiger
2057 *Arctia caja* (L.)

County status: Fairly widespread but becoming less common.
Flight: Late June to August.
Larval foodplants: Docks*, nettles*, Dandelion*, Hollyhock*, and many other herbaceous plants.

The Garden Tiger is found throughout Warwickshire in a wide range of open habitats, but long term recorders all report a reduction in numbers over the last 20 years (Fig. 17). It has been well documented that this decline is due to a combination of tidying and spraying of weedy areas and climate change producing mild and wet winters that are unsuitable for overwintering larvae.

An unusually late adult was caught on 1/10/1989 at Charlecote (AFG).

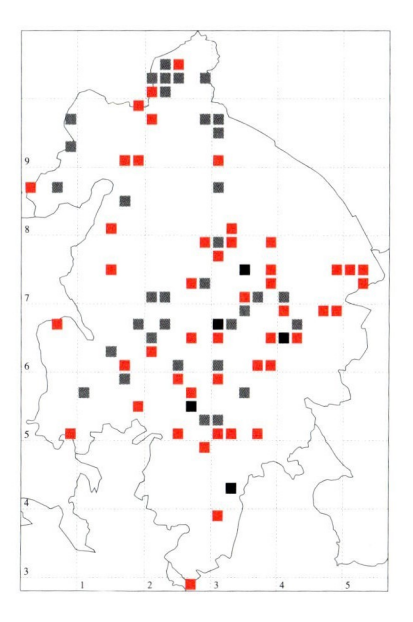

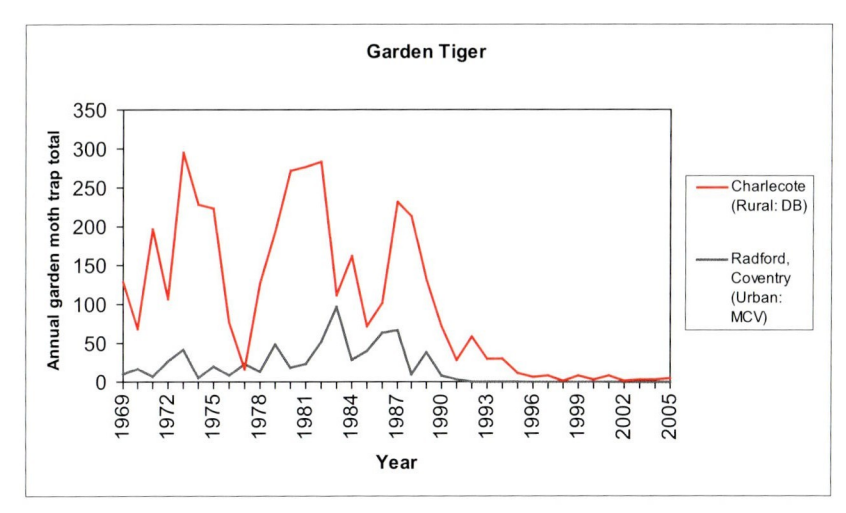

Figure 17. The decline of *A. caja* in both rural and urban districts.

VCH 1904: *'Common everywhere.'*

Cream-spot Tiger
2058 *Arctia villica britannica* Ob.

Nationally Local

County status: Extinct.
Flight: No dates available.
Larval foodplants: A wide range of herbaceous plants, including chickweeds and ragworts.

Rugby, pre-1883, (A. Sidgwick, 1893).

Clouded Buff
2059 *Diacrisia sannio* (L.)

Nationally Local

County status: Extinct.
Flight: June. Males observed by day.
Larval foodplants: Polyphagous on herbaceous plants.

Sutton Park was the only known site for this colourful moth, last seen in 1916.

Records:
Sutton Park, 1890–1900 (WGB, HML, CJW, GWW), 10/6/1911, 16/6/1915, 1916 several males and one female (SEWC).

VCH 1904: *'Sutton Park - occasionally seen.'*

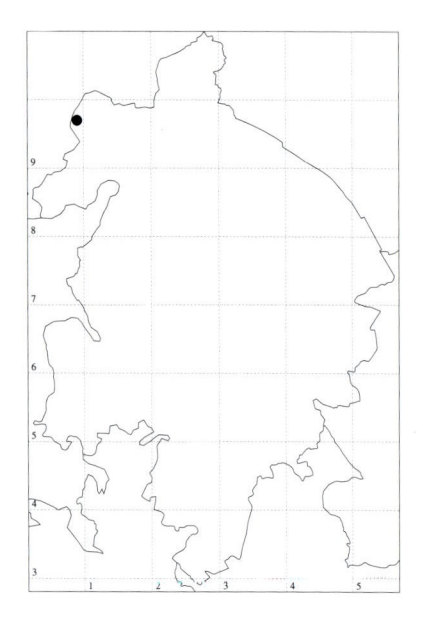

White Ermine
2060 *Spilosoma lubricipeda* (L.)

County status: Widespread and fairly common.
Flight: Mid-May to mid-July.
Larval foodplants: A wide range of herbaceous plants, including docks*, Common Nettle and chickweeds*.

The White Ermine is found in a wide range of habitats, including woodland, wetland, road and railway cuttings, and gardens. It appears to be less common than *luteum* in urban environments.

The conspicuous dark-brown, hairy caterpillar with a red dorsal stripe is often observed crawling rapidly across open ground prior to pupation. The adult is usually out by the middle of May but occasionally much earlier; for instance, Lillington 27/4/1953 (WTT). Specimens are sometimes caught in August; for example, Charlecote, 17/8/2005, 18/8/2005 (DB).

VCH 1904: *'Common everywhere.'*

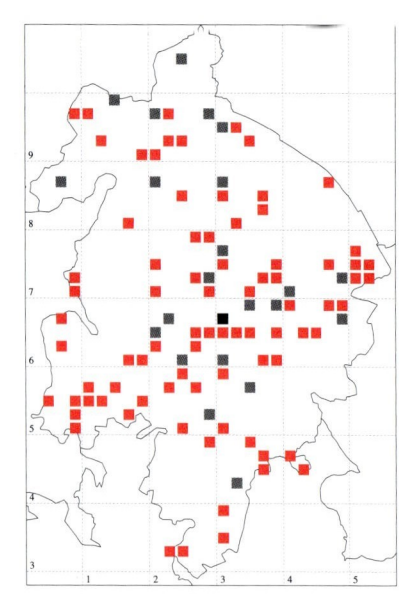

Buff Ermine
2061 *Spilosoma luteum* (Hufn.)

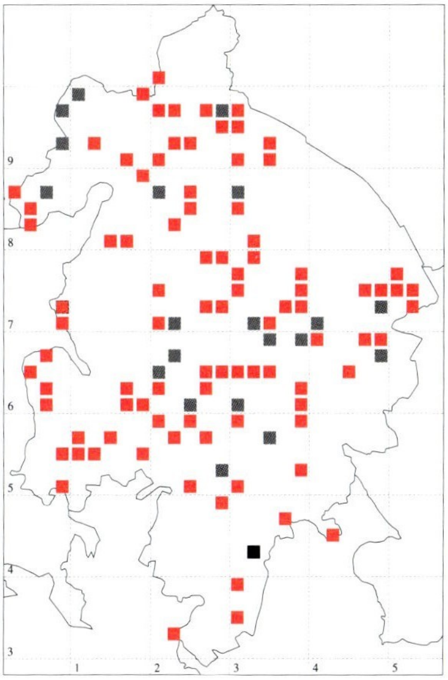

County status: Widespread and fairly common.
Flight: Mid-May to late July.
Larval foodplants: A wide range of herbaceous plants, including plantains*, chickweeds*, docks* and White Bryony*.

The Buff Ermine is another widespread moth found in similar habitats to the preceding species. Like its congener, the moth is occasionally encountered well into August; for example, Water Orton, 15/8/1994 (KM).

It is sometimes fairly plentiful in urban districts, as the following garden moth trap tallies illustrate:
Radford, Coventry: 1979 (55), 1980 (70), 1993 (88), 2002 (47) (MCV). Interestingly, no White Ermine were recorded at this site during these years.

The table below compares frequency of the two species in the suburban district of **Hillmorton, Rugby**, (DIP):

Species	1982	1985	1990	1995	2000
Buff Ermine	44	41	120	76	35
White Ermine	62	23	29	29	3

VCH 1904: *'Common everywhere.'*

Muslin Moth
2063 *Diaphora mendica* (Cl.)

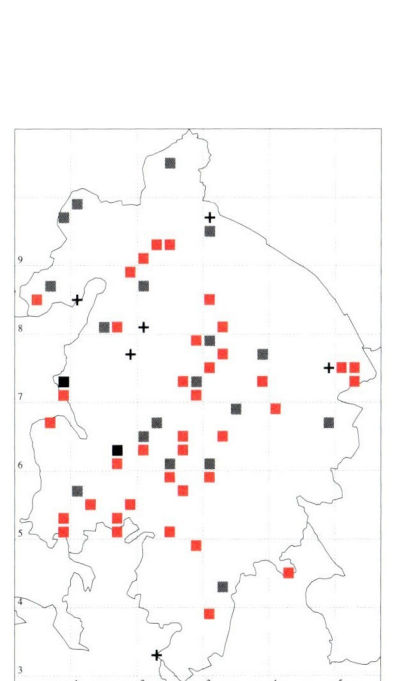

County status: Widespread and usually fairly common.
Flight: Mid-April to mid-June.
Larval foodplants: Many herbaceous plants, including docks and plantains.

The Muslin Moth is generally not as numerous as the two previous species, but is found over a wide area of the County. It frequents a range of habitats, including open woodland, railway cuttings, heathland and gardens.

The male comes regularly to moth traps but the chiefly day-flying white female is only very occasionally observed.

Some unusually early and late records of the adult are: Charlecote, 19/10/1995 (AFG); Kenilworth Road, Coventry, 12/8/2001 (MA); Radford, Coventry, 26/3/2003 (MCV); Brailes, 6/4/2003 (CI); Pillerton Priors, 23/9/2004 (CI); Temple Grafton, 2/11/2005 (AFG).

The table below compares rural and suburban garden moth trap totals:

Habitat	Location	1982	1985	1990	1995	2000
Suburban	Hillmorton, Rugby (DIP)	7	5	35	6	1
Rural	Charlecote (AFG)	43	108	139	31	130

VCH 1904: *'Not common.'*
Hampton-in-Arden, Knowle, Small Heath, Overslade, Atherstone, Wolford.

Ruby Tiger
2064 *Phragmatobia fuliginosa fuliginosa* (L.)

County status: Widespread and fairly common.
Flight: Two generations. Late April to June, and mid-July to mid-September.
Larval foodplants: Many herbaceous plants, including Dandelion*.

Ruby Tiger is found in an extensive range of habitats throughout the County. The second generation is generally much more plentiful.

Frequent in garden moth traps, as these figures indicate:
Pillerton Priors: 1992 (15), 1993 (11), 2002 (14), 2003 (24), 2004 (24), 2005 (30) (CI).

VCH 1904: *'Not common.'*
Sutton Park, Knowle, Atherstone, Wolford.

Scarlet Tiger
2068 *Callimorpha dominula* (L.)

Nationally Local

County status: Status uncertain. Suspected vagrant.
Flight: Late June to July. Flies by day and at night.
Larval foodplants: A wide range of plants, including Hollyhock*, Common Comfrey, Hemp-agrimony, Common Nettle, brambles, sallows and Honeysuckle.

This attractive species is associated with riverbanks and marshy areas containing large amounts of Common Comfrey. The few recent records of Scarlet Tiger are assumed to be vagrants from the neighbouring Counties of Gloucestershire or Oxfordshire.

It is unlikely that such a large and colourful day-flying moth could be overlooked if it was breeding in Warwickshire, as the County has only a limited number of suitable locations for colonisation.

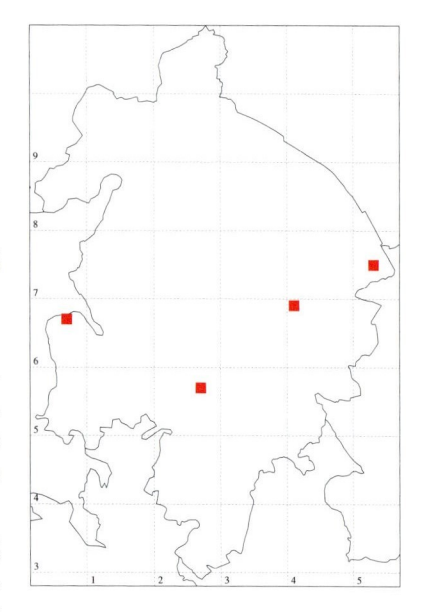

Records:
Matchborough, Redditch, 29/6/1992 MV (SD); **Charlecote,** 19/7/1996 MV (DB); **Rugby,** May 1997 larva on Hollyhock in urban garden (IGMR); **Marton,** 1/7/2001 flying in daytime (RA).

Cinnabar
2069 *Tyria jacobaeae* (L.)

County status: Widespread and fairly common.
Flight: Day- and night-flying. May to mid-August.
Larval foodplants: Ragworts* and groundsels*.

The Cinnabar is widely distributed and often common on light well-drained soils where the larval foodplant, Common Ragwort, grows in profusion. The yellow and black banded larvae are a familiar sight and may be seen in very large numbers in most years at favoured locations, such as Brandon Marsh.

It has not always been so plentiful and the VCH 1904 commented *'Rare, has not been taken anywhere near Birmingham for many years.'* Brandon Wood, Atherstone, Wolford.

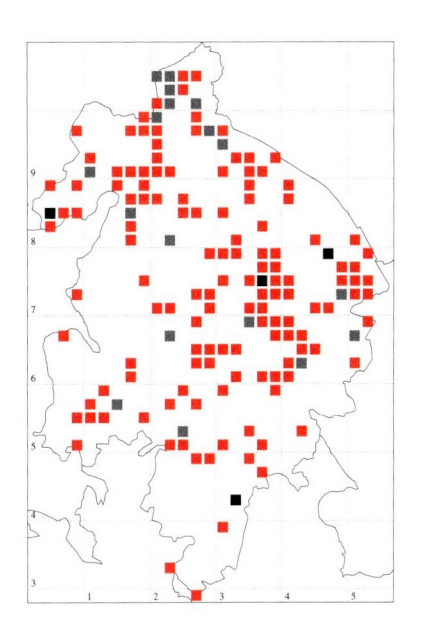

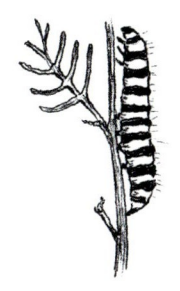

Family: Nolidae

The Nolidae is a family of just four resident British species, two of which are found in Warwickshire. They are generally small, white or grey nocturnal moths and are often mistaken for microlepidoptera.

Short-cloaked Moth
2077 *Nola cucullatella* (L.)

County status: Widespread and fairly common.
Flight: June to mid-August.
Larval foodplants: Blackthorn*, hawthorns, apple, pear and plum.

The Short-cloaked Moth frequents woodland, disused railway embankments, quarries, orchards and gardens. Owing to its small size it could well be under-recorded.

The adults are frequently noted in rural areas, as the following garden moth trap totals show:
Pillerton Priors: 1992 (9), 1993 (28), 1994 (10), 2002 (11), 2003 (10), 2004 (9), 2005 (11) (CI).

Numbers in urban districts are generally lower:
Radford, Coventry: 1992 (2), 1993 (4), 1994 (6), 2002 (0), 2003 (1), 2004 (2), 2005 (1) (MCV).

VCH 1904: *'Generally common, mainly in the north.'*

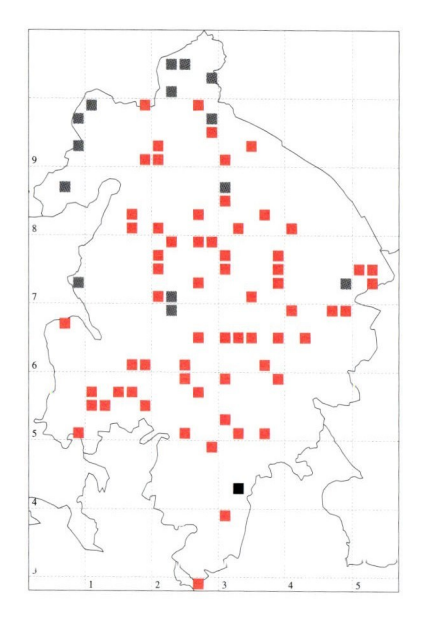

Least Black Arches
2078 *Nola confusalis* H.-S.

Nationally Local

County status: Widespread and fairly common.
Flight: Late April to early July.
Larval foodplants: Many deciduous trees, including Field Maple*, birches*, Purging Buckthorn, and Blackthorn.

This diminutive species has proved to be widespread in the south of the County but is more sparsely distributed in the north. The adult visits MV in generally low numbers but is often noted resting on tree trunks and palings. Favoured habitats include woodland, overgrown quarries, scrub and railway embankments.

Typical totals at garden moth traps are shown below:
Pillerton Priors: 1992 (3), 1993 (7), 1994 (3), 2002 (1), 2003 (2), 2004 (3) (CI);
Bidford-on-Avon: 1989 (8), 1990 (1), 1992 (5), 1993 (3), 1994 (1), 1995 (6) (RMC).

VCH 1904: *Coombe Wood, Brandon Wood, Wolford Wood.*

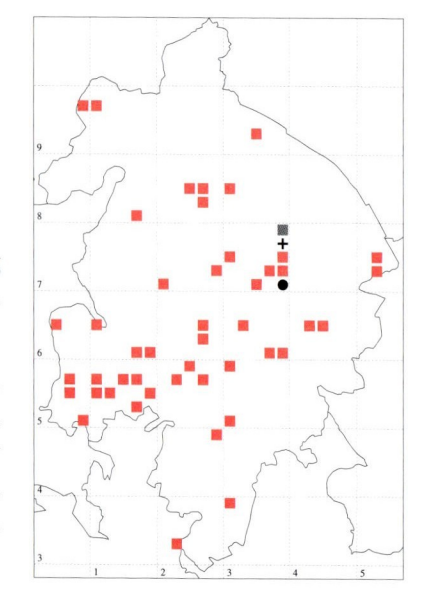

Family: Noctuidae

The Noctuidae is the largest family of macro-moths with approximately 400 species on the British list, of which almost 200 are currently known to occur in Warwickshire.

Most species in the family are nocturnal and freely attracted to light, whilst many are also attracted to sugar. There are a few day-flying species, of which Mother Shipton and Burnet Companion are the most familiar in the County. The majority of long distance immigrant moths are noctuids, 19 species having been recorded in Warwickshire during the last 35 years.

The Noctuidae are a diverse family but are generally medium-sized with stout bodies. At rest the forewings are held roof-like to cover the hindwings and body, whilst in other species the wings partially or completely overlap. The snouts, fan-foots and closely related species, such as Waved Black, are more slender than a typical noctuid and generally rest with wings spread flat, thus creating difficulties for beginners in separation from Geometers. The forewing pattern of many noctuids includes a conspicuous kidney-shaped marking, the reniform stigma, and an adjacent oval orbicular stigma. Often the stigmata are well defined and their form plays an important role in the identification of difficult species. These features are, however, obsolete or entirely absent on the majority of wainscots and plusias. The latter possess forewings displaying metallic silver or gold markings, making them one of the most popular sub-families.

The larvae of the Noctuidae, as might be expected of such a large family, are highly variable but generally rather fleshy with few hairs, except for the daggers. Most have five pairs of prolegs but in the Herminiinae (fan-foots), Catocalinae (red underwings), Hypeninae (snouts) and Plusiinae (plusias) these are often reduced to three or four pairs, including the anal claspers.

Foodplants are varied with the leaves of trees, shrubs and grasses being utilised. A few species, such as Bulrush Wainscot, feed internally within stems whilst a small minority, including Turnip Moth and Light Arches, eat roots and are subterranean.

Square-spot Dart
2080 *Euxoa obelisca grisea* (Tutt)

Nationally Scarce B

County status: Very local and scarce.
Flight: August to early September.
Larval foodplants: Various low-growing plants, including Lady's Bedstraw.

This almost entirely coastal species is frequently recorded from the Hillmorton district of Rugby. It has also been noted at Coventry and on heathland in the north of the County.

Records:
Sutton Park, 1893 (PWA), 1895 (GWW); **Gravelly Hill, Birmingham**, 1920s (GPS); **Hillmorton, Rugby**, 25/8/1981, 1/8/1984 (2), 8/8/1984, 15/8/1984, 8/9/1985, 13/8/1986, 17/8/1988, 3/8/1990, 19/8/1991, 24/8/1992, 17/8/1996, 10/9/2000, 11/9/2000, 10/8/2002 (DIP); 3/9/1986 (PN, confirmed D. Carter), 26/8/1987, 18/8/1988, 26/8/1988, 6/9/1988, 23/8/1990, 14/8/1991, 15/8/1991, 20/8/1991, 17/8/1995, 19/8/1996,

3/9/1998, 24/8/2000, 18/8/2002, 28/8/2003 (PN); **Parkside**, **Coventry**, 16/8/1986 (MB); **Grendon Common**, 18/8/1990 (2) (DB, RGB, AFG).

VCH 1904: *'This species, usually associated with the sea coast occurs in Sutton Park, where a few specimens have been taken.'*

White-line Dart
2081 *Euxoa tritici* (L.)

County status: Very local and uncommon.
Flight: Late July to early September.
Larval foodplants: A wide range of herbaceous plants, including bedstraws.

The White-line Dart is most frequently observed on heathland in the north of the County. It is fairly common at Sutton Park, otherwise rarely seen.

Records:
Solihull, 31/7/1946 (SEWC); **Edgbaston, Birmingham**, Aug. 1946 (MWB); **Earlsdon, Coventry**, 1955, 11/8/1978 (LEM); **Erdington**, 22/8/1956 (LJE); **Nuneaton**, 1970s (RJT); **Marton**, 1970s (RA); **Sutton Park** 1970s (LJE), 18/8/1983 (AN), 17/8/2002 (12), 13/8/2005 (24) (Warks Moth Group); **Hartshill Hayes**, 1975–79 (RJT); **Harborne**, 1974 (DWB); **Oakfield (football ground), Rugby**, 1975 (A. Seats); **Charlecote**, 23/7/1976, 5/8/1976, 3/8/1998 (DB, AFG); **Hatton Green**, 20/8/1977 (AP); **Bolehall**, 9/9/1977 (WA); **Wilmcote Rough**, 1977–79 (JMP); **Claverdon**, 14/8/1982 (IGMR); **Stretton-under-Fosse**, 1/8/1995 (J. Wallace); **Hillmorton, Rugby**, 11/8/1997 (DIP).

VCH 1904: *'Very rare.'*
Hampton-in-Arden, Rugby.

Garden Dart
2082 *Euxoa nigricans* (L.)

County status: Very local and becoming scarce.
Flight: July to mid-September.
Larval foodplants: Herbaceous plants, including clovers, docks and plantains.

The Garden Dart has been recorded in a number of habitats other than gardens, including disused railway embankments, calcareous grassland, heathland, and open woodland.

It is a species subject to periodic fluctuations and range expansions followed by sudden contractions. There is, however, evidence of a more serious decline since 1980 (Fig. 18).

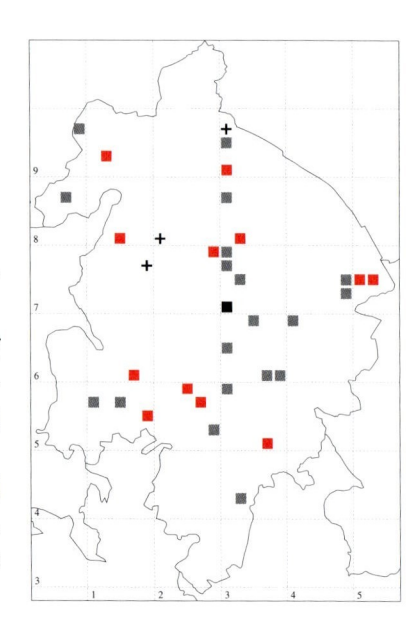

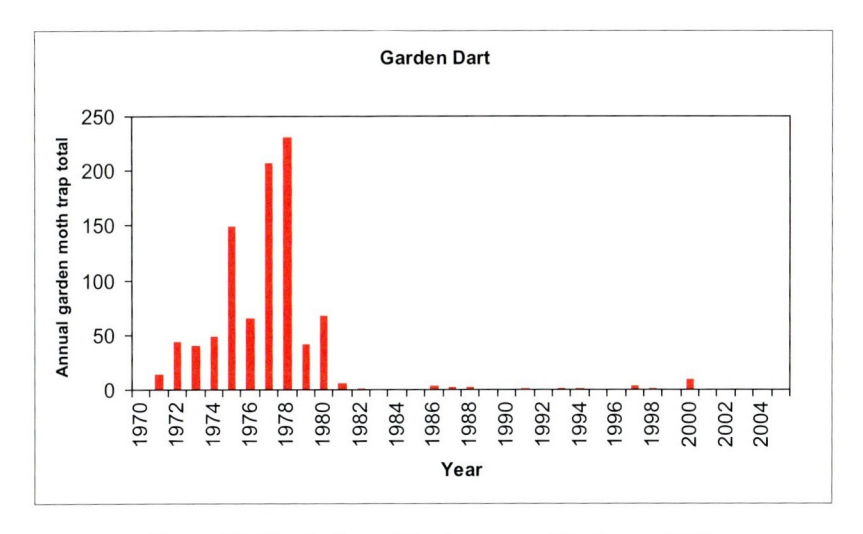

Figure 18. The decline of *E. nigricans* at Charlecote (DB).

VCH 1904: *Birmingham (very rare), Knowle, Hampton-in-Arden (a few), Atherstone, Rugby.*

Light Feathered Rustic
2084 *Agrotis cinerea* ([D. & S.])

Nationally Scarce B

County status: Possibly extinct. Formerly very local.
Flight: May.
Larval foodplants: Wild Thyme and possibly other low-growing plants.

This chalk and limestone grassland species has only been recorded from Nelson's Quarry, Stockton, where it was discovered in 1990 (DB, AFG). Unfortunately in recent years much of the area has become enveloped with hawthorn scrub and the status of the Light Feathered Rustic is now uncertain.

Records:
Nelson's Quarry, Stockton, 6/5/1990 (45) (DB, AFG), 24/5/1991 (12) (DB, PJR), 29/5/1991 (26) (DB, RMC), 30/5/1992 (2) (Warks Moth Group).

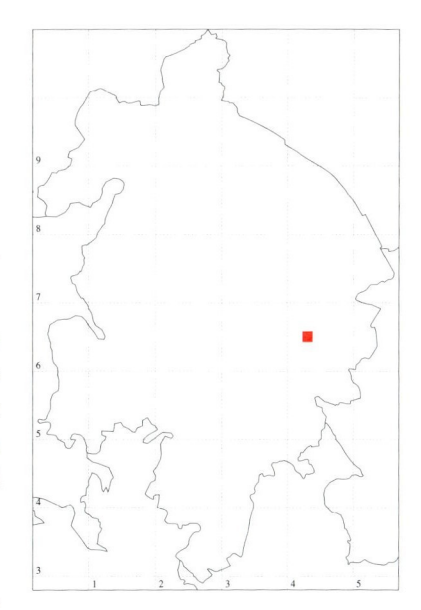

Turnip Moth
2087 *Agrotis segetum* ([D. & S.])

County status: Widespread and common.
Flight: Two overlapping generations. May to November.
Larval foodplants: The roots and lower stems of various herbaceous plants, including Turnip*, Carrot*, Beet*, Swede* and Cabbage*.

The Turnip Moth thrives in a variety of habitats, especially gardens and cultivated areas. The larvae are a pest of root crops. It is common at moth traps in both rural and suburban districts.

Numbers at **Hillmorton, Rugby**, are as follows: 1982 (83), 1985 (119), 1990 (452), 1995 (515), 2000 (32), 2004 (42) (DIP). Melanic forms are plentiful in most Warwickshire populations.

VCH 1904: *'Common everywhere.'*

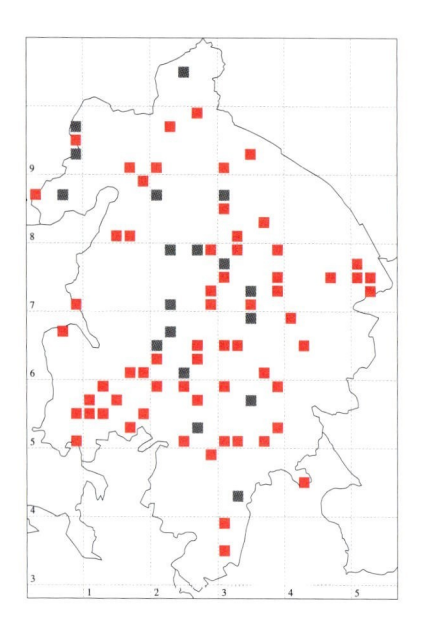

Heart and Club
2088 *Agrotis clavis* (Hufn.)

County status: Local and sometimes common.
Flight: June and July.
Larval foodplants: A wide range of herbaceous plants, including Dandelion, docks, clovers and Knotgrass.

The Heart and Club favours dry, open, calcareous grassland where plants grow in a sparse sward. Such conditions can be found at Bishops Hill, Burton Dassett Hills C.P. and Cross Hands Quarry. Healthy populations are established at these sites, as reflected by the following moth trap figures: Bishops Hill, 20/6/2005 (250) (Warks Moth Group); Burton Dassett Hills C.P., 19/6/2004 (16) (Warks Moth Group); Cross Hands Quarry, 9/7/2005 (20) (CI, RGB). Wanderers are occasionally noted in garden moth traps, usually on or near calcareous soils.

VCH 1904: *'Rare with us.'*
Marston Green, Lapworth, Hampton-in-Arden, Overslade.

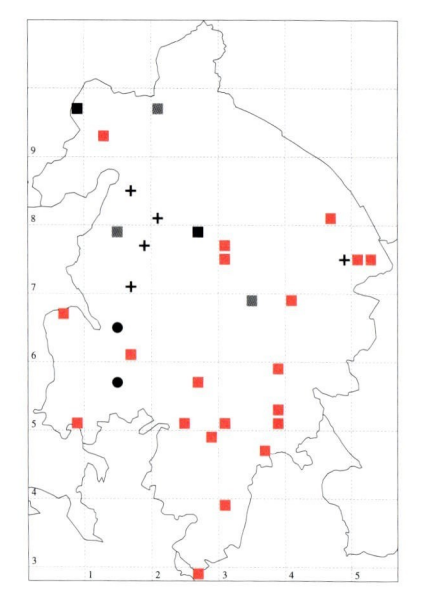

Heart and Dart
2089 *Agrotis exclamationis* (L.)

County status: Widespread and abundant.
Flight: Possibly two generations. May to August, and occasionally September.
Larval foodplants: Polyphagous on herbaceous plants.

The Heart and Dart is an abundant species throughout the County, appearing in large numbers in both rural and urban districts.

Examples of totals in an urban garden moth trap at **Radford, Coventry**, are: 1970 (1,152), 1975 (330), 1980 (427), 1985 (513), 1990 (443), 1995 (627), 2000 (683) (MCV).

The following late examples may represent individuals of a partial second generation: Styvechale, Coventry, 21/9/2001 (NJS); Warwick, 15/9/2003 (SDT).

VCH 1904: *'Very common everywhere.'*

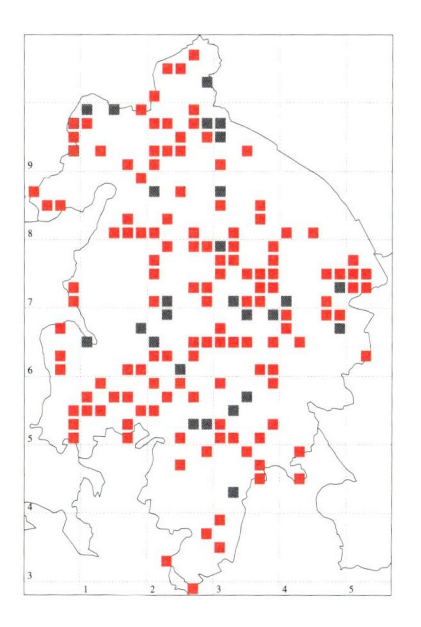

Dark Sword-grass
2091 *Agrotis ipsilon* (Hufn.)

Common immigrant, possible transitory resident: Southern and central Europe

County status: Annual immigrant.
Flight: March to November.
Larval foodplants: Polyphagous on herbaceous plants.

The Dark Sword-grass occurs annually in Warwickshire but with considerable variation in numbers. The peak time of occurrence is usually between mid-August and late September. The table below gives the garden moth trap totals at Charlecote and Hillmorton, Rugby, from 1985 to 2005.

Habitat	Location	1985–89	1990–94	1995–99	2000–05
Suburban	Hillmorton, Rugby (DIP)	46	13	23	22
Rural	Charlecote (DB)	81	39	138	58

VCH 1904: *'Not common.'*
Sutton, Knowle, Hampton-in-Arden, Overslade, Atherstone, Birmingham.

Shuttle-shaped Dart
2092 *Agrotis puta puta* (Hb.)

County status: Widespread and common.
Flight: Two or possibly three overlapping generations in warm years, April to November.
Larval foodplants: Polyphagous on herbaceous plants, including docks*.

This species is found commonly in a wide range of habitats in both rural and urban districts. During warm years there is evidence of a partial third generation, peaking at the end of September and continuing throughout November.

Garden moth trap counts in built-up districts are as follows:

Radford, Coventry: 1982 (141), 1985 (42), 1990 (541), 1995 (218), 2000 (74), 2004 (329) (MCV); **Hillmorton, Rugby:** 1982 (348), 1985 (238), 1990 (274), 2000 (743), 2004 (805) (DIP).

VCH 1904: *'Not common'.*
Waverley Wood, Wolford, Atherstone, Rugby, Knowle.

Flame
2098 *Axylia putris* (L.)

County status: Widespread and common.
Flight: May to end of July with individuals of a partial second generation in September.
Larval foodplants: Polyphagous on herbaceous plants.

Another widespread and common species occurring in numerous habitats, including agricultural land and gardens. Generally univoltine in Warwickshire but occasional examples representing a small second generation are noted: Charlecote, 16-25/9/1971 (3) (AFG), 28-30/9/1992 (2) (AFG); Central Rugby, 22/9/2004 (IGMR); Hillmorton, Rugby, 25/9/2004 (DIP).

Typical garden moth trap totals at **Bidford-on-Avon** are as follows: 1988 (137), 1989 (323), 1992 (282), 1993 (126), 1994 (133) (RMC).

VCH 1904: *'Not common.'*
Atherstone, Rugby, Overslade, Knowle, Waverley Wood, Wolford.

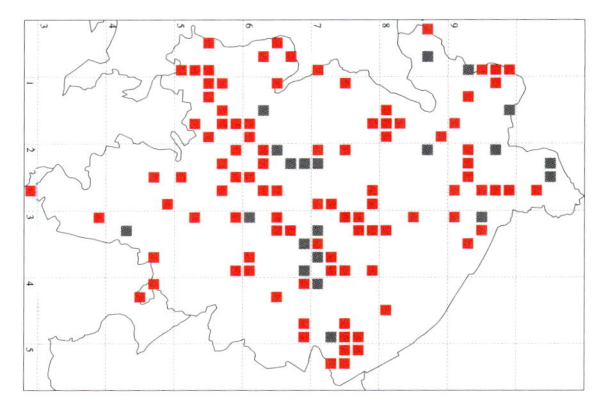

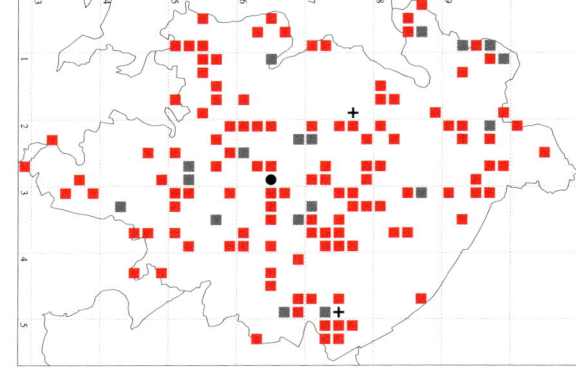

Eversmann's Rustic
2100 *Actebia fennica* (Tausch.)

Very rare immigrant: Northern Europe

County status: Very rare immigrant.
Flight: July and August.
Larval foodplants: Bilberry, willowherbs and other herbaceous plants.

A specimen of this very rare immigrant was caught in a garden moth trap at Hillmorton, Rugby on 14/8/1983 (DIP). The latest of only six British records (Bretherton, Chalmers-Hunt, 1984).

Flame Shoulder
2102 *Ochropleura plecta* (L.)

County status: Widespread and common.
Flight: Two overlapping generations. May to September.
Larval foodplants: Polyphagous on herbaceous plants.

The Flame Shoulder is found commonly in diverse habitats with smaller numbers in built-up areas. There are two overlapping broods, peaking in late June and mid-August. The table below compares rural and urban trap sites:

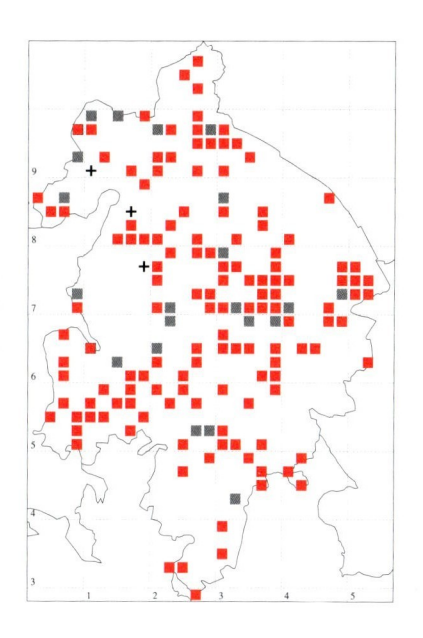

Habitat	Location	1988	1992	1993	1994	1995
Urban	Radford, Coventry (MCV)	12	8	10	6	7
Rural	Bidford-on-Avon (RMC)	184	73	122	82	31

VCH 1904: *Sutton, Knowle, Hampton-in-Arden, Marston Green, Overslade, Atherstone.*

Dotted Rustic
2105 *Rhyacia simulans* (Hufn.)

Nationally Local

County status: Fairly widespread but becoming scarce.
Flight: Late June to early October with a period of summer dormancy (aestivation) during August and part of September.
Larval foodplants: Unknown in the wild.

There were no records of Dotted Rustic in the County before the 1970s, during which decade the species spread across the region and became reasonably plentiful in the 1980s. This was linked to a national range expansion. Frequenting open woodland, calcareous grassland and gardens, adults could often be observed at night feeding on valerian and buddleia flowers. Since the beginning of the 1990s, however, this moth has undergone a sudden and widespread decline in Warwickshire (Fig. 19).

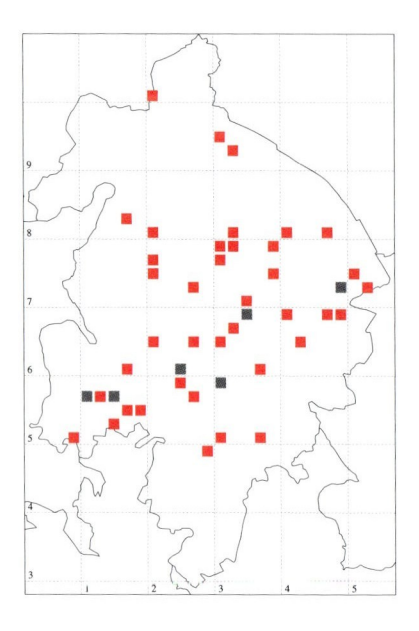

The imago has a period of aestivation and is relatively easy to locate when in this quiescent condition. In the 1980s many were found behind curtains or under boxes in outdoor buildings, summer-houses and garages. This summer dormancy has been observed well into September and a late solitary example was discovered under a carpet in a house in Charlecote on 28/9/2003 (PG).

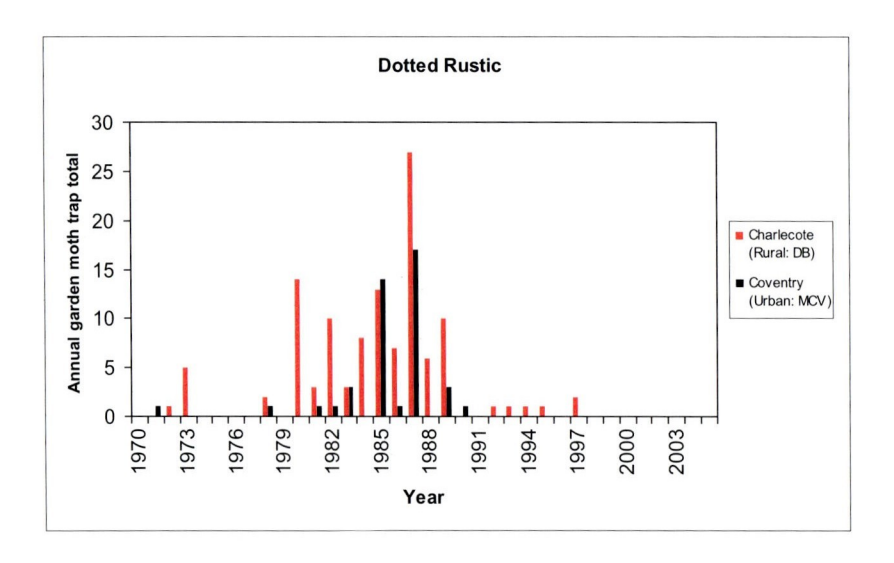

Figure 19. Fluctuations and recent decline of *R. simulans* in rural and urban districts.

Large Yellow Underwing
2107 *Noctua pronuba* (L.)

County status: Widespread and abundant.
Flight: May to November.
Larval foodplants: Polyphagous on herbaceous plants and grasses, including docks* and Dandelion*.

A ubiquitous species in the County and often the commonest Noctuid at moth traps.

The adult is a regular visitor to the sugar patch and is frequently disturbed from vegetation during the daytime. The Large Yellow Underwing has been found in every conceivable type of habitat in both rural and urban districts.

It is on the wing from May until December in one protracted generation. A particularly late specimen was captured on the cold night of 18/12/2004 at Solihull (RL).

An example of the unusual pale yellow form of the larva was found in Lillington, Royal Leamington Spa, on 14/4/2003 (EMR).

VCH 1904: *'Abundant everywhere.'*

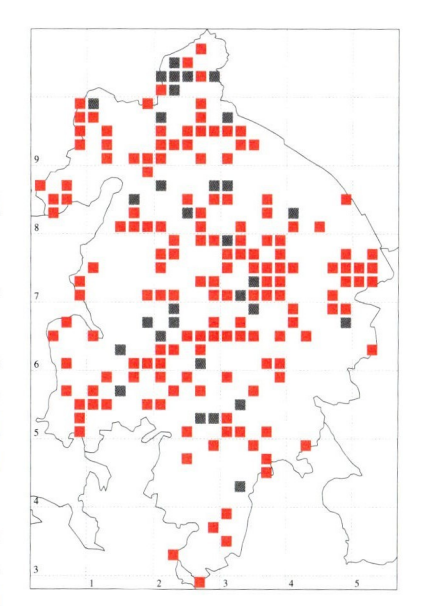

Lunar Yellow Underwing
2108 *Noctua orbona* (Hufn.)

Nationally Scarce B

County status: Extinct.
Flight: July.
Larval foodplants: Various herbaceous plants and grasses.

Edgbaston, 23/7/1870 (F. Enock).
Tile Hill Wood, 1949 (GW) unconfirmed record.

Lesser Yellow Underwing
2109 *Noctua comes* Hb.

County status: Widespread and common.
Flight: June to October.
Larval foodplants: Polyphagous on herbaceous plants, including docks*, trees and shrubs.

Another very common species but not as abundant as its congener, *pronuba*. It is similarly found in all types of habitats.

Large numbers occur in urban districts as garden moth trap figures at **Radford, Coventry**, illustrate: 1970 (25), 1975 (232), 1980 (370), 1985 (493), 1990 (278), 1995 (290), 2000 (168) (MCV).

VCH 1904: *'Common everywhere.'*

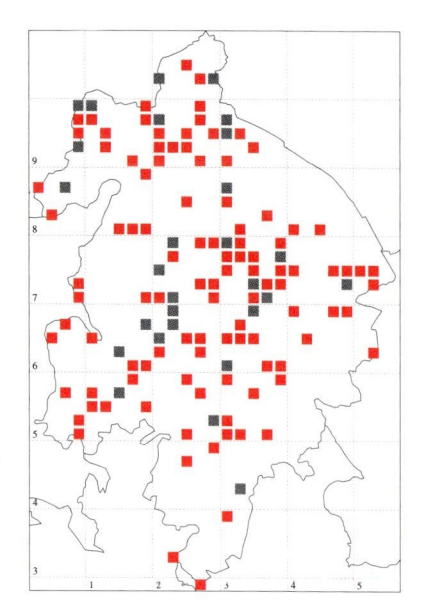

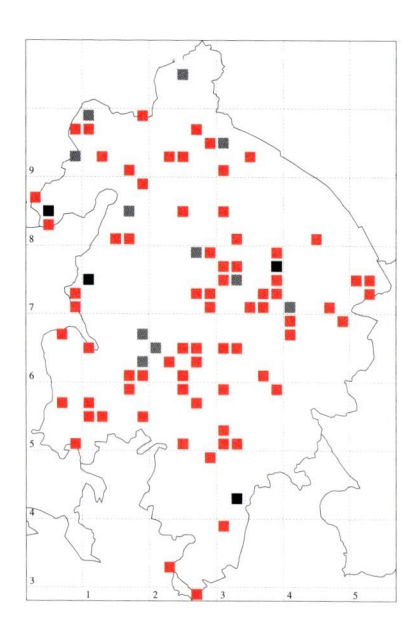

Broad-bordered Yellow Underwing
2110 *Noctua fimbriata* (Schreb.)

County status: Widespread and fairly common.
Flight: July to October.
Larval foodplants: A wide range of herbaceous plants, including docks*; also the young buds and foliage of various trees during the spring.

Although considerably less common than the preceding species, this attractive moth is a regular visitor to garden moth traps well into the autumn. Peak numbers occur in late July, the latter part of August and early September.

It is plentiful in wooded districts, and occasionally visits moth traps in large quantities; for example, Waverley Wood, 20/7/1990 (40) (Warks Moth Group).

VCH 1904: *'Not uncommon. Occurs in nearly every list, but is never abundant.'*

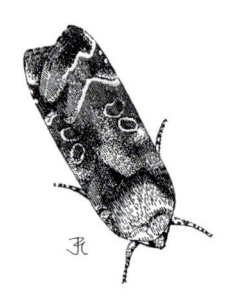

Lesser Broad-bordered Yellow Underwing
2111 *Noctua janthe* (Borkh.)

County status: Widespread and common.
Flight: July to mid-September.
Larval foodplants: A wide range of herbaceous plants and the young buds and foliage of trees in the spring.

This species is found commonly in a variety of habitats, including woodland, heathland and gardens.

The type of frequency it may reach is shown by the following garden moth trap counts:
Hillmorton, Rugby: 1982 (92), 1985 (166), 1990 (302), 1995 (377), 2000 (83), 2004 (236) (DIP);
Radford, Coventry: 1982 (26), 1985 (26), 1990 (54), 1995 (62), 2000 (22), 2004 (33) (MCV).

VCH 1904: *'Common throughout the district.'*

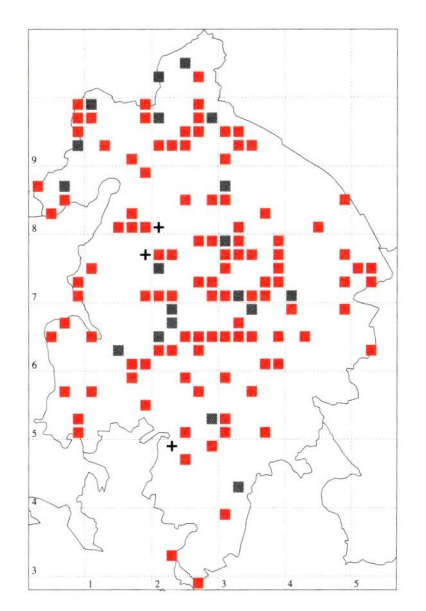

Least Yellow Underwing
2112 *Noctua interjecta caliginosa* Schaw.

County status: Widespread and fairly common.
Flight: Mid-July to late August.
Larval foodplants: A wide range of herbaceous plants and the young buds and foliage of trees in spring.

The Least Yellow Underwing is widespread and found in similar habitats to the last species with good numbers in marshy areas. Generally the least frequent of the *Noctua* species but, nevertheless, fairly plentiful in most years as the following figures show:
Radford, Coventry: 1982 (7), 1985 (4), 1990 (32), 1995 (42), 2000 (0), 2004 (2) (MCV);
Hillmorton, Rugby: 1982 (54), 1985 (1), 1990 (88), 1995 (143), 2000 (2), 2004 (10) (DIP).

VCH 1904: *'Rare.'*
Knowle, Hampton-in-Arden, Overslade, Atherstone, Wolford.

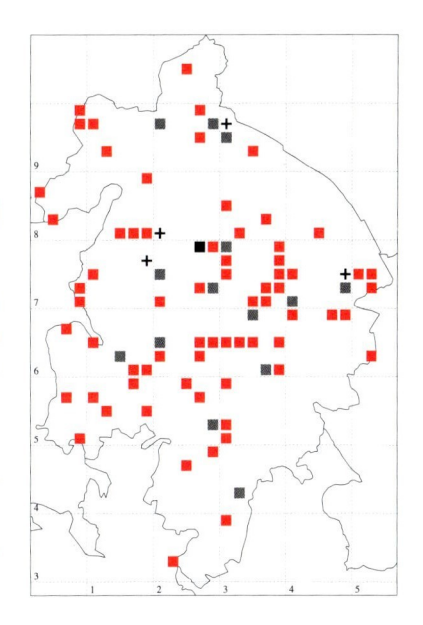

Stout Dart
2113 *Spaelotis ravida* ([D. & S.])
Nationally Local

County status: Possibly extinct. Formerly very local.
Flight: Late June to September.
Larval foodplants: Unknown in the wild.

The Stout Dart is similar to the Dotted Rustic in experiencing periodic fluctuations and range expansions followed by contractions. Having been fitfully recorded in the County during the first half of the twentieth century, the species experienced a dramatic increase during the 1970s. It became locally plentiful in river valleys, damp woodland and gardens over a broad band of central and southern Warwickshire. By the mid-1980s a serious decline had commenced and this unpredictable moth has not been observed since 1988 (Fig. 20).

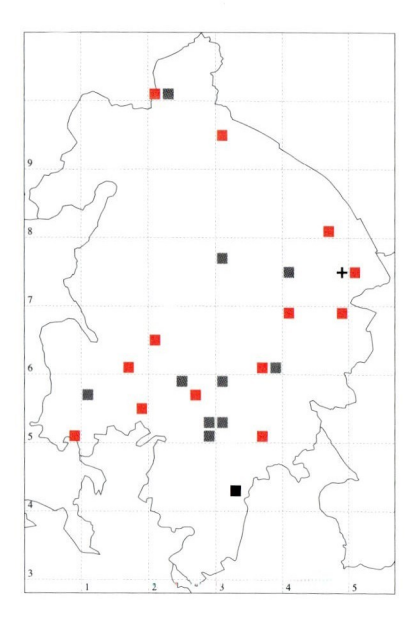

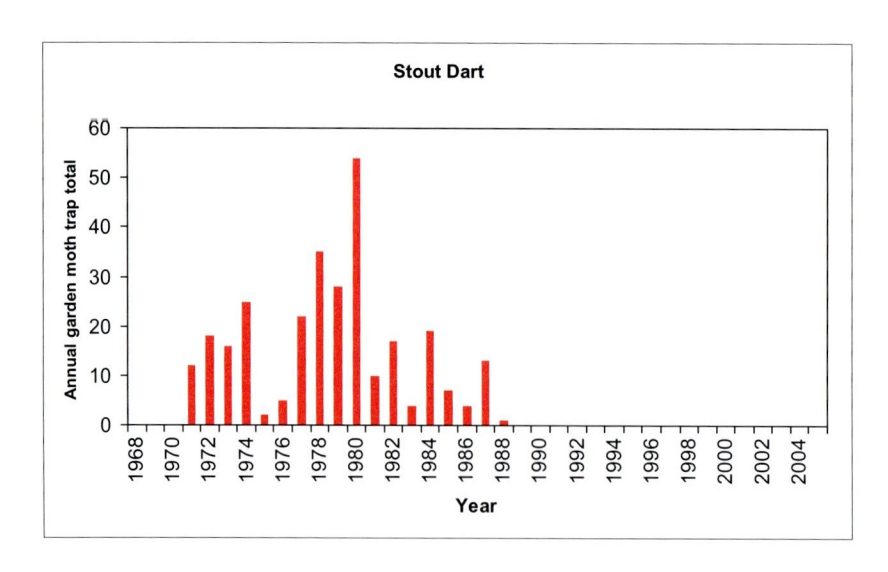

Figure 20. The changes in fortune of *S. ravida* at Charlecote (DB).

Records:
Tysoe, July 1947 (TT); **Ufton Fields**, 15/8/1964 (ANT), 9/8/1985 (CDNHSS); **Wilnecote**, 1965 (RGW); **Earlsdon, Coventry**, 1968 (PC); **Bowshot Wood**, 1970, 1971 (DB); **Charlecote**, 1970–88 Last record 9/9/1988 (DB, AFG); **Hampton Wood**, 1972 (23), 1973 (3), 1974 (7) (AFG); **Oakley Wood**, 24/7/1973 (DB), 18/9/1976 (DB, AFG), 26/7/1977 (DB, WF), 29/8/1978 (2) (DB, WF); **Walton**, 8/8/1973 (2) (DB, PR, ES), 9/8/1973 one at sugar (DB), 25/8/1973 (DB, BE, JC); **Marton**, 1970s (RA); **Wolston**, 5/8/1977 (KAM); **Walton Wood railway embankment**, 27/8/1978 (3) (DB, RHS, AFG); **Toft Farm, Dunchurch**, 14/7/1979 (AFG); **Oversley Wood**, 2/8/1980, 28/8/1987 (AFG, DB); **Hartshill Hayes**, 1980 (RJT); **Hillmorton, Rugby**, 1982 (4), 1983, 1984 (3), 1985 (9), 1986 (2), 1987 (3) (DIP); **Dosthill**, 1982 (PAD); **Evesham Road, Stratford-upon-Avon**, 5/8/1983 (DB); **Pailton**, 1984–85 (KCG);

Bidford-on-Avon, 1980s until 4/9/1988 (RMC); **Claverdon**, 14/8/1985, 13/9/1985 (IGMR); **CAD Kineton**, 7/8/1987 (2) (Warks Moth Group).

VCH 1904: *'Very rare.'*
Rugby, Overslade.

Double Dart
2114 *Graphiphora augur* (Fabr.)

County status: Fairly widespread but becoming uncommon.
Flight: June to August.
Larval foodplants: Various herbaceous plants in the autumn and the young foliage of hawthorns, Blackthorn, birches and sallows in the spring.

The Double Dart has been recorded from a large part of the County in a variety of habitats, including woodlands, marshes and gardens. Many local populations have surprisingly plummeted during the last 25 years (Fig. 21).

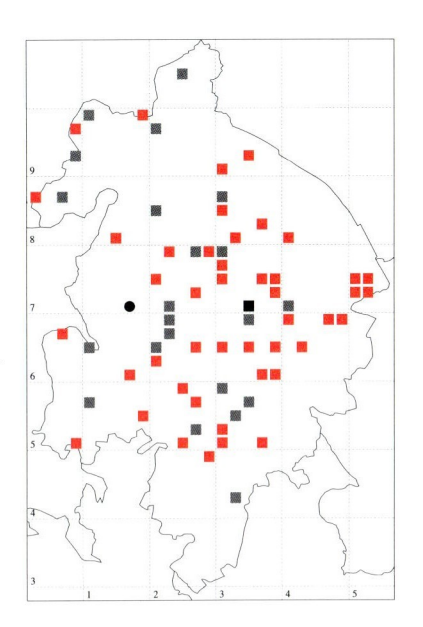

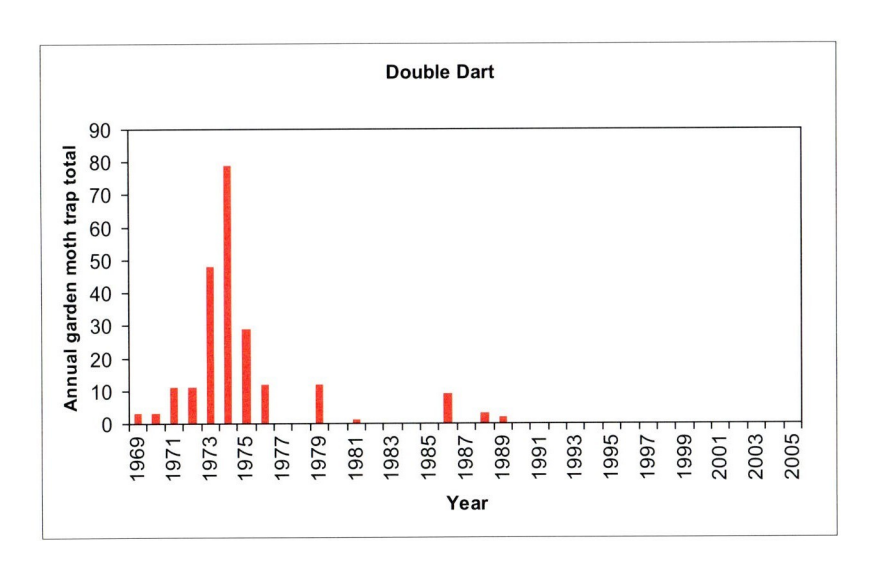

Figure 21. Diminishing population of *G. augur* at Charlecote (DB).

VCH 1904: *'Common throughout the district.'*

Autumnal Rustic
2117 *Eugnorisma glareosa* (Esp.)

County status: Local and fairly common on heathland.
Flight: Late August to September.
Larval foodplants: Low-growing plants, including heathers, bedstraws, and Bluebell; also birches and sallows.

The Autumnal Rustic is found on heathland and open woodland with light, well-drained soils. Sites include Sutton Park, Grendon Common, Windmill Hill, Crackley Wood, Close Wood, Hay Wood and Oversley Wood. Occasionally observed at light in good numbers; for example, Sutton Park, 29/8/1992 (20) (Warks Moth Group). Individuals are sometimes noted in garden moth traps.

VCH 1904: *Sutton Park, Knowle, Hampton-in-Arden.*

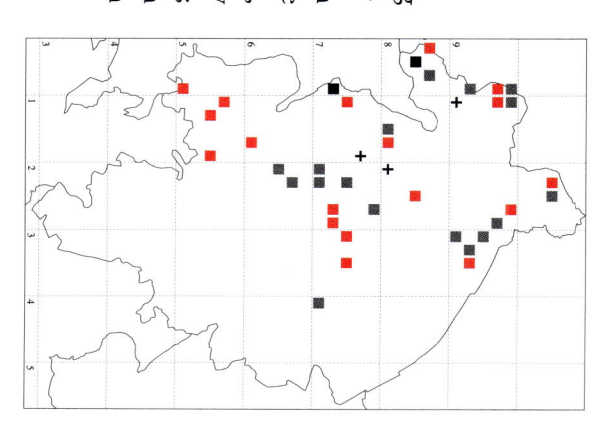

Plain Clay
2103 *Eugnorisma depuncta* (L.)
Nationally Scarce B

County status: Presumed extinct.
Flight: July and August.
Larval foodplants: A wide range of low-growing plants, including Primrose, Cowslip, sorrels, nettles and stitchworts.

The Plain Clay was included in A. Sidgwick's 1893 list for the Rugby district and subsequently recorded in Sutton Park during the 1960s (JB). It has since contracted northwards in the British Isles and become Nationally Scarce.

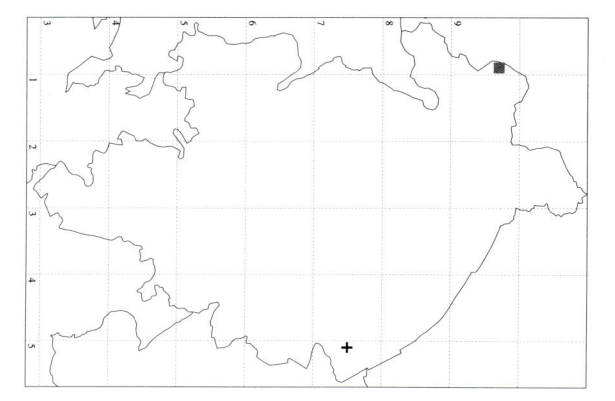

True Lover's Knot
2118 *Lycophotia porphyrea* ([D. & S.])

County status: Local and common on heathland.
Flight: Late June to end of August.
Larval foodplants: Heathers*.

The True Lover's Knot is a common species on heather terrain at Grendon Common, and in Sutton Park; for example, at the latter site 150 were recorded on 5/8/2000 (DB, DG). Small numbers occur in woodland containing sparse heather at Hay Wood, Wainbody Wood, Waverley Wood, Whitacre Heath and Coughton Park. Less frequently observed in gardens, usually as singletons, where it is associated with ornamental heathers.

VCH 1904: *Sutton Park, Hay Wood.*

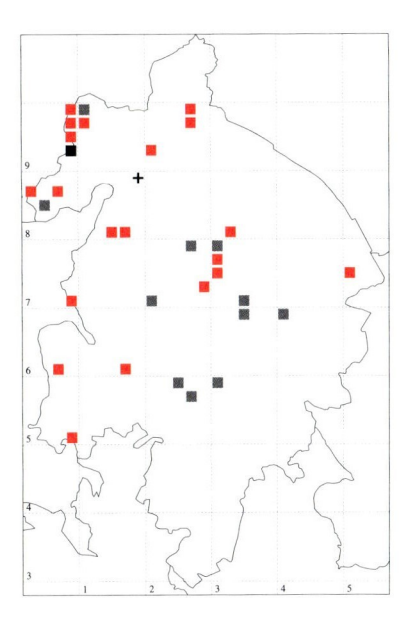

Pearly Underwing
2119 *Peridroma saucia* (Hb.)

Common immigrant, possible transitory resident: Europe and North Africa

County status: Almost annual immigrant.
Flight: April to November.
Larval foodplants: Polyphagous on herbaceous plants.

The Pearly Underwing reaches Warwickshire in most years but rarely in any numbers.

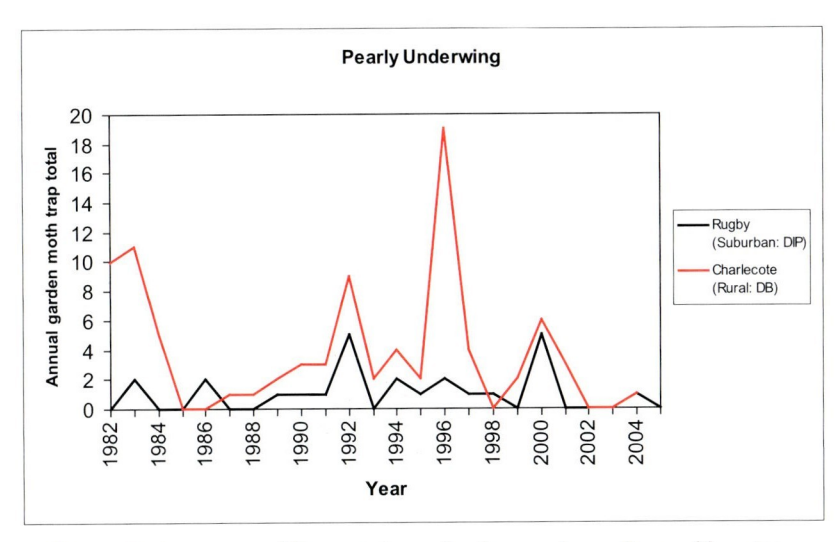

Figure 22. Frequency of *P. saucia* in a suburban garden and a rural location.

VCH 1904: *'Not common'*
Sutton, Knowle, Small Heath, Overslade.

Ingrailed Clay
2120 *Diarsia mendica mendica* (Fabr.)

County status: Widespread and fairly common.
Flight: Late May to early August.
Larval foodplants: Herbaceous plants, including Primrose and violets; also woody species such as brambles, sallows, hawthorns, Blackthorn and Hazel.

The Ingrailed Clay is a highly polymorphic species in which the markings and ground colour are subject to extensive variation. It occurs over a large area of the County but is most common in broadleaved woodlands.

Good numbers exist in the partially wooded outskirts of Coventry as garden moth trap counts illustrate:
Kenilworth Road: 2001 (71), 2002 (78), 2003 (102), 2004 (61), 2005 (73) (MA).

VCH 1904: *'Common everywhere.'*

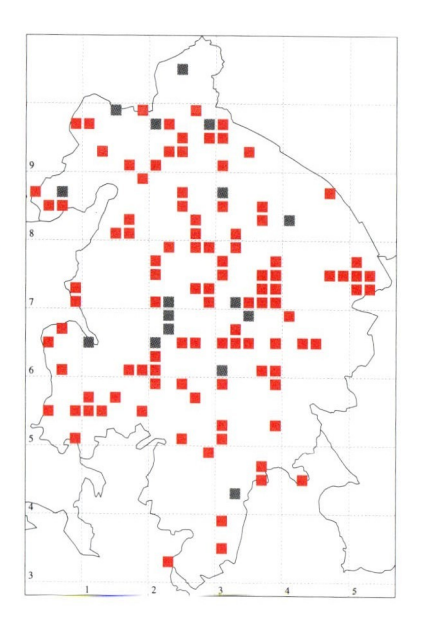

Barred Chestnut
2121 *Diarsia dahlii* (Hb.)

Nationally Local

County status: Very local and fairly common.
Flight: August and September.
Larval foodplants: Brambles, sallows, Bilberry, birches and a variety of herbaceous plants.

The Barred Chestnut is confined to the acidic soils of north-west Warwickshire where healthy colonies exist on the heather terrain of Sutton Park. Good numbers are usually attracted to MV; for example, 29/8/1992 (12), 17/8/2002 (10) (Warks Moth Group).

Records:
Sutton Park, 1960s (JB), 1970s (LJE), 29/8/1992, 17/8/2002, 13/8/2005 (Warks Moth Group).

VCH 1904: *'Not common.'*
Sutton Park, Knowle, Overslade.

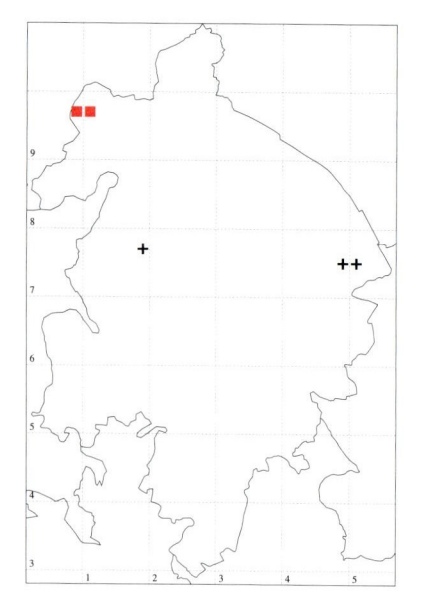

Purple Clay
2122 *Diarsia brunnea* ([D. & S.])

County status: Fairly widespread and fairly common.
Flight: June to August.
Larval foodplants: A wide range of herbaceous plants in the autumn, and woody species such as Heather, sallows, brambles and birches in the spring.

The Purple Clay is primarily a woodland species. It is well established and plentiful at Wolford Wood, Oversley Wood, Snitterfield Bushes, Hampton Wood, Oakley Wood, Ryton Wood, Waverley Wood, Kingsbury Wood and Sutton Park.

VCH 1904: *Sutton Park, Knowle, Brandon Wood, Marston Green, Hampton-in-Arden.*

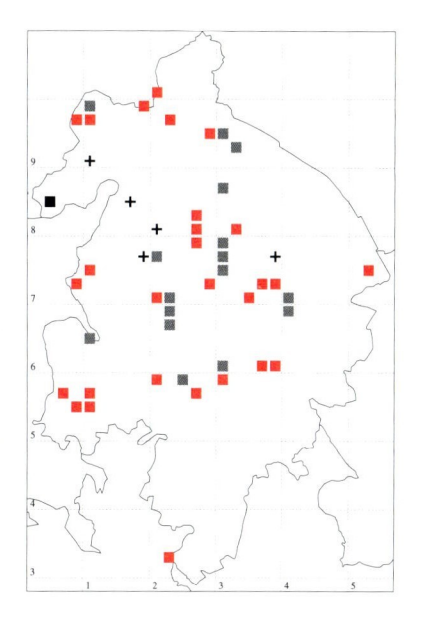

Small Square-spot
2123 *Diarsia rubi* (View.)

County status: Widespread and fairly common, but beginning to show signs of decline.
Flight: Two generations. May to June, and August to September.
Larval foodplants: Polyphagous on herbaceous plants.

The Small Square-spot is widely distributed and found in all types of habitats. The second generation has usually finished by the end of September, but occasional stragglers are recorded in October; for example, Charlecote, 19/10/1995 (DB).

Typical numbers in urban and rural garden moth traps are:
Radford, Coventry: 1988 (8), 1989 (39), 1994 (12), 1995 (25) (MCV);
Bidford-on-Avon: 1988 (361), 1989 (510), 1994 (189), 1995 (144) (RMC).

VCH 1904: *Sutton Park, Knowle, Hampton-in-Arden, Overslade, Atherstone.*

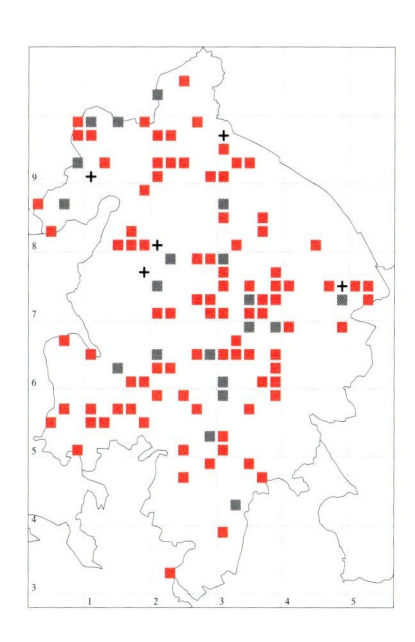

Setaceous Hebrew Character
2126 *Xestia c-nigrum* (L.)

County status: Widespread and abundant.
Flight: Two generations. May to July, and August to October.
Larval foodplants: Polyphagous on herbaceous plants.

An abundant species found in all types of habitats, but especially plentiful in gardens, cultivated areas and waste-ground. There are two distinct broods, the second being much more numerous and peaking in late August to early September.

Annual garden moth trap totals in rural areas often exceed 1,000 individuals.

Lesser quantities occur in built-up districts, as the following counts from **Radford, Coventry**, show: 1975 (37), 1980 (10), 1985 (17), 1990 (36), 1995 (48), 2000 (45) (MCV).

VCH 1904: *'Common everywhere.'*

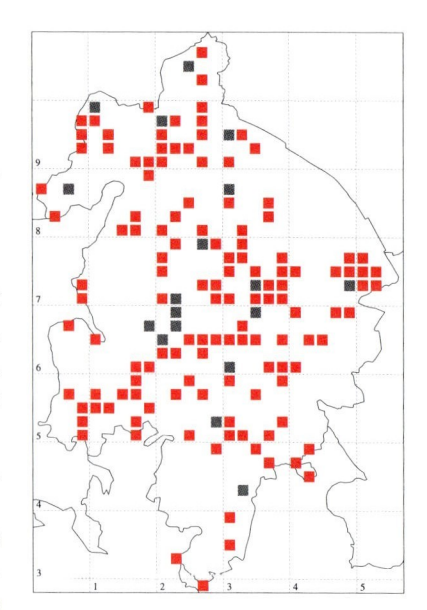

Triple-spotted Clay
2127 *Xestia ditrapezium* ([D. & S.])

Nationally Local

County status: Very local and scarce.
Flight: Mid-June to July.
Larval foodplants: Herbaceous plants, including Primrose and, after hibernation, the buds and young foliage of birches, sallows, Blackthorn and brambles.

The Triple-spotted Clay was first recorded in Warwickshire during the 1970s, in which decade it became locally established. It is most often observed in well-wooded districts, but occasionally noted in built-up areas.

Records:
Hampton Wood, 26/7/1972 (AFG); **Edgbaston, Birmingham**, 1972 (MRY); **Tile Hill Wood**, 28/7/1973 (DB); **Charlecote**, 1/7/1976, 10/7/1985, 4/7/1986, 11/7/1986 (DB, AFG); **Broad Street, Warwick**, 17/6/1990 (RGB); **Hillmorton, Rugby**, 16/7/2000, 29/6/2001, 12/7/2005, 3/8/2005 (PN).

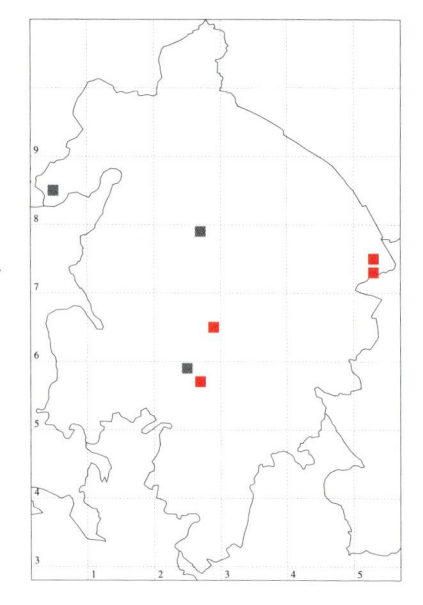

Double Square-spot
2128 *Xestia triangulum* (Hufn.)

County status: Widespread and fairly common.
Flight: June to early August.
Larval foodplants: Polyphagous on herbaceous plants, including valerians*, docks* and in the spring on the buds and young foliage of woody plants and shrubs.

The Double Square-spot is a widespread species found in a range of habitats, including woodland, open waste-ground and gardens.

The following garden moth trap counts give an idea of frequency:
Hillmorton, Rugby: 1982 (166), 1985 (138), 1990 (223), 1995 (222), 2000 (114), 2004 (68) (DIP).

VCH 1904:
Sutton Park, Knowle, Marston Green, Small Heath, Atherstone, Overslade, Yardley, Hampton-in-Arden.

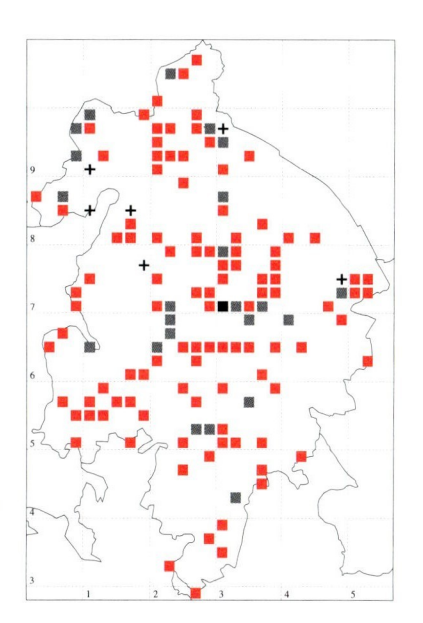

Dotted Clay
2130 *Xestia baja* ([D. & S.])

County status: Very local and sometimes fairly common.
Flight: Late July to late August.
Larval foodplants: Polyphagous on herbaceous plants during the autumn, and the young foliage of woody species such as birches, sallows and Blackthorn in the spring.

This woodland and heathland species can be found in Waverley Wood, Hay Wood, Oakley Wood, Brandon Marsh and Grendon Common. However, the largest numbers are usually observed at Sutton Park; for example, 5/8/2000 (40) (Warks Moth Group). It is occasionally noted in garden moth traps.

Records since 1980:
Dosthill, 1981 (RJT); **Hillmorton**, **Rugby**, 1980s (DIP); **Thickthorn Wood**, **Kenilworth**, 20/8/1982 (CDNHSS); **Sutton Park**, 11/8/1983 (AN), 28/8/1993, 5/8/2000 (40) (Warks Moth Group), 18/8/2001 (2) (DG), 17/8/2002 (10), 13/8/2005 (4) (Warks Moth Group); **Waverley Wood**, 18/8/1983 (CDNHSS), 19/8/1989 (5), 20/7/1990, 28/7/2001 (12) (Warks Moth Group); **Pailton**, 1986 (KCG); **Oakley Wood**, 5/8/1988, 2/8/1989, 3/8/1989 (DB); **Brandon Marsh**, 12/8/1988 (SAL); **Cheylesmore**, **Coventry**, Aug. 1990 (RCK); **Grendon Common**, 18/8/1990 (DB, AFG, RGB), 24/8/1990 (DB, RMC, BM).

VCH 1904: *'Common everywhere.'*

Square-spotted Clay
2131 *Xestia rhomboidea* (Esp.)

Nationally Scarce B

County status: Presumed extinct.
Flight: No details known.
Larval foodplants: Common Nettle, Dog's Mercury and probably other herbaceous plants.

This species was recorded in Bannam's Wood (mature broadleaved woodland on chalk soil) during the 1960s (FAN). Unfortunately no exact dates or indication of numbers are available. Subsequent fieldwork has proved negative and it is assumed this moth has now disappeared.

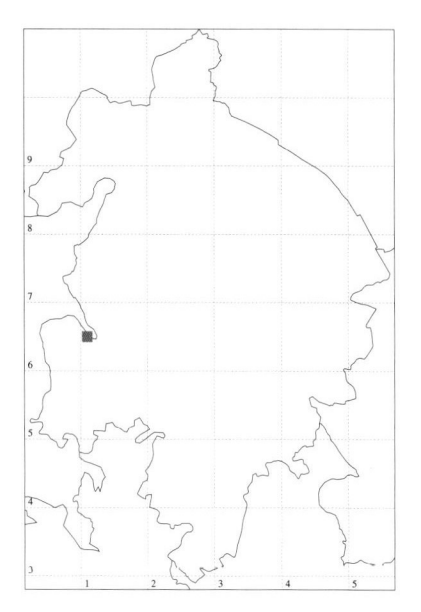

Neglected Rustic
2132 *Xestia castanea* (Esp.)

Nationally Local

County status: Status uncertain. Presumed extinct.
Flight: August and September.
Larval foodplants: Heather.

This Nationally Local heathland species was recorded in Sutton Park until the 1970s (LJE, JB). There have been no recent sightings and its present status is uncertain; further fieldwork is required.

VCH 1904:
Birmingham, Atherstone, Frankton, Overslade 5/9/1893 (RNHS).

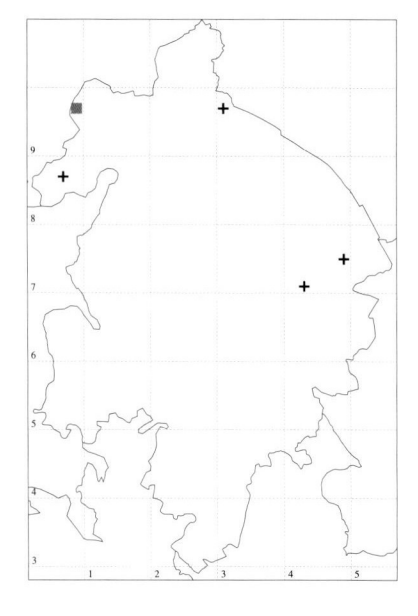

Six-striped Rustic
2133 *Xestia sexstrigata* (Haw.)

County status: Widespread and fairly common.
Flight: Late July to early September.
Larval foodplants: Various herbaceous plants, including Bluebell, Hedge Bedstraw and Ribwort Plantain.

The Six-striped Rustic is widely distributed and found in a number of open grassy habitats, including woodland rides and clearings, road and railway cuttings and wetlands.

The adult is a regular visitor to garden moth traps with varying frequency as the following figures show:

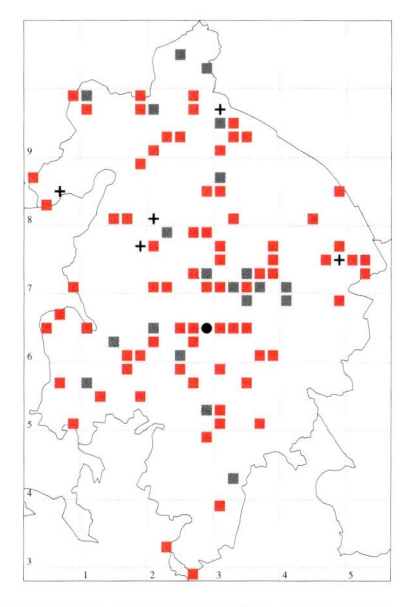

Habitat	Location	1982	1985	1990	1995	2000
Suburban	Hillmorton, Rugby (DIP)	11	6	119	54	5
Rural	Charlecote (DB)	176	59	122	79	61

VCH 1904: *Yardley, Hampton-in-Arden, Knowle, Atherstone, Overslade, Wolford.*

Square-spot Rustic
2134 *Xestia xanthographa* ([D. & S.])

County status: Widespread and sometimes abundant.
Flight: Late July to mid-October.
Larval foodplants: Various grasses, including Couch Grass*, and herbaceous plants.

The Square-spot Rustic is one of the commonest of the early autumn species in moth traps. It is found in almost any type of rural or urban habitat where grasses grow. It is highly polymorphic with dark forms predominating in Warwickshire.

Garden moth trap counts compare rural, urban and suburban districts:

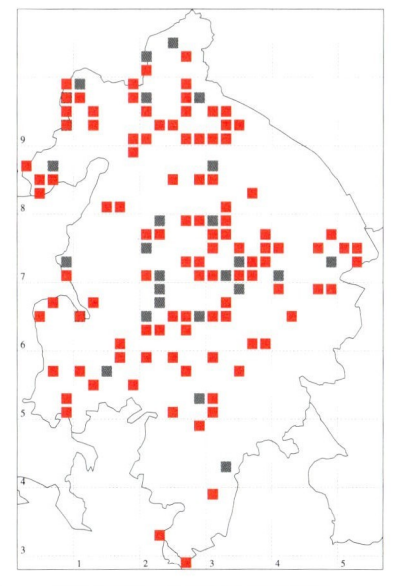

Habitat	Location	1982	1985	1990	1995	2000
Urban	Radford, Coventry (MCV)	87	98	389	352	450
Suburban	Hillmorton, Rugby (DIP)	103	120	885	408	243
Rural	Charlecote (DB)	477	171	462	531	363

VCH 1904: *'Very common everywhere.'*

Heath Rustic
2135 *Xestia agathina agathina* (Dup.)
Nationally Local

County status: Very local and fairly common at one location.

Flight: Mid-August to September.

Larval foodplants: Heather*.

Populations of the Heath Rustic are restricted to the heather terrain of Sutton Park and Grendon Common. This species has occasionally been observed in garden moth traps where ornamental heathers may have been utilised as a larval foodplant.

Records:
Charlecote, 27/8/1991 (DB), 30/8/1999 (AFG), 28/8/2002 (DB); **Sutton Park**, 28/8/1993 (6) including a very dark melanic specimen (Warks Moth Group), 2/9/2000 (3) (DG), 13/8/2005 (SDT); **Grendon Common**, 19/8/1994 (BS, DB); **Hillmorton, Rugby**, 29/8/2002, 31/8/2002 (PN).

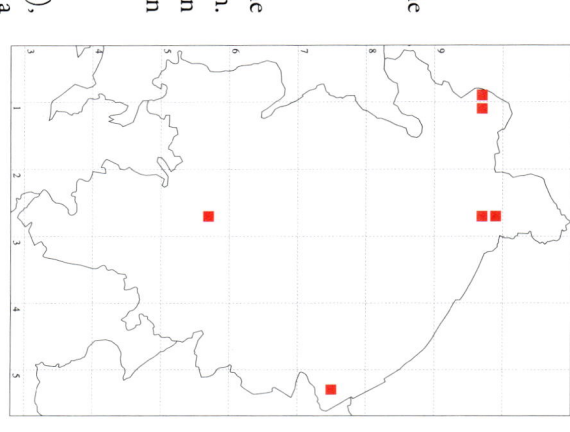

VCH 1904: *Sutton Park – 'only taken once'*.

Gothic
2136 *Naenia typica* (L.)
Nationally Local

County status: Widespread and generally fairly common.

Flight: Late June to mid-August.

Larval foodplants: A wide range of wild and cultivated herbaceous and woody plants, including willowherbs, sallows, apple, buddleias and Lupin*.

The Gothic is found in a number of rural and urban habitats. It favours river banks, flood meadows, marshes and damp woodland. The adult visits the sugar patch more readily than MV.

Larvae have been found feeding on Lupin in built-up districts; for example, Birmingham, 7/5/1949, 4/5/1951 (HEH).

It is a fairly frequent visitor to urban garden moth traps as the following records illustrate:
Radford, Coventry: 1975 (5), 1980 (3), 1985 (2), 1990 (6), 1995 (1), 2000 (4), 2005 (7) (MCV).

VCH 1904: *'Common everywhere'*.

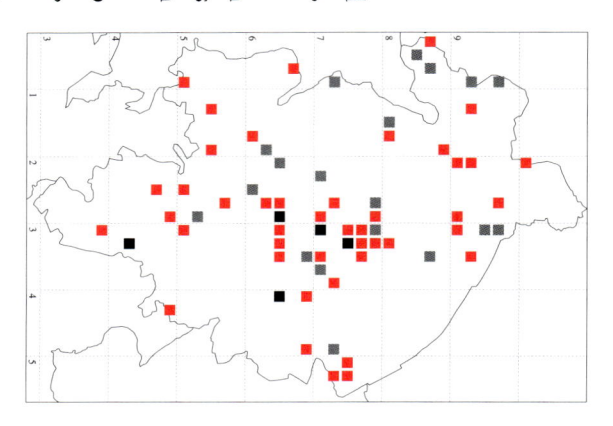

Great Brocade
2137 *Eurois occulta* (L.)

Resident in Scotland (Nationally Scarce B) and immigrant from Europe

County status: Scarce immigrant.
Flight: July to early September.
Larval foodplants: Bog-myrtle, birches and sallows and other herbaceous plants.

This species is an occasional visitor to Warwickshire and the examples observed are of the pale grey Scandinavian form.

Records:

1927—**Birmingham,** (recorder unknown).
1955—**Tile Hill Wood**, 9/7, 31/7 (CDNHSS).
1960—**Tile Hill Wood**, (FWS).
1976—**Charlecote**, 28/8 (AFG).
1977—**Charlecote**, 18/7 (DB) (Brown, 1977).
1982—**Charlecote**, 29/7, 31/7 (AFG).
1983—**Radford, Coventry**, 9/8 (MCV).
1995—**Charlecote**, 7/7 (DB); **Bidford-on-Avon**, 4/8 (RMC); **Solihull**, 6/8 (AP).
1996—**Hillmorton, Rugby**, 15/8, 5/9 (DIP).
1997—**Walsgrave, Coventry**, August (TRG).

Green Arches
2138 *Anaplectoides prasina* ([D. & S.])

County status: Fairly widespread but generally uncommon.
Flight: June and July.
Larval foodplants: Many herbaceous and woody plants, including Primrose, docks, Honeysuckle, brambles and Bilberry.

The Green Arches frequents broadleaved woodland and well-wooded rural and suburban districts over a large part of Warwickshire. Typical sites include Waverley Wood, Kingsbury Wood, Ryton and Wappenbury Woods, Hay Wood, Snitterfield Bushes, Hampton Wood, Oversley Wood, Wolford Wood and Whichford Wood.

VCH 1904: *'Not common.'*
Hay Wood, Sutton Park, Knowle, Frankton Wood, Atherstone.

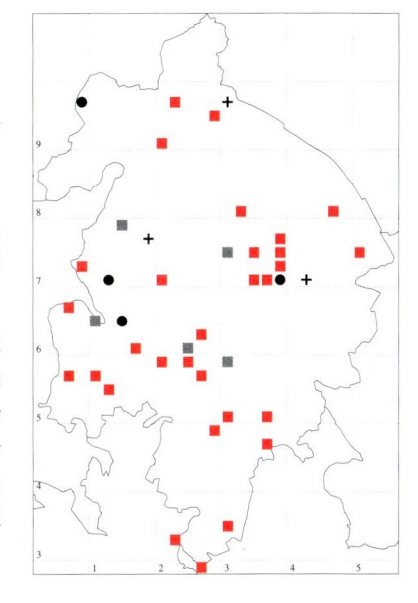

Red Chestnut
2139 *Cerastis rubricosa* ([D. & S.])

County status: Widespread and fairly common.
Flight: Early March to late May.
Larval foodplants: Herbaceous and woody plants, including bedstraws, docks, chickweeds, groundsels and sallows.

The Red Chestnut shows a preference for open woodland containing an abundance of sallows, on which blossom it has frequently been found feeding in the springtime. The adult can be numerous at MV; for example, Oversley Wood: 10/4/1976 (42), (AFG, DB); Oakley Wood, 19/3/1977 (24), (DB).

It is by no means restricted to wooded areas and visits garden moth traps, as the following trap counts illustrate:
Pillerton Priors: 1992 (16), 1993 (23), 1994 (8), 2002 (0), 2003 (4), 2004 (11), 2005 (15) (CI);
Hillmorton, Rugby: 1982 (7), 1985 (10), 1990 (15), 1995 (7), 2000 (2), 2004 (2) (DIP).

VCH 1904: *'Common throughout the County.'*

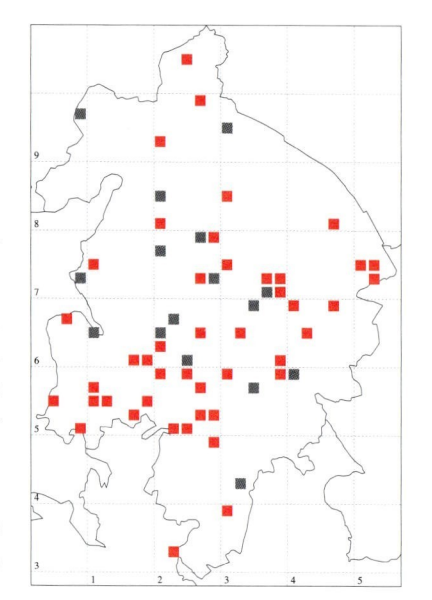

Beautiful Yellow Underwing
2142 *Anarta myrtilli* (L.)

County status: Very local and fairly common at one site.
Flight: Two generations. May, and July to August. Flies in sunshine and at night.
Larval foodplants: Heather.

The Beautiful Yellow Underwing is restricted to the heather-clad areas of Sutton Park where it is found in fairly good numbers. It may be observed during the daytime feeding on, and rapidly flying over the flowers of heathers. The adults later visit MV freely.

Records:
Sutton Park, 1960s, 1970s (LJE, JB), 1987, 1988 (SAL), 3/8/1995 (MCV); **Sutton Park, Little Bracebridge**, 12/7/1990 (RJB), 23/5/1997 (MS); **Sutton Park, Boldmere Gate**, 17/8/2002 (12 at MV) (Warks Moth Group).

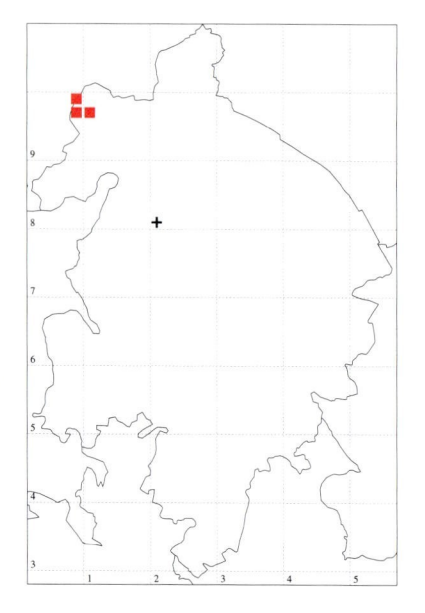

VCH 1904: *'Common in Sutton Park and also recorded from Hampton-in-Arden.'*

Nutmeg
2145 *Discestra trifolii* (Hufn.)

County status: Fairly widespread and fairly common.
Flight: Two generations. Early May to mid-July, and August to October.
Larval foodplants: Herbaceous plants, including goosefoots, Common Orache, docks and Dandelion.

The Nutmeg is now far more plentiful than in the VCH 1904 and is found fairly commonly in central and southern Warwickshire. Gardens, woodland and waste-ground are favoured habitats. The adult is occasionally observed in November; for example, Charlecote, 11/11/1990 (DB).
   Typical garden moth trap figures are as follows:
Bidford-on-Avon: 1992 (188), 1993 (68), 1994 (58), 1995 (72) (RMC).

VCH 1904: *'Rare.'*
Rugby, Overslade, Knowle

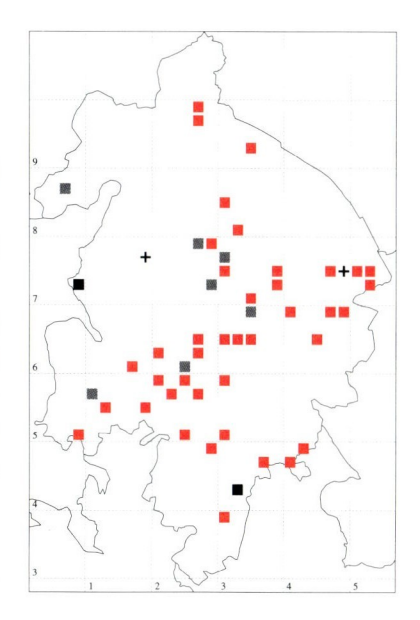

Shears
2147 *Hada plebeja* (L.)

County status: Fairly widespread and occasionally fairly common.
Flight: May to July.
Larval foodplants: Various herbaceous plants, including Knotgrass, chickweeds, Dandelion and Mouse-ear Hawkweed.

The Shears has a preference for rough open ground on well-drained soils. It is found on post-industrial brownfield sites and heathland in north Warwickshire, and calcareous waste-ground in the south. Established sites include Windmill Hill, Draycote Water, Grendon Common, Sutton Park and Wilmcote Rough. This species also visits garden moth traps in both rural and urban districts.

VCH 1904: *'Common everywhere.'*

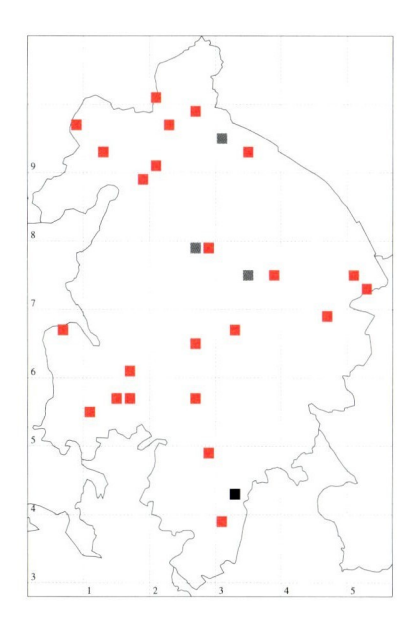

Pale Shining Brown
2148 *Polia bombycina* (Hufn.)

pRDB

County status: Presumed extinct.
Flight: June to early August.
Larval foodplants: Unconfirmed, but in captivity will feed on various herbaceous plants, including docks, Knotgrass, Dandelion and Sow-thistle.

The VCH 1904 classified the Pale Shining Brown as 'very rare' and only noted from Wolford and Overslade. Sightings in the first part of the twentieth century were sparse but frequency had increased by the 1940s. This impressive moth enjoyed a period of comparative plenty during the 1970s and became established in the southern half of the County. However, by the 1980s it was considered Nationally Scarce and suffered a similar fate locally. Since the 1990s it has undergone a massive decline in Britain and is now chiefly restricted to the Salisbury Plain area. The last sighting in Warwickshire was at Bidford-on-Avon on 3/7/1995 (RMC).

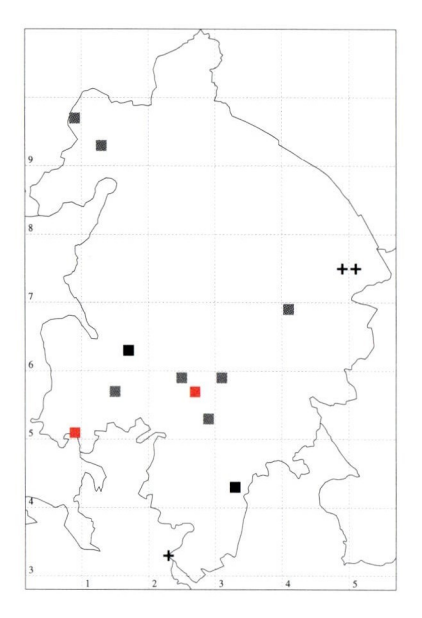

Records:
Rugby district, pre-1893, (A. Sidgwick, 1893); **Sutton Park**, 1911, 1913 (WB), 1961 (LJE); **Wilmcote Rough**, 1928 two at sugar (SEWC), 1958–59 (5) (SEWC, FAN); **Austy Wood**, 1941 (HEH); **Tysoe**, 6/6/1946, 13/7/1946, 4/8/1946, 30/6/1948 (TT); **NVRS, Wellesbourne**, 7/7/1956 (JAH); **Erdington**, 4/6/1968 (LJE); **Walton**, 1970–73 (DB); **Charlecote**, 8/7/1971–19/6/1982; annual totals: 1971 (4), 1972 (4), 1973 (3), 1974 (2), 1975 (8), 1976 (23), 1977, 1981 (2), 1982 (DB, AFG); **Hampton Wood**, 1972 (2), 1973 (3), 1974 (5) (AFG); **Oakley Wood**, 29/7/1972 (AFG); **Marton**, June 1976 (RA); **Bidford-on-Avon**, 26/6/1984, 9/7/1985, 10/7/1986, 2/7/1989, 8/7/1992, 3/7/1994, 3/7/1995 (RMC).

VCH 1904: *'Very rare.' Wolford, Overslade.*

Silvery Arches
2149 *Polia trimaculosa* (Esp.)

Nationally Scarce B

County status: Presumed extinct.
Flight: No dates available.
Larval foodplants: Various herbaceous plants; also birches, sallows and hawthorns in the spring.

Earlswood, 1957 (BNHS) unconfirmed record.

VCH 1904: *Knowle 1890 (WGB).*

Grey Arches
2150 *Polia nebulosa* (Hufn.)

County status: Fairly widespread and locally fairly common.
Flight: June to early August.
Larval foodplants: Woody plants, including Hazel*, oaks*, Honeysuckle*, birches, sallows and brambles.

The Grey Arches is fairly common in broadleaved woodland and less plentiful in open countryside and suburban districts. Good populations are established in Whichford Wood, Wolford Wood, Coughton Park, Clowes Wood, Oversley Wood, Hay Wood, Wappenbury Wood, Ryton Wood and Kingsbury Wood. The distinctive larva has been found several times during the spring by night-time searching in sheltered woodland.

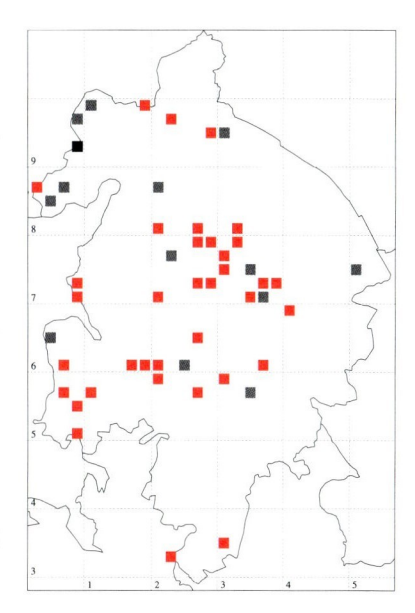

VCH 1904: *'Common throughout the County.'*

Bordered Gothic
2153 *Heliophobus reticulata marginosa* (Haw.)

pRDB

County status: Extinct.
Flight: No dates available.
Larval foodplants: Unrecorded in the wild, accepting Knotgrass and Soapwort in captivity.

VCH 1904: *'Rare.'* Whitchurch, Overslade, Wolford.

Cabbage Moth
2154 *Mamestra brassicae* (L.)

County status: Widespread and fairly common.
Flight: Two overlapping generations. May to September.
Larval foodplants: Various wild and cultivated plants, including Lupin* but especially Cabbage* and other brassicas.

This species has been recorded in an extensive range of habitats, including open woodland and waste-ground, but more commonly from gardens and cultivated areas. The larvae are a pest of brassicas on allotments. The imago can be seen anytime from May to October, peaking in late July.

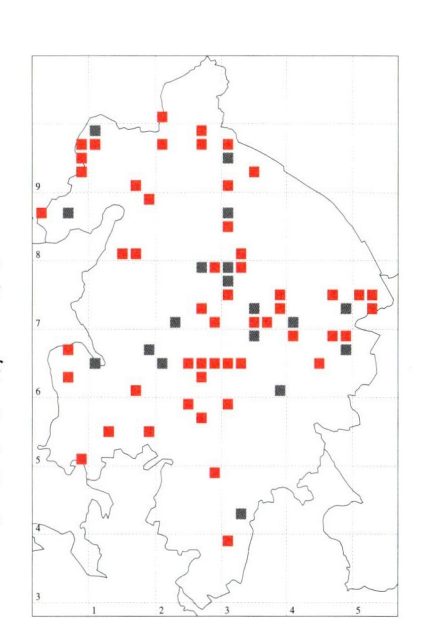

Garden moth trap counts reflect larger populations in suburban districts:

Habitat	Location	1982	1985	1990	1995	2000
Urban	Radford, Coventry (MCV)	54	96	31	44	55
Suburban	Hillmorton, Rugby (DIP)	128	120	149	116	15
Rural	Charlecote (AFG)	57	14	68	7	23

VCH 1904: *'Common everywhere.'*

Dot Moth
2155 *Melanchra persicariae* (L.)

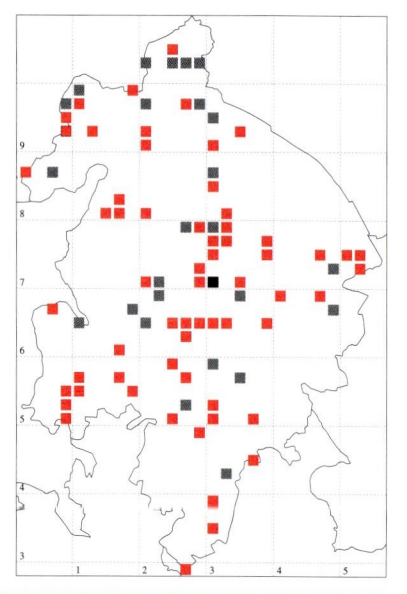

County status: Widespread and fairly common.
Flight: Mid-June to early August.
Larval foodplants: Polyphagous on wild and cultivated herbaceous and woody plants, including sallows*.

This distinctive moth is found in numerous habitats throughout the County and, like the last species, is commonest in suburban districts.

The following table compares urban, suburban and rural garden moth traps:

Habitat	Location	1982	1985	1990	1995	2000
Urban	Radford, Coventry (MCV)	74	37	17	12	3
Suburban	Hillmorton, Rugby (DIP)	–	–	307	381	147
Rural	Charlecote (DB)	93	19	13	28	12

VCH 1904: *'Common, particularly in gardens.'*

Broom Moth
2163 *Melanchra pisi* (L.)

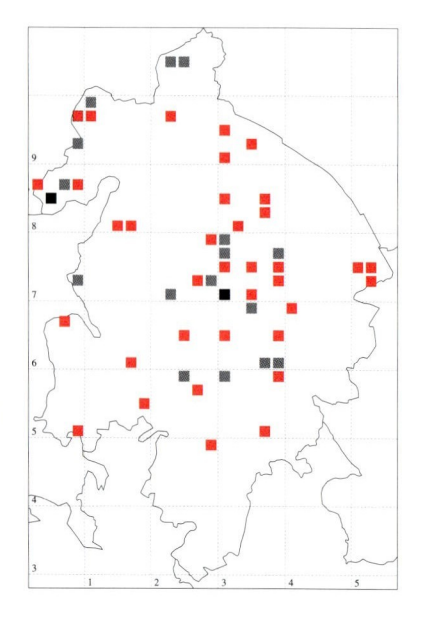

County status: Fairly widespread and fairly common.
Flight: Late May to July.
Larval foodplants: A number of herbaceous and woody plants, including Broom*, groundsels*, Bracken*, brambles and sallows.

The Broom Moth favours open terrain and has been recorded frequently in railway cuttings, disused quarries, gravel pits and heathland. Smaller numbers are observed from open woodland and gardens.

Garden moth trap totals at **Charlecote** are generally low: 1973 (2), 1983 (3), 1993 (1), 2003 (0) (DB).

VCH 1904: *'Common everywhere.'*

Beautiful Brocade
2156 *Lacanobia contigua* ([D. & S.])

Nationally Local

County status: Extinct.
Flight: No dates available.
Larval foodplants: A wide range of woody plants, including, oaks, birches and Heather.

VCH 1904: *Sutton Park, Knowle, Hampton-in-Arden, Rugby.*

Light Brocade
2157 *Lacanobia w-latinum* (Hufn.)

Nationally Local

County status: Very local and scarce.
Flight: May and June.
Larval foodplants: Various plants, including Broom, Knotgrass, docks, brambles and Common Persicaria.

The Light Brocade is only very rarely noted in Warwickshire, usually on or near calcareous soil. All recent records are from garden moth traps.

Records:
Tile Hill Wood, 1/6/1935 (JWS); **Mappleborough Green**, 1940–60 (FHL); **Austy Wood**, 1949 (HEH); **Tysoe**, 12/6/1950 (TT); **Wilmcote Rough**, 19/6/1956 (SEWC); **Bidford-on-Avon**, 23/5/1989 (RMC); **Hillmorton**, **Rugby**, 18/5/1991, 26/5/1997, 6/6/1997, 24/5/1998 (DIP); **Central Rugby**, 29/5/2004 (IGMR); **Charlecote**, 9/6/2005 (DB).

VCH 1904: *'Not common.'*
Knowle, Kingswood, Rugby, Atherstone, Sutton Park.

Pale-shouldered Brocade
2158 *Lacanobia thalassina* (Hufn.)

County status: Widespread and fairly common.
Flight: Early May to late July.
Larval foodplants: A variety of trees and woody plants, including oaks, birches, sallows, hawthorns, Blackthorn, Honeysuckle, Aspen, apple and Broom.

The Pale-shouldered Brocade is evenly distributed over central and southern Warwickshire but dwindles northwards. It frequents a diversity of habitats and displays a predilection for wooded areas.

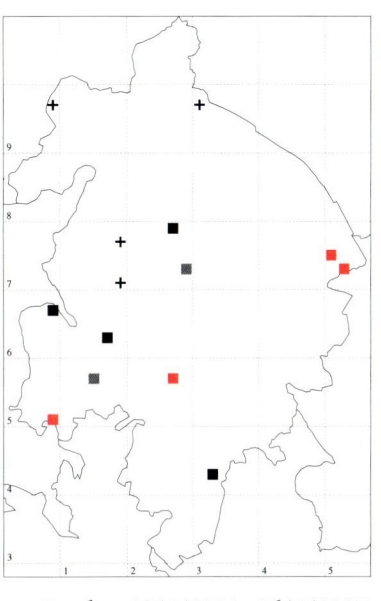

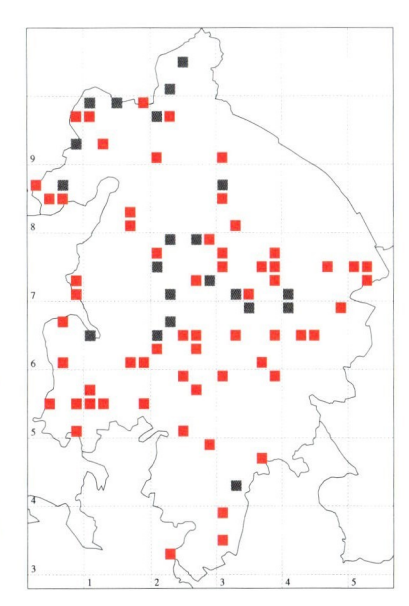

Dog's Tooth
2159 *Lacanobia suasa* (D.&S.)

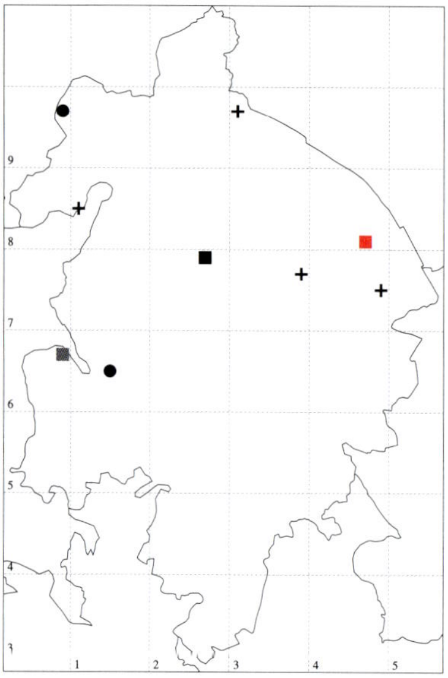

Nationally Local

County status: Status uncertain.

Flight: June.

Larval foodplants: Various low-growing plants, such as docks, Dandelion, plantains and Knotgrass.

With no recent records, the status of this moth is not clear. Although there are inland populations of Dog's Tooth it is primarily a salt-marsh and coastal grassland species.

Records:
Sutton Park, 1930 (FHLs); **May's Wood**, 1930s annually (GBM); **Mappleborough Green**, 1950–1960, 1956 (2) (FHL); **Tile Hill Wood**, 29/6/1935 (JWS); **Pailton**, 1984 (KCG).

VCH 1904: *'Rare' Small Heath, Overslade, Brandon Wood, Atherstone.*

This species is generally univoltine with the occasional individual representing a partial second generation; for example, Hillmorton, Rugby, 3/10/1982, 18/9/1989 (DIP).

VCH 1904: *'Common everywhere'.*

Bright-line Brown-eye
2160 *Lacanobia oleracea* (L.)

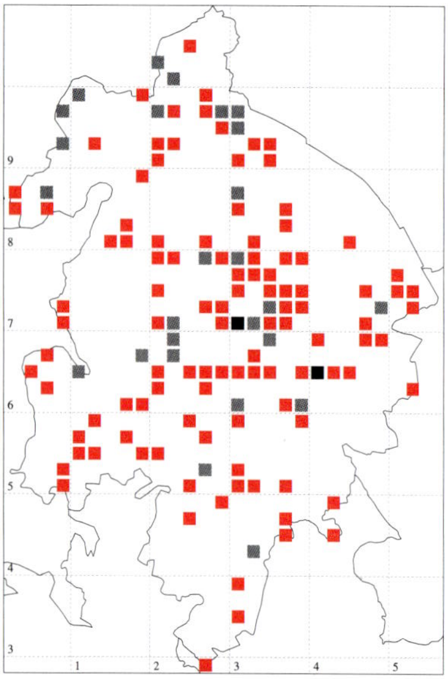

County status: Widespread and common.

Flight: Late April to September, and occasionally October.

Larval foodplants: A variety of wild and cultivated herbaceous and woody plants, including Common Nettle, willowherbs, Hazel, Hop, Traveller's-joy, Forsythia* and Tomato*.

The Bright-line Brown-eye is the most widespread and commonest member of the genus. It is found in many types of habitats, especially gardens and cultivated land. The larvae are a constant pest of Tomato plants.

The adult is plentiful at garden moth traps in both rural and built-up districts, as the figures below illustrate:

Habitats	Location	1980	1985	1990	1995	2000
Urban	Radford, Coventry (MCV)	205	211	104	203	365
Rural	Charlecote (DB)	266	84	315	336	167

VCH 1904: *'Common everywhere.'*

Glaucous Shears
2162 *Papestra biren* (Goeze)

Nationally Local

County status: Very local and scarce.
Flight: May to June; once recorded in August.
Larval foodplants: A wide range of herbaceous and woody plants, including Meadowsweet, Heather and sallows.

Historically, Glaucous Shears is best known from Sutton Park and the VCH 1904 reported *'of regular occurrence although not abundant.'*

It was observed intermittently at this site until the 1970s, by which time a transient population had appeared in mid-Warwickshire. Always rare and of uncertain appearance, this moth has not been recorded since 1992.

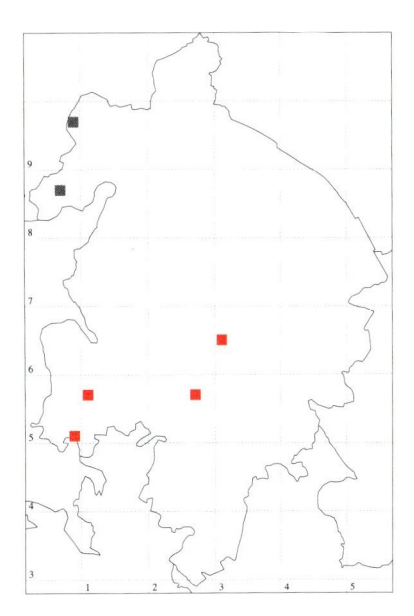

Records:
Sutton Park, 1911, 1913, 16/6/1956, 15/8/1956 (WB), 1960s, 1970s LJE); **Birmingham**, 1960s (LJE); **Charlecote**, 4/6/1977, 20/5/1982 (AFG); **Oversley Wood**, 19/5/1982 (AFG); **Bidford-on-Avon**, 25/5/1988 (RMC); **Royal Leamington Spa**, 26/5/1992 (PhP).

VCH 1904: *Sutton Park 'of regular occurrence although not abundant.'*

Broad-barred White
2164 *Hecatera bicolorata* (Hufn.)

County status: Fairly widespread and fairly common, especially on calcareous soils.
Flight: Late May to July.
Larval foodplants: The buds and flowers of hawkweeds, hawk's-beards and other related plants.

The Broad-barred White is found over a large area of Warwickshire and has a particular penchant for dry open terrain on calcareous soil.

Habitats include disused railway cuttings, quarries and open waste-ground. The species is not restricted to rural areas and occurs in urban districts in small numbers, as garden moth trap figures from Rugby and Coventry show:

Hillmorton: 1982 (5), 1985 (18), 1990 (9), 1995 (0), 2000 (1), 2004 (3) (DIP);
Radford: 1982 (0), 1985 (1), 1990 (4), 1995 (5), 2000 (7), 2004 (2) (MCV).

VCH 1904: *'Not common, occurs occasionally in Sutton Park.'*
Wolford, Brandon Wood, Atherstone.

Campion
2166 *Hadena rivularis* (Fabr.)

County status: Local and uncommon.
Flight: Two generations. May to June, and late July to August.
Larval foodplants: The ripening seeds of White Campion*, Red Campion* and Ragged-Robin.

Although associated with open grassy places the vast majority of records for this species are from static garden moth traps. It is noted infrequently in both rural and urban districts. Easily distinguished from the Lychnis when fresh by the purplish-pink marbling on the forewing. In faded specimens the lower parts of the reniform and orbicular stigmata need to be checked, being united in the Campion.

VCH 1904: *'Not uncommon.'*
Knowle, Birmingham, Overslade, Atherstone.

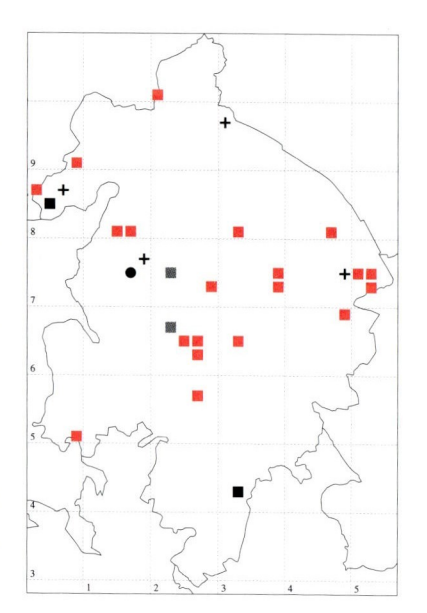

Tawny Shears
2167 *Hadena perplexa perplexa* ([D. & S.])

County status: Very local and scarce.
Flight: May to August.
Larval foodplants: The ripening seeds of White Campion* and Bladder Campion.

The majority of records for Tawny Shears are from garden moth traps on or near calcareous soils, though it has also been noted in woodland rides and field margins. Further recording on chalk soils in south Warwickshire may prove this species to have a wider distribution than the map shows.

Records:
Rugby district, pre-1893, (A. Sidgwick, 1893); **Birmingham**, 1930s occasional larvae and adults (GPS); **Tysoe**, 13/5/1949 (TT); **Mappleborough Green**, 1956 (FHL); **Edgbaston, Birmingham**, 1956–58 (4) (FAN); **Charlecote**, 10/6/1975, 7/6/1976, 4/6/1978, 5/7/1983, 9/8/1983, 4/6/1984, 10/6/1984, 4/7/1985, 18/5/1990, 13/5/1992, 23/5/1993, 26/5/1995, 10/6/1997 (DB, AFG); **Radford, Coventry**, 21/5/1976 (MCV); **Hillmorton, Rugby**, 1980s plentiful, 1990s–2000s sporadic (DIP); **Ryton Wood**, 31/7/1992 (RCK, LB); **Bidford-on-Avon**, 24/5/1992 (RMC); **Edgehill**, 8/6/1996 (CI, RGB); **Pillerton Priors**, 7/6/2003 (CI).

Varied Coronet
2170 *Hadena compta* ([D. & S.])

County status: Widespread and generally fairly common.
Flight: May to mid-August.
Larval foodplants: The ripening seed pods of Sweet-William*.

The Varied Coronet first became established in Britain during 1948 when several were recorded breeding in Dover. It was first noted in Warwickshire during the 1970s and began to spread throughout the County.

Gardens containing Sweet-William plants harbour this species, which is more frequently observed in built-up areas (Fig. 23).

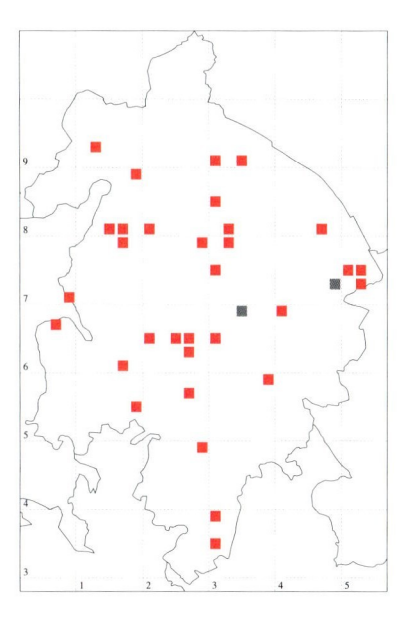

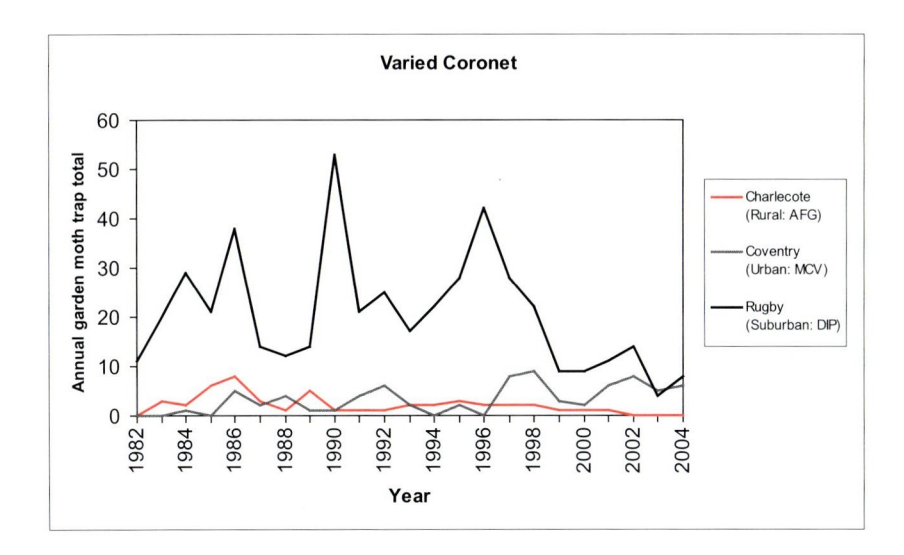

Figure 23. Frequency of *H. compta* in urban, suburban and rural districts.

NB. No recording took place during the flight period at the Rugby site in 1994 so an assumed value has been used.

Marbled Coronet
2171 *Hadena confusa* (Hufn.)

Nationally Local

County status: Exact status uncertain. Very local and scarce.
Flight: June.
Larval foodplants: The ripening seed-pods of Bladder Campion.

Little is known of this rare Warwickshire species, which is strictly confined to calcareous soil. Fieldwork in disused quarries or open waste-ground may help to discover colonies.

Records:
Tysoe, 1950s (TT); **Southam**, 1970; **Hillmorton, Rugby**, 24/6/1986, 5/6/1990 (DIP).

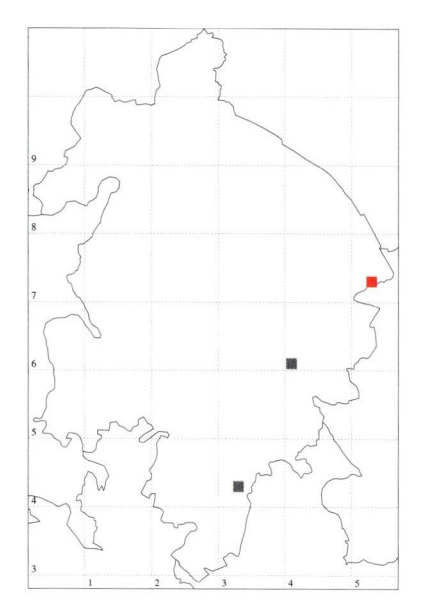

Lychnis
2173 *Hadena bicruris* (Hufn.)

County status: Widespread and fairly common.
Flight: Two generations. May to July, and August to September.
Larval foodplants: The ripening seeds of White Campion*, Red Campion, Sweet William and Soapwort*.

The Lychnis is the commonest of its genus in Warwickshire. Recorded from a variety of habitats, including disused quarries, railway cuttings, field margins and woodland, but especially in the vicinity of gardens.

Garden moth trap counts at **Charlecote** are as follows: 1980 (49), 1985 (25), 1990 (28), 1995 (32), 2000 (6) (AFG).

VCH 1904: *'Common.'*
Marston Green, Small Heath, Knowle, Rugby and Edgbaston.

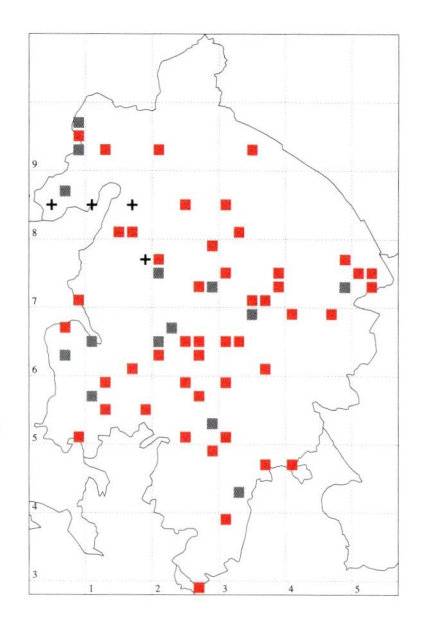

Antler Moth
2176 *Cerapteryx graminis* (L.)

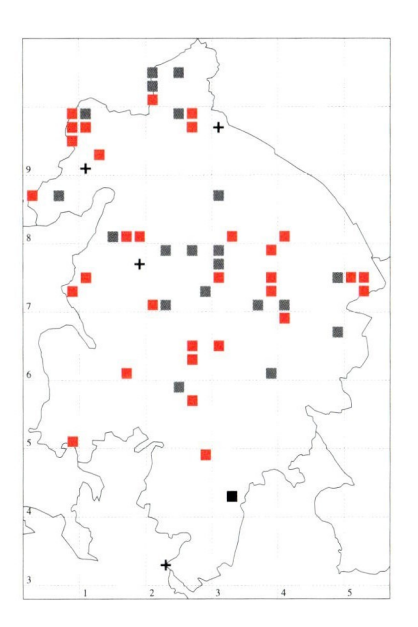

County status: Fairly widespread but generally uncommon.
Flight: July to mid-September.
Larval foodplants: Hard-bladed grasses, including Sheep's-fescue.

The Antler Moth is associated with various types of grassland; although at times reported to be a pest on the hills of northern England, it is never very abundant in Warwickshire. Generally more plentiful on heathland; for example, Grendon Common, 18/8/1990 (23) (DB, AFG) and Sutton Park, 17/8/2002 (40), 13/8/2005 (70) (Warks Moth Group).

Decidedly uncommon and of sporadic appearance in the southern half of the County.

VCH 1904: *'Not uncommon.'*
Sutton Park, Knowle, Overslade, Atherstone, Wolford.

Hedge Rustic
2177 *Tholera cespitis* ([D. & S.])

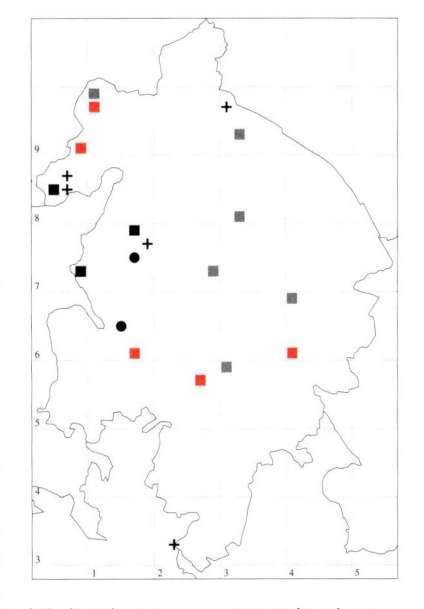

County status: Very local and scarce.
Flight: Mid-August to mid-September.
Larval foodplants: Hard-bladed grasses, including Mat-grass and Wavy Hair-grass.

The Hedge Rustic is an inhabitant of open grassland areas but has declined in Warwickshire during the last 20 years.

Records:
May's Wood, 20/8/1910 (GBM); **Dorridge**, 17/9/1923 (SEWC); **Solihull**, August 1945 (SEWC); **Edgbaston, Birmingham**, 1950s (FAN); **Windmill Naps**, 20/8/1955 (FAN); **Four Oaks**, 26/8/1960 (EVW); **Charlecote**, 7/9/1969, 9/9/1969, 23/8/1976, 17/8/1984–28/8/1984 (3), 25/8/1992 (AFG, DB); **Radford, Coventry**, 1/9/1970 (MCV); **Oakley Wood**, 16/8/1971–17/8/1971 (5) (DB); **Marton**, 1976 (RA); **Fen End, Kenilworth**, 1976 (DC); **Camp Hill, Nuneaton**, 1978 (Anon); **Claverdon**, 23/8/1981, 15/8/1983 (IGMR); **Southam**, 8/9/1982 (JWW); **Sutton Park**, 24/8/1983 (AN); **Witton**, 1984–1987 (TEG).

VCH 1904: *'Not common.'*
Knowle, Yardley, Birmingham, Atherstone, Wolford.

Feathered Gothic
2178 *Tholera decimalis* (Poda)

County status: Fairly widespread and fairly common.
Flight: Mid-August to late September.
Larval foodplants: Hard-bladed grasses, including Mat-grass and Sheep's-fescue.

The Feathered Gothic is found over a large part of central and southern Warwickshire in grassy woodland rides, railways cuttings, waste-ground, parkland and gardens.

Garden moth trap figures are as follows:
Charlecote: 1982 (10), 1985 (32), 1990 (21), 1995 (15) (AFG);
Hillmorton, Rugby: 1982 (15), 1985 (2), 1990 (37), 1995 (6) (DIP).

VCH 1904: '*Not common but occurs in every list.*'

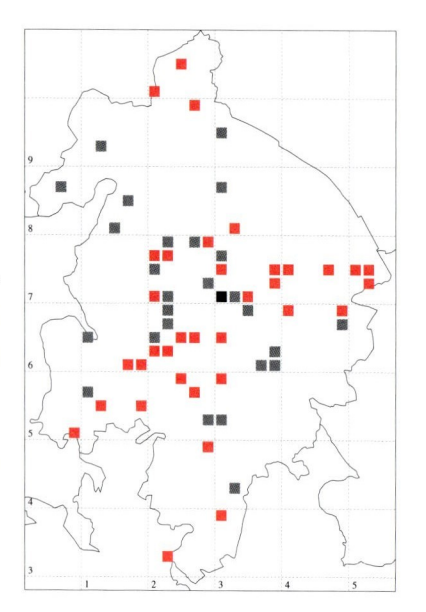

Pine Beauty
2179 *Panolis flammea* ([D. & S.])

County status: Fairly widespread and locally fairly common.
Flight: March to May.
Larval foodplants: Pines*.

The Pine Beauty occurs fairly commonly in pine plantations at Hay Wood, Oakley Wood and Oversley Wood. Mixed woodlands with sparse pine, such as Snitterfield Bushes, Wellesbourne Wood, Bentley Park Wood and Sutton Park, contain smaller numbers. This species also survives at low density in rural and urban districts with isolated pines.

The flight period is long and in some years good numbers may be observed well into May; for example, Oversley Wood, 24/5/1980 (15) (DB, AFG).

VCH 1904: '*Very local, occurs regularly in Sutton Park. Also recorded from Marston Green and Rugby.*'

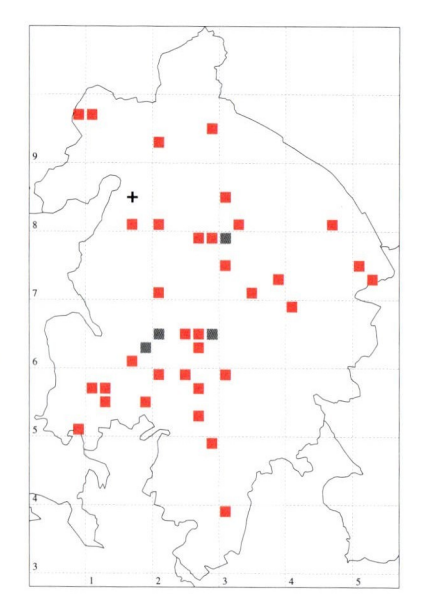

Silver Cloud
2181 *Egira conspicillaris* (L.)

Nationally Scarce A

County status: Very local and generally uncommon.
Flight: April to early June.
Larval foodplants: Unconfirmed in the wild. In captivity it accepts docks, Common Nettle, oaks, elms, Blackthorn and other plants.

The range of this nationally restricted species extends into south-west Warwickshire, where it can be locally fairly plentiful in some years. Garden moth traps at Bidford-on-Avon (RMC) and Temple Grafton (AFG) regularly record the moth. Apart from a stray specimen during the 1980s at Marton (RA), Charlecote and Pillerton Priors mark the eastern limit of its extent, although appearances are erratic. The Silver Cloud is found in open countryside, woodland rides, clearings and gardens. Other than a solitary example in 1953 at Long Marston, just within Gloucestershire, there appear to be no records of this moth in Vice-County 38 before the 1970s.

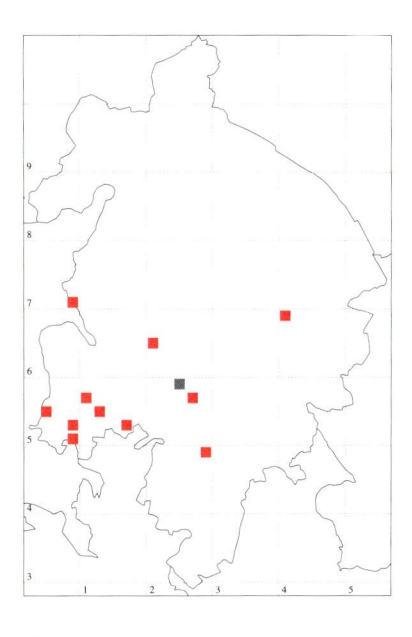

The predominant form within the County is f. *melaleuca* View. with black forewings, whilst the typical form is only occasionally recorded.

Records:
Charlecote, 20/5/1971, 3/5/1972 to 7/6/1972 (6), 12/5/1974, 26/5/1974, 21/5/1976–23/5/1976 (3), 12/5/1977, 26/5/1978, 6/5/1981, 23/5/1982, 1/5/1994*, 18/5/2003, 27/5/2003, 6/5/2004, 10/5/2004 (DB, AFG); **Hampton Wood**, 19/5/1973 (AFG); **Marton**, 1980s (RA); **Oversley Wood**, 24/5/1980, 14/5/1982 (2), 21/5/1982, 21/5/1992 (AFG, DB), 1/5/2004 (DG, MK, AJP, VW, J. Rush); **Broom Gravel Pits**, 20/5/1985, 24/4/1987 (2) (RMC); **Claverdon**, 28/5/1986 (IGMR); **Bidford-on-Avon**, 26/4/1983*, 15/5/1984*–23/5/1984 (3), 11/5/1985, 6/5/1991, 9/5/1991, 27/5/1992, 2/5/1995, 4/5/1995, 4/5/1996 to 5/6/1996 (4), 15/4/1997* (both forms), 21/4/1997–17/5/1997 (8), 15/8/1998, 18/8/1998, 25/4/1999 to 5/5/1999 (4), 1/5/2001 to 4/6/2001 (7), 19/4/2002–23/4/2002 (4), 20/4/2003 to 7/5/2003 (3), 25/5/2003*, 13/4/2004–14/4/2004 (2), 25/4/2004 (4), 26/4/2004–12/5/2004 (3), 12/4/2005–25/4/2005 (7), 10/5/2005–24/5/2005 (5) (RMC); **Weethley Wood**, 12/5/1990 (DB, AFG, PJR, SD); **Luddington**, 17/5/1991* (Warks Moth Group); **Tanworth-in-Arden**, 7/5/2004 (SW); **Pillerton Priors**, 14/5/2004 (CI); **Temple Grafton**, 24/4/2004–25/4/2004 (2), 8/5/2004–19/5/2004 (13), 29/4/2005–18/5/2005 (39 including 2*) (AFG).

* = Typical Form.

Small Quaker
2182 *Orthosia cruda* (D. & S.)

County status: Widespread and sometimes abundant in oak woodland.
Flight: Late February to May.
Larval foodplants: Oaks*, sallows* and a number of other broadleaved trees.

The Small Quaker is found over most of the County, especially where oak is well-established. Extremely large populations are found in Oversley Wood, Ryton Wood, Snitterfield Bushes, Rough Hill Wood, and Wolford Wood.

On mild spring evenings huge numbers of individuals congregate in moth traps: Oversley Wood, 31/3/1975 (450) (DB, AFG), 8/4/1980 (950) (DB); Ryton Wood and Meadows 18/3/2005 (1523) (CJ, MK, AJP, NJS, JWkn, VW).

VCH 1904: '*Very common.*'

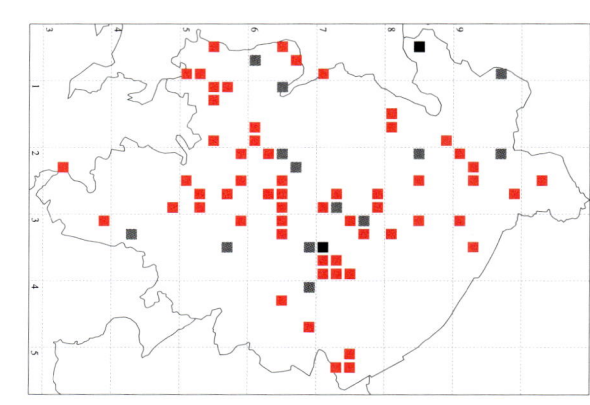

Blossom Underwing
2183 *Orthosia miniosa* (D. & S.)

Nationally Local

County status: Very local and becoming scarce.
Flight: Late March to early May.
Larval foodplants: Oaks*.

An oak woodland species with small populations in Ryton Wood, Oversley Wood and Oakley Wood. More fieldwork is required to find out the present status in Austy Wood and Ufton Wood. During the 1980s the Blossom Underwing experienced a temporary expansion in range and was captured in moth traps long distances from known colonies. Its range has since contracted and there are few recent records.

Records:
Nettle Hill, 29/4/1946 (LR); **Austy Wood**, 1949 three larvae beaten from oak (HEH); **Ufton Wood**, 1950 (GCG); **Oversley Wood**, 19/4/1979 (DB); **Charlecote**, 8/5/1983, 29/3/1989, 16/4/2003 (AFG, DB); **Parkside, Coventry**, 18/4/1987 (MB); **Shottery, Stratford-upon-Avon**, 22/4/1987 (RGB); **Oakley Wood**, 24/4/1987 (2), 5/4/1988 (AFG), 7/4/1988 (2) (DB), 27/3/1989 (4) (DB, AFG, PJR), 3/4/1991 (DB), 9/4/1993 (AJK); **Bidford-on-Avon**, 31/3/1990, 3/4/1999 (RMC); **Ryton Wood**, 30/3/1991 (RCK).

VCH 1904: *Princethorpe Wood, Marston Green.*

Northern Drab
2184 *Orthosia opima* (Hb.)

Nationally Local

County status: Exact status uncertain. Very local and scarce.
Flight: April and May.
Larval foodplants: A range of woody and herbaceous plants, including sallows, birches, ragworts and Mugwort.

The true status of this species is uncertain as no current sites are known, but very occasional specimens appear in garden moth traps.

Records:
Earlswood, 4/5/1924 (WB); **Umberslade**, April 1928 (2) at sallow blossom (SEWC); **Coleshill**, 1930s odd specimens (GPS); **Hampton Wood**, 22/4/1975, 26/4/1975 (AFG); **Charlecote**, 11/5/1983, 28/4/1997 (AFG); **Pailton**, 1987 (KCG).

VCH 1904: *'Only a single record at Kenilworth, 1899' (EAL).*

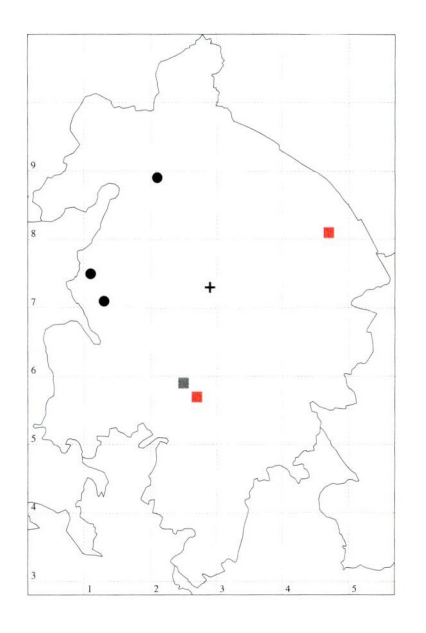

Lead-coloured Drab
2185 *Orthosia populeti* (Fabr.)

Nationally Local

County status: Fairly widespread and locally fairly common.
Flight: March to May.
Larval foodplants: Aspen* and poplars*.

The Lead-coloured Drab is found over a large part of Warwickshire where Aspen and poplar occur. Typical sites include Ryton Wood, Waverley Wood, Oakley Wood, Snitterfield Bushes, Wellesbourne Wood, Ufton Fields and Rough Hill Wood. Healthy populations are present in Oversley Wood, where it is sometimes abundant at light; for example, 19/4/1979 (345), 18/4/1980 (410), 16/4/1983 (255) (DB, AFG, RMC). This species is occasionally noted in garden moth traps.

VCH 1904: '*Not common.*'
Marston Green, Overslade.

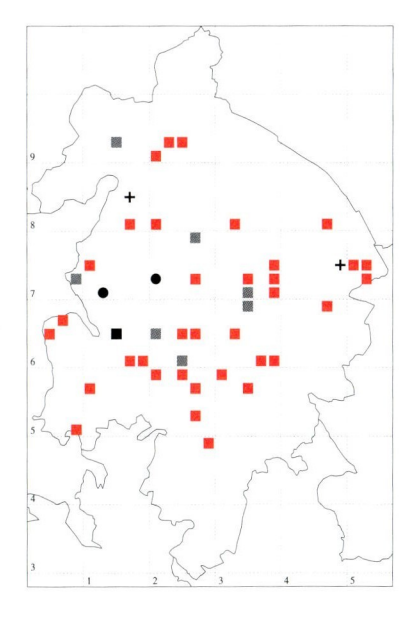

Powdered Quaker
2186 *Orthosia gracilis* ([D. & S.])

County status: Fairly widespread but becoming uncommon.
Flight: Late March to May.
Larval foodplants: Willows, Black Poplar, Blackthorn and also herbaceous plants such as Purple-loosestrife and Meadowsweet.

The Powdered Quaker is associated with marshy areas, river valleys and damp woodland. There is evidence of a steady decline over the last 30 years as the following garden moth trap totals illustrate:
Pillerton Priors: 1992 (7), 1993 (13), 1994 (10), 2002 (1), 2003 (3), 2004 (7), 2005 (8) (CI);
Hillmorton, Rugby: 1982 (42), 1985 (43), 1990 (37), 1995 (19), 2000 (3), 2004 (5), 2005 (4) (DIP).

VCH 1904: '*Not common but well distributed.*'
Marston Green, Hampton-in-Arden, Knowle, Olton, Yardley, Overslade, Atherstone.

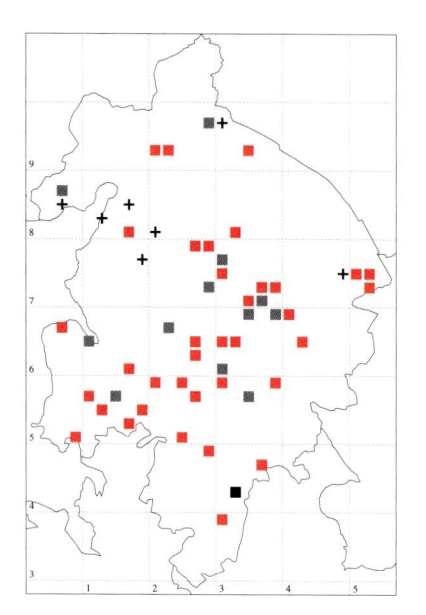

Common Quaker
2187 *Orthosia cerasi* (Fabr.)

County status: Widespread and abundant.
Flight: February to late May.
Larval foodplants: Oaks*, hawthorns*, Field Maple*, sallows*, Rowan*, limes* and many other deciduous trees.

The Common Quaker is a common species in many habitats, but is most abundant in broadleaved woodland where vast numbers can be attracted to light; for example, Oversley Wood, 19/4/1979 (900) (DB); Oakley Wood, 6/4/1996 (620) (DB).

The following garden moth trap totals give an idea of frequency in suburban districts:
Hillmorton, Rugby: 1982 (294), 1985 (351), 1990 (686), 1995 (809), 2000 (188), 2004 (309) (DIP).

VCH 1904: '*Abundant, especially at Sallow blossom.*'

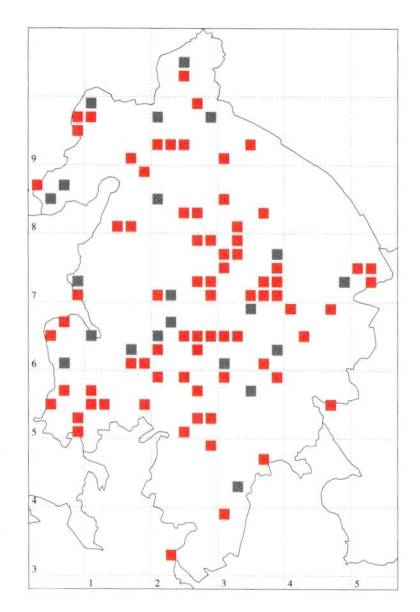

Clouded Drab
2188 *Orthosia incerta* (Hufn.)

County status: Widespread and common.
Flight: February to June.
Larval foodplants: Oaks*, limes*, poplars*, sallows*, Rowan* and many other deciduous trees.

The Clouded Drab is a dominant species in moth traps during the springtime. It has a long flight period and worn individuals may sometimes be noticed amongst summer species; for example, Hillmorton, Rugby, 28/6/1986 (PN).

Black and dark reddish-brown specimens prevail with pale grey forms less frequent.

The following garden moth trap figures give an idea of abundance:
Hillmorton, Rugby: 1982 (201), 1985 (220), 1990 (213), 1995 (160), 2000 (83) (DIP);
Charlecote: 1982 (292), 1985 (146), 1990 (129), 1995 (89), 2000 (168) (AFG)

VCH 1904: *'Abundant, especially at Sallow blossom in the spring and in the pupal stage at the feet of trees in the autumn'.*

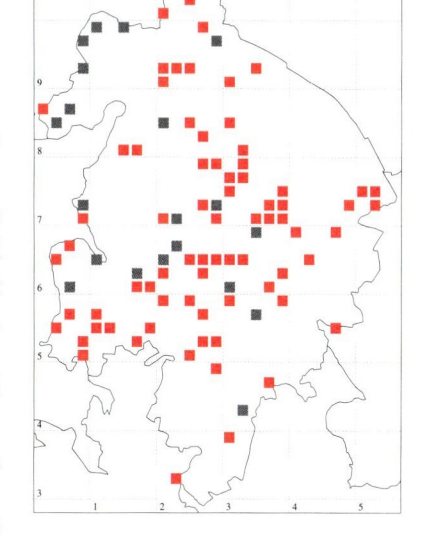

Twin-spotted Quaker
2189 *Orthosia munda* ([D. & S.])

County status: Widespread and fairly common in woodland.
Flight: March and April.
Larval foodplants: Oaks*, poplars*, sallows*, Hazel*, Field Maple*, birches*, and many other deciduous trees and shrubs.

The Twin-spotted Quaker is less numerous than *cerasi* and *cruda*, but is still observed in fairly good numbers in many broadleaved woodlands, as the following moth trap figures illustrate: Oversley Wood, 5/4/1977 (23), 8/4/1980 (35), 7/4/1984 (29) (DB, AFG); Oakley Wood, 9/4/1979 (34) (DB); Snitterfield Bushes, 31/3/1995 (22) (DB, AFG, RMC).

Ab. *immaculata* Staudinger, in which the twin spots are absent, is frequent in Oversley Wood and occasionally noted elsewhere.

VCH 1904: *'Not common but well distributed.'*
Sutton Park, Marston Green, Knowle, Overslade, Kenilworth, Wolford Wood.

Hebrew Character
2190 *Orthosia gothica* (L.)

County status: Widespread and abundant.
Flight: January to early June.
Larval foodplants: Polyphagous on deciduous trees and bushes, including hawthorns*, limes*, Field Maple*, Elder*, Aspen* and oaks*.

The Hebrew Character is one of the most prevalent springtime species in all types of habitats. It is subject to variation, chiefly in the ground colour, which ranges from reddish to dark grey. The occasional ab. *gothicina* (H.&S.) is reported, and a perfect specimen of ab. *obsolescens* (Lonz.) was caught at Charlecote on 29/4/2001 (DB).

There is one prolonged generation lasting up to five months, usually peaking in early to mid-April. Perhaps as a result of climate change there is evidence that the imago is emerging earlier: Charlecote, 9/2/1989, 22/2/1990 (3), 23/2/1990 (2), 14/1/2005, 31/1/2005 (DB).

The following moth trap figures indicate frequency:

Habitat	Location	1982	1985	1990	1995	2000
Urban	Radford, Coventry (MCV)	23	5	22	44	23
Suburban	Hillmorton, Rugby (DIP)	206	170	451	265	208
Rural	Charlecote (AFG)	608	246	436	208	272

VCH 1904: *'Very common.'*

Brown-line Bright-eye
2192 *Mythimna conigera* ([D. & S.])

County status: Widespread and fairly common.
Flight: June to August.
Larval foodplants: Grasses, including Cock's-foot* and Common Couch.

The Brown-line Bright-eye is associated with grassy areas and has been recorded from a variety of habitats, including road and railway cuttings, marshes, parkland, open woodland and gardens.

A particularly late specimen was recorded at Hillmorton, Rugby, on 16/9/1984 (DIP).

Garden moth trap counts are as follows:
Hillmorton, Rugby: 1982 (16), 1985 (14), 1990 (19), 1995 (9), 2000 (5) (DIP);
Bidford-on-Avon: 1990 (73), 1991 (78), 1992 (21), 1994 (102), 1995 (148) (RMC).

VCH 1904: *'Hampton-in-Arden, Knowle, Solihull, Overslade, Wolford'.*

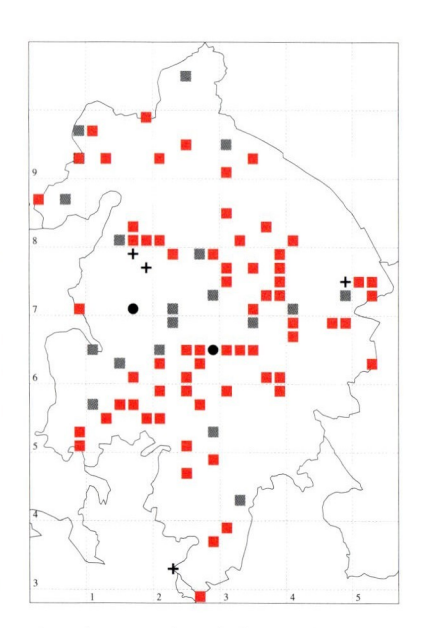

Clay
2193 *Mythimna ferrago* (Fabr.)

County status: Widespread and fairly common.
Flight: Late June to August.
Larval foodplants: Grasses, especially Cock's-foot* and meadow-grasses.

The Clay is generally more widespread than the preceding species and found in similar grassy locations. It appears to be more plentiful in built-up districts than *conigera*.

Urban and suburban garden moth trap counts show:
Radford, Coventry: 1982 (21), 1985 (40), 1990 (33), 1995 (62), 2000 (31) (MCV);
Hillmorton, Rugby: 1982 (137), 1985 (124), 1990 (242), 1995 (223), 2000 (79) (DIP).

VCH 1904: '*Found throughout the County.*'

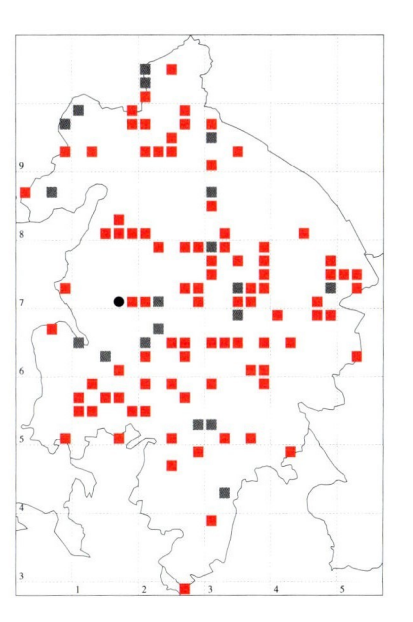

Delicate
2195 *Mythimna vitellina* (Hb.)

Regular immigrant: Southern Europe and North Africa

County status: Scarce immigrant.
Flight: Late August to October.
Larval foodplants: Various grasses, including Cock's-foot and Annual Meadow-grass.

The Delicate sometimes reaches Warwickshire in small numbers during good immigrant years. There were no records until 1977 when individuals were recorded at Marton on 19 October (GR) and Charlecote on 20 October (AFG). This was followed by a further brace in 1978 at Hampton Lucy and Charlecote on 14 October (DB). 1992 remains the best year to date with 10 records.

Records:

1977—**Marton** 19/10 (GR);
  Charlecote 20/10 (AFG).
1978—**Charlecote** 14/10 (DB);
  Hampton Lucy 14/10 (DB).
1982—**Marton** (GR).
1983—**Charlecote** 8/9 (DB).
1992—**Pillerton Priors** 12/9, 20/9, 21/9, 26/9, 28/9, 29/9 (CI);
  Charlecote 25/8 (AFG), 13/9 (DB), 16/9, 29/9 (AFG).
1996—**Charlecote** 24/10 (DB).
2005—**Temple Grafton** 29/9 (AFG).

Southern Wainscot
2197 *Mythimna straminea* (Treit.)

Nationally Local

County status: Very local and occasionally fairly common.
Flight: July and August.
Larval foodplants: Common Reed and Reed Canary-grass.

The Southern Wainscot is a fairly recent coloniser of Warwickshire, being first noticed in a restricted area of Common Reed at Wootton Wawen, on 10/8/1973 (DB). Populations have since become established at Brandon Marsh, Alvecote Pools, Coombe Abbey, Middleton Hall, Bradnock's Marsh and Nelson's Quarry.

Isolated individuals have been recorded in garden moth traps, suggesting undetected colonies.

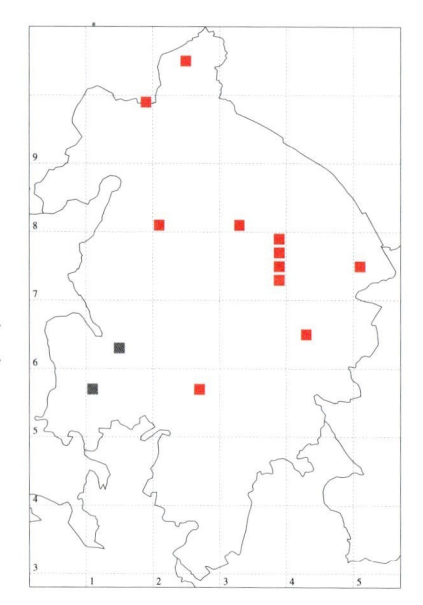

Records:
Wootton Wawen, 10/8/1973 (DB); **Charlecote**, 16/7/1974 (DB), 19/7/1986 (AFG), 18/7/1987 (DB), 9/7/1992, 17/7/1996 (AFG), 10/7/2000 (DB); **Oversley Wood**, 15/8/1974 (DB); **Nelson's Quarry**, **Stockton**, 5/7/1986 (4) (DB, IGMR, RMC); **Hillmorton, Rugby**, 3/8/1986 (DIP); **Brandon Wood**, 9/8/1988 (SAL); **Brandon Marsh**, 15/6/1989 (AFG, CP), 3/7/1992 (5) (DB, RGB), 25/7/1992 (3) (Warks Moth Group), 28/6/1993 (5) (DB, CI, RGB, RCK), 30/6/1995, 19/7/1996 (PC, NWH, CW), 4/8/2000 (25) (Warks Moth Group), 30/7/2005 (30) (Warks Moth Group); **Ryton Wood**, 1992 (LB, CE); **Alvecote Pools**, 18/7/1994 (DB, RCK, BM); **Middleton Hall**, 2/7/1995 (25) (Warks Moth Group), 9/7/2005 (4) (AJP, NJS); **Radford, Coventry**, 19/7/1997 (MCV); **Coombe Abbey**, 1/8/1997 (5) (Warks Moth Group); **Bidford-on-Avon**, 5/7/2001 (RMC); **Bradnock's Marsh**, 5/7/2003 (Warks Moth Group).

Smoky Wainscot
2198 *Mythimna impura* (Hb.)

County status: Widespread and sometimes abundant.
Flight: June to August with an occasional second generation during September to October.
Larval foodplants: Grasses, including Cock's-foot and Common Reed.

The Smoky Wainscot occurs in all types of grassland habitats, especially marshland. It is plentiful in both rural and built-up districts. Garden moth trap counts at **Hillmorton, Rugby,** however, illustrate a recent local decline: 1982 (236), 1985 (105), 1990 (445), 1995 (411), 2000 (69), 2004 (47) (DIP).

VCH 1904: *'Common everywhere.'*

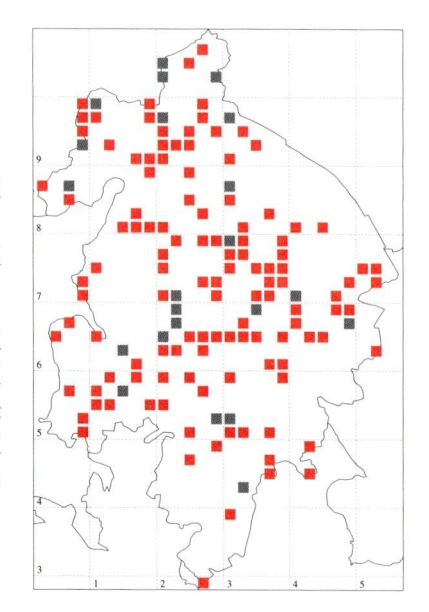

Common Wainscot
2199 *Mythimna pallens* (L.)

County status: Widespread and abundant.
Flight: Two generations. June to July, and August to October.
Larval foodplants: Grasses, including Annual Meadow-grass, Common Couch, Cock's-foot and Tufted Hair-grass.

The Common Wainscot is found commonly throughout Warwickshire in a wide range of habitats. It is equally plentiful in dry and damp grasslands.

Garden moth trap counts at **Hillmorton, Rugby**, are as follows: 1982 (286), 1985 (47), 1990 (287), 1995 (419), 2000 (49) 2004 (116) (DIP).

VCH 1904: *'Common everywhere.'*

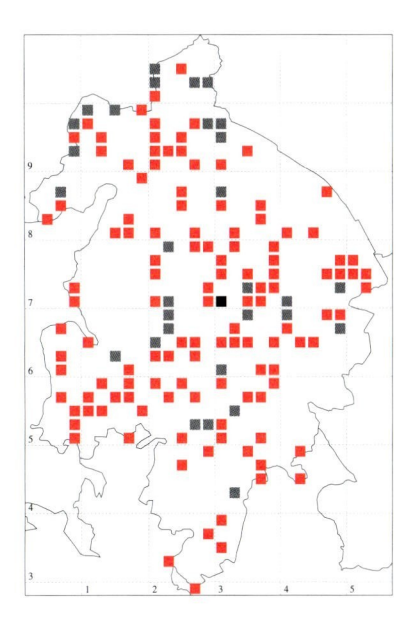

White-speck
2203 *Mythimna unipuncta* (Haw.)

Regular immigrant: Southern Europe and North Africa

County status: Scarce immigrant.
Flight: Late September to November.
Larval foodplants: Grasses, including Cock's-foot and Common Couch.

The White-speck was first recorded in Warwickshire in 1978, when three were caught during a period of significant immigrant activity in the British Isles. Since then it has only very occasionally been observed.

Records:
1978—**Marton** 25/10 (RA);
      Charlecote 9/11 (AFG), 11/11 (DB).
1979—**Radford, Coventry** 16/10 (MCV).
1984—**Hillmorton, Rugby** 31/10 (DIP).
1989—**Bidford-on-Avon** 14/10 (RMC).
2000—**Rugby** 29/9, 6/10 (IGMR);
      Charlecote 16/10 (AFG).

Obscure Wainscot
2204 *Mythimna obsoleta* (Hb.)
Nationally Local

County status: Very local and uncommon.
Flight: Late May to early July.
Larval foodplants: Common Reed.

First recorded at Rugby in 1899, this species endured a long absence before the next sighting in 1979 at Charlecote. Colonies have since been discovered at Brandon Marsh, Nelson's Quarry, Stockton and Bishops Bowl, Bishops Itchington. Occasional specimens in garden moth traps suggest further undiscovered colonies.

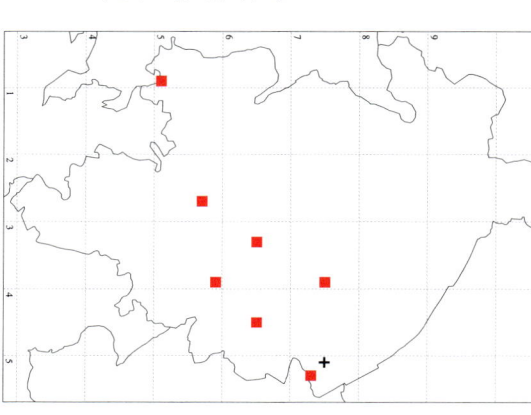

Records:
Charlecote, 6/7/1979 (DB), 20/6/1984, 9/6/2000, 7/6/2003 (AFG), 28/6/2005 (DB); **Hillmorton, Rugby**, 17/6/1990, 14/6/1992, 27/6/1992, 29/6/1992, 8/7/1997, 5/7/1998 (DIP); **Nelson's Quarry, Stockton**, 30/5/1992 (2 on BENHS field meeting PS, CW); **Steedey Meadows**, 18/6/1993, 16/6/1995 (PC, CW); **Brandon Marsh**, 25/6/1993 (PC, NWH, CW), 28/6/1993 (DB), 24/6/1994, 8/7/1994 (PC, NWH, CW), 4/8/2000 (AFG), 5/6/2001 (DB); **Bishops Bowl, Bishops Itchington**, 14/6/1997 (MA); **Bidford-on-Avon**, 29/6/2004 (RMC); **Royal Leamington Spa**, 6/7/2005 (JWkn).

VCH 1904: *Rugby 1899.*

Shoulder-striped Wainscot
2205 *Mythimna comma* (L.)

County status: Widespread and fairly common.
Flight: Late May to early August.
Larval foodplants: Grasses, including Cock's-foot.

The Shoulder-striped Wainscot has been recorded in all types of habitats from woodland rides to gardens. An unusually late individual occurred at Pillerton Priors on 2/10/2003 (CI).

Although this species is never as plentiful as *impura* or *pallens*, reasonable numbers are recorded in garden moth traps, as the following figures illustrate:
Pillerton Priors: 1992 (30), 1993 (30), 1994 (33), 2002 (15), 2003 (17), 2004 (22), 2005 (85) (CI).
Hillmorton, Rugby: 1982 (85), 1985 (12), 1990 (54), 1995 (39), 2000 (8), 2004 (15) (DIP).

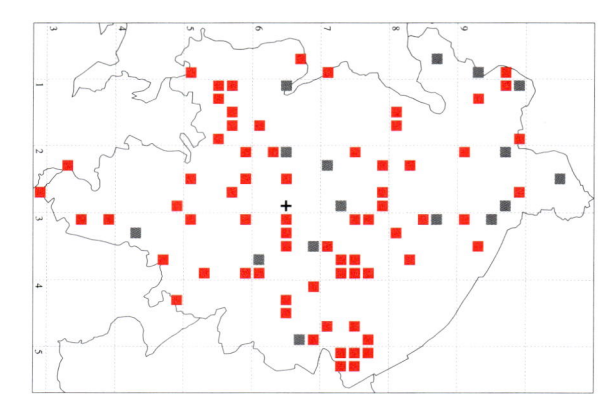

VCH 1904: *'Common everywhere.'*

Cosmopolitan
2208 *Mythimna loreyi* (Dup.)

Scarce immigrant, occasionally common: Southern Europe and North Africa

County status: Rare immigrant.
Flight: September to November.
Larval foodplants: Grasses, including Cock's-foot.

The first Cosmopolitan to be recorded in the County at Charlecote on 23/10/2000 (AFG) was connected to an unusual immigration of the species, covering a more extensive radius than usual. Two further specimens were subsequently caught in Warwickshire during the exceptionally mild autumn of 2005.

Records:
2000—**Charlecote**, 23/10 (AFG).
2005—**Temple Grafton**, 13/9 (AFG).
 Charlecote, 2/11 (DB).

Wormwood
2211 *Cucullia absinthii* (L.)

Nationally Scarce B

County status: Very local and scarce.
Flight: July and August.
Larval foodplants: The flowers and seeds of Wormwood* and Mugwort*.

In the early part of the twentieth century the Wormwood was essentially a coastal species, but in the late 1940s it colonised bomb sites and other waste places in Birmingham and Coventry. The beautifully cryptic larvae could be found commonly and an unprecedented 66 were collected at Lea Hall, Birmingham, during 1948 (SEWC). Now, following clearance and development of such areas, the species is only found in small numbers. The moth continues, however, to be an opportunist and will quickly colonise suitable terrain as it develops, including gravel pits, quarries and other post-industrial brownfield sites.

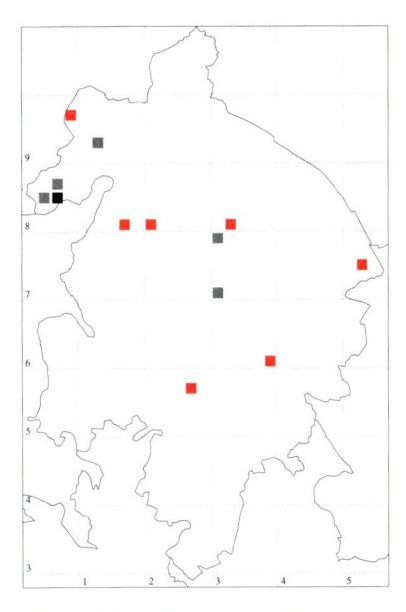

Records:
Lea Hall, 1948 larvae (66) (SEWC); **Birmingham**, 1949 several larvae (FAN); **South Yardley**, 1950 several larvae on waste-ground (HEH); **Edgbaston, Birmingham**, 1956 (FAN); **N.E. Birmingham**, 1960s (LJE); **Erdington**, 1960s (JB); **Earlsdon, Coventry**, 20/7/1961 (LEM); **Charlecote**, 31/7/1980 (DB), 20/7/1996 adult netted on Buddleia flowers (AFG), 23/7/2003 (DB); **Radford, Coventry**, 12/8/1984, 8/8/1998 (MCV); **Hampton-in-Arden** 1985 (MCV); **Hillmorton, Rugby**, 19/8/1991 (DIP); **Ufton Fields**, 1991 (RCK); **Charlecote/Wasperton**, disused gravel pit 9/8/1995 larvae on Mugwort (4) (AFG); **Sutton Park**, 17/8/2002 (Warks Moth Group); **Solihull**, 2002 (RL).

Chamomile Shark
2214 *Cucullia chamomillae* ([D. & S.])

Nationally Local

County status: Local and uncommon.
Flight: April and May.
Larval foodplants: Chamomiles* and mayweeds*.

This species has a somewhat restricted distribution and the largest nucleus of sightings is from the south-west of the County. It frequents open grassy areas on or near chalky soils, favouring wide field edges and marginal waste-ground. The adult visits garden moth traps in generally low numbers, as the following figures illustrate:
Bidford-on-Avon: 1988 (1), 1990 (2), 1991 (2), 1992 (4), 1993 (1), 1997 (3) (RMC);
Charlecote: 1988 (3), 1990 (1), 1991 (5), 1992 (1), 1993 (3), 1997 (2) (AFG).

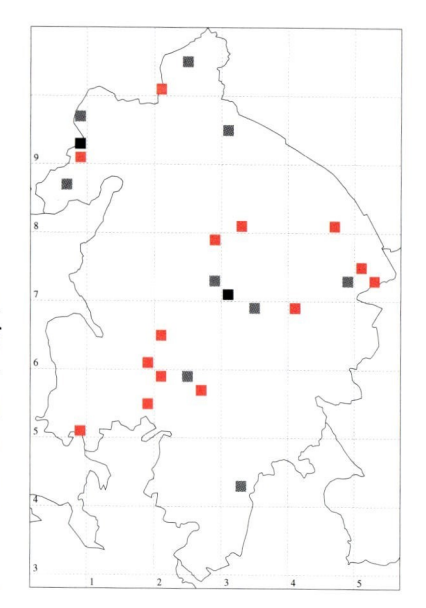

VCH 1904: '*Occurs throughout the County.*'

Shark
2216 *Cucullia umbratica* (L.)

County status: Widespread and fairly common.
Flight: June to August.
Larval foodplants: Sow-thistles, wild lettuces, hawk's-beards and hawkweeds.

The Shark is fairly widely distributed in Warwickshire but is rarely seen in large numbers. It is only occasionally recorded from woodland, preferring open terrain, including disused quarries, railway embankments and rough waste-ground.

A particularly late specimen was caught at Hillmorton, Rugby, on 2/9/1989 (DIP).

The following moth trap totals illustrate generally low frequency:
Pillerton Priors: 1992 (3), 1993 (1), 1994 (0), 2002 (1), 2003 (0), 2004 (4) (CI);
Bidford-on-Avon: 1992 (20), 1993 (0), 1994 (2), 1995 (9) (RMC).

VCH 1904: '*Occurs throughout the County.*'
Knowle, 1898 (HWE).

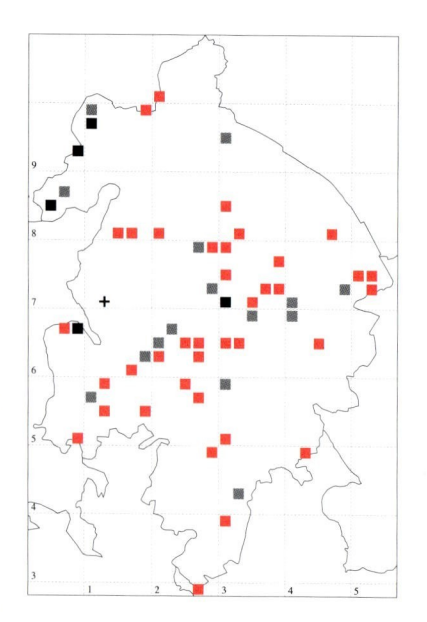

Mullein
2221 *Shargacucullia verbasci* (L.)

County status: Fairly widespread and generally fairly common.
Flight: April to early June.
Larval foodplants: Wild and cultivated mulleins*, Common and Water Figwort*, buddleias*.

The Mullein is fairly widespread over the southern half of the County but dwindles further north. It has been recorded from a number of woodland and grassland sites but is more frequently noted in gardens. The conspicuous larvae are often found on cultivated mulleins and buddleias, but the adult is only sparingly attracted to light.

VCH 1904: *'Not common.'*
Knowle, Rugby, Wolford.

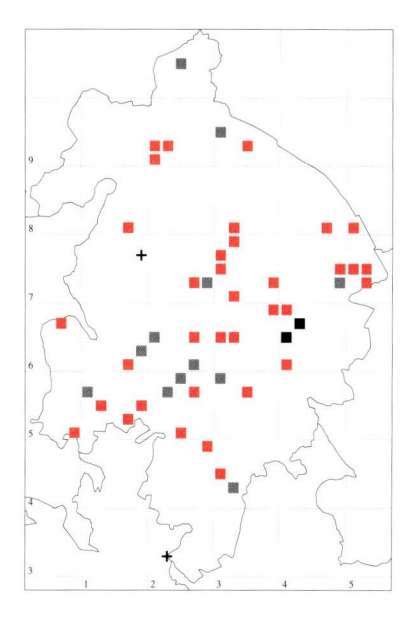

Minor Shoulder-knot
2225 *Brachylomia viminalis* (Fabr.)

County status: Fairly widespread and locally common.
Flight: Late June to August.
Larval foodplants: Sallows*, willows and Aspen.

The Minor Shoulder-knot favours damp woodland and marshy areas containing an abundance of sallows. Choice sites include Waverley Wood, Brandon Marsh, Wappenbury Wood and Oversley Wood, where prodigious numbers of adults have been recorded at MV; for example, 3/7/1976 (45), 28/7/1978 (53), 2/8/1980 (86) (DB, AFG).

Melanic forms regularly occur in all Warwickshire populations.

VCH 1904: *Wolford Wood, Knowle, Rugby, Atherstone.*

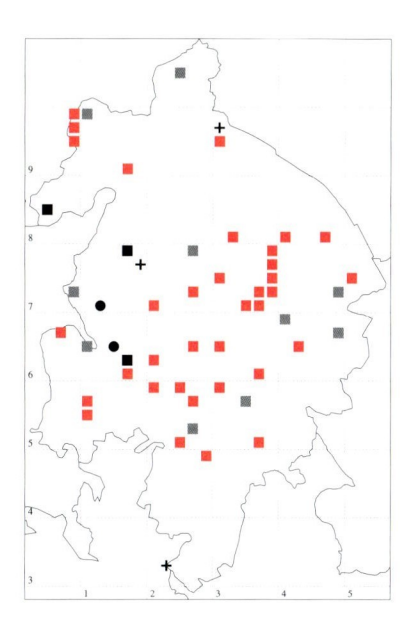

Sprawler
2227 *Asteroscopus sphinx* (Hufn.)

County status: Local and sometimes fairly common.
Flight: Late October to early December.
Larval foodplants: Various trees and bushes, including Ash*, buckthorns*, elms*, oaks*, limes*, Field Maple*, Blackthorn*, apple* and Wild Privet*.

The Sprawler is on the wing late in the season and does not usually respond to light until after 11.00 p.m. which may partly account for a lack of records.

It is most plentiful in well-wooded areas, particularly on calcareous soils containing copious amounts of Blackthorn and Wild Privet.

Although a wide range of larval foodplants are known, Wild Privet, which appears to be favoured in Warwickshire, is not generally recognised. The following are examples of final instar larvae beaten from Wild Privet: Chesterton Wood, 7/6/1983 (2), Gospel Oak, 12/6/1984, 23/6/1985 (2), Harbury Spoilbank, 2/6/1985, 22/5/2993 and Ladies Wood, Ragley Hall, 23/5/1992 (2) (MCV).

VCH 1904: *'Wolford Wood – occasionally'.*

Deep-brown Dart
2231 *Aporophyla lutulenta* ([D. & S.])

County status: Local and uncommon.
Flight: September and October.
Larval foodplants: Various grasses, Broom, hawthorns, Blackthorn and herbaceous plants, including plantains.

The Deep-brown Dart frequents a range of open habitats, including woodland clearings, railway cuttings, meadows and gardens. There is evidence of a decline in some populations since the 1980s.

Typical garden moth trap figures in rural areas are as follows:
Pillerton Priors: 1992 (14), 1993 (3), 1994 (0), 2002 (3), 2003 (14), 2004 (13), 2005 (7) (CI);
Charlecote: 1981 (16), 1982 (32), 1991 (8), 1992 (3), 2001 (3), 2002 (6), 2005 (40) (DB).

VCH 1904: *'Very rare.'* Knowle, 1898 (HWE)

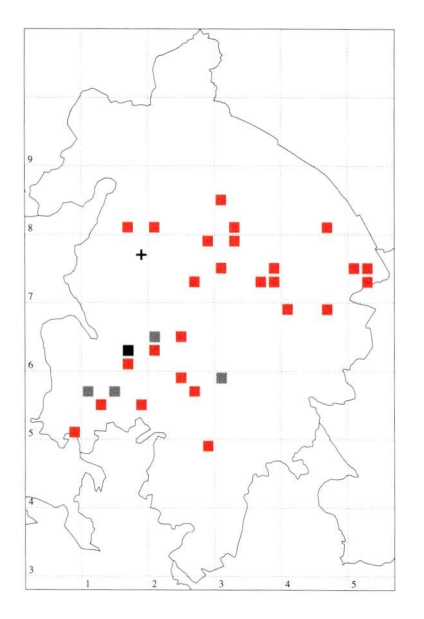

Black Rustic
2232 *Aporophyla nigra* (Haw.)

County status: Widespread and common.
Flight: Late August to November.
Larval foodplants: A variety of woody and herbaceous plants, including docks, Dandelion, clovers, Tufted Hair-grass and Heather.

There was a gap of exactly 100 years between the first and second records of this species in Warwickshire: Rugby, 30/9/1875 (WSE) and Charlecote, 20/9/1975 (DB).

Linked to a national extension in range during the 1970s the Black Rustic spread into the County from the south-west, reaching north Warwickshire by the 1980s (Fig. 24). It is now a widespread and common species, being found in a vast range of urban and rural habitats.

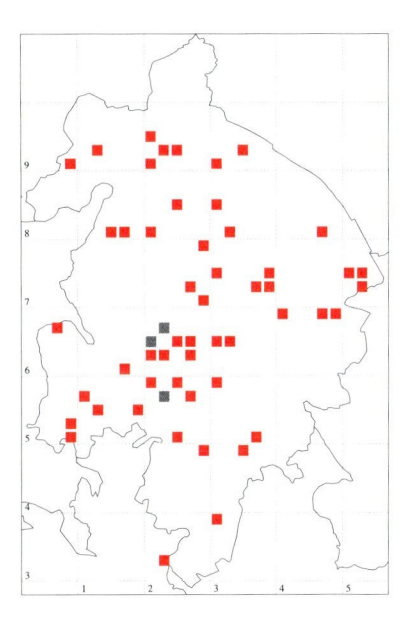

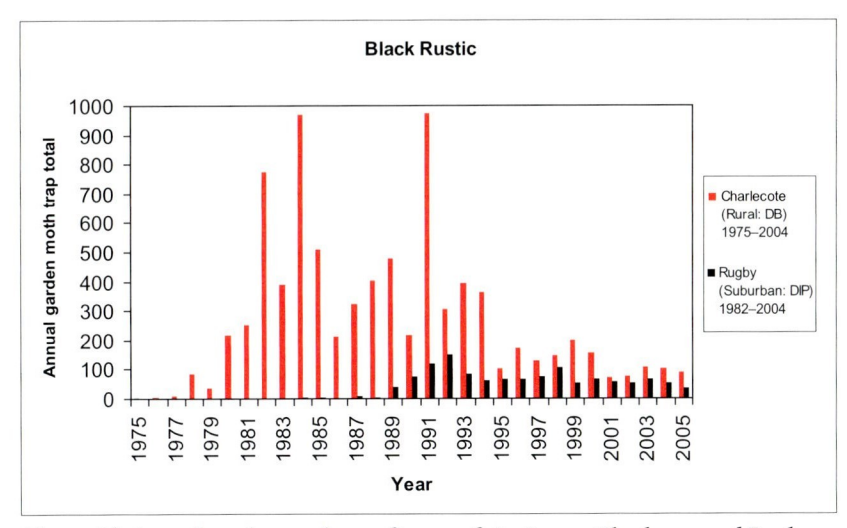

Figure 24. Annual garden moth trap figures of *A. nigra* at Charlecote and Rugby.

Golden-rod Brindle
2233 *Lithomoia solidaginis* (Hb.)

Resident (Nationally Local). Occasional immigrant: Northern Europe

County status: Rare immigrant.
Flight: August and September.
Larval foodplants: Heather, Bilberry, birches and willows.

Five examples of this chiefly moorland species have been caught in Warwickshire. There is very little potentially suitable habitat for colonisation and it is assumed that these isolated individuals were immigrants.

Records:
1969—**Charlecote**, 2/9, 3/9 (DB).
1982—**Hillmorton, Rugby**, 11/8, 15/8, 22/8 (DIP).

Tawny Pinion
2235 *Lithophane semibrunnea* (Haw.)

Nationally Local

County status: Fairly widespread but uncommon.
Flight: Late September to November and after hibernation in March to mid-May.
Larval foodplants: Ash.

The Tawny Pinion was first recorded in Warwickshire at May's Wood in 1909 (GBM). It is now found locally over a fairly large area of the County in the vicinity of Ash. The adult is never seen in any numbers and the majority of records are of singletons. Favoured habitats include broadleaved woodland, hedgerows, scrub, disused quarries and railway embankments containing a plentiful supply of regenerating Ash. Typical sites are Oversley Wood, Wellesbourne Wood, Hampton Wood, Ryton Wood, Nelson's Quarry and Bearley Station. It is occasionally noted in garden moth traps.

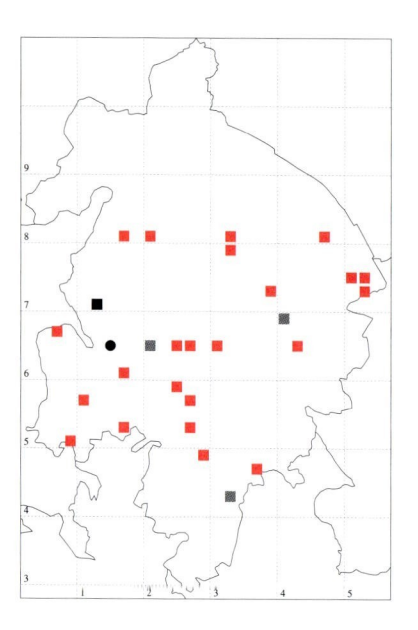

Pale Pinion
2236 *Lithophane hepatica* (Cl.)

Nationally Local

County status: Fairly widespread and becoming more common.
Flight: Late September to October and after hibernation in March to late May.
Larval foodplants: A variety of trees and shrubs, including oaks, sallows, birches, brambles and Wild Privet.

Following an extension in range from south-west England the Pale Pinion was first recorded in Warwickshire on 6/4/1984 at Oversley Wood (RMC). It spread slowly north-eastwards across the County and reached the Rugby district during the 1990s. This species frequents broadleaved woodland and choice locations include Oakley Wood and Ryton Wood. It is also found in well-wooded rural and suburban areas where it has become an annual visitor to many static garden moth traps.

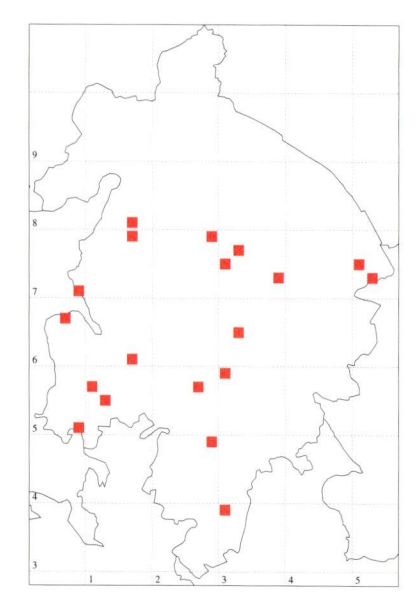

Grey Shoulder-knot
2237 *Lithophane ornitopus lactipennis* (Dadd)

County status: Fairly widespread and becoming fairly common.

Flight: Late September to November; after hibernation in March to late May. It may be seen as early as January in mild winters.

Larval foodplants: Oaks*.

The Grey Shoulder-knot is subject to periodic fluctuations and range expansions. During the 1970s there was a paucity of records linked to a national decline. There followed a substantial recovery throughout the next two decades and this species has now become fairly common in many woodlands. It has dispersed widely into parks and gardens in both rural and urban districts (Fig. 25).

The adult is frequently observed at rest during the daytime on walls, posts, and tree trunks.

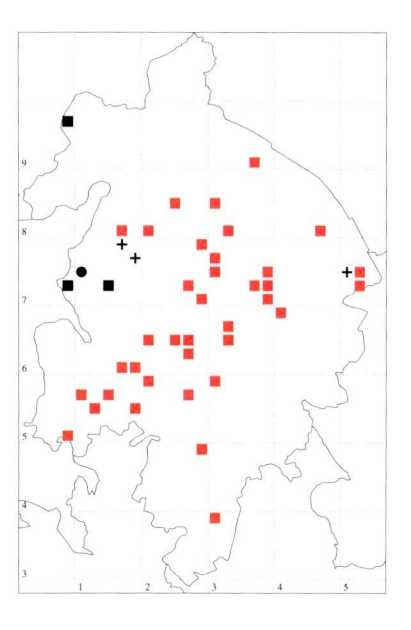

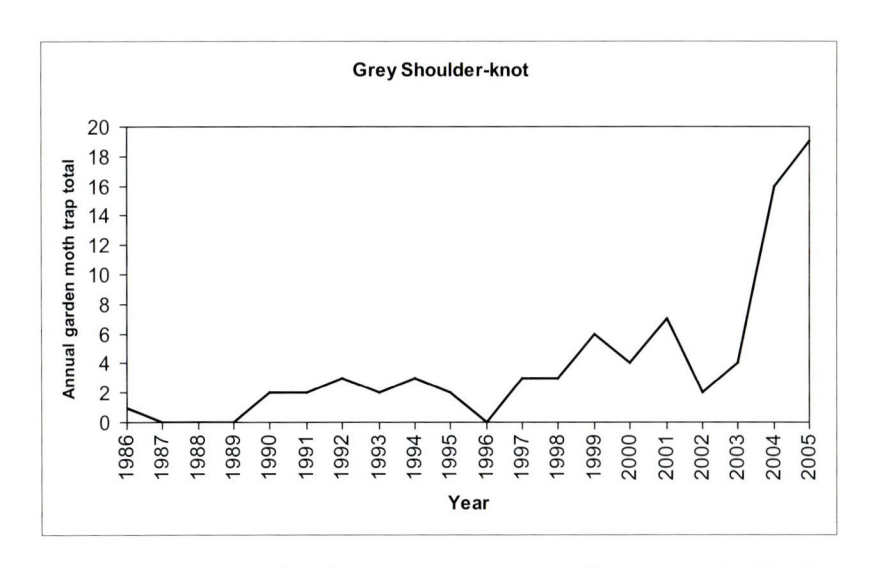

Figure 25. Increasing abundance in *L. ornitopus* at Hillmorton, Rugby (DIP).

VCH 1904: *'Not common.'*
Knowle, Solihull, Rugby.

Blair's Shoulder-knot
2240 *Lithophane leautieri hesperica* Bours.

County status: Widespread and common.
Flight: Mid-September to November.
Larval foodplants: Monterey, Lawson's* and Leyland* Cypress.

Blair's Shoulder-knot was first seen in this country in 1951 on the Isle of Wight. By the late 1960s, assisted by further immigrations, it had colonised many parts of southern England. The ensuing years saw a northward incursion with the first Warwickshire specimen at Charlecote on 8/10/1978 (DB; Brown, 1979b).

By the early 1990s populations had become established in parks and gardens throughout much of the County. The expeditious proliferation of this species has been assisted by an increasing popularity in the use of Cypress cultivars for privacy in residential districts and shelter-belts in rural areas.

The first emergents are usually noted in mid-September but a particularly early specimen was caught at Hillmorton, Rugby, on 27/8/2004 (DIP).

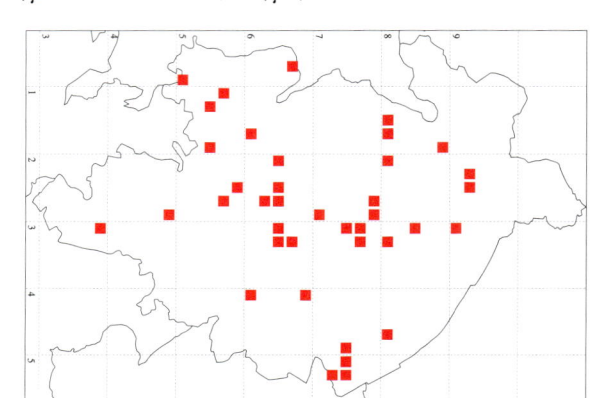

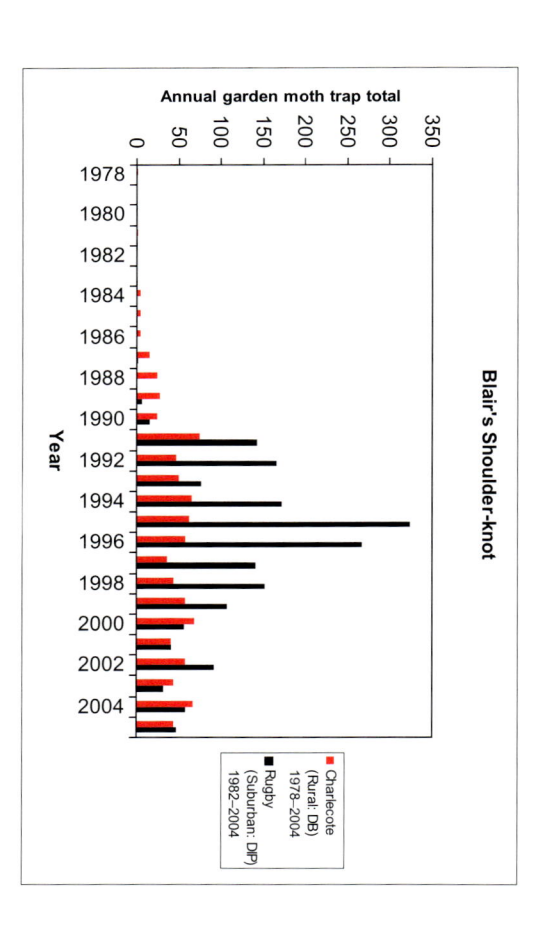

Figure 26. Annual garden moth trap figures illustrating the establishment of *L. leautieri* in a rural and a suburban area.

Red Sword-grass
2241 *Xylena vetusta* (Hb.)

Nationally Local

County status: Status uncertain. Possible vagrant.
Flight: October and, after hibernation, in March.
Larval foodplants: Heather, Yellow Iris, the flower heads of rushes and other herbaceous and woody plants.

With only three modern day records the status of Red Sword-grass in Warwickshire is uncertain. Individuals noted could either be vagrants or may represent small transient populations.

Records:
Hampton Wood, 16/10/1974 (AFG); **Charlecote,** 25/10/1978 (AFG); **Ryton Meadows,** 18/3/2005 (CJ, JWkn).

VCH 1904: *'Not common.'*
Sutton Park, Knowle, Rugby, Overslade.

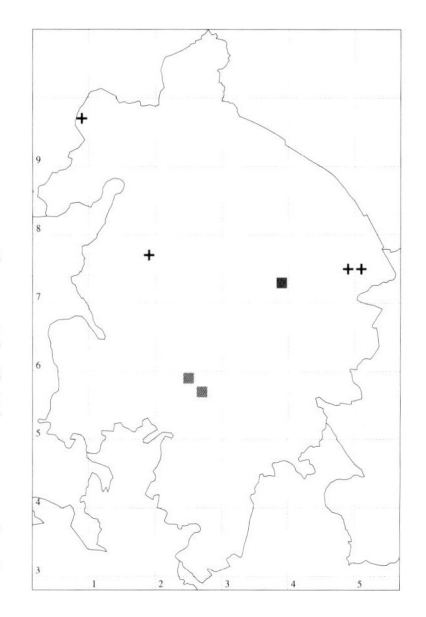

Sword-grass
2242 *Xylena exsoleta* (L.)

Nationally Scarce B

County status: Extinct.
Flight: October and in April, after hibernation.
Larval foodplants: Many low-growing herbaceous plants, including groundsels, docks and thistles.

This species has contracted northwards in the British Isles during recent decades, becoming extinct in many counties, including Warwickshire.

Records:
Rugby district, 1874 (RNHS); **Packwood,** April 1911 (SEWC); **East Birmingham,** 1920s annually (GPS); **Long Lawford, Townsend Lane Nurseries,** 1948 (AGB); **Monkspath, Solihull,** 20/10/1948 (SEWC); **Four Oaks,** 2/10/1950 single to sugar (EVW).

VCH 1904: *'Not uncommon.'*
Marston Green, Knowle, Birmingham, Sutton Park, Solihull, Overslade.

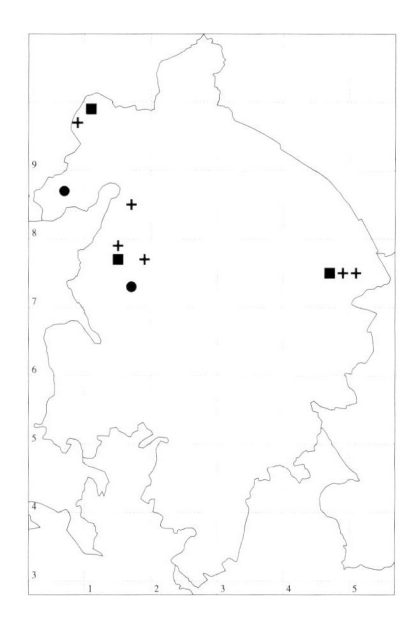

Early Grey
2243 *Xylocampa areola* (Esp.)

County status: Widespread and fairly common.
Flight: March to May.
Larval foodplants: Honeysuckle*.

The Early Grey is a familiar species in both woodlands and gardens as a consequence of using wild and cultivated varieties of Honeysuckle as a larval food source.

The largest populations occur in woodland. Quantities can be seen in Oversley Wood, Ryton Wood, Wappenbury Wood, Oakley Wood, Hampton Wood, Snitterfield Bushes and Wolford Wood.

Emergence periods are normally in March and April but individuals are sometimes caught much earlier; for example, Hillmorton, Rugby, 16/1/1989 (DIP).

VCH 1904: *'Not common'.*
Knowle, Sutton Park, Coleshill, Overslade, Wolford.

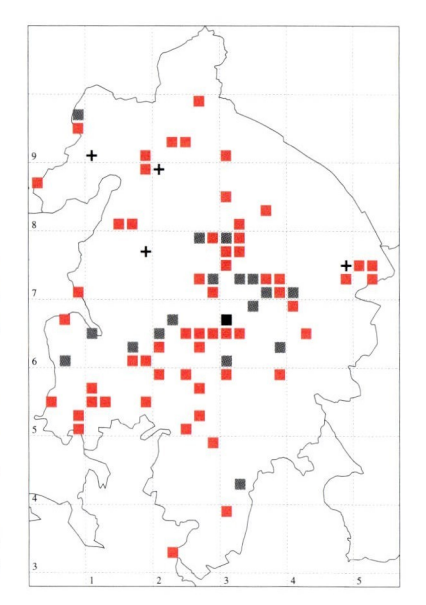

Green-brindled Crescent
2245 *Allophyes oxyacanthae* (L.)

County status: Fairly widespread and fairly common.
Flight: September to November.
Larval foodplants: Hawthorns*, Blackthorn* and apple*.

The Green-brindled Crescent is locally common in deciduous woodland but less plentiful in open terrain. It is a frequent visitor to the sugar patch and has often been observed feeding on Ivy blossom by torchlight.

The melanic form ab. *capucina* is of frequent occurrence in urban districts. In rural areas it is less common and represents approximately 10% of the population.

An unusual intensively black specimen was caught at Tile Hill, Coventry, on 14/10/2004 (AJK).

VCH 1904: *'Common everywhere with ab. capucina.'*

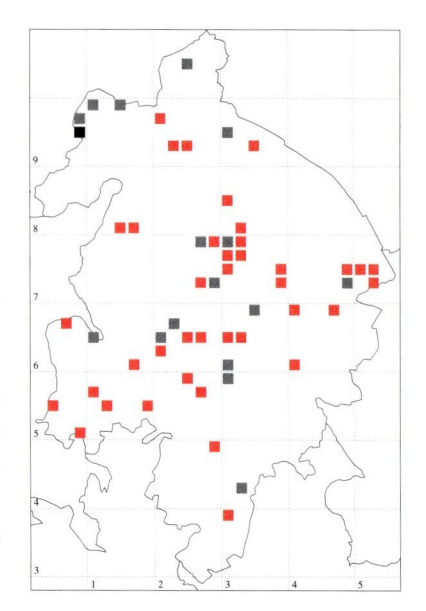

Merveille du Jour
2247 *Dichonia aprilina* (L.)

County status: Widespread and fairly common.
Flight: September to early November.
Larval foodplants: Oaks*.

This attractive species is well established in deciduous and mixed woods throughout the County. It is also associated with hedgerow and roadside oaks, parkland and gardens. The adult has been noted feeding at Ivy flowers and visits MV light in generally low numbers.

The following garden moth trap counts give an illustration of frequency:
Hillmorton, Rugby: 1982 (8), 1985 (3), 1990 (10), 1995 (4) (DIP);
Charlecote: 1982 (9), 1985 (4), 1990 (14), 1995 (10), (AFG).

VCH 1904: '*Occurs throughout the County.*'

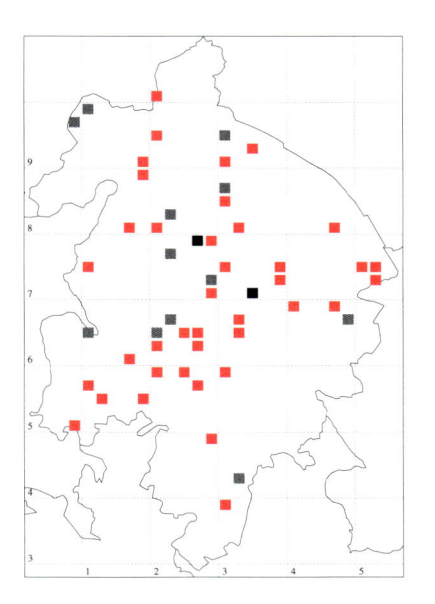

Brindled Green
2248 *Dryobotodes eremita* (Fabr.)

County status: Widespread and fairly common.
Flight: Late August to late October.
Larval foodplants: Oaks*.

The Brindled Green has a similar distribution to the preceding species and is found in mixed woodland and open terrain with isolated oaks. Dark green and blackish-green forms represent a higher percentage in urban districts, but long-term recorders report a reduction of melanic specimens during the last 30 years.

The following garden moth trap totals reflect larger numbers than *aprilina*:
Hillmorton, Rugby: 1982 (3), 1985 (14), 1990 (25), 1995 (9), 2000 (8) (DIP);
Charlecote: 1982 (60), 1985 (129), 1990 (54), 1995 (119), 2000 (48) (AFG).

VCH 1904: '*Common throughout the County.*'

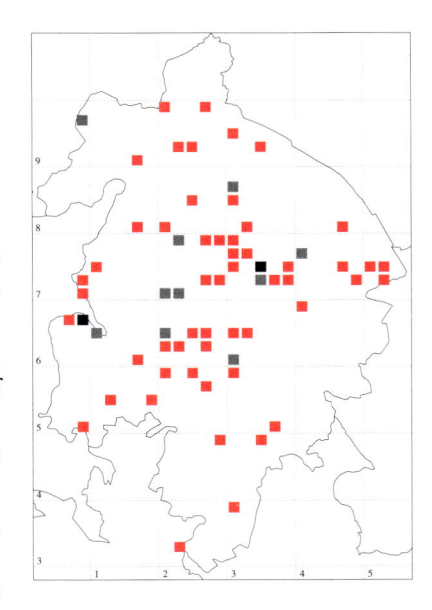

Dark Brocade
2250 *Blepharita adusta* (Esp.)

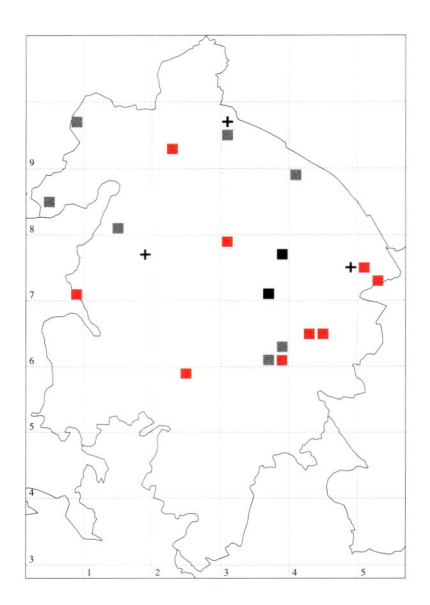

County status: Very local and scarce, but fairly common at one site.
Flight: Early May to mid-August.
Larval foodplants: A wide range of woody and herbaceous plants, including Heather, Bladder Campion and Alder.

The Dark Brocade is occasionally fairly common at Nelson's Quarry, Stockton, but is otherwise scarcely observed. This species shows a preference for calcareous soils.

Records:
Rugby district, 1893, (A. Sidgwick, 1893); **Brandon Wood**, 23/6/1936 (LR); **Wappenbury Wood**, 1940s (APll); **Edgbaston, Birmingham**, July 1946 (MWB), 1956 (FAN); **Ufton Wood**, (1959 survey); **Sutton Park**, 11/6/1966, 1970s (LJE); **Ufton Fields**, 29/6/1968 (ANT), 16/6/1989 (MB); **Hartshill Hayes**, 1975–79 (RJT); **Bramcote Canal, Bramcote**, 28/6/1976 (BBr); **Solihull**, 1976 (CD); **Chapelfields, Coventry**, 5/7/1982 (CW); **Stockton Cutting**, 27/7/1984 (CDNHSS); **Hampton Wood**, 17/8/1984 (ANT, CW, PC); **Hillmorton, Rugby**, 2/7/1985, 2/6/1992, 7/6/1992, 10/6/1992, 28/6/1992, 19/7/1995 (DIP); **Nelson's Quarry, Stockton**, 6/5/1990 (7) (DB, AFG), 24/5/1991 (3) (DB, PJR), 29/5/1991 (3) (DB, RMC), 30/5/1992 (3) (Warks Moth Group); **Central Rugby**, 23/6/2001 (IGMR); **Nether Whitacre**, 30/5/2003 (JBt).

VCH 1904: *'Very local and not at all common.'*
Sutton Park, Knowle, Overslade, Atherstone.

Grey Chi
2254 *Antitype chi* (L.)

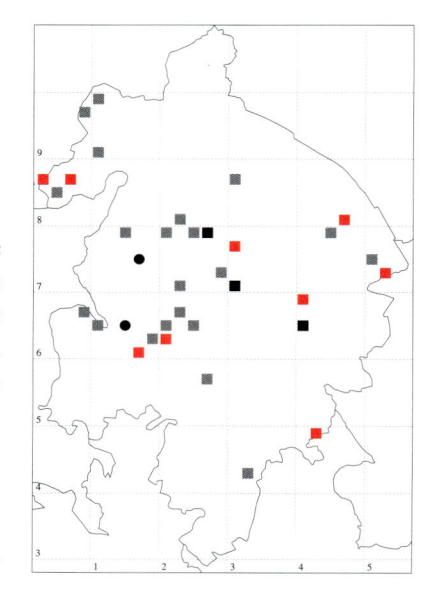

County status: Very local and scarce.
Flight: August and September.
Larval foodplants: Sorrels, docks and Dandelion.

The Grey Chi favours high ground and has therefore been largely absent from river valleys. Prior to the 1980s it was frequently recorded in north and west Warwickshire but a serious decline has been experienced and there has only been one record of this species since 1992 (Fig. 27).

Records since 1980:
Claverdon, 22/8/1980 (5), 29/8/1980 (3), 10/9/1981 (6, including f. *olivacea* Steph.), 16/8/1982 (4), 14/8/1983 (3), 22/8/1983 (5), 24/8/1983 (3), 28/8/1983 (2), 30/8/1984 (3), 4/9/1985, 8/9/1985, 24/8/1986, 26/8/1986, 31/8/1986, 9/9/1986, 11/9/1986, 13/9/1986 (IGMR);

Wolverton, Aug. 1980 (DS), **Marton**, 1980 (RA); **Hillmorton**, **Rugby**, 1982–1990 annual, not seen since 1990 (DIP), 2/9/1986 to 4/9/1986 (3) (PN); **Birmingham**, 1983 (DV); **Pailton**, 1984–88 (KCG); **Farnborough Hall N.T**, 6/9/1986 specimen at rest on wall (AFG); **Bearley Station**, 2/8/1992 (IGMR); **Earlsdon, Coventry**, 3/9/2005 (PC).

VCH 1904: *'Occurs throughout the County.'*

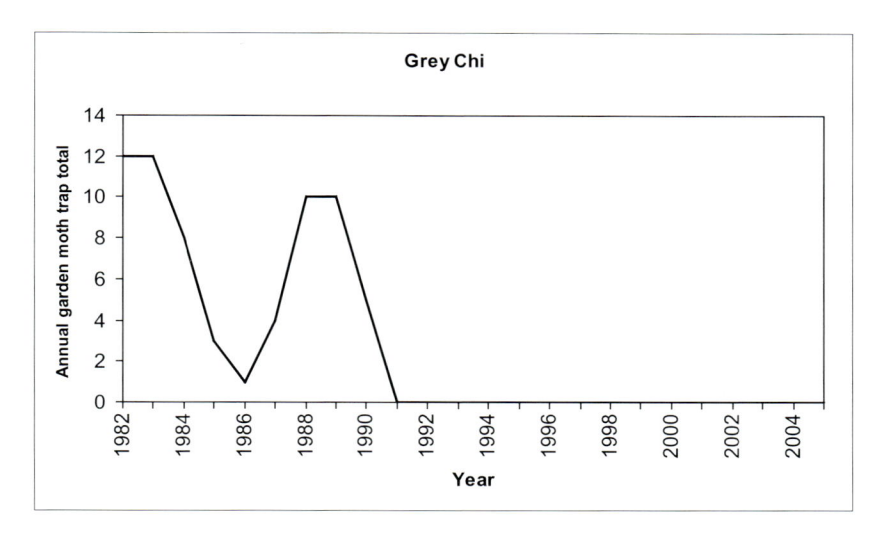

Figure 27. The sudden decline of *A. chi* at Hillmorton, Rugby (DIP).

Large Ranunculus
2252 *Polymixis flavicincta* ([D. & S.])

Nationally Local

County status: Very local and uncommon.

Flight: September to late October.

Larval foodplants: Various low-growing plants, including Dandelion, Red Valerian, Rosebay Willowherb and sometimes woody species such as currants and plum.

The Large Ranunculus is a scarce moth in Warwickshire, rarely straying from calcareous soils. It has been recorded in open woodland, waste-ground and gardens.

Records:
Tysoe, 1950–60 (TT); **Oakley Wood**, 24/9/1976 (DB); **Marton**, 29/9/1976 (RA); **Charlecote**, 23/9/1977 (DB), 11/10/1978 (AFG), 26/9/1980 (DB); **Hillmorton, Rugby**, 27/9/1982, 20/10/1987, (DIP), 1/10/2000 (PN); **Pailton**, 1986 (KCG); **CAD Kineton**, 1/11/1987 (RJB); **Central Rugby**, 26/9/1999 (IGMR); **Warwick**, 6/10/2004 (AV); **Brailes**, 24/9/2005 (2), 1/10/2005 (CI).

VCH 1904: *'Very rare.'* Rugby 1867, Wolford.

Feathered Ranunculus
2255 *Polymixis lichenea lichenea* (Hb.)

Nationally Local

County status: Status uncertain.
Flight: August and September.
Larval foodplants: A variety of herbaceous plants, including Dandelion, plantains, ragworts, docks and trefoils.

This mainly coastal species has been recorded from a small number of inland counties where it is associated with chalk and limestone slopes. The exact status of *lichenea* remains uncertain in this region with single records from Bidford-on-Avon (RMC) and Charlecote (AFG).

It is possible that small populations may exist on the calcareous escarpments in the Stratford-upon-Avon/Alcester district.

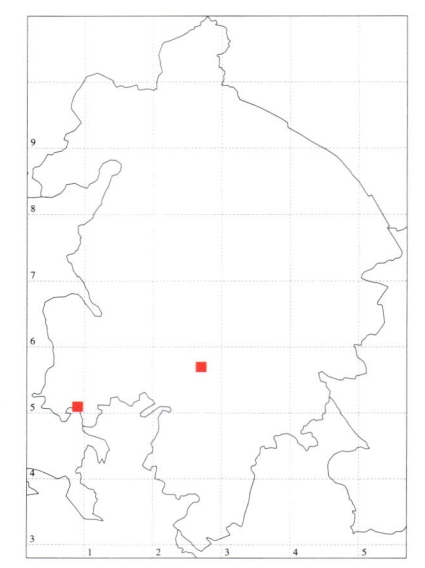

Records:
Bidford-on-Avon, 23/9/1983 (RMC); **Charlecote,** 26/8/1998 (AFG).

Satellite
2256 *Eupsilia transversa* (Hufn.)

County status: Widespread and fairly common.
Flight: Late September to early May.
Larval foodplants: Oaks*, Beech*, Aspen*, sallows* and hawthorns*.

The Satellite is a widely distributed species, plentiful in wooded districts. The adult hibernates but becomes active during mild weather and visits MV. It became the final moth of the twentieth century to enter the author's garden moth trap at Charlecote, when a specimen arrived at 11.50 p.m. on 31/12/1999!

VCH 1904: *'Common everywhere.'*

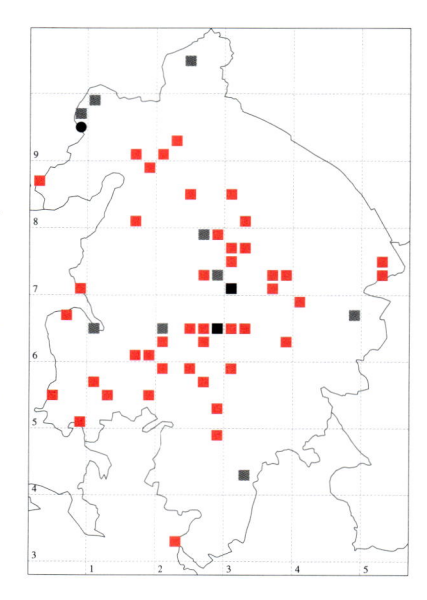

Chestnut
2258 *Conistra vaccinii* (L.)

County status: Widespread and locally common.
Flight: Late September to May.
Larval foodplants: Oaks*, Blackthorn*, Alder*, sallows*, elms*, Aspen*, and other deciduous trees and shrubs.

The Chestnut is found throughout the County, being particularly numerous in woodlands.
During the last two decades, perhaps linked to climate change, there has been a substantial increase in sightings during late February and early March. This pre-springtime escalation is highlighted by the following single night moth trap figures: Oversley Wood, 28/2/1987 (95), (DB, AFG); Ryton Wood, 23/2/1991 (34) (DB, PJR); Oversley Wood, 11/3/1991 (180) (DB, AFG, RMC).

The colour and pattern of specimens is very variable and dark forms are fairly frequent.

VCH 1904: *'Common everywhere.'*

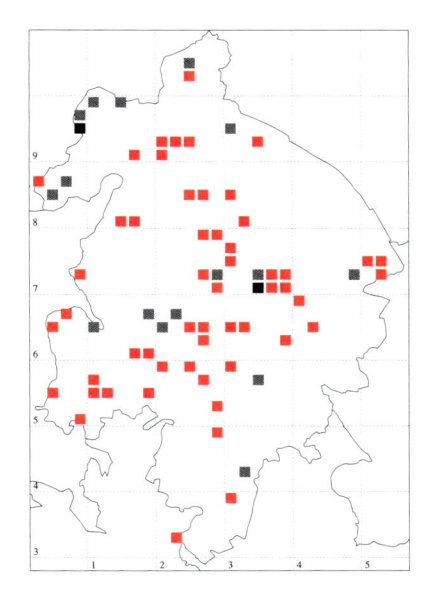

Dark Chestnut
2259 *Conistra ligula* (Esp.)

County status: Fairly widespread and generally uncommon.
Flight: October to mid-March.
Larval foodplants: Hawthorns*, Blackthorn*, sallows*, and other deciduous trees and low-growing plants.

This species is far less frequently observed than its congener, the Chestnut, and appears to be only thinly distributed. The Dark Chestnut displays a predilection for more open habitat and has been noted in garden moth traps in both rural and urban districts.

The adult is often seen during the mid-winter but has usually ceased by mid-March.

VCH 1904: *'Not as common as **vaccinii** but generally occurs with it.'*

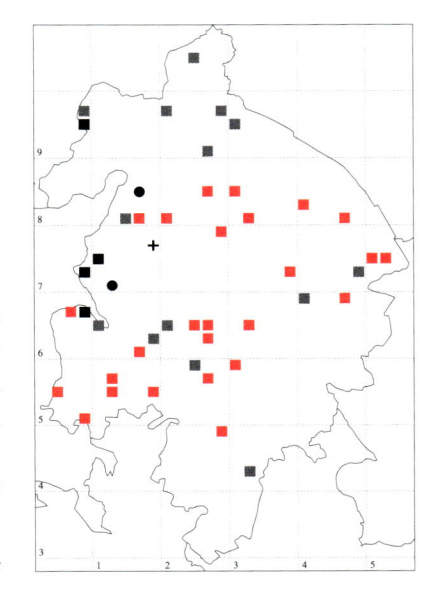

Dotted Chestnut
2260 *Conistra rubiginea* ([D. & S.])

Nationally Scarce B

County status: Recent coloniser. Very local.
Flight: October and March to April after hibernation.
Larval foodplants: In captivity will eat apple, sallows, Blackthorn and plum.

The Dotted Chestnut experienced a national expansion in range during the 1990s. Formerly established on heathland in central southern England, *rubiginea* dispersed northwards and westwards across several counties, reaching Warwickshire in 2003. The erstwhile Rugby record had remained in isolation for 117 years.

Records:
Barby Road, **Rugby**, 6/10/1886 (RNHS); **Charlecote**, 28/3/2003 gravid female (DB; Brown, 2003), 29/3/2005, 10/4/2005 (DB); **Bidford-on-Avon**, 17/3/2004 (2) (RMC, WC), 10/3/2005 (RMC), 28/10/2005 (DCr); **Temple Grafton**, 24/4/2004, 21/3/2005 (AFG); **Oversley Wood**, 25/3/2005 (G&AF); **Pillerton Priors**, 29/4/2005 (CI).

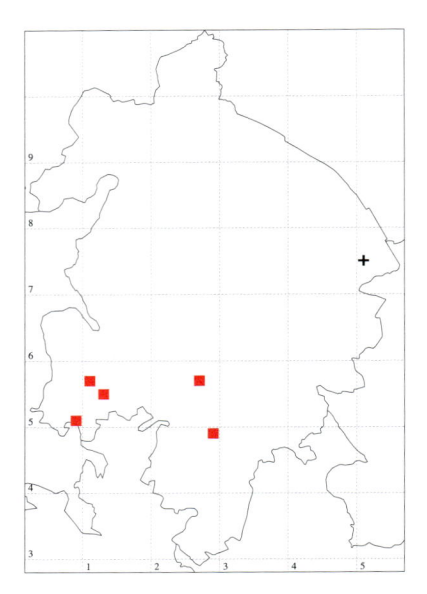

Brick
2262 *Agrochola circellaris* (Hufn.)

County status: Fairly widespread but becoming less common.
Flight: September to early December.
Larval foodplants: Sallows*, Wych Elm*, Aspen*, poplars, Ash.

The Brick frequents varied habitats where the foodplants grow, including woodland, parks and gardens. During the last 40 years, perhaps linked to Dutch elm disease in rural districts, there has been a steady decline.

Garden moth trap figures are as follows:
Hillmorton, Rugby: 1982 (21), 1985 (12), 1990 (1), 1995 (4), 2000 (1), 2004 (10), 2005 (1) (DIP).

VCH 1904: '*Common everywhere.*'

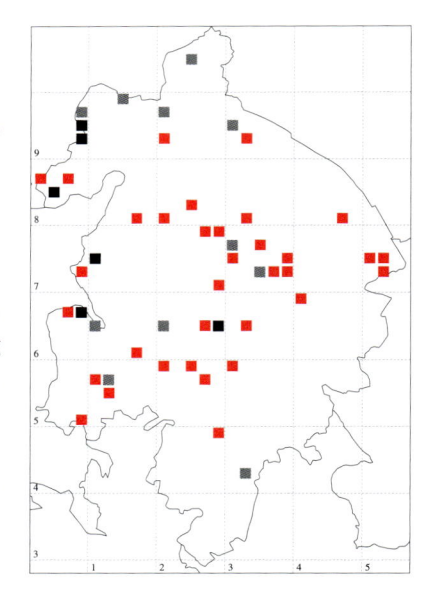

Red-line Quaker
2263 *Agrochola lota* (Cl.)

County status: Widespread and fairly common.
Flight: September to November.
Larval foodplants: Sallows* and willows.

The Red-line Quaker is plentiful in river valleys and damp woodlands containing the larval foodplants. It is a frequent visitor to garden moth traps in rural and suburban districts. Warwickshire specimens tend to be generally quite dark. The first ab. *rufa* in the County (forewings suffused reddish) was taken at Packwood in 1908 (EWC) and this attractive form is still occasionally encountered.

Garden moth trap totals are as follows:
Bidford-on-Avon: 1990 (72), 1991 (139), 1992 (29), 1993 (119) (RMC).

VCH 1904: *'Generally distributed but not abundant.'*

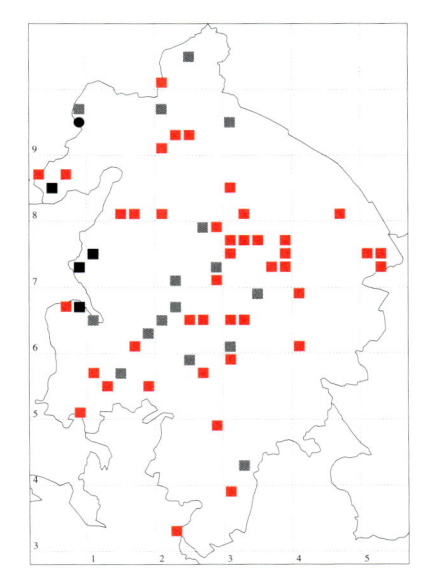

Yellow-line Quaker
2264 *Agrochola macilenta* (Hb.)

County status: Widespread but uncommon.
Flight: September to November.
Larval foodplants: Oaks*, Beech*, hawthorn blossom* and poplar catkins*.

The Yellow-line Quaker has a wide distribution in the County but is far less plentiful than the Red-line Quaker. Favoured habitats are broad-leaved woodlands, scrub, mature hedgerows, sheltered gardens and orchards. The imago is partial to overripe apples and plums and has often been observed feeding on windfalls.

It visits MV in small numbers, as the following moth trap figures indicate:
Pillerton Priors: 1992 (7), 1993 (1), 1994 (0), 2002 (5), 2003 (12), 2004 (8), 2005 (4) (CI).

VCH 1904: *'Rare.'*
Knowle, Saltley, Chelmsley Wood, Overslade, Wolford Wood.

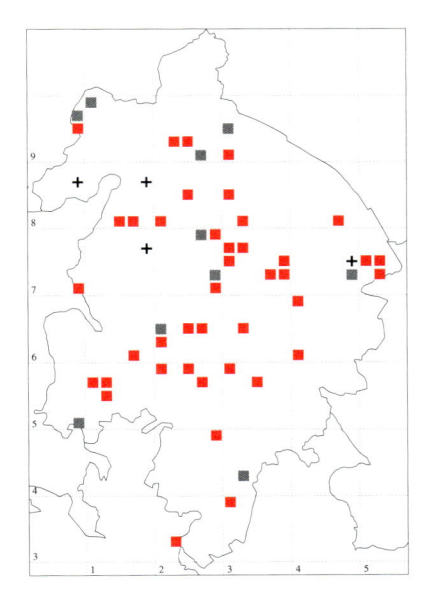

Flounced Chestnut
2265 *Agrochola helvola* (L.)

County status: Local and uncommon.
Flight: September and October.
Larval foodplants: A range of deciduous trees, including oaks, birches, sallows, elms and hawthorns.

The Flounced Chestnut is an inhabitant of broadleaved woodland, being only very occasionally recorded in garden moth traps. Good populations were established in Hampton Wood, Oakley Wood, Oversley Wood and Tile Hill Wood during the 1970s and 1980s, but there is evidence of a major decline.

Fieldwork is required to confirm presence and monitor population levels at these sites and other former locations.

VCH 1904: *'Not uncommon.'*
Sutton Park, Hampton-in-Arden, Marston Green, Knowle, Overslade, Atherstone.

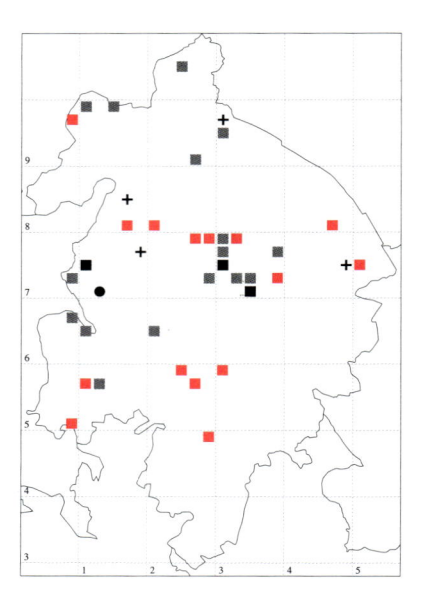

Brown-spot Pinion
2266 *Agrochola litura* (L.)

County status: Widespread but becoming uncommon.
Flight: Late August to October.
Larval foodplants: Docks*, Common Sorrel, chickweeds and other herbaceous plants and trees, including sallows and oaks.

The Brown-spot Pinion is found in a range of habitats, including broadleaved woodland, heathland, rough waste-ground and gardens. As with the preceding species, there has been a sharp decline in abundance since the 1980s.

The following garden moth trap totals reflect the sudden decrease:
Charlecote: 1971 (292), 1982 (255), 1985 (202), 1990 (117), 1995 (56), 2000 (2), 2004 (9), 2005 (1) (DB);
Hillmorton, Rugby: 1982 (46), 1985 (53), 1990 (14), 1995 (12), 2000 (0), 2004 (0), 2005 (0) (DIP).

VCH 1904: *'Common everywhere.'*

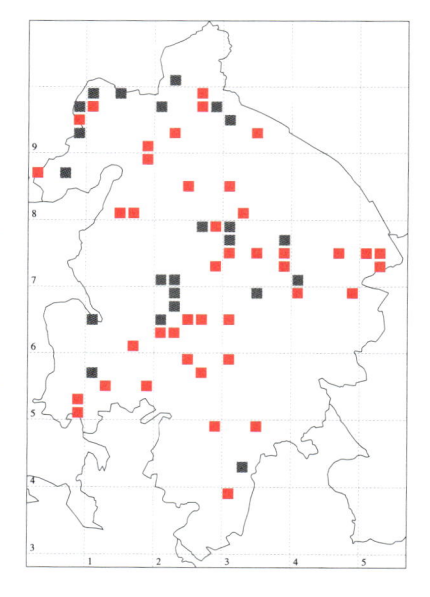

Beaded Chestnut
2267 *Agrochola lychnidis* ([D. & S.])

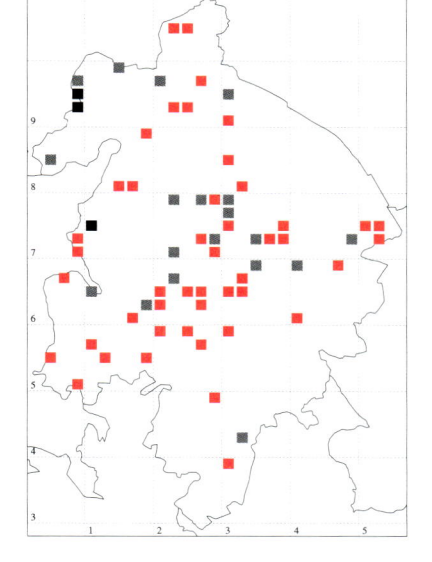

County status: Widespread and common.
Flight: September to late November.
Larval foodplants: Docks*, Dandelion, chickweeds, buttercups, clovers, grasses and larger deciduous trees and shrubs, including hawthorns.

The Beaded Chestnut is the most common member of the genus and found in all types of habitats in both town and countryside.

It is subject to much colour variation from greyish-ochreous to chestnut or reddish-brown. Very dark melanic forms occur in urban and, less frequently, in rural districts. An extreme uniform black specimen was caught at Charlecote, 27/9/2004 (DB).

Garden moth trap counts show a general decline in numbers:
Hillmorton, Rugby: 1982 (297), 1985 (178), 1990 (144), 1995 (128) (DIP);
Charlecote: 1982 (772), 1985 (314), 1990 (430), 1995 (257), 2005 (151) (DB).

VCH 1904: '*Common everywhere.*'

Centre-barred Sallow
2269 *Atethmia centrago* (Haw.)

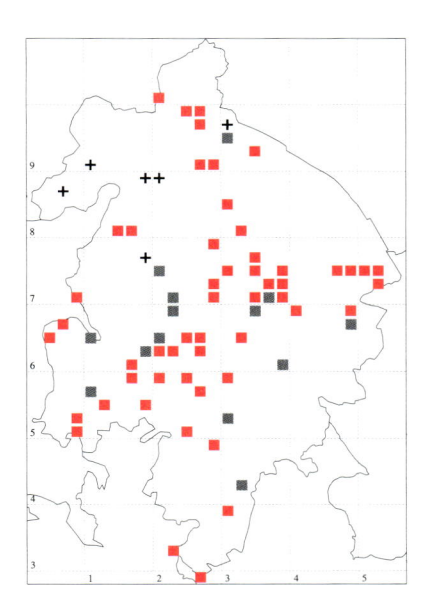

County status: Widespread and fairly common.
Flight: Late August to early October.
Larval foodplants: Ash*.

A widely-distributed species in both wooded and open terrain where isolated Ash trees grow. The larvae feed on the opening buds during the spring.

Garden moth trap records at **Pillerton Priors** are as follows: 1992 (8), 1993 (18), 2002 (12), 2003 (20), 2005 (41) (CI).

VCH 1904: '*Rare.*'
Knowle (1), Atherstone, Coleshill, Sutton, Rugby.

Lunar Underwing
2270 *Omphaloscelis lunosa* (Haw.)

County status: Widespread and common, sometimes abundant.
Flight: September to late October.
Larval foodplants: Various grasses, including Annual Meadow-grass*.

The Lunar Underwing is one of the commonest of the autumnal species but was curiously described as '*rare*' in the VCH 1904.

It is particularly plentiful in open grassy wasteground, railway cuttings, field edges and extensive woodland clearings. Various colour forms have been noted, from pale ochreous-brown to dark brownish-grey and reddish-brown to dark brown. Dark blackish-grey forms predominate in urban districts.

Garden moth trap totals at **Hillmorton, Rugby**, are as follows: 1982 (119), 1985 (169), 1990 (218), 1995 (226), 2000 (298), 2004 (234) (DIP).

VCH 1904: '*Rare.*'
Sutton Park, Knowle, Yardley, Atherstone.

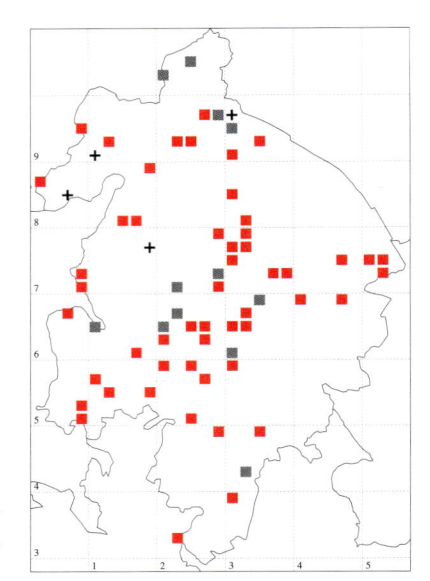

Orange Sallow
2271 *Xanthia citrago* (L.)

County status: Fairly widespread and locally fairly common.
Flight: August to early October.
Larval foodplants: Limes*.

Colonies of Orange Sallow are found locally in central and north Warwickshire. In urban districts, lime trees situated along pavements and in recreation parks are utilised. Results from trapping suggest the moth is scarce, but larvae are not difficult to find. A total of 26 was found on ancient limes in Charlecote Park between 9.00 p.m. and 10.00 p.m. on 17/5/1975 (DB, AFG). This contrasts sharply with a mere 17 adults from 38 consecutive years of light trapping in a nearby garden.

Fieldwork using sugar or wine ropes as a lure may prove a more effective method of monitoring, especially in the south of the County where there is a lack of records.

VCH 1904: '*Not common.*'
Sutton, Knowle, Hay Wood, Overslade.

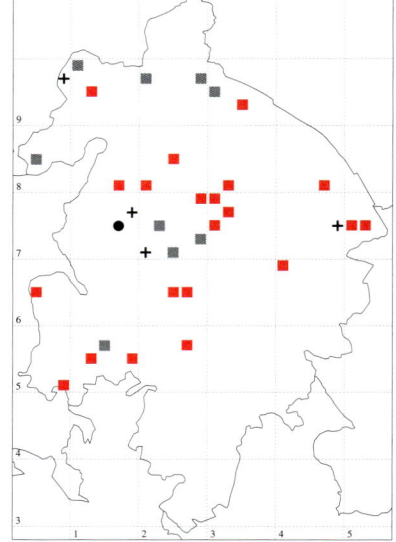

Barred Sallow
2272 *Xanthia aurago* ([D. & S.])

County status: Fairly widespread and fairly common.
Flight: September to early November.
Larval foodplants: Field Maple* and Beech.

The Barred Sallow has increased in both range and frequency since 1980 and is now established in a number of woodlands and hedgerows in open countryside containing Field Maple. Select locations include Bannam's Wood, Tocil Wood, Hampton Wood, Snitterfield Bushes and Oversley Wood.

It is a regular visitor to many garden moth traps, as the following totals illustrate:
Kenilworth Road, Coventry: 2001 (20), 2002 (6), 2004 (9), 2005 (52) (MA);
Pillerton Priors: 1992 (9), 1993 (1), 1994 (0), 2002 (5), 2003 (11), 2004 (9), 2005 (11) (CI).

VCH 1904: '*Rare.*'
One record from Knowle (WGB)

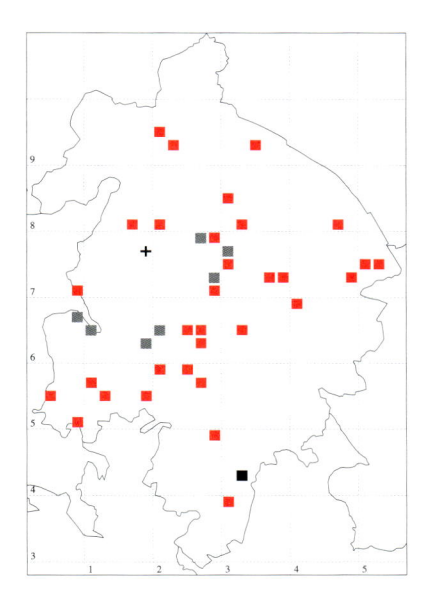

Pink-barred Sallow
2273 *Xanthia togata* (Esp.)

County status: Widespread and fairly common.
Flight: Late August to late October.
Larval foodplants: Sallow* and Aspen* catkins.

This attractive moth is found over the greater part of the County amongst sallows and poplars, in the catkins of which the larvae occur in early spring. It is well established and plentiful in the damp woodlands of Clowes Wood, Wappenbury Wood, Brandon Marsh and Oversley Wood.

The Pink-barred Sallow also occurs on drier ground and is an occasional visitor to garden moth traps, as the following figures show:
Charlecote: 1994 (3), 1995 (1), 1996 (5), 1997 (7), 1998 (3), 1999 (2), 2000 (4) (AFG).

VCH 1904: '*Common everywhere.*'

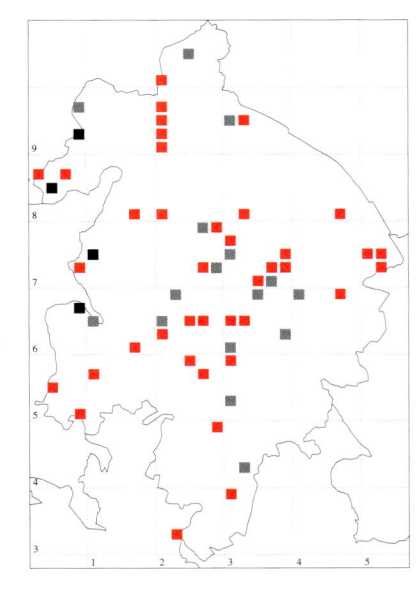

Sallow
2274 *Xanthia icteritia* (Hufn.)

County status: Widespread and fairly common.
Flight: August to late October.
Larval foodplants: Sallow* and poplar catkins.

The Sallow frequents similar habitats to the previous species and records show it to be generally more plentiful. It is subject to considerable variation in markings, including f. *flavescens* Esp. (almost pure yellow forewing with very faint orange cross-lines), which was first seen at Sutton Park in 1893 (PWA) and is now recorded frequently.

Garden moth trap counts at **Charlecote** provide a comparison with those for *togata*:
1994 (26), 1995 (9), 1996 (21), 1997 (17), 1998 (4), 1999 (3), 2000 (6) (AFG).

VCH 1904: *'Common everywhere.'*

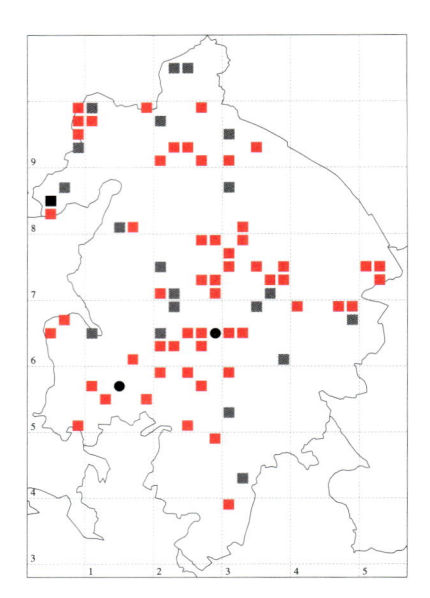

Dusky-lemon Sallow
2275 *Xanthia gilvago* ([D. & S.])

Nationally Local

County status: Very local and scarce.
Flight: Late August to late October.
Larval foodplants: The seeds and flowers of Wych Elm* and sometimes English Elm.

The Dusky-lemon Sallow has drastically declined since the advent of Dutch elm disease in the early 1970s. Prior to the epidemic the species was widely distributed and reasonably plentiful. The Charlecote figures below highlight just how severely populations of *gilvago* were affected. The data suggests that mature, heavily flowering English Elms had formerly been used for breeding. The majority of existing hedgerow saplings, including Wych Elms, are of insufficient age to produce the abundance of flowers critical for the development of the larvae during the early summer.

Annual garden moth trap totals at **Charlecote**, 1970 to 1980 (DB), clearly illustrate a diminishing population:
1970 (42), 1971 (196), 1972 (36), 1973 (2), 1974 (1), 1975 (0), 1976 (2), 1977 (1), 1978 (0), 1979 (5), 1980 (0).

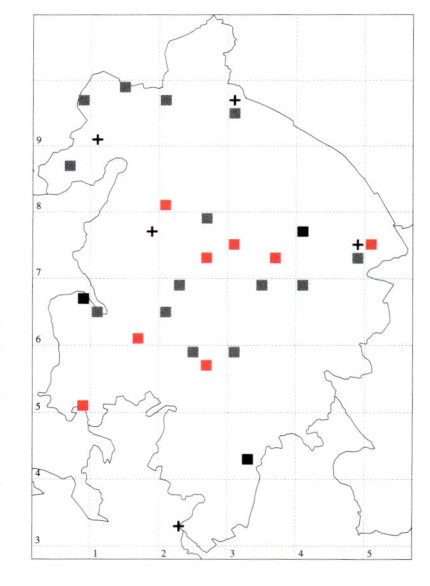

Records:
Brandon, 16/9/1946 (LR); **Tysoe**, 31/8/1947, 22/9/1948, 12/9/1949, 8/10/1949 (TT); **Mappleborough Green**, 1950–60 (FHL); **Wainbody Wood**, 1956 (STm); **Sutton Park**, 1960s (JB); **Bannam's Wood**, 1964–79 (FAN); **New Park Wood**, 1970s (LJE); **Cubbington**, 1970s (AFG); **Hampton Wood**, 1972 (10), 1973 (2), 1974 (4) (AFG); **Marton**, 1970s (RA); **Oakley Wood**, 1970s (DB); **N.E. Birmingham**, 1970s (LJE); **Hartshill Hayes**, 1970s (RJT); **Kingsbury**, 1970s (KEH); **Charlecote**, 1970s, 1983 (3), 1985, 1989, 1990, 1991, 1992 (2), 1997 (4), 1998 (4), 2000 (2), 2001, 2003 (3), 2005 (DB); **Haseley Green**, 26/8/1976 (DB); **Claverdon**, 1978–79 (IGMR); **Bilton**, 1978 (BB); **Bidford-on-Avon**, 1980s, 22/9/1994, 20/9/1998, 29/9/1999 (RMC); **Hillmorton, Rugby**, 4/10/1981 (DIP); **Hampton-in-Arden**, 1983 (MCV); **Bearley**, 1992, 1993 (IGMR); **Kenilworth**, 27/9/1998 (PA); **Kenilworth Road, Coventry**, 27/9/2003, 28/10/2005 (MA); **Ryton Meadows**, 11/10/2005 (MA, AJP).

VCH 1904: *'Not common.'*
Sutton, Knowle, Hampton-in-Arden, Overslade, Atherstone, Wolford.

Poplar Grey
2278 *Acronicta megacephala* ([D. & S.])

County status: Widespread and fairly common.
Flight: Possibly two generations. Mid-May to mid-September.
Larval foodplants: Aspen*, poplars* and willows*.

The Poplar Grey has a wide distribution in the County; it frequents woodland, marshes and many other habitats in rural and urban areas where the foodplants occur. The adult is noted continuously from May until the middle of August with individuals representing a possible second generation during September. A particularly late specimen was caught at Hillmorton, Rugby, on 5/10/1982 (DIP).

Garden moth trap counts at **Pillerton Priors** are as follows: 1992 (3), 1993 (14), 1994 (11), 2002 (9), 2003 (9), 2004 (5), 2005 (19) (CI).

VCH 1904: '*Common in the Birmingham suburbs'.*
Knowle, Rugby, Warwick.

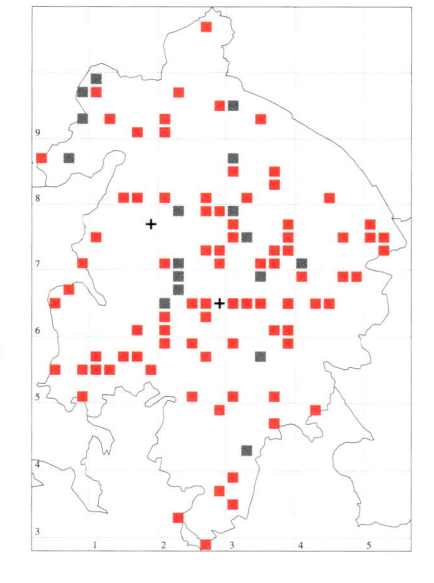

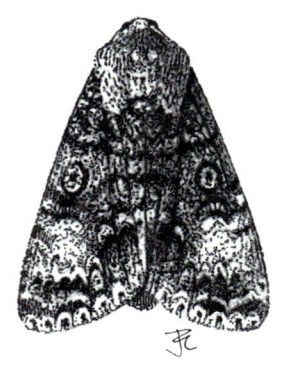

Sycamore
2279 *Acronicta aceris* (L.)

Nationally Local

County status: Fairly widespread and fairly common.
Flight: June to early August.
Larval foodplants: Sycamore*, Field Maple and Horse Chestnut*.

Before 1990 this species had only been recorded twice in the County: Small Heath, 1870 specimen found at rest on palings (WGB), and Bannam's Wood, 1979 (FAN).

During the 1990s the Sycamore experienced a dramatic increase to become locally plentiful in gardens, parks, hedgerows and woodlands Fig. 28). The dark grey form *infuscata* Haw. occurs occasionally in both urban and rural districts.

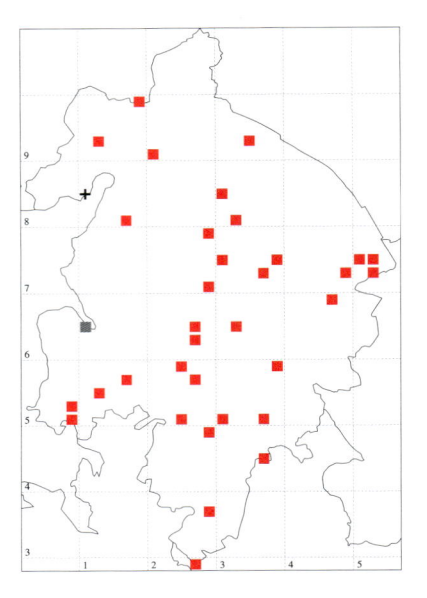

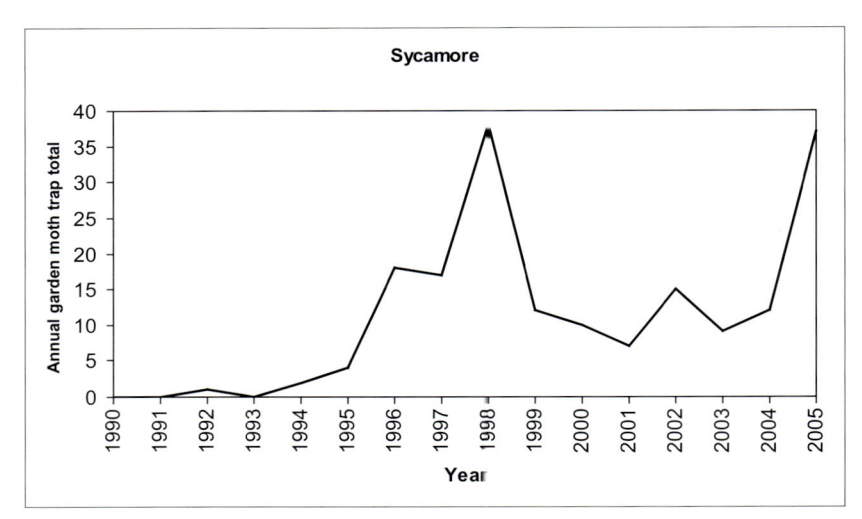

Figure 28. Annual totals of *A. aceris* in a garden moth trap at Hillmorton, Rugby (DIP).

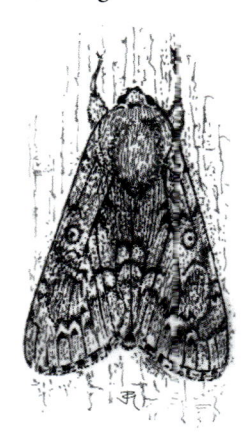

Miller
2280 *Acronicta leporina* (L.)

County status: Widespread and fairly common.
Flight: Mid-May to mid-August.
Larval foodplants: Birches*, Alder* and poplars*.

The Miller is widely distributed and locally fairly common in woodland containing a predominance of birch. Healthy populations exist in Waverley Wood, Ryton Wood, Sutton Park, Hay Wood, Oakley Wood, Snitterfield Bushes and Oversley Wood.

Occasional specimens of the dark form *melanocephala* (Mansbridge) have been taken at Hampton-in-Arden (MCV), and one was recorded in Hampton Magna, 1991 (PJR).

VCH 1904: *'Not uncommon.'*
Larvae frequent on poplars at Sutton Park and Knowle. Also recorded from Yardley, Brandon Wood and Atherstone.

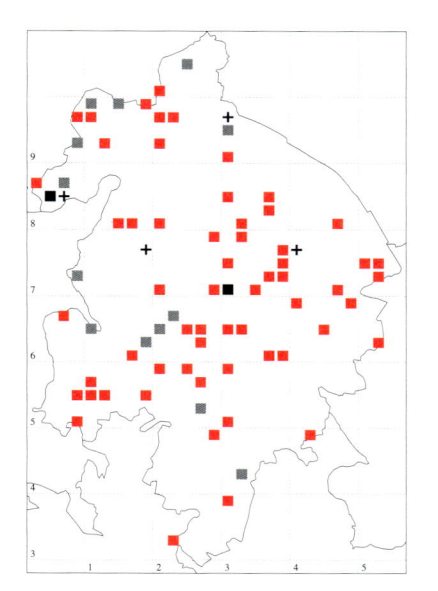

Alder Moth
2281 *Acronicta alni* (L.)

Nationally Local

County status: Fairly widespread and locally fairly common.
Flight: May to mid-July.
Larval foodplants: Birches*, oaks*, Rowan*, Field Maple*, Alder, willows, hawthorns and many other trees.

In the days before the widespread use of mercury vapour light the Alder Moth was considered to be a rarity. Today it is found over much of the County and is locally plentiful in woodlands with a mixture of birches, oaks and sallows.

VCH 1904: *'Occurs throughout the district, but never more than one specimen seems to be taken at one time or place, so it must be considered very rare.'*
Wylde Green, Rugby, Brandon Wood, Overslade, Atherstone, Sutton Park, Knowle, Solihull, Small Heath, Edgbaston, Yardley.

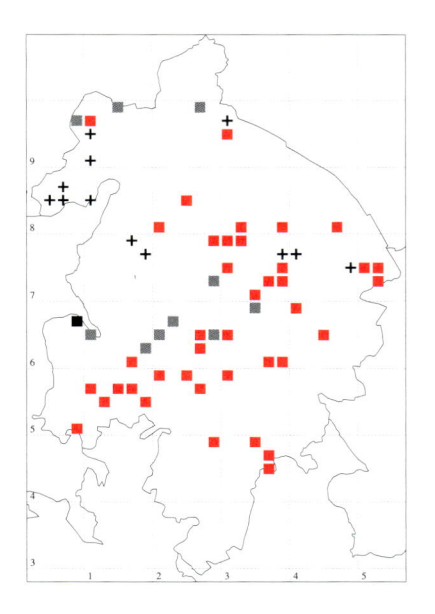

Dark Dagger
2283 *Acronicta tridens* ([D. & S.])

County status: Status uncertain, but available evidence suggests it is 'very local and scarce'.
Flight: June and July.
Larval foodplants: Hawthorns*, apple*, sallows*, Blackthorn*, elms*, and many other trees and shrubs.

Due to identification problems the distribution of this species is unclear. The Dark Dagger adult can only reliably be separated from the Grey Dagger by genitalia dissection. However, the larvae of the two species are easily distinguishable. The lack of larval records for *tridens* compared to *psi* does indicate that it is much less common. The following records are of larvae, or adults determined by genitalia dissection:

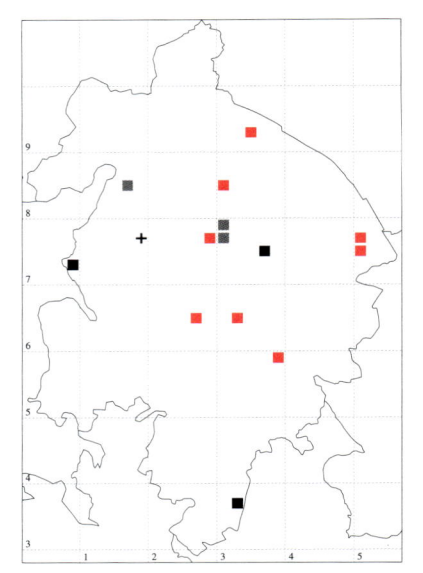

Clowes Wood, 24/9/1939 larva (BNHS); **Forshaw Heath,** 1939 larva (HEH); **Windmill Naps,** 1939 larva (HEH); **Traitors Ford,** 18/9/1948 larva (TT); **Ryton-on-Dunsmore,** Aug. 1951 larva (PC); **Marston Green,** 1964 larva (LEM); **Earlsdon, Coventry,** 1964 larva (LEM); **Charlecote,** 1982 larva (AFG, DB); **Hillmorton, Rugby,** 3/7/1999 (DIP); **Keresley, Coventry,** 3/6/2004 (NJS); **Kirby Corner, Coventry,** 29/8/2004 larva (RR); **Swift Valley, Rugby,** 2/6/2005 (NJS, AJP, PN); **Sydenham, Royal Leamington Spa,** 9/6/2005 (MK); **Bishops Hill,** 14/7/2005 (AJP); **Windmill Hill, Nuneaton,** 23/7/2005 (DG).

VCH 1904: *'Very doubtfully distinguished from the next species. It is probably not uncommon, but records cannot be trusted. Larvae taken on elms at Knowle (WGB), Rugby (NVS).'*

Grey Dagger
2284 *Acronicta psi* (L.)

County status: Widespread and fairly common.
Flight: May to August with occasional individuals of a partial second generation in September and October.
Larval foodplants: Apple*, oaks*, elms*, willows*, poplars*, hawthorns*, Beech*, birches*, limes*, Hornbeam*, Rowan*, Blackthorn* and *Photinia fraseri* 'Red Robin'*.

The Grey Dagger is found over a large part of the County in most types of urban and rural habitats. There is evidence of a small second generation in some years and the latest date for the adult is 8/10/1955, Tile Hill Wood (GW).

As the vast majority of records relate to adults without examination of the genitalia it is likely that examples of *A. tridens* are included.

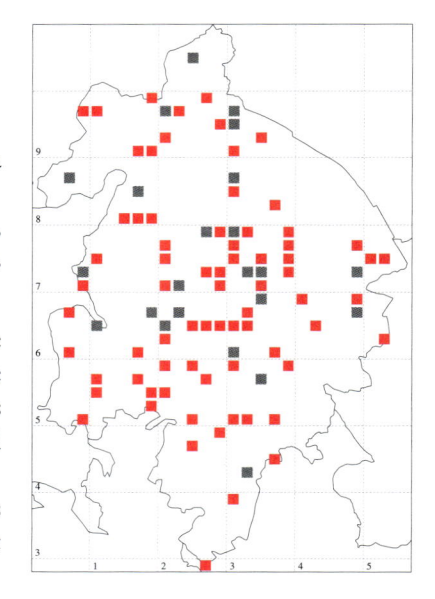

VCH 1904: *'Very common everywhere.'*

Light Knot Grass
2286 *Acronicta menyanthidis menyanthidis* (Esp.)

Nationally Local

County status: Extinct.
Flight: No dates available.
Larval foodplants: Heather, birches, sallows and other plants.

VCH 1904: *Richmond Hill, Edgbaston 1899.*

Knot Grass
2289 *Acronicta rumicis* (L.)

County status: Widespread and fairly common.
Flight: Two generations. May to October.
Larval foodplants: Herbaceous and woody plants, including Silverweed*, plantains*, Knotgrass*, birches* and poplars*.

The Knot Grass is a widespread species, occurring in a diversity of habitats. The larvae are very conspicuous, often being observed at ground level amongst herbaceous plants. In rural districts pale forms of the adult are dominant but in built-up areas melanic specimens are equally plentiful.

Garden moth trap totals are generally low:
Pillerton Priors: 1992 (1), 1993 (2), 1994 (0), 2002 (7), 2003 (12), 2004 (10) (CI);

This species was not mentioned in the VCH 1904 and there appear to be no Warwickshire records until 1931, in which year three were caught at Tile Hill Wood (DCbll, JWSt, JTS).

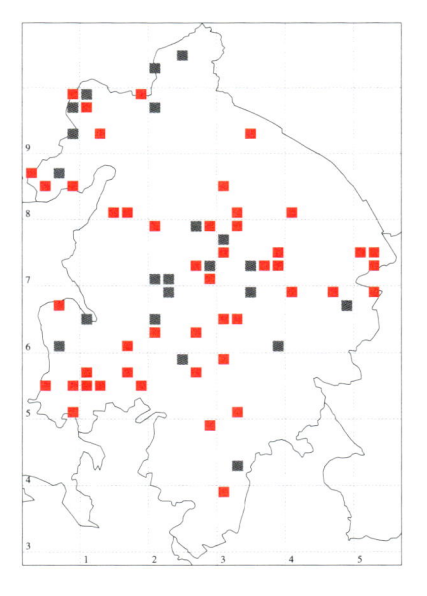

Coronet
2291 *Craniophora ligustri* ([D. & S.])

Nationally Local

County status: Very local and scarce.
Flight: June and July.
Larval foodplants: Ash and Wild Privet.

Formerly recorded in the Victoria County History and again in 1965, this species made a comeback in Warwickshire during 2005 with four sightings at widely separated locations in the south of the County.

Records:
Earlsdon, Coventry, 31/7/1965 (LEM); **Pillerton Priors**, 19/6/2005 (CI); **Whichford Wood**, 25/6/2005 (DB, IGMR); **Shottery, Stratford-upon-Avon**, 3/7/2005 (RGB); **Cross Hands Quarry**, 9/7/2005 (CI, RGB).

VCH 1904: *Coombe Wood, Atherstone 1889.*

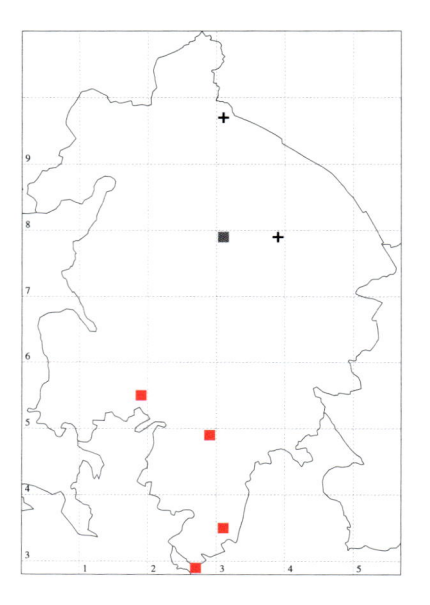

Marbled Beauty
2293 *Cryphia domestica* (Hufn.)

County status: Widespread and common in urban districts.
Flight: Late June to early September.
Larval foodplants: Lichens growing on walls and roofs, including *Lecidea confluens** and *Xanthoria parietina*.

The Marbled Beauty is strongly associated with built-up areas, where it may be very common. Some of the largest annual garden moth trap totals in the County have been noted in Central Rugby where counts show: 2000 (343), 2001 (553), 2003 (506), 2004 (308) (IGMR).

It is an extremely variable moth in colouration and in the extent of the forewing markings. Greyish-green forms prevail in rural districts with yellow, dull orange and melanic specimens frequent in urban areas. An attractive form with bright orange markings has been reported from Radford, Coventry (MCV).

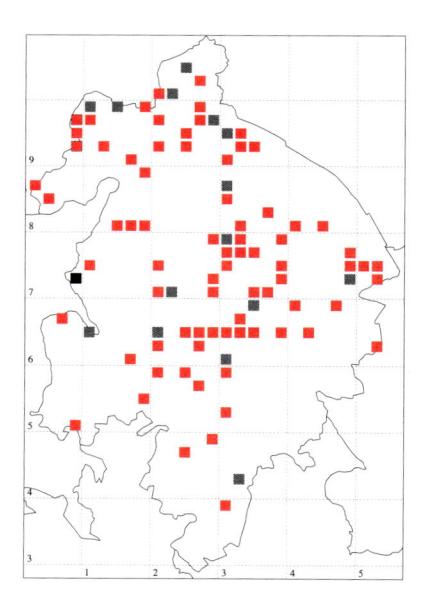

The table below highlights sharply contrasting garden moth trap totals in urban and rural districts.

Habitat	Location	1982	1988	1990	1995	2000	2004
Urban	Radford, Coventry (MCV)	85	82	279	259	136	218
Rural	Charlecote (AFG)	2	0	0	6	1	0

VCH 1904: *'Common throughout the County in suitable spots, but of course local.'*

Marbled Green
2295 *Cryphia muralis muralis* (Forst.)

Nationally Local

County status: Status uncertain.
Flight: July.
Larval foodplants: Lichens such as *Xanthoria* and *Caloplaca* species growing on walls.

Two recent records within fairly close proximity of one another in the south of the County suggest that the Marbled Green may have colonised locally. Although chiefly a coastal species, there are nearby colonies in west Oxfordshire and Gloucestershire. More fieldwork is needed in south Warwickshire to ascertain the true status of this attractive moth.

Records:
Ettington Park, 30/7/1994 (RGB and Warks Moth Group); **Charlecote,** 24/7/2001 (AFG).

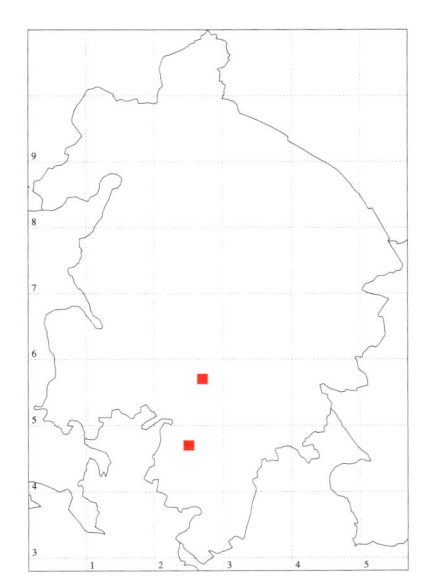

Copper Underwing
2297 *Amphipyra pyramidea* (L.)

County status: Widespread and fairly common.
Flight: Late July to early October.
Larval foodplants: Ash*, Hornbeam*, willows*, *Berberis* (cultivated forms)*, oaks*, Field Maple*, hawthorns*, Bilberry*, Hazel*, apple* and many other broadleaved trees and shrubs.

The Copper Underwing is found throughout the County in a number of habitats with good populations in deciduous woodland. The adult has a stronger attraction to the sugar patch than MV.

VCH 1904: *'Common locally.'*
Atherstone, Knowle, Overslade, Coventry, Warwick, Idlicote, Wolford Wood.

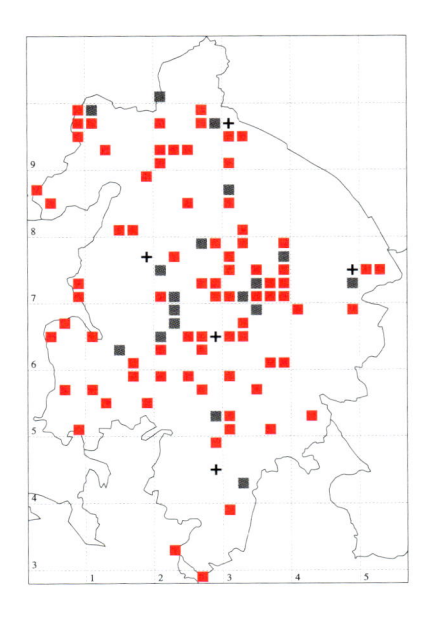

Svensson's Copper Underwing
2298 *Amphipyra berbera svenssoni* Fletch.

County status: Fairly widespread and fairly common.
Flight: Late July to mid-September.
Larval foodplants: Oaks*, Field Maple*, Blackthorn*, apple*, elms* and many other broadleaved trees.

Svensson's Copper Underwing shares the same habitat preferences with its congener, the Copper Underwing, but so far has not been recorded as widely.

The two species were only separated as distinct in 1968, before which all records could apply to either. There have been a limited number of genitalia dissections to determine catches and most recorders have identified each by using the generally reliable external characteristic features.

The larva of *berbera* is quite distinctive in possessing a red-tipped hump on the dorsal segment. It is habitually obtained from higher vegetation and mature trees.

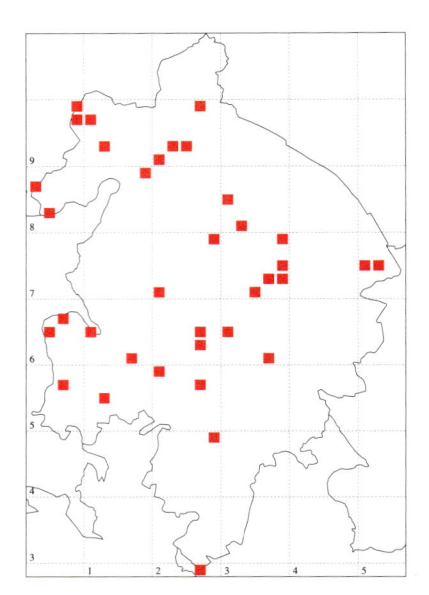

Mouse Moth
2299 *Amphipyra tragopoginis* (Cl.)

County status: Widespread and fairly common.
Flight: July to early October.
Larval foodplants: Elms*, hawthorns, sallows, and a wide range of herbaceous plants, including Salad Burnet and Mugwort.

The Mouse Moth is found in a wide range of habitats and may be just as common in suburban districts as in open countryside. Like other *Amphipyra* species it is more plentiful at sugar than light.

VCH 1904: *'Common everywhere.'*

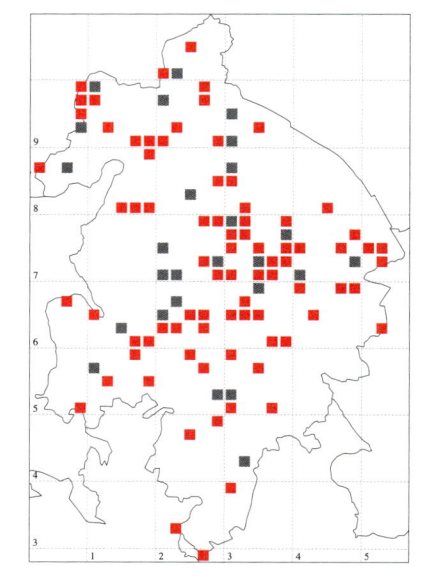

Old Lady
2300 *Mormo maura* (L.)

Nationally Local

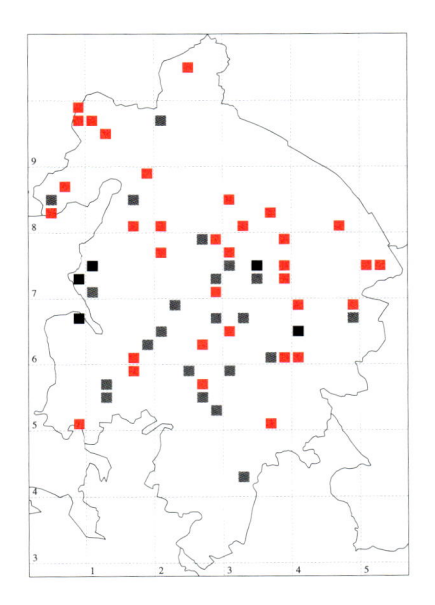

County status: Fairly widespread and sometimes fairly common.
Flight: July to early September.
Larval foodplants: Herbaceous plants during the autumn, such as chickweeds and docks, and woody plants after hibernation, including sallows, Blackthorn, hawthorns and birches.

The Old Lady is found over a wide area of the County with the majority of more recent records from the north. It seems equally at home in built-up districts as in the tranquil surroundings of rural riverbanks, but is rarely seen in woodland. This species has often been perceived by the more discerning clientele of the Saxon Mill public house in Warwick, as the moths fly gracefully around a partially lit waterwheel on warm summer evenings. Generally, however, *maura* shies away from the bright lights and is more strongly attracted to sugar.

An amazing 60 specimens were observed on a small number of sugared tree trunks along the banks of the River Dene, Walton, on 8/8/1973 (DB, PR, ES).

VCH 1904: *'Occurs throughout the County not uncommonly.'*

Bird's Wing
2301 *Dypterygia scabriuscula* (L.)

Nationally Local

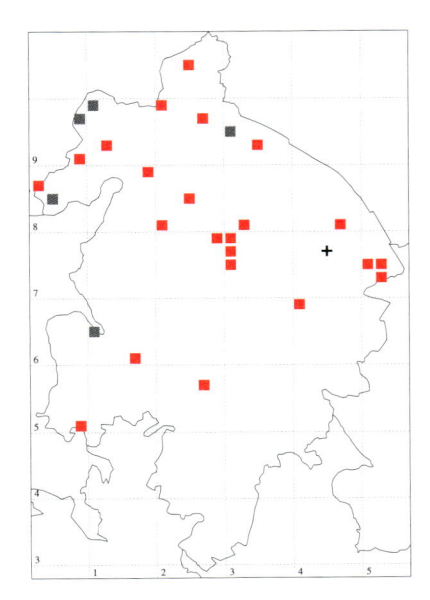

County status: Fairly widespread but generally uncommon.
Flight: June to August.
Larval foodplants: Docks, sorrels and Knotgrass.

The Bird's Wing is chiefly restricted to the northern half of the County, where it is generally uncommon and usually observed as singletons. It frequents open woodland and scrub, disused quarries, railway embankments and heathland. It is often noted in garden moth traps in built-up districts.

This species has undergone a general decline in mid- and south Warwickshire since the 1990s.

VCH 1904: *'Once taken at Kings Newnham, Nr Rugby.'*

Brown Rustic
2302 *Rusina ferruginea* (Esp.)

County status: Widespread and fairly common.
Flight: June and July.
Larval foodplants: A variety of low-growing herbaceous plants, including Dandelion*, plantains*, docks and vetches.

The Brown Rustic is found in a vast range of habitats in both wooded and open terrain. An unusually late individual was recorded on 8/9/1979 in Tile Hill Wood (PC).
 Suburban garden moth trap totals are as follows:
Hillmorton, Rugby: 1982 (27), 1985 (28), 1990 (11), 1995 (11), 2000 (16), 2004 (16) (DIP).

VCH 1904: *'Common everywhere.'*

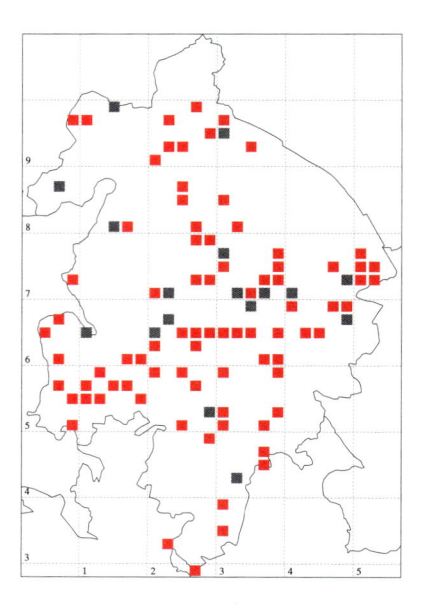

Straw Underwing
2303 *Thalpophila matura* (Hufn.)

County status: Widespread and fairly common.
Flight: July and August.
Larval foodplants: Grasses, including Annual Meadow-grass and Mat-grass.

The Straw Underwing is a widespread species that frequents open grassy habitats, including railway cuttings, woodland rides and clearings, heathland and gardens.
 Garden moth trap figures are as follows:
Pillerton Priors: 1992 (30), 1993 (31), 1994 (5) 2002 (21), 2003 (28), 2004 (19) (CI);
Hillmorton, Rugby: 1982 (13), 1985 (7), 1990 (21), 1995 (19), 2000 (2), 2004 (0) (DIP).

VCH 1904: *'Well distributed but not common.'*
Knowle, Hampton-in-Arden, Overslade, Atherstone, Wolford.

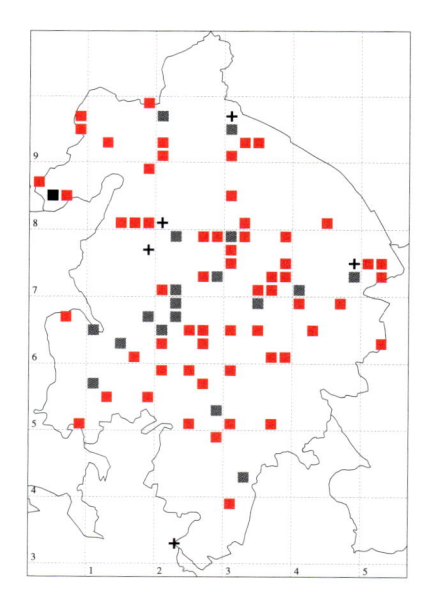

Small Angle Shades
2305 *Euplexia lucipara* (L.)

County status: Widespread and fairly common.

Flight: Late May to early August. Occasionally individuals of a possible second generation occur in August to September.

Larval foodplants: Mostly Bracken and other ferns, but also a wide range of woody and herbaceous plants, including *Antirrhinum* (Snapdragon)*.

The Small Angle Shades is most often recorded in woodland, but is also frequently noted in open habitats, including gardens.

This species is normally univoltine but late specimens caught at Tile Hill Wood on 25/8/1962 (ANT) and Hillmorton, Rugby, on 8/9/1989 (DIP) may represent individuals of a partial second generation.

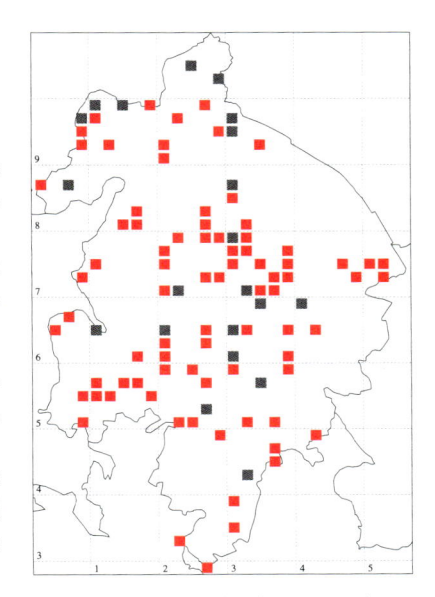

The larva is one of the few species to feed on Bracken and ferns, but other herbaceous plants are utilised outside woodland. Larvae were found feeding on Snapdragon plants in a Birmingham garden on 23/9/1955 (HEH).

VCH 1904: *'Common everywhere.'*

Angle Shades
2306 *Phlogophora meticulosa* (L.)

County status: Widespread and common.

Flight: Recorded all year round, but mainly in two generations: May to July and August to October.

Larval foodplants: Polyphagous on herbaceous plants and vegetables, including Dandelion*, Tangerine Sage*, and Cabbage*. Sometimes a pest, damaging greenhouse plants, including Tomatoes*.

The Angle Shades has been caught in garden moth traps during every month of the year, even in mid-winter. Examples include Charlecote, 8/1/1981, 27/12/1984 (DB) and Hillmorton, Rugby, 4/1/1991 (DIP).

A small peak occurs during June, followed by a larger surge in late August and early September, which is sometimes reinforced by immigration.

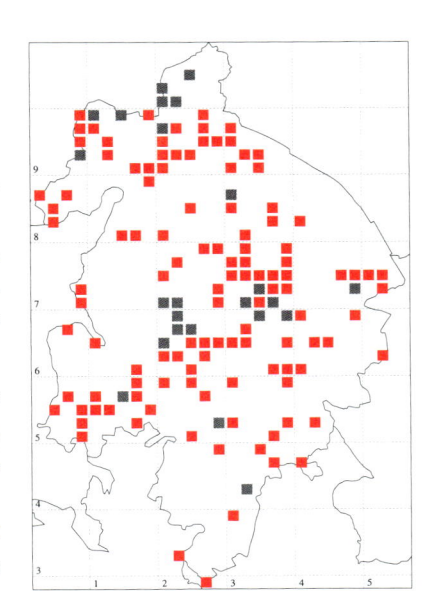

The adult is often observed during the daytime at rest on ground vegetation, walls and various other vertical objects. It later arrives freely at MV in every type of habitat.

VCH 1904: *'Common everywhere.'*

Olive
2312 *Ipimorpha subtusa* ([D. & S.])

Nationally Local

County status: Widespread and sometimes locally fairly common.
Flight: July to late August.
Larval foodplants: Poplars* and Aspen*.

The Olive has become established at a number of sites since 1980. Strongholds include Ufton Fields, Cubbington Wood, Bowshot Wood and Oakley Wood.

Smaller populations exist in urban districts where poplars in recreation parks and gardens are utilised. The larva feeds amongst leaves spun together and is consequently easy to locate.

VCH 1904: *'Rare.'*
Hampton-in-Arden, Knowle, Small Heath, Rugby.

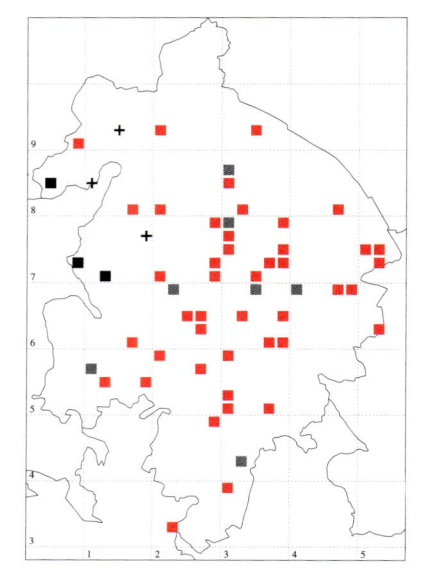

Angle-striped Sallow
2313 *Enargia paleacea* (Esp.)

Nationally Scarce B

County status: Very local and occasionally fairly common.
Flight: Late July to August.
Larval foodplants: Birches.

This impressive species is well established at three sites in the west of the County. It is associated with mature birches growing on open heathland and in oak woodland.

The Angle-striped Sallow has been known to occur at Oversley Wood and Old Park Wood for many years, but the Sutton Park records are suspected to be the result of recent colonisation, perhaps emanating from nearby populations in Cannock Chase, Staffordshire or Wyre Forest, Worcestershire.

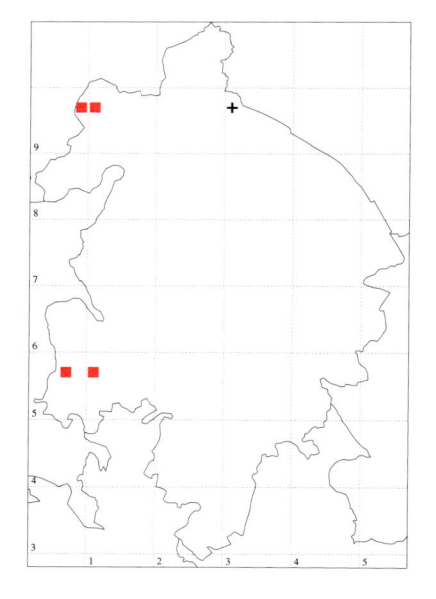

Records:
Oversley Wood, 26/7/1974 (DB), 2/8/1980 (DB, AFG), 30/7/2004 (RMC, DG, MA, AJP, VW, R&SW); **Old Park Wood**, 17/8/1988 (3) (RMC), 16/8/2003 (7) (Warks Moth Group); **Sutton Park, Boldmere Gate**, 5/8/2000 (2) (DB, DG), 18/8/2001 (6) (DG), 17/8/2002 (17) (Warks Moth Group), 13/08/2005 (3) (Warks Moth Group).

VCH 1904: *'Reported to occur at Atherstone (CB).'*

Suspected
2268 *Parastichtis suspecta* (Hb.)

Nationally Local

County status: Local and generally uncommon.
Flight: July and August.
Larval foodplants: Birches.

The Suspected is found chiefly in the north of Warwickshire, where it frequents heathy woodland with an abundance of birch. Typical sites include Whitacre Heath, Sutton Park, Hay Wood, Waverley Wood, Clowes Wood, Ryton Wood, Wappenbury Wood and Oakley Wood.

Although generally uncommon, it is sometimes attracted to MV in good numbers; for example, Hay Wood, 2/8/1975 (12) (DB); Oversley Wood, 3/7/1976 (14) (DB, AFG); Waverley Wood, 20/7/1990 (20) (Warks Moth Group). Wanderers have occasionally been noted in garden moth traps.

VCH 1904: *'Rare.'*
Sutton Park, Coventry, Whitchurch.

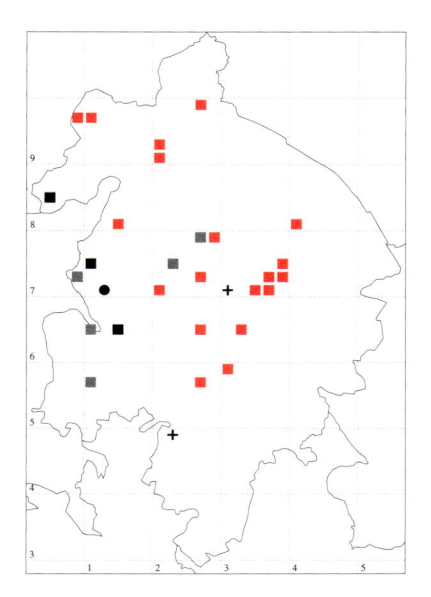

Dingy Shears
2314 *Parastichtis ypsillon* ([D. & S.])

Nationally Local

County status: Widespread and fairly common.
Flight: Late June to mid-August.
Larval foodplants: Sallows*, willows* and poplars*.

The Dingy Shears is fairly common along willow-lined river banks and in damp woodlands. Good sites include Whitacre Heath, Alvecote Pools, Brandon Marsh, Waverley Wood and Hampton Wood. It also occurs more widely in river valleys, especially on the floodplains encompassing the River Avon.

Final instar larvae can easily be found under the bark of willows in late May and early June.

VCH 1904: *'Rare.'*
Sutton Park, Rugby.

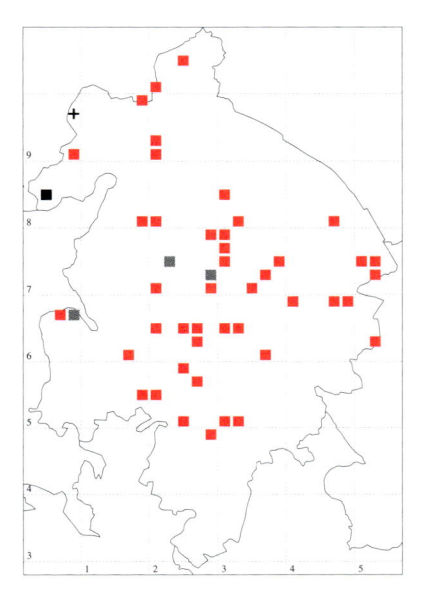

Lesser-spotted Pinion
2316 *Cosmia affinis* (L.)

Nationally Local

County status: Very local and scarce.
Flight: Mid-July to September.
Larval foodplants: English Elm* and Wych Elm.

Dutch Elm disease during the 1970s severely affected populations of the elm-feeding *Cosmia* species. Formerly, the Lesser-spotted Pinion was locally fairly common in central and south Warwickshire, where once countless mature English Elms bordered lanes and fields. The total absence of records during the 1980s and early 1990s suggested *affinis* had become extinct, but recent individuals from Charlecote and Rugby give an indication that the species may be surviving at low density on elm re-growth (Fig. 29).

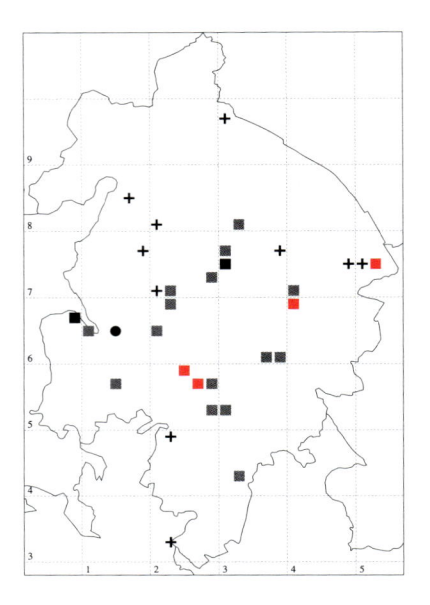

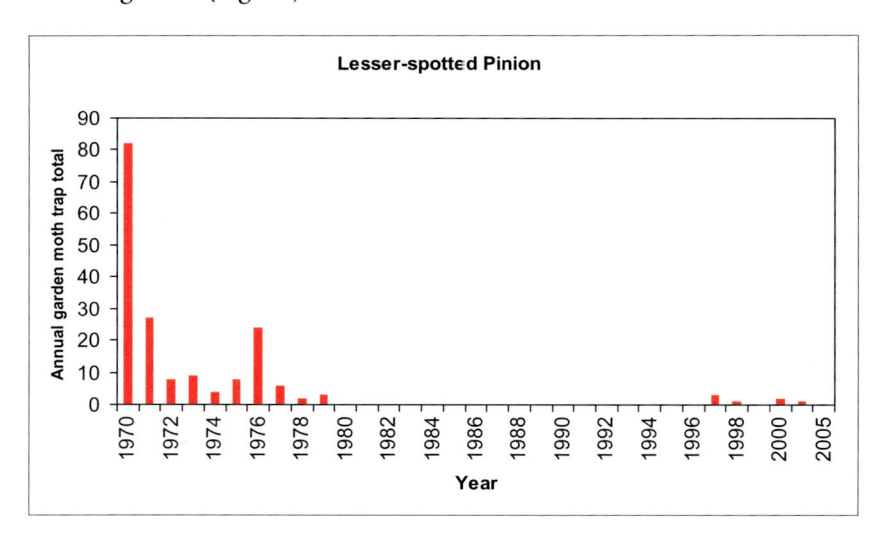

Figure 29. Annual numbers of *C. affinis* in a garden moth trap at Charlecote (DB).

Records:
May's Wood, 1911–30 occasionally at sugar (GBM, GPS); **Mappleborough Green**, 1940–60 (FHL); **Tysoe**, 1940–60 (TT); **Gibbet Hill, Coventry**, 17/8/1955 (JEF, MEC); **Wilmcote**, 1959 (2) (FAN); **Bannam's Wood**, 1964–70 (FAN); **Haseley Knob**, 1970 (CDNHSS); **Newbold Pacey**, 1970s (DB); **Princethorpe**, 1970s (RA); **Charlecote**, 1970–1979 annually (DB, AFG), 5/8/1998, 14/8/2000, 25/8/2000 (AFG), 5/8/2004 (DB); **Kenilworth**, 1970 (DC); **Marton**, 1970s, 1980 (RA); **Bowshot Wood**, 1970s (DB). **Radford, Coventry**, 1970s (MCV); **Hampton Wood**, 1972 (11), 1973 (2), 1974 (12), 1975 (12) (AFG), 1985 (RGB); **Walton**, 9/8/1973 (PR, ES), 25/8/1973 (BE, JC), 13/8/1975 (2) (DB); **Ufton Fields**, 24/8/1974 (LEM), 7/8/1975 (DB), 11/8/1979 (CDNHSS); **Claverdon**, 1979 (IGMR); **Hillmorton, Rugby**, 25/7/2001 (PN).

VCH 1904: *'Well distributed but not common.'*
Rugby, Hampton-in-Arden, Knowle, Hay Wood, Marston Green, Atherstone, Wolford, Whitchurch.

White-spotted Pinion
2317 *Cosmia diffinis* (L.)

pRDB

County status: Presumed extinct.
Flight: Late July to September.
Larval foodplants: English Elm* and Wych Elm.

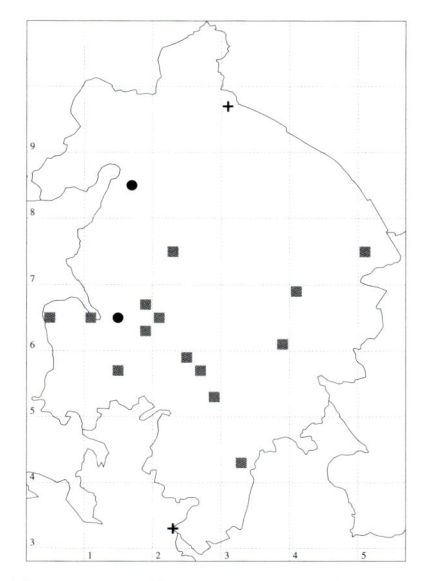

During its heyday in the late 1960s and early 1970s this species was locally plentiful in Warwickshire and greatly admired by visiting lepidopterists.

The ravages of Dutch elm disease, however, have had a greater impact on the White-spotted Pinion than its congener, the Lesser-spotted Pinion, and it is feared this attractive moth is now extinct in the County. The last to be recorded was at Yarningale Common on 4/9/1979 (IGMR). The larval requirement for epicormic foliage (shoots growing directly from the trunk) creates difficulties in the absence of mature elms and consequently any immediate chances of a recovery are unlikely.

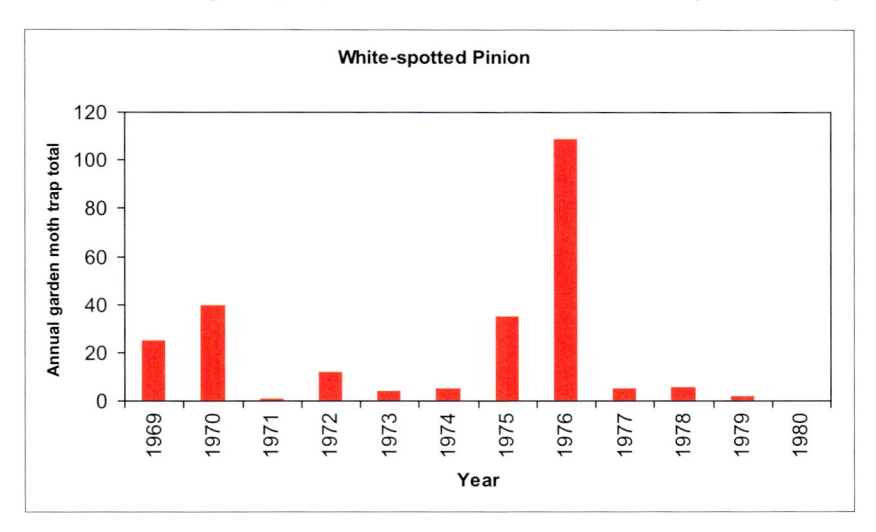

Figure 30. Annual numbers of *C. diffinis* in a garden moth trap, Charlecote 1969–1979 (DB).

Records:
Marston Green, 1910 (WHF); **May's Wood,** 20/8/1913 (GBM); **Wilmcote,** 1955 (GCG, WTT), 1956 (SEWC, FAN); **Tysoe,** 3/8/1956, 10/8/1956, 8/9/1956 (TT); **NVRS, Wellesbourne,** 10/8/1956 (JAH); **Charlecote,** 1969–79 Last record 31/8/1979 (AFG); **Marton,** 1970s (RA); **Hampton Wood,** 1972 (10), 1973 (3), 1974 (4), 1975 (3) (AFG); **Walton,** 3/9/1972 (19) (BS), 4/9/1972 (2) (DB), 8/8/1973 (2) (ES, PR, DB), 25/8/1973 (6) (BE, JC), 13/8/1975 (2) (DB); **Ufton Fields,** 7/8/1975 (DB); **Rugby town centre,** 1976 (A Seats, MAA); **Claverdon,** 1977–1978 (IGMR); **Fen End, Kenilworth,** 1977 (DC); **Bannam's Wood,** 1979 (FAN); **Yarningale Common,** 4/9/1979 (IGMR).

VCH 1904: *'Much less common than **affinis**.'* *Atherstone, Wolford, Rugby.*

Dun-bar
2318 *Cosmia trapezina* (L.)

County status: Widespread and common.
Flight: Late June to mid-September.
Larval foodplants: Polyphagous on broadleaved trees and shrubs, including oaks*, elms*, Field Maple*, sallows*, Beech*, hawthorns*, birches* and poplars*.

The Dun-bar is the commonest member of the genus *Cosmia*, being found throughout the County in a wide range of habitats. Largest populations occur in areas of broadleaved woodland.

An idea of frequency in garden moth traps can be gained from the following figures:
Hillmorton, Rugby: 1982 (37), 1985 (28), 1990 (53), 1995 (60), 2000 (27), 2004 (26) (DIP);
Kenilworth Road, Coventry: 2001 (197), 2002 (30), 2003 (65), 2004 (104) (MA).

VCH 1904: *'Common everywhere.'*

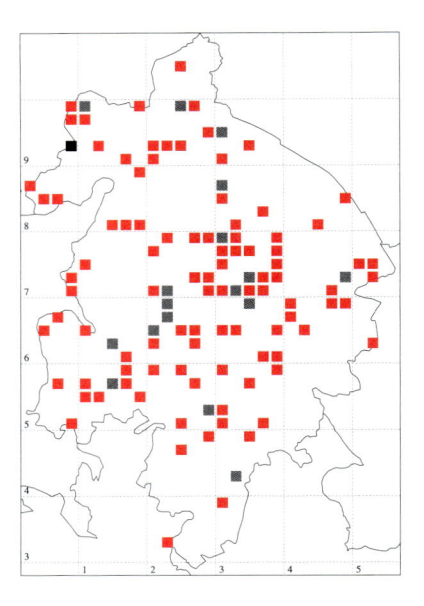

Lunar-spotted Pinion
2319 *Cosmia pyralina* ([D. & S.])

Nationally Local

County status: Fairly widespread and fairly common.
Flight: Late June to August.
Larval foodplants: Apple*, Bullace, Blackthorn, hawthorns, and elms.

The larva of this species is known to feed on a range of trees other than elms; consequently the moth has not suffered as badly as its elm-feeding congeners. It is currently locally plentiful in orchards, gardens, woodland edges, hedgerows and parkland over a large part of the County. There is, however, a distinct lack of records in the north.

Before 1970 the Lunar-spotted Pinion was considered rare in Warwickshire with only a handful of sightings spanning the previous 80 years: Rugby district, pre-1893 (ASk); Tysoe, 4/8/1946, 28/7/1947, 3/8/1947 (TT); Gibbet Hill, Coventry, 17/8/1955 (JEF, MEC); Wilmcote, 8/8/1959 (FAN); Charlecote, 20/7/1968 (DB).

A dramatic increase occurred in 1969 and 1970. This resurgence was curbed during the Dutch elm epidemic but numbers are now fairly constant, as shown by the following figures:
Charlecote: 1971 (198), 1981 (26), 1991 (18), 2001 (24) (DB);
Pillerton Priors: 1992 (11), 1993 (15), 2002 (12), 2003 (11), 2004 (13) (CI).

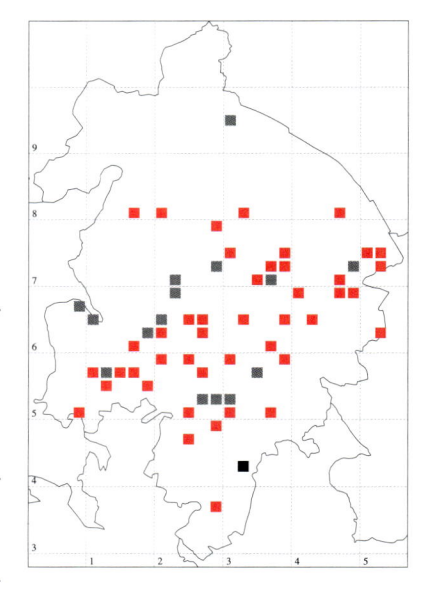

Dark Arches
2321 *Apamea monoglypha* (Hufn.)

County status: Widespread and abundant.
Flight: June to September and, occasionally, October.
Larval foodplants: Grasses, including Common Couch and Cock's-foot.

The Dark Arches is a dominant summer species in moth traps, being equally abundant in rural and suburban districts.

Dark brown and blackish examples represent approximately 5% of totals in the Birmingham area (DG). The first known example of ab. *aethiops* Stdgr. in the County (all markings obscured by dense blackish ground colour) was recorded in 1952 at Solihull (SEWC).

Late individuals well outside the normal flight period have occasionally been noted; for example, Hillmorton, Rugby, 30/11/2005 (DIP); Pillerton Priors, 20/11/2003 (CI), Warwick, 11/11/2005 (AV).

VCH 1904: *'Extremely common everywhere.'*

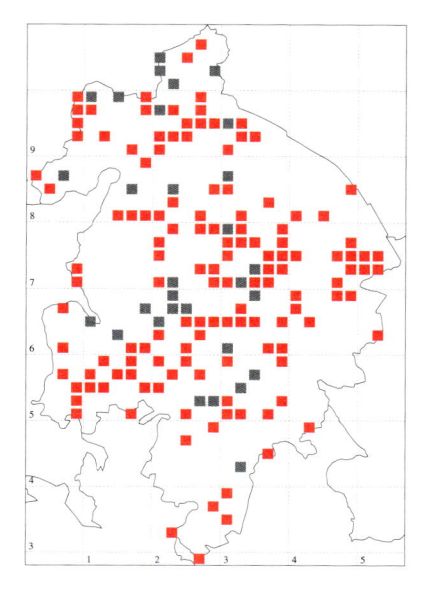

Light Arches
2322 *Apamea lithoxylaea* ([D. & S.])

County status: Widespread and locally common.
Flight: June to August.
Larval foodplants: Grasses, including Annual Meadow-grass.

The Light Arches is considerably less common than the preceding species, but nevertheless is a fairly common moth, especially in open grassy habitats. Generally lower numbers occur in built-up districts, but in some years it may be common in suburban garden moth traps as the following figures illustrate:
Hillmorton, Rugby: 1982 (214), 1985 (158), 1990 (135) (DIP).

VCH 1904: *'Common, occurs in every list.'*

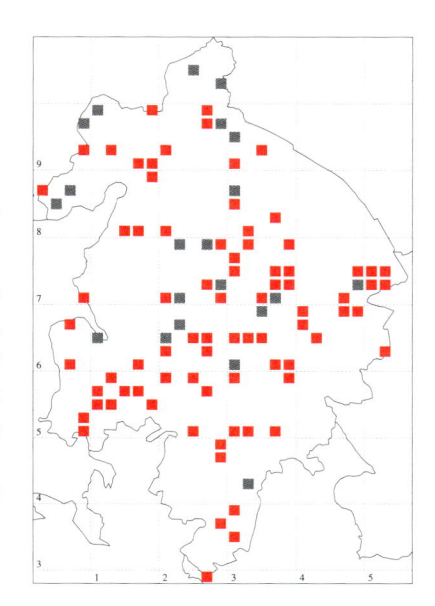

Reddish Light Arches
2323 *Apamea sublustris* (Esp.)

Nationally Local

County status: Very local and scarce.
Flight: June and July.
Larval foodplants: Unknown in the wild. In captivity the lower stems and roots of grasses.

The Reddish Light Arches is a Nationally Local moth associated with calcareous grassland. It is evident that the species wanders widely during hot weather to occasionally visit garden moth traps, whilst exact breeding grounds remain undetected.

Records:
Hampton-in-Arden, 1920, 1922 (GWW); **Cubbington**, 22/6/1970 (AFG); **Bidford-on-Avon**, 29/6/1995, 1/7/1995 (RMC); **Oxhouse Farm, Combrook**, 22/6/1997 (DB); **Brailes**, 30/6/2004 (CI).

VCH 1904: *Hampton-in-Arden (a few in 1900), Knowle, Overslade.*

Clouded-bordered Brindle
2326 *Apamea crenata* (Hufn.)

County status: Widespread and fairly common.
Flight: May to early August.
Larval foodplants: Grasses, including Cock's-foot.

The Clouded-bordered Brindle is plentiful in a variety of grassland habitats. It is particularly numerous in woodland rides and clearings.

The paler typical form is generally dominant but the melanic f. *combusta* (Haw.) is very frequent in urban populations. Within the suburban district of Hillmorton, Rugby, MV records show that since 1992 f. *combusta* represents 45.7% of the population. There is, however, evidence of an overall decline in numbers of *crenata* in this district as the following garden moth trap figures illustrate: 1982 (157), 1988 (67), 1990 (154), 1992 (115), 1995 (76), 1999 (11), 2003 (11), 2005 (7) (DIP).

VCH 1904: *'Common everywhere.'*

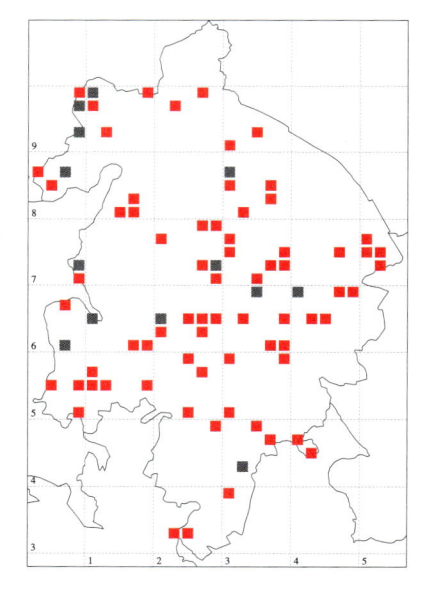

Clouded Brindle
2327 *Apamea epomidion* (Haw.)

County status: Fairly widespread and fairly common.
Flight: Late May to July.
Larval foodplants: Grasses, including Cock's-foot and Tufted Hair-grass.

This species is found over a large part of the County and appears to have increased since the VCH 1904. Favoured habitats include broadleaved woodland, scrub, disused railway cuttings and well-established gardens. The Clouded Brindle is, however, far less plentiful in suburban districts than the preceding species, as the following garden moth trap figures show:
Hillmorton, Rugby, 1982 (9), 1988 (7), 1990 (4), 1992 (5), 1995 (2), 1999 (0) (DIP).

VCH 1904: *'Not common.'*
Hampton-in-Arden (once, in 1900), Knowle, Rugby, Atherstone.

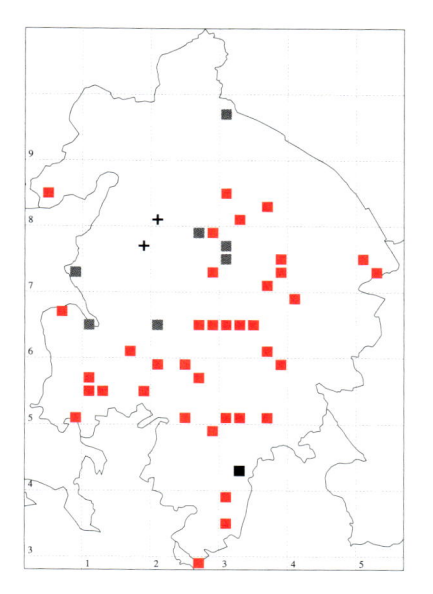

Dusky Brocade
2330 *Apamea remissa* (Hb.)

County status: Widespread and fairly common.
Flight: Late May to August.
Larval foodplants: Grasses, including Common Couch.

The Dusky Brocade occurs in a variety of grassy places, including marginal wetland, woodland clearings and rides, waste-ground and gardens.

The commonest form is f. *obscura* (Haw.) with the distinctively marked typical form being decidedly uncommon compared to f. *submissa* (Treit.).

Garden moth trap counts show the species to be fairly plentiful in both urban and rural districts:
Radford, Coventry: 1982 (67), 1990 (57), 1992 (52), 1993 (35) (MCV);
Charlecote: 1982 (146), 1990 (19), 1992 (98), 1993 (76) (AFG).

VCH 1904: *'Common.'*
Knowle, Small Heath, Sutton Park, Hampton-in-Arden, Rugby, Overslade, Wolford.

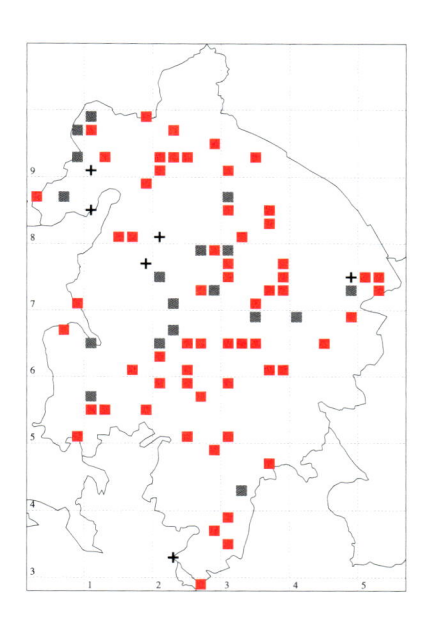

Small Clouded Brindle
2331 *Apamea unanimis* (Hb.)

County status: Fairly widespread and occasionally fairly common.
Flight: Late May to July.
Larval foodplants: Grasses, including Reed Canary-grass and Wavy Hair-grass.

The Small Clouded Brindle frequents wetland habitats. Typical sites include the reedbeds of Brandon Marsh, the moist rides of Ryton and Waverley Wood and the damp margins of ponds, rivers and streams over a large part of the County. There has been a significant increase in the range of this species since 1980.

It is occasionally attracted to garden moth traps and, in some years, noted frequently in urban districts as the following figures indicate:
Radford, Coventry: 1983 (17), 1986 (10), 1988 (13), 1994 (10) (MCV).

VCH 1904: *'Rare.'*
Birmingham area.

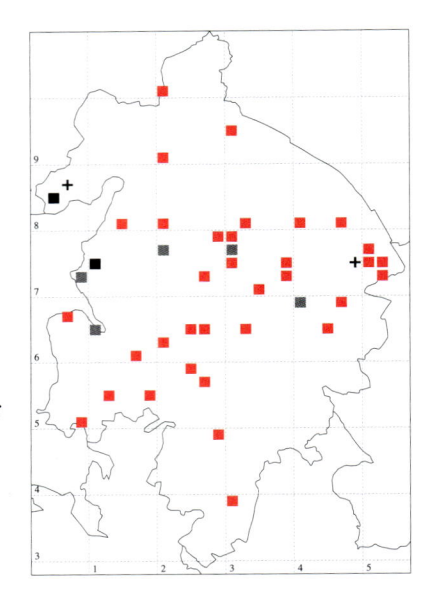

Large Nutmeg
2333 *Apamea anceps* ([D. & S.])

Nationally Local

County status: Widespread and becoming common.
Flight: Late May to July.
Larval foodplants: Grasses, including Cock's-foot and Common Couch.

This species is widely distributed in Warwickshire on well-drained grasslands. Typical habitats include road and railway embankments, disused quarries, broad field margins and open woodland. There is evidence of a substantial increase during the last 20 years.

Very large numbers may sometimes be attracted to MV on calcareous grassland; for example, Oxhouse Farm, Combrook, 26/6/1994 (85) (DB); Grove Hill, 18/6/2005 (150+) (Warks Moth Group).

Totals in suburban and rural moth traps also reach large figures:
Hillmorton, Rugby: 1988 (62), 1990 (60), 1996 (53), 2005 (49) (DIP);
Charlecote: 1988 (506), 1990 (525), 1996 (630), 2005 (235) (DB).

VCH 1904: *'Not common.'*
Sutton Park, Coventry, Hampton-in-Arden, Small Heath, Knowle, Overslade.

Rustic Shoulder-knot
2334 *Apamea sordens* (Hufn.)

County status: Widespread and common.
Flight: May to July.
Larval foodplants: Grasses, including Cock's-foot* and Common Couch.

The Rustic Shoulder-knot is generally distributed, but records are fewer from the north of the County. It is common in a variety of rural and urban habitats, including railway embankments, disused quarries, woodland, marshland, and gardens.

Populations in built-up districts are generally large, as garden moth trap counts from **Radford, Coventry**, show: 1980 (44), 1985 (36), 1990 (43), 1995 (109), 2000 (82) (MCV).

VCH 1904: *'Common everywhere.'*

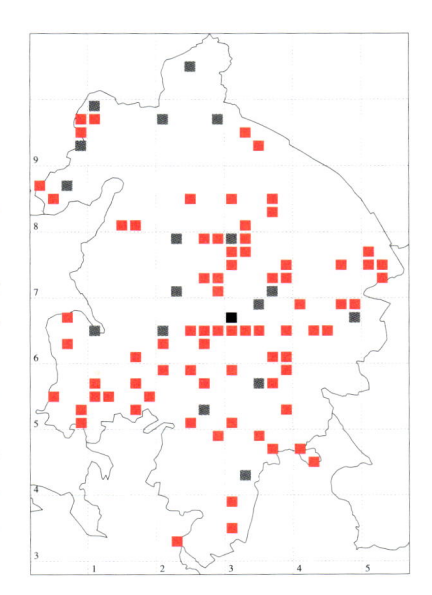

Slender Brindle
2335 *Apamea scolopacina* (Esp.)

County status: Fairly widespread and fairly common.
Flight: Late June to mid-August.
Larval foodplants: Woodland grasses, including Wood Melick, Wood Meadow-grass, False Brome and wood-rushes.

The Slender Brindle frequents damp woodland rides and clearings. It is fairly common at Oversley Wood, Snitterfield Bushes, Bowshot Wood, Clowes Wood, Waverley Wood, Tile Hill Wood, Hay Wood, Ryton Wood and Wappenbury Wood.

In years of high density dispersal proceeds into more open country and occasionally urban centres.

VCH 1904: *'Not common.'*
Hay Wood, Wolford Wood, Knowle, Atherstone.

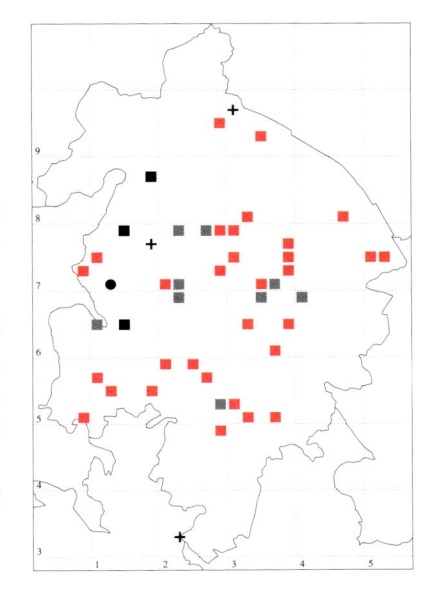

Double Lobed
2336 *Apamea ophiogramma* (Esp.)

County status: Local and occasionally fairly common.
Flight: July and August.
Larval foodplants: Reed Canary-grass, Reed Sweet-grass and cultivated Pampas-grass.

The Doubled Lobed was first recorded in Warwickshire at May's Wood on 31/7/1910 (GBM). This species has a thin and patchy distribution in Warwickshire with the largest concentration of records from the Coventry district. There are good populations in the wetlands of Brandon Marsh and smaller numbers frequent gardens of the city conurbation, where it is associated with ornamental Pampas-grass. Similarly, other parts of the County contain a mixture of scattered garden and wetland colonies.

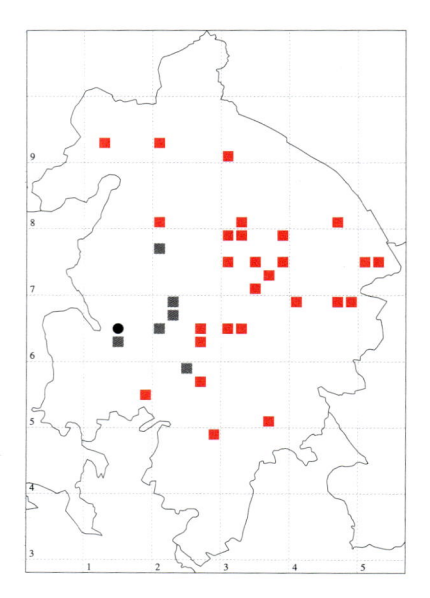

Genus: *Oligia*—Minors

A genus of four species, three of which (*strigilis*, *versicolor* and *latruncula*) are very hard to separate and superficial characteristics are often masked by melanism. Microscopic examination of the genitalia is therefore required to determine accurate identification.

Marbled Minor
2337 *Oligia strigilis* (L.)

County status: Widespread and fairly common.
Flight: Late May to early August.
Larval foodplants: Grasses, including Cock's-foot and Common Couch.

Annual counts of *Oligia* species at most garden moth traps run into hundreds and it would seem that this moth is both widespread and fairly common. It is equally frequent in both rural and urban districts. The melanic form f. *aethiops* (Osthelder) occurs in built-up areas.

The vast majority of specimens have been identified by using external characteristics; therefore the distribution maps may be inaccurate.

VCH 1904: '*Very common throughout the district.*'

Note—this statement would include *strigilis*, *latruncula* and *versicolor*.

Rufous Minor
2338 *Oligia versicolor* (Borkh.)

Nationally Local

County status: Widespread and locally fairly common.
Flight: June and July.
Larval foodplants: Unknown in the wild. In captivity Cock's-foot and other grasses.

The Rufous Minor was considered to be generally less common than other *Oligia* species, but genitalia dissections from random samples during 2005 (N.J. Stone) has shown the species to be more plentiful than realised. For example, from a selection of 23 *Oligia* specimens captured at Charlecote between 7–15 July, results showed the sample to consist of 9% Marbled Minor, 26% Tawny Marbled Minor and 65% Rufous Minor. Favoured habitats include grassy waste-ground, woodland rides and clearings and well-established gardens.

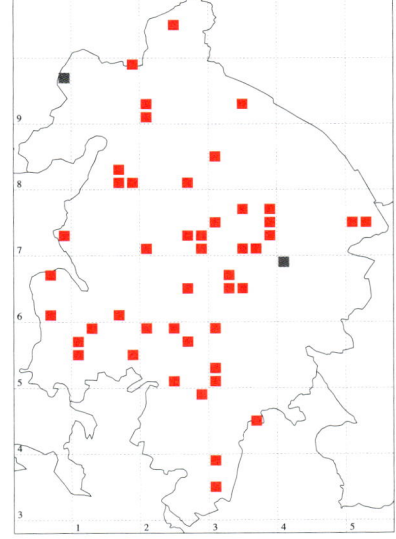

VCH 1904: Not recognised as a separate species.

Tawny Marbled Minor
2339 *Oligia latruncula* ([D. & S.])

County status: Widespread and fairly common.
Flight: Late May to early August.
Larval foodplants: Grasses, including Cock's-foot.

The range of this species has been derived chiefly from recorders using external characteristics for identification. It appears to have a wider distribution than *strigilis* and is noted in generally larger numbers.

A considerable proportion of most populations are blackish, obscurely-marked melanics.

VCH 1904: Not recognised as a separate species from *strigilis*.

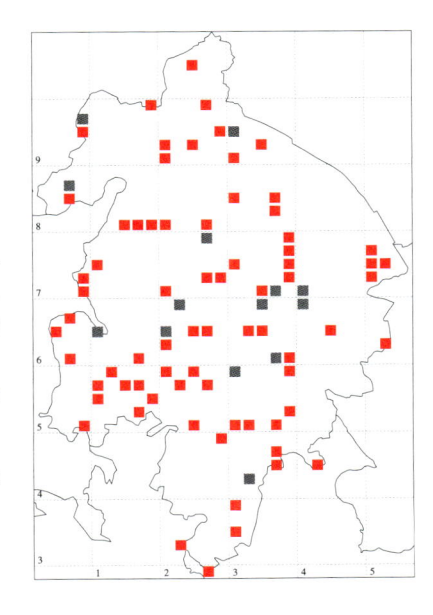

Middle-barred Minor
2340 *Oligia fasciuncula* (Haw.)

County status: Widespread and fairly common.
Flight: Mid-May to July.
Larval foodplants: Grasses, especially Tufted Hair-grass.

The Middle-barred Minor is one of the more distinctive species in this genus and is widespread throughout the County. It is particularly plentiful in river valleys, open woodland and gardens.

The results of static moth trapping in built-up districts show reasonable populations:
Radford, Coventry: 1980 (16), 1985 (18), 1990 (21), 1995 (6), 2000 (14) (MCV).

VCH 1904: *'Common, occurs in every list and nearly always found with* **strigilis** *but less commonly.'*

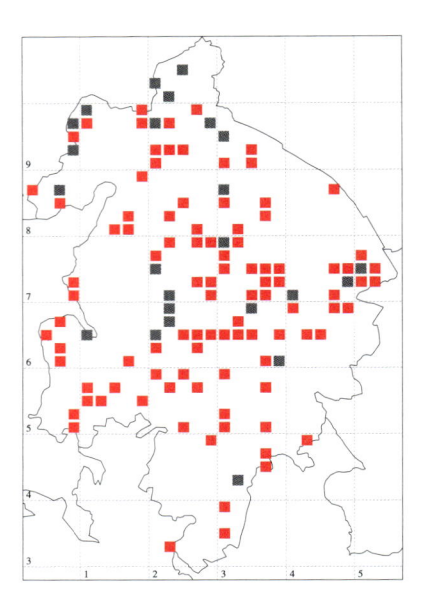

Cloaked Minor
2341 *Mesoligia furuncula* ([D. & S.])

County status: Widespread and fairly common.
Flight: Late June to early September.
Larval foodplants: Grasses, including Sheep's-fescue, Tufted Hair-grass and False Oat-grass.

The Cloaked Minor has a wide distribution, frequenting an extensive range of habitats but with the largest populations occurring on calcareous soils.

The adult has normally stopped flying by early September, but occasional stragglers are recorded; for example, Hillmorton, Rugby, 15/9/1985 (DIP).

Garden moth trap totals at **Pillerton Priors** are as follows: 1992 (11), 1993 (16), 2002 (12), 2003 (13), 2004 (15), 2005 (13) (CI).

VCH 1904: *Sutton Park, Yardley, Hampton-in-Arden (very common in 1900), Rugby.*

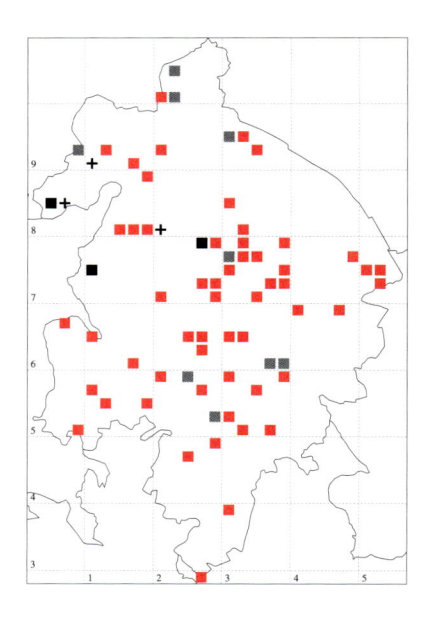

Rosy Minor
2342 *Mesoligia literosa* (Haw.)

County status: Fairly widespread and fairly common.
Flight: June to August.
Larval foodplants: Grasses, including Cock's-foot, cereal crops and sedges.

The Rosy Minor is well established in north Warwickshire, where good populations exist on many post-industrial brownfield sites, including disused quarries, railway tracks, heathland and scrub. It was formerly plentiful in urban districts of Coventry, but is now far less frequently seen. This moth has traditionally been uncommon in the rural southern half of the County.

Garden moth trap figures from **Radford, Coventry**, illustrate urban decline: 1970 (112), 1975 (137), 1980 (72), 1985 (32), 1990 (28), 1995 (14), 2000 (10) melanic forms dominant (MCV).

VCH 1904: *Knowle, Small Heath, Hampton-in-Arden, Atherstone.*

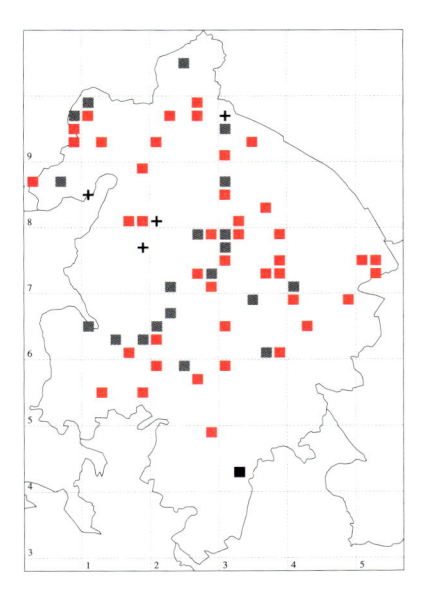

Genus: *Mesapamea*—Common Rustics

In 1983 the genus *Mesapamea*, following research on the Continent, was shown to contain two species (Remm 1983). Genitalic examination is essential for proper determination, although Lesser Common Rustic *M. didyma* is generally smaller than Common Rustic *M. secalis*, and black examples with a distinctive chalky white reniform stigma are usually the former species. Both are polymorphic, which adds to the confusion.

Remm's Rustic *Mesapamea remmi* (Rézb-Res.) is probably a hybrid between *secalis* and *didyma*. It is listed as a distinct species in both the British and European checklists but recent authors are doubtful of its validity. A *Mesapamea* species caught at Charlecote on 18/7/1994 (DB) and dissected (M. Bailey) was found to have identical genitalia structure to that described by Jordan and illustrated by Nowacki (1998) for *M. remmi* (Jordan, 1987).

Common Rustic
2343 *Mesapamea secalis* (L.)

County status: Widespread and abundant.
Flight: July to early September.
Larval foodplants: Grasses, including Cock's-foot, Tufted Hair-grass and cereals.

The Common Rustic is a dominant species in moth traps throughout the County. Found in a wide range of habitats in rural and urban districts, it is a frequent visitor to sugar and may be seen feeding on buddleia flowers and grasses.

Extremely variable in ground colour and the extent of the dark transverse markings. Many colour forms occur in Warwickshire, from pale grey to yellow or reddish-brown, with darker melanic forms predominating.

Numbers at a garden moth trap in **Radford, Coventry**, are as follows: 1973 (199), 1983 (584), 1993 (449), 2003 (253) (MCV).

VCH 1904: *'Occurs in various forms commonly everywhere.'*

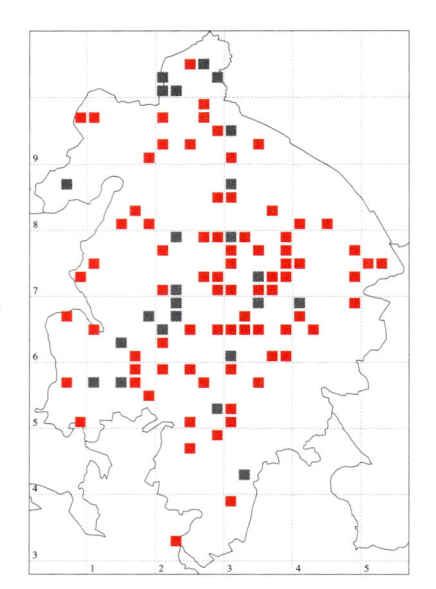

Lesser Common Rustic
2343a *Mesapamea didyma* (Esp.)

County status: Local and generally uncommon.
Flight: July and August.
Larval foodplants: Grasses, including Cock's-foot.

The Lesser Common Rustic appears in most samples of *Mesapamea* specimens that have been critically examined, and its distribution may eventually prove to be as widespread as *secalis*. Evidence has shown *didyma* to be far less common, however; for example, out of 47 random *Mesapamea* specimens selected from Charlecote for genitalia dissection, between 15–29 July 2005, *didyma* represented only 6% of the sample (DB, NJS gen. det.). Open grassy habitats are favoured, including woodland rides, parkland, meadows, wetland, heathland and gardens.

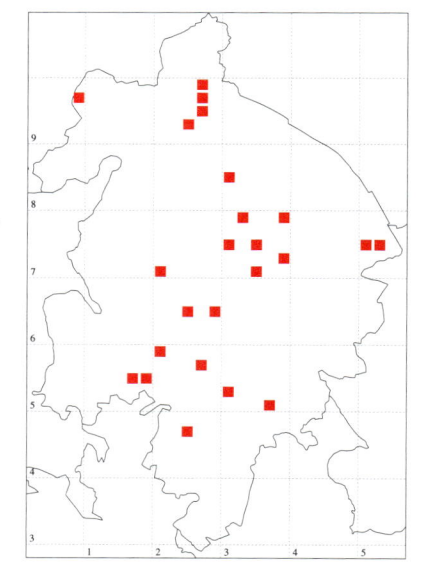

Small Dotted Buff
2345 *Photedes minima* (Haw.)

County status: Widespread and fairly common.
Flight: June to August.
Larval foodplants: Tufted Hair-grass.

The Small Dotted Buff is found over a large part of the County, frequenting damp terrain in open woodland, meadows and marshes. Although dependent upon poorly drained grassland where the larval foodplant grows, the adult is regularly observed in garden moth traps.

The following garden counts give an idea of frequency:
Pillerton Priors: 1992 (17), 1993 (19), 1994 (15), 2002 (6), 2003 (15), 2004 (15) (CI);

VCH 1904: *'Common everywhere'.*

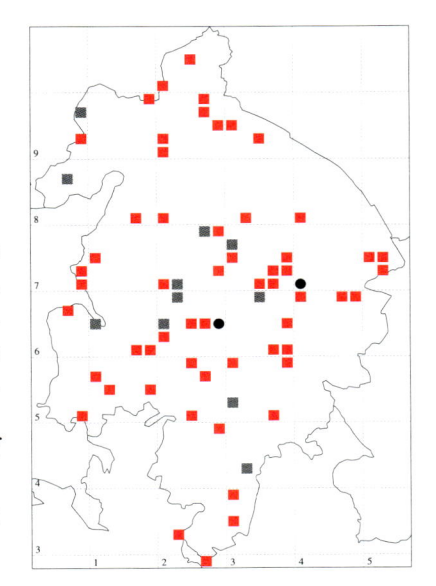

Mere Wainscot
2349 *Chortodes fluxa* (Hb.)

Nationally Scarce B

County status: Very local and occasionally fairly common.
Flight: Late June to August.
Larval foodplants: Wood Small-reed.

The Mere Wainscot is a relatively recent addition to Warwickshire and four distinct populations have been identified. The largest nucleus is found within the Princethorpe woodland complex, with smaller numbers at Ladywalk, Bowshot Wood and Oversley Wood. This species frequents damp, sheltered woodland rides containing a good supply of the larval foodplant. There have been two instances of stray individuals in garden moth traps within 5 km of known colonies.

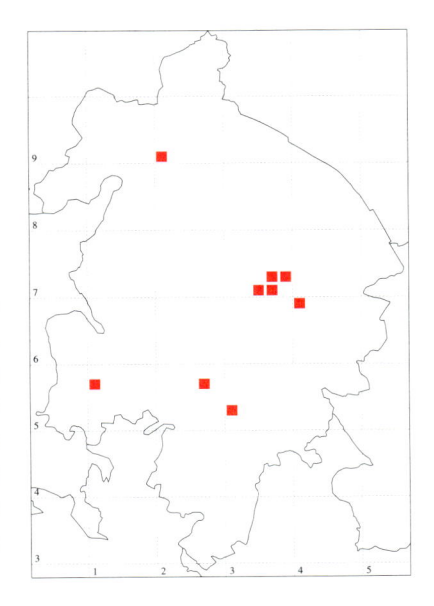

Records:
Bowshot Wood, 27/8/1972, 29/8/1972 (7), 5/9/1972, 5/8/1974 (12), 17/8/1974 (4), 18/8/1974 (9), 19/8/1974 (4), 20/8/1974 (5) (DB), 10/8/1988 (3) (RGB, DB); **Marton**, Aug. 1974 (RA); **Wappenbury Wood**, 30/7/1975 (18), (DB, RHS, RA, GR), 5/7/1997 (3) (Warks Moth Group); **Charlecote**, 13/8/1986 (AFG); **Ryton Wood**, 10/8/1988 (SAL), 1990s (LB, CE); **Oversley Wood**, 27/6/2000 (DB, RGB, MA); **Waverley Wood**, 28/7/2001 (12) (Warks Moth Group); **Ladywalk**, 15/7/2002, 25/7/2002 (JBt), 25/6/2005 (DG); **Ryton Meadows**, 16/7/2005 (DB).

Small Wainscot
2350 *Chortodes pygmina* (Haw.)

County status: Fairly widespread and locally fairly common.
Flight: Late July to September.
Larval foodplants: Sedges, including Lesser Pond-sedge, grasses and possibly rushes.

The Small Wainscot frequents damp woodland rides, marshes and marginal wetland habitats by rivers and streams. Typical sites include Sutton Park, Brandon Marsh, Ufton Fields, Ryton Wood, Waverley Wood, Hampton Wood, Bowshot Wood and Wolford Wood. The adult sometimes visits light in good quantity; for example, Oversley Wood, 6/9/1973 (14 in Heath trap) (DB).

Occasional individuals are noted in garden moth traps.

VCH 1904: *Sutton Park, Knowle, Hampton-in-Arden, Rugby.*

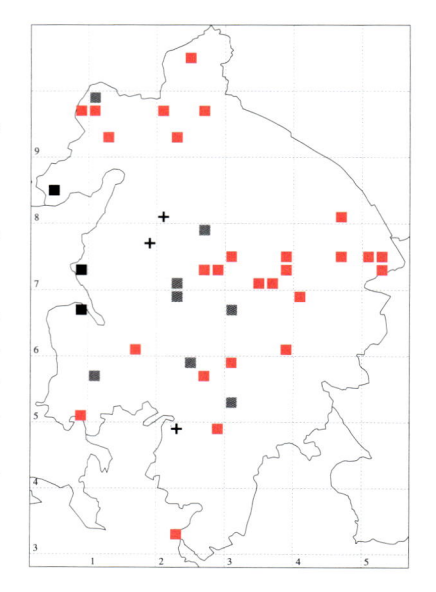

Dusky Sallow
2352 *Eremobia ochroleuca* ([D. & S.])

County status: Widespread and fairly common.
Flight: Mid-July to early September. Occasionally observed flying in hot sunshine.
Larval foodplants: The flowers and seeds of grasses, including Cock's-foot, Common Couch and sometimes cereal crops.

The Dusky Sallow was a very rare species in the VCH 1904 with a solitary record from Small Heath. Apart from an early 1960s specimen taken at MV in Tysoe (TT), there appear to be no further records until the 1970s. During this decade *ochroleuca* experienced a rapid increase and subsequent dispersal across the County.

It is habitually noted in sandy districts or on chalk and limestone, but in Warwickshire has adapted to other soil types and utilises a diversity of habitats, including woodland and wetlands as well as calcareous grasslands.

Garden moth trap totals are as follows:
Pillerton Priors: 1992 (5), 1993 (2), 2002 (11), 2003 (16), 2004 (14), 2005 (8) (CI).

VCH 1904: '*One specimen is in the Blatch collection which has been recorded as having occurred near Small Heath. According to the Blatch catalogue of the collection it was taken by Mr James Madison.*'

Flounced Rustic
2353 *Luperina testacea* ([D. & S.])

County status: Widespread and abundant.
Flight: Late July to late September.
Larval foodplants: The roots and stem bases of grasses, including Common Couch, fescues and sometimes cereal crops.

The Flounced Rustic is found throughout the County in numerous open habitats and is one of the commonest species of the early autumn.
  Garden moth trap counts from an urban site are as follows:
Radford, Coventry: 1970 (46), 1975 (230), 1980 (41), 1985 (58), 1990 (100), 1995 (87), 2000 (86) (MCV).

VCH 1904: '*Common everywhere*'.

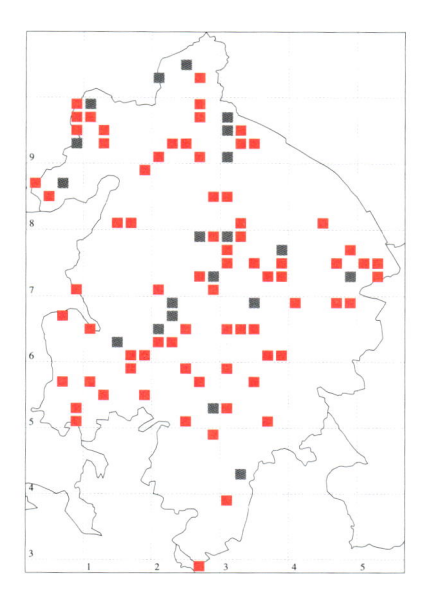

Genus: *Amphipoea*—Ear Moths

There are four species of this genus in Britain, all of which are sufficiently similar to require genitalic examination for accurate determination. Three of the four have been recorded in Warwickshire.

Large Ear
2357 *Amphipoea lucens* (Freyer)

Nationally Local

County status: Very local and scarce.
Flight: August.
Larval foodplants: Purple Moor-grass.

This species is normally associated with wet acid moorland and marshes, but has been recorded intermittently in the north and west of the County.

Records (all determined by genitalia dissection):
Birmingham, 1956 (FAN); **Sutton Park**, 1960s (LJE); **N.E. Birmingham**, 1970s (LJE); **Claverdon**, 4/8/1983 (IGMR) (gen. det. M. Bailey); **Bearley**, 21/8/1987 (IGMR) (gen. det. M. Bailey).

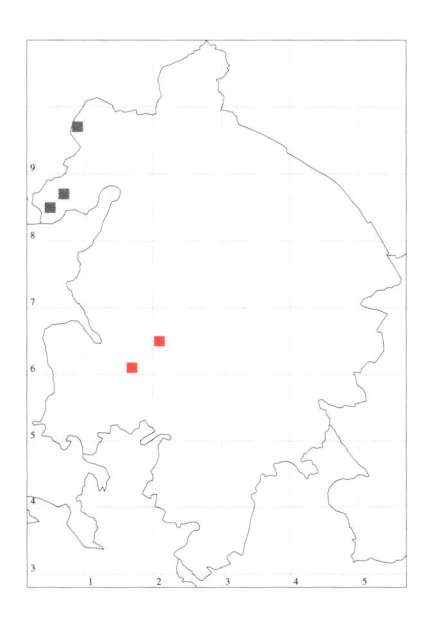

Saltern Ear
2358 *Amphipoea fucosa paludis* (Tutt)

Nationally Local

County status: Status uncertain. No recent records.
Flight: July and August.
Larval foodplants: In captivity, the stems and roots of grasses.

This Nationally Local moth, associated with coastal habitats and damp moorland, was surprisingly recorded a few times in the Birmingham district between 1920 and 1964.

Records (all determined by genitalia dissection):
Gravelly Hill, Birmingham, 1920s (GPS); **Erdington, Birmingham,** July 1941 (GPS) (gen. det. M. D. Bryan); **Hampton Railway Cutting, Stonebridge,** 1956 (STm); **Edgbaston, Birmingham,** 10/8/1957 (FAN) (gen. det. M. D. Bryan); **N.E. Birmingham,** 1960s (LJE); **Birmingham,** (west of centre) 1964 (FAN).

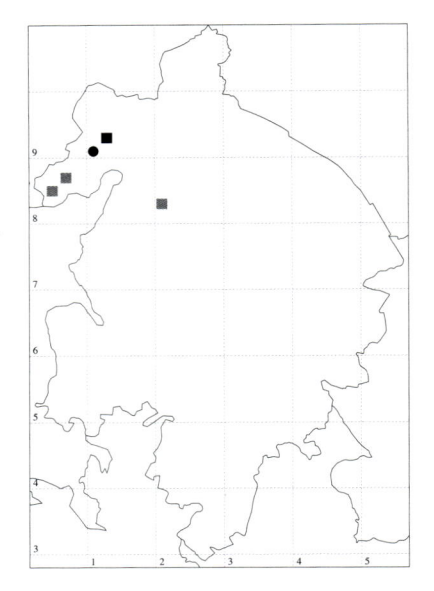

Ear Moth
2360 *Amphipoea oculea* (L.)

County status: Local and uncommon.
Flight: Late July to September.
Larval foodplants: The lower stem and roots of grasses, including Tufted Hair-grass.

The Ear Moth is found locally in open habitats over a fairly large part of the County. It is most frequently recorded on heathland in north Warwickshire; for example, Grendon Common, 18/8/1990 (3) (DB, AFG, RGB), 24/8/1990 (2) (DB, RMC, BM). This species also exists in suitable grassy habitats throughout the large urban conurbations of Birmingham and Coventry.

The moth is an occasional visitor to garden moth traps in rural areas.

VCH 1904: *'Common everywhere.'*

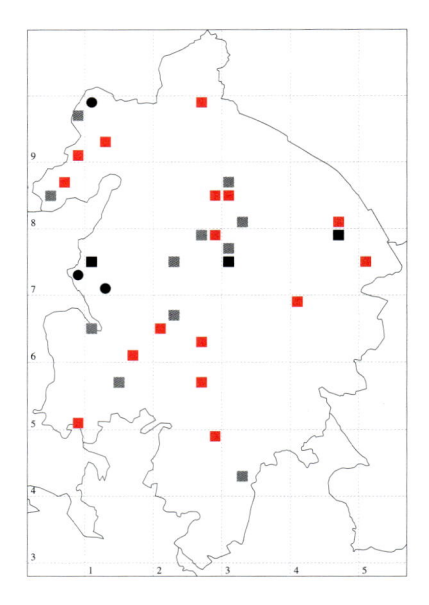

Rosy Rustic
2361 *Hydraecia micacea* (Esp.)

County status: Widespread and fairly common.
Flight: Late July to early November.
Larval foodplants: A variety of low-growing plants, including docks, plantains, Burdock and horse-tails.

The Rosy Rustic has a wide distribution in Warwickshire.

It is found in a diversity of open sites with a preference for damper habitats, especially river valleys. This species varies considerably in size with some females being particularly large. The forewings are generally of a pinkish-brown colouration but occasional specimens are much darker.

Garden moth trap counts are as follows:
Pillerton Priors: 1992 (19), 1993 (9), 2002 (9), 2003 (16), 2004 (8), 2005 (27) (CI).

VCH 1904: *'Common'.*
Sutton Park, Knowle, Small Heath, Atherstone, Rugby, Hampton-in-Arden, Wolford.

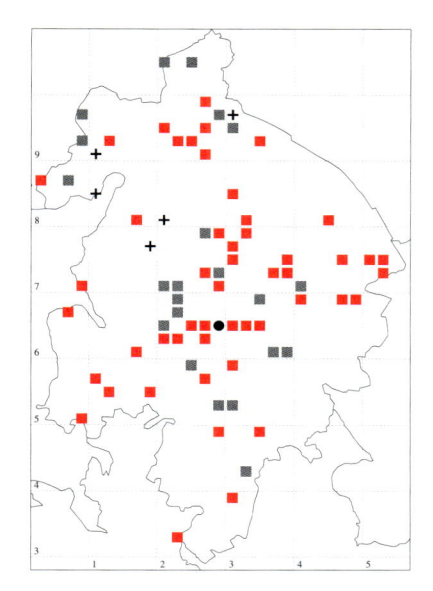

Frosted Orange
2364 *Gortyna flavago* ([D. & S.])

County status: Fairly widespread and fairly common.
Flight: Late August to October.
Larval foodplants: The inner stems and roots of thistles, Burdock, Foxglove*, Hemp-agrimony, Common Nettle and other plants.

Although found over a wide area of the County, with the largest concentration of records in the south-west section, this species has a rather linear distribution elsewhere. It appears to have no specific requirements other than favouring slightly moist ground, and is to be found in many open woodland and rough grassland habitats.

Garden moth trap totals fluctuate as the following results show:
Bidford-on-Avon: 1989 (50), 1990 (19), 1994 (7), 1995 (4), 1996 (4) (RMC);
Pillerton Priors: 1992 (7), 1993 (2), 2002 (6), 2003 (28), 2004 (6), 2005 (20) (CI).

VCH 1904: '*Not uncommon.*'
Sutton Park, Knowle, Small Heath, Hay Mills, Overslade.

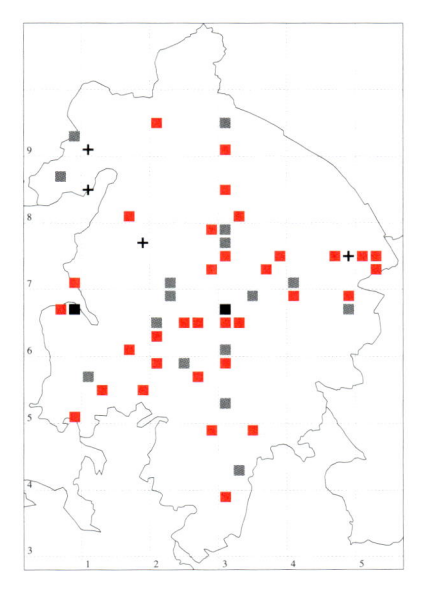

Crescent
2368 *Celaena leucostigma leucostigma* (Hb.)
Nationally Local

County status: Local and occasionally fairly common.
Flight: July to early September.
Larval foodplants: Yellow Iris, Great Fen-sedge and other similar plants.

This Nationally Local wetland species was first noted in Warwickshire in 1938 at Tile Hill Wood (CDNHSS). Healthy colonies are now established in Brandon Marsh, Wyken Slough and Coombe Abbey. It is generally observed in low numbers, but occasionally seen in double figures; for example, Brandon Marsh, 30/7/2005 (18) (Warks Moth Group). Individuals captured in garden moth traps from time to time suggest the presence of undiscovered colonies.

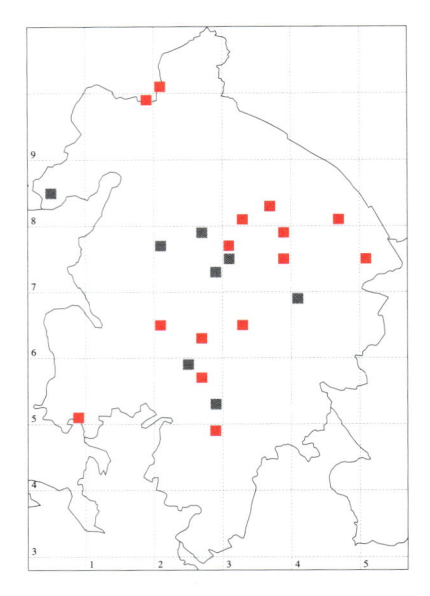

Bulrush Wainscot
2369 *Nonagria typhae* (Thunb.)

County status: Fairly widespread and locally fairly common.
Flight: Late July to early October.
Larval foodplants: Reed-mace*.

The VCH 1904 described this species as *'local but probably occurring wherever its foodplant grows freely'*. This statement is an accurate assessment of its present day status.

The Bulrush Wainscot frequently wanders long distances from wetland habitats and is often noted in garden moth traps. It is capable of quickly colonising new sites as they become suitable. Large colonies have developed in former gravel extraction sites at Brandon Marsh, Ufton Fields, Whitacre Heath and Alvecote Pools. Sometimes large numbers of adults arrive at light: Brandon Marsh, 27/8/1991 (10) (Warks Moth Group).

VCH 1904: *'Local but probably occurring wherever its foodplant grows freely.'* Sutton Park, Whitacre, Knowle, Rugby.

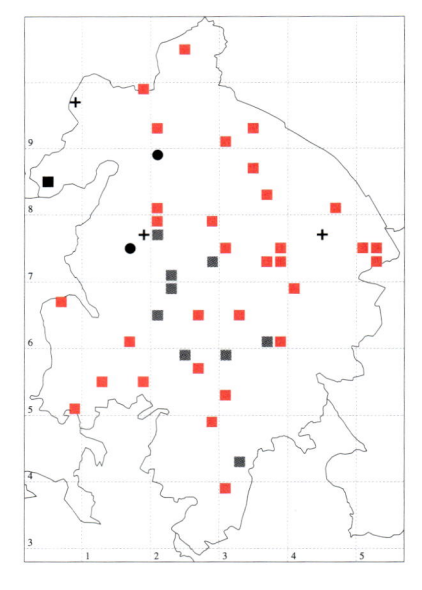

Twin-spotted Wainscot
2370 *Archanara geminipuncta* (Haw.)
Nationally Local

County status: Very local and occasionally fairly common.
Flight: Early August to September.
Larval foodplants: Common Reed.

The Twin-spotted Wainscot is a reedbed species that was first recorded in a garden moth trap at Bidford-on-Avon on 15/8/1984 (RMC). This was followed by others at static traps in the district as the week progressed. During the ensuing years, emanating from further dispersals, it has been observed at several more locations in the County. Established colonies have now been confirmed at Brandon Marsh, Broom and Compton Verney.

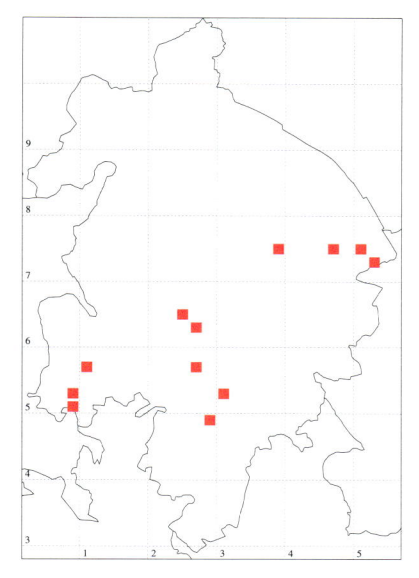

Records:
Bidford-on-Avon, 15/8/1984, 22/8/1984, 22/8/1988, 15/8/1996, 18/8/1996, Aug. 1997, 10/8/1998, 5/8/2000, 6/8/2003 (RMC); **Charlecote**, 19/8/1984, 21/8/1984 (2), 22/8/1984, 20/8/1991, 16/8/1996 (DB, AFG); **Broom Gravel Pits**, 29/8/1985 (3), 8/9/1985 (12), 9/9/1985 (RMC); **Brandon Marsh**, 27/8/1991 (4), 25/7/1992 (3) (Warks Moth Group); **Long Lawford**, 2/9/1991 (AFG); **Oversley Wood**, 1/8/1992 (2) (Warks Moth Group); **Steetley Meadows**, 11/8/1995 (PC, CW); **Hillmorton**, **Rugby**, Aug. 1997 (DIP), 20/8/1998 (PN); **Compton Verney**, 7/8/1999 (3) (RMC, DB, Warks Moth Group); **Pillerton Priors**, 7/8/2002 (CI); **Warwick**, 3/8/2005 (SDT); **Hampton Magna**, 15/8/2005 (PJR).

Brown-veined Wainscot
2371 *Archanara dissoluta* (Treit.)
Nationally Local

County status: Very local and occasionally fairly common.
Flight: August to early September.
Larval foodplants: Common Reed*.

The Brown-veined Wainscot was first discovered in Warwickshire as recently as 1967 at Alvecote Pools (ANT) and Sutton Park (DTG). Large colonies of this marshland species now exist at Brandon Marsh and Coombe Abbey. Generally, however, it is uncommon. During warm summers it is prone to wander widely.

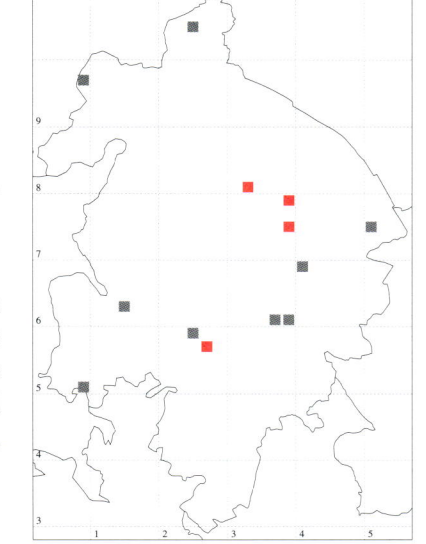

Records:
Pooley Fields, **Alvecote Pools**, 4/8/1967 (ANT), 10/8/1968 (MAA); **Sutton Park**, Aug. 1967 (DTG), 1970s (LJE); **Wootton Wawen**, 10/8/1973 (DB); **Ufton Fields**, 24/8/1974 (LEM); 10/8/1975 (DB); **Charlecote**, 6/8/1975 (2) (DB), 18/8/1983, 19/8/1983, 20/8/1987 (AFG); **Hampton Wood**, 7/8/1975 (AFG); **Brandon Marsh**,

1980s (MB), 12/8/1986 (AFG), 4/8/2000 (12) (Warks Moth Group) 30/7/2005 (12) (Warks Moth Group); **Marton**, Aug. 1976 (RA); **Radford**, **Coventry**, 5/9/1979, 17/8/1983 (MCV); **Bidford-on-Avon**, 1/9/1991 (RMC); **Hillmorton**, **Rugby**, 14/8/1981, 13/8/1983 (DIP); **Coombe Abbey**, 8/8/1988 (SAL), 1/8/1997 (8) (Warks Moth Group).

Large Wainscot
2375 *Rhizedra lutosa* (Hb.)

County status: Local and uncommon.
Flight: August to October.
Larval foodplants: Common Reed.

This marginal wetland species is very much a wanderer, being observed every so often in garden moth traps across the County, whilst exact breeding grounds remain undetected. It has been noted in both rural and urban districts. Large Wainscot is very variable in size with occasional individuals no larger than the *Mythimna* species; the ground colour also varies from light greyish-straw to reddish-ochreous, whilst some specimens are heavily dusted with black.

VCH 1904: *'One taken at light in signal box, Knowle railway station (RCB).'*

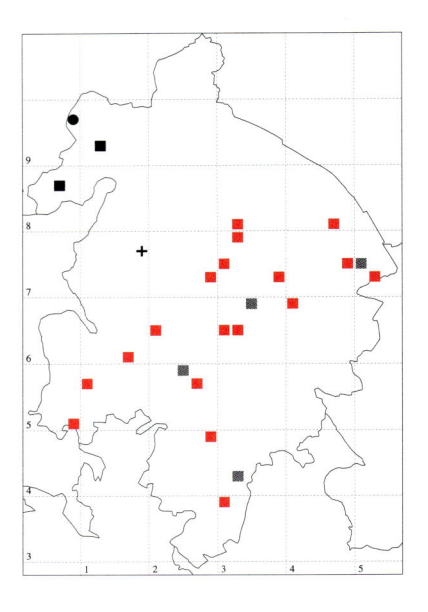

Fen Wainscot
2377 *Arenostola phragmitidis* (Hb.)

Nationally Local

County status: Very local and fairly common at one site.
Flight: Late July to August.
Larval foodplants: Common Reed.

A small colony of this Nationally Local reedbed species was discovered at Brandon Marsh on 4/8/2000 (Warks Moth Group). Previously a vagrant individual had been captured in a garden moth trap at Charlecote on 9/8/1996 (DB).

Records:
Charlecote, 9/8/1996 (DB); **Brandon Marsh**, 4/8/2000 (5), 30/7/2005 (10) (Warks Moth Group).

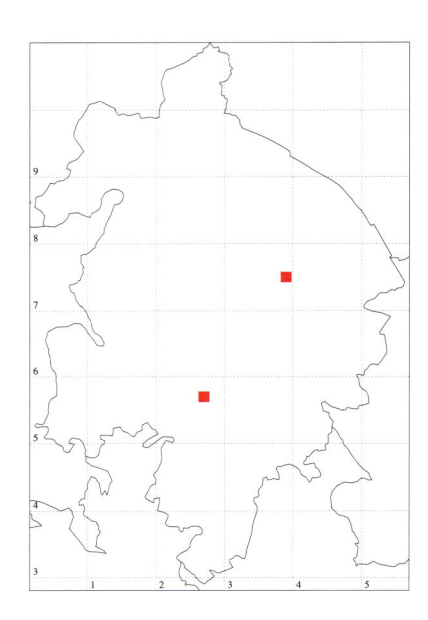

Small Rufous
2379 *Coenobia rufa* (Haw.)

Nationally Local

County status: Local and sometimes fairly common.
Flight: Late July to mid-September.
Larval foodplants: Jointed Rush and Soft Rush.

The Small Rufous, first recorded in Tile Hill Wood in 1937 (ANT), is an inhabitant of marshy areas in woodland, heathland, and marginal wetland bordering ponds, rivers and streams. There are established colonies in Sutton Park, Hay Wood, Ryton/Wappenbury Wood, Waverley Wood, Brandon Marsh and Coombe Abbey. It is generally uncommon but is sometimes observed at light in numbers; for example, Brandon Marsh 4/8/2000 (15) (Warks Moth Group); Sutton Park 5/8/2000 (5) (DB, DG). Occasionally noted in garden moth traps in both rural and urban districts.

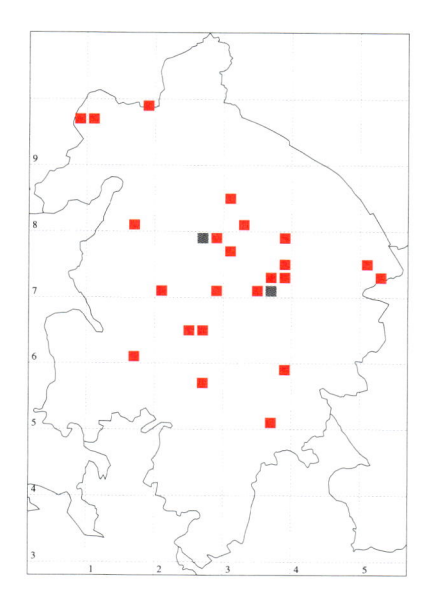

Treble Lines
2380 *Charanyca trigrammica* (Hufn.)

County status: Widespread and fairly common.
Flight: May to July.
Larval foodplants: A wide range of herbaceous plants, including plantains, knapweeds, Knotgrass and Dandelion.

The Treble Lines is found in a large part of central and south Warwickshire but dwindles northwards. A vast range of grassy habitats are utilised. There is evidence of a substantial increase in numbers during the last five years.

It is very variable in ground colour, ranging from whitish or greyish-brown to reddish-ochreous; ab. *bilinea* (Haw.), a melanic form, occurs occasionally at Charlecote and in other populations.

The figures below show moth trap counts at **Charlecote** (DB) and highlight the recent escalation: 1977 (3), 1983 (3), 1988 (10), 1998 (17), 1999 (19), 2001 (54), 2002 (140), 2003 (103), 2004 (118).

VCH 1904: '*Occurs throughout the County*'.

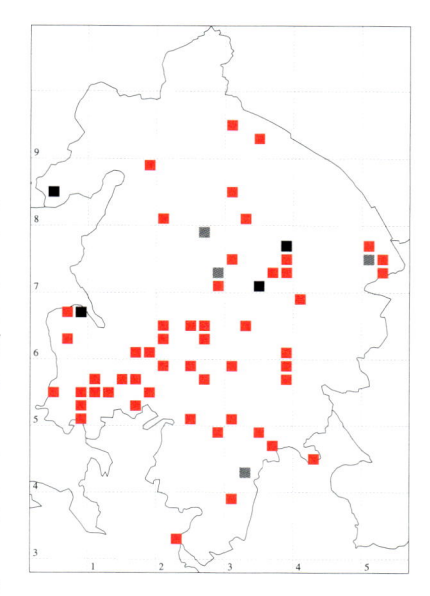

Uncertain
2381 *Hoplodrina alsines* (Brahm)

County status: Widespread and common.
Flight: Mid-June to mid-August.
Larval foodplants: A wide range of herbaceous plants, including docks, chickweeds, Dandelion, dead-nettles and Primrose.

The separation of this species and the next has caused some difficulties for beginners, but most recorders have shown themselves competent to distinguish each and it is clear that both are widespread and common throughout the County.

The Uncertain appears to be more plentiful in urban districts but rural populations of the two species are considered to be almost equal.

VCH 1904: *Knowle, Hampton-in-Arden, Rugby, Atherstone, Wolford.*

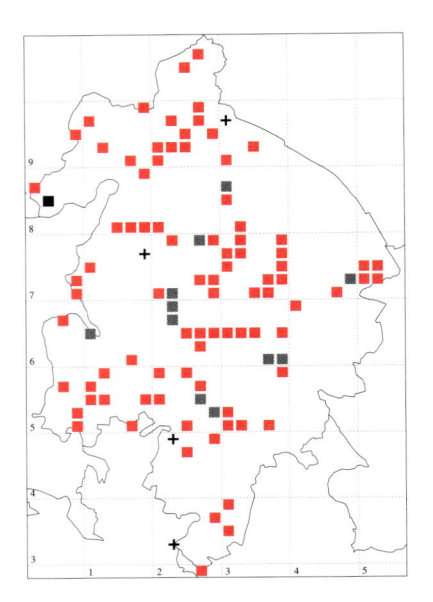

Rustic
2382 *Hoplodrina blanda* ([D. & S.])

County status: Widespread and common.
Flight: Late June to late August.
Larval foodplants: A wide range of herbaceous plants, including docks, chickweeds, Dandelion, plantains and Knotgrass.

The Rustic is found in a similar wide range of habitats to the preceding species, including open woodland, marshland, heathland, gardens and all types of grassland.

The table below compares garden moth trap numbers of Rustic and Uncertain in the urban district of **Radford, Coventry** (MCV):

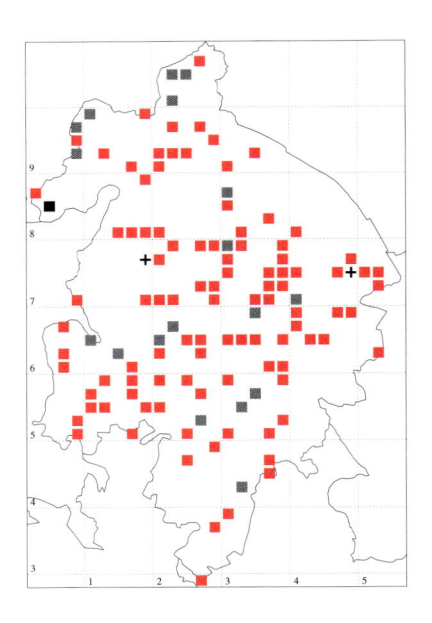

Species	1982	1983	1986	1988	1995	1999	2000	2002
Rustic	4	7	9	6	34	47	96	99
Uncertain	20	23	27	15	77	147	195	172

VCH 1904: *Knowle, Hampton-in-Arden, Overslade.*

Vine's Rustic
2384 *Hoplodrina ambigua* ([D. & S.])

County status: Local but becoming fairly common.
Flight: Two generations. Late May to June, and August to early October.
Larval foodplants: A wide range of herbaceous plants, including Dandelion, docks and Primrose.

The first British specimen of this species was taken at sugar, near Shoreham, Sussex in 1879. Regarded as an immigrant in the nineteenth and early twentieth centuries, it gradually became established along the south coast and then spread rapidly in the 1940s.

First noted in Warwickshire during 1976, it initially became installed slowly across the County but momentum has increased since 2000, perhaps augmented by immigrants. It has been recorded from open grassy habitats, including railway cuttings, quarries, waste-ground and gardens.

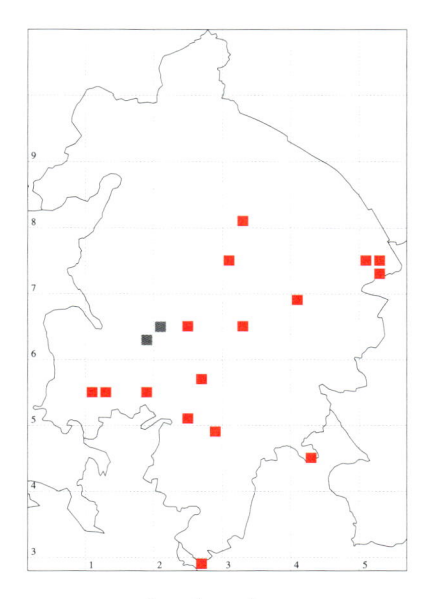

Garden moth trap totals at **Charlecote** (DB) clearly illustrate the recent proliferation: 1976 (2), 1977 (14), 1982 (1), 1992 (2), 2002 (1), 2003 (1), 2004 (17), 2005 (126).

Small Mottled Willow
2385 *Spodoptera exigua* (Hb.)
Regular immigrant, sometimes common: Europe and North Africa

County status: Regular immigrant.
Flight: May to October.
Larval foodplants: Probably herbaceous plants in the wild. In captivity it will eat Dandelion, docks, groundsels and many other low-growing plants.

Since 1980 the Small Mottled Willow has become a regular visitor to Warwickshire; 1996 was a record year, in which 23 individuals were noted.

Records:

1956—**Erdington, Birmingham**, 28/5 (LJE).
1958—**Edgbaston, Birmingham**, (FAN).
1961—**Birmingham**, (LJE).
1979—**Fen End, Kenilworth**, (DC).
1982—**Charlecote**, 8/7, 21/8 (AFG), 17/9 (2), 18/9, 19/9 (DB).
1983—**Charlecote**, 15/6, 17/8, 24/8 (AFG).
1984—**Charlecote**, 6/8 (2) (AFG), 13/9 (DB).
1985—**Charlecote**, 21/8 (DB).
1986—**Charlecote**, 4/7 (DB).
1988—**Charlecote**, 29/8 (DB).
1994—**Charlecote**, 18/8, 20/8 (DB), **Hillmorton, Rugby**, 22/8 (PN).
1995—**Charlecote**, 30/8, 1/9 (AFG).
1996—**Charlecote**, 7/6–30/6 (7), 10/8–28/8 (14) (AFG, DB); **Bidford-on-Avon**, 9/8 (RMC); **Radford, Coventry**, 19/9 (MCV).
1998—**Charlecote**, 15/5, 25/7 (AFG).
2000—**Oversley Wood**, 27/6 (DB, RGB, MA); **Charlecote**, 27/6, 23/8–12/9 (4) (DB, AFG); **Hillmorton, Rugby**, 30/6, 19/9 (PN).
2003—**Charlecote**, 30/6 (AFG), 17/8, 18/8 (DB); **Bidford-on-Avon**, 12/8 (RMC).

2004—**Royal Leamington Spa**, 14/6 (JWkn);
Temple Grafton, 5/8 (AFG).

2005—**Pillerton Priors**, 11/10 (CI).

Mottled Rustic
2387 *Caradrina morpheus* (Hufn.)

County status: Widespread and fairly common.

Flight: Late May to early August.

Larval foodplants: A wide range of herbaceous plants, including dead-nettles*, Common Nettle, docks, goosefoots, teasels, plantains and Knotgrass.

The Mottled Rustic is found in a wide range of habitats, including woodland, marshland, railway cuttings, quarries, heathland and gardens.

It is plentiful in both rural and built-up districts, as the table below illustrates.

VCH 1904: '*Common everywhere.*'

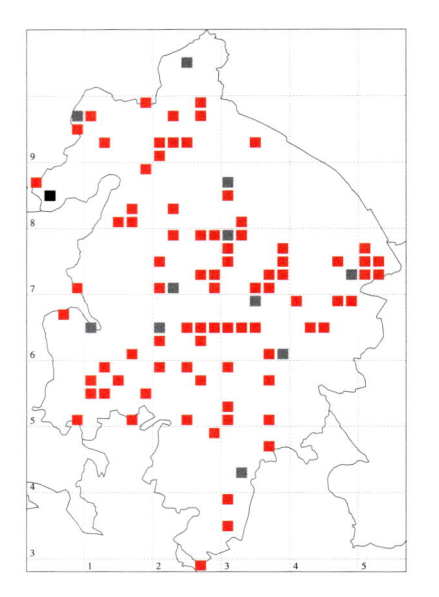

Habitat	Location	1983	1991	1992	1998	2000
Urban	Radford, Coventry (MCV)	239	157	139	78	84
Rural	Charlecote (DB)	127	237	375	166	105

Pale Mottled Willow
2389 *Paradrina clavipalpis* (Scop.)

County status: Widespread and fairly common.

Flight: Probably two or three overlapping generations. February to November.

Larval foodplants: Grass seeds, including cereal grains, both growing and stored.

A widespread species found in all types of habitats, including gardens and cultivated land, as well as wasteground. The adult has been recorded in Warwickshire in every month from February to November, usually peaking in late June to July and mid-September

The earliest specimen recorded was on 13/2/2004 at Keresley, Coventry (NJS). This may have been an immigrant, occurring as it did during a period of intense immigrant activity.

VCH 1904: '*Common generally.*'

Silky Wainscot
2391 *Chilodes maritimus* (Tausch.)

Nationally Local

County status: Very local and fairly common at three sites.
Flight: Mid-June to early August.
Larval foodplants: A variety of vegetable and animal matter, feeding on living and dead invertebrates and the inner tissues of dead Common Reed stems.

The Silky Wainscot was first recorded in the County in 1970 at Ufton Fields (LEM). Populations now exist in the reedbeds at Brandon Marsh, Coombe Abbey and Whitacre Heath.

As is the tendency with many wetland species, especially in hot, dry summers, individuals are prone to wander and are occasionally noted in garden moth traps.

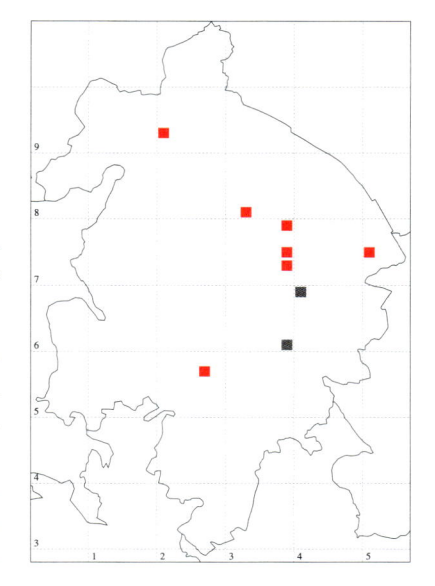

Records:
Ufton Fields, 1970 (LEM); **Charlecote**, 22/6/1976, 17/6/1983, 24/7/2001, 26/6/2003, 20/7/2003, 29/7/2003, 1/8/2003 (AFG, DB); **Marton**, July 1976 (RA); **Radford, Coventry**, 25/7/1985 (MCV); **Ryton Wood**, 1992 (CE, LB); **Hillmorton, Rugby**, 4/8/1992 (DIP); **Brandon Marsh**, 25/7/1992 (3) (Warks Moth Group), 28/6/1993 (DB, CI, RGB, RCK); 4/8/2000 (AFG, Warks Moth Group), 30/7/2005 (8) (Warks Moth Group); **Steetley Meadows**, 18/6/1993 (PC, CW); **Coombe Abbey**, 1/8/1997 (6) (Warks Moth Group); **Whitacre Heath**, 17/7/1999 (3) (Warks Moth Group).

Small Yellow Underwing
2397 *Panemeria tenebrata* (Scop.)

Nationally Local

County status: Fairly widespread and fairly common.
Flight: Day-flying. May to early June.
Larval foodplants: The seed capsules of Common Mouse-ear and Field Mouse-ear.

Despite its small size and erratic flight this day-flying moth has been noted throughout Warwickshire in a variety of grassy habitats, including meadows, road and railway embankments, woodland clearings and disused quarries. Some of the colonies comprise small self-contained populations existing in restricted pockets of flowery grassland such as churchyards. Further fieldwork may prove *tenebrata* to be even more widespread.

VCH 1904: *'Common locally throughout the County.'*

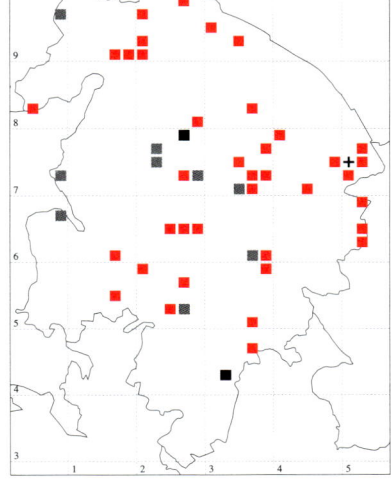

Bordered Sallow
2399 *Pyrrhia umbra* (Hufn.)

Nationally Local

County status: Very local and scarce, but fairly common at one site.
Flight: June and July.
Larval foodplants: The flowers and seeds of rest-harrows.

The Bordered Sallow is associated with calcareous grassland and open woodland. It is fairly common on the vegetated spoilheaps from limestone quarrying at Bishops Hill, but is otherwise rarely seen.

Records:
Wappenbury Wood, 17/7/1965 (MJL); **Sutton Park**, 1960s (JB); **NVRS, Wellesbourne**, 1970 (JAH); **Charlecote**, 14/7/1968, 14/7/1971, 22/7/1972 (3), 5/7/1973, 11/8/1977, 13/8/1977, 26/7/1981, 30/7/1981, 9/7/1983, 13/7/1996, 6/7/1999, 15/7/2003, 3/7/2005 (DB, AFG); **Marton**, July 1976 (RA); **Dosthill**, 28/6/1983 (MAA); **Stockton Cutting**, 27/7/1984 (CDNHSS); **Draycote Water**, 30/7/1984 (AFG); **Royal Leamington Spa**, 9/6/1992 (PhP); **Warwick**, 27/6/2004 (SDT); **Pillerton Priors**, 6/7/2004, 12/7/2005 (CI); **Bishops Hill**, 20/6/2005 (15) (MA, DB, SDT J.Wkn), 14/7/2005 (12) (MA, DB, AJP, NJS); **Cross Hands Quarry**, 9/7/2005 (CI, RGB).

VCH 1904: *'Very rare.'*
Coleshill, Knowle, Overslade.

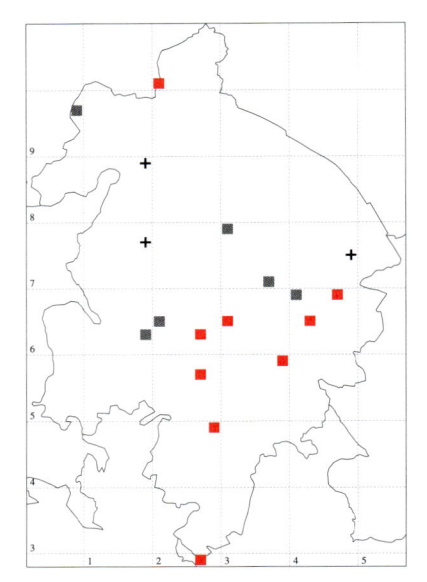

Scarce Bordered Straw
2400 *Helicoverpa armigera* (Hb.)

Regular immigrant, occasionally imported: Southern Europe and North Africa

County status: Regularly observed in recent years.
Flight: May, July to November.
Larval foodplants: In captivity the flowers, leaves and fruits of various plants, including garden *Geranium*, marigold, carnation and Tomato.

The record year for Scarce Bordered Straw was 1996 when approximately 300 were noted in Britain, of which three were caught in Warwickshire. 1992 was the best year locally with a reported seven specimens.

Records:

1859—**Edgbaston, Birmingham**, 11/10 (GTBB).
1976—**Charlecote**, 17/10 (AFG).
1980—**Marton,** 21/9 (GR).
1982—**Charlecote**, 23/9 (DB), 27/9 (AFG).
1985—**Charlecote**, 15/10 (AFG).
1988—**Charlecote**, 9/11 (DB).
1992—**Bearley Station**, 28/5 (IGMR); **Charlecote**, 24/7, 7/8, 21/9 (AFG); **Tile Hill, Coventry**, 30/7 (AJK); **Pillerton Priors**, 7/8 (CI); **Hillmorton, Rugby**, 29/8 (DIP).
1994—**Charlecote**, 29/9 (AFG).
1995—**Charlecote**, 13/10 (AFG).
1996—**Hillmorton, Rugby**, 15/6 (DIP); **Bidford-on-Avon**, 30/8 (RMC); **Charlecote**, 29/9, 19/10, 1/11 (AFG);
Solihull, 30/9 (AP); **Kenilworth Road, Coventry**, 23/10 (MA).
1998—**Charlecote**, 27/9 (DB), 6/10 (AFG), 7/10 (2) (AFG, DB).
1999—**Charlecote**, 13/9 (AFG), 14/9 (DB), 9/10 (AFG).
2000—**Charlecote**, 29/9, 30/9 (AFG).
2003—**Charlecote**, 21/8 (DB); **Rugby**, 20/9 (IGMR).
2004—**Bidford-on-Avon**, 1/8 (RMC); **Charlecote**, 10/9 (DB); **Hillmorton, Rugby,** 1/11 (DIP).
2005—**Tile Hill, Coventry**, 11/10 (AJK). **Charlecote,** 23/10 (DB). **Guys Cliffe, Warwick,** 26/10 (MWsh).

Bordered Straw
2403 *Heliothis peltigera* ([D. & S.])

Regular immigrant, occasionally common: Southern Europe and North Africa

County status: Regular immigrant.
Flight: May to September.
Larval foodplants: The flowers of garden marigolds, Common Restharrow and others.

The Bordered Straw has been recorded more times over the years in Warwickshire than the preceding species, and similarly enjoyed good years in 1992 and 1996.

Records:

1947—**Tysoe**, 11/8 (TT).
1958—**Erdington, Birmingham**, (LJE); **Mappleborough Green**, 18/5 (FHL).
1963—**Solihull**, 16/7 (JSB)
1968—**Charlecote**, 2/7, 9/7 (DB).
1970—**NRVS, Wellesbourne**, 5/8 (RAW).
1975—**Charlecote**, 12/8 (DB).
1981—**Dosthill**, (RJT); **Gravel Pit, Charlecote**, 4/10 disturbed in daytime (DB, AFG).
1984—**Marton**, 1/8 (RA).
1986—**Bidford-on-Avon**, 9/7 (RMC); **Marton**, 21/7 (RA).
1987—**Shottery, Stratford-upon-Avon**, 20/7 (RGB).
1992—**Bidford-on-Avon**, 22/5–27/5 (4) (RMC); **Royal Leamington Spa**, 23/5 (PhP); **Bearley Station**, 28/5 (IGMR); **Charlecote**, 28/5, 29/5 (DB, AFG); **Shottery, Stratford-upon-Avon**, 15/8 (RGB); **Hillmorton, Rugby**, 28/8 (DIP).

1994—**Charlecote**, 1/6 (AFG), 10/9, 11/9 (DB);
Tile Hill, Coventry, 26/8 (AJK);
Radford, Coventry, 27/8 (MCV);
Sutton Park, 2/9 (MCV).
1996—**Radford, Coventry**, 9/6, 10/6 (MCV);
Charlecote, 9/6–12/7 (14) (AFG, DB), 5/8–24/8 (7) (AFG, DB), 1/9–18/9 (3) (AFG);
Walsgrave, Coventry, June (TRG);
Tile Hill, Coventry, 6/6 (AJK);
Hillmorton, Rugby, 15/6, 19/8 (DIP);
Solihull, 15/6 (AWD);
Hampton Magna, 17/6 (PJR);
Kenilworth Road, Coventry, 19/6 (MA);
Bidford-on-Avon, 18/8 (RMC).
1997—**Hillmorton, Rugby**, 19/8 (DIP).
2000—**Radford, Coventry**, 19/6 (MCV);
Charlecote, 23/6 (2), 22/9 (DB).
2001—**Rugby**, 11/10 (IGMR).
2002—**Charlecote**, 28/6 (DB);
Rugby, 9/9 (IGMR).
2003—**Charlecote**, 17/6–29/6 (3), 3/7, 1/8–17/8 (3), 14/9, 30/9 (DB, AFG);
Rugby, 7/8 (IGMR);
Bidford-on-Avon, 9/8 (RMC);
Tile Hill, Coventry, 27/8 (AJK);
Radford, Coventry, 2/9, 8/9 (MCV).
2004—**Sydenham, Royal Leamington Spa**, 10/9 (MK).

Marbled White Spot
2410 *Protodeltote pygarga* (Hufn.)

County status: Very local and uncommon.
Flight: June to August.
Larval foodplants: Grasses such as False Brome.

Oversley Wood is the only woodland site with recent records of this species. Occasional specimens in garden moth traps may be a clue to the presence of undetected colonies elsewhere.

Records:
Bickenhill, 1940s annually (GPS); **Waverley Wood**, 24/6/1941 (RFB), 6/7/1954 (AHK); **Coleshill Bog**, 1955–56 several on trunks of hawthorn and pine (SEWC), 1960s (LJE); **NVRS, Wellesbourne**, 6/8/1970 (RAW); **Charlecote**, 19/7/1981 (DB), 29/6/1986, 1/7/1998 (AFG), 11/7/2005 (DB); **Hillmorton, Rugby**, 10/7/1985, 1/7/1986, 3/7/1993 (DIP); **Solihull**, 12/6/2003, 14/6/2004 (RL); **Oversley Wood**, 7/6/2004 (RMC, DG, AJP), 20/7/2004 (DG, AJP, NJS), 4/6/2005 (Warks Moth Group), 18/6/2005 (DG, AJP, VW); **Temple Grafton**, 18/6/2005, 19/6/2005, 23/6/2005 (AFG); **Pillerton Priors**, 3/7/2005 (CI).

VCH 1904: *'Twice recorded at Waverley Wood in 1882.'*

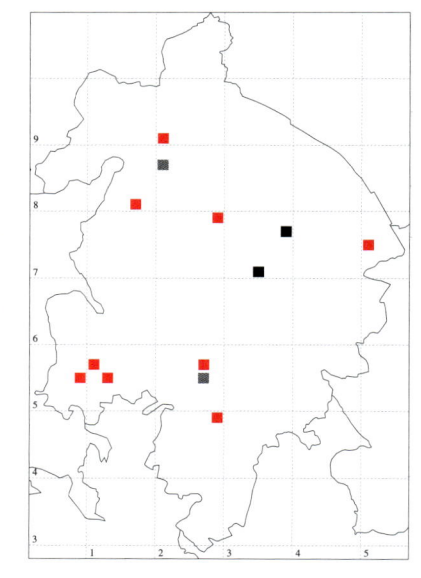

Silver Barred
2413 *Deltote bankiana* (Fabr.)

RDB

County status: Extinct.
Flight: No dates available.
Larval foodplants: Purple Moor-grass, Smooth Meadow-grass and other grasses.

VCH 1904: *'Very rare', Bubbenhall Wood, Waverley Wood.*

Cream-bordered Green Pea
2418 *Earias clorana* (L.)

Nationally Scarce B

County status: Very local and scarce.
Flight: June and July.
Larval foodplants: Sallows, willows and Osier.

The Cream-bordered Green Pea was first recorded at Brandon Marsh on 24/6/1994 (CW, PC) in a typical wetland habitat with an abundance of larval foodplants.

Four specimens caught more recently in static garden moth traps suggest further undetected colonies.

Records:
Brandon Marsh, 24/6/1994 (CW, PC); **Charlecote**, 28/7/2002, 10/6/2004 (DB); **Hillmorton**, **Rugby**, 29/6/2005 (PN); **Warwick**, 27/8/2005 (SDT).

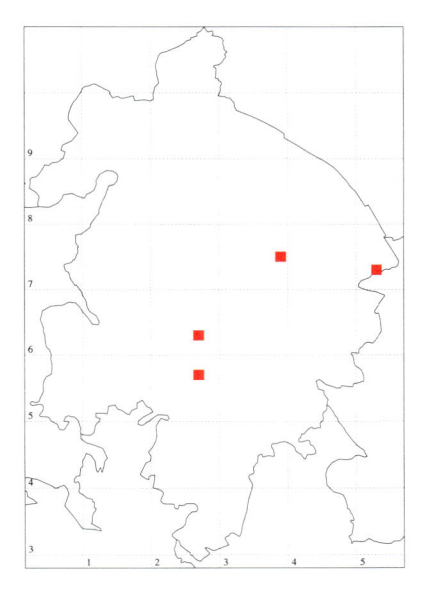

Scarce Silver-lines
2421 *Bena bicolorana* (Fuess.)

Nationally Local

County status: Widespread and fairly common.
Flight: Late June to early August.
Larval foodplants: Oaks* and occasionally birches.

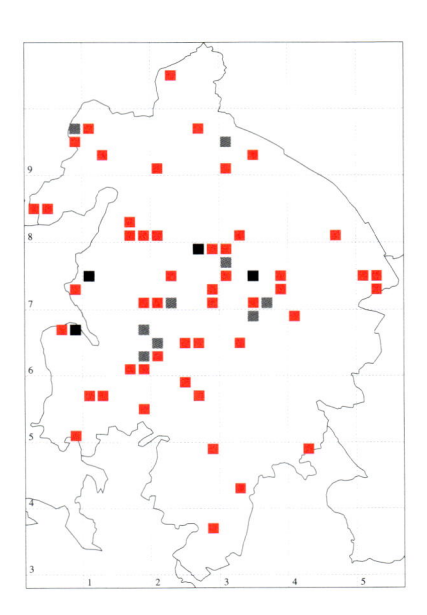

Scarce Silver-lines is most frequently seen in broadleaved woodland containing mature oak. Locations include Ryton Wood, Wappenbury Wood, Waverley Wood, Clowes Wood, Hay Wood, Snitterfield Bushes and Oversley Wood. The moth is also found in open countryside near ancient hedgerows containing isolated oaks, parkland and gardens. It is surprisingly able to exist in urban parts of Coventry and has been noted in a garden moth trap at Radford on 15 occasions between 1971 and 2004 (MCV).

There was no mention of this handsome moth in the VCH 1904 and the earliest records appear to be from Tile Hill Wood and Clowes Wood during the 1930s (CDNHSS, BNHS).

Green Silver-lines
2422 *Pseudoips prasinana britannica* (Warr.)

County status: Widespread and fairly common; presently increasing.
Flight: May to July.
Larval foodplants: Usually oaks*, birches* and Beech, but sometimes Hazel, Sweet Chestnut, Aspen and elm.

In addition to the localities mentioned for the Scarce Silver-lines this species is also well established at Brandon Wood, Bentley Park Wood, Kingsbury Wood, Ufton Wood, Coughton Park, Rough Hill Wood, Wolford Wood and many other sites. The Green Silver-lines has a larger range of foodplants and is consequently the commoner of the two species. There is evidence of a general increase in numbers (Fig. 31) and a record 16 imagines were attracted to light at Oversley Wood, 7/6/2004 (RMC, DG, AJP).

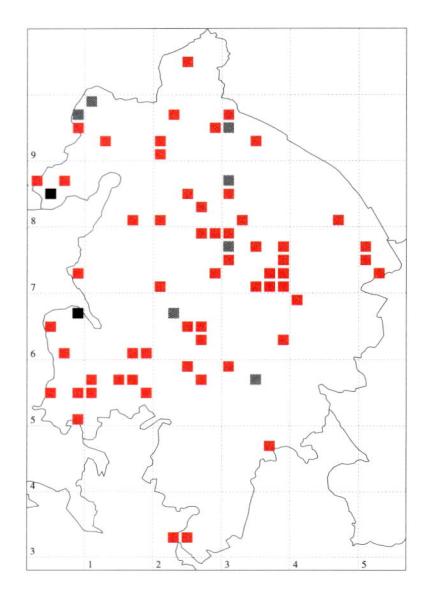

As with Scarce Silver-lines, examples have been noted in urban Coventry (Radford) but not since 1992 (MCV). Although this species is not mentioned in the VCH 1904 it was included in A. Sidgwick's 1893 list for the Rugby district.

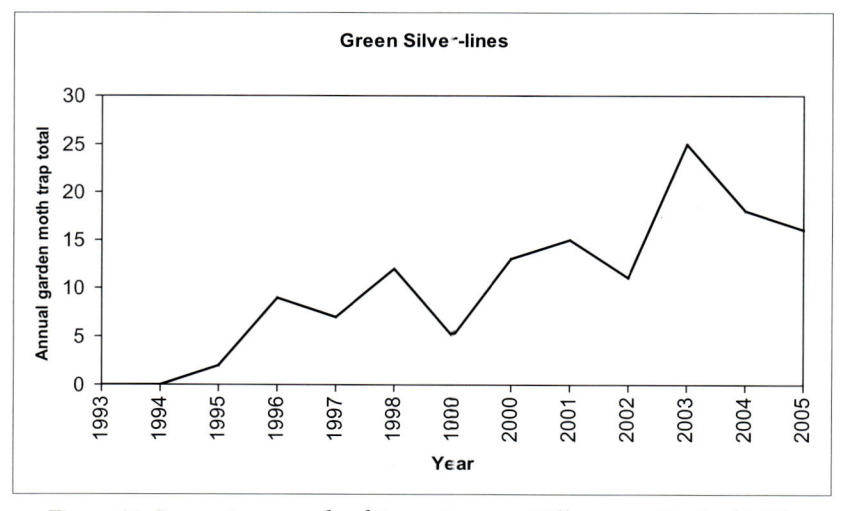

Figure 31. Increasing records of *P. prasinana* at Hillmorton, Rugby (DIP).

Oak Nycteoline
2423 *Nycteola revayana* (Scop.)

Nationally Local

County status: Fairly widespread but uncommon.
Flight: Probably two generations. Most frequent after hibernation in late March and again during July, but has been recorded in every month of the year.
Larval foodplants: Oaks*.

The Oak Nycteoline was first noted in the County at Umberslade on 19/10/1935 (SEWC). This species is possibly overlooked due to its variations and resemblance to a tortricid and may well have a wider distribution than the map suggests. Associated with woodlands, parks and hedgerows containing oaks.

It is occasionally recorded at light in small numbers; for example, Wellesbourne Wood, 28/3/1998 (4) (DB), but usually observed as singletons. A very variable moth with dark forms predominating in Warwickshire.

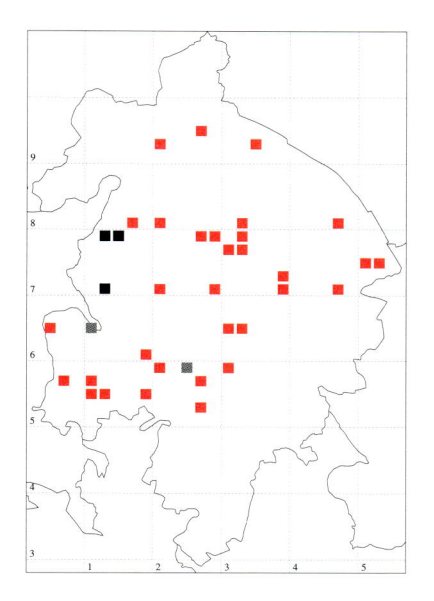

Nut-tree Tussock
2425 *Colocasia coryli* (L.)

County status: Very local and scarce.
Flight: May to mid-July.
Larval foodplants: Birches, Beech, Hazel, oaks, Field Maple and other broadleaved trees.

The Nut-tree Tussock, a species of broadleaved woodland, is surprisingly rare in Warwickshire considering that it is locally plentiful in the neighbouring counties of Worcestershire, Gloucestershire and Oxfordshire. There are no recent records from Ryton Wood despite much fieldwork. The discovery of a colony in Wolford Wood in 2005 gives hope of further undetected colonies in the south of the County.

Records:
Oversley Wood, 1961–1970 (GCG, WTT), 26/5/2005 (J. Rush); **Ryton Wood**, 15/5/1992 (LB, CE), 7/6/1992 (AJK); **Sydenham**, **Royal Leamington Spa**, 11/7/2004 (MK); **Wolford Wood**, 21/5/2005 (2) (RMC, AJP).

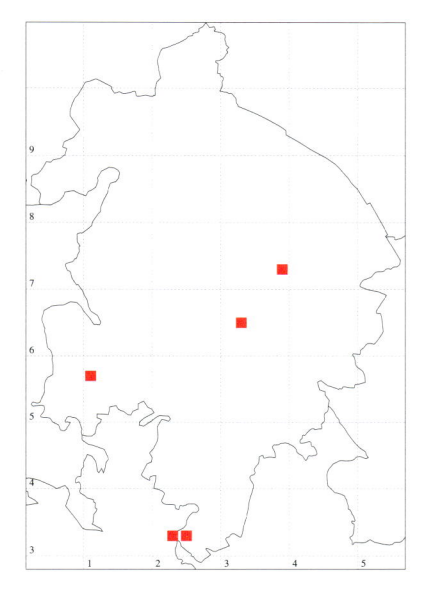

Ni Moth
2432 *Trichoplusia ni* (Hb.)

Scarce but regular immigrant: Southern Europe and North Africa

County status: Scarce immigrant.
Flight: June, August and September.
Larval foodplants: Garden Marigold and abroad many other plants.

The Ni Moth was first noted in Warwickshire in 1982 and this remains its best year locally with five records.

Records:
1982—**Hartshill Hayes** 17/9 (RJT);
    Charlecote 18/9, 19/9 (DB; Brown, 1982);
    Radford, Coventry 19/9 (MCV);
    Marton 20/9 (RA).
1985—**Pailton** 27/9 netted at dusk (KCG).
1992—**Pillerton Priors** 2/8 (CI).
1996—**Charlecote** 11/6, 23/6 (DB), 9/8 (AFG);
    Tile Hill, Coventry 22/8 (AJK).

Slender Burnished Brass
2433 *Thysanoplusia orichalcea* (Fabr.)

Rare immigrant: Mediterranean and North Africa

County status: Very rare immigrant.
Flight: July
Larval foodplants: In captivity Woody Nightshade, Potato and Tomato plants.

A female of this rare immigrant was captured in a Heath trap operated on an area of wasteland at Stratford-upon-Avon, 30/7/1983 (RGB), one of 10 to be recorded in Great Britain during 1983. A perfect specimen, and a gravid female, from which many offspring were successfully bred for the first time from a British immigrant (Brown & Gardner, 1984).

Burnished Brass
2434 *Diachrysia chrysitis* (L.)

County status: Widespread and fairly common.
Flight: Two generations. June to early August, and late August to early October.
Larval foodplants: Common Nettle and other herbaceous plants.

The Burnished Brass is plentiful in a diversity of habitats in rural and urban districts. The second brood, occurring from late August to early October, is only partial, considerably smaller numbers being involved than in the main generation. Very late individuals are sometimes noted; for example, Kenilworth Road, Coventry, 19/10/2001 (MA).

Garden moth trap records at **Hillmorton, Rugby**, are as follows: 1982 (261), 1985 (47), 1990 (175), 1995 (154), 2000 (31), 2004 (17), 2005 (57) (DIP).

VCH 1904: '*Throughout the County, not uncommon.*'

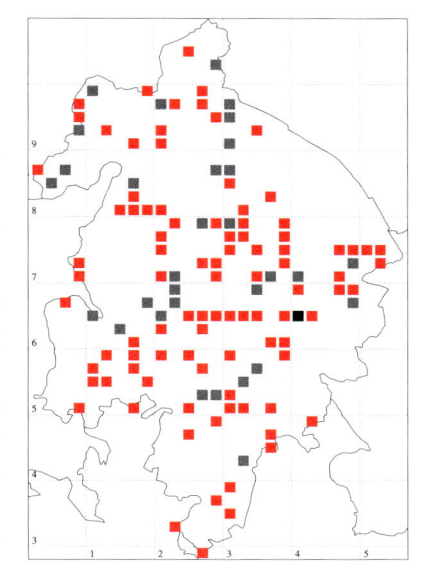

Dewick's Plusia
2436 *Macdunnoughia confusa* (Steph.)

Scarce immigrant: Southern, central and northern Europe

County status: Rare immigrant.
Flight: August to October.
Larval foodplants: In captivity Common Nettle, wormwoods and other herbaceous plants.

Three examples of this scarce immigrant have been caught in Warwickshire. The 1983 individual was netted feeding on Sow-thistle flowers in sunshine.

Records:
1977—**Marton,** 24/10 (GR; Gardner, 1978).
1983—**Stockton Cutting,** 31/8 (DW).
1991—**Bearley Station,** 4/9 (IGMR; Brown, 1992).

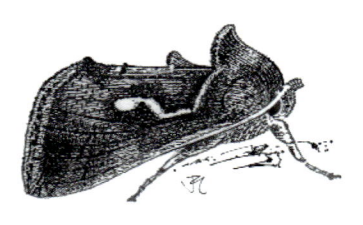

Golden Plusia
2437 *Polychrysia moneta* (Fabr.)

County status: Fairly widespread but becoming uncommon.
Flight: June to early August with occasional individuals in September.
Larval foodplants: Garden Delphinium* and Monks'-hood*.

The Golden Plusia was first recorded in Britain in 1890, following a northward expansion of its range in mainland Europe; it subsequently spread throughout England and Wales. The earliest Warwickshire records were from Brandon Wood on 6/7/1938 (LF) and Mappleborough Green in 1940 (FHL). By the mid-1950s *moneta* had increased in abundance and 125 were recorded between 1954 and 1958 at Edgbaston, Birmingham (FAN).

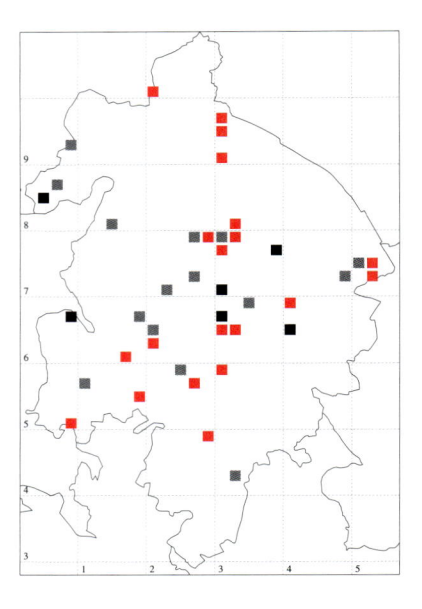

During the 1960s and early 1970s it became fairly widespread in the County, frequenting gardens with Monk's-hood and *Delphinium*. Since 1990 there has been a noticeable decline in most districts. Garden moth trap records from **Hillmorton, Rugby**, (DIP) provide an example of this:
1982 (16), 1985 (33), 1990 (18), 1995 (14), 2000 (1), 2004 (1), 2005 (5).

Gold Spot
2439 *Plusia festucae* (L.)

County status: Fairly widespread but generally uncommon.
Flight: Two overlapping generations. June to mid-August, and late August to September.
Larval foodplants: Various sedges, grasses and other plants, including Yellow Iris.

The Gold Spot is thinly distributed over a fairly wide area of the County; it appears to have small populations in damp areas near watercourses and in moist woodland and heathland. Larger concentrations are known to be present at Brandon Marsh, Alvecote Pools and Middleton Hall.

The adult is an occasional visitor to garden moth traps, especially those situated in river valleys.

VCH 1904: *'One record only from Sutton Park and Wolford.'*

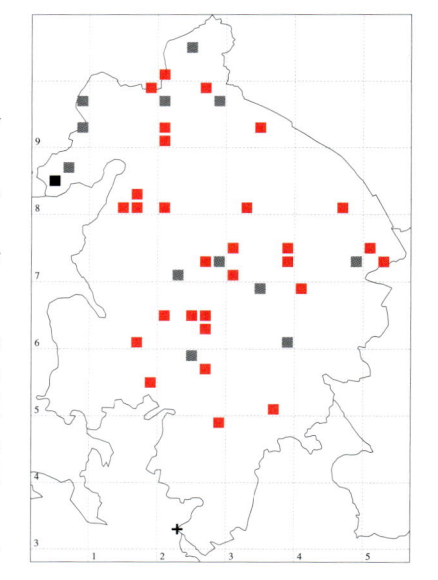

Silver Y
2441 *Autographa gamma* (L.)

Common immigrant, sometimes abundant: Europe and North Africa

County status: Annual immigrant. Often common.
Flight: Several generations. May to October.
Larval foodplants: Polyphagous on herbaceous plants.

The Silver Y is an annual immigrant to Warwickshire, sometimes in large quantities. Peak numbers are usually observed in late August; numbers are often augmented by local breeding and further incursions during the autumn. Individuals have occasionally been noted during the winter; for example, Charlecote, 6/1/1989, 2/12/1994, 9/12/1999 (DB).

VCH 1904: '*Abundant.*'

Beautiful Golden Y
2442 *Autographa pulchrina* (Haw.)

County status: Widespread but becoming uncommon.
Flight: Late May to August.
Larval foodplants: Herbaceous plants, including Common Nettle and Common Ragwort.

The Beautiful Golden Y is found in a vast range of habitats, including woodland, gardens and all types of grassland.

There is evidence of a decline in numbers over the last 20 years. The following garden moth trap results highlight declining numbers:
Hillmorton, Rugby, 1982 (121), 1985 (6) 1990 (33), 1995 (11), 2000 (2), 2004 (0), 2005 (2) (DIP).

VCH 1904: '*Not uncommon throughout the County.*'

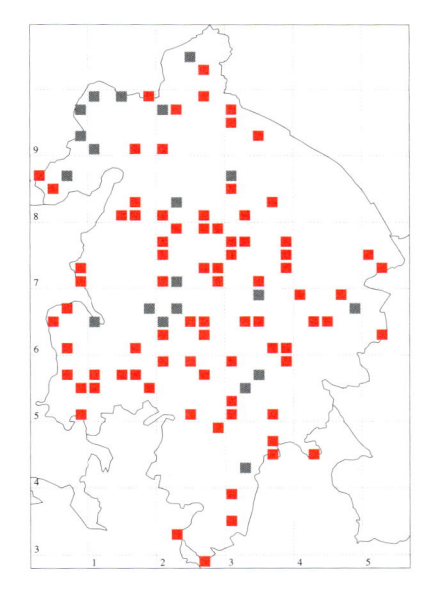

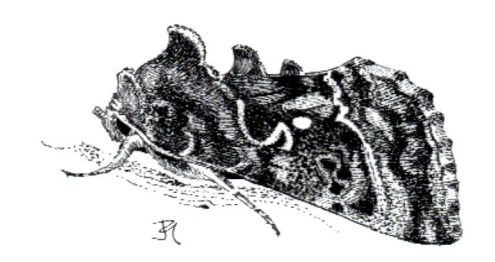

Plain Golden Y
2443 *Autographa jota* (L.)

County status: Widespread and fairly common. Declining.
Flight: Early June to early August
Larval foodplants: Herbaceous plants, including Common Nettle, White and Red Dead-nettles.

The Plain Golden Y is generally more plentiful than *pulchrina* but has also experienced a decline in numbers during the last decade. It is found in a wide range of habitats, from woodlands to gardens.

Garden moth trap figures are as follows:
Hillmorton, Rugby: 1982 (212), 1985 (106), 1990 (69), 1995 (61), 2000 (17), 2004 (5), 2005 (4) (DIP).

VCH 1904: '*Not uncommon throughout the County.*'

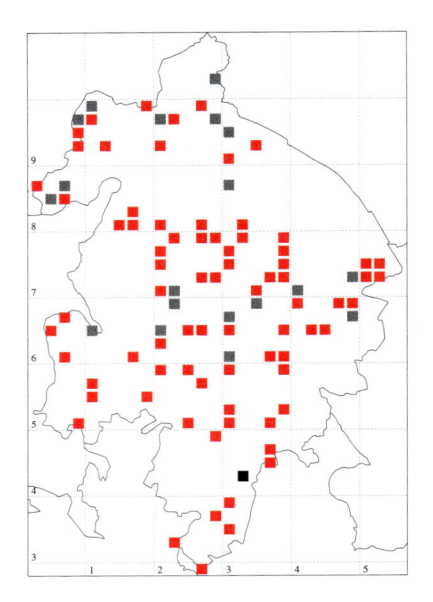

Gold Spangle
2444 *Autographa bractea* ([D. & S.])

County status: Status uncertain. No recent records.
Flight: July to early August.
Larval foodplants: Various herbaceous plants, including Common Nettle* and White Dead-nettle.

The Gold Spangle is a resident species in Scotland, Ireland, Wales and northern England. Warwickshire marks the southern extent of its distribution, which fluctuates periodically. During the 1970s this attractive moth was caught frequently in mid-Warwickshire, but has since contracted northwards and consequently there have been no records since 1994.

An out of season specimen was caught on 2/9/1993 at Hillmorton, Rugby (DIP).

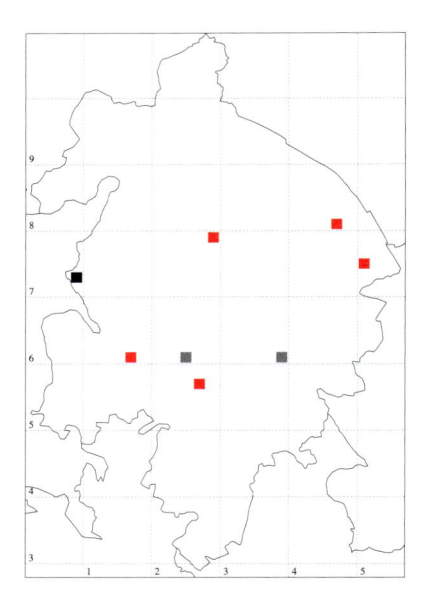

Records:
Clowes Wood, 1946 larva on Common Nettle (HR); **Charlecote**, 10/7/1973, 14/7/1973 (DB), 5/8/1981, 12/7/1982 (AFG); **Ufton Fields**, 2/8/1974 (AFG); **Hampton Wood**, 4/7/1975 (AFG); **Hillmorton, Rugby**, 22/7/1981, 2/9/1993 (DIP); **Pailton**, 1987 (KCG); **Tile Hill, Coventry**, 6/7/1988 (AJK); **Bearley Station**, 5/8/1994 (IGMR).

Scarce Silver Y
2447 *Syngrapha interrogationis* (L.)
Resident (Nationally Local) and occasional immigrant: Northern Europe
County status: Very rare immigrant.
Flight: August.
Larval foodplants: Heather and Bilberry.

The Scarce Silver Y is a resident species in northern and western Britain but occurs very occasionally in southern and eastern England as an immigrant. It was therefore of some surprise that a specimen of the Continental form was caught in a garden moth trap at Shottery, Stratford-upon-Avon, on 4/8/1995 (RGB). There was considerable immigrant activity at the time with other examples of Continental *interrogationis* reported from Hampshire, Nottinghamshire and Norfolk (Skinner & Parsons, 1998).

Dark Spectacle
2449 *Abrostola triplasia* (L.)

County status: Very local and scarce.
Flight: May to June and mid-July to early September.
Larval foodplants: Common Nettle* and Hop.

The Dark Spectacle was formerly found over a large part of Warwickshire in a variety of open and wooded habitats, including gardens. It has suffered a dramatic decline during the last three decades and is now only very occasionally observed.

Records since 1970:
Charlecote, 22/7/1972, 11/8/1977, 2/8/2002 (DB); **Hampton Wood**, 18/7/1974 (AFG); **Kingsbury**, 1976 (KEH); **Chapelfields, Coventry**, 3/8/1982 (CW); **Middleton Hall**, 9/7/2005 (R&SW); **Solihull**, 9/7/2005 (RL).

VCH 1904: *'Not common.'*
Yardley, Knowle, Overslade, Atherstone, Wolford.

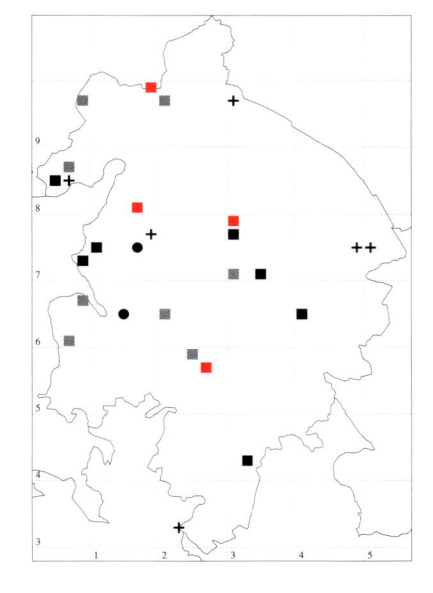

Spectacle
2450 *Abrostola tripartita* (Hufn.)

County status: Widespread and fairly common.
Flight: Two overlapping generations. Mid-April to mid-September.
Larval foodplants: Common Nettle*.

The Spectacle, in contrast to the last species, seems to have become more plentiful and widespread since 1980. It is found in all types of habitats where the foodplant, Common Nettle, grows.

Numbers at garden moth traps in built-up districts are as follows:
Radford, Coventry: 1982 (9), 1985 (8), 1990 (7), 1995 (20), 2000 (41), 2004 (39) (MCV);
Hillmorton, Rugby: 1982 (133), 1985 (62), 1990 (90), 1995 (137), 2000 (50), 2004 (103) (DIP).

VCH 1904: '*Not common.*'
Yardley, Knowle, Overslade, Atherstone, Wolford.

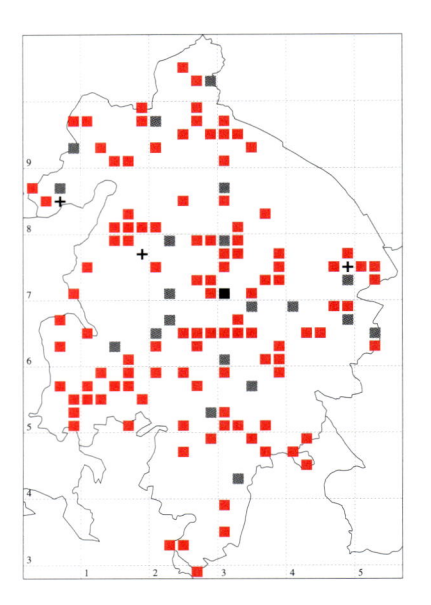

Clifden Nonpareil
2451 *Catocala fraxini* (L.)

Scarce immigrant and transitory resident: Northern, central and southern Europe

County status: Very rare immigrant.
Flight: August and September.
Larval foodplants: Aspen.

This magnificent moth has only been recorded twice in Warwickshire with a gap of 122 years separating the two captures. The most recent, a male, was found resting on a garden wall illuminated by MV at Southcrest, Redditch, on 14/9/2002 (AFG). During that week there had been a major influx of Scandinavian immigrants, including the third Eastern Nycteoline *Nycteola asiatica* (Krul.) for the British Isles at Spurn, East Yorkshire (Spence, 2003).

Records:
1880—**Lower Hillmorton Road, Rugby,** 31/8 specimen taken at sugar (TWW; Wratislaw, 1880).
2002—**Southcrest, Redditch,** 14/9 (AFG).

Red Underwing
2452 *Catocala nupta* (L.)

County status: Widespread and usually fairly common.
Flight: August to October.
Larval foodplants: Willows*, poplars* and Aspen.

The Red Underwing is widely distributed throughout the County and is particularly plentiful in river valleys. This species is less common in built-up districts, where it is associated with poplars growing in recreation parks and waste-ground. Frequently encountered during the daytime at rest on palings, tree trunks, and walls.

VCH 1904: *'Not common.'*
Hampton-in-Arden, Knowle, Rugby, Warwick, Baddesley Clinton, Wolford.

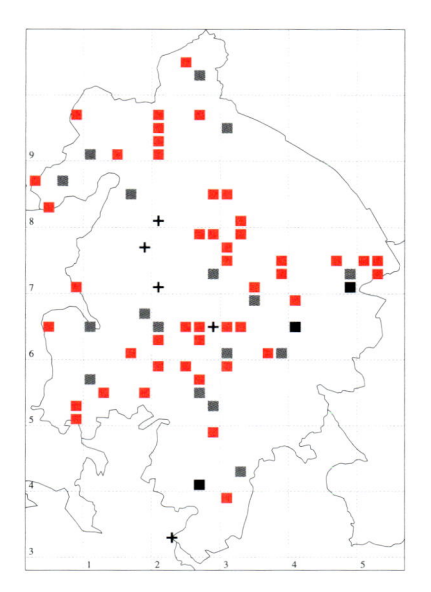

Light Crimson Underwing
2454 *Catocala promissa* ([D. & S.])

RDB

County status: Extinct.
Flight: No dates available.
Larval foodplants: Pedunculate Oak.

VCH 1904: *Brandon Wood 1888.*

Dark Crimson Underwing
2455 *Catocala sponsa* (L.)

RDB

County status: Extinct.
Flight: No dates available.
Larval foodplants: Pedunculate Oak.

VCH 1904: *Wolford Wood.*

Mother Shipton
2462 *Callistege mi* (Cl.)

County status: Widespread and locally fairly common.
Flight: Day-flying. May to early July.
Larval foodplants: Clovers, trefoils and Black Medick.

Mother Shipton is found in a varied range of grassy habitats, including woodland rides at Brandon and Ryton Wood, and heathland at Grendon Common and Sutton Park. It is, however, most plentiful on railway embankments with a calcareous flora, disused quarries and vegetated spoilheaps.

VCH 1904: *'Recorded from most parts of the County but local.'*

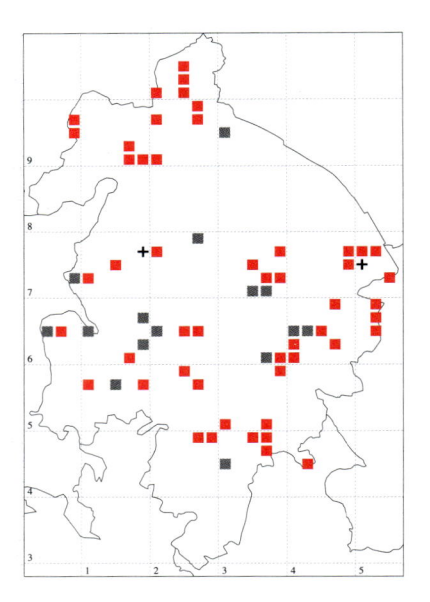

Burnet Companion
2463 *Euclidia glyphica* (L.)

County status: Fairly widespread and locally fairly common.
Flight: Day-flying. Mid-May to early July.
Larval foodplants: Clovers, trefoils, vetches and Black Medick.

The Burnet Companion is locally fairly common on calcareous grassland. The adult becomes very active in warm sunshine and is easily disturbed during overcast, humid weather, embarking on short rapid flights before resettling. Bishops Hill and Ashlawn Cutting contain particularly healthy populations.

VCH 1904: *'Usually occurs with Mother Shipton, but there are fewer records for it.'*

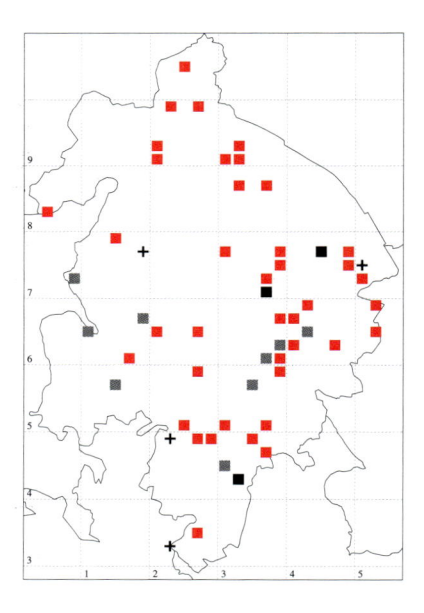

Four-spotted
2465 *Tyta luctuosa* ([D. & S.])

Nationally Scarce A

County status: Extinct. Formerly very local.
Flight: Two generations. May and August.
Larval foodplants: Field Bindweed.

The Four-spotted began to decline nationally in the 1950s and 1960s, which was reflected in Warwickshire. It was formerly very restricted with colonies on calcareous grassland at Wilmcote Rough and Bishops Itchington Quarry.

A small population on rough pasture at Mappleborough Green suffered habitat destruction in the late 1950s.

Records:
Wilmcote Rough, 1939–41 (SEWC); **Harbury and Bishops Itchington Quarries,** 17/5/1951 (AHK); **Mappleborough Green,** 7/8/1957 (FHL).

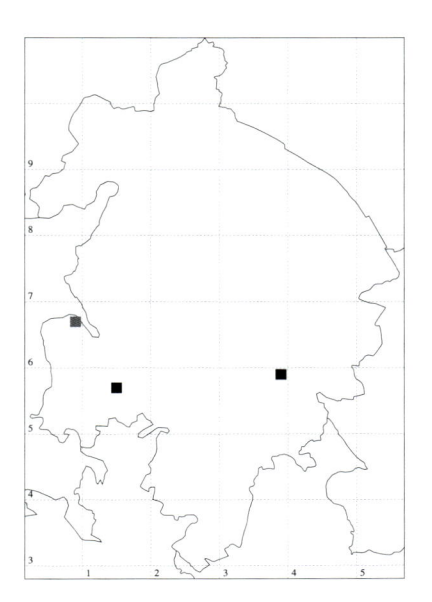

Blackneck
2466 *Lygephila pastinum* (Treit.)

Nationally Local

County status: Fairly widespread and locally fairly common.
Flight: Mid-June to late July.
Larval foodplants: Tufted Vetch*.

Colonies of Blackneck can be found in two types of habitat in Warwickshire—calcareous grassland and woodland rides. The species is well established in disused railway cuttings at Goldicote Cutting, Oxhouse Farm, Combrook and Ashlawn Cutting, with good numbers being recorded at the latter site; for example, 21/6/1997 (10) (Warks Moth Group).

Woodland populations occur at Clowes Wood and Kingsbury Wood, where three were recorded on 23/6/1989 (Warks Moth Group).

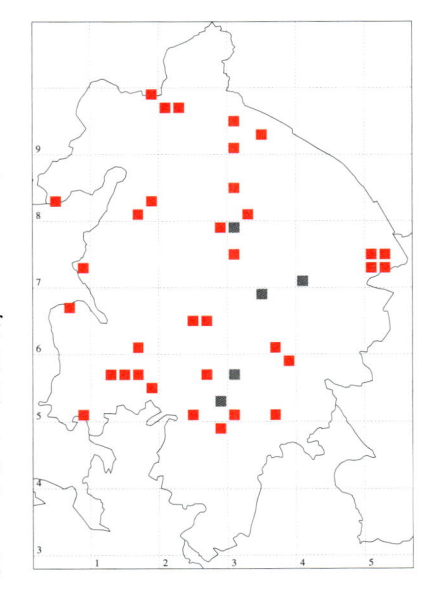

Stray individuals are occasionally noted in garden moth traps at distances from known colonies, usually during hot weather.

There was no mention of this species in the VCH 1904 and the earliest record is from Wilmcote Rough in 1928 (SEWC), where reasonable numbers are still present; for example, 10/7/1998 (6) (Warks Moth Group).

Herald
2469 *Scoliopteryx libatrix* (L.)

County status: Widespread and fairly common.
Flight: July to late October and, after hibernation April to June.
Larval foodplants: Poplars*, including Western Balsam Poplar*, willows* and sallows*.

The Herald is found throughout the County in both rural and urban areas. It is particularly plentiful in broadleaved woodlands and willow-lined river banks. Numbers have often been observed huddled together in outbuildings; for example, six in a wooden shed at Chesterton Wood on 15/8/1992 (Warks Moth Group).

Confirmation that the species is bivoltine in Warwickshire was provided with the discovery of fully grown larvae on coppiced poplar in August 2004 at Newbold Comyn (JWkn), and on Purple Willow at Lillington, Royal Leamington Spa (EMR), producing offspring in October.

VCH 1904: '*Generally distributed and fairly common.*'

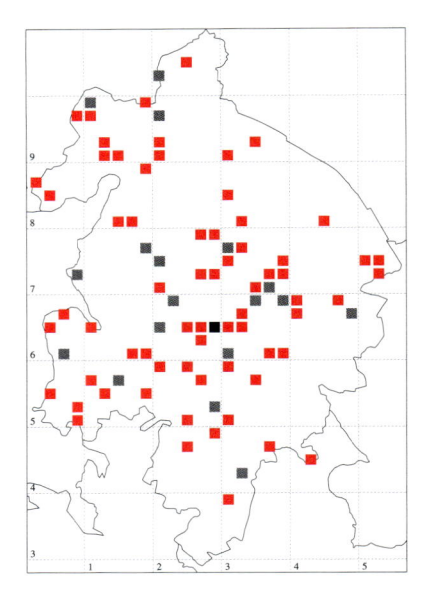

Small Purple-barred
2470 *Phytometra viridaria* (Cl.)

Nationally Local

County status: Status uncertain. No recent records.
Flight: Mainly day-flying. Late May to July.
Larval foodplants: Milkworts.

The Small Purple-barred has not been recorded in Warwickshire since the 1970s and its status is uncertain. Frequenting calcareous grassland and heathy woodland, this diminutive species is easily overlooked.

Records:
Brandon Wood, 20/6/1889 (RNHS); **May's Wood,** 1920s annually (GBM); **Clowes Wood,** 1938–53 (SEWC); **Wilmcote Rough,** 1916 common (SEWC), 1977 (JMP), 17/6/1972 (DB, RHS); **Nelson's Quarry, Stockton,** 1970s (RHS).

VCH 1904: '*Common at Knowle, Coleshill, Sutton Park and Wolford Wood.*'

Beautiful Hook-tip
2473 *Laspeyria flexula* ([D. & S.])

Nationally Local

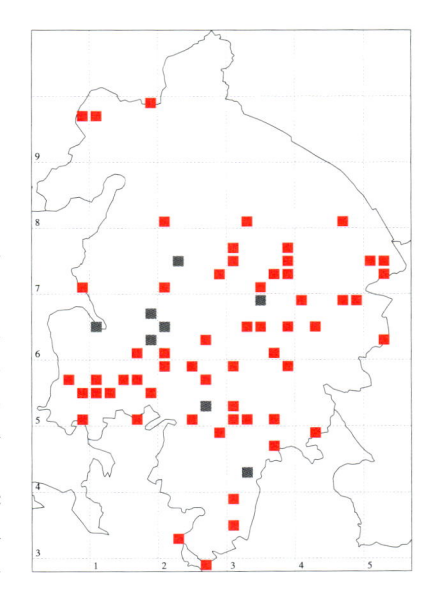

County status: Widespread and locally fairly common.
Flight: June to mid-August.
Larval foodplants: Lichens growing on twigs and branches of trees.

The Beautiful Hook-tip favours damp woodlands with plentiful lichens. Typical sites include Brandon Marsh, Sutton Park, Ryton Wood, Waverley Wood, Wellesbourne Wood, Bowshot Wood, Snitterfield Bushes and Hampton Wood.

Some orchards and gardens also provide suitable conditions for breeding and the adult visits MV in small numbers. A particularly late individual was caught on 18/10/1997 at Hillmorton, Rugby (DIP).

The following garden moth trap counts from **Kenilworth Road, Coventry**, give an illustration of frequency: 2001 (7), 2002 (3), 2003 (12), 2004 (18), 2005 (6) (MA).

VCH 1904: *Rugby only.*

Straw Dot
2474 *Rivula sericealis* (Scop.)

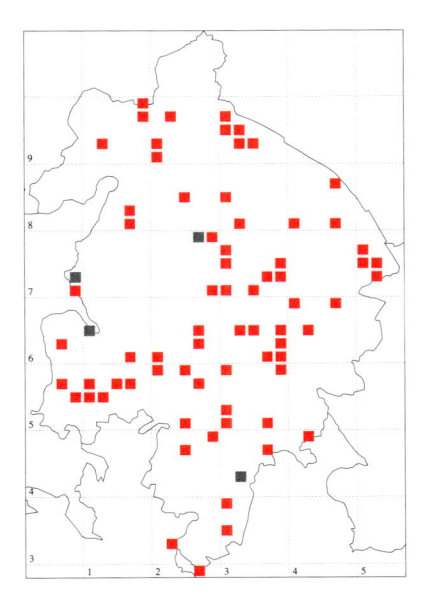

County status: Widespread and fairly common.
Flight: Two generations. June to late July, and August to October.
Larval foodplants: Grasses, including False Brome.

Similar to the preceding species, the Straw Dot had only been observed as a singleton from Rugby in the VCH 1904. It continued to be very local and uncommon during the first half of the twentieth century with records from Wainbody Wood in 1956 (ANT), Clowes Wood on 6/7/1956 (HEH) and Ufton Wood, (1959 Survey). A slow resurgence began during the 1960s with sightings at Tysoe (TT) and Bannam's Wood (FAN). The momentum continued into the 1970s as colonies were discovered at Oakley Wood, Oversley Wood (DB), Hampton Wood (AFG) and Tile Hill Wood (DB).

During the next 30 years the Straw Dot multiplied and dispersed to become increasingly widespread in a diverse range of grassy habitats throughout the County. Moth trap totals highlight a further escalation in numbers:

Hillmorton, Rugby: 1986 (1), 1995 (0), 2000 (0), 2004 (45), 2005 (71) (DIP).

VCH 1904: *Rugby (one).*

Waved Black
2475 *Parascotia fuliginaria* (L.)

Nationally Scarce B

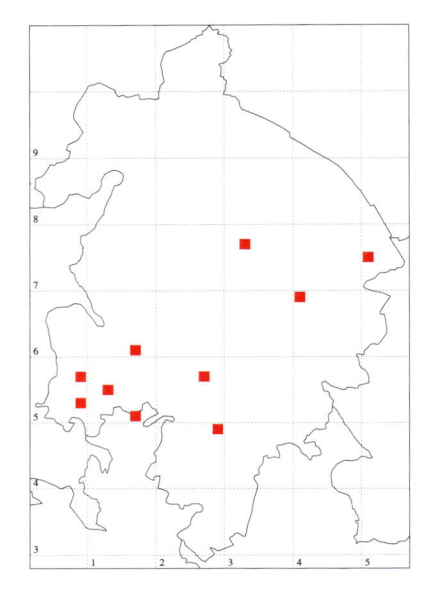

County status: Very local and uncommon.
Flight: July and August.
Larval foodplants: Various fungi growing on fallen logs, tree stumps and rotting timber.

The Waved Black was considered a great rarity in the nineteenth century and associated with the dockland area of London. During the first part of the twentieth century its range extended into many of the neighbouring counties. The species continued to progress northward and was first noted in Warwickshire in 1984 at Marton, near Rugby (RA), but was not observed again in the County for a further seven years. Suspected to be breeding on bracket fungi growing on a stored pile of birch logs, adults were attracted to MV at Bearley Station during the early 1990s (IGMR).

It has subsequently been seen with increasing regularity at widely separated sites, showing that the Waved Black is slowly becoming established.

Records:
Marton, July 1984 (RA); **Bearley Station**, 27/7/1991, 6/7/1993, 21/7/1995 (IGMR); **Rugby**, 27/7/1998 (IGMR); **Bidford-on-Avon**, 9/7/2003 (RMC); **Charlecote**, 19/7/2003 (AFG); **Pillerton Priors**, 14/7/2003, 6/7/2004, 11/7/2004 (CI); **The Greenway, Stratford-upon-Avon**, 10/7/2004 (RGB); **Alcester**, 21/7/2004 (MPW); **Temple Grafton**, 31/7/2004, 11/7/2005, 21/7/2005, 2/8/2005, 26/8/2005 (AFG); **Cheylesmore, Coventry**, 26/7/2005 (MD).

Beautiful Snout
2476 *Hypena crassalis* (Fabr.)

Nationally Local

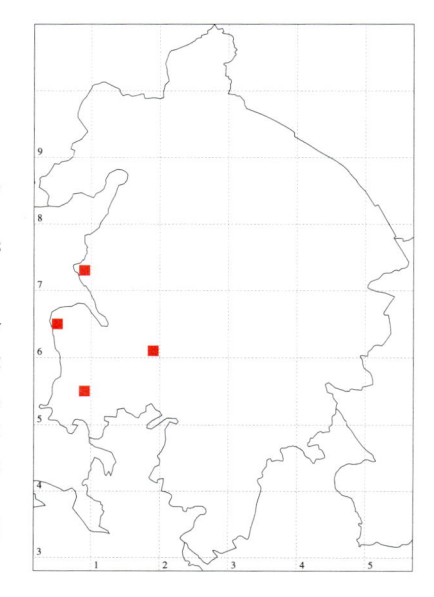

County status: Very local and fairly common at one site.
Flight: June and July.
Larval foodplants: Bilberry*. At sites where Bilberry is absent the foodplant is unknown.

The Beautiful Snout is usually associated with Bilberry growing in open heathy woodland. The largest population is found in a restricted area of Clowes Wood, where the adults are sometimes attracted to light in numbers; for example, 18/6/1993 (12) (Warks Moth Group).

This species has also been recorded at Snitterfield Bushes and Oversley Wood, where there is no Bilberry.

Records:
Snitterfield Bushes, 1/7/1989 (AFG; Gardner, 1989), 23/6/1994 (AFG, BS); **Clowes Wood**, 25/6/1992 specimen on tree trunk (MCV), 1/9/1992 larva, 4/9/1992 larva (MCV), 18/6/1993 (12) (Warks Moth Group); **Rough Hill Wood**, 25/6/1993 (CI, RGB); **Oversley Wood**, 18/6/2005 (DG).

Snout
2477 *Hypena proboscidalis* (L.)

County status: Widespread and common.
Flight: Two generations. June to early August, and late August to October.
Larval foodplants: Common Nettle*.

The Snout is a common species throughout the County in all types of habitats where Common Nettle grows in profusion. MV does not reflect the true status of this moth, which can often be seen in much larger numbers at dusk flying over the foodplant.

The second generation consists of many undersized individuals. It is occasionally noted in early November; for example, Charlecote, 1/11/1982 (2) (AFG).

VCH 1904: *'Common.'*

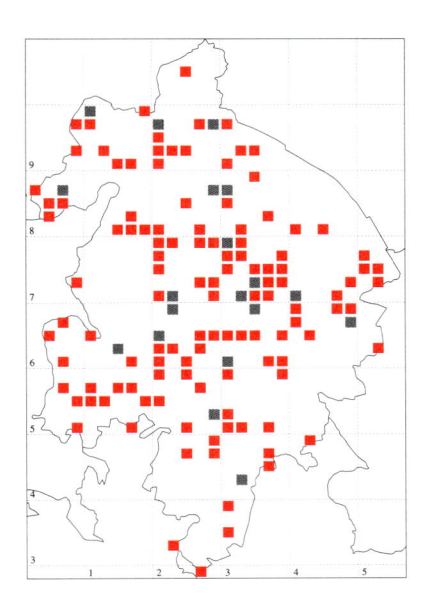

Paignton Snout
2479 *Hypena obesalis* (Treit.)

Very rare immigrant: Central, eastern and southern Europe

County status: Very rare immigrant.
Flight: August.
Larval foodplants: Common Nettle.

A female of this very rare immigrant was caught in a garden moth trap at Charlecote on 26/8/1973 (DB). This was the third of only five British records to date (Brown, 1973). A considerable immigration was in progress between 20–28 August, when examples of Death's-head Hawk-moth and Convolvulus Hawk-moth were recorded in the Midlands (Heath, 1983).

Pinion-streaked Snout
2484 *Schrankia costaestrigalis* (Steph.)

Nationally Local

County status: Very local and usually scarce.
Flight: July to mid-August; occasionally individuals of a partial second generation occur in late September.
Larval foodplants: Unknown in the wild. In captivity eats Wild Marjoram, Wild Thyme and Heather flowers.

The Pinion-streaked Snout is certainly under-recorded, owing to its small size and resemblance to a pyralid moth. First noted in Bannam's Wood (FAN) during the 1960s, this species has only ever been recorded in numbers at Oversley Wood.

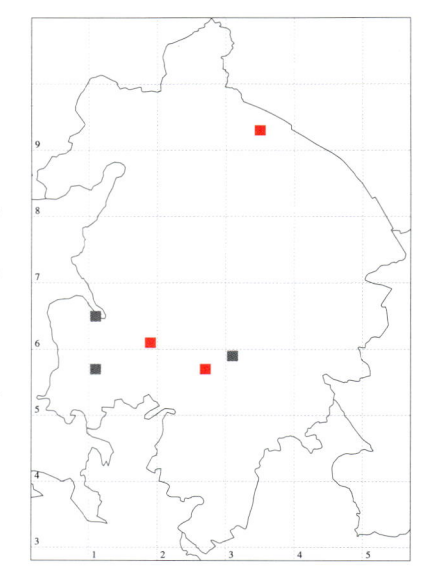

Records:
Bannam's Wood, 1963 (FAN); **Oakley Wood**, 24/7/1973 (DB); **Oversley Wood**, 15/8/1974, 28/7/1975 (4) (DB), 3/7/1976 (5), 2/8/1980 (3), 17/7/1981 (DB, AFG), 28/7/1982 (2) (DB); **Snitterfield Bushes**, 3/8/1988 (DB, AFG, RMC), 17/8/1988 (AFG); **Charlecote**, 20/7/1989 (2), 30/9/1989, 6/8/2000 (DB); **Windmill Hill, Nuneaton**, 7/6/2003 (NJS, DG).

Common Fan-foot
2488 *Pechipogo strigilata* (L.)

Nationally Scarce A

County status: Presumed extinct.
Flight: Late May to June.
Larval foodplants: Oaks. Damaged branches with withering leaves.

The English name belies the true status of this moth as it is a much declined species and now Nationally Scarce. Formerly restricted to a small number of woodland sites, it continued to be recorded sporadically until the early 1960s, after which time it has not been recorded from Warwickshire.

Records:
Knowle, 1880 (WGB); **Rugby**, 1893 (AS); **Bickenhill**, 1930–40 odd specimens (GPS); **Sutton Park**, 1960s (JB); **Four Oaks**, 1961 (EVW); **Arley Wood**, 1962 (EABS).

VCH 1904: *Brandon Wood, Princethorpe Wood, Atherstone.*

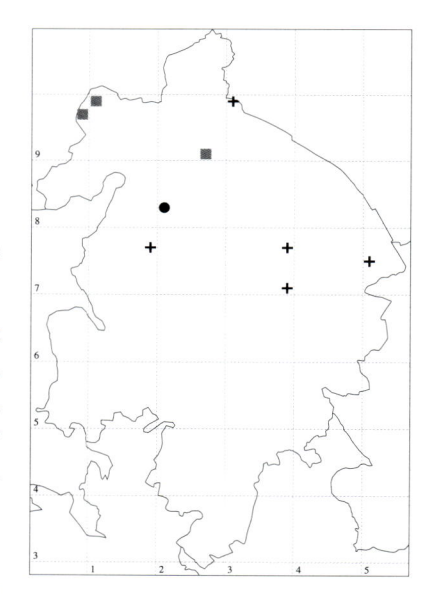

Plumed Fan-foot
2488a *Pechipogo plumigeralis* (Hb.)

Rare immigrant: Central and southern Europe, northern Africa

County status: Very rare immigrant.
Flight: July.
Larval foodplants: Unknown in Britain. In mainland Europe roses, Broom, Ivy and probably other plants.

A worn male of this very rare immigrant was caught in a garden moth trap at Hillmorton, Rugby, on 23/7/2005 (DIP), the first to be recorded away from the Kent and Sussex coast. An example of the Vestal was noted at Charlecote (DB) on the same evening, suggesting a widespread immigration of moths into Warwickshire.

Fan-foot
2489 *Zanclognatha tarsipennalis* (Treit.)

County status: Widespread and fairly common.
Flight: June to early August.
Larval foodplants: Withered leaves of oaks, Beech, brambles and other plants.

The Fan-foot is found over a large part of Warwickshire, frequenting broadleaved woodlands, scrub and sheltered gardens. Small numbers have been recorded in urban districts.

VCH 1904: *'Not uncommon.'*
Brandon Wood, Princethorpe Wood, Knowle, Atherstone, Coventry, Overslade.

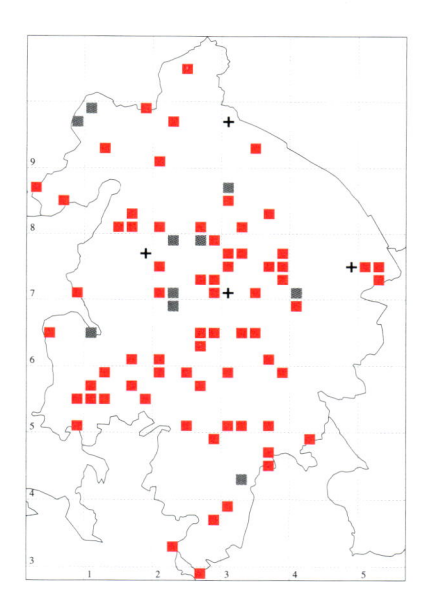

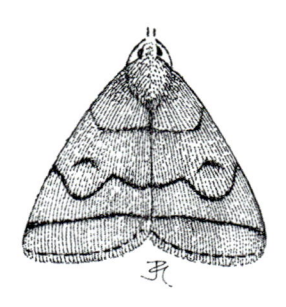

Small Fan-foot
2492 *Herminia grisealis* ([D. & S.])

County status: Widespread and fairly common.
Flight: Early June to mid-August.
Larval foodplants: Small-leaved Lime*, oaks, Alder and brambles—feeding on the living leaves as well as the withered foliage of broken branches.

The Small Fan-foot is found in a varied range of wooded habitats throughout the County. It is particularly plentiful along woodland edges and amongst scrub on disused railway embankments and in old quarries. As with the preceding species, greater numbers are attracted to lower wattage actinic tubes than bright MV.

VCH 1904: *'Not uncommon.'*
Sutton Park, Knowle, Overslade.

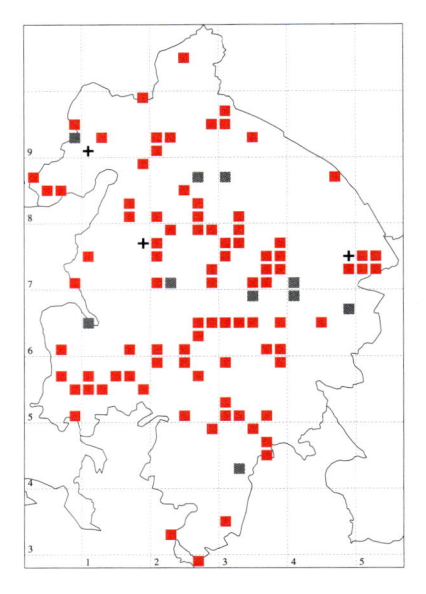

Appendix 1. Species Doubtfully Recorded in Warwickshire or Recorded as Probable Imports Only

1670 Small Grass Emerald *Chlorissa viridata* (L.)
National status: Nationally Scarce A.

A doubtful record of this damp heathland and moss species from Tile Hill Wood on 1/6/1935 (JWSt) is unconfirmed.

1694 Smoky Wave *Scopula ternata* (Schr.)
National status: Local.

A doubtful record of this essentially heathland and moorland species from Tile Hill Wood on 13/6/1931 (CDNHSS) is unconfirmed.

1701 Dotted Border Wave *Idaea sylvestraria* (Hb.)
National status: Nationally Scarce B.

A doubtful record of this heathland species from Tile Hill Wood on 13/6/1931 (CDNHSS) is unconfirmed.

1704 Silky Wave *Idaea dilutaria* (Hb.)
National status: RDB.

This species was included in the VCH 1904 with records from Brandon and Newbold, near Rugby. It was almost certainly mistaken for Dwarf Cream Wave *Idaea fuscovenosa* (Goeze) which was not mentioned.

1737 Small Argent & Sable *Epirrhoe tristata* (L.)
There is an unconfirmed record of this species at Fosters Pool, Leicester Grange, in 1977 (HDNHS).

1744 Grey Mountain Carpet *Entephria caesiata* ([D. & S.])
A specimen of this mountain and moorland species was caught in a garden moth trap at Radford, Coventry, on 6/7/1986 (MCV). It is possible this specimen emerged locally, having been transported to the neighbourhood on a Heather plant.

1966 Black-veined Moth *Siona lineata* (Scop.)
National status: RDB.

Birmingham 24/5/1870 (F. Enock)
A puzzling record from an experienced observer.

1967 Straw Belle *Aspitates gilvaria gilvaria* ([D. & S.])
National status: RDB.

There is a curious 1961 record given for north-west Warwickshire from the Biological Records Centre (ITE Monks Wood). No further detail is given.

1968 Yellow Belle *Semiaspilates ochrearia* (Rossi)
National status: Local.

A rather dubious record from Oversley Wood in 1960 (GCG, WTT) of this chiefly coastal species was never fully confirmed.

2013 Plumed Prominent *Ptilophora plumigera* ([D. & S.])
National status: Nationally Scarce A.

There is a curious record of an adult reared from a larva found in Austy Wood in 1940 (HEH).

2067 Jersey Tiger *Euplagia quadripunctaria* (Poda)
National status: Nationally Scarce B.

An example of this large and colourful species was noted resting on low vegetation, and confirmed with a photograph, in a garden at Bearley Station on 8/8/1993 (IGMR), before flying away. It is not clear if this specimen was a release, an escapee from Stratford Butterfly House, or a genuine immigrant/vagrant.

2074a Banana Stowaway *Antichloris eriphia* (Fabr.)
Status: Import, with bananas.

Two cocoons of this adventive species were found in a box of bananas from Guadeloupe at Barras Heath Wholesale Market, Stoke Heath, Coventry, on 14/2/2000 (IGMR). One perfect male specimen subsequently emerged.

2085 Archer's Dart *Agrotis vestigialis* (Hufn.)
National status: Local.

A single 1960–1980 record from the Bedworth area was obtained from the Biological Records Centre (ITE Monks Wood). No further detail is given.

2152 White Colon *Sideridis albicolon* (Hb.)
National status: Nationally Scarce B.

A rather dubious record of this chiefly coastal species from Tile Hill Wood on 1/7/1950 (CDNHSS) is unconfirmed.

2329 Confused *Apamea furva britannica* (Cock.)
National status: Local.

VCH 1904: *Atherstone (unconfirmed).*
There are unconfirmed records from Tile Hill Wood in 1956 (STm) and Hartshill Hayes in 1978 (RJT).

2359 Crinan Ear *Amphipoea crinanensis* (Burr.)
National status: Local.

Two Noctuids of the genus *Amphipoea* taken in the 1980s at Charlecote (DB) and Claverdon (IGMR) were believed to be of this species and included in *The Lepidoptera of Warwickshire, Part Two* (Smith & Brown, 1987). Although superficial characteristics originally suggested *crinanensis*, subsequent genitalia dissection (M. Bailey) proved these specimens to be *oculea* and *lucens* respectively.

2440 Lempke's Gold Spot *Plusia putnami gracilis* (Lempke)
National status: Local.

There are no confirmed records of this species in Warwickshire. Although mentioned in *The Lepidoptera of Warwickshire, Part Two* (Smith & Brown, 1987) the Charlecote specimen of 1970 (DB) has proved through genitalia dissection (M. Bailey) to be *festucae*, and there appears to be no voucher specimen to validate the Sutton Park records of 1983 (AN).

2493 Dotted Fan-foot *Macrochilo cribrumalis* (Hb.)
National status: Nationally Scarce B.

A record of this wetland species from Tysoe on 3/8/1956 (TT) was never fully confirmed and no voucher specimen has been located in the collection of Trevor Trought.

Appendix 2. Authors' Names which have been Abbreviated

Barrett	Barr.	Mabille	Mab.
Bastelberger	Bast.	Metcalfe	Metc.
Boheman	Boh.	Millière	Mill.
Boisduval	Boisd.	Müller	Müll.
Borkhausen	Borkh.	Newman	Newm.
Boursin	Bours.	Oberthür	Ob.
Brünnich	Brünn.	Ochsenheimer	Ochs.
Bytinski-Satz	Byt.-Satz.	Osbeck	Osb.
Clerk	Cl.	Pallas	Pall.
Cockayne & Williams	Cock. & Will.	Philpott	Philp.
Cockayne	Cock.	Piller	Pill.
Cockerell	Cockll.	Prunner, de	Prunn.
Curtis, W. Parkinson	W. P. Curt.	Rambur	Ramb.
Curtis, W.	Curt.	Rézbanyai-Reser	Rézb.-Res.
DeGeer	DeG.	Richardson	Rich.
Dennis & Schiffermüller	D. & S.	Rothschild	Roths.
Donovan	Don.	Rottemburg	Rott.
Doubleday	Doubl.	Rowland-Brown	Rowl.-Br.
Duponchel	Dup.	Scharfenburg	Scharf.
Esper	Esp.	Scheven	Schev.
Eversmann, von	Eversm.	Schrank	Schr.
Fabricius	Fabr.	Schreber	Schreb.
Fletcher	Fletch.	Scopoli	Scop.
Forster	Forst.	Sheldon	Sheld.
Fuessly	Fuessl.	Sparre-Schneider	Sp.-Schn.
Graslin	Grasl.	Spuler	Spul.
Gregson	Gregs.	Stainton	Stt.
Guenée	Guen.	Staudinger	Stdgr.
Harrison	Harr.	Stephens	Steph.
Haworth	Haw.	Tauscher	Tausch.
Hering	Her.	Thunberg	Thunb.
Herrich-Schäffer	H.-S.	Treitschke	Treit.
Hohenwarth	Hohen.	Tremewan	Trem.
Hübner	Hb.	Turner	Turn.
Hufnagel	Hufn.	Verity	Ver.
Humphreys & Westwood	Humph. & Westw.	Vieweg	View.
Joannis, de	Joann.	Villers	Vill.
Jordan	Jord.	Walker	Walk.
La Harpe, de	La Harpe.	Warren	Warr.
Laspeyres	Lasp.	Werneburg	Werneb.
Lederer	Led.	Wnukoqaky	Wnuk.
Lefebvre	Lefeb.	Wollaston	Woll.
Linnaeus	L.	Zeller	Zell.
		Zincken	Zinck.

Appendix 3. Scientific Names of Plants

Alder	*Alnus glutinosa*
Almond	*Prunus dulcis*
Alyssum	*Alyssum* sp.
Alyssum, Golden	*Alyssum saxatile*
Angelica, Wild	*Angelica sylvestris*
Apple (cultivated)	*Malus pumila*
Apple, Crab	*Malus sylvestris*
Ash	*Fraxinus excelsior*
Aspen	*Populus tremula*
Barberry	*Berberis vulgaris*
Bartsia, Red	*Odontites vernus*
Bedstraw, Hedge	*Galium mollugo*
Bedstraw, Lady's	*Galium verum*
Beech	*Fagus sylvatica*
Beet	*Beta* sp.
Bellflower, Giant	*Campanula latifolia*
Bellflower, Nettle-leaved	*Campanula trachelium*
Berberis	*Berberis* sp.
Bilberry	*Vaccinium myrtillus*
Bindweed	*Convolvulus* sp.
Bindweed, Field	*Convolvulus arvensis*
Birch	*Betula* sp.
Birch, Downy	*Betula pubescens*
Birch, Silver	*Betula pendula*
Bird's-foot-trefoil, Common	*Lotus corniculatus*
Bird's-foot-trefoil, Greater	*Lotus pedunculatus*
Blackthorn	*Prunus spinosa*
Bluebell	*Hyacinthoides non-scripta*
Bog-myrtle	*Myrica gale*
Bracken	*Pteridium aquilinum*
Bramble	*Rubus fruticosus* agg.
Broom	*Cytisus scoparius*
Bryony, White	*Bryonia dioica*
Buckthorn	*Rhamnus* sp.
Buckthorn, Alder	*Frangula alnus*
Buckthorn, Purging	*Rhamnus cathartica*
Buddleia	*Buddleia* sp.
Bullace	*Prunus institia*
Burdock	*Arctium* sp.
Burnet, Salad	*Sanguisorba minor* ssp. *minor*
Burnet-saxifrage	*Pimpinella saxifrage*
Buttercup	*Ranunculus* sp.
Cabbage	*Brassica oleracea*
Campion, Bladder	*Silene vulgaris*
Campion, Red	*Silene dioica*
Campion, White	*Silene latifolia*
Canary-grass, Reed	*Phalaris arundinacea*
Carnation	*Dianthus* sp.
Carrot	*Daucus carota*
Carrot, Wild	*Daucus carota* ssp. *carota*
Chamomile	*Chamaemelum nobile*
Cherry	*Prunus* sp.
Chestnut, Sweet	*Castanea sativa*
Chickweed	*Stellaria* sp.
Clematis (cultivated)	*Clematis* sp.
Clover	*Trifolium* sp.
Cock's-foot	*Dactylis glomerata*
Comfrey, Common	*Symphytum officinale*
Couch, Common	*Elytrigia repens*
Cowslip	*Primula veris*
Cow-wheat, Common	*Melampyrum pratense*
Currant, Black	*Ribes nigrum*
Currant, Red	*Ribes rubrum*
Cypress, Lawson's	*Chamaecyparis lawsoniana*
Cypress, Leyland	*Cupressus macrocarpa* x *Chamaecyparis nootkatensis* = x *Cupressocyparis leylandii*
Cypress, Monterey	*Cupressus macrocarpa*
Cypress, Swamp	*Taxodium distichum*
Dandelion	*Taraxacum officinale* agg.
Dead-nettle, Red	*Lamium purpureum*
Dead-nettle, White	*Lamium album*
Delphinium, Garden	*Delphinium* x *cultorum*
Dock	*Rumex* sp.
Dog's Mercury	*Mercurialis perennis*
Dog-rose	*Rosa canina*
Dogwood	*Cornus sanguinea*
Dyer's Greenweed	*Genista tinctoria*
Elder	*Sambucus nigra*
Elm, English	*Ulmus procera*
Elm, Wych	*Ulmus glabra*
Eyebright	*Euphrasia* sp.
False-brome	*Brachypodium sylvaticum*
Fen-sedge, Great	*Cladium mariscus*
Figwort, Common	*Scrophularia nodosa*
Figwort, Water	*Scrophularia auriculata*
Fir, Douglas	*Pseudotsuga menziesii*
Forsythia	*Forsythia suspensa* x *viridissima* = F. x *intermedia*

Foxglove	*Digitalis purpurea*	Lupin	*Lupinus* sp.
Fuschia	*Fuchsia magellanica*	Madder, Wild	*Rubia peregrina*
Garden Mint	*Mentha* sp.	Mallow, Common	*Malva sylvestris*
Geranium	*Geranium* sp.	Maple, Field	*Acer campestre*
Goldenrod	*Solidago virgaurea*	Marigold	*Calendula* sp.
Gooseberry	*Ribes uva-crispa*	Marjoram, Wild	*Origanum vulgare*
Goosefoot	*Chenopodium* sp.	Mat-grass	*Nardus stricta*
Goosegrass (Common Cleavers)	*Galium aparine*	Mayweed	*Matricaria* sp.
		Meadow-grass, Annual	*Poa annua*
Gorse	*Ulex europaeus*	Meadow-grass, Smooth	*Poa pratensis*
Grape Vine	*Vitis vinifera*	Meadow-grass, Wood	*Poa nemoralis*
Groundsel	*Senecio vulgaris*	Meadow-rue, Common	*Thalictrum flavum*
Guelder Rose	*Viburnum opulus*	Meadowsweet	*Filipendula ulmaria*
Hair-grass, Tufted	*Deschampsia cespitosa* ssp. *cespitosa*	Medic, Black	*Medicago lupulina*
		Melick, Wood	*Melica uniflora*
Hair-grass, Wavy	*Deschampsia flexuosa*	Milkwort	*Polygala* sp.
Hawk's-beard	*Crepis* sp.	Monks'-hood	*Aconitum* sp.
Hawkweed	*Hieracium* sp.	Moor-grass, Purple	*Molinia caerulea*
Hawthorn	*Crataegus* sp.	Mouse-ear, Common	*Cerastium fontanum*
Hawthorn, Common	*Crataegus monogyna*	Mouse-ear, Field	*Cerastium arvense*
Hawthorn, Midland	*Crataegus laevigata*	Mouse-ear-hawkweed	*Pilosella officinarum*
Hazel	*Corylus avellana*	Mugwort	*Artemis vulgaris*
Heather	*Calluna vulgaris*	Mullein	*Verbascum* sp.
Hemp-agrimony	*Eupatorium cannabinum*	Mustard, Garlic	*Alliaria petiolata*
Hemp-nettle, Common	*Galeopsis tetrahit*	Nasturtium	*Tropaeolum majus*
Himalayan Balsam	*Impatiens glandulifera*	Nettle, Common	*Urtica dioica*
Hogweed	*Heracleum sphondylium*	Nightshade, Woody	*Solanum dulcamara*
Holly	*Ilex aquifolium*	Oak	*Quercus* sp.
Hollyhock	*Alcea rosea*	Oak, Evergreen	*Quercus ilex*
Honeysuckle	*Lonicera periclymenum*	Oak, Pedunculate	*Quercus robur*
Hop	*Humulus lupulus*	Oak, Sessile	*Quercus petraea*
Hornbeam	*Carpinus betulus*	Oat-grass, False	*Arrhenatherum elatius*
Horse Chestnut	*Aesculus hippocastanum*	Oleander	*Nerium* sp.
Horse-tail	*Equisetum* sp.	Orache	*Atriplex* sp.
Iris, Yellow	*Iris pseudacorus*	Orache, Common	*Atriplex patula*
Ivy	*Hedera helix* ssp. *helix*	Osier	*Salix viminalis*
Jasmine	*Jasminum* sp.	Pampas-grass	*Cortaderia selloana*
Juniper	*Juniperus* sp.	Parsley, Cow	*Anthriscus sylvestris*
Knapweed	*Centaurea nigra*	Parsnip, Wild	*Pastinaca sativa*
Knotgrass	*Polygonum aviculare*	Pear	*Pyrus* sp.
Larch	*Larix* sp.	Periwinkle, Lesser	*Vinca minor*
Laurel, Portugal	*Prunus lusitanica*	Persicaria, Common	*Persicaria persicaria*
Lettuce, Wild	*Lactuca* sp.	Petty Whin	*Genista anglica*
Lilac	*Syringa vulgaris*	Pignut	*Conopodium majus*
Lime	*Tilia* sp.	Pine, Corsican	*Pinus nigra* ssp. *laricio*
Lime, Small-leaved	*Tilia cordata*	Pine, Lodgepole	*Pinus contorta*
Lucerne	*Medicago sativa* ssp. *sativa*	Pine, Scots	*Pinus sylvestris*

Common name	Scientific name
Plantain	*Plantago* sp.
Plantain, Ribwort	*Plantago lanceolata*
Plum	*Prunus* sp.
Pond-sedge, Lesser	*Carex acutiformis*
Poplar	*Populus* sp.
Poplar, Black	*Populus nigra*
Poplar, Western Balsam	*Populus trichocarpa*
Potato	*Solanum tuberosum*
Primrose	*Primula vulgaris*
Privet, Garden	*Ligustrum ovalifolium*
Privet, Wild	*Ligustrum vulgare*
Purple-loosestrife	*Lythrum salicaria*
Ragged-Robin	*Lychnis flos-cuculi*
Ragwort	*Senecio* sp.
Ragwort, Common	*Senecio jacobaea*
Raspberry	*Rubus idaeus*
Red Robin	*Photinia* x *fraseri*
Reed, Common	*Phragmites australis*
Reed-mace	*Typha latifolia*
Restharrow	*Ononis* sp.
Restharrow, Common	*Ononis repens*
Rose	*Rosa* sp. including cultivars
Rose, Burnet	*Rosa spinosissima*
Rose, Wild	*Rosa* sp.
Rowan	*Sorbus aucuparia*
Rush	*Juncus* sp.
Rush, Jointed	*Juncus articulatus*
Rush, Soft	*Juncus effusus*
Sage, Wood	*Teucrium scorodonia*
Sallow	*Salix* sp.
Scabious, Devil's-bit	*Succisa pratensis*
Scabious, Field	*Knautia arvensis*
Sedge	*Carex* sp.
Sheep's-fescue	*Festuca ovina*
Silverweed	*Potentilla anserine*
Sloe	*Prunus spinosa*
Small-reed, Wood	*Calamagrostis epigejos*
Snapdragon	*Antirrhinum* sp.
Sneezewort	*Achillea ptarmica*
Soapwort	*Saponaria officinalis*
Sorrel	*Rumex* sp.
Sorrel, Common	*Rumex acetosa* ssp. *acetosa*
Sorrel, Sheep's	*Rumex acetosella*
Sow-thistle	*Sonchus* sp.
Spindle	*Euonymus europaeus*
Spruce	*Picea* sp.
Spruce, Norway	*Picea abies*
Spurge-laurel	*Daphne laureola*
St. John's-wort	*Hypericum* sp.
Stitchwort	*Stellaria* sp.
Strawberry, Wild	*Fragaria vesca*
Swede	*Brassica napus* ssp. *rapifera*
Sweet William	*Dianthus barbatus*
Sweet-grass, Reed	*Glyceria maxima*
Sycamore	*Acer pseudoplatanus*
Tangerine Sage	*Salvia elegans*
Teasel	*Dipsacus* sp.
Thistle	*Carduus, Cirsium, Silybum,* or *Onopordum* sp.
Thyme, Wild	*Thymus polytrichus*
Toadflax, Common	*Linaria vulgaris*
Toadflax, Pale	*Linaria repens*
Tomato	*Lycopersicon esculentum*
Traveller's-joy	*Clematis vitalba*
Trefoil	*Lotus* sp.
Turnip	*Brassica rapa*
Valerian, Common	*Valeriana officinalis*
Valerian, Marsh	*Valeriana dioica*
Valerian, Red	*Centranthus rubra*
Vetch	*Vicia* sp.
Vetch, Kidney	*Anthyllis vulneraria*
Vetch, Tufted	*Vicia cracca*
Vetchling, Meadow	*Lathyrus pratensis*
Violet	*Viola* sp.
Virginia Creeper	*Parthenocissus quinquefolia*
Wallflower	*Erysimum cheiri*
Water Lily	*Nuphar* sp.
Wayfaring Tree	*Viburnum lantana*
Willow	*Salix* sp.
Willow, Creeping	*Salix repens*
Willowherb	*Epilobium* sp.
Willowherb, Great	*Epilobium hirsutum*
Willowherb, Rosebay	*Chamerion angustifolium*
Wood-rush	*Luzula* sp.
Wormwood	*Artemisia absinthium*
Wych Hazel	*Hamamelis* sp.
Yarrow	*Achillea millefolium*
Yellow-rattle	*Rhinanthus minor*
Yew	*Taxus baccata*

Appendix 4. Site Gazetteer

Site	Grid Ref
Alcester	SP0856
Alvecote, Pooley Fields (WWT, SSSI)	SK2504
Alveston	SP2356
Amington	SK2304
Ansty	SP4182
Arley Wood (FC)	SP2790
Ashlawn Cutting (WWT)	SP5172
Ashorne House	SP3158
Ashorne Wood	SP2858
Atherstone	SP3096
Austrey	SK2906
Austy Wood	SP1662
Baddesley Clinton (NT)	SP2070
Baddesley Ensor	SP2798
Baginton	SP3474
Bannam's Wood (SSSI)	SP1164
Barford	SP2760
Barton	SP1051
Bearley	SP1760
Bentley Park Wood (SSSI)	SP2895
Bickenhill	SP1983
Bidford on Avon	SP0951
Billesley	SP1456
Bilton	SP4873
Birmingham	SP0787
Birmingham, Castle Bromwich	SP1589
Birmingham, Edgbaston	SP0484
Birmingham, Erdington	SP1292
Birmingham, Gravelly Hill	SP1090
Birmingham, Handsworth	SP0490
Birmingham, Harborne	SP0284
Birmingham, Lea Hall	SP1486
Birmingham, Pype Hayes	SP1392
Birmingham, Saltley	SP0987
Birmingham, Selly Oak	SP0482
Birmingham, Shirley	SP1178
Birmingham, Small Heath	SP1085
Birmingham, Ward End	SP1188
Birmingham, Witton	SP0789
Birmingham, Yardley	SP1284
Bishops Bowl	SP3858
Bishops Hill	SP3958
Bishops Itchington	SP3957
Bishops Tachbrook	SP3161
Bishopton	SP1856
Bodymoor Heath	SP2096
Bolehall	SK2103
Bonehill	SK1902
Bowshot Wood	SP3052
Bradnock's Marsh	SP2180
Brailes	SP3037
Bramcote Canal	SP4089
Brandon Marsh (WWT, SSSI)	SP3875
Brandon Wood	SP3876
Brick Kiln Coppice	SP3251
Broom	SP0953
Broom Gravel Pits	SP0953
Brownsover	SP5076
Bubbenhall Glade	SP3671
Burton Dassett Hills (CP)	SP3952
CAD Kineton (MOD)	SP3650
Camp Hill, Nuneaton	SP3392
Castle Hills, Solihull	SP1782
Cawston	SP4672
Chalcot Wood	SP1272
Charlecote	SP2656
Charlecote, Old Gravel Pit	SP2657
Chase Wood	SP2572
Chelmsley Wood	SP1886
Cherington	SP2936
Chesterton Wood	SP3357
Claverdon	SP2064
Close Wood (FC)	SP2584
Clowes Wood (WWT, SSSI)	SP0973
Coleshill	SP1888
Coleshill Bog	SP2086
Compton Verney	SP3152
Compton Wynyates	SP3342
Coombe Abbey	SP3879
Coombe Wood	SP3878
Corley	SP2985
Coughton Park	SP0660
Coventry, Allesley	SP2981
Coventry, Bell Green	SP3581
Coventry, Canley	SP3077
Coventry, Chapelfields	SP3178
Coventry, Cheylesmore	SP3377
Coventry, Earlsdon	SP3177
Coventry, Flints Green	SP2680
Coventry, Hall Green	SP3582
Coventry, Holbrooks	SP3383
Coventry, Kenilworth Road	SP3074
Coventry, Keresley	SP3184
Coventry, Kirby Corner	SP2976
Coventry, Parkside	SP3378
Coventry, Radford	SP3280
Coventry, Stoke	SP3678
Coventry, Styvechale	SP3276
Coventry, Tamworth Road	SP3083
Coventry, Tile Hill	SP2878
Coventry, Tile Hill Wood (LNR, SSSI)	SP2778
Coventry, Walsgrave on Sowe	SP3880
Coventry, Whitley	SP3576
Coventry, Wyken Slough (WWT)	SP3683
Crackley Wood, Kenilworth (WWT)	SP2873
Cross Hands Quarry (SSSI)	SP2629

Site	Grid Ref	Site	Grid Ref
Cubbington	SP3468	Ladies Wood	SP0755
Danzey	SP1269	Ladywalk (WMBC)	SP2091
Dordon	SK2600	Lapworth	SP1670
Dorridge	SP1675	Lighthorne	SP3355
Dosthill	SP2199	Lillington, Leamington Spa	SP3367
Draycote Meadows (WWT, SSSI)	SP4570	Little Alne	SP1461
Draycote Water	SP4568	Little Aston	SK0999
Dunchurch	SP4871	Little Bracebridge, Sutton Park	SP0998
Earlswood	SP1074	Long Itchington	SP4165
Easenhall	SP4679	Long Itchington Quarry	SP4163
Eathorpe	SP3868	Long Lawford	SP4775
Edgehill	SP3747	Lower Haselor	SP1257
Elmdon Manor	SP1682	Loxley	SP2453
Ettington Park	SP2447	Luddington	SP1652
Ettington Road Cutting	SP2648	Malpass Quarry	SP4876
Farnborough Hall	SP4349	Mappleborough Green	SP0867
Fen End, Kenilworth	SP2274	Marston Green	SP1785
Fenny Compton	SP4152	Marton	SP4068
Forshaw Heath	SP0873	Matchborough, Redditch	SP0766
Four Oaks	SP1099	May's Wood	SP1464
Frankton	SP4270	Meigh's Wood (FC)	SP2684
Frankton Wood	SP4171	Merevale	SP2997
Galley Common, Nuneaton	SP3191	Meriden	SP2482
Goldicote Cutting (WWT)	SP2351	Meriden Shafts (FC)	SP2583
Gospel Oak	SP2693	Middle Tysoe	SP3444
Grendon Common	SP2798	Middleton	SP1698
Grove Hill (WWT)	SP1154	Middleton Hall	SP1998
Guys Cliffe, Warwick	SP2966	Middleton Woods	SP1696
Hampton Lucy	SP2557	Minworth	SP1592
Hampton Magna	SP2665	Monks Park Wood	SP2996
Hampton Wood (WWT)	SP2560	Monkspath, Solihull	SP1476
Hampton-in-Arden	SP2080	Moreton Morrell	SP3055
Harbury	SP3658	Navigation Cutting, Willoughby	SP5268
Harbury Spoilbank (WWT, SSSI)	SP3859	Nelson's Quarry	SP4365
Hartshill	SP3293	Nether Whitacre	SP2393
Hartshill Hayes (CP)	SP3194	Nettle Hill	SP4182
Haseley	SP2267	New Fallings Coppice (WWT, SSSI)	SP1074
Haseley Knob	SP2371	New Park Wood	SP1598
Haselor	SP1257	Newbold Comyn, Leamington Spa	SP3465
Hatton	SP2466	Newbold on Avon	SP4876
Hatton Green	SP2367	Newbold Quarry (WWT)	SP4976
Hay Wood (FC)	SP2071	Newton Regis	SK2707
Henley-in-Arden	SP1565	Norton Lindsey	SP2263
Hillmorton Ballast Pits	SP5473	Nuneaton	SP3090
Hillmorton, Rugby	SP5274	NVRS (National Vegetable Research Station), Wellesbourne	SP2757
Hockley Heath	SP1572		
Judkins Quarry, Nuneaton	SP3493	Oakfield, Rugby	SK4974
Kenilworth	SP2672	Oakley Wood	SP3058
Kings Newnham	SP4477	Old Nun Wood (WWT)	SP3870
Kingsbury	SP2196	Old Park Wood	SP0657
Kingsbury Water Park (CP)	SP2096	Olton	SP1382
Kingsbury Wood (SSSI)	SP2397	Overslade	SP4874
Kingswood	SP1871	Oversley Wood (FC)	SP1056
Kite's Hardwick	SP4768	Oxhouse Farm, Combrook (WWT, SSSI)	SP2950
Knowle	SP1876	Packington Park	SP2283

Site	Grid Ref	Site	Grid Ref
Packwood	SP1772	Walton	SP2852
Pailton	SP4781	Walton Wood, Disused Railway track	SP2850
Pathlow	SP1758	Wappenbury Wood (WWT)	SP3771
Pig Wood (LNR)	SP2878	Warwick	SP2864
Piles Coppice, Brandon Wood	SP3876	Warwick University Campus, Coventry	SP2976
Pillerton Priors	SP2947	Wasperton	SP2658
Polesworth	SK2602	Water Orton	SP1690
Princethorpe Wood	SP3870	Waverley Wood	SP3570
Print Wood	SP3865	Weddington, Nuneaton	SP3694
Purley Chase, Mancetter	SP3095	Weethley Wood, Alcester	SP0455
Radford Semele	SP3464	Welford-on-Avon	SP1452
Radway	SP3546	Wellesbourne	SP2855
Red Hill, Alcester	SP1356	Wellesbourne Wood	SP2653
Rough Hill Wood, Redditch (WWT, SSSI)	SP0564	Weston Park	SP2834
Royal Leamington Spa	SP3165	Whichford Wood (SSSI)	SP3034
Rugby	SP5075	Whitacre Heath (WWT, SSSI)	SP2092
Rugby Cement Works	SP4875	Whitchurch	SP2248
Ryton Meadows (BC)	SP3772	Whittleford Park	SP3392
Ryton Organic Gardens	SP4074	Wilmcote Rough	SP1557
Ryton Pools Country Park	SP3772	Windmill Hill, Nuneaton	SP3493
Ryton Wood (WWT, SSSI)	SP3772	Windmill Naps (SSSI)	SP0972
Ryton-on-Dunsmore	SP3774	Withycombe Wood (SSSI)	SP1457
Salford Priors	SP0650	Wolford	SP2434
Shipston on Stour	SP2640	Wolford Wood (SSSI)	SP2333
Shottery	SP1854	Wolverton	SP2062
Shotteswell	SP4245	Woodlands Quarry, Hartshill	SP3293
Snitterfield Bushes (WWT, SSSI)	SP1860	Woodloes, Warwick	SP2866
Solihull	SP1679	Woodrow North, Redditch	SP0565
Southam	SP4060	Wootton Green	SP2278
Southcrest, Redditch	SP0466	Wootton Wawen	SP1563
Stareton	SP3371	Wylde Green	SP1194
Steetley Meadows	SP3875	Yarningale Common	SP1866
Stockton Cutting (WWT, SSSI)	SP4364		
Stonebridge Meadows (WWT)	SP3475		
Stoneleigh	SP3272	BC	Butterfly Conservation reserve
Stratford-upon-Avon	SP1954	CP	Country Park
Stretton-under-Fosse	SP4481	FC	Forestry Commission
Studley	SP0763	LNR	Local Nature Reserve
Sutton Coldfield	SP1090	MOD	Ministry of Defence
Sutton Park (NNR)	SP0896	NNR	National Nature Reserve
Sutton-under-Brailes	SP3037	NT	National Trust
Swift Valley, Rugby (WWT)	SP5077	SSSI	Site of Special Scientific Interest
Tamworth	SK2104	WMBC	West Midland Bird Club reserve
Tanworth in Arden	SP1170	WWT	Warwickshire Wildlife Trust reserve
Temple Balsall (WWT)	SP2076		
Temple Grafton	SP1254		
Thickthorn Wood	SP3070		
Tocil Wood (WWT)	SP3075		
Traitor's Ford	SP3336		
Tysoe	SP3343		
Tysoe Island (WWT)	SP3343		
Ufton Fields (WWT, SSSI)	SP3761		
Ufton Wood (SSSI)	SP3862		
Umberslade	SP1270		
Wainbody Wood (LNR)	SP3175		

No right of public access should be assumed to any of the sites mentioned in this list.

Appendix 5. Contributors of Warwickshire Macro-moth Records

Apart from the recorders mentioned in the text for specific records of very local and scarce species in the County, there have been a significant number of recorders contributing macro-moth records over a period of almost 150 years. Without their records the comprehensive distribution maps in this volume would not have been possible:

Alexander, K., Allan, A.P., Allan, W.C., Allen, C.P., Bailey, N. & J., Billing, K., Blair, S., Bloxham, K., Bloxham, M.G., Blythe, R., Bott, V.M., Bough, K., Burgess, F., Burnett, W.E., Cain, J., Campbell, J.L., Carvell, G., Chadwick, L., Cheshire, S., Chetwynd, H., Childs, J.M., Churms, R., Clarke, Dr. J.H., Clement, P., Cole, D., Cooke, R., Cooper, D., Copson, P., Cowley, M. J., Cox, W., Cronin, J., Crowther, C. M., Davis, I.G., Davison, K., Dawson, D.A., Derry, S., Doyle, P., Dudley, L., Dukes, R., Durham, A., Eagleton, J., Eccleston, D.B., Edwards, C., Elstubb, G.F., Emery, J., Faulkner, A., Fletcher, D.S., Forsyth, T., Fortey, J., Fountain, J.T., Freeman, M., Gibbs, R., Goldingay, S., Gosling, W., Grant, C., Grant, J.H., Greaves, A., Gregory, N. & C., Hajok, A., Hall, N.M., Hancox, J.A., Harcourt-Bath, W., Harper, Dr. M., Harris, M., Harrison, D., Harvey, P.H., Hayston, W., Hilcox, P., Hill, L., Hooper, G.N., Horton, J.G., Housey, M., Jardine, N., Johnson, M., Jones, D.A., Jones, P., Juckes, D.J., Justice, J., Kenrick, G.H., Kirk, J., Kleeton, J., Lamb, R.G., Laney, B., Langdon, R., Lees, D.R., Leonard, D., Lewis, E., Lewis, G.E, Lewis, J, Linder, G., Longstaff, G.B., Madison, J., Malkin, W., Marriott, D., McPhail, J., Measures, D.G., Meredith, R.M., Milton, P. & M., Morris, R., Moseley, I., Moughtin, T., Needle, J., Newell, H., Normand, R., Oki, T., Oliver, R., Osborne, M., Oswin, R., Owen, W., Parry, C.R., Partridge, D.S., Penton, D. & M., Perkins, M., Perry, B., Pheasey, P., Picherozyk, J., Pickvance, A.E.E., Pisolkar, E., Pitt, R., Poulton, M., Purley, P., Pyke, P., Rake, J.S., Righton, R.H., Roberts, J. & V., Robinson, J., Sadler, A., Seeley, W.F.E., Shepherd, M., Sidgwick, N.V., Sills, E.H., Simmons, A., Simper, I.J., Simpson, A.N.B., Siviter-Smith, P., Slawson, G.C., Sloan, S., Smiles, M., Smith, A., Smith, D., Smith, J. & T., Smith, P., Smith, R., Soden, G., Solliss, D., Stanton, W., Stephenson, M., Stephenson, P., Stradan, R., Street, P., Sutherland, C., Taylor, D., Terence, T., Thomas, S., Thorpe, G., Thorpe, J., Trowell, E., Tucker, R.J., Turner, J., Turner, T., Tyler, J.A., Vernon, M., Wager, S., Walker, S., Wallace, J., Ward, A.E., Ward, J.J., Ware, T., Watkins, E.P., Watkins, I., Watson, W., Wells, M., Wheeler, G., Wheeler, P., Wheeler, W.C.E., Whiston, F.C., White, R., Wilkinson, C., Williams, B. & S., Wilson, B., Woodhams, M., Wright, A., Wrigley, P., Wynn, A., Yates, G., Young, J.

Appendix 6. Published Works on Warwickshire's Larger Moths

Sidgwick, A., 1893. *Rugby Past and Present*. Rugby (This publication included a list of Lepidoptera found in the Rugby district.)

Doubleday, A. & Page, W., 1904. *The Victoria History of the County of Warwick, Volume 1 (Lepidoptera)*. Constable, London.

Arnold, G.A. & M.A., 1979. *Alvecote Pools Nature Reserve, Lists of Flora and Fauna 1946–1978*. Warwickshire Museum Service, Warwick.

Arnold, G.A. & M.A. & Thomas, R.J., 1981. *A Provisional List of the Macro Lepidoptera of Nuneaton, Tamworth, Hinckley, Bedworth, Atherstone and Market Bosworth Area*. Warwickshire Museum Service, Warwick.

Thomas, R.J. and Arnold, G.A. & M.A., 1982. *The Flora and Fauna of Hartshill Hayes Wood and Neighbourhood (plus Addenda)*. Warwickshire Museum Service, Warwick.

Cooke, P. *et al*., 1986. Warwickshire moths: Part I: The macro moths. *Proceedings Coventry Natural History and Scientific Society*. Vol. 5, no.10: 375–401, 407.

Smith, R. & Brown, D.C.G. (Eds. Hough, N., & Copson, P.), 1987. *The Lepidoptera of Warwickshire, Parts One and Two*. Warwickshire Museum Service, Warwick.

Price, J.M., 1990. *Lepidoptera of the Midland (Birmingham) Plateau, A Concise History 1890–1990*. Birmingham Natural History Society.

Arnold, G.A. & M.A. and Mitchell, B.R., 1992. *The Macromoths of Alvecote Pools N.R. SSSI*. Privately published and circulated.

Emms, C. & Barnett, L.K., 1994. *The Lepidoptera of Ryton Wood Nature Reserve*. Warwickshire Wildlife Trust, Butterfly Conservation.

Robbins, J., 1997. *The Lepidoptera of Warwickshire, Part Three: The Smaller Moths and the more Primitive Larger Moths*. Warwickshire Museum Service, Warwick.

Smith, R., 1998. *The Lepidoptera of Warwickshire 1900–1995, An Historical Summary*. Warwickshire Museum Service, Warwick.

Price, J.M., 2002. *Stratford-upon-Avon, A Flora and Fauna*. Gem Publishing Company, Wallingford.

Warmington, K. & Vickery, M., 2003. *Warwickshire's Butterflies—Their Habitats and Where to Find Them*. Warwickshire Branch of Butterfly Conservation. (This publication contains a section on Warwickshire's day-flying moths by D.C.G. Brown).

Grundy, D., 2004. *A Provisional List of the Lepidoptera of Birmingham*. Birmingham City Council.

Prior, A. & Weston, V., 2005. *Warwickshire Branch Moth Equipment, 2004—The First Year*. Warwickshire Branch of Butterfly Conservation. (This publication contains detailed accounts of moth field excursions in Warwickshire and neighbouring counties during 2004. Illustrated by John Reeve and Rita Ruban)

Coxhead, P. & Fowkes, H. (in prep.). *A Natural History of Sutton Park, Part 4: Animals*. Sutton Coldfield Natural History Society. (This publication will contain a list of the larger moths with brief comments on each species.)

In addition to the above publications, and too numerous to include in this book, are lists, articles and annual reports of the larger moths of Warwickshire in the proceedings of natural history societies, wildlife group newsletters and entomological journals. The very first of these was F. Enock's list of moths for the Birmingham district which appeared in the *Proceedings of Birmingham Natural History and Microscopial Society* in 1869.

Appendix 7. Most Recently Published Lists for Adjoining Counties

VC23—Oxfordshire

Bretherton, R.F., 1940. A list of the macrolepidoptera of the Oxford district. *Proceedings of the Ashmolean Natural History Society of Oxfordshire.* 1939: 25–70.

Bretherton, R.F., 1941. Additions to the list of macrolepidoptera of the Oxford district. *Proceedings of the Ashmolean Natural History Society of Oxfordshire.* 1940: 22–23.

Emmet, A.M., 1948. Second supplement to the list of macrolepidoptera of the Oxford district by R. F. Bretherton. *Proceedings of the Ashmolean Natural History Society of Oxfordshire.* 1941–1947: 47–55.

Work is underway towards putting together an up-to-date list (M. Townsend in prep.).

VC32—Northamptonshire

Goss, H., Briggs, T.H., Vipan, J.A.W. & Bankes E.R., 1902. Ryland, W. *et al.* (Eds). *The Victoria History of the County of Northamptonshire* 1: 94–100.

Slater, H.H., 1906. *Victoria County History – Northants Lepidoptera.* Northampton Natural History Society 13: 178–180.

There are no recent lists, but a comprehensive and regularly updated account of each species, together with records, photographs and distribution maps by County Recorder J. Ward, can be located on the following website:

http://www.northamptonshirewildlife.co.uk/nmoths/nmothsindex.htm

VC33 & VC34—Gloucestershire

Gaunt, R., 2000. *Gloucester Moths – An Account.* R. Gaunt, St Briavels. To be updated in 2006.

VC37—Worcestershire

Harper, M. & Simpson, T., 2001. *Larger Moths and Butterflies of Herefordshire and Worcestershire. An Atlas.* The West Midlands branch of Butterfly Conservation.

VC39—Staffordshire

Emley, D.W. & Warren, R.G., 2001. *The Larger Moths of Staffordshire.* Staffordshire Ecological Record, Stoke-on-Trent.

VC55—Leicestershire

Bouskell, F. & Page, W. (Ed)., 1907. *The Victoria History of the County of Leicestershire* 1: 78–89.

Work is continuing towards the publication of *The Butterflies and Moths of Leicestershire and Rutland* (A. Russell in prep.).

The Leicestershire and Rutland Moth Group have a website, created and maintained by Mark Skevington. This includes a County moth list, photographs, news and detailed information on habitats:

http://www.pintail-close.freeserve.co.uk/vc55mothgroup

Appendix 8. Details of Local Societies, Groups and Organisations

Atherstone Natural History Society
　For details contact John Walton. Tel: 01827 712455.

Birmingham Natural History Society
　For details contact Jean Osbourne. Tel: 0121 477 7550.
　Website: http://freespace.virgin.net/clare.h/br_hs.htm

Butterfly Conservation, Warwickshire branch
　For details contact Margaret Vickery. Tel: 01926 512343.

Butterfly Conservation, West Midlands Branch
　For details contact Richard Southwell. Tel: 01384 397066.
　Website: http://www.westmidlandsbutterflyconservation.org.uk

Coventry & District Natural History and Scientific Society
　For details contact Mrs R. Cooke. Tel: 02476 676756.
　Website: http://www.cdnhss.org.uk

Hinckley & District Natural History Society
　For details contact David Goldsmith. Tel: 01455 613920.

Rugby Natural History Society
　For details contact Paul Hodges. Tel: 01788 522758.

Sutton Coldfield Natural History Society
　For details contact Peter Coxhead. Tel: 0121 353 5044.

Warwickshire Moth Group
　For details contact David Brown. Tel: 01789 840295.

Warwickshire Museum
　Website: http://www.warwickshire.gov.uk/museum

Local Biodiversity Action Plans
　Many important moth habitats can be viewed at:
　http://www.warwickshire.gov.uk/biodiversity

Warwick Natural History Society
　For details contact June Read. Tel: 01926 842476.
　Website: http://warkcom.net/wnhs

Warwick University Open Studies
　For details ring: 02476 573739.
　Website: http://www2.warwick.ac.uk/study/cll/OpenStudies

Warwickshire Wildlife Trust
　For details ring: 02476 302912
　Website: http://www.warwickshire-wildlife-trust.org.uk

Bibliography and References

Allan, P.B.M., 1947. *A Moth Hunter's Gossip*. Watkins and Doncaster, London.

Allan, P.B.M., 1949. *Larval Foodplants*. Watkins and Doncaster, London.

Arnold, G.A. & M.A. *Alvecote Pools Annual Reports 1959–1980*. Warwickshire Nature Conservation Trust Ltd., Warwick.

Arnold, G.A. & M.A., 1979. *Alvecote Pools Nature Reserve, Lists of Flora and Fauna 1946–1978*. Warwickshire Museum Service, Warwick.

Arnold, G.A. & M.A. & Thomas, R.J., 1981. *A Provisional List of the Macrolepidoptera of Nuneaton, Tamworth, Hinckley, Bedworth, Atherstone and Market Bosworth Area*. Warwickshire Museum Service, Warwick.

Arnold, G.A. & M.A. & Mitchell, B.R., 1992. *The Macromoths of Alvecote Pools N.R. SSSI*. Privately published and circulated.

Arnold, V.W., Baker, C.R.B., Manning, D.V. & Woiwod, I.P., 1997. *The Butterflies and Moths of Bedfordshire*. Bedfordshire Natural History Society.

Bailey, M.A. & Brown, D.C.G., 2005. A possible female Remm's Rustic *Mesapamea remmi* (Rézbanyai-Reser) (Lep.: Noctuidae) in Warwickshire. *Entomologist's Record and Journal of Variation* Vol. 117: 140–141.

Baker, C., 1899. *Chaerocampa porcellus*. *Entomologist* Vol. 32: 213.

Baker, C., 1903. *Sphinx convolvuli* and *Chaerocampa nerii* in Warwickshire. *Entomologist* Vol. 36: 292.

Bradley, J.D., 2000. *Checklist of Lepidoptera Recorded from the British Isles*. Bradley, Fordingbridge.

Bretherton, R.F. & Chalmers-Hunt, J.M., 1984. Immigration of Lepidoptera to the British Isles, 1983. *Entomologist's Record and Journal of Variation* Vol. 96: 147–196.

British Entomological & Natural History Society., 1981. *An Identification Guide to the British Pugs (Lepidoptera: Geometridae)*. British Entomological & Natural History Society, London.

Brown, D.C.G., 1969. Warwickshire M.V. recordings 1968. *Entomologist's Record and Journal of Variation* Vol. 81: 167–168.

Brown, D.C.G., 1973. Warwickshire and beyond, 1972. *Entomologist's Record and Journal of Variation* Vol. 85: 94–98.

Brown, D.C.G., 1973. *Autographa bractea* ([D. & S.]) in Warwickshire. *Entomologist's Record and Journal of Variation* Vol. 85: 270.

Brown, D.C.G., 1973. *Hypena obesalis* (Treit.) in Warwickshire. *Entomologist's Record and Journal of Variation* Vol. 85: 240.

Brown, D.C.G., 1975. An excess of *Orgyia antiqua* (L.). *Entomologist's Record and Journal of Variation* Vol. 87: 276.

Brown, D.C.G., 1977. *Hyles gallii* (Rott.) and *Eurois occulta* (L.) in Warwickshire. *Entomologist's Record and Journal of Variation* Vol. 89: 283.

Brown, D.C.G., 1979a. Warwickshire and Northamptonshire migrants. *Entomologist's Record and Journal of Variation* Vol. 91: 17.

Brown, D.C.G., 1979b. *Lithophane leautieri* (Boisd.) in Warwickshire. *Entomologist's Record and Journal of Variation* Vol. 91: 29.

Brown, D.C.G., 1982. The first recording of *Trichoplusia ni* (Hbn.) in Warwickshire. *Entomologist's Record and Journal of Variation* Vol. 94: 239.

Brown, D.C.G. & Gardner, A.F.J., 1984. Rearing the Slender Burnished Brass *Diachrysia orichalcea* (Fabr.). *Entomologist's Record and Journal of Variation* Vol. 96: 220–221.

Brown, D.C.G., 1992. *Macdunnoughia confusa* Stephens (Lep.: Noctuidae) in Warwickshire. *Entomologist's Record and Journal of Variation* Vol. 104: 159.

Brown, D.G.G., 1993. A splendid year (1992) for Warwickshire moths. *Warwickshire Wildlife Trust Magazine.* Issue 82: 4–7.

Brown, D.C.G., 1997. County focus—Lepidoptera in Warwickshire (V.C. 38). *Atropos* 3: 16–22.

Brown, D.C.G., 1999. Identification workshop—separating Lesser-spotted Pinion, White-spotted Pinion and Lunar-spotted Pinion. *Atropos* 7: 21–23.

Brown, D.C.G., 2000. Cloaked Pug *Eupithecia abietaria* in Warwickshire (V.C. 38). *Atropos* 11: 57.

Brown, D.C.G., 2003. Dotted Chestnut *Conistra rubiginea* ([D. & S.]) (Lep.: Noctuidae) in Warwickshire. *Entomologist's Record and Journal of Variation* Vol. 115: 176.

Brown, D.C.G., 2005. Confluent form of Narrow-bordered Five-spot Burnet *Zygaena lonicerae* ssp. *latomarginata*. *Proceedings British Entomological and Natural History Society* Vol. 18, part 3: 175, plate 2, fig. 9.

Brown, D.C.G., 2005. Confluent form of Narrow-bordered Five-spot Burnet *Zygaena lonicerae* ssp. *latomarginata*. *Atropos* 25: 64 Plate 4, Fig. 13.

Carter, D.J. & Hargreaves, B., 1986. *A Field Guide to Caterpillars of Butterflies and Moths in Britain and Europe.* Collins, London.

Chalmers-Hunt, J.M., 1989. *Local Lists of Lepidoptera.* Hedera Press Oxfordshire.

Chinery, M., 1989. *Butterflies & Day-Flying Moths of Britain and Europe.* Collins New Generation Guide, London

Clark, M.C., 1986/7. Obituary—Francis Anthony Noble. *Birmingham Natural History Society Proceedings* Vol. 25, No. 4: 220–221.

Collins, A., 2002. Clearwing recording using pheromones in 2001. *Atropos* 16: 64–72.

Collins, G.A., 1997. *Larger Moths of Surrey.* Surrey Wildlife Trust.

Conrad, K.F., Woiwod, I. P. & Perry, J.N., 2003. East Atlantic teleconnection pattern and the decline of a common arctiid moth. *Global Change Biology* 9: 125–130.

Cooke, P. *et al.*, 1986. Warwickshire moths: Part I: The macro moths. *Proceedings Coventry Natural History and Scientific Society.* Vol. 5, No.10: 375–401, 407.

Cooke, P., 1990. Professor F.W. Shotton—An appreciation. *Proceedings Coventry Natural History and Scientific Society.* Vol. 6, No. 4: 174.

Cooke, P., 2005. Arthur Norman Thomas (obituary) *Proceedings Coventry Natural History and Scientific Society.* Vol. 7, No. 9: 447.

Crafer, T., 2005. *Foodplant List for the Caterpillars of Britain's Butterflies and Larger Moths.* Atropos Publishing, Holmfirth.

Davey, P., 2004. The winter immigration of 2004. *Atropos* 22: 3–10.

Emms, C. & Barnett, L.K., 1994. *The Lepidoptera of Ryton Wood Nature Reserve.* Warwickshire Wildlife Trust & Butterfly Conservation.

Enock, F., 1870. A list of Lepidoptera captured within ten miles of Birmingham during the years 1867, '68 & '69. *Birmingham Natural History & Microscopial Society Proceedings* 1869: 101–105.

Enock, F., c.1890. *Butterflies and moths.* In: *The Birmingham Saturday half-holiday Guide.* pp 41–45.

Evans, L.J., 1969. West Midlands records of *Hydraecia, Procus* and *Oporinia* species. *Entomologist's Record and Journal of Variation* Vol. 81: 199–200.

Ford, R.L.E., 1963. *Practical Entomology.* Warne, London.

Fox, R., Conrad, K.F., Parsons, M.S., Warren, M.S. & Woiwod, I.P., 2006. *The State of Britain's Larger Moths*. Butterfly Conservation and Rothamsted Research, Wareham, Dorset.

French, R.A., 1953. List of immigrant Lepidoptera to the British Isles. *Entomologist* Vol. 87: 62.

Fry, R. & Waring, P., 1996. *A Guide to Moth Traps and Their Use.* The Amateur Entomologist's Society, London.

Gardner, A.F.J., 1974. M.V. recordings, Hampton Wood, Warwickshire. *Entomologist's Record and Journal of Variation* Vol. 86: 163–164.

Gardner, A.F.J., 1976. *Orthosia opima* (Hübn.) and *Lygris prunata* (L.) in Warwickshire, 1975. *Entomologist's Record and Journal of Variation* Vol. 88: 50.

Gardner, A.F.J., 1977. *Acherontia atropos* (L.) and other immigrants in Warwickshire in 1976. *Entomologist's Record and Journal of Variation* Vol. 89: 84.

Gardner, A.F.J., 1978. Dewick's Plusia *Macdunnoughia confusa* (Steph.) and other rare migrant moths in Warwickshire. *Entomologist's Record and Journal of Variation* Vol. 90: 81.

Gardner, A.F.J., 1981. The Death's-head Hawkmoth and other immigrants in Warwickshire in 1980. *Entomologist's Record and Journal of Variation* Vol. 93: 21.

Gardner, A.F.J., 1989. *Hypena crassalis* (Fab.), the Beautiful Snout (Lep.: Noctuidae) new to Warwickshire. *Entomologist's Record and Journal of Variation* Vol. 101: 275.

Goater, B., illustrated by Senior, G. & Dyke, R., 1986. *British Pyralid Moths. A Guide to their Identification.* Harley Books, Colchester.

Goater, B., 1986. A new technique of sugaring. *Entomologist's Record and Journal of Variation* Vol. 98: 37.

Goater, B. & Norris, T., 2001. *Moths of Hampshire and the Isle of Wight.* Pisces Publications, Newbury.

Grundy, D., 2004. *A Provisional List of the Lepidoptera of Birmingham.* Birmingham City Council, Birmingham.

Hammond, H.E., 1951. The Lepidoptera of a Birmingham garden. *Entomologist's Gazette*, Vol. 2: 169–172.

Hammond, H.E., 1957. A survey of the Lepidoptera of a small oak-beech wood on the midland kuyper marl with ecological notes on the species and two appendices. *Birmingham Natural History Society Proceedings* Vol. 18, No. 16: 147–173.

Harper, M. & Simpson, T., 2005. *Larger Moths and Butterflies of Herefordshire and Worcestershire. An Atlas.* West Midlands Branch of Butterfly Conservation.

Heath, J. & Emmet, A.M. (eds), 1976–1991. *The Moths and Butterflies of Great Britain and Ireland.* Vols. 1, 2, 7, 9, 10. Harley Books, Colchester.

Jordan, M.J.R., 1987. *Mesapamea remmi* Rézbanyai-Reser, 1985, (Lep: Noctuidae) a species new to Britain. *Entomologist's Record and Journal of Variation* Vol. 101: 161–165.

Kolaj, A.J., 1993. Unusual aberration of Scalloped Oak *Crocallis elinguaria* (L.). *Proceedings British Entomological and Natural History Society* Vol. 6, part 2: 55, plate III, fig. 18.

Leverton, R., 2001. *Enjoying Moths.* Poyser Natural History, London.

Mabbett, R. & Williams, M., 1992. *The Butterflies and Moths of the West Midlands and Gloucestershire. A Five Year Review.* West Midlands branch of Butterfly Conservation.

Majerus, M., 2002. *Moths.* The New Naturalist. Harper Collins, London.

McCormick, R., 2001. *The Moths of Devon.* Various publishers.

Mitchell, B., 1993. The Cinnabar *Tyria jacobaeae* (L.) (Lep.: Arctiidae) in North Warwickshire, 1992. *Entomologist's Record and Journal of Variation* Vol. 105: 181.

Newman, L.H., 1965. *Hawkmoths of Great Britain and Europe.* Cassell, London.

Newman, L.W. & Leeds, H.A., 1913. *Text Book of British Butterflies and Moths*. Gibbs & Bamforth Ltd, St. Albans.

Noble, F.A., 1963. Stuart E. Wace Carlier—An appreciation. *Birmingham Natural History Society Proceedings* Vol. 20, No. 2: 39–40.

Noble, F.A., 1964. The Lepidoptera of the Birmingham Plateau. *Birmingham Natural History Society Proceedings* Vol. 20, No. 3: 3–13.

Noble, F.A., 1974. Obituary—Lt. Colonel William Bowater M.C., T.D., D.L., F.R.E.S. 1880–1973. *Birmingham Natural History Society Proceedings* Vol. 22, No. 4: 230–231.

Nowacki, J., 1998. *The Noctuids (Lepidoptera, Noctuidae) of Central Europe*. Slamka, Bratislava.

Palmer, S., 2004. *Lancashire Moths, Newsletter Issue 11*. (Autumn 2004).

Parsons, M.S., Green, D. & Waring, P., 2000. The Action for Threatened Moths Project. *Atropos* 10: 34–38.

Parsons, M.S., Davis, T., Green, D. & Waring, P., 2003. A brief review of the UK Biodiversity Action Plan for Moths and Butterfly Conservation's Action for Threatened Moths Project (1999–2002). *Atropos* 20: 3–11.

Parsons, M.S., Hoare, D., Davis, T. & Green, D., 2005. The distribution of the UK Biodiversity Action Plan Priority Moth Species 1999–2004. *Atropos* 25: 5–20.

Parsons, M.S., Fox, R., Conrad, K.F., Woiwod, I.P. & Warren, M.S., 2005 British moths: throwing light on a new conservation challenge. *British Wildlife* 16: 386–394.

Platts, J., 2005. Barred Hook-tip *Watsonalla cultraria* larva feeding on oak. *Atropos* 26: 50.

Porter, D., 2000. My Warwickshire garden. *Atropos* 10: 28–31.

Porter, D., 2004. Moth populations in a Warwickshire garden. *Atropos* 22: 44–50.

Porter, J., 1997. *The Colour Identification Guide to Caterpillars of the British Isles*. Viking, Middlesex.

Pratt, C., 1981. *A History of the Butterflies and Moths of Sussex*. Booth Museum Brighton.

Pratt, C., 2006, in press. An investigation into the traditional numerical fluctuations within the Garden Tiger *Arctia caja* (Linn.). *Atropos*.

Price, J.M., 1981. Wilmcote Rough, Warwickshire – Part 2. Report on moths, with additional notes on butterflies and vascular plants. *Birmingham Natural History Society Proceedings* Vol. 24, No. 3: 157–174.

Price, J.M., 1983. Frederick Henry Latham—An appreciation. *Birmingham Natural History Society Proceedings* Vol. 25, No. 1: 49–52.

Price, J.M., 1990. *Lepidoptera of the Midland (Birmingham) Plateau. A Concise History 1890–1990*. Birmingham Natural History Society.

Price, J.M., 2002. *Stratford-upon-Avon, A Flora and Fauna*. Gem Publishing Company, Wallingford.

Prior, A. & Weston, V., 2005. *Warwickshire Branch Moth Equipment, 2004—The First Year*. Warwickshire Branch of Butterfly Conservation.

Remm, H., 1983. New species of Noctuidae (Lepidoptera) from the U.S.S.R. *Entomologicheskoe Obozrenie* 62: 596–600.

Riley, A.M., 1991. *A Natural History of the Butterflies and Moths of Shropshire*. Swan Hill Press, Shrewsbury.

Riley, A.M. & Prior, G., 2003. *British and Irish Pug Moths. A Guide to their Identification and Biology*. Harley Books, Colchester.

Robbins, J. 1997., *The Lepidoptera of Warwickshire, Part Three: The Smaller Moths and the more Primitive Larger Moths*. Warwickshire Museum Service, Warwick.

Royal Horticultural Society, 1996. *New Encyclopedia of Garden Plants*. Dorling Kindersley, London

Saunt, J.W., 1937. The Lepidoptera of the Tile Hill Nature Reserve: records for the period 1931–1936. *Proceedings Coventry Natural History and Scientific Society.* Vol. 1, 145–151.

Sidgwick, A., 1893. *Rugby Past and Present.* Rugby.

Skinner, B., 1984. *Colour Identification Guide to Moths of the British Isles.* Viking, Middlesex.

Skinner, B. & Parsons, M., 1998. The immigration of Lepidoptera to the British Isles in 1994. *Entomologist's Record and Journal of Variation* Vol. 110: 1, 197.

Smith, F.H.N., 1997. *The Moths and Butterflies of Cornwall and The Isles of Scilly.* Gem Publishing Company, Wallingford.

Smith, R., 1980. *Thera juniperata* (L.) Juniper Carpet in Warwickshire. *Entomologist's Record and Journal of Variation* Vol. 92: 24.

Smith, R., 1998. *Lepidoptera in Warwickshire 1900–1995. An Historical Summary.* Warwickshire Museum Service, Warwick.

Smith, R. & Brown, D.C.G., 1979. *The Lepidoptera of Warwickshire, A Provisional List. Part One. Butterflies 1900–1977.* Warwickshire Biological Records Centre & Warwickshire Museum Service, Warwick.

Smith, R. & Brown, D.C.G., 1986–2005. *Warwick NHS Annual Reports.* Containing annual Lepidoptera reports.

Smith, R. & Brown, D.C.G. (Eds. Hough, N., and Copson, P.), 1987. *The Lepidoptera of Warwickshire. Parts One and Two.* Warwickshire Museum Service, Warwick.

South, R., 1948. *The Moths of the British Isles. Series I and II.* Wayside and Woodland. Warne, London.

Spalding, A., Tunmore, M., Parsons, M. & Fox, R., 2005. The state of moth recording in Britain: The results of the national macro-moth recording scheme consultation questionnaire. *Atropos* 24: 9–19.

Spence, B., 2003. Eastern Nycteoline *Nycteola asiatica* (Krul) in Yorkshire—a moth previously unrecorded in Britain. *Atropos* 19: 9–10.

Stace, C., 1997. *New Flora of the British Isles. Second Edition.* Cambridge University Press, Cambridge.

Stevens, C. & Warwickshire Museum., 1995. *Rocks and Fossils of Warwickshire.* Warwickshire Museum, Warwick.

Sutton, S.L. & Beaumont, H.E., 1989. *Butterflies and Moths of Yorkshire. Distribution and Conservation.* Yorkshire Naturalist's Union.

Tasker, Dr. A., 1990. *The Nature of Warwickshire.* Barracuda Books Limited, Buckingham.

Thomas, R.J. and Arnold, G.A. & M.A., 1982. *The Flora and Fauna of Hartshill Hayes Wood and Neighbourhood.* Warwickshire Museum Service, Warwick.

Trought, T., 1956–58. Lepidoptera recorded in the parish of Tysoe, 1955–57. *Warwick NHS Annual Reports.* 2, 21; 3, 35–36; 4, 27–28.

Vice, M., 1969. M.V. records for industrial Warwickshire. *Entomologist's Record and Journal of Variation* Vol. 81: 265.

Wainwright, H.A., 1904. *Lepidoptera.* In: Doubleday, H.A. & Page, W. (Eds). *The Victoria History of the County of Warwickshire* 1: 124–158. Constable, London.

Wale, C., 1983 & 1986. Moths in a Coventry (Chapelfields) garden. *Proceedings Coventry Scientific and Natural History Society*, Vol. 7: 235–240; Vol. 10: 405–407.

Waring, P., 1987–1992. *Moth conservation project news bulletin.* No.'s 1–4. Nature Conservancy Council, Joint Nature Conservation Committee.

Waring, P., 1993. Annotated list of the macro-moths recorded in the British Isles, showing the current status of each species. *National Moth Conservation Project; News bulletin 5.* Butterfly Conservation.

Waring, P., 1995. 'Wine-roping' for moths. *Butterfly Conservation News* 60: 23.

Waring, P., 1997. National moth conservation project. *Butterfly Conservation News* 64: 16–17.

Waring, P., 1999. The national recording network for the rarer British moths. *Atropos* 6: 19–27.

Waring, P., 2002. Some observations on False Mocha (*Cyclophora porata* (Linn.) in Oakley Wood, Buckinghamshire and Waterperry Wood, Oxfordshire. *Atropos* 15: 19–24.

Waring, P., Townsend, M. & Lewington, R., 2003 *Field Guide to the Moths of Great Britain and Ireland.* British Wildlife Publishing, Hook, Hampshire.

Warmington, K. & Vickery, M., 2003. *Warwickshire's Butterflies. Their Habitats and Where to Find Them.* Warwickshire branch of Butterfly Conservation.

Warren, R.G., 1979. *Atlas of the Lepidoptera of Staffordshire.* The City Museum and Art Gallery, Stoke-on-Trent

Warren, R.G., 1979. *Thera juniperata* (L.) (Juniper Carpet) in Warwickshire. *Entomologist's Record and Journal of Variation* Vol. 91: 142.

Warren, R.G., 1983. *Staffordshire Butterflies and Moths. A Revised Checklist.* The City Museum and Art Gallery, Stoke-on-Trent.

Williams, C.B., 1958. *Insect Migration.* The New Naturalist. Collins, London.

Williams, M., 1998. *West Midlands Branch of Butterfly Conservation Regional Action Plan. Annual Review 1998.*

Woiwod, I., Gould, P. & Conrad, K., 2005. The Rothamsted light-trap network—shedding light on a common moth problem. *Atropos* 26: 5–18.

Wratislaw, T.W., 1880. Clifden Nonpareil *Catocala fraxini* (L.) at Rugby, Warwickshire. *Entomologist* Vol. 13: 310.

Young, M., 1997. *The Natural History of Moths.* Poyser Natural History, London.

Index of English Names

Numbers in bold refer to colour plates.

Alder Kitten, 19, 188
Alder Moth, 285
Angle Shades, 293
Angle-striped Sallow, 8, 10, 25, 294, **7**
Annulet, 13, 176, **22**
Antler Moth, 249
Archer's Dart, 346
Argent & Sable, 15, 16, 24, 104
Ash Pug, 131
August Thorn, 153
Autumn Green Carpet, 17, 18, 95
Autumnal Moth, 109, 110
Autumnal Rustic, 228, **18**
Banana Stowaway, 346
Barred Chestnut, 9, 13, 230, **17**
Barred Hook-tip, 12, 55
Barred Red, 175
Barred Rivulet, 112
Barred Sallow, 19, 281
Barred Straw, 93
Barred Tooth-striped, 15, 16, 24, 142, **24**
Barred Umber, 150
Barred Yellow, 96
Beaded Chestnut, 17, 279
Beautiful Brocade, 15, 243, **1**
Beautiful Carpet, 89
Beautiful Golden Y, 17, 331
Beautiful Hook-tip, 339
Beautiful Snout, 11, 20, 340
Beautiful Yellow Underwing, 9, 13, 238, **17**
Bedstraw Hawk-moth, 22, 185
Beech-green Carpet, 16, 100
Birch Mocha, 67
Bird's Wing, 291, **22**
Black Arches, 202
Black Rustic, 19, 265
Blackneck, 11, 337, **15**
Black-veined Moth, 345
Blair's Mocha, 21, 67
Blair's Shoulder-knot, 19, 20, 268
Bleached Pug, 125
Blood-vein, 69
Blossom Underwing, 17, 252
Blotched Emerald, 18, 64, **13**
Blue-bordered Carpet, 18, 97
Bordered Beauty, 152
Bordered Gothic, 15, 241, **1**

Bordered Pug, 128
Bordered Sallow, 322, **15**
Bordered Straw, 22, 323
Bordered White, 172
Brick, 17, 276
Bright-line Brown-eye, 244
Brimstone Moth, 151
Brindled Beauty, 17, 161
Brindled Green, 271
Brindled Pug, 132
Brindled White-spot, 170
Broad-barred White, 245, **22**
Broad-bordered Bee Hawk-moth, 15, 16, 183, **1**
Broad-bordered Yellow Underwing, 224
Broken-barred Carpet, 99
Broom Moth, 242
Broom-tip, 25, 138
Brown Rustic, 292
Brown Scallop, 107
Brown Silver-line, 150
Brown-line Bright-eye, 256
Brown-spot Pinion, 17, 278
Brown-tail, 200
Brown-veined Wainscot, 14, 315
Brussels Lace, 15, 168, **1**
Buff Arches, 56, 57
Buff Ermine, 211
Buff Footman, 20, 207
Buff-tip, 196
Bulrush Wainscot, 215, 314, **19**
Burnet Companion, 215, 336
Burnished Brass, 329
Cabbage Moth, 241
Campanula Pug, 20, 25, 127
Campion, 246
Canary-shouldered Thorn, 154
Centre-barred Sallow, 279
Chalk Carpet, 10, 12, 24, 25, 83, **15**
Chamomile Shark, 262
Chestnut, 275
Chevron, 91
Chimney Sweeper, 139
Chinese Character, 56
Chocolate-tip, 195
Cinnabar, 213, **23**
Clay, 257
Clay Triple-lines, 18, 69, **7**

Clifden Nonpareil, 22, 334
Cloaked Carpet, 11, 20, 25, 108, **8**
Cloaked Minor, 306
Cloaked Pug, 117
Clouded Border, 146
Clouded Brindle, 301
Clouded Buff, 15, 210, **1**
Clouded Drab, 255
Clouded Magpie, 11, 12, 17, 145
Clouded Silver, 18, 174
Clouded-bordered Brindle, 300
Common Carpet, 85, 86
Common Emerald, 65
Common Fan-foot, 15, 16, 342
Common Footman, 208
Common Heath, 171
Common Lutestring, 59
Common Marbled Carpet, 95, 96
Common Pug, 125
Common Quaker, 254
Common Rustic, 307, 308
Common Swift, 38
Common Wainscot, 259
Common Wave, 173
Common White Wave, 172
Confused, 347
Convolvulus Hawk-moth, 2, 21, 177, 341, **3**
Copper Underwing, 289, 290
Coronet, 288
Cosmopolitan, 21, 22, 261
Coxcomb Prominent, 192
Cream Wave, 72
Cream-bordered Green Pea, 20, 25, 325, **20**
Cream-spot Tiger, 209
Crescent, 314, **21**
Crinan Ear, 347
Currant Clearwing, 25, 44
Currant Pug, 124
Cypress Pug, 20, 134
Dark Arches, 31, 299
Dark Brocade, 272
Dark Chestnut, 275
Dark Crimson Underwing, 14, 15, 335, **1**
Dark Dagger, 286
Dark Marbled Carpet, 95
Dark Spectacle, 17, 333
Dark Spinach, 17, 18, 89
Dark Sword-grass, 21, 22, 219
Dark Tussock, 14, 15, 199, **1**
Dark Umber, 107
Dark-barred Twin-spot Carpet, 81

Death's-head Hawk-moth, 21, 22, 178, 341, **4**
December Moth, 49
Deep-brown Dart, 17, 264
Delicate, 22, 257
Dewick's Plusia, 22, 329
Dingy Footman, 206
Dingy Mocha, 15, 66, **1**
Dingy Shears, 295
Dingy Shell, 140
Dog's Tooth, 244
Dot Moth, 242
Dotted Border, 164
Dotted Border Wave, 345
Dotted Chestnut, 10, 19, 25, 276, **6**
Dotted Clay, 233
Dotted Fan-foot, 347
Dotted Rustic, 17, 222
Double Dart, 17, 227
Double Lobed, 304
Double Square-spot, 233
Double-striped Pug, 18, 137
Drinker, 48, 52, **21**
Dun-bar, 298
Dusky Brocade, 301
Dusky Sallow, 19, 310
Dusky Thorn, 154
Dusky-lemon Sallow, 12, 17, 282
Dwarf Cream Wave, 20, 73, 345
Dwarf Pug, 135
Ear Moth, 312
Early Grey, 270
Early Moth, 174
Early Thorn, 155
Early Tooth-striped, 143
Eastern Nycteoline, 334
Elephant Hawk-moth, 186
Emperor Moth, 17, 53, **16**
Engrailed, 169
Eversmann's Rustic, 22, 134, 221
Eyed Hawk-moth, 181
False Mocha, 10, 17, 25, 68
Fan-foot, 343
Feathered Gothic, 250
Feathered Ranunculus, 21, 274
Feathered Thorn, 159
Fen Wainscot, 14, 20, 316, **20**
Fern, 103
Festoon, 43
Figure of Eight, 17, 197, 198
Figure of Eighty, 57
Five-spot Burnet, 42

Flame, 220
Flame Carpet, 80
Flame Shoulder, 221
Flounced Chestnut, 17, 278
Flounced Rustic, 311
Forester, 12, 40, 41
Four-dotted Footman, 205
Four-spotted, 16, 337, **1**
Fox Moth, 48, 51
Foxglove Pug, 118
Freyer's Pug, 19, 20, 122
Frosted Green, 60
Frosted Orange, 313
Galium Carpet, 16, 86
Garden Carpet, 82
Garden Dart, 17, 18, 216, 217
Garden Tiger, 17, 18, 209
Gem, 21, 22, 61, 79, **3**
Ghost Moth, 37
Glaucous Shears, 17, 245
Goat Moth, 17, 25, 40, **5, 23**
Gold Spangle, 17, 332
Gold Spot, 330, **21**
Gold Swift, 38
Golden Plusia, 17, 18, 330
Golden-rod Brindle, 22, 265
Golden-rod Pug, 132
Gothic, 236
Grass Emerald, 63
Grass Rivulet, 113
Grass Wave, 13, 177, **17**
Great Brocade, 22, 237
Great Oak Beauty, 8, 11, 25, 167, **8**
Great Prominent, 197, **9**
Green Arches, 237, **10**
Green Carpet, 101
Green Pug, 136
Green Silver-lines, 19, 326
Green-brindled Crescent, 270
Grey Arches, 241
Grey Birch, 171
Grey Chi, 17, 272, 273
Grey Dagger, 286
Grey Mountain Carpet, 345
Grey Pine Carpet, 98,
Grey Pug, 127
Grey Scalloped Bar, 15, 16, 176, **1**
Grey Shoulder-knot, 18, 19, 267, **2**
Gypsy Moth, 202
Haworth's Pug, 116
Heart and Club, 218

Heart and Dart, 219
Heath Rustic, 236, **18**
Hebrew Character, 256
Hedge Rustic, 17, 249
Herald, 338
Hornet Moth, 25, 43
Humming-bird Hawk-moth, 21, 22, 184
Ingrailed Clay, 230
Iron Prominent, 189
Jersey Tiger, 346
July Belle, 84
July Highflyer, 101
Juniper Carpet, 18, 19, 99
Juniper Pug, 17, 133
Knot Grass, 287
Lace Border, 12, 16, 70, **1**
Lackey, 17, 50
Lappet, 17, 52, **11**
Larch Pug, 134
Large Ear, 311
Large Emerald, 64
Large Nutmeg, 19, 302
Large Ranunculus, 273
Large Red-belted Clearwing, 25, 47
Large Twin-spot Carpet, 18, 81
Large Wainscot, 316
Large Yellow Underwing, 31, 223
Latticed Heath, 149
Lead Belle, 84
Lead-coloured Drab, 253
Lead-coloured Pug, 15, 16, 116
Least Black Arches, 214
Least Carpet, 20, 72
Least Yellow Underwing, 225
Lempke's Gold Spot, 347
Leopard Moth, 39
Lesser Broad-bordered Yellow Underwing, 225
Lesser Common Rustic, 19, 20, 307, 308
Lesser Cream Wave, 71
Lesser Swallow Prominent, 191
Lesser Treble-bar, 139
Lesser Yellow Underwing, 224
Lesser-spotted Pinion, 12, 17, 296, 297
Light Arches, 215, 299
Light Brocade, 243
Light Crimson Underwing, 14, 335
Light Emerald, 175
Light Feathered Rustic, 12, 16, 217
Light Knot Grass, 15, 287
Light Orange Underwing, 10, 11, 12, 25, 62, **9**
Lilac Beauty, 153, **13**

Lime Hawk-moth, 12, 181, **23**
Lime-speck Pug, 121
Ling Pug, 124
Little Emerald, 66
Little Thorn, 10, 20, 149
Lobster Moth, 16, 196, **1**
Lunar Hornet Moth, 44, **11**
Lunar Marbled Brown, 194
Lunar Thorn, 17, 156
Lunar Underwing, 280
Lunar Yellow Underwing, 14, 223, **1**
Lunar-spotted Pinion, 298
Lychnis, 246, 248
Magpie, 17, 144, 145
Maiden's Blush, 68
Mallow, 87
Maple Pug, 115
Map-winged Swift, 9, 39
Marbled Beauty, 288, **24**
Marbled Brown, 194
Marbled Coronet, 248
Marbled Green, 21, 289
Marbled Minor, 304, 305
Marbled White Spot, 324
March Moth, 61, 63
Marsh Carpet, 15, 114, **1**
Marsh Pug, 120
May Highflyer, 102
Mere Wainscot, 10, 11 20, 25, 309
Merveille du Jour, 271
Middle-barred Minor, 306
Miller, 285
Minor Shoulder-knot, 263
Mocha, 25, 66
Mother Shipton, 215, 336
Mottled Beauty, 167
Mottled Grey, 100
Mottled Pug, 118
Mottled Rustic, 320
Mottled Umber, 165
Mouse Moth, 290
Mullein, 10, 263
Mullein Wave, 70
Muslin Footman, 204
Muslin Moth, 211
Narrow-bordered Bee Hawk-moth, 15, 183
Narrow-bordered Five-spot Burnet, 40, 42, **24**
Narrow-winged Pug, 10, 131
Neglected Rustic, 16, 234
Netted Pug, 120
Ni Moth, 21, 22, 328, **3**

Northern Drab, 253
Northern Spinach, 92
Northern Winter Moth, 111
November Moth, 109
Nutmeg, 239
Nut-tree Tussock, 327
Oak Beauty, 162
Oak Eggar, 48, 51
Oak Hook-tip, 18, 54
Oak Lutestring, 59
Oak Nycteoline, 327
Oak-tree Pug, 133
Oblique Carpet, 78
Obscure Wainscot, 14, 19, 260
Ochreous Pug, 130
Old Lady, 291
Oleander Hawk-moth, 22, 184
Olive, 294
Orange Footman, 19, 206, **8**
Orange Moth, 17, 159, **11**
Orange Sallow, 280
Orange Swift, 37
Orange Underwing, 61, 62
Orange-tailed Clearwing, 25, 46, **6**
Paignton Snout, 22, 341
Pale Brindled Beauty, 161
Pale Eggar, 49
Pale Mottled Willow, 320
Pale November Moth, 109
Pale Oak Beauty, 20, 168
Pale Pinion, 20, 266
Pale Prominent, 193
Pale Shining Brown, 16, 240, **1**
Pale Tussock, 200
Pale-shouldered Brocade, 243
Peach Blossom, 4, 56
Peacock Moth, 20, 147
Pearly Underwing, 22, 229
Pebble Hook-tip, 18, 55, **9**
Pebble Prominent, 191
Peppered Moth, 162, 163
Phoenix, 18, 91
Pimpinel Pug, 13, 20, 130
Pine Beauty, 250
Pine Carpet, 97
Pine Hawk-moth, 21, 180, **2**
Pinion-spotted Pug, 10, 25, 119, **7**
Pinion-streaked Snout, 342
Pink-barred Sallow, 281
Plain Clay, 15, 16, 228, **1**
Plain Golden Y, 17, 332

Plain Pug, 129
Plain Wave, 77
Plumed Fan-foot, 22, 343
Plumed Prominent, 346
Poplar Grey, 283
Poplar Hawk-moth, 181, 182
Poplar Kitten, 189
Poplar Lutestring, 58, **11**
Powdered Quaker, 17, 254
Pretty Chalk Carpet, 8, 104
Privet Hawk-moth, 180
Purple Bar, 90
Purple Clay, 231
Purple Thorn, 157
Puss Moth, 187, **13**, **23**
Red Chestnut, 238
Red Sword-grass, 269
Red Twin-spot Carpet, 80
Red Underwing, 335
Red-belted Clearwing, 25, 46
Reddish Light Arches, 300
Red-green Carpet, 18, 94, **2**
Red-line Quaker, 277
Red-necked Footman, 20, 205, **2**
Red-tipped Clearwing, 25, 47, **20**
Remm's Rustic, 307
Riband Wave, 76
Rivulet, 111
Rosy Footman, 204, **7**
Rosy Minor, 307, **22**
Rosy Rustic, 313
Round-winged Muslin, 19, 203
Royal Mantle, 14, 85, **1**
Ruby Tiger, 212
Ruddy Carpet, 8, 12, 25, 85, **15**
Ruddy Highflyer, 102
Rufous Minor, 304, 305
Rush Veneer, 21
Rustic, 318
Rustic Shoulder-knot, 303
Sallow, 282
Sallow Kitten, 188
Saltern Ear, 312
Sandy Carpet, 18, 113
Satellite, 274
Satin Beauty, 18, 166
Satin Lutestring, 58
Satin Wave, 75
Satyr Pug, 123
Scallop Shell, 106
Scalloped Hazel, 3, 157

Scalloped Hook-tip, 54
Scalloped Oak, 158
Scarce Bordered Straw, 22, 322
Scarce Footman, 19, 207
Scarce Prominent, 15, 16, 193
Scarce Silver Y, 22, 333
Scarce Silver-lines, 325, 326, **10**
Scarce Tissue, 105
Scarce Umber, 164
Scarce Vapourer, 14, 198, **1**
Scarlet Tiger, 20, 212, **2**
Scorched Carpet, 146
Scorched Wing, 151
September Thorn, 155
Seraphim, 141
Setaceous Hebrew Character, 232
Shaded Broad-bar, 83
Shaded Pug, 8, 20, 129
Shark, 262
Sharp-angled Carpet, 108
Shears, 239
Short-cloaked Moth, 214
Shoulder Stripe, 88
Shoulder-striped Wainscot, 260
Shuttle-shaped Dart, 220
Silky Wainscot, 14, 20, 321
Silky Wave, 345
Silver Barred, 15, 325, **1**
Silver Cloud, 10, 25, 251, **5**
Silver Y, 21, 22, 331
Silver-ground Carpet, 82
Silver-striped Hawk-moth, 21, 22, 187
Silvery Arches, 15, 240, **1**
Single-dotted Wave, 74
Six-belted Clearwing, 10, 25, 48, **15**
Six-spot Burnet, 40, 41
Six-striped Rustic, 235
Slender Brindle, 303
Slender Burnished Brass, 21, 22, 134, 328, **3**
Slender Pug, 115,
Sloe Pug, 19, 20, 136
Small Angle Shades, 293
Small Argent & Sable, 345
Small Blood-vein, 71
Small Brindled Beauty, 160
Small Chocolate-tip, 14, 195, **1**
Small Clouded Brindle, 19, 302
Small Dotted Buff, 309
Small Dusty Wave, 74,
Small Eggar, 15, 16, 50, **1**
Small Elephant Hawk-moth, 186, **15**

Small Emerald, 65
Small Engrailed, 169
Small Fan-foot, 344
Small Fan-footed Wave, 73
Small Grass Emerald, 345
Small Mottled Willow, 22, 319, 320
Small Phoenix, 93
Small Purple-barred, 17, 338
Small Quaker, 252
Small Rivulet, 112
Small Rufous, 19, 317
Small Scallop, 76,
Small Seraphim, 143, **13**
Small Square-spot, 17, 231
Small Wainscot, 310
Small Waved Umber, 103
Small White Wave, 140
Small Yellow Underwing, 321, 322
Small Yellow Wave, 141
Smoky Wainscot, 258
Smoky Wave, 345
Snout, 341
Southern Wainscot, 14, 20, 258
Speckled Yellow, 15, 16, 152, **1**
Spectacle, 334
Spinach, 17, 18, 91, 92
Sprawler, 264, **23**
Spring Usher, 163
Spruce Carpet, 98
Square Spot, 170
Square-spot Dart, 13, 25, 215, **5**
Square-spot Rustic, 235
Square-spotted Clay, 15, 16, 234, **1**
Stout Dart, 16, 226, **1**
Straw Belle, 346
Straw Dot, 19, 339
Straw Underwing, 292
Streak, 10, 137
Streamer, 88
Striped Hawk-moth, 22, 185, **4**
Suspected, 295
Svensson's Copper Underwing, 19, 20, 290
Swallow Prominent, 192
Swallow-tailed Moth, 158
Sword-grass, 16, 269, **1**
Sycamore, 19, 284
Tawny Marbled Minor, 304, 305
Tawny Pinion, 266
Tawny Shears, 246
Tawny Speckled Pug, 128
Tawny-barred Angle, 147

Tissue, 17, 106
Toadflax Pug, 117
Transparent Burnet, 42
Treble-bar, 138
Treble Brown Spot, 18, 75
Treble Lines, 19, 317
Triangle, 14, 15, 43
Triple-spotted Clay, 17, 232
Triple-spotted Pug, 12, 121
True Lover's Knot, 10, 229, **17**
Turnip Moth, 215, 218
Twin-spot Carpet, 114
Twin-spotted Quaker, 255
Twin-spotted Wainscot, 14, 20, 315
Uncertain, 318
Valerian Pug, 10, 20, 25, 119
Vapourer, 199
Varied Coronet, 20, 247
Vestal, 21, 22, 61, 77, 343, **3**
Vine's Rustic, 20, 319, **2**
V-Moth, 17, 18, 91, 148
V-Pug, 135
Water Carpet, 90,
Waved Black, 20, 25, 215, 340, **6**
Waved Carpet, 14, 15, 141
Waved Umber, 165
White Colon, 346
White Ermine, 210, 211
White Satin Moth, 19, 201, **12**
White-barred Clearwing, 15, 16, 45
White-line Dart, 216
White-pinion Spotted, 18, 173
White-speck, 22, 259
White-spotted Pinion, 12, 15, 16, 297, **1**
White-spotted Pug, 126
Willow Beauty, 166
Winter Moth, 110
Wood Carpet, 86
Wood Tiger, 15, 16, 208, **1**
Wormwood, 25, 261, **5**
Wormwood Pug, 123
Yellow Belle, 346
Yellow Horned, 60
Yellow Shell, 87
Yellow-barred Brindle, 144
Yellow-legged Clearwing, 25, 45, **6**
Yellow-line Quaker, 277
Yellow-tail, 201

Index of Scientific Names

Numbers in bold refer to colour plates.

abbreviata, Eupithecia, 132
abietaria, Eupithecia, 117
Abraxas, 144–145
Abrostola, 333–334
abruptaria, Menophra, 165
absinthiata, Eupithecia, 123
absinthiata f. goossensiata, Eupithecia, 124
absinthii, Cucullia, 25, 261, **5**
Acasis, 144
aceris, Acronicta, 19, 284
Acherontia, 178
Achlya, 60
Acronicta, 283–287
Actebia, 221
Adscita, 41
adusta, Blepharita, 272
adustata, Ligdia, 146
advenaria, Cepphis, 10, 20, 149
aescularia, Alsophila, 61, 63
aestivaria, Hemithea, 65
Aethalura, 171
affinis, Cosmia, 12, 17, 296, 297
affinitata, Perizoma, 111
agathina, Xestia, 236, **18**
Agriopis, 163–164
Agrius, 177
Agrochola, 276–279
Agrotis, 217–220
albicilla, Salebriopsis, 10
albicillata, Mesoleuca, 89
albicolon, Sideridis, 346
albipunctata, Cyclophora, 67
albulata, Perizoma, 113
albulata, Asthena, 140
alchemillata, Perizoma, 112
Alcis, 167
Allophyes, 270
alni, Acronicta, 285
alniaria, Ennomos, 154
alsines, Hoplodrina, 318
Alsophila, 63
alternata, Epirrhoe, 85, 86
ambigua, Hoplodrina, 20, 319, **2**
Amphipoea, 311–312
Amphipyra, 289–290
Anaplectoides, 237
Anarta, 238

anceps, Peridea, 197, **9**
anceps, Apamea, 19, 302
andrenaeformis, Synanthedon, 25, 46, **6**
Angerona, 159
annularia, Cyclophora, 25, 66
Antichloris, 346
Anticlea, 88
antiqua, Orgyia, 199
Antitype, 272
Apamea, 299–304
Apeira, 153
apiformis, Sesia, 25, 43
Aplocera, 138–139
Apocheima, 160
Aporophyla, 264–265
aprilina, Dichonia, 271
Archanara, 315
Archiearis, 61–62
Arctia, 209
ARCTIIDAE, 203
Arenostola, 316
areola, Xylocampa, 270
armigera, Helicoverpa, 22, 322
asella, Heterogenea, 14, 15, 43
asiatica, Nycteola, 334
Aspitates, 346
assimilata, Eupithecia, 124
Asteroscopus, 264
Asthena, 140
Atethmia, 279
Atolmis, 205
atomaria, Ematurga, 171
atrata, Odezia, 139
atropos, Acherontia, 21, 22, 178, 341, **4**
augur, Graphiphora, 17, 227
aurago, Xanthia, 19, 281
aurantiaria, Agriopis, 164
Autographa, 331–332
autumnata, Epirrita, 109, 110
aversata, Idaea, 76
Axylia, 220
badiata, Anticlea, 88
baja, Xestia, 233
bajularia, Comibaena, 18, 64, **13**
bankiana, Deltote, 15, 325, **1**
batis, Thyatira, 4, 56
Bembecia, 48

bembeciformis, Sesia, 44, **11**
Bena, 325
berbera svenssoni, Amphipyra, 19, 20, 290
betularia, Biston, 162, 163
biangulata, Euphyia, 11, 20, 25, 108, **8**
bicolorana, Bena, 325, 326, **10**
bicolorata, Hecatera, 245, **22**
bicruris, Hadena, 246, 248
bicuspis, Furcula, 19, 188
bidentata, Odontopera, 3, 157
bifaciata, Perizoma, 112
bifida, Furcula, 189
bilineata, Camptogramma, 87
bimaculata, Lomographa, 18, 173
binaria, Watsonalla, 18, 54
bipunctaria cretata, Scotopteryx, 10, 12, 24, 25, 83, **15**
biren, Papestra, 17, 245
biselata, Idaea, 73
Biston, 162
bistortata, Ectropis, 169
blanda, Hoplodrina, 318
Blepharita, 272
bombycina, Polia, 16, 240, **1**
Brachylomia, 263
bractea, Autographa, 17, 332
brassicae, Mamestra, 241
britannica, Thera, 18, 98
brumata, Operophtera, 110
brunnea, Diarsia, 231
bucephala, Phalera, 196
Bupalus, 172
Cabera, 172–173
caeruleocephala, Diloba, 17, 197, 198
caesiata, Entephria, 345
caja, Arctia, 17, 18, 209
Callimorpha, 212
Callistege, 336
Calliteara, 200
Campaea, 175
Camptogramma, 87
capucina, Ptilodon, 192
Caradrina, 320
carmelita, Odontosia, 15, 16, 193
carpinata, Trichopteryx, 143
castanea, Xestia, 16, 234
Catarhoe, 85
Catocala, 334–335
Celaena, 314
celerio, Hippotion, 21, 22, 187
centaureata, Eupithecia, 121
centrago, Atethmia, 279

Cepphis, 149
Cerapteryx, 249
cerasi, Orthosia, 254
Cerastis, 238
Cerura, 187
cervinalis, Rheumaptera, 105
cespitis, Tholera, 17, 249
chamomillae, Cucullia, 262
Charanyca, 317
Charissa, 176
chenopodiata, Scotopteryx, 83
Chesias, 137–138
chi, Antitype, 17, 272, 273
Chiasmia, 149
Chilodes, 321
chloerata, Pasiphila, 19, 20, 136
Chlorissa, 345
Chloroclysta, 94–96
Chloroclystis, 135
chlorosata, Petrophora, 150
Chortodes, 309–310
christyi, Epirrita, 109
chrysitis, Diachrysia, 329
chrysoprasaria, Hemistola, 65
chrysorrhoea, Euproctis, 200
Cidaria, 96
Cilix, 56
cinerea, Agrotis, 12, 16, 217
circellaris, Agrochola, 17, 276
cirrago, Xanthia, 280
cirrata, Chloroclysta, 95
clathrata, Chiasmia, 149
clavaria, Larentia, 87
clavipalpis, Paradrina, 320
clavis, Agrotis, 218
Cleorodes, 168
clorana, Earias, 20, 25, 325, **20**
Clostera, 195
c-nigrum, Xestia, 232
Coenobia, 317
Colocasia, 327
Colostygia, 100–101
Colotois, 159
comae, Timandra, 69
comes, Noctua, 224
Comibaena, 64
comitata, Pelurga, 17, 18, 89
comma, Mythimna, 260
complana, Eilema, 19, 207
compta, Hadena, 20, 247
confusa, Macdunnoughia, 22, 329

confusa, Hadena, 248
confusalis, Nola, 214
conigera, Mythimna, 256
Conistra, 275–276
consonaria, Paradarisa, 170
conspicillaris, Egira, 10, 25, 251, **5**
contigua, Lacanobia, 15, 243, **1**
convolvuli, Agrius, 2, 21, 177, 341, **3**
corylata, Electrophaes, 99
coryli, Colocasia, 327
Cosmia, 296–298
Cosmorhoe, 90
COSSIDAE, 39
cossus, Cossus, 17, 25, 40, **5**, **23**
Cossus, 40
costaestrigalis, Schrankia, 342
Craniophora, 288
crassalis, Hypena, 11, 20, 340
crataegi, Trichiura, 49
crenata, Apamea, 300
crepuscularia, Ectropis, 169
cribrumalis, Macrochilo, 347
crinanensis, Amphipoea, 347
Crocallis, 158
cruda, Orthosia, 252
Cryphia, 288–289
cuculata, Catarhoe, 14, 85, **1**
cucullatella, Nola, 214
Cucullia, 261–262
culiciformis, Synanthedon, 25, 47
cultraria, Watsonalla, 12, 55
curtula, Clostera, 195
Cybosia, 205
Cyclophora, 66–69
Cymatophorima, 59
dahlii, Diarsia, 9, 13, 230, **17**
Daphnis, 184
decimalis, Tholera, 250
defoliaria, Erannis, 165
Deilephila, 186
Deileptenia, 166
Deltote, 325
denotata, Eupithecia, 20, 25, 127
dentaria, Selenia, 155
depressa, Eilema, 20, 207
depuncta, Eugnorisma, 15, 16, 228, **1**
derivata, Anticlea, 88
designata, Xanthorhoe, 80
Diachrysia, 329
Diacrisia, 210
Diaphora, 211

Diarsia, 230–231
Dicallomera, 199
Dichonia, 271
didyma, Mesapamea, 19, 20, 307, 308
didymata, Perizoma, 114
diffinis, Cosmia, 12, 15, 16, **1**, 297
Diloba, 197
diluta hartwiegi, Cymatophorima, 59
dilutaria, Idaea, 345
dilutata, Epirrita, 109
dimidiata, Idaea, 74
Discestra, 239
dispar, Lymantria, 202
dissoluta, Archanara, 14, 315
ditrapezium, Xestia, 17, 232
dodonaea, Drymonia, 194
dodoneata, Eupithecia, 133
dolabraria, Plagodis, 151
domestica, Cryphia, 288, **24**
dominula, Callimorpha, 20, 212, **2**
Drepana, 55
DREPANIDAE, 54
dromedarius, Notodonta, 189
Drymonia, 194
Dryobotodes, 271
dubitata, Triphosa, 17, 106
duplaris, Ochropacha, 59
Dypterygia, 291
Dyscia, 176
Earias, 325
Ecliptopera, 93
Ectropis, 169
efformata, Aplocera, 139
Egira, 251
Eilema, 206–208
Electrophaes, 99
elinguaria, Crocallis, 158
elpenor, Deilephila, 186
emarginata, Idaea, 76
Ematurga, 171
Enargia, 294
Ennomos, 153–155
Entephria, 345
Epione, 152
Epirrhoe, 85–86
Epirrita, 109–110
epomidion, Apamea, 301
Erannis, 165
eremita, Dryobotodes, 271
Eremobia, 310
Eriogaster, 50

eriphia, Antichloris, 346
erosaria, Ennomos, 155
Euchoeca, 140
Euclidia, 336
Eugnorisma, 228
Eulithis, 91–93
Euphyia, 108
Eupithecia, 114–135
Euplagia, 346
Euplexia, 293
Euproctis, 200–201
Eupsilia, 274
Eurois, 237
Euthrix, 52
Euxoa, 215–216
exanthemata, Cabera, 173
exclamationis, Agrotis, 219
exigua, Spodoptera, 22, 319, 320
exiguata, Eupithecia, 118
expallidata, Eupithecia, 125
exsoleta, Xylena, 16, 269, **1**
fagaria, Dyscia, 15, 16, 176, **1**
fagata, Operophtera, 111
fagi, Stauropus, 16, 196, **1**
Falcaria, 54
falcataria, Drepana, 18, 55, **9**
fascelina, Dicallomera, 14, 15, **1**, 199
fasciaria, Hylaea, 175
fasciuncula, Oligia, 306
fennica, Actebia, 22, 134, 221
ferrago, Mythimna, 257
ferrugata, Xanthorhoe, 81
ferruginea, Rusina, 292
festucae, Plusia, 330, **21**
filipendulae, Zygaena, 40, 41
fimbriata, Noctua, 224
firmata, Thera, 97
flammea, Panolis, 250
flammeolaria, Hydrelia, 141
flavago, Gortyna, 313
flavicincta, Polymixis, 273
flavicornis, Achlya, 60
flavofasciata, Perizoma, 18, 113
flexula, Laspeyria, 339
floslactata, Scopula, 72
fluctuata fluctuata, Xanthorhoe, 82
fluctuosa, Tetheella, 58
fluxa, Chortodes, 10, 11 20, 25, 309
formicaeformis, Synanthedon, 25, 47, **20**
fraxinata, Eupithecia, 131
fraxini, Catocala, 22, 334

fuciformis, Hemaris, 15, 16, 183, **1**
fucosa paludis, Amphipoea, 312
fuliginaria, Parascotia, 20, 25, 215, 340, **6**
fuliginosa, Phragmatobia, 212
fulvata, Cidaria, 96
furcata, Hydriomena, 101
furcula, Furcula, 188
Furcula, 188–189
furuncula, Mesoligia, 306
furva britannica, Apamea, 347
fuscantaria, Ennomos, 154
fusconebulosa, Hepialus, 9, 39
fuscovenosa, Idaea, 20, 73, 345
galiata, Epirrhoe, 16, 86
gallii, Hyles, 22, 185
gamma, Autographa, 21, 22, 331
Gastropacha, 52
geminipuncta, Archanara, 14, 20, 315
Geometra, 64
GEOMETRIDAE, 61
gilvago, Xanthia, 12, 17, 282
gilvaria gilvaria, Aspitates, 346
glareosa, Eugnorisma, 228, **18**
glaucata, Cilix, 56
glyphica, Euclidia, 215, 336
gnoma, Pheosia, 191
Gortyna, 313
gothica, Orthosia, 256
gracilis, Orthosia, 17, 254
graminis, Cerapteryx, 249
Graphiphora, 227
grisealis, Herminia, 344
griseola, Eilema, 206
grossulariata, Abraxas, 17, 144, 145
Gymnoscelis, 137
Habrosyne, 57
Hada, 239
Hadena, 246–248
halterata, Lobophora, 141
hastata, Rheumaptera, 15, 16, 24, 104
haworthiata, Eupithecia, 116
Hecatera, 245
hecta, Hepialus, 38
Helicoverpa, 322
Heliophobus, 241
Heliothis, 323
helvola, Agrochola, 17, 278
Hemaris, 183
Hemistola, 65
Hemithea, 65
hepatica, Lithophane, 20, 266

HEPIALIDAE, 37
Hepialus, 37–39
Herminia, 344
Heterogenea, 43
Hippotion, 187
hirtaria, Lycia, 17, 161
hispidaria, Apocheima, 160
Hoplodrina, 318–319
Horisme, 103
humuli, Hepialus, 37
Hydraecia, 313
Hydrelia, 141
Hydriomena, 101–102
Hylaea, 175
Hyles, 185
Hyloicus, 180
Hypena, 340–341
Hypomecis, 167–168
ichneumoniformis, Bembecia, 10, 25, 48, **15**
icterata subfulvata, Eupithecia, 128
icteritia, Xanthia, 282
Idaea, 72–77
imitaria, Scopula, 71
immutata, Scopula, 71
impluviata, Hydriomena, 102
impura, Mythimna, 258
incerta, Orthosia, 255
indigata, Eupithecia, 130
insigniata, Eupithecia, 10, 25, 119, **7**
interjecta calignosa, Noctua, 225
interrogationis, Syngrapha, 22, 333
intricata, Eupithecia, 19, 20, 122
inturbata, Eupithecia, 115
Ipimorpha, 294
ipsilon, Agrotis, 21, 22, 219
jacobaeae, Tyria, 213, **23**
janthe, Noctua, 225
Jodis, 66
jota, Autographa, 17, 332
juniperata, Thera, 18, 19, 99
Lacanobia, 243–244
lacertinaria, Falcaria, 54
lactearia, Jodis, 66
Lampropteryx, 90
lanestris, Eriogaster, 15, 16, 50, **1**
Laothoe, 182
Larentia, 87
lariciata, Eupithecia, 134
Lasiocampa, 51
LASIOCAMPIDAE, 48
Laspeyria, 339

latruncula, Oligia, 304, 305
leautieri hesperica, Lithophane, 19, 20, 268
legatella, Chesias, 10, 137
leporina, Acronicta, 285
Leucoma, 201
leucophaearia, Agriopis, 163
leucostigma, Celaena, 314, **21**
libatrix, Scoliopteryx, 338
lichenaria, Cleorodes, 15, 168, **1**
lichenea, Polymixis, 21, 274
Ligdia, 146
ligula, Conistra, 275
ligustri, Craniophora, 288
ligustri, Sphinx, 180
limacodes, Apoda, 43
LIMACODIDAE, 43
linariata, Eupithecia, 117
linearia, Cyclophora, 18, 69, **7**
lineata, Siona, 345
literosa, Mesoligia, 307, **22**
Lithomoia, 265
Lithophane, 266–268
lithoxylaea, Apamea, 215, 299
litura, Agrochola, 17, 278
liturata, Macaria, 147
livornica, Hyles, 22, 185, **4**
Lobophora, 141
Lomaspilis, 146
Lomographa, 173–174
lonicerae, Zygaena, 40, 42, **24**
loreyi, Mythimna, 21, 22, 261
lota, Agrochola, 277
lubricipeda, Spilosoma, 210, 211
lucens, Amphipoea, 311
lucipara, Euplexia, 293
luctuosa, Tyta, 16, 337, **1**
lunosa, Omphaloscelis, 280
lunularia, Selenia, 17, 156
Luperina, 311
lupulinus, Hepialus, 38
luridata plumbaria, Scotopteryx, 84
lurideola, Eilema, 208,
luteolata, Opisthograptis, 151
luteum, Spilosoma, 211
lutosa, Rhizedra, 316
lutulenta, Aporophyla, 17, 264
lychnidis, Agrochola, 17, 279
Lycia, 161
Lycophotia, 229
Lygephila, 337
Lymantria, 202

LYMANTRIIDAE, 198
Macaria, 147–148
Macdunnoughia, 329
macilenta, Agrochola, 277
Macrochilo, 347
Macroglossum, 184
Macrothylacia, 51
macularia, Pseudopanthera, 15, 16, 152, **1**
Malacosoma, 50
Mamestra, 241
margaritata, Campaea, 175
marginaria, Agriopis, 164
marginata, Lomaspilis, 146
marginepunctata, Scopula, 70
maritimus, Chilodes, 14, 20, 321
matura, Thalpophila, 292
maura, Mormo, 291
megacephala, Acronicta, 283
Melanchra, 242
Melanthia, 104
mellinata, Eulithis, 17, 18, 91, 92
mendica, Diaphora, 211
mendica mendica, Diarsia, 230
Menophra, 165
menyanthidis, Acronicta, 15, 287
Mesapamea, 307–308
Mesoleuca, 89
Mesoligia, 306–307
mesomella, Cybosia, 205
meticulosa, Phlogophora, 293
mi, Callistege, 215, 336
miata, Chloroclysta, 17, 18, 95
micacea, Hydraecia, 313
Miltochrista, 204
Mimas, 181
miniata, Miltochrista, 204, **7**
minima, Photedes, 309
miniosa, Orthosia, 17, 252
monacha, Lymantria, 202
moneta, Polychrysia, 17, 18, 330
monoglypha, Apamea, 31, 299
montanata, Xanthorhoe, 82
Mormo, 291
morpheus, Caradrina, 320
mucronata, Scotopteryx, 84
multistrigaria, Colostygia, 100
munda, Orthosia, 255
mundana, Nudaria, 204
muralis, Cryphia, 21, 289
myopaeformis, Synanthedon, 25, 46
myrtilli, Anarta, 9, 13, 238, **17**

Mythimna, 256–261
Naenia, 236
nanata, Eupithecia, 10, 131
nebulata, Euchoeca, 140
nebulosa, Polia, 241
nerii, Daphnis, 22, 184
neustria, Malacosoma, 17, 50
ni, Trichoplusia, 21, 22, 328, **3**
nigra, Aporophyla, 19, 265
nigricans, Euxoa, 17, 18, 216, 217
Noctua, 223–225
noctuella, Nomophila, 21
NOCTUIDAE, 215
Nola, 214
NOLIDAE, 214
Nonagria, 314
notata, Macaria, 20, 147
notha, Archiearis, 10, 11, 12, 25, 62, **9**
Notodonta, 189–191
NOTODONTIDAE, 187
Nudaria, 204
nupta, Catocala, 335
Nycteola, 327
obelisca grisea, Euxoa, 13, 25, 215, **5**
obeliscata, Thera, 98,
obesalis, Hypena, 22, 341
obscurata, Charissa, 13, 176, **22**
obsoleta, Mythimna, 14, 19, 260
obstipata, Orthonama, 21, 22, 61, 79, **3**
occulta, Eurois, 22, 237
ocellata, Smerinthus, 181
ocellata, Cosmorhoe, 90
ochrearia, Semiaspilates, 346
ochroleuca, Eremobia, 19, 310
Ochropacha, 59
Ochropleura, 221
ocularis octogesimea, Tethea, 57
oculea, Amphipoea, 312
Odezia, 139
Odontopera, 157
Odontosia, 193
oleracea, Lacanobia, 244
Oligia, 304–307
olivata, Colostygia, 16, 100
Omphaloscelis, 280
Operophtera, 110–111
ophiogramma, Apamea, 304
opima, Orthosia, 253
Opisthograptis, 151
or, Tethea, 58, **11**
orbona, Noctua, 14, 223, **1**

Orgyia, 198–199
orichalcea, Thysanoplusia, 21, 22, 134, 328, **3**
ornata, Scopula, 12, 16, 70, **1**
ornitopus lactipennis, Lithophane, 18, 19, 267, **2**
Orthonama, 78–79
Orthosia, 252–256
Ourapteryx, 158
oxyacanthae, Allophyes, 270
paleacea, Enargia, 8, 10, 25, 294, **7**
pallens, Mythimna, 259
palpina, Pterostoma, 193
Panemeria, 321
Panolis, 250
Papestra, 245
papilionaria, Geometra, 64
Paradarisa, 170
Paradrina, 320
Parascotia, 340
Parasemia, 208
Parastichtis, 295
Parectropis, 170
parthenias, Archiearis, 61, 62
Pasiphila, 136
pastinum, Lygephila, 11, 337, **15**
pavonia, Saturnia, 17, 53, **16**
Pechipogo, 342–343
pectinataria, Colostygia, 101
peltigera, Heliothis, 22, 323
Pelurga, 89
pendularia, Cyclophora, 15, 66, **1**
pennaria, Colotois, 159
Perconia, 177
Peribatodes, 166
Peridea, 197
Peridroma, 229
Perizoma, 111–114
perplexa, Hadena, 246
persicariae, Melanchra, 242
Petrophora, 150
Phalera, 196
Pheosia, 191–192
Phigalia, 161
Philereme, 107
Phlogophora, 293
phoeniceata, Eupithecia, 20, 134
Photedes, 309
Phragmatobia, 212
phragmitidis, Arenostola, 14, 20, 316, **20**
Phyllonorycter, 10
Phytometra, 338
pigra, Clostera, 14, 195, **1**

pilosaria, Phigalia, 161
pimpinellata, Eupithecia, 13, 20, 130
pinastri, Hyloicus, 21, 180, **2**
piniaria, Bupalus, 172
pisi, Melanchra, 242
plagiata plagiata, Aplocera, 138
Plagodis, 150–151
plantaginis, Parasemia, 15, 16, 208, **1**
plebeja, Hada, 239
plecta, Ochropleura, 221
Plemyria, 97
plumbeolata, Eupithecia, 15, 16, 116
plumigera, Ptilophora, 346
plumigeralis, Pechipogo, 22, 343
Plusia, 330, 347
Poecilocampa, 49
Polia, 240–241
Polychrysia, 330
polycommata, Trichopteryx, 15, 16, 24, 142, **24**
Polymixis, 273–274
Polyploca, 60
populata, Eulithis, 92
populeti, Orthosia, 253
populi, Poecilocampa, 49
populi, Laothoe, 181, 182
porata, Cyclophora, 10, 17, 25, 68
porcellus, Deilephila, 186, **15**
porphyrea, Lycophotia, 10, 229, **17**
potatoria, Euthrix, 48, 52, **21**
prasina, Anaplectoides, 237, **10**
prasinana britannica, Pseudoips, 19, 326
primaria, Theria, 174
proboscidalis, Hypena, 341
procellata, Melanthia, 8, 104
promissa, Catocala, 14, 335
pronuba, Noctua, 31, 223
Protodeltote, 324
pruinata atropunctaria, Pseudoterpna, 63
prunaria, Angerona, 17, 159, **11**
prunata, Eulithis, 18, 91
Pseudoips, 326
Pseudopanthera, 152
Pseudoterpna, 63
psi, Acronicta, 286
Pterapherapteryx, 143
Pterostoma, 193
Ptilodon, 192
Ptilophora, 346
pudibunda, Calliteara, 200
pulchellata, Eupithecia, 118
pulchrina, Autographa, 17, 331

pulveraria, Plagodis, 150
punctaria, Cyclophora, 68
punctinalis, Hypomecis, 20, 168
punctulata, Aethalura, 171
puppillaria, Cyclophora, 21, 67
purpuralis, Zygaena, 42
pusaria, Cabera, 172
pusillata, Eupithecia, 17, 133
puta, Agrotis, 220
putnami gracilis, Plusia, 347
putris, Axylia, 220
pygarga, Protodeltote, 324
pygmaeata, Eupithecia, 120
pygmina, Chortodes, 310
pyraliata, Eulithis, 93
pyralina, Cosmia, 298
pyramidea, Amphipyra, 289, 290
pyrina, Zeuzera, 39
pyritoides, Habrosyne, 56, 57
Pyrrhia, 322
quadrifasiata, Xanthorhoe, 18, 81
quadripunctaria, Euplagia, 346
quercifolia, Gastropacha, 17, 52, **11**
quercinaria, Ennomos, 153
quercus, Lasiocampa, 48, 51
ravida, Spaelotis, 16, 226, **1**
recens, Orgyia, 14, 198, **1**
rectangulata, Pasiphila, 136
remissa, Apamea, 301
remmi, Mesapamea, 307
repandaria, Epione, 152
repandata, Alcis, 167
reticulata, Heliophobus, 15, 241, **1**
revayana, Nycteola, 327
Rheumaptera, 104–106
Rhizedra, 316
Rhodometra, 77
rhomboidaria, Peribatodes, 166
rhomboidea, Xestia, 15, 16, 234, **1**
Rhyacia, 222
ribeata, Deileptenia, 18, 166
ridens, Polyploca, 60
rivata, Epirrhoe, 86
Rivula, 339
rivularis, Hadena, 246
roboraria, Hypomecis, 8, 11, 25, 167, **8**
ruberata, Hydriomena, 102
rubi, Macrothylacia, 48, 51
rubi, Diarsia, 17, 231
rubidata, Catarhoe, 8, 12, 25, 85, **15**
rubiginata rubiginata, Plemyria, 18, 97

rubiginea, Conistra, 10, 19, 25, 276, **6**
rubricollis, Atolmis, 20, 205, **2**
rubricosa, Cerastis, 238
rufa, Coenobia, 19, 317
rufata, Chesias, 25, 138
ruficornis, Drymonia, 194
rufifasciata, Gymnoscelis, 18, 137
rumicis, Acronicta, 287
Rusina, 292
rusticata atrosignaria, Idaea, 20, 72
sacraria, Rhodometra, 21, 22, 61, 77, 343, **3**
sagittata, Perizoma, 114, **1**
Salebriopsis, 10
salicis, Leucoma, 19, 201, **12**
sambucaria, Ourapteryx, 158
sannio, Diacrisia, 15, 210, **1**
Saturnia, 53
SATURNIIDAE, 53
satyrata, Eupithecia, 123
saucia, Peridroma, 22, 229
scabriuscula, Dypterygia, 291, **22**
Schrankia, 342
Sciota, 10
Scoliopteryx, 338
scolopacina, Apamea, 303
Scopula, 70–72
Scotopteryx, 83–84
secalis, Mesapamea, 307, 308
segetum, Agrotis, 215, 218
Selenia, 155–157
Semiaspilates, 346
semibrunnea, Lithophane, 266
senex, Thumatha, 19, 203
seriata, Idaea, 74
sericealis, Rivula, 19, 339
Sesia, 43–44
SESIIDAE, 43
sexalata, Pterapherapteryx, 143, **13**
sexstrigata, Xestia, 235
Shargacucullia, 263
Sideridis, 346
silaceata, Ecliptopera, 93
similaria, Parectropis, 170
similis, Euproctis, 201
simpliciata, Eupithecia, 129
simulans, Rhyacia, 17, 222
Siona, 345
siterata, Chloroclysta, 18, 94, **2**
Smerinthus, 181
solidaginis, Lithomoia, 22, 265
sordens, Apamea, 303

sororcula, Eilema, 19, 206, **8**
spadicearia, Xanthorhoe, 80
Spaelotis, 226
spheciformis, Synanthedon, 15, 16, 45
SPHINGIDAE, 177
sphinx, Asteroscopus, 264, **23**
Sphinx, 180
Spilosoma, 210–211
Spodoptera, 319
sponsa, Catocala, 14, 15, 335, **1**
statices, Adscita, 12, 40, 41
Stauropus, 196
stellatarum, Macroglossum, 21, 22, 184
straminata, Idaea, 77
straminea, Mythimna, 14, 20, 258
strataria, Biston, 162
strigilata, Pechipogo, 15, 16, 342
strigilis, Oligia, 304, 305
strigillaria, Perconia, 13, 177, **17**
suasa, Lacanobia, 244
subfuscata, Eupithecia, 127
sublustris, Apamea, 300
subsericeata, Idaea, 75
subtusa, Ipimorpha, 294
subumbrata, Eupithecia, 8, 20, 129
succenturiata, Eupithecia, 128
suffumata, Lampropteryx, 90,
suspecta, Parastichtis, 295
sylvata, Abraxas, 11, 12, 17, 145
sylvata, Hydrelia, 14, 15, 141
sylvestraria, Idaea, 345
sylvina, Hepialus, 37
Synanthedon, 44–47
Syngrapha, 333
syringaria, Apeira, 153, **13**
tantillaria, Eupithecia, 135
tarsipennalis, Zanclognatha, 343
temerata, Lomographa, 18, 174,
tenebrata, Panemeria, 321, 322
tenuiata, Eupithecia, 115,
ternata, Scopula, 345
tersata, Horisme, 103
testacea, Luperina, 311
testata, Eulithis, 91
Tethea, 57–58
Tetheella, 58
tetralunaria, Selenia, 157
thalassina, Lacanobia, 243
Thalpophila, 292
Thera, 97–99
Theria, 174

Tholera, 249–250
Thumatha, 203
Thyatira, 56
THYATIRIDAE, 56
Thysanoplusia, 328
tiliae, Mimas, 12, 181, **23**
Timandra, 69
tipuliformis, Synanthedon, 25, 44
tityus, Hemaris, 15, 183
togata, Xanthia, 281
tragopoginis, Amphipyra, 290
transversa, Eupsilia, 274
transversata britannica, Philereme, 107
trapezina, Cosmia, 298
tremula, Pheosia, 192
triangulum, Xestia, 233
Trichiura, 49
Trichoplusia, 328
Trichopteryx, 142–143
tridens, Acronicta, 286
trifolii, Zygaena, 42
trifolii, Discestra, 239
trigeminata, Idaea, 18, 75
trigrammica, Charanyca, 19, 317
trimaculosa, Polia, 15, **1**, 240
tripartita, Abrostola, 334
Triphosa, 106
triplasia, Abrostola, 17, 333
tripunctaria, Eupithecia, 126
trisignaria, Eupithecia, 12, 121
tristata, Epirrhoe, 345
tritici, Euxoa, 216
truncata, Chloroclysta, 95, 96
typhae, Nonagria, 215, 314, **19**
typica, Naenia, 236
Tyria, 213
Tyta, 337
umbra, Pyrrhia, 322, **15**
umbratica, Cucullia, 262
unangulata, Euphyia, 108
unanimis, Apamea, 19, 302
undulata, Rheumaptera, 106
unipuncta, Mythimna, 22, 259
vaccinii, Conistra, 275
valerianata, Eupithecia, 10, 20, 25, 119
v-ata, Chloroclystis, 135
venosata, Eupithecia, 120
verbasci, Shargacucullia, 10, 263
versicolor, Oligia, 304, 305
vespiformis, Synanthedon, 25, 45, **6**
vestigialis, Agrotis, 346

vetulata, Philereme, 107
vetusta, Xylena, 269
villica britannica, Arctia, 209
viminalis, Brachylomia, 263
vinula, Cerura, 187, **13**, **23**
viretata, Acasis, 144
virgaureata, Eupithecia, 132
viridaria, Phytometra, 17, 338
viridata, Chlorissa, 345
vitalbata, Horisme, 103
vitellina, Mythimna, 22, 257
vittata, Orthonama, 78
vulgata, Eupithecia, 125
Watsonalla, 54–55
wauaria, Macaria, 17, 18, 91, 148
w–latinum, Lacanobia, 243
Xanthia, 280–282
xanthographa, Xestia, 235
Xanthorhoe, 80–82
Xestia, 232–236
Xylena, 269
Xylocampa, 270
ypsillon, Parastichtis, 295
Zanclognatha, 343
Zeuzera, 39
ziczac, Notodonta, 191
Zygaena, 41–42
ZYGAENIDAE, 40

Acknowledgements

As with all major county publications, there are numerous individuals who have worked tirelessly in the background with great commitment to ensure the smooth running and success of the project.

One person who deserves special mention is Nigel Stone, whose dedicated input throughout has been immense and invaluable. His combination of computer skills, efficiency in processing records and willingness to devote unlimited hours has enabled the entire Warwickshire moth database to be computerised from the original card index system. Nigel has consequently produced the distribution maps, charts and graphs published in this book. He has also spent countless hours, along with Heather Warmington and Kath Gardner (née Brown), word processing the text from an original handwritten format.

I would also like to thank Mark Tunmore of *Atropos*, the publishers, for devoting so much time and effort to this project. His help, advice and experience have been invaluable. A number of people have spent many hours proofreading and provided useful comments, including Sean Clancy, Kath Gardner (née Brown), Andrew Gardner, Patricia Gardner, Mark Parsons, Jim Porter, Iain Reid, Bernard Skinner, Michael Slater, Catherine Wellings and Sue Wharam.

The following have also given help and advice or provided valuable information: Roy Allen, Michael Astley, Mike Bailey, Ray Barnett, Stephan Bodnar, John Bates, Ray Bliss, Graham Collins, Peter Davey, Les Evans, Richard Gardner, Dave Grundy, Martin Kennard, Alec Kolaj, Lucy Kolaj, Roy Ledbury, Ian Maclean, Brian Mitchell, Paul Nicholas, Steve Palmer, Jim Porter, John M. Price, Philip Robbins, Rita Ruban, Elaine Rumary, Peter Sharp, Roger Smith, Chris Sumner, Charles Wale, Paul Waring, Keith Warmington and Matthew Willmott.

Special thanks are conveyed to John Radley and Steven Falk for writing the geology section and further thanks to Martyn Bradley for additional help and comments. The author is extremely grateful to Andy Tasker of Warwickshire Wildlife Trust for permission to reproduce the County geology map. Barbara Davies, Lorna Dudley and Jane O'Dell are acknowledged for the help given with plants.

I would like to extend thanks to the hundreds of contributors of records for this book and impart my special gratitude to Michael Astley, Robert Cox, Andrew Gardner, Chris Ivin, Paul Nicholas, David Porter, Iain Reid and Martyn Vice, who provided such immaculate garden moth trap records. In an age when most lepidopterists rely heavily upon mercury vapour light, I would like to give Martyn Vice a special mention for the enormous amount of detailed information he has provided on larval foodplants attained by years of dedicated and diligent fieldwork.

Many people have helped with the photographic section of this book but I am especially grateful to Robert Thompson, who not only provided such an excellent photograph and design for the cover but has also offered much help and advice overall. The book has been greatly enhanced by the inclusion of colour photographs of representative species. I am greatly indebted to the following for providing such marvellous photographs for this book: Steven Falk, Paul Harris, Roy Ledbury, Roy Leverton, Paul Nicholas, David Porter, Jim Porter, John Roberts, Robert Thompson, Mark Tunmore, and Keith Warmington. My thanks are extended to Geoffrey Senior and Peter Theideke for the work involved in the production of the specimen plate and the use of their studio in London.

I would like to thank Roger Gaunt, Dave Grundy, Adrian Russell, Bernard Skinner, Martin Townsend, John Ward and Paul Waring for help and information on adjoining county publications.

I would especially like to acknowledge Catherine Wellings for producing the plant list and the index and Nigel Stone for working on the site gazetteer. Both tackled these unenviable tasks with a determined efficiency. Keith Warmington also deserves a special mention for so willingly giving help and advice.

Turning to the funding of the endeavour, the author is very grateful to the British Entomological and Natural History Society and Birmingham Natural History Society for loan finance. Thanks are also due to the Centre for Lifelong Learning and Open Studies department of Warwick University, not only for assistance with funding but also for encouragement and help throughout. Sincere thanks also to the numbers of individuals who kindly contributed donations to this publication. Special thanks must go to Val Weston who worked so hard to raise funds, which were then matched by Barclays Bank Plc. I would like to express thanks to Chris Johnson who pulled the finances together and always displayed eternal optimism for this project.

Thanks also go to John Reeve and George Higgs for their excellent artistic sketches included in this work, and to Debbie Hibbitt, Steven Cheshire and John Williamson for scanning of some monochrome images. I am very grateful to Jim Porter for agreeing to write a Foreword.

As with all projects that take years to complete, inspiration is a much needed quality which, although imparted unwittingly, is truly appreciated by the recipient. For this I owe special thanks to Lorna Dudley, Jane O'Dell, Winklet Smith, Catherine Wellings and Sue Wharam. Whilst on a personal note, I would like to thank two further people; firstly, Geoffrey Thorpe, to whom I owe much gratitude for initiating my interest in moths. On a mild March day in 1968 as Geoffrey lent me his moth trap, I was unaware of the profound effect it would have on the rest of my life. Secondly, I wish to thank Roger Smith, who, in 1971 recognised enough potential in an eighteen year old to forward him as the County Recorder.

Thanks also go to the colleagues who have, over many years, accompanied me on numerous moth field nights (sometimes at very short notice) to far corners of Warwickshire, in varying climatic conditions. Gratitude is further extended to the exclusive band of individuals who have accompanied me to a local hostelry to provide convivial evenings with a wealth of absorbing conversation, banter and humour. Such special occasions would arise when the night had become too cold, wet and windy, or on evenings when it was parchingly hot and dry; or indeed, simply to satisfy a desire to try out the local ale!

David Brown
December 2005